Table of Contents

VB.NET LANGUAGE
IN A NUTSHELL

A Desktop Quick Reference

Second Edition

Steven Roman, Ron Petrusha & Paul Lomax

O'REILLY®

Beijing • Cambridge • Farnham • Köln • Paris • Sebastopol • Taipei • Tokyo

VB.NET Language in a Nutshell, Second Edition

by Steven Roman, Ron Petrusha, and Paul Lomax

Editor: Ron Petrusha

Production Editor: Catherine Morris

Cover Designer: Pam Spremulli

Interior Designer: David Futato

Printing History:

August 2001:	First Edition.
April 2002:	Second Edition.

Library of Congress Cataloging-in-Publication Data

Roman, Steven.
   VB .NET language in a nutshell / Steven Roman & Paul Lomax.--2nd ed.
     p. cm.
   ISBN 0-596-00308-0
   1. Microsoft Visual BASIC. 2. BASIC (Computer program language) I. Petrusha,
     Ronald, 1951- II. Lomax, Paul. III. Title.

QA76.73.B3 R657 2002
005.26'8--dc21   2002023324

[M]

Part II: Reference

Part III: Appendixes

Preface

Microsoft Visual Basic began its life just eleven years ago as a kind of amalgamation of Microsoft's QBasic programming language and a graphical interface design program developed in part by Alan Cooper. Since then, it has become by far the most popular programming language in the world, with an installed base that is estimated at five to eight million developers worldwide.

The tenth anniversary of Visual Basic coincided with the announcement of Microsoft's new .NET platform, and with a totally revised and revamped version of VB named Visual Basic .NET. The language has been streamlined and modernized, and many old "compatibility" elements have been dropped from the language, while other language elements that were implemented as statements are now either functions or procedures.

In addition, many of you will be glad to hear that Visual Basic is now a fully object-oriented programming language, with the inclusion of the long sought-after class inheritance, as well as other OOP features.

We suspect that many of you will greet with mixed emotions, as do we, the fact that Microsoft's Component Object Model (COM), the technology that was at the core of Visual Basic since the release of Version 4.0, has been abandoned in favor of the .NET platform. On the one hand, we find this to be a great relief, because COM can be so complex and confusing. On the other hand, we find this somewhat irritating, because we have invested so much time and effort in learning and using COM. Finally, we find this change somewhat frightening; who knows what pitfalls await us as we become more familiar with this new technology?

The best news of all is that, whereas in the past, Visual Basic served as a "wrapper" that simplified and hid much of the complexity of Windows and the Windows operating system, at long last Visual Basic is an "equal player" in the .NET Framework; Visual Basic programmers have full and easy access to the features of the .NET platform, just as Visual C++ and C# programmers do.

The extensive changes to the language and the introduction of the .NET platform make a reference guide to the Visual Basic language more essential than ever. At the same time, they make it easy to delineate this book's subject matter. This is a book that focuses on the language elements of Visual Basic .NET—on its statements, functions, procedures, directives, and objects (notably the Err and Collection objects).

While it's important to emphasize that this book focuses on the Visual Basic language components for the .NET platform, it's also important to emphasize what this book is not:

- It is not a reference guide to Visual Basic for Applications (VBA), the programming language used in all of the major applications in the Microsoft Office suite, as well as in dozens of other third-party applications. As you probably know, VBA is the programming language in previous versions of Visual Basic and in the major Office applications. However, VBA is not the programming language for VB.NET. Indeed, until VB.NET is incorporated into a release of Microsoft Office for .NET, the two languages will differ significantly.

- It is not a reference guide to the .NET Framework Class Library. To be sure, the Framework Class Library is discussed in these pages, and a number of its classes and their members are documented in this book's reference section. But that documentation just scratches the surface; the Framework Class Library consists of over 90 namespaces (one of which, incidentally, is Microsoft.VisualBasic, the namespace that defines the objects of the Visual Basic language), several thousand types (classes, interfaces, delegates, and enumerations), and an enormous number of members. In selecting the .NET Framework classes to document in this book, we've tried to focus on .NET elements that replace commonly used features in previous versions of Visual Basic, as well as on .NET elements that expand and enhance the functionality of existing Visual Basic .NET elements in significant ways.

- It is not a reference guide to the attributes that you can apply to program elements. To be sure, Chapter 8 introduces attribute-based programming, and there are entries for important language-based attributes in the reference section. But of the more than 200 attributes available in the .NET Framework Class Library, only language-related attributes and the general-purpose attributes VB developers are most likely to use are documented in this book.

- It is not a guide to developing applications or components using Visual Basic . NET. In documenting the language, we'll show you some simple code fragments that illustrate the relevant issues and show you how a language element works. On the other hand, we won't show you, for example, how to use the Windows Forms package to build a Windows application, how to develop a web application using ASP.NET, or how to implement a web service.

Why Another VB Book?

There are literally hundreds of books lining the shelves on how to program using Visual Basic, and they will no doubt be joined by a flood of books on how to program in VB.NET. The majority of these books assume that you're a complete novice and slowly introduce you to such concepts as variables, arrays, and looping structures.

This is a different kind of book, however. It is a detailed, professional reference to the VB.NET language—a reference that you can turn to if you want to jog your memory about a particular language element or a particular parameter. You're also looking for a reference that you can turn to when you're having difficulty programming and need to review the rules for using a particular language element, or when you want to check that there isn't some "gotcha" you've over-looked that is associated with a particular language element.

In addition, we believe this book will serve as the main reference for VB 6 programmers who are upgrading to VB.NET. To this end, we have devoted consid-erable space to the extensive language differences between VB 6 and VB.NET. For each relevant language entry, we have included a "VB.NET/VB 6 Differences" section that details the differences in the operation of the language element between VB 6 and VB.NET.

Who This Book Is For

Just like any reference (such as a dictionary), this book will be useful to many types of readers:

* Developers who have used previous versions of Visual Basic

* Developers who are new to Visual Basic, but who have been developing applications in other programming languages, such as C++

* Those who are learning VB.NET as their first language and would like to have a definitive language reference on their shelf

Readers New to Visual Basic

If you are new to the Visual Basic language, then you will want to pay particular attention to the first half of the book, which discusses many important areas of programming under VB.NET, including variables, data types, the basic principles of object-oriented programming, and error-handling techniques.

VB and VBScript Developers New to VB.NET

Some critics have argued that VB.NET is an entirely new language. While we wouldn't go quite that far, we do agree not only that the language changes have been extensive, but that the new .NET platform will result in a paradigm shift that affects the way we think about application development. So in many ways, as a VB or VBScript developer new to VB.NET, you may find yourself in a position similar to that of a developer who is new to all forms of VB.NET.

However, one of our goals was to develop a book that will ease the thorny transi-tion to VB.NET from earlier versions of VB. In particular, the first nine chapters of the book offer a rapid introduction to VB.NET and its new features. Appendix A discusses many of the major language changes between VB 6 and VB.NET, while Appendix F lists VB 6 language elements that are no longer supported in VB.NET.

Finally, if version differences exist in a language element, we include a "VB.NET/ VB 6 Differences" section that shows you precisely how the behavior of that element has changed from VB 6 to VB.NET.

Existing VB.NET Developers

As we write the second edition of this book, VB.NET is brand new (the initial version of the .NET Framework and Visual Studio .NET have just been released to manufacturing), so existing VB.NET developers are a rarity. But we believe that, given the strengths of VB.NET, this situation will change quickly. As you continue to develop in VB.NET, we believe you will find that *VB.NET Language in a Nutshell* retains its value. As an experienced developer, you can delve into the book to get the lowdown on a language element that interests you or that seems to be behaving erratically or unexpectedly in your code. Appendix B details all of the language elements by category to help you find the relevant entry in the language reference more easily.

How This Book Is Structured

VB.NET Language in a Nutshell is divided into three parts. The first part of the book, *The Basics*, is an introduction to the main features and concepts of Visual Basic programming. Given the newness of VB.NET, even seasoned VB professionals should find items of interest here. If you're new to VB, this part of the book is essential reading. It's divided into the following chapters:

Chapter 1, *Introduction*
In this chapter, you'll see how Visual Basic has evolved into the VB.NET language of today and get some sense of how and why VB.NET is different from previous versions of Visual Basic.

Chapter 2, *Program Structure*
This chapters discusses the entry points that allows the .NET runtime to execute your code and shows how to structure the code in a Visual Basic program.

Chapter 3, *Variables and Data Types*
This chapter looks at the standard Visual Basic data types and how you use them. Behind the scenes, Visual Basic takes advantage of the .NET Framework's common type system, so the chapter also examines the .NET data types and the way in which VB wraps these data types.

Chapter 4, *Introduction to Object-Oriented Programming*
With the release of its .NET version, Visual Basic finally becomes a fully object-oriented programming language. This chapter discusses the basic concepts of object-orientated programming and shows how you implement VB's object-oriented features in your programming.

Chapter 5, *The .NET Framework: General Concepts*
This chapter surveys some of the new features of the .NET Framework that most impact the VB developer. These include namespaces, the Common Language Runtime (CLR), and assemblies.

Chapter 6, *The .NET Framework Class Library*

The .NET Framework Class Library replaces portions of the Win32 API, as well as many of the individual object models that VB programmers have worked with over the past five years, with a single class library. This chapter offers a very fast-paced overview of the Framework Class Library and some of its features.

Chapter 7, *Delegates and Events*

While handling events was more or less automatic in previous versions of VB and even in VBScript, you typically have to "wire" events to your code in VB. NET. This chapter shows how to do that.

Chapter 8, *Attributes*

The .NET Framework supports attributes, an extensible mechanism that allows you to store customized items of information about a particular program element in an assembly's metadata. This makes it possible to modify the behavior of the compiler, of a design time environment, or of the runtime environment if a particular attribute is present. This chapter explains what attributes are in greater detail, introduces the syntax of attribute-based programming, and shows you how to define and consume custom attributes.

Chapter 9, *Error Handling in VB.NET*

Visual Basic now offers two techniques for error handling. The first, which uses the On Error statement, is termed *unstructured error handling* and is a traditional part of VB. The second, which uses the Try...Catch...Finally construct, is termed *structured exception handling* and is new to VB.NET. In this chapter, we'll show you how to use both.

The second part of this book, *The Reference*, consists of one large chapter, Chapter 10, *The Language Reference*, which thoroughly details all the functions, statements, directives, objects, and object members that make up the VB.NET language.

The third and final section consists of the following appendixes:

Appendix A, *What's New and Different in VB.NET*

A discussion of language changes from VB 6 to VB.NET.

Appendix B, *Language Elements by Category*

A listing of all VB.NET functions, statements, and major keywords by category.

Appendix C, *Operators*

A list of the operators supported by VB.NET, along with a slightly more detailed treatment of the Boolean and bitwise operators.

Appendix D, *Constants and Enumerations*

A list of VB.NET intrinsic constants, as well as VB.NET enumerations and their members.

Appendix E, *The VB.NET Command-Line Compiler*

For the first time, Visual Basic includes a command-line compiler—you can actually use NotePad as your primary "development environment" for Visual Basic (although we are not necessarily recommending this approach) and use the compiler to compile your code. This appendix documents the operation of the Visual Basic command-line compiler.

Appendix F, *VB 6 Language Elements Not Supported by VB.NET*
> A list of the language elements that have dropped out of the Visual Basic language as a result of its transition to the .NET Framework.

The Format of the Language Reference

The following template has been used in preparing the entries for functions, procedures, statements, properties, and methods that appear in Chapter 10:

Class
> For functions, procedures, classes, or class members, the class to which the item belongs.

Named Arguments
> Typically, we indicate if a function, procedure, or method does *not* accept named arguments. Otherwise, you can assume that the language element supports both named and positional arguments.

Syntax
> This section uses standard conventions to give a synopsis of the syntax used for the language item. It also lists parameters and replaceable items (and indicates whether they're optional or not), lists their data types, and provides a brief description.

Return Value
> For functions, this section provides a brief description of the value or data type returned by the function. For properties, it describes the data type of the property.

Description
> A short description of what the language element does, and when and why it should be used.

Rules at a Glance
> This section describes the main points of how to use the function. The dos and don'ts are presented in the form of a bulleted list to let you quickly scan through the list of rules. In the vast majority of cases, this section goes well beyond the basic details found in the VB documentation.

Example
> We've tried to avoid the kind of gratuitous examples commonly found in documentation that only manage to illustrate the obvious. Instead, we've used short code fragments that help to enhance your understanding of how the language element is used.

Programming Tips and Gotchas
> This is the most valuable section of Chapter 10, in our opinion, and it is gained from years of experience using the VB language in a variety of projects and applications. The information included here will save you countless hours of head scratching and experimentation. Often, this is the stuff Microsoft doesn't tell you!

See Also
> A simple cross-reference list of related or complimentary language elements.

A modified version of the template has been used for statements and attributes.

What's on the CD

The CD in the back of this book contains a version of the *VB.NET Language in a Nutshell* Language Reference (Chapter 10) and Operators reference (Appendix C) that can be plugged directly into the online Help system of your copy of Microsoft Visual Studio .NET. Once installed, this material becomes a fully integrated part of Visual Studio .NET Dynamic Help available to you as you program along with the built-in Microsoft online documentation.

By making *VB.NET Language in a Nutshell* a part of your online development environment, you gain the following benefits:

- Continuous access to the contents of the book as you work in the online Visual Studio .NET development environment

- Ability to interactively browse the contents of the book through the Visual Studio .NET Help Contents window

- Constantly refreshed links to relevant entries in the book that appear in the Help Dynamic Help window as you write your Microsoft Visual Basic .NET code (these links appear in a separate Dynamic Help window link group named O'Reilly Help)

- Links to both *VB.NET Language in a Nutshell* topics as well as Microsoft documentation topics when you use either the Help Search facility or interactive Index

- Access to the O'Reilly web site, *http://www.oreilly.com*, for additional books and articles on Visual Basic .NET and the .NET Framework

To use *VB.NET Language in a Nutshell for Visual Studio .NET*, you must have already installed a version of Visual Basic .NET or Visual Studio .NET on your computer or laptop. Once you have done so, you may add the book to your Visual Studio .NET Help collection by completing the following steps:

1. Place the CD in the CD player.

2. Double-click on the installation file (*VB.NETLanguageinaNutshell.msi*).

3. Follow the instructions contained in the install program windows. You must read and accept the terms of the software license before proceeding. For up-to-date information on the book, be sure to read the release notes, which include a quick tour of Dynamic Help.

To uninstall *VB.NET Language in a Nutshell for Visual Studio .NET*, repeat the above procedure, but select the Remove option when the program prompts you to select an install option.

Making *VB.NET Language in a Nutshell* available as a Visual Studio .NET plug-in is an experiment for both O'Reilly and Microsoft, and we want very much to hear your comments before deciding how to enhance this offering and whether to extend it to additional titles in our .NET Nutshell series. Please send your comments to:

bookquestions@oreilly.com

If you discover errors in content or encounter any problems in using this product, please report them to:

> *bookquestions@oreilly.com*

Conventions Used in This Book

Throughout this book, we've used the following typographic conventions:

Constant width

> Constant width in body text indicates a language construct, such as a VB.NET statement (like `For` or `Do While`), an enumeration, an intrinsic or user-defined constant, a structure (i.e., a user-defined type), an operator, a declaration, a directive, or an expression (like `dblElapTime = Timer - dblStartTime`). Code fragments and code examples appear exclusively in constant-width text. In syntax statements and prototypes, text set in constant width indicates such language elements as the function or procedure name and any invariable elements required by the syntax.

Constant width italic

> Constant width italic in body text indicates parameter names. In syntax statements or prototypes, constant width italic indicates replaceable parameters. In addition, constant width italic is used in both body text and code fragments to denote variables.

Italic

> Italicized words in the text indicate intrinsic or user-defined functions and procedure names. Many system elements, such as paths and filenames, are also italicized. In addition, URLs and email address are italicized. Finally, italics are used the first time a term is used.

How to Contact Us

We have tested and verified all the information in this book to the best of our ability, but you may find that features have changed (or even that we have made mistakes). Please let us know about any errors you find, as well as your suggestions for future editions, by writing to:

> O'Reilly & Associates, Inc.
> 1005 Gravenstein Highway North
> Sebastopol, CA 95472
> (800) 998-9938 (in the United States or Canada)
> (707) 829-0515 (international/local)
> (707) 829-0104 (fax)

You can also send messages electronically. To be put on our mailing list or to request a catalog, send email to:

> *info@oreilly.com*

To ask technical questions or comment on the book, send email to:

> *bookquestions@oreilly.com*

It's our hope that as the Visual Basic language continues to grow and evolve, so too will *VB.NET Language in a Nutshell*, and that the book will come to be seen by VB developers as the official (so to speak) unofficial documentation on the Visual Basic language. To do that, we need your help. If you see errors here, we'd like to hear about them. If you're looking for information on some VB language feature and can't find it in this book, we'd like to hear about that, too. And finally, if you would like to contribute your favorite programming tip or gotcha, we'll do our best to include it in the next edition of this book. You can request these fixes, additions, and amendments to the book at our web site, *http://www.oreilly.com/ catalog/vbdotnetnut2/*.

In addition, Steven Roman maintains a web site at *www.romanpress.com* that includes information on his other books published by O'Reilly (and others), articles on VB/VBA and VB.NET, and a variety of software.

Acknowledgments

Writing a book always requires a substantial commitment of time and effort, and for that we are grateful to our spouses and families for their support in helping to bring this project through to completion. Steve would like to thank Donna; Ron would like to thank Vanessa, Sean and Ami; and Paul would like to thank Deb, Russel, and Victoria.

In commemorating the tenth anniversary of Visual Basic, we would also like to acknowledge the contributions of the designers and developers who transformed Visual Basic from an idea into a reality. Truly, it has been a monumental accomplishment that has transformed the way in which applications are created.

We'd also like to thank the book's technical reviewers, Daniel Crecron, Budi Kurniawan, and Matt Childs, for their thoughtful, careful reviews of our work. We'd also like to thank Alan Carter, Chris Dias, Amanda Silver, and Sam Spencer at Microsoft for their help in answering our annoying questions and for reviewing portions of the manuscript.

The on-line Visual Studio .NET edition of this book was made possible by the work of many individuals. Mike Sierra of O'Reilly converted the Language Reference to Microsoft Help 2.0 format and did the work necessary to make its content available through the Visual Studio .NET dynamic help system. Kipper York, Shane McRoberts, and Etka Mittal of the Microsoft Help team provided invaluable technical assistance at crucial moments in the project, and Eric Promislow and Vladimir Baikalov of ActiveState built the install package that plugs our Help collection into Visual Studio .NET. Frank Gocinski of the Visual Studio .NET Integration Program was instrumental in helping us become full partners in the program. A special tip of the hat to Rob Howard of Microsoft who supported our original vision and helped us make the right connections with the Visual Studio .NET team to get this project off the ground.

PART I

The Basics

This section serves as a general introduction to Visual Basic .NET, Microsoft's version of Visual Basic for the .NET platform. Taken together, these chapters form an extremely fast-paced introduction to the most critical VB.NET programming topics. If you're an experienced programmer who is learning VB.NET as a second (or additional) programming language, the material should familiarize you with VB.NET in as short a time as possible.

In addition to its role as a tutorial, Chapter 3 is an essential reference to the data types supported by VB.NET.

Part I consists of the following chapters:

- Chapter 1, *Introduction*
- Chapter 2, *Program Structure*
- Chapter 3, *Variables and Data Types*
- Chapter 4, *Introduction to Object-Oriented Programming*
- Chapter 5, *The .NET Framework: General Concepts*
- Chapter 6, *The .NET Framework Class Library*
- Chapter 7, *Delegates and Events*
- Chapter 8, *Attributes*
- Chapter 9, *Error Handling in VB.NET*

CHAPTER 1

Introduction

Since its introduction in 1991, Microsoft Visual Basic has enjoyed unprecedented success. In fact, in slightly more than a decade, it has become the world's most widely used programming language, with an installed base of somewhere between three and five million developers (depending on the particular source you use and whether the estimate includes only the retail versions of the Visual Basic product or the hosted version of Visual Basic for Applications (VBA) as well).

The reason for this success is twofold. First, Visual Basic has excelled as a rapid application development (RAD) environment for corporate and commercial applications. Second, Visual Basic offers a programming language and development environment noted for its simplicity and ease of use, making it an extremely attractive choice for those new to programming.

With the release of its new .NET platform, Microsoft also released a new version of the Visual Basic language, Visual Basic .NET. VB.NET is a from-the-ground-up rewrite of Visual Basic that not only adds a number of new features, but also differs significantly from previous versions of Visual Basic. From a high-level view, two of these differences are especially noteworthy:

- Until the release of VB.NET, Microsoft focused on creating a unified version of VBA, the language engine used in Visual Basic, which could serve as a "universal batch language" for Windows and Windows applications. With Version 6 of Visual Basic, this goal was largely successful: VB 6.0 featured VBA 6.0, the same language engine that drives the individual applications in the Microsoft Office 2000 suite, Microsoft Project, Microsoft FrontPage, Microsoft Visio, and a host of popular third-party applications such as AutoDesk's AutoCAD and Corel's WordPerfect Office 2000. With the release of VB.NET, this emphasis on a unified programming language has, for the moment at least, faded into the background, as the hosted version of Visual Basic continues to be VBA rather than VB.NET.

- Since Version 4, Visual Basic had increasingly been used as a kind of "glue language" to access COM components and their object models, such as ActiveX Data Objects (ADO), Collaborative Data Objects (CDO), or the Outlook object model. Although VB.NET supports COM for reasons of backward compatibility, VB.NET is designed primarily to work with the .NET Framework rather than with COM.

You may be wondering why Microsoft would totally redesign a programming language and development environment that is so wildly successful. As we shall see, there is some method to this madness.

Why VB.NET?

When Visual Basic was introduced in 1991, Windows 3.0 was a fairly new operating system in need of application and utility software. Although Windows 3.0 itself had proven successful, the graphical applications that offered native support for Windows—and upon whose release the ultimate success or failure of Windows would depend—were slow in coming. The major problem was that C and C++ programmers, who had produced the majority of applications for the MS-DOS operating system, were faced with a substantial learning curve in writing Windows applications and adapting to Windows' event-driven programming model.

The introduction of Visual Basic immediately addressed this problem by offering a programming model that was thoroughly consistent with Windows' graphical nature. Although Windows marked a radical change in the way programs were written, C and C++ programmers continued to produce code as they always had: a text editor was used to write source code, the source code was compiled into an executable, and the executable was finally run under Windows. Visual Basic programmers, on the other hand, worked in a programming environment that its critics derisively labeled a "drawing program." Visual Basic automatically created a form (or window) whenever the developer began a new project. The developer would then "draw" the user interface by dragging and dropping controls from a toolbox onto the form. Finally, the developer would write code snippets that responded to particular events (such as the window loading or the window being resized). In other words, Visual Basic's initial success was due to its ease of use, which in turn reflected that Visual Basic offered a graphical programming environment that was entirely consistent with the graphical character of Windows itself.

To get some sense of the revolutionary character of Visual Basic, it is instructive to compare a simple "Hello World" program for Windows 3.0 written in C (see Example 1-1) with one written in Visual Basic (see Example 1-2). While the former program is over two pages long, its Visual Basic counterpart takes only three lines of code—and two of them are provided automatically by the Visual Basic environment itself.

Example 1-1: "Hello World" in C

```
// "Hello World" example
//
// The user clicks a command button, and a "Hello World"
// message box appears.
#include <windows.h>
```

Example 1-1: "Hello World" in C (continued)

```
LRESULT CALLBACK WndProc (HWND, UINT, WPARAM, LPARAM);

int WINAPI WinMain (HINSTANCE hInstance, HINSTANCE hPrevInstance,
                    PSTR szCmdLine, int iCmdShow)
   {
   static char szAppName[] = "SayHello" ;
   HWND hwnd ;
   MSG msg ;
   WNDCLASSEX wndclass ;

   wndclass.cbSize        = sizeof (wndclass) ;
   wndclass.style         = CS_HREDRAW | CS_VREDRAW ;
   wndclass.lpfnWndProc   = WndProc ;
   wndclass.cbClsExtra    = 0 ;
   wndclass.cbWndExtra    = 0 ;
   wndclass.hInstance     = hInstance ;
   wndclass.hIcon         = LoadIcon(NULL, IDI_APPLICATION) ;
   wndclass.hCursor       = LoadCursor(NULL, IDC_ARROW) ;
   wndclass.hbrBackground = (HBRUSH) GetStockObject(WHITE_BRUSH) ;
   wndclass.lpszMenuName  = NULL ;
   wndclass.lpszClassName = szAppName ;
   wndclass.hIconSm       = LoadIcon(NULL, IDI_APPLICATION) ;

   RegisterClassEx(&wndclass) ;

   hwnd = CreateWindow(szAppName, "Hello World",
                       WS_OVERLAPPEDWINDOW,
                       CW_USEDEFAULT, CW_USEDEFAULT,
                       CW_USEDEFAULT, CW_USEDEFAULT,
                       NULL, NULL, hInstance, NULL) ;

   ShowWindow(hwnd, iCmdShow) ;
   UpdateWindow(hwnd) ;

   while (GetMessage(&msg, NULL, 0, 0))
      {
      TranslateMessage(&msg) ;
      DispatchMessage(&msg) ;
      }
   return msg.wParam ;
   }

LRESULT CALLBACK WndProc(HWND hwnd, UINT iMsg, WPARAM wParam,
                    LPARAM lParam)
   {
   int wNotifyCode ;
   HWND hwndCtl ;
   static HWND  hwndButton ;
   static RECT  rect ;
   static int   cxChar, cyChar ;
   HDC          hdc ;
```

Example 1-1: "Hello World" in C (continued)

```
    PAINTSTRUCT  ps ;
    TEXTMETRIC   tm ;

    switch (iMsg)
        {
        case WM_CREATE :
            hdc = GetDC(hwnd) ;
            SelectObject(hdc, GetStockObject (SYSTEM_FIXED_FONT)) ;
            GetTextMetrics(hdc, &tm) ;
            cxChar = tm.tmAveCharWidth ;
            cyChar = tm.tmHeight + tm.tmExternalLeading ;
            ReleaseDC(hwnd, hdc) ;
            GetClientRect( hwnd, &rect ) ;

            hwndButton = CreateWindow("BUTTON", "&Say Hello",
                        WS_CHILD | WS_VISIBLE | BS_PUSHBUTTON,
                        (rect.right-rect.left)/20*9,
                        (rect.bottom-rect.top)/10*4,
                        14 * cxChar, 3 * cyChar,
                        (HWND) hwnd, 1,
                        ((LPCREATESTRUCT) lParam) -> hInstance, NULL) ;

            return 0 ;

        case WM_SIZE :
            rect.left   = 24 * cxChar ;
            rect.top    =  2 * cyChar ;
            rect.right  = LOWORD (lParam) ;
            rect.bottom = HIWORD (lParam) ;
            return 0 ;

        case WM_PAINT :
            InvalidateRect(hwnd, &rect, TRUE) ;

            hdc = BeginPaint(hwnd, &ps) ;
            EndPaint(hwnd, &ps) ;
            return 0 ;

        case WM_DRAWITEM :
        case WM_COMMAND :
            wNotifyCode = HIWORD(wParam) ;
            hwndCtl = (HWND) lParam ;

            if ((hwndCtl == hwndButton) && (wNotifyCode == BN_CLICKED))
                MessageBox(hwnd, "Hello, World!", "Greetings", MB_OK) ;

            ValidateRect(hwnd, &rect) ;

            break ;

        case WM_DESTROY :
            PostQuitMessage (0) ;
```

Example 1-1: "Hello World" in C (continued)

```
        return 0 ;
    }
    return DefWindowProc (hwnd, iMsg, wParam, lParam) ;
    }
```

Example 1-2: "Hello World" in Visual Basic

```
Private Sub Command1_Click()

MsgBox "Hello, World", vbOKOnly Or vbExclamation, "Hi!"

End Sub
```

While Version 1.0 of Visual Basic was relatively underpowered, Microsoft displayed a firm commitment to Visual Basic and worked very hard to increase its power and flexibility with each new release. By the time Version 3.0 was released, Visual Basic offered a programming paradigm that was completely intuitive, making it easy for novice programmers to get started and produce simple applications very quickly. At the same time, particularly through its ability to access the Windows Application Programming Interface (API) and through its support for add-on controls, Visual Basic had become a programming tool capable of creating applications of considerable sophistication and complexity.

Like VB.NET, Visual Basic Version 4.0, which was released in 1995 to support Microsoft's 32-bit family of operating systems, was a complete rewrite of Visual Basic. It featured limited support for object-oriented programming in the form of class modules (CLS files) and the ability to generate not only Windows executables, but ActiveX DLLs (also known as COM components) as well.

In the periods shortly before and after the release of VB 4, the character of programming changed dramatically. The rise of the Internet as an application platform meant that standalone Windows applications were becoming less and less necessary. The increased prominence of distributed applications that assumed the presence of the Internet marked another change in programming paradigms. Yet Visual Basic's real strength remained as it always had been: a great platform for developing standalone Windows applications.

This disparity between Visual Basic's strengths and the prevailing programming paradigm, which emphasized distributed applications and the Internet, created something of a contradiction. On the one hand, Visual Basic excelled at graphically depicting the Windows interface. On the other hand, developers were creating fewer and fewer Windows interfaces. Instead, they were now using Visual Basic primarily to write source code that would eventually be compiled into middle-tier components. Ironically, a programming environment whose real strength and point of departure was its graphical character was now being used as a text editor, in very much the same way the first generation of Windows programmers used text editors to create C source code for Windows applications.

Moreover, as the popularity of the Internet grew, it became clearer that Visual Basic was not a particularly good platform for developing Internet applications. With VB 6, Microsoft introduced Web Classes as the preferred technology for

Internet application development. Yet, the metaphor presented by Web Classes (which focused on separating a web application's presentation from its programmatic functionality) was confusing to developers, and, as a result, Web Classes never became popular. While VB remained critically important for developing middle-tier components for distributed applications, both it and the Visual Basic community that grew up around it remained strangely isolated from the Internet as an application platform.

Numerous detractors have labeled VB.NET as an entirely new language with little relationship to previous versions of Visual Basic—a dubious innovation foisted on the Visual Basic community by Microsoft in an attempt to sell a new version of its development products. However, we don't agree. Instead, we view the introduction of VB.NET as a logical and even necessary step forward in the development of Visual Basic as a premier programming language. The goal of VB.NET is to address the limitations of Visual Basic as a development environment and bring it into the Internet age so that it can remain the major platform for developing applications of all kinds. Very much like Visual Basic 1.0 offered a graphical interface that was suitable for Windows applications, VB.NET and Visual Studio .NET aim to provide a graphical interface that is suitable for developing web applications and for taking full advantage of the Internet as an application-development platform, as well as for developing Windows applications and components.

What Is VB.NET?

VB.NET is a programming language designed to create applications that work with Microsoft's new .NET Framework. The .NET platform in turn addresses many of the limitations of "classic" COM, Microsoft's Component Object Model, which provided one approach toward application and component interoperability. These limitations included type incompatibilities when calling COM components, versioning difficulties ("DLL hell") when developing new versions of COM components, and the need for developers to write a certain amount of code (mostly in C++) to handle the COM "plumbing." In contrast to VB, with its reliance on COM, VB.NET offers a number of new features and advantages. Let's take a look at some of these.

Object Orientation

With the release of Version 4, Visual Basic added support for classes and class modules and in the process became an object-oriented programming language. Yet the debate persists about whether Visual Basic is a "true" object-oriented language or whether it only supports limited features of object orientation.

The debate centers around Visual Basic's support for *inheritance*, an object-oriented programming concept that allows a class to derive its properties and its functionality from another class. Proponents of the view that Visual Basic is object-oriented point to Visual Basic's support for interface-based programming and the use of virtual base classes. Yet relatively few VB programmers take advantage of interface-based programming. And interface-based programming itself does not allow a derived class to inherit the functionality of a base class; only virtual base classes can be inherited using the Implements keyword.

While the object-oriented character of previous versions of VB may be in doubt, there is no question that VB.NET is an object-oriented programming language. In fact, even if VB.NET is used to write what appears to be procedural code, it is object-oriented "under the hood," so to speak. Let's take as a simple example the clearly procedural, nonobject-oriented program shown in Example 1-3. If we use ILDASM (.NET's intermediate language disassembler) to look at the IL generated for this source code (see Figure 1-1), we see that internally, modMain is in fact defined as a class that has two methods, Increment and Main.

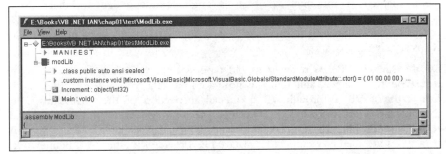

Figure 1-1: A procedural program shown using ILDASM

Example 1-3: A procedural program for VB.NET .

```
Public Module modMain

Public Sub Main()
    Dim x As Integer
    x = 10
    MsgBox(Increment(x))
End Sub

Private Function Increment(iVar As Integer)
    Return(iVar+1)
End Function

End Module
```

A Common Type System

Traditionally, one of the problems of calling routines written in other languages from Visual Basic or of calling Visual Basic routines from other languages is that such inter-language calls presuppose a common type system. This is the case when calling Win32 API functions from Visual Basic, but it is also applies to attempts to call methods in a VB COM component from other languages or to call methods in a non-VB COM component from VB.

For instance, until the addition of the **AddressOf** operator, which allows us to pass a pointer to a function or subroutine, there was no way to provide a callback function, which is required by most Win32 API enumeration functions. As another example, it is expected that members of structures passed to Win32 API functions be aligned on their natural boundaries, something that VB programmers had great difficulty accomplishing.

Problems of type compatibility tended to occur most often when scripted applications were used to call and pass arguments to COM components. An excellent example is the attempt to pass an array from a script written in JScript to a COM component, since COM sees JScript arrays as a string of comma-delimited values rather than a COM-compatible array (called a SafeArray).

The .NET platform removes these difficulties by providing a common type system. Ultimately, all data types are either classes or structures defined by or inherited from the .NET Framework Class Library. This common type system means that .NET components will be truly language-independent and that a .NET component written in one language will be seamlessly interoperable with .NET components written in any other .NET language. The problem of incompatible types simply disappears.

On the surface, VB has retained its old type system. VB still supports the Long data type, for instance, although it is now a 64-bit data type instead of the 32-bit data type of VB 4 through VB 6. Casual inspection of the code shown in Example 1-4 suggests that VB has retained its type system. However, if we use ILDASM to examine the IL generated from this Visual Basic code, we see that VB data types are merely wrappers for data types provided by the .NET Framework. (See Figure 1-2.)

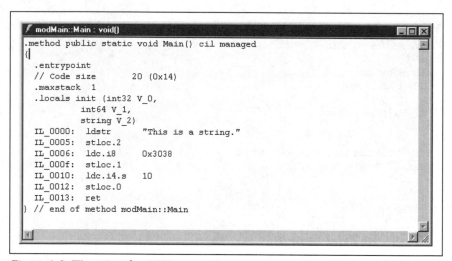

Figure 1-2: Wrapping the .NET type system

Example 1-4: Using the Visual Basic type system

```
Public Module modMain

Public Sub Main()

Dim s As String = "This is a string."
Dim l As Long = 12344
Dim i As Integer = 10
```

Example 1-4: Using the Visual Basic type system (continued)

```
End Sub

End Module
```

The simple program in Example 1-5 also supports this conclusion. The program instantiates an integer of type Long, a standard Visual Basic data type. It then calls the ToString method—a method of the Int64 class—to convert that number to its string representation. In other words, the variable 1 in Example 1-5 is really an Int64 data type masquerading as a traditional VB Long data type.

Example 1-5: Calling .NET type methods from a VB data type

```
Public Module modMain

Public Sub Main()

Dim l As Long = 64.31245
Dim s As String

s = l.ToString
MsgBox(s)

End Sub

End Module
```

Access to System Services: The Framework Class Library

Ever since VB added support for calls to routines in the Windows and Win32 APIs, many Visual Basic programmers came to regard API programming as a kind of black art. Not only was there a confusing and seemingly limitless array of functions that might be called, but also passing parameters to routines and receiving their return values often seemed to be a mysterious process. Moreover, with the growing emphasis on object-oriented programming, the Win32 API, with its function-based approach to programming, seemed more and more archaic.

Although the Declare statement remains in VB and programmers can still call the Win32 API and routines in other external Windows DLLs, many of the common system services provided by the Win32 API, as well as by some COM components, are now provided by the .NET Framework Class Library. The Framework Class Library is a collection of types (classes, structures, interfaces, delegates, and enumerations) organized into namespaces.

To get some sense of the difference in programming style between the Win32 API and the .NET Framework Class Library, as well as to appreciate the simplicity and ease with which the Framework Class Library can be accessed, compare Examples 1-6 and 1-7. Example 1-6 is a VB 6 routine that creates a value entry in the registry to load a particular program on Windows startup. Note that all API constants must be defined, as must the API functions themselves.

In addition, the API functions must be called correctly. In particular, to avoid passing a BSTR rather than a C null-terminated string to the *RegSetValueEx* function, the string must be passed using the ByVal keyword. This is a common oversight that usually causes an application crash. In contrast, Example 1-7 shows the comparable VB.NET code that uses the RegistryKey class in the Microsoft.Win32 namespace of the .NET Framework Class Library. Note that the code is short and simple and, therefore, far less error-prone.

Example 1-6: Writing to the registry using the Win32 API

```
Private Const ERROR_SUCCESS = 0&

Private Const HKEY_CLASSES_ROOT = &H80000000
Private Const HKEY_CURRENT_CONFIG = &H80000005
Private Const HKEY_CURRENT_USER = &H80000001
Private Const HKEY_DYN_DATA = &H80000006
Private Const HKEY_LOCAL_MACHINE = &H80000002
Private Const HKEY_PERFORMANCE_DATA = &H80000004
Private Const HKEY_USERS = &H80000003

Private Const REG_SZ = 1

Private Const KEY_SET_VALUE = &H2

Private Declare Function RegCloseKey Lib "advapi32.dll" _
        (ByVal hKey As Long) As Long
Private Declare Function RegOpenKeyEx Lib "advapi32.dll" _
        Alias "RegOpenKeyExA" _
        (ByVal hKey As Long, ByVal lpSubKey As String, _
        ByVal ulOptions As Long, ByVal samDesired As Long, _
        phkResult As Long) As Long
Private Declare Function RegSetValueEx Lib "advapi32.dll" _
        Alias "RegSetValueExA" _
        (ByVal hKey As Long, ByVal lpValueName As String, _
        ByVal Reserved As Long, ByVal dwType As Long, lpData As Any, _
        ByVal cbData As Long) As Long

Private Sub LoadByRegistry()

   Const cPGM As String = "C:\Test\TestStartup.exe"

   Dim hKey As Long, nResult As Long

   nResult = RegOpenKeyEx(HKEY_CURRENT_USER, _
            "Software\Microsoft\Windows\CurrentVersion\Run", 0, _
            KEY_SET_VALUE, hKey)

   If nResult = ERROR_SUCCESS Then
      RegSetValueEx hKey, "MyVBApp", 0, REG_SZ, ByVal cPGM, Len(cPGM)
      RegCloseKey hKey
   End If

End Sub
```

Example 1-7: -Writing to the registry using the Framework Class Library

```
Private Const cPGM As String = "C:\VB Forum\startup\TestStartup.exe"

Private Shared Sub LoadByRegistry()

    Dim oReg As RegistryKey = Registry.CurrentUser
    Dim oKey as RegistryKey = _
        oReg.OpenSubKey("Software\Microsoft\Windows\CurrentVersion\Run", _
        True)

    oKey.SetValue("MyVBApp", cPGM)

End Sub
```

A Common Runtime Environment

Although VB had traditionally shielded the developer from many of the intricacies of Windows as an operating system or of COM as a method for interoperability, nevertheless, some slight knowledge of how the system worked was essential, or the developer was sure to run into trouble sooner or later. For instance, consider the following code fragment for VB 6:

```
Dim oObj As New cSimpleClass

Set oObj = Nothing

If oObj Is Nothing Then
    ' Perform Cleanup
End If
```

Because of an idiosyncrasy of VB, objects declared and instantiated using the New keyword on the same line of code are not actually created until the first reference to that object. As a result, our attempt to determine if the object oObj is Nothing instead recreates the object, and our cleanup code never executes.

This, at least, is usually a relatively benign error. Much more pernicious, however, are circular object references, where COM objects hold references to one another and therefore cannot be released, even though they've been set to Nothing in code. This situation creates a memory leak that eventually can result in a General Protection Fault.

Under .NET, many problems like these are eliminated because of the .NET platform's Common Language Runtime (CLR). The CLR, as its name clearly implies, provides a variety of services to applications and processes running under the .NET platform, regardless of the language in which they were originally written. These services include memory management and garbage collection. They also include a unified system of exception handling, which makes it possible to use the same set of debugging tools on all code, regardless of the particular .NET language in which it was written.

What Can You Do with VB.NET?

With its language enhancements and its tight integration into the .NET Framework, Visual Basic is a thoroughly modernized language that will likely become the premier development tool for creating a wide range of .NET applications. In the past, Visual Basic was often seen as a "lightweight" language that could be used for particular kinds of tasks, but was wholly unsuitable for others. (It was often argued, sometimes incorrectly, that you couldn't create such things as Windows dynamic link libraries or shell extensions using Visual Basic.) In the .NET Framework, VB.NET emerges as an equal player; Microsoft's claim of language independence—that programming language should be a lifestyle choice, rather than a choice forced on the developer by the character of a project—is realized in the .NET platform.

This means that VB.NET can be used to create a wide range of applications and components, including the following:

- Windows console mode applications
- Standard Windows applications
- Windows services
- Windows controls and Windows control libraries
- Web (ASP.NET) applications
- Web services
- Web controls and web control libraries
- .NET classes and namespaces
- Accessing application object models (such as those of the individual applications in the Microsoft Office suite) using COM automation

Most importantly, for the first time with the release of VB.NET, Visual Basic becomes an all-purpose development environment for building Internet applications, an area in which it has traditionally been weak. This means that the release of this newest version should revitalize Visual Basic, allowing it to remain the tool of choice for developing state-of-the-art software for the next generation of software development.

CHAPTER 2

Program Structure

VB.NET, unlike previous versions of Visual Basic, is fully object-oriented. Also unlike previous versions, VB.NET is fully integrated with its underlying platform, the .NET Framework and the .NET Common Language Runtime. As shown in this chapter, these two factors, perhaps more than any others, influence the structure of a VB.NET program.

Getting a VB Program to Run

Any Visual Basic executable—i.e., a Windows Forms or Windows console application—has a single application-level entry point, a subroutine named *Main*. *Main* must be a method of the executed class.

 The web applications (either ASP.NET applications or web service applications) that you develop with Visual Studio are not executables. They exist as dynamic link libraries (DLLs) in the system's disk storage. ASP.NET applications may also rely on just-in-time compilation and be resident solely in memory.

Main must not only exist, it must also be:

A public routine
  In VB 6, *Main* could be either public or private. In VB.NET, it must be public to be visible as an entry point.

A static or shared routine
  Its declaration must include the Shared keyword. A single Main method must be shared by all application instances; it cannot be an instance method. Thus, all methods called by Main must also be static (or shared) methods; a shared method is unable to invoke an instance method.

15

This section focuses on executable programs. These programs exclude code libraries, as well as ASP.NET applications and web service applications, all of which are compiled as dynamic link libraries.

Console Applications

The requirement that there must be a subroutine named *Main* capable of serving as the executable's entry point is clear in a console application like the one shown in Example 2-1. The routine creates a module named modMain; that module in turn contains a subroutine named *Main*, which is the sole executable routine in the application. At runtime, *Main* serves as the program entry point; the Common Language Runtime finds the *Main* procedure, displays a message to the console, and then terminates the program.

Example 2-1: A simple console application

```
Option Strict On
Imports Microsoft.VisualBasic
Imports System

Public Module modMain

Public Sub Main
    Console.WriteLine("This is a console application.")
End Sub

End Module
```

The code in Example 2-1 should be familiar to Visual Basic programmers, since it depicts one of the methods used to define a program entry point in VB 6. In VB 6, this program would be stored in a separate standard module (*.bas*) file, which is shown in Example 2-2. As long as *Main* is identified as the startup point for the Visual Basic project, the VB runtime would find *Main* and execute it.

Example 2-2: A VB 6 version of a simple console application

```
Option Explicit

Private Sub Main()
    MsgBox "A simple console application."
End Sub
```

Although the VB.NET program in Example 2-1 seems similar to the VB 6 program in Example 2-2, under the hood, we would find important differences. If we use ILDASM to graphically depict the members of the VB.NET console application, as Figure 2-1 shows, we see that the VB.NET compiler translates our code module into a public class and gives it a single method, *Main*. If we examine the intermediate language (or IL) for Main (see Figure 2-2), we see that it is marked as the program entry point and that it is a shared method, rather than an instance method. The VB.NET compiler and the .NET Common Language Runtime, it would seem, have transformed our simple code module into a self-executing class.

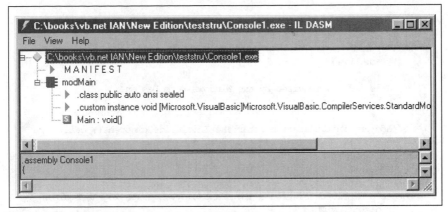

Figure 2-1: The modMain module in ILDASM

```
/ modMain::Main : void()                                              _ □ ×
.method public static void  Main() cil managed
{
  .entrypoint
  .custom instance void [mscorlib]System.STAThreadAttribute::.ctor() = ( 01 0
  // Code size       11 (0xb)
  .maxstack  8
  IL_0000:  ldstr       "This is a console application."
  IL_0005:  call        void [mscorlib]System.Console::WriteLine(string)
  IL_000a:  ret
} // end of method modMain::Main
```

Figure 2-2: IL for the Main procedure

Windows Forms Applications

The notion of a self-executing class is novel.[*] However, if we use Visual Studio .NET to create the simple Windows Forms application shown in Example 2-3, it is unclear exactly how the application is able to start, since the only entry point appears to be *New*, the class constructor. Because *New* executes when the New keyword is encountered (and as a result, the class is instantiated), it clearly cannot serve as a program entry point.

---

[*] If you designate a form as an application's startup object, previous versions of Visual Basic *appear* to create self-executing forms. This appearance applies only to forms, not to other Visual Basic classes (*.cls* files). In fact, it's not really true of forms; Visual Basic supplies the startup code, which includes the code used to instantiate the startup form. The program entry point is not located in the form.

Example 2-3: A simple Windows Forms application

```
Public Class Form1
    Inherits System.Windows.Forms.Form

#Region " Windows Form Designer generated code "

    Public Sub New()
        MyBase.New()

        'This call is required by the Windows Form Designer.
        InitializeComponent()

        'Add any initialization after the InitializeComponent() call

    End Sub

    'Form overrides dispose to clean up the component list.
    Protected Overloads Overrides Sub Dispose(ByVal disposing As Boolean)
        If disposing Then
            If Not (components Is Nothing) Then
                components.Dispose()
            End If
        End If
        MyBase.Dispose(disposing)
    End Sub

    'Required by the Windows Form Designer
    Private components As System.ComponentModel.IContainer

    'NOTE: The following procedure is required by the Windows Form Designer
    'It can be modified using the Windows Form Designer.
    'Do not modify it using the code editor.
    Friend WithEvents Button1 As System.Windows.Forms.Button

    <System.Diagnostics.DebuggerStepThrough()> _
    Private Sub InitializeComponent()
        Me.Button1 = New System.Windows.Forms.Button()
        Me.SuspendLayout()
        '
        'Button1
        '
        Me.Button1.Location = New System.Drawing.Point(104, 48)
        Me.Button1.Name = "Button1"
        Me.Button1.Size = New System.Drawing.Size(88, 48)
        Me.Button1.TabIndex = 0
        Me.Button1.Text = "Button1"
        '
        'Form1
        '
        Me.AutoScaleBaseSize = New System.Drawing.Size(5, 13)
        Me.ClientSize = New System.Drawing.Size(292, 165)
        Me.Controls.AddRange(New System.Windows.Forms.Control() {Me.Button1})
        Me.Name = "Form1"
```

Example 2-3: A simple Windows Forms application (continued)

```
    Me.Text = "Form1"
    Me.ResumeLayout(False)

End Sub

#End Region

Private Sub Button1_Click(ByVal sender As System.Object, _
                    ByVal e As System.EventArgs) _
                    Handles Button1.Click
    MsgBox("This is a Windows Forms application.")
End Sub
End Class
```

However, ILDASM gives a slightly different picture of this Windows Forms application. In Figure 2-3, we see that in addition to the methods defined in the source code either by us or in the code autogenerated by Visual Studio, the VB.NET compiler has generated a Main method automatically and transparently.

When examining the IL for the Main method (see Example 2-4), it becomes clear why code for the Main method is not more obvious and how the method itself works. As Example 2-4 shows, the method is declared public but is marked as hidden. Once again, the method is declared static or shared. The method operates by invoking the class constructor, then calling the Application object's Run method to launch an instance of the form. Note that the Application object's Run method is a shared or static method, rather than an instance method.

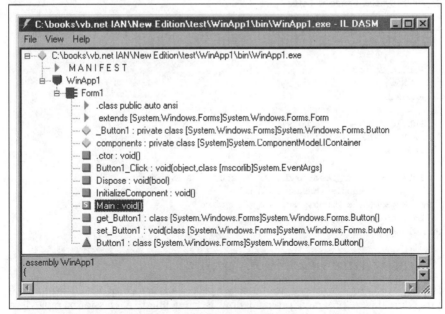

Figure 2-3: The Windows Forms application in ILDASM

Example 2-4: IL for the Main method

```
.method public hidebysig static void  Main() cil managed
{
  .entrypoint
  .custom instance void
          [mscorlib]System.STAThreadAttribute::.ctor() = ( 01 00 00 00 )
  // Code size       14 (0xe)
  .maxstack  8
  IL_0000:  nop
  IL_0001:  newobj instance void WinApp1.Form1::.ctor()
  IL_0006:  call    void
          [System.Windows.Forms]System.Windows.Forms.Application::Run(
          class [System.Windows.Forms]System.Windows.Forms.Form)
  IL_000b:  nop
  IL_000c:  nop
  IL_000d:  ret
} // end of method Form1::Main
```

We can simplify our Windows Forms application by coding outside of Visual Studio. The result is shown in Example 2-5.

Example 2-5: A simple Windows forms application created without Visual Studio

```
Option Strict On

Imports Microsoft.VisualBasic
Imports System
Imports System.ComponentModel
Imports System.Windows.Forms

Public Class MyForm
   Inherits Form

   Public Shared Sub Main()
       Application.Run(New MyForm)
   End Sub

   Public Sub New()
      MyBase.New()
   End Sub

   Public Sub Form_Load(sender As Object, e As EventArgs) _
            Handles MyBase.Load
      MsgBox("The Windows Forms application.")
   End Sub
End Class
```

The Structure of a VB Program

Broadly speaking, programs can be either *procedure driven* or *event driven*. In a procedure-driven program, program flow is predefined. A classic example is a console application: program flow begins at the program entry point (in the case of a .NET console application, it begins with the *Main* routine) and proceeds along a predictable path until it reaches program termination. In an event-driven program, on the other hand, program flow is not predetermined and is instead controlled by external events (i.e., by the program's interaction with the user and the system), and possibly by internal events as well.

From the perspective of program structure, the difference between procedure-driven and event-driven programs is less sharp than is usually thought. Both rely on a procedure as an entry point, which in turn can call other functions and subroutines that are visible to it. The major difference is that a procedure-driven program has a single entry point, whereas an event-driven program has multiple entry points. For event-driven programs, these entry points (in addition to the required *Main* procedure) are *event handlers*, which are invoked automatically by the .NET Common Language Runtime in response to an event within the code itself or in its environment.

Therefore, regardless of whether an application is procedure driven or event driven, Visual Basic code can be divided into three main categories:

Entry point code
> For procedural applications, this code is a routine named *Main*. For an event-driven application, it is a routine named *Main*, supplemented by code that you write to handle events such as a button being clicked by the user. These latter procedures are called event handlers.

Custom procedures
> In these procedures, you create the main functionality of your application. When these custom procedures are located within a class, they are termed methods and are typically used to perform an operation.

Property procedures
> These procedures are used in form and class modules, typically to retrieve or set the value of a class attribute.

For the rest of this section, we'll discuss program structure by focusing on applications that fire events, which ultimately control program flow.

Events: The Starting Point

Aside from the obligatory Sub *Main*, which serves as the initial entry point for an application, an event provides an entry point into your code for any event-driven program. In other words, once the application is launched and the code in the application entry point has executed, an application can have numerous entry points that are invoked by the Common Language Runtime in response to particular events. An event can be system generated, such as the Load event of a form or a Timer control event, or it can be a user-generated event, such as the Click event on a command button. In can also be a custom event that you define in your code. For example, a stock monitoring application might generate a Positive event when a stock's value changes from negative to positive, and a Negative event when its value changes from positive to negative.

For a discussion of events and the way in which procedures can be defined to handle events, see Chapter 7.

Windows Forms events

For a Windows Form application in which a form serves as the startup object, the order of execution of code is as follows:

The Main procedure
The New constructor
The Load event
The Activated event
The Closing event
The Closed event
The Dispose event

Individual controls also expose events.

ASP.NET events

ASP.NET exposes a more complex event model, in which events can be trapped at the application, session, and page level. Table 2-1 illustrates the sequence of application, session, and page events for an ASP.NET application.

Table 2-1: ASP.NET events

Event	Type	Description
Start	Application	Fired when the application starts. The event handler must reside in *global.asaz*.
Start	Session	Fired when a user session is created. The event handler must reside in *global.asaz*.
Init	Page	Fired when the page is initialized.
Load	Page	Fired when the page is loaded.
PreRender	Page	Fired when the page is about to be rendered.
Unload	Page	Fired when the page is unloaded.
Disposed	Page	Fired when the page is released from memory.
End	Session	Fired when a user session ends or times out.
End	Application	Fired when an application ends. The event handler must reside in *global.asaz*.

Individual controls also expose events.

 For a full discussion of the events that fire when an object reference becomes null or when an application ends, see the section "Finalize, Dispose, and Garbage Collection" in Chapter 4.

Event arguments

Typically, when an event is fired, the CLR passes two arguments to the event handler:

sender
> An object of type Object that represents the instance of the class raising the event

e
> An object of type EventArgs or of a type derived from EventArgs that contains information about the event

For example, Example 2-6 shows an event handler for a Button object's Click event in a Windows application.

Example 2-6: A Button object's event handler

```
Option Strict On
Imports Microsoft.VisualBasic
Imports System
Imports System.Drawing
Imports System.Windows.Forms

Public Class CEvent
    Inherits System.Windows.Forms.Form

Friend WithEvents oBtn As Button

Private Sub New()
    oBtn = New Button

    Dim x As Integer = CInt(Me.Width/2 - oBtn.Width / 2)
    Dim y As Integer = CInt(Me.Height/2 - oBtn.Height / 2)

    Me.oBtn.Location = New System.Drawing.Point(x, y)
    Me.oBtn.Text = "Event Information"

    Me.Controls.Add(oBtn)
End Sub

Public Shared Sub Main
    Application.Run(New CEvent)
End Sub

Private Sub oBtn_Click(sender As Object, e As EventArgs) _
                Handles oBtn.Click
    MsgBox(sender.GetType.ToString & vbCrLf & _
        e.GetType.ToString)
End Sub
End Class
```

When the event is fired, the dialog shown in Figure 2-4 is displayed.

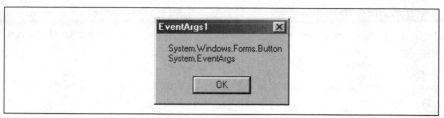

Figure 2-4: A dialog box displaying event information

The EventArgs class itself has no useful members; all of its members are inherited from the Object class. Most event handlers are passed an instance of the Event-Args class. Sometimes, however, the event handler is passed useful information about the event. In this case, the event handler's second parameter is an instance of a class derived from EventArgs; its added members provide information about the event. For example, the Button and ImageButton controls in the System.Web. UI.WebControls namespace raise a Command event that is fired when the control is clicked. Instead of an instance of the EventArgs class, the CLR passes the event handler an instance of the CommandEventArgs class. It has the following properties:

CommandName property
> The name of the command to be executed. It corresponds to the Button or ImageButton control's CommandName property.

CommandArgument property
> Any optional arguments passed along with the command.

In some cases, an event's default action can be cancelled by modifying the member of the class instance derived from EventArgs. For instance, the Cancel-EventArgs class is derived from EventArgs and is the base class of InputLanguageChangingEventArgs, TreeViewCancelEventArgs, and PrintEvent-Args. By setting its Cancel property to True, you can cancel a pending application print job programmatically, cancel a change of language, or cancel the checking, expansion, collapse, or selection of a TreeView item.

Calling Routines from Event Handlers

An event handler, in turn, can call methods, functions, or procedures and can set and retrieve property values. These values can reside in the .NET Framework Class Library, or they can be custom functions in code modules or methods in custom classes that you wrote. For example, in Example 2-7, the Click event from a Button control named btnSave demonstrates this approach to event handling.

Example 2-7: Calling an external routine from an event handler

```
Private Sub btnSave_Click(sender As Object, e As EventArgs) _
                    Handles btnSave.Click

Try
   If SaveDetails(strFileName) Then
```

```
    MsgBox("Details Saved OK", vbInformation)
Else
    MsgBox("Details have not been saved", vbCritical)
End If
Catch ex As Exception
    MsgBox(ex.Message)
End Try

End Sub
```

Because the SaveDetails method contains all the code to actually save the details, the function can be called from anywhere in the class.

Writing Custom Procedures

Placing all code in event handlers is often inconvenient. Particularly when more than one event handler needs to execute the same code, it is preferable to write that code only once and call it from each event handler or any other routine that needs to access it. For this purpose, Visual Basic supports custom procedures. To create a new procedure, move to the bottom of the code window and type the Function or Sub definition before the **End Module** or **End Class** statement.

The three main types of custom procedures in Visual Basic include:

- Functions
- Sub procedures
- Properties

Functions

A function is a collection of related statements and expressions used to perform a particular task. When it completes execution, the function returns a value to the calling statement. If you don't specify an explicit return value for the function, the default value of the return data type is returned. If you write a custom function in a class module and declare it as **Public**, it will become a class method.

Here's a quick example of a function used to provide a minimum number:

```
Private Function MinNumber(ByVal iNumber As Integer) As Integer

    If iNumber >= 500 Then
        MinNumber = iNumber
    Else
        MinNumber = 500
    End If

End Function
```

Because functions return a value, you can use them as part of an expression in place of a value. In the following snippet, the string passed to the VB *Instr* function is a custom function that returns the customer name corresponding to a customer code:

```
If InStr(1, GetCustomerName(sCustCode), "P") > 0 Then
```

For full details on the syntax and use of functions, see the entry for the Function statement in Chapter 10.

Sub procedures

A Sub procedure is used just like a function, except it does not return a value and therefore cannot be used as part of an argument. Visual Basic uses Sub procedures to provide event handling.

Generally, you should use functions rather than Subs to create custom procedures. Functions allow you to return a value, which, minimally, could be a Boolean True or False, to inform the caller that the function has succeeded or failed. Tests indicate that there is no performance hit for coding a routine as a function instead of a procedure.

Like a function, if you write a custom Sub in a class module and declare it as Public, it will become a class method.

For full details of the syntax and use of Sub procedures, see the entry for the Sub statement in Chapter 10.

Property procedures

Property procedures are specialized procedures used to assign and retrieve custom property values. They can only be included in class definitions marked by the Class...End Class statement. Property procedures are defined within a Property...End Property statement and can take either of two forms:

Property accessors
   Retrieve the value of a property, returning it to the caller

Property mutators
   Assign a value to or modify a property's value

Example 2-8, which defines a simple class with only one property, illustrates the syntax for property procedures.

Example 2-8: A property

```
Public Class CPerson

Dim sName As String

Public Property Name As String
    Get             ' Property accessor
        Return sName
    End Get
    Set             ' Property mutator
```

Example 2-8: A property (continued)

```
      sName = Value
   End Set
End Property

End Class
```

Internally, properties are implemented as methods. Visual Basic implements each property accessor as a get_*propertyname* method, while each mutator is implemented as a set_*propertyname* method. This implementation is evident in Figure 2-5, in which ILDASM displays two additional methods for the CPerson class that we created in Example 2-8, and Figure 2-6, in which ILDASM displays the IL for the Name property and shows that property references are resolved as separate calls to the get_Name and set_Name methods.

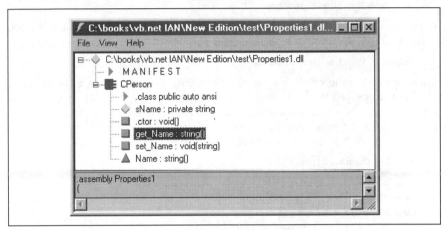

Figure 2-5: CPerson class members

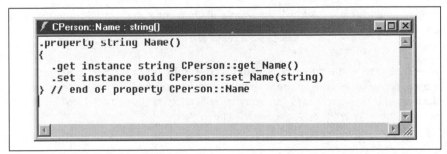

Figure 2-6: IL for the Name property

Controlling Execution Flow

Now you've got your event handlers. These handlers will spring into life when the user clicks a button or a form loads. You've also written some useful functions that do all the work behind the scenes. How do you link the two together?

Calling sub and function procedures

Methods and functions or procedures can be called in one of two ways. In the case of a procedure, or in the case of a method or function whose return value is to be discarded, the `Call` statement can be used. Its syntax is:

```
Call routine([argumentlist])
```

where *routine* is the name of the function, procedure, or a class or class instance along with the name of its method, and *argumentlist* is a comma-delimited list of arguments expected by the routine. The argument list must always be enclosed in parentheses. For example:

```
Call Console.WriteLine("The Save operation completed successfully.")
```

or

```
Call SaveDetails(sFileName)
```

The `Call` statement can also be omitted. If it is omitted, the syntax for a method or function whose return value is being stored to a variable is:

```
retval = routine([argumentlist[)
```

where *retval* is the function or method's return value, *routine* is the name of the function, procedure, or a class (or class instance along with its method), and *argumentlist* is a comma-delimited list of arguments expected by the routine. The argument list must always be enclosed in parentheses. The syntax for a method or procedure that does not return a value is:

```
routine([argumentlist])
```

Note again that the argument list must be enclosed in parentheses. This requirement contrasts with VB 6, which allows only a single parameter to be enclosed in parentheses in this instance.

Setting and retrieving property values

Property values can be set using a simple assignment statement with the property on the left side of the equals sign. The syntax is:

```
object.property = value
```

where *object* is the name of a shared class or an object instance, *property* is the property name, and *value* is the value to be assigned to the property. When dealing with property arrays (an array or collection of property values), an index into the property array is also required. The syntax is:

```
object.property(index) = value
```

where *index* is the zero-based ordinal position of the property array element whose value is to be changed, or the key value if the property array supports access by keys.

Property values can also be retrieved by using a simple assignment statement with the property on the right side of the equals sign. The syntax is:

```
value = object.property
```

where *value* is the value of the property, *object* is the name of a shared class or an object instance, and *property* is the property name. When dealing with property arrays (an array or collection of property values), an index into the property array is also required. The syntax is:

```
value = object.property(index)
```

where *index* is the zero-based ordinal position of the property array element whose value is to be changed, or the key value if the property array supports access by keys.

CHAPTER 3

Variables and Data Types

Many programmers take the concept of a variable for granted. In this chapter, we take a close look at variables and their properties, discussing such things as the scope and lifetime of a variable.

Variables

A *variable* can be defined as an entity that has the following six properties:

Name

A variable's name is used to identify the variable in code. In VB.NET, a variable name can start with a Unicode alphabetic character or an underscore, and can be followed by additional underscore characters or various Unicode characters, such as alphabetic, numeric, formatting, or combined characters.

Address

Every variable has an associated memory address, which is the location in memory at which the variable's value is stored. Note that in many circumstances, the address of a variable will change during its lifetime, so it would be dangerous to make any assumptions about this address.

Type

The *type* of a variable, also called its *data type*, determines the possible values that the variable can assume. We discuss data types in detail later in the chapter.

Value

The value of a variable is the contents of the memory location at the address of the variable. This is also sometimes referred to as the *r-value* of the variable, since it is what really appears on the right side of an assignment statement. For instance, in the code:

```
Dim i As Integer
Dim j As Integer
i = 5
j = i
```

the final statement can be read as "assign the *value* of i to memory at the address of j." For similar reasons, the address of a variable is sometimes called its *l-value.*

Scope

The scope of a variable determines where in a program that variable is visible to the code. Scope is discussed in detail in the next section.

Lifetime

A variable's lifetime determines when and for how long a particular variable exists. It may or may not be visible (that is, be in scope) for that entire period. For a detailed discussion of lifetime, see the "Variable Lifetime" section later in this chapter.

Variable Scope

Variables (and constants) have a *scope*, which indicates where in the program the variable is recognized or *visible* to the code—that is, where it can be referred to in code.

Local variables: block-level and procedure-level scope

If a variable is declared inside a *code block* (a set of statements that is terminated by an End..., Loop, or Next statement), then the variable has *block-level scope*; that is, it is visible only within that block.

For example, consider the following code:

```
If x <> 0 Then
    Dim rec As Integer
    rec = 1/x
End If
MsgBox CStr(rec)
```

In this code, the variable *rec* is not recognized outside the block in which it is defined, so the final statement produces an error.

It is important to note that the *lifetime* of a variable always refers to the entire procedure, even if the variable's scope is block-level. (We discuss this in the "Variable Lifetime" section later in this chapter.) This implies that if a block is entered more than once, a block-level variable will retain its value from the previous time the block code was executed.

A variable declared using the Dim keyword within a Visual Basic procedure but not within a code block has *procedure-level scope*. Its scope consists of the procedure in which it is declared.

A variable that has block-level scope or procedure-level scope is called a *local* variable. One of the advantages of local variables is that the same name can be used in different procedures without conflict, since each variable is visible only to its own procedure. Another is that the memory allocated to the variable can be released as soon as control leaves the procedure, making our code easier to maintain.

Module-level and project-level scope

There are differences in the way scope is handled for variables declared in the Declarations section of a standard module and a class module. We restrict our discussion here to standard modules, postponing a discussion of class modules until Chapter 4.

We first note that a standard module itself can be declared using one of the access modifiers Public, Friend, or Private (this is the default). Using such a modifier simply restricts the individual members to that level of access at most. Thus, for instance, a Public variable declared in a Friend module has only Friend scope.

Private access. A variable declared in the Declarations section of a *standard* module using the Private access modifier has *module-level scope*; that is, it is visible in the entire module, but nowhere else. Using the Dim keyword also gives the variable module-level scope, but its use is not as clear and should be avoided for readability sake.

Friend access. A variable declared in the Declarations section of a standard module using the Friend access modifier is visible in the entire project and thus has *project-level scope.* However, it is not visible to other projects.

Public access. A variable declared in the Declarations section of a Public standard module using the Public access modifier is visible not only to the project in which it is declared, but also to any external project that holds a reference to the project. For instance, consider the following module declared in Project1:

```
Public Module Module1
    Public iModulePublic As Integer
    Friend iModuleFriend As Integer
End Module
```

If Project2 has a reference to Project1, then we can write:

```
Project1.Module1.iModulePublic = 100
```

However, the code:

```
Project1.Module1.iModuleFriend = 100
```

generates a "not accessible" syntax error.

Variable Lifetime

Variables also have a *lifetime*. The difference between lifetime and scope is quite simple. Lifetime refers to *when*, or at what time during program execution the variable is valid; scope refers to *where* in the program the variable is recognized by (visible to) the code.

To illustrate the difference, consider the following procedure:

```
Sub ProcedureA()
    Dim LocalVar As Integer = 0
    Call ProcedureB
    LocalVar = 1
End Sub
```

Note that *LocalVar* is a local variable. When the line:

```
Call ProcedureB
```

is executed, execution switches to *ProcedureB*. While the lines of *ProcedureB* are being executed, the variable *LocalVar* is out of scope since it is local to *ProcedureA*. But it is still valid. In other words, the variable still exists and has a value. It is simply not accessible to the code in *ProcedureB*. In fact, *ProcedureB* could also have a local variable named *LocalVar*, which would have nothing to do with the variable of the same name in *ProcedureA*.

Once *ProcedureB* has completed, execution continues in *ProcedureA* with the line:

```
LocalVar = 1
```

which is a valid instruction, since the variable *LocalVar* is back in scope.

Thus, the lifetime of the local variable *LocalVar* extends from the moment *ProcedureA* is entered to the moment it is terminated, including the period during which *ProcedureB* is being executed as a result of the call to this procedure, even though during that period, *LocalVar* is out of scope.

We mention again that the lifetime of a block-level variable is the lifetime of the procedure in which it is defined.

Static variables

We have seen that a variable may go in and out of scope during its lifetime. However, once the lifetime of a variable expires, the variable is destroyed and its value is lost. It is the lifetime that determines the *existence* of a variable; its scope determines its visibility.

Thus, consider the following procedures:

```
Sub ProcedureA()
    Call ProcedureB
    Call ProcedureB
    Call ProcedureB
    Call ProcedureB
    Call ProcedureB
End Sub

Sub ProcedureB()
    Dim x As Integer
    x = 5
    . . .
End Sub
```

When *ProcedureA* is executed, it simply calls *ProcedureB* five times. Each time *ProcedureB* is called, the local variable *x* is created anew and destroyed at the end of that call. Thus, *x* is created and destroyed five times.

Normally, this is just what we want. However, there are times when we would like the lifetime of a local variable to persist longer than the lifetime of the procedure in which it is declared. For example, we may want a procedure to do something special the first time it is called, but not in subsequent times.

A *static variable* is a local variable whose lifetime is the lifetime of the entire program. The following VB code shows how one might use a static variable:

```
Sub test()

Static bFirstTime As Boolean = True

If bFirstTime Then
    Debug.WriteLine("first time")
    bFirstTime = False
Else
    Debug.WriteLine("not first time")
End If

End Sub
```

Note that we can initialize a static variable, provided that we do so *within the variable declaration*. The following code illustrates this point:

```
Sub StaticTest()
    Static st As Boolean = True    ' initialize static variable
    MsgBox(st)
    st = False
End Sub

Private Sub button1_Click(ByVal sender As System.Object, _
    ByVal e As System.EventArgs) Handles button1.Click
    StaticTest()
End Sub
```

The first time we hit the button1 command button, *StaticTest* displays the message True, because the static variable *st* has been initialized to True. However, all subsequent times we hit the button, *StaticTest* returns False. This ability to initialize a static variable was missing and was a very annoying oversight in earlier versions of VB.

We could accomplish the same effect by using a module-level variable to keep a record of whether the procedure has been called, instead of a static local variable. However, it is considered better programming style to use the most restrictive scope possible, which, in this case, is a local variable with an "extended" lifetime. This helps prevent accidental alteration of the variable in other portions of the code. (Remember that this code may be part of a much larger code module, with a lot of things going on.)

Declaring Variables and Constants

A *variable declaration* is an association of a variable name with a data type. In and of itself, this does not imply variable creation. However, for nonobject variables, a variable declaration does create a variable. A declaration such as:

```
Dim x As Integer
```

creates an Integer variable named *x*. We can also write:

```
Dim x As Integer = New Integer()
```

which emphasizes the role of the constructor function for the Integer data type. (The *constructor* is the function that VB.NET uses to create the variable.)

When multiple variables are declared on the same line, if a variable is not declared with an explicit type declaration, then its type is that of the next variable with an explicit type declaration. Thus, in the line:

```
Dim x As Long, i, j, k As Integer, s As String
```

the variables i, j, and k have type Integer. (In VB 6, the variables i and j would have type Variant, which is VB 6's default data type.)

VB.NET permits the initialization of variables in the same line as their declaration (at long last!). Thus, we may write:

```
Dim x As Integer = 5
```

to declare an Integer variable and initialize it to 5. Similarly, we can declare and initialize more than one variable on a single line:

```
Dim x As Integer = 6, y As Integer = 9
```

Note that in this case, each variable that you declare must explicitly be assigned a data type. You cannot assign each variable an explicit value without explicitly declaring the data type of each variable.

Object variables are declared in the same manner:

```
Dim obj As MyClass
```

However, this declaration does not create an object variable, and the variable is equal to Nothing at this point. Object creation requires an explicit call to the object's constructor, as in:

```
Dim obj As New MyClass()
```

or:

```
Dim obj As MyClass = New Myclass()
```

or:

```
Dim obj As MyClass
obj = New MyClass()
```

Variables and constants can be declared with any of the following *access modifiers*:

- `Public`
- `Private`
- `Friend`
- `Protected`
- `Protected Friend`

Note also that the Dim keyword can be used as well, but it often defaults to one of the previously mentioned access modifiers. This is potentially confusing, so the Dim keyword should be used only when required, as it is for local variables.

Access modifiers help to specify the scope and accessibility of the variable. We discuss the meaning of these access variables in detail in Chapter 4.

Constant declarations are analogous to variable declarations and have the form:

```
AccessModifier Const Name As Type = Value
```

where *AccessModifier* is one of the access modifiers defined earlier. Note that when Option Strict is On (the default), all constant declarations must have a declared type.

Data Types

The .NET Common Language Runtime (CLR) includes the *Common Type System* (CTS), which defines the data types that are supported by the CLR. Thus, each of the languages in the .NET Framework (VB, C#, JScript, and Managed C++) implements a subset of a common set of data types. We say subset because, unfortunately, not all of the CTS types are implemented by VB.NET. For instance, the CTS includes some unsigned integer data types that are not implemented in VB.

As an aside, it is possible to use the VB-unsupported data types in VB by direct use of the corresponding Framework Class Library class. Here is an example illustrating the ability to use the unsigned 16-bit integer data type, whose range of values is 0 to 65,535. Note the use of the ToUInt16 method of the Convert class to actually get an unsigned 16-bit integer:

```
Dim ui As UInt16
ui = Convert.ToUInt16(65535)
MsgBox(ui.ToString)
```

Thus, the native VB data types are wrappers for the CTS data types. To illustrate, the VB Integer data type is a wrapper for the Int32 structure that is part of the .NET Framework's System namespace. One of the members of the Int32 structure is MaxValue, which returns the maximum value allowed for this data type. Thus, even though MaxValue is not officially part of VB.NET (nor is it mentioned in the VB documentation), we can write:

```
Dim i As Integer
MsgBox(i.Maxvalue)    ' Displays 2147483647
```

Value and Reference Types

The types defined in the CTS fall into three categories:

- Value types
- Reference types
- Pointer types

However, pointer types are not implemented in VB, so we will not discuss these types.

The difference between value and reference types is how variables of the corresponding type represent that type. When a value-type variable is defined, as in:

```
Dim int As Integer = 5
```

a memory location is set aside to hold the actual data (in this case the number 5). In contrast, when a reference-type variable is defined, as in:

```
Dim obj As New CEmployee
```

the VB compiler creates the object in memory, but then sets the variable *obj* to a 4-byte memory location that contains the address of the object.

In short, value-type variables *contain* the data, whereas reference-type variables *point to* the data.

The distinction between value type and reference type has several consequences, one of which is in the way assignments work. To illustrate, consider the following class, which has a single property:

```
Public Class MyClass
    Public Age As Short
End Class
```

and the structure **MyStruct**, also with a single property:

```
Structure MyStruct
    Public Age As Short
End Structure
```

Classes are reference types, whereas structures are value types. Now consider the following code, which is thoroughly commented:

```
' Declare two class variables and two structure variables.
Dim objRef1 As MyClass
Dim objRef2 As MyClass
Dim objValue1 As MyStruct
Dim objValue2 As MyStruct

' Instance the class.
objRef1 = New MyClass()
' Set the Age property to 20.
objRef1.Age = 20
' Set the second variable to the first variable.
' This is an equating of object *references* because
' classes are reference types.
objRef2 = objRef1
' Set the Age property of objRef2 to 30.
objRef2.Age = 30
' Check the values of the Age property.
Debug.WriteLine(objRef1.Age)
Debug.WriteLine(objRef2.Age)

' Do the same thing with the structure

' Instance the structure.
objValue1 = New MyStruct()
' Set the Age property to 20.
objValue1.Age = 20
' Set the second variable to the first variable.
' This is an equating of object *values* because
' structures are value types.
```

```
objValue2 = objValue1
' Set the Age property of objValue2 to 30.
objValue2.Age = 30
' Check the values of the Age property.
Debug.Writeline(objValue1.Age)
Debug.Writeline(objValue2.Age)
```

Now, the output is:

```
30
30
20
30
```

To understand what is happening, we need to realize that the reference assignment:

```
objRef2 = objRef1
```

sets both variables to the same value. But that value is the address of the object, and so both variables point to the same object. Hence, when we change the Age property using the second variable, this change is also reflected in the first variable.

On the other hand, the value assignment:

```
objValue2 = objValue1
```

causes a second structure to be created, setting the new structure's properties to the same value as the original structure. Thus, changing one structure's Age property does not affect the other structure's Age property.

Note that the VB Array type is also a reference type. To illustrate, consider the following code:

```
Dim iArray1() As Integer = {1, 2, 3}
Dim iArray2() As Integer

iArray2 = iArray1
iArray1(0) = 100
msgbox(iArray2(0))
```

The message box displays 100, indicating that both array variables point to the same array.

The String data type is a reference type, implemented by the String class. However, it has some characteristics of a value type. To illustrate, consider the following code:

```
Dim s1, s2 As String
s1 = "String 1"
s2 = s1
s2 = "String 2"
MsgBox(s1)
```

Since this is a reference type, we would expect the last line to produce the message "String 2", but instead we get "String 1". The reason can be found in Microsoft's documentation:

An instance of String is "immutable" because its value cannot be modified once it has been created. Methods that appear to modify a String actually return a new instance of String containing the modification.

Thus, the code:

```
s2 = s1
```

points s2 to the same string as s1, as is usual with reference types. Then the attempt to modify the string in the code:

```
s2 = "String 2"
```

does not produce the expected result because strings are immutable. Instead, we get a new string pointed to by s2, while s1 retains its value.

The following code supports this conclusion:

```
Dim s1, s2 As String
s1 = "String 1"
' s2 poitns to same string as s1
s2 = s1
' Show s2 before any changes to the string
MsgBox(s2)       ' Displays "String1"
' Change the string
s2 = "String 2"
' Set s1 to Nothing
s1 = Nothing
' Now s1 is nothing and displays accordingly
MsgBox(s1)       ' Displays nothing
' s2 is a new string
MsgBox(s2)       ' Displays "String 2"
```

Enjoy!

VB Data Types: A Summary

The following lists the data types supported by VB.NET, along with their underlying .NET type, storage requirements, and range of values:

Boolean

> .NET CTS type: System.Boolean
>
> Type: Value (Structure)
>
> Storage: 2 bytes
>
> Value range: **True** or **False**

Byte

> .NET CTS type: System.Byte
>
> Type: Value (Structure)
>
> Storage: 1 byte
>
> Value range: 0 to 255 (unsigned)

Char

> .NET CTS type: System.Char

Type: Value (Structure)

Storage: 2 bytes

Value range: A character code from 0 to 65,535 (unsigned)

Date
.NET CTS type: System.DateTime

Type: Value (Structure)

Storage: 8 bytes

Value range: January 1, 1 CE to December 31, 9999

Decimal
.NET CTS type: System.Decimal

Type: Value (Structure)

Storage: 12 bytes

Value range: +/–79,228,162,514,264,337,593,543,950,335 with no decimal point; +/–7.9228162514264337593543950335 with 28 places to the right of the decimal; smallest nonzero number is +/–0.0000000000000000000000000001

Double (double-precision floating point)
.NET CTS type: System.Double

Type: Value (Structure)

Storage: 8 bytes

Value range: –1.79769313486231E308 to –4.94065645841247E–324 for negative values; 4.94065645841247E–324 to 1.79769313486232E308 for positive values

Integer
.NET CTS type: System.Int32

Type: Value (Structure)

Storage: 4 bytes

Value range: –2,147,483,648 to 2,147,483,647

Long (long integer)
.NET CTS type: System.Int64

Type: Value (Structure)

Storage: 8 bytes

Value range: –9,223,372,036,854,775,808 to 9,223,372,036,854,775,807

Object
.NET CTS type: System.Object

Type: Reference (Class)

Storage: 4 bytes

Value range: Any type can be stored in an Object variable.

Short
.NET CTS type: System.Int16

Type: Value (Structure)

Storage: 2 bytes

Value range: –32,768 to 32,767

Single (single precision floating point)
.NET CTS type: System.Single

Type: Value (Structure)

Storage: 4 bytes

Value range: –3.402823E38 to –1.401298E–45 for negative values; 1.401298E–45 to 3.402823E38 for positive values

String (variable-length)
.NET CTS type: System.String

Type: Reference (Class)

Storage: 10 bytes + (2 * string length)

Value range: 0 to approximately 2 billion Unicode characters

User-Defined Type (structure)
.NET CTS type: (inherits from System.ValueType)

Type: Value (Structure)

Storage: Sum of the sizes of its members

Value range: Each structure member has range determined by its data type and is independent of the ranges of the other members.

Note that the CTS data types are either structures (which are value types) or classes (which are reference types) and are located within the .NET System namespace.

Simple Data Types in Visual Basic

In this section, we discuss data types in general and VB.NET data types in particular.

Simple data types can be classified into groups as follows. Note that these groups are *not* mutually exclusive:

Numeric data type
A data type in which the underlying set is a set of numbers and for which the set of operations includes the arithmetic operations.

Integer data type
A numeric data type in which the underlying set is a set of integers. (As we will see, VB has several integer data types.)

Floating-point data type
A noninteger data type whose underlying set is a subset of the rational numbers.

Boolean data type
A data type whose underlying set has size 2. This set is usually thought of as {True, False}.

Character data type

A data type whose underlying set is a set of characters. Of course, each value must be represented in memory as a binary string, which can also be interpreted as a number. Nevertheless, this interpretation is not part of a character data type.

Let us consider the Visual Basic .NET data types individually.

Boolean data type

The Boolean is a 16-bit data type that can only represent two values: `True` and `False`. The VB keywords `True` and `False` are used to assign these values to a Boolean variable.

When a numeric value is converted to Boolean, any nonzero value is converted to `True`, and zero is converted to `False`. In the other direction, `False` is converted to zero, and `True` is converted to –1. (Incidentally, in C, C#, and C++, `True` is converted to 1. This change was made in Beta 1 of VB.NET to bring it in line with the other languages, but was subsequently changed back in Beta 2.)

The underlying .NET data type for Boolean is System.Boolean.

Byte data type

The Byte data type is an 8-bit unsigned data type whose range is the set of integers from 0 to 255. According to the documentation, the Byte data type "is used for containing binary data." Since ordinary arithmetic operations can be used with Byte variables, the data type is, in this sense, an integer data type. Also, there do not appear to be any special operators, such as shift operators, that would give the type a "binary data" flavor. Oh well.

The underlying .NET data type for Byte is System.Byte.

Char data type

The Char data type is a 16-bit character data type with a character code ranging from 0 to 65,535, which represent a single Unicode character. As a data type, Char is new to VB.NET; there was no equivalent in previous versions of Visual Basic.

It is important not to confuse the Char and String data types. (We discuss this data type in the "String data type" section.) A string consisting of a single character is *not* the same as a Char. To illustrate, consider defining a new string and initializing it to a sequence consisting of a repeated single character, for example, "AAAAA." In earlier versions of VB, this was done as follows:

```
Dim s As String
s = String$(5, "A")
```

In VB.NET, this is done using the String class constructor, which has the syntax:

```
Dim variable As New String(Character, Integer)
```

If we turn strict type checking on with the `Option Strict On` statement, the code:

```
Dim s As New String("A",5)
```

produces the error message, "Option Strict disallows implicit conversions from String to Char."

To get a Char, we must append a c to the end of the string literal. Thus, the following works:

```
Dim s As New String("A"c, 5)
```

The underlying .NET data type for Char is System.Char.

Date data type

Date values are stored as IEEE 64-bit long integers that can represent dates in the range January 1, 0001 to December 31, 9999 (which should be plenty), and times from 0:00:00 to 23:59:59.

Literal strings must be enclosed in number signs (#) to be recognized as dates. The VB.NET compiler changes date formats automatically. For instance, if we enter the code:

```
Dim d As Date
d = #November 9, 1948#
Msgbox(d)
```

the compiler changes the second line to:

```
d = #11/9/1948#
```

or whatever the regional settings on the host system dictate. The .NET equivalent of Date is System.DateTime.

Decimal data type

Values of the Decimal data type are stored as 96-bit (12-byte) signed integers, along with an internal scale factor ranging from 0 to 28, which is applied automatically when we set a value for a Decimal variable. This allows us to enter values from a number of different ranges.

For instance, we can use *integers* (no decimal part) in the range:

+/–79,228,162,514,264,337,593,543,950,335

in which case the scale factor is set to 0. On the other extreme, we can use values in the range:

–7.9228162514264337593543950335 to –0.0000000000000000000000000001

on the negative side, or:

0.0000000000000000000000000001 to 7.9228162514264337593543950335

on the positive side. In this case, the scale factor is set to 28.

To write a literal Decimal, append a D, as in:

```
123456.789D
```

The type identifier for Decimal is the symbol @, as in:

```
Dim dec@
```

The underlying .NET data type for Decimal is System.Decimal. This class has some useful members, such as MaxValue and MinValue, which give the maximum and minimum values of the decimal type.

By the way, in previous versions of VB, the Decimal existed only as a Variant data subtype—there were no variables of type Decimal.

Double data type

Values of type Double are IEEE 64-bit (8-byte) floating-point numbers with the range:

$-1.79769313486231E308$ to $-4.94065645841247E{-}324$

on the negative side, and:

$4.94065645841247E{-}324$ to $1.79769313486232E308$

on the positive side.

To write a literal Double, we must append an R, as in:

    12345.678R

The type identifier for a Double is #, as in:

    Dim dbl#

The underlying .NET data type for Double is System.Double.

Integer data type

The Integer data type is a 32-bit data type that stores signed integers ranging from:

$-2{\wedge}31$ to $2{\wedge}31{-}1$

or:

$-2,147,483,648$ to $2,147,483,647$

Note that this is the native word size on a 32-bit processor, and so the Integer data type provides superior performance as compared to integer data types of other sizes.

Note also that this data type size is new for VB.NET. In VB 6 and earlier, the Integer data type was a 16-bit data type.

To define a literal Integer, append an I, as in:

    123I

The Integer type identifier is the percent sign (%), as in:

    Dim int%

The underlying .NET data type for Integer is System.Int32.

Long data type

The Long data type is a 64-bit integer data type that stores signed integers ranging from:

-2^63 to 2^63-1

or:

$-9{,}223{,}372{,}036{,}854{,}775{,}808$ to $9{,}223{,}372{,}036{,}854{,}775{,}807$

Note that this data type size is new for VB.NET. In VB 6 and earlier, the Long data type was a 32-bit data type.

To define a literal Long, append an L, as in:

```
123L
```

The Long type identifier is the ampersand sign (&), as in:

```
Dim lng&
```

The underlying .NET data type for Long is System.Int64.

Object data type

The Object data type is a pointer data type. That is, a value of type Object is an address that references the object in memory. In VB.NET, the Object data type is the universal data type; an Object variable can refer to (point to) data of any other data type. For instance, the following code places a Long value in an Object variable:

```
Dim obj As Object
obj = 123L
```

The underlying .NET data type for Object is System.Object.

It is worth noting that when we use variables of type Object, we do pay a performance penalty because VB.NET cannot bind the object's method invocations to the actual method code until runtime. This is referred to as *late binding*. On the other hand, declaring variables of a specific object type allows early binding at compile time, which is much more efficient. Thus, code such as:

```
Dim obj As Object
. . .
obj.AMethod
```

is much less efficient than:

```
Dim obj As System.Data.DataSet
. . .
obj.AMethod
```

We revisit this issue in more detail later in this chapter.

As we have seen, the Object data type is universal. Just as in VB 6, in which you can use the *VarType* function to determine the data subtype of a Variant, in VB.NET you can use the *VarType* function to determine the data subtype of an object.

In addition, the Object class in the Framework Class Library's System namespace has a method named GetType that returns an object of type Type. Thus, if *obj* is a variable of type Object, then the code:

```
obj.GetType
```

returns a Type object. In turn, the Type class, which is also a member of the Framework Class Library's System namespace, has two methods that return information about the subtype of the object:

- ToString returns a string that describes the subtype of the data. It is roughly equivalent to calling the VB.NET *TypeName* function, except that the former method uses the data type name from the .NET Framework Class Library, whereas the latter function uses the Visual Basic name.

- GetTypeCode returns an enumeration value from the TypeCode enumeration. It is roughly equivalent to calling the VB6 *VarType* function, which, as we have said, is no longer supported in VB.NET.

For reference, the following code generates the values in Table 3-1:

```
Dim obj As Object
obj = ???
debug.write(obj.GetType.ToString)
Debug.Write(TypeName(obj))
debug.writeline(Type.GetTypeCode(obj.GetType))
```

Table 3-1: Values of ToString and GetTypeCode

obj = ???	ToString	TypeName	GetType
obj = True	System.Boolean	Boolean	3
obj = CByte(100)	System.Byte	Byte	6
obj = #1/1/2000#	System.DateTime	Date	16
obj = CDec(100)	System.Decimal	Decimal	15
obj = CDbl(100)	System.Double	Double	14
obj = CInt(100)	System.Int32	Integer	9
obj = CLng(100)	System.Int64	Long	11
obj = CShort(100)	System.Int16	Short	7
obj = CSng(100)	System.Single	Single	13
obj = "Donna"	System.String	String	18

Short data type

The Short data type is a 16-bit integer data type that stores signed integers ranging from:

-2^{15} to $2^{15}-1$

or:

$-32,768$ to $32,767$

Note that in earlier versions of Visual Basic, the Short data type is called the Integer data type.

To define a literal Short, append an S, as in:

123S

The underlying .NET data type for Short is System.Int16.

Single data type

Values of type Single are IEEE 32-bit (4-byte) floating-point numbers with the range:

−3.402823E38 to −1.401298E−45

on the negative side, and:

1.401298E−45 to 3.402823E38

on the positive side.

To write a literal Single, we must append an `F` (for floating point), as in:

```
12345.678F
```

The type identifier for a Single is an exclamation point (!), as in:

```
Dim sng!
```

The underlying .NET data type for Single is System.Single.

String data type

The String data type represents Unicode strings of up to approximately 2 billion characters. The type identifier for the string data type is a dollar sign ($). The underlying .NET data type for this type is System.String.

To create a new string, we can declare a variable and assign it a string as follows:

```
Dim sName As String
sName = "Donna"
```

or equivalently, in one statement:

```
Dim sName As String = "Donna"
```

The type identifier for a String is a dollar sign ($), as in:

```
Dim str$
```

Structure data type: user-defined types

In VB.NET, the Structure type is a powerful data type that has many properties in common with classes.

To declare a structure, we use the **Structure** statement, whose syntax is:

```
[Public|Private|Friend] Structure StructureName
    Nonmethod member declarations
    Method member declarations
End Structure
```

The members of a structure can be variables, properties, methods, or events. Note, however, that each member must be declared with an access modifier: **Public** (or **Dim**), **Private**, or **Friend**.

The simplest and most common use of structures is to encapsulate related variables. For instance, we might define a structure as follows:

```
Structure strPerson
```

```
        Public Name As String
        Public Address As String
        Public City As String
        Public State As String
        Public Zip As String
        Public Age As Short
    End Structure
```

To define a variable of type **strPerson**, we write (as usual):

```
    Dim APerson As strPerson
```

To access a member of a structure, we use the dot syntax, as in:

```
    APerson.Name = "Beethoven"
```

Note that structure members can be other structures or other objects. Structures can also be passed as arguments to functions, or as the return type of a function.

As mentioned, structures are similar to classes. For instance, consider the following structure:

```
    Structure strTest
        ' A public nonmethod member
        Public Name As String
        ' A private member variable
        Private msProperty As String
        ' A public method member
        Public Sub AMethod()
            Msgbox("Structure method. Property is: " & msProperty)
        End Sub
        ' A public property member
        Public Property AProperty() As String
            Get
                AProperty = msProperty
            End Get
            Set
                msProperty = Value
            End Set
        End Property
    End Structure
```

Now we can set the structure's property and invoke its method as follows:

```
    Dim str As strTest
    str.AProperty = "Donna"
    str.AMethod()
```

Although structures are similar to classes, they do not support the following class features:

- Structures cannot explicitly inherit, nor can they be inherited.
- All constructors for a structure must be parameterized.
- Structures cannot define destructors.
- Member declarations cannot include initializers nor can they use the **As New** syntax or specify an initial array size.

For a reference to the object-oriented terminology, see Chapter 4.

Data Type Conversion

The process of converting a value of one data type to another is called *conversion* or *casting*. A *cast operator* can be applied to a literal value or to a variable of a given type. For instance, we have:

```
Dim lng As Long
Dim int As Integer = 6
' Cast an Integer variable to a Long
lng = CLng(Int)
' Cast a literal integer to a Long
lng = CLng(12)
```

A cast can be widening or narrowing. A *widening cast* is one in which the conversion is to a target data type that can accommodate all values in the source data type, such as casting from Short to Integer or Integer to Double. In such a case, no data is ever lost, and the cast will not generate an error. A *narrowing cast* is one in which the target data type cannot accommodate all values in the source data type. In this case, data may be lost, and the cast may not succeed.

Under VB.NET, conversions are made in two ways: implicitly and explicitly. An *implicit conversion* is done by the compiler when circumstances warrant it (and if it is legal). For instance, if we write:

```
Dim lng As Long
lng = 54
```

then the compiler casts the Integer 54 as a Long.

The type of implicit conversion that the compiler will do depends in part on the setting of the `Option Strict` value. For instance, if `Option Strict` is On, only widening casts can be implicit; so then the following code:

```
Dim b As Boolean
b = "True"
```

generates a type conversion error, whereas if we add the line:

```
Option Strict Off
```

to the beginning of the module, then the previous code executes without error.

Explicit conversion requires explicitly calling a conversion function (or cast operator). The type conversion functions supported by VB.NET all have the form:

```
Cname(expression)
```

where *expression* is an expression that is in the range of the target data type. Specifically, we have the following conversion functions:

CBool
> Converts any valid String or numeric expression to Boolean. When a numeric value is converted to Boolean, any nonzero value is converted to `True`, and zero is converted to `False`.

CByte

Converts any numeric expression in the range 0 to 255 to Byte, while rounding any fractional part.

CChar

Takes a string argument and returns the first character of the string as a Char data type.

CDate

Converts any valid representation of a date or time to Date.

CDbl

Converts any expression that can be evaluated to a number in the range of a Double to Double.

CDec

Converts any expression that can be evaluated to a number in the range of a Decimal to Decimal.

CInt

Converts any numeric expression in the range of Integer (−2,147,483,648 to 2,147,483,647) to Integer, while rounding any fractional part.

CLng

Converts any expression that can be evaluated to a number in the range of a Long to Long, while rounding any fractional part.

CObj

Converts any expression that can be interpreted as an object to Object. For instance, the code:

```
Dim obj As Object
obj = CObj("test")
```

casts the string "test" to type Object and places it in the Object variable *obj*.

CShort

Converts any numeric expression in the range −32,768 to 32,767 to Short, while rounding any fractional part.

CSng

Converts any expression that can be evaluated to a number in the range of a Single to Single. If the numeric expression is outside the range of a Single, an error occurs.

CStr

If the expression input to *CStr* is Boolean, the function returns one of the strings "True" or "False." For an expression that can be interpreted as a date, the return value is a string representation of that date, in the date format defined by the regional settings of the host computer. For a numeric expression, the return value is a string representing the number.

CType

A general-purpose conversion function, *CType* has the following syntax:

```
CType(expression, typename)
```

where **expression** is an expression or variable, and **typename** is the data type to which it will be converted. The function supports conversions to and from the standard data types, as well as to and from object data types, structures, and interfaces.

Arrays

The array data type is a fundamental data type in most languages, including Visual Basic. An array is used to store a collection of similar data types or objects.

Many authors of programming books misuse the terms associated with arrays, so let's begin by establishing the correct terminology. In fact, if you will indulge us, we would like to begin with a formal definition of the term array.

Definition of Array

Let S^1, S^2 ..., S^N be finite sets, and let T be a data type (such as Integer). Then an *array* of type T is a function:

```
arr:S¹ · S² · ... · SN   T
```

where $S^1 \cdot S^2 \cdot \ldots \cdot S^N$ is the Cartesian product of the sets S^1, S^2 ..., S^N. (This is the set of all n-tuples whose coordinates come from the sets S^i.)

For arrays in VB.NET (and the other languages that implement the Common Language Runtime), the sets S^i must have the form:

```
Si={0,1,...,Ki}
```

In other words, each set S^i is a finite set of consecutive integers starting with 0.

Each position in the Cartesian product is referred to as a *coordinate* of the array. For each coordinate, the integer K^i is called the upper bound of the coordinate. The lower bound is 0 for all arrays in VB.NET.

Dimension of an Array

The number N of coordinates in the domain of the function *arr* is called the *dimension* (or sometimes *rank*) of the array. Thus, every array has a dimension (note the singular); it is *not* correct to refer to the dimensions of an array (note the plural). An array of dimension 1 is called a *one-dimensional array*, an array of dimension 2 is called a *two-dimensional array*, and so on.

Size of an Array

Along with a dimension, every array has a *size*. For instance, the one-dimensional array:

```
arr:{0,1,...,5}   T
```

has size 6. The two-dimensional array:

```
arr:{0,1,...,5}·{0,1,...,8}   T
```

has size 6·9. The three-dimensional array:

```
arr:{0,1,...,5}·{0,1,...,8}·{0,1}   T
```

has size 6·9·2.

Arrays in VB.NET

In VB.NET, all arrays have lower bound 0. This is a change from earlier versions of VB, where we could choose the lower bound of an array.

The following examples show various ways to declare a one-dimensional array:

```
' Implicit constructor: No initial size and no initialization
Dim Days() As Integer

' Explicit constructor: No initial size and no initialization
Dim Days() As Integer = New Integer() {}

' Implicit constructor: Initial size but no initialization
Dim Days(6) As Integer

' Explicit constructor: Initial size but no initialization
Dim Days() As Integer = New Integer(6) {}

' Implicit constructor: Initial size implied by initialization
Dim Days() As Integer = {1, 2, 3, 4, 5, 6, 7}

' Explicit constructor, Initial size and initialization
Dim Days() As Integer = New Integer(6) {1, 2, 3, 4, 5, 6, 7}
```

Note that an array declaration can:

- Call the array's constructor implicitly or explicitly. (The constructor is the function that VB.NET uses to create the array.)
- Specify an initial size for each dimension or leave the initial size unspecified.
- Initialize the elements of the array or not.

It is important to note that in the declaration:

```
Dim ArrayName(X) As ArrayType
```

the number X is the *upper bound* of the array. Thus, the array elements are ArrayName(0) through ArrayName(X), and the array has X+1 elements.

Multidimensional arrays are declared similarly. For instance, the following example declares and initializes a two-dimensional array:

```
Dim X(,) As Integer = {{1, 2, 3}, {4, 5, 6}}
```

and the following code displays the contents of the array:

```
Debug.Write(X(0, 0))
Debug.Write(X(0, 1))
Debug.Writeline(X(0, 2))
Debug.Write(X(1, 0))
Debug.Write(X(1, 1))
Debug.Write(X(1, 2))

123
456
```

In VB.NET, all arrays are dynamic; there is no such thing as a fixed-size array. The declared size should be thought of as simply as the initial size of the array, which is subject to change using the ReDim statement. Note, however, that the dimension of an array cannot be changed.

Moreover, unlike with VB 6, the ReDim statement cannot be used for array declaration, but can be used only for array redimensioning. All arrays must be declared initially using a Dim (or equivalent) statement.

Redimensioning arrays

The ReDim statement is used to change the size of an array. This is referred to as *redimensioning*—a term no doubt invented by someone who didn't know the difference between the dimension of an array and the size of an array! In any case, redimensioning changes the size of the array, not its dimension. In fact, as we have already mentioned, the dimension of an array cannot be changed.

The *UBound* function returns the upper limit of an array coordinate. Its syntax is:

```
UBound(MyArray, CoordinateIndex)
```

where *CoordinateIndex* is the index of the coordinate for which we want the upper bound.

Here is an example of array redimensioning:

```
Dim MyArray(10, 10) As Integer
Msgbox(UBound(MyArray, 2))          ' Displays 10
ReDim MyArray(15, 20)
Msgbox(UBound(MyArray, 2))          ' Displays 20
```

When an array is redimensioned using the ReDim statement without qualification, all data in the array is lost; that is, the array is reinitialized. However, the Preserve keyword, when used with ReDim, redimensions the array while retaining all current values. Note that when using the Preserve keyword, only the last coordinate of an array can be changed. Thus, referring to the array defined earlier, the following code generates an error:

```
ReDim Preserve MyArray(50, 20)
```

You will probably not be surprised to learn that redimensioning an array is a time-intensive process. Hence, when redimensioning, we face the ubiquitous dichotomy between saving space and saving time. For instance, consider the code segment used to populate an array:

```
Dim MyArray(100) As Integer
Dim i As Integer, iNext As Integer

iNext = 0
Do While (Some condition)
    If (some condition here) Then
        ' Add element to array
        If ubound(MyArray) < iNext Then
            ReDim Preserve MyArray(iNext + 100)
        End If
        MyArray(iNext) = (whatever)
```

```
            iNext = iNext + 1
        End If
    Loop
```

The key issue here is to decide how much to increase the size of the array each time resizing is necessary. If we want to avoid using any extra space, we could increase the size of the array by 1 each time:

```
ReDim Preserve MyArray(iNext + 1)
```

But this would be very inefficient. Alternatively, we could kick up the size by 1,000:

```
ReDim Preserve MyArray(iNext + 1000)
```

But this uses a lot of extra space. Sometimes experimentation is required to find the right compromise between saving space and saving time.

Object Variables and Their Binding

In VB.NET, classes and their objects are everywhere. Of course, there are the classes and objects that we create in our own applications. There are also the classes in the .NET Framework Class Library. In addition, many applications take advantage of the objects that are exposed by other applications, such as ActiveX Data Objects (ADO), Microsoft Word, Excel, Access, various scripting applications, and more. The point is that for each object we want to manipulate, we will need to declare a variable of that class type. For instance, if we create a class named CPerson, then in order to instantiate a CPerson object, we must declare a variable:

```
Dim APerson As CPerson
```

Similarly, if we decide to use the ADO Recordset object, we will need to declare a variable of type ADO.Recordset:

```
Dim rs As ADO.Recordset
```

Even though object variables are declared in the same manner as nonobject variables, there are some significant differences. In particular, the declaration:

```
Dim obj As MyClass
```

does not *create* an object variable—it only binds a variable name with a class name. To actually construct an object and set the variable to refer to that object, we need to call the *constructor* of the class. This function, discussed in detail in Chapter 4, is responsible for creating objects of the class.

Constructors are called using the New keyword, as in:

```
Dim obj As MyClass = New MyClass()
```

or:

```
Dim obj As MyClass
obj = New MyClass()
```

VB.NET also provides a shortcut that does not mention the constructor explicitly:

```
Dim obj As New MyClass()
```

(In earlier versions of VB, we use the Set statement, which is no longer supported.)

Late Binding Versus Early Binding

The object-variable declaration:

```
Dim obj As Class1
```

explicitly mentions the class from which the object will be created (in this case it is Class1). Because of this, VB can obtain and display information about the class members, as we can see in VB's Intellisense, shown in Figure 3-1.

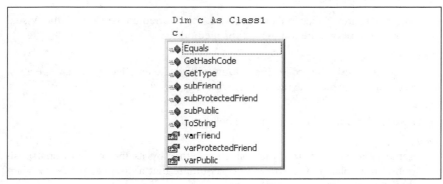

Figure 3-1: Intellisense showing member list

As you know, Intellisense also shows the signature of a method, as shown in Figure 3-2.

```
Dim c As Class1
c.ShowSig(
```
ShowSig (**x As Integer**) As String

Figure 3-2: Intellisense showing method signature

Of course, Intellisense is very helpful during program development. However, more important is that the previous object-variable declaration allows VB to bind the object's methods to actual function addresses *at compile time*. This is known as *early binding*.

An alternative to using a declaration that specifically mentions that class is a *generic* object-variable declaration that uses the As Object syntax:

```
Dim obj As Object
```

While it is true that *obj* can hold a reference to any object, we pay a major penalty for this privilege. VB can no longer get information about the class and its members because it does not know which class the object *obj* belongs to!

As a result, VB's Intellisense cannot help us with member syntax. More importantly, we pay a large performance penalty because VB cannot bind any of the

Variables and
Data Types

classes, properties, or methods at compile time—it must wait until runtime. This is referred to as *late binding*.

In summary, explicit object-variable declarations allow for early binding and thus are much more efficient than generic declarations, which use late binding. Hence, explicit object-variable declarations should be used whenever possible.

The Collection Object

VB.NET implements a special object called the Collection object that acts as a container for objects of all types. In fact, Collection objects can hold other objects, as well as nonobject data.

In some ways, the Collection object is an object-oriented version of the Visual Basic array. It supports the following four methods:

Add
> Adds an item to the collection. Along with the data itself, you can specify a key value by which the member can be referenced.

Count
> Returns the number of items in the collection.

Item
> Retrieves a member from the collection either by its index (or ordinal position in the collection) or by its key (assuming that a key was provided when the item was added to the collection).

Remove
> Deletes a member from the collection using the member's index or key.

For example, the following code defines a collection object named colStates to hold information about U.S. states and then adds two members to it, using the state's two-letter abbreviation as a key:

```
Dim colStates As New Collection
colStates.Add("New York", "NY")
colStates.Add("Michigan", "MI")
```

Like members of an array, the members of a collection can be iterated using the **For Each...Next** construct. Also like arrays, collection members are accessible by their index value, although the lower bound of a collection object's index is always 1.

Arrays and collections each have advantages and disadvantages. Some of the advantages of collections over arrays are:

- New collection members can be inserted before or after an existing member in index order. Moreover, indexes are maintained automatically by VB, so we don't need to adjust the indexes manually.

- Collection members can be referenced by key value. This feature makes collections similar to associative arrays (which are used by languages such as Perl).

Note that when deleting collection members by index, it is important to iterate though the indexes *in reverse order* because member deletion changes the indexes of other members.

Parameters and Arguments

The terms *parameter* and *argument* are often used interchangeably, although they have entirely different meanings. Let us illustrate with an example. Consider the following function, which replicates a string a given number of times:

```
Function RepeatString(ByVal sInput As String, ByVal iCount As Integer) _
                      As String
    Dim i As Integer
    For i = 1 To iCount
        RepeatString = RepeatString & sInput
    Next
End Function
```

The variables *sInput* and *iCount* are the parameters of this function. Note that each parameter has an associated data type.

Now, when we call this function, we must replace the parameters by variables, constants, or literals, as in:

```
s = RepeatString("Donna", 4)
```

The items that we use in place of the parameters are called arguments.

Passing Arguments

Arguments can be passed to a function in one of two ways: by value or by reference. Incidentally, argument passing is often called parameter passing, although it is the arguments and not the parameters that are being passed.

The declaration of *RepeatString* given earlier contains the keyword **ByVal** in front of each parameter. This specifies that arguments are passed by value to this function. Passing by value means that the actual value of the argument is passed to the function. This is relevant when an argument is a variable. For instance, consider the following code:

```
Sub Inc(ByVal x As Integer)
    x = x + 1
End Sub

Dim iAge As Integer = 20
Inc(iAge)
Msgbox(iAge)
```

The final line:

```
Msgbox(iAge)
```

actually displays the number 20. In other words, the line:

```
Inc(iAge)
```

does nothing. The reason is that the argument *iAge* is passed to the procedure Inc by value. Since only the value (in this case 20) is passed, that value is assigned to a local variable named *x* within the procedure. This local variable is increased to 21, but once the procedure ends, the local variable is destroyed. The variable *iAge* is not passed to the procedure, so its value is not changed.

On the other hand, if we modify the definition of the procedure Inc, replacing ByVal with ByRef, the story is different:

```
Sub Inc(ByRef x As Integer)
    x = x + 1
End Sub
```

In this case, what is passed to the procedure Inc is a reference to the argument *iAge*. Hence, the procedure actually operates on the variable passed to it, incrementing the value of *iAge* to 21. Put another way, the variable represented by the parameter *x* is actually the passed variable *iAge*.

In VB.NET, the default method of argument passing for arguments is by value. This is a change from earlier versions of VB, in which the default method was by reference.

Passing Objects

There is a subtlety in argument passing with parameters of any object type. Actually, the subtlety occurs because an object variable is a *pointer*; that is, it contains a reference to (or the address of) the object.

If we pass an object variable by value, we are passing the contents of the variable, which is the address of the object. Thus, any changes made in the called procedure affects the object itself, not a copy of the object. This seems like passing by reference, but it is not. Think of it this way: passing the *value* of an object's address is passing a *reference* to the object.

On the other hand, if we pass an object variable by reference, we are passing the address of the variable. In other words, we are passing the address of the address of the object! In languages that support pointers, this is referred to as a *double pointer*.

Let us illustrate with an example. Consider the following code, and imagine that the form containing this code has two textboxes: TextBox1 with text "TextBox1" and TextBox2 with text "TextBox2":

```
Public Function GetText(ByVal txt As TextBox) As String
    ' Change reference to textbox
    txt = Textbox2
End Function

Sub Doit
    Dim t As TextBox
    t = TextBox1
    GetText(t)
    msgbox(t.Text)     ' Displays TextBox1 when ByVal, _
                       ' TextBox2 when ByRef
End Sub
```

Now, here is what happens when we execute *DoIt*. Note that the argument is passed to *GetText* by value in this case.

- The TextBox variable *t* is assigned to TextBox1, as shown in Figure 3-3.

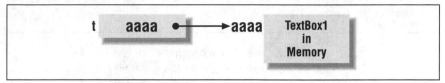

Figure 3-3: Assigning an object reference

- GetText is called, passing *t* by value. Since *t* contains the address aaaa of the TextBox1 object, the local variable *txt* is given the value aaaa, as shown in Figure 3-4.

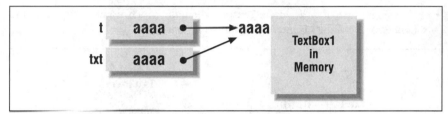

Figure 3-4: Passing an object by value

- The single line of code in GetText is executed, which now causes *txt* to point to TextBox2, as shown in Figure 3-5.

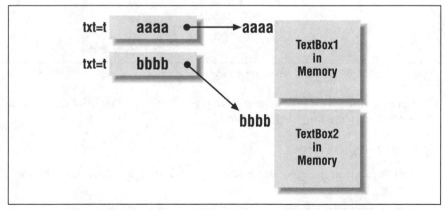

Figure 3-5: Assigning a new object reference

- Upon return from GetText, *t* is unaffected, so the *MsgBox* function displays the string "TextBox1."

Now suppose we change the ByVal keyword to ByRef in *GetText*. Here is what happens:

- The TextBox variable *t* is assigned to TextBox1, as shown previously in Figure 3-3.

- GetText is called, passing *t* by reference. Hence, txt is *t*. This is quite different from *txt* and *t* containing the same value, as in the ByVal case. The situation is shown in Figure 3-6.

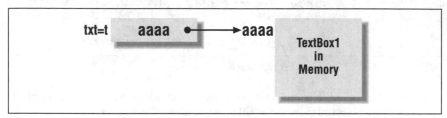

Figure 3-6: Passing an object by reference

- The single line of code in GetText is executed, which now causes *txt* (and hence *t*) to point to TextBox2, as shown in Figure 3-7.

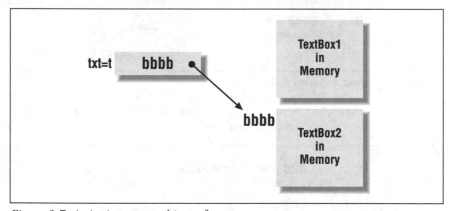

Figure 3-7: Assigning a new object reference

- Upon return from GetText, *t* is now pointing to TextBox2, so the *MsgBox* function displays the string "TextBox2."

Optional Arguments

In VB.NET, parameters can be declared as optional using the Optional keyword, as shown in the following code:

```
Sub Calculate(Optional ByVal Switch As Boolean = False)
```

In VB.NET, all optional parameters must declare a default value, which is passed to the procedure if the calling program does not supply that parameter.

The following rules apply to optional arguments:

- Every optional argument must specify a default value, and this default must be a constant expression (not a variable).

- Every argument following an optional argument must also be optional.

Note that in earlier versions of VB, you could omit the default value and, if the parameter was of type Variant, you could use the *IsMissing* function to determine if a value was supplied. This is not possible in VB.NET, and the *IsMissing* function is not supported.

ParamArray

Normally, a procedure definition specifies a fixed number of parameters. However, the `ParamArray` keyword, which is short for Parameter Array, permits us to declare a procedure with an unspecified number of parameters. Therefore, each call to the procedure can use a different number of parameters.

Suppose, for instance, that we want to define a function to take the average of a number of test scores, but the number of scores may vary. Then we declare the function as follows:

```
Function GetAverage(ByVal ParamArray Scores() As Single) As Single
    Dim i As Integer
    For i = 0 To UBound(Scores)
        GetAverage = GetAverage + CSng(Scores(i))
    Next
    GetAverage = GetAverage / (UBound(Scores) + 1)
End Function
```

Now we can make calls to this function with a varying number of arguments:

```
Msgbox(GetAverage(1, 2, 3, 4, 5))
Msgbox(GetAverage(1, 2, 3))
```

The following rules apply to the use of `ParamArray`:

- A procedure can only have one parameter array, and it must be the last parameter in the procedure.
- The parameter array must be passed by value, and you must explicitly include `ByVal` in the procedure definition.
- The parameter array must be a one-dimensional array. If the type is not declared, it is assumed to be Object.
- The parameter array is automatically optional. Its default value is an empty one-dimensional array of the parameter array's data type.

CHAPTER 4

Introduction to Object-Oriented Programming

In this chapter, we present a brief and succinct introduction to object-oriented programming. Since this is not a book on object-oriented programming per se, we will confine our attention to those topics that are important to VB.NET programming.

Why Learn Object-Oriented Techniques?

As you may know, Visual Basic has implemented some features of object-oriented programming since Version 4. However, in terms of object-orientation, the move from Version 6 to VB.NET has been dramatic. Many people did not consider VB 6 (or earlier versions) to be a truly object-oriented programming language. Whatever your thoughts may have been on this matter, it seems clear that VB.NET is an object-oriented programming language by any reasonable definition of the term.

You may be saying to yourself: "I prefer not to use object-oriented techniques in my programming." This is something you could easily have gotten away with in VB 6. But in VB.NET, the structure of the .NET Framework—specifically the .NET Framework Class Library—as well as the documentation, is so object-oriented that you can no longer avoid understanding the basics of object-orientation, even if you decide not to use them in your applications.

Principles of Object-Oriented Programming

It is often said that there are four main concepts in the area of object-oriented programming:

- Abstraction
- Encapsulation
- Inheritance
- Polymorphism

Each of these concepts plays a significant role in VB.NET programming at one level or another. Encapsulation and abstraction are "abstract" concepts providing motivation for object-oriented programming. Inheritance and polymorphism are concepts that are directly implemented in VB.NET programming.

Abstraction

Simply put, an *abstraction* is a view of an entity that includes only those aspects that are relevant for a particular situation. For instance, suppose that we want to create a software component that provides services for keeping a company's employee information. For this purpose, we begin by making a list of the items relevant to our entity (an employee of the company). Some of these items are:

- FullName
- Address
- EmployeeID
- Salary
- IncSalary
- DecSalary

Note that we include not only *properties* of the entities in question, such as FullName, but also *actions* that might be taken with respect to these entities, such as IncSalary, to increase an employee's salary. Actions are also referred to as methods, operations, or behaviors. We will use the term methods, since this term is used by VB.NET.

Of course, we would never think of including an IQ property, since this would not be politically correct, not to mention discriminatory and therefore possibly illegal. Nor would we include a property called HairCount, which gives the number of hairs on the employee's right arm, because this information is of absolutely no interest to us, even though it is part of every person's being.

In short, we have abstracted the concept of an employee—we have included only those properties and methods of employees that are relevant to our needs. Once the abstraction is complete, we can proceed to *encapsulate* these properties and methods within a software component.

Encapsulation

The idea of encapsulation is to contain (i.e., encapsulate) the properties and methods of an abstraction, and expose only those portions that are absolutely necessary. Each property and method of an abstraction is called a *member* of the abstraction. The set of exposed members of an abstraction is referred to collectively as the *public interface* (or just *interface*) of the abstraction (or of the software component that encapsulates the abstraction).

Encapsulation serves three useful purposes:

- It permits the protection of these properties and methods from any outside tampering.

- It allows the inclusion of validation code to help catch errors in the use of the public interface. For instance, it permits us to prevent the client of the employee software component from setting an employee's salary to a negative number.

- It frees the user from having to know the details of how the properties and methods are implemented.

Let us consider an example that involves the Visual Basic Integer data type, which is nicely encapsulated for us by VB. As you undoubtedly know, an integer is stored in the memory of a PC as a string of 0s and 1s called a *binary string*. In Visual Basic, integers are interpreted in a form called *two's-complement representation*, which permits the representation of both negative and non-negative values.

For simplicity, let us consider 8-bit binary numbers. An 8-bit binary number has the form $a_7a_6a_5a_4a_3a_2a_1a_0$, where each of the $a$xs is a 0 or a 1. We can think of it as appearing in memory as shown in Figure 4-1.

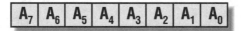

Figure 4-1: An 8-bit binary number

In the two's-complement representation, the leftmost bit, a_7 (called the most significant bit), is the *sign bit*. If the sign bit is 1, the number is negative. If the sign bit is 0, the number is positive.

The formula for converting a two's-complement representation $a_7a_6a_5a_4a_3a_2a_1a_0$ of a number to a decimal representation is:

```
decimal rep. = -128a7 + 64a6 + 32a5 + 16a4 + 8a3 + 4a2 + 2a1 + a0
```

To take the negative of a number when it is represented in two's-complement form, we must take the complement of each bit (that is, change each 0 to a 1 and each 1 to a 0) and then add 1.

At this point you may be saying to yourself, "As a programmer, I don't have to worry about these details. I just write code like:

```
x = -16
y = -x
```

and let the computer and the programming language worry about which representation to use and how to perform the given operations."

This is precisely the point behind encapsulation. The details of how signed integers are interpreted by the computer (and the compiler), as well as how their properties and operations are implemented, are encapsulated in the integer data type itself and are thus hidden from us, the users of the data type. Only those portions of the properties and operations that we need in order to work with integers are exposed outside of the data type. These portions form the public interface for the Integer data type.

Moreover, encapsulation protects us from making errors. For instance, if we had to do our own negating by taking Boolean complements and adding 1, we might forget to add 1! The encapsulated data type takes care of this automatically.

Encapsulation has yet another important feature. Any code that is written using the exposed interface remains valid even if the internal workings of the Integer data type are changed for some reason, as long as the interface is not changed. For instance, if we move the code to a computer that stores integers in one's-complement representation, then the *internal* procedure for implementing the operation of negation in the integer data type will have to be changed. However, from the programmer's point of view, nothing has changed. The code:

```
x = -16
y = -x
```

is just as valid as before.

Interfaces

As VB programmers, we must implement encapsulation through the use of software components. For instance, we can create a software component to encapsulate the Employee abstraction discussed earlier.

In VB.NET, the methods of an interface are realized as *functions*. On the other hand, a property, as we see later in this chapter, is realized as a *private* variable that stores the property's value together with a pair of *public* functions—one to set the variable and one to retrieve the variable. These functions are sometimes referred to as *accessor methods* of the property. It is the set of exposed functions (ordinary methods and accessor methods) that constitute the *interface* for an abstraction.

In general, a software component may encapsulate and expose more than one abstraction—hence, more than one interface. For example, in a more realistic setting, we might want a software component designed to model employees to encapsulate an interface called `IIdentification` (the initial "I" is for interface) that is used for identification purposes. This interface might have properties such as name, Social Security number, driver's license number, age, birthmarks, and so on. Moreover, the software component might also encapsulate an interface called IEducation for describing the employee's educational background. Such an interface might implement properties such as education level, degrees, college attended, and so on.

The interface of each abstraction exposed by a software component is also referred to as an interface of the software component. Thus, the Employee component implements at least two interfaces: `IIdentification` and `IEducation`. Note, however, that the term interface is often used to refer to the set of *all* exposed properties and methods of a software component, in which case a component has only one interface.

Referring to our original Employee abstraction, its interface might consist of the functions shown in Table 4-1. (Of course, this interface is vastly oversimplified, but it is more than sufficient to illustrate the concepts.)

Table 4-1: Members of the Employee interface

Type	Name
Property	FullName: GetFullName(), SetFullName()
Property	Address: GetAddress(), SetAddress()

Table 4-1: Members of the Employee interface (continued)

Type	Name
Property	EmployeeID: GetEmployeeID(), SetEmployeeID()
Property	Salary: GetSalary(), SetSalary()
Method	IncSalary()
Method	DecSalary()

Using the term interface as a set of functions, while quite common, poses a problem. Just listing the functions of the interface by name (as done previously) does not provide enough information to call those functions. Thus, a more useful definition of interface would be the set of signatures of the public functions of a software component.

To clarify this, let us discuss one of the most important distinctions in object-oriented programming—the distinction between a function *declaration* and an *implementation* of that function.

By way of example, consider the following sorting function:

```
Function Sort(a() as Integer, iSize as Integer) as Boolean
    For i = 1 to iSize
        For j = i+1 to iSize
            If a(j) < a(i) Then swap a(i), a(j)
        Next j
    Next I
    Sort = True
End Function
```

The first line in this definition:

```
Function Sort(a() as Integer, iSize as Integer) as Boolean
```

is the *function declaration*. It supplies information on the number and types of parameters and the return type of the function. The body of the function:

```
    For i = 1 to iSize
        For j = i+1 to iSize
            If a(j) < a(i) Then swap a(i), a(j)
        Next j
    Next i
    Sort = True
```

represents the *implementation* of the function. It describes how the function carries out its intended purpose.

Note that it is possible to alter the implementation of the function without changing the declaration. In fact, the current function implementation sorts the array a using a simple selection-sort algorithm, but we could replace that sorting method with any one of a number of other methods (bubble sort, insertion sort, quick sort, and so on).

Now consider a client of the *Sort* function. The client only needs to know the function declaration in order to use the function. It need not know (and probably doesn't want to know) anything about the implementation. Thus, it is the function declaration, and not the implementation, that forms the interface for the function.

The *signature* of a function is the function name and return type, as well as the names, order, and types of its parameters. A function declaration is simply a clear way of describing the function's signature. Note that Microsoft does not consider the return type of a function to be part of the function's signature. By signature, they mean what is generally termed the function's *argument signature*. The reasons for doing this become clearer later in the chapter when we discuss overloading, although it would have been better (as usual) if they were more careful with their terminology.

Under this more specific definition of interface, the interface for our employee component might be as follows (in part):

```
Function GetFullName(lEmpID As Long) As String
Sub SetFullName(lEmpID As Long, sName As String)
. . .
Sub IncSalary(sngPercent As Single)
Sub DecSalary(sngPercent As Single)
```

Classes and Objects

Generally speaking, a *class* is a software component that defines and implements one or more interfaces. (Strictly speaking, a class need not implement all the members of an interface. We discuss this later when we talk about abstract members.) In different terms, a class combines data, functions, and types into a new type. Microsoft uses the term *type* to include classes.

Class Modules in VB.NET

Under Visual Studio.NET, a VB class module is inserted into a project using the Add Class menu item on the Project menu. This inserts a new module containing the code:

```
Public Class ClassName

End Class
```

Although Visual Studio stores each class in a separate file, this isn't a requirement. It is the **Class...End Class** construct that marks the beginning and end of a class definition. Thus, the code for more than one class as well as one or more code modules (which are similarly delimited by the **Module...End Module** construct) can be contained in a single source code file.

The CPerson class defined in the next section is an example of a VB class module.

Class Members

In VB.NET, class modules can contain the following types of members:

Data members
> This includes member variables (also called *fields*) and constants.

Event members
> Events are procedures that are called automatically by the Common Language Runtime in response to some action that occurs, such as an object being

created, a button being clicked, a piece of data being changed, or an object going out of scope.

Function members

This refers to both functions and subroutines. A function member is also called a method. A class' constructor is a special type of method. We discuss constructors in detail later in this chapter.

Property members

A property member is implemented as a Private member variable together with a special type of VB function that incorporates both accessor functions of the property. We discuss the syntax of this special property function in the "Properties" section later in the chapter.

Type members

A class member can be another class, which is then referred to as a nested class.

The following CPerson class illustrates some of the types of members:

```
Public Class CPerson

    ' -------------
    ' Data Members
    ' -------------
    ' Member variables
    Private msName As String
    Private miAge As Integer

    ' Member constant
    Public Const MAXAGE As Short = 120

    ' Member event
    Public Event Testing()


    ' ----------------
    ' Function Members
    ' ----------------

    ' Method
    Public Sub Test()
        RaiseEvent Testing()
    End Sub

    Property Age() As Integer
        Get
            Age = miAge
        End Get
        Set(ByVal Value As Integer)
            ' Some validation
            If Value < 0 Then
                MsgBox("Age cannot be negative.")
            Else
                miAge = Value
```

```
            End If
        End Set
    End Property

    ' Property
    Property Name() As String
        ' Accessors for the property
        Get
            Name = msName
        End Get
        Set(ByVal Value As String)
            msName = Value
        End Set
    End Property

    ' Overloaded constructor
    Overloads Sub New()

    End Sub

    ' Constructor that initializes name
    Overloads Sub New(ByVal sNewName As String)
        msName = sNewName
    End Sub

    Sub Dispose()
        ' Code here to clean up
    End Sub

End Class
```

The Public Interface of a VB.NET Class

We have seen that, when speaking in general object-oriented terms, the exposed members of a software component constitute the component's public interface (or just interface). Now, in VB.NET, each member of a class module has an access type, which may be Public, Private, Friend, Protected, or Protected Friend. We discuss each of these in detail later in this chapter. Suffice it to say, a VB.NET class module may accordingly have Public, Private, Friend, Protected, and Protected Friend members.

Thus, we face some ambiguity in defining the concept of the public interface of a VB.NET class. The spirit of the term might indicate that we should consider any member that is exposed outside of the class itself as part of the public interface of the class. This would include the Protected, Friend, and Protected Friend members, as well as the Public members. On the other hand, some might argue that the members of the public interface must be exposed outside of the project in which the class resides, in which case only the Public members would be included in the interface. Fortunately, we need not make too much fuss over the issue of what exactly constitutes a VB.NET class' public interface, as long as we remain aware that the term may be used differently by different people.

Objects

A class is just a description of some properties and methods and does not have a life of its own (with the exception of shared members, which we discuss later). In general, to execute the methods and use the properties of a class, we must create an instance of the class, officially known as an object. Creating an instance of a class is referred to as *instancing*, or *instantiating*, the class.

There are three ways to instantiate an object of a VB.NET class. One method is to declare a variable of the class' type:

```
Dim APerson As CPerson
```

and then instantiate the object using the New keyword as follows:

```
APerson = New CPerson()
```

We can combine these two steps as follows:

```
Dim APerson As New CPerson()
```

or:

```
Dim APerson As CPerson = New CPerson()
```

The first syntax is considered shorthand for the second.

Properties

Properties are members that can be implemented in two different ways. In its simplest implementation, a property is just a public variable, as in:

```
Public Class CPerson

    Public Age As Integer

End Class
```

The problem with this implementation of the Age property is that it violates the principle of encapsulation; anyone who has access to a CPerson object can set its Age property to any Integer value, even negative integers, which are not valid ages. In short, there is no opportunity for data validation. (Moreover, this implementation of a property does not permit its inclusion in the public interface of the class, as we have defined that term.)

The "proper" object-oriented way to implement a property is to use a Private data member along with a special pair of function members. The Private data member holds the property value; the pair of function members, called *accessors*, are used to get and set the property value. This promotes data encapsulation, since we can restrict access to the property via code in the accessor functions, which can contain code to validate the data. The following code implements the Age property:

```
Private miAge As Integer

Property Age() As Integer
    Get
        Age = miAge
```

```
          End Get
      Set(ByVal Value As Integer)
          ' Some validation
          If Value < 0 Then
              MsgBox("Age cannot be negative.")
          Else
              miAge = Value
          End If
      End Set
  End Property
```

As you can see from the previous code, VB has a special syntax for defining the property accessors. As soon as we finish typing the line:

```
Property Age() As Integer
```

the VB IDE automatically creates the following template:

```
Property Age() As Integer
   Get

   End Get
   Set(ByVal Value As Integer)

   End Set
End Property
```

Note the *Value* parameter that provides access to the incoming value. Thus, if we write:

```
Dim cp As New CPerson()
cp.Age = 20
```

then VB passes the value 20 into the Property procedure in the *Value* argument.

Instance and Shared Members

The members of a class fall into two categories:

Instance members
> Members that can only be accessed through an instance of the class, that is, through an object of the class. To put it another way, instance members "belong" to an individual object rather than to the class as a whole.

Shared (static) members
> Members that can be accessed without creating an instance of the class. These members are shared among all instances of the class. More correctly, they are independent of any particular object of the class. To put it another way, shared members "belong" to the class as a whole, rather than to its individual objects or instances.

Instance members are accessed by qualifying the member name with the object's name. Here is an example:

```
Dim APerson As New CPerson()
APerson.Age = 50
```

To access a shared member, we simply qualify the member with the class name. For instance, the String class in the System namespace of the .NET Framework Class Library has a shared method called Compare that compares two strings. Its syntax (in one form) is:

```
Public Shared Function Compare(String, String) As Integer
```

This function returns 0 if the strings are equal, −1 if the first string is less than the second, and 1 if the first string is greater than the second. Since the method is shared, we can write:

```
Dim s As String = "steve"
Dim t As String = "donna"
MsgBox(String.Compare(s, t))    ' Displays 1
```

Note the way the Compare method is qualified with the name of the String class.

Shared members are useful for keeping track of data that is independent of any particular instance of the class. For instance, suppose we want to keep track of the number of CPerson objects in existence at any given time. Then we write code such as the following:

```
' Declare a Private shared variable to hold the instance count
Private Shared miInstanceCount As Integer

' Increment the count in the constructor
' (If there are additional constructors,
' this code must be added to all of them.)
Sub new()
    miInstanceCount += 1
End Sub

' Supply a function to retrieve the instance count
Shared Function GetInstanceCount() As Integer
    Return miInstanceCount
End Function

' Decrement the count in the destructor
Overrides Protected Sub Finalize()
    miInstanceCount -= 1
    MyBase.Finalize
End Sub
```

Now, code such as the following accesses the shared variable:

```
Dim steve As New CPerson()
MsgBox(CPerson.GetInstanceCount)        ' Displays 1
Dim donna As New CPerson()
MsgBox(CPerson.GetInstanceCount)        ' Displays 2
```

Class Constructors

When an object of a particular class is created, the compiler calls a special function called the class' *constructor* or *instance constructor*. Constructors can be used to initialize an object when necessary. (Constructors take the place of the Class_ Initialize event in earlier versions of VB.)

We can define constructors in a class module. However, if we choose not to define a constructor, VB uses a default constructor. For instance, the line:

```
Dim APerson As CPerson = New CPerson()
```

invokes the default constructor of our CPerson class simply because we have not defined a custom constructor.

To define a custom constructor, we just define a subroutine named *New* within the class module. For instance, suppose we want to set the Name property to a specified value when a CPerson object is first created. Then we can add the following code to the CPerson class:

```
' Custom constructor
Sub New(ByVal sName As String)
    Me.Name = sName
End Sub
```

Now we can create a CPerson object and set its name as follows:

```
Dim APerson As CPerson = New CPerson("fred")
```

or:

```
Dim APerson As New CPerson("fred")
```

Note that because VB.NET supports function overloading (discussed later in this chapter), we can define multiple constructors in a single class, provided each constructor has a unique argument signature. We can then invoke any of the custom constructors simply by supplying the correct number and type of arguments for that constructor.

Note also that once we define one or more custom constructors, we can no longer invoke the default (that is, parameterless) constructor with a statement such as:

```
Dim APerson As New CPerson()
```

Instead, to call a parameterless constructor, we must specifically add the constructor to the class module:

```
' Default constructor
Sub New()
    ...
End Sub
```

Finalize, Dispose, and Garbage Collection

In VB 6, a programmer can implement the Class_Terminate event to perform any clean up procedures before an object is destroyed. For instance, if an object held a reference to an open file, it might be important to close the file before destroying the object itself.

In VB.NET, the Terminate event no longer exists, and things are handled quite differently. To understand the issues involved, we must first discuss garbage collection.

When the garbage collector determines that an object is no longer needed (which it does, for instance, when the running program no longer holds a reference to the object), it automatically runs a special *destructor method* called Finalize. However, it is important to understand that, unlike with the Class_Terminate event, we have no way to determine exactly when the garbage collector will call the Finalize method. We can only be sure that it will be called at some time after the last reference to the object is released. Any delay is due to the fact that the .NET Framework uses a system called *reference-tracing garbage collection*, which periodically releases unused resources.

Finalize is a Protected method. That is, it can be called from a class and its derived classes, but it is not callable from outside the class, including by clients of the class. (In fact, since the Finalize destructor is automatically called by the garbage collector, a class should never call its own Finalize method directly.) If a class' Finalize method is present, then it should explicitly call its base class' Finalize method as well. Hence, the general syntax and format of the Finalize method is:

```
Overrides Protected Sub Finalize()
    ' Cleanup code goes here
    MyBase.Finalize
End Sub
```

The benefits of garbage collection are that it is automatic and it ensures that unused resources are always released without any specific interaction on the part of the programmer. However, it has the disadvantages that garbage collection cannot be initiated directly by application code and some resources may remain in use longer than necessary. Thus, in simple terms, we cannot destroy objects on cue.

We should note that not all resources are managed by the Common Language Runtime. These resources, such as Windows handles and database connections, are thus not subject to garbage collection without specifically including code to release the resources within the Finalize method. But, as we have seen, this approach does not allow us or clients of our class to release resources on demand. For this purpose, the Framework Class Library defines a second destructor called Dispose. Its general syntax and usage is:

```
Class classname
    Implements IDisposable

Public Sub Dispose() Implements IDisposable.Dispose
    ' cleanup code goes here
    ' call child objects' Dispose methods, if necessary, here
End Sub

' Other class code

End Class
```

Note that classes that support this callable destructor must implement the IDisposable interface—hence the Implements statement just shown. IDisposable has just one member, the Dispose method.

It is important to note that it is necessary to inform any clients of the class that they must call this method specifically in order to release resources. (The technical term for this is the *manual approach*!)

Inheritance

Perhaps the best way to describe inheritance as it is used in VB.NET is to begin with an example.

The classes in a given application often have relationships to one another. Consider, for instance, our Employee information application. The Employee objects in the class CEmployee represent the general aspects common to all employees—name, address, salary, and so on.

Of course, the executives of the company will have different prerequisites than, say, the secretaries. So it is reasonable to define additional classes named CExecutive and CSecretary, each with properties and methods of its own. On the other hand, an executive is also an employee, and there is no reason to define different Name properties in the two cases. This would be inefficient and wasteful.

This situation is precisely what inheritance is designed for. First, we define the CEmployee class, which implements a Salary property and an IncSalary method:

```
' Employee class
Public Class CEmployee
    ' Salary property is read/write
    Private mdecSalary As Decimal
    Property Salary() As Decimal
        Get
            Salary = mdecSalary
        End Get
        Set
            mdecSalary = Value
        End Set
    End Property
    Public Overridable Sub IncSalary(ByVal sngPercent As Single)
        mdecSalary = mdecSalary * (1 + CDec(sngPercent))
    End Sub
End Class
```

Next, we define the CExecutive class:

```
' Executive Class
Public Class CExecutive
    Inherits CEmployee
    ' Calculate salary increase based on 5% car allowance as well
    Overrides Sub IncSalary(ByVal sngPercent As Single)
        Me.Salary = Me.Salary * CDec(1.05 + sngPercent)
    End Sub
End Class
```

There are two things to note here. First, the line:

```
Inherits CEmployee
```

indicates that the CExecutive class *inherits* the members of the CEmployee class. Put another way, an object of type CExecutive is also an object of type CEmployee. Thus, if we define an object of type CExecutive:

```
Dim ceo As New CExecutive
```

then we can invoke the Salary property, as in:

```
ceo.Salary = 1000000
```

Second, the keyword **Overrides** in the IncSalary method means that the implementation of IncSalary in CExecutive is called instead of the implementation in CEmployee. Thus, the code:

```
ceo.IncSalary
```

raises the salary of the CExecutive object **ceo** based on a car allowance. Note also the presence of the **Overridable** keyword in the definition of IncSalary in the CEmployee class, which specifies that the class inheriting from a base class is allowed to override the method of the base class.

Next, we define the CSecretary class, which also inherits from CEmployee but implements a different salary increase for secretary objects:

```
' Secretary Class
Public Class CSecretary
    Inherits CEmployee
    ' Secretaries get a 2% overtime allowance
    Overrides Sub IncSalary(ByVal sngPercent As Single)
        Me.Salary = Me.Salary * CDec(1.02 + sngPercent)
    End Sub
End Class
```

We can now write code to exercise these classes:

```
' Define new objects
Dim ThePresident As New CExecutive()
Dim MySecretary As New CSecretary()

' Set the salaries
ThePresident.Salary = 1000000
MySecretary.Salary = 30000

' Set Employee to President and inc salary
Debug.Writeline("Pres before: " & CStr(ThePresident.Salary))
ThePresident.IncSalary(0.4)
Debug.WriteLine("Pres after: " & CStr(ThePresident.Salary))

Debug.Writeline("Sec before: " & CStr(MySecretary.Salary))
MySecretary.IncSalary(0.3)
Debug.Writeline("Sec after: " & CStr(MySecretary.Salary))
```

The output in this case is:

```
Pres before: 1000000
Pres after: 1450000
Sec before: 30000
Sec after: 39600
```

The notion of inheritance is quite simple, as put forth in Microsoft's documentation:

> If Class B inherits from Class A, then any object of Class B is also an object of Class A and so includes the public properties and methods (that is, the public interface) of Class A. In this case, Class A is called the *base class* and Class B is called the *derived*

class. On the other hand, in general, the derived class can *override* the implementation of a member of the base class for its own use.

We have seen in the previous example that inheritance is implemented using the `Inherits` keyword.

Permission to Inherit

There are two keywords used in the base class definition that affect the ability to inherit from a base class:

NotInheritable

When this is used to define a class, as in:

```
Public NotInheritable Class InterfaceExample
```

the class cannot be used as a base class.

MustInherit

When this is used to define a class, as in:

```
Public MustInherit Class InterfaceExample
```

objects of this class cannot be created directly. Objects of a derived class can be created, however. In other words, `MustInherit` classes can be used as base classes and *only* as base classes.

Overriding

There are several keywords that control whether a derived class can override an implementation in the base class. These keywords are used in the declaration of the member in question, rather than in the class definition:

Overridable

Allows but does not require a member to be overridden. Note that the default for a `Public` member is `NotOverridable`. Here is an example:

```
Public Overridable Sub IncSalary()
```

NotOverridable

Prohibits overriding of the member. This is the default for `Public` members of a class.

MustOverride

Must be overridden. When this keyword is used, the member definition is restricted to just the declaration line, with no implementation and no `End Sub` or `End Function` line. For example:

```
Public MustOverride Sub IncSalary()
```

Note also that when a class module contains a `MustOverride` member, then the class itself must be declared as `MustInherit`.

Overrides

Unlike the other modifiers, this modifier belongs in the derived class and indicates that the modified member is overriding a base class member. For example:

```
Overrides Sub IncSalary()
```

Rules of Inheritance

In many object-oriented languages, such as C++, a class can inherit directly from more than one base class. This is referred to as *multiple inheritance*. VB.NET does not support multiple inheritance, and so a class can inherit directly from at most one other class. Thus, code such as the following is not permitted:

```
' Executive Class
Public Class CExecutive      'INVALID
    Inherits CEmployee
    Inherits CWorker
    . . .
End Class
```

On the other hand, Class C can inherit from Class B, which, in turn, can inherit from Class A, thus forming an inheritance hierarchy. Note also that a class can implement multiple interfaces through the **Interface** keyword. We discuss this issue later in this chapter.

MyBase, MyClass, and Me

The keyword **MyBase** provides a reference to the base class from within a derived class. If you want to call a member of the base class from within a derived class, you can use the syntax:

```
MyBase.MemberName
```

where *MemberName* is the name of the member. This will resolve any ambiguity if the derived class also has a member of the same name.

The **MyBase** keyword can be used to call the constructor of the base class in order to instantiate a member of that class, as in:

```
MyBase.New(...)
```

Note that **MyBase** cannot be used to call **Private** class members.

Visual Basic looks for the most immediate version in parent classes of the procedure in question. Thus, if Class C derives from Class B, which derives from Class A, a call in Class C to:

```
MyBase.AProc
```

first looks in Class B for a matching procedure named *AProc*. If none is found, then VB looks in Class A for a matching procedure. (By *matching*, we mean a method with the same argument signature.)

The keyword **MyClass** provides a reference to the class in which the keyword is used. It is similar to the **Me** keyword, except when used to call a method. To illustrate the difference, consider a class named Class1 and a derived class named Class1Derived. Note that each class has an IncSalary method:

```
Public Class Class1

    Public Overridable Function IncSalary(ByVal sSalary As Single) _
                                          As Single
        IncSalary = sSalary * CSng(1.1)
    End Function
```

```
    Public Sub ShowIncSalary(ByVal sSalary As Single)
        MsgBox(Me.IncSalary(sSalary))
        MsgBox(MyClass.IncSalary(sSalary))
    End Sub

End Class

Public Class Class1Derived
    Inherits Class1
    Public Overrides Function IncSalary(ByVal sSalary As Single) _
                                        As Single
        IncSalary = sSalary * CSng(1.2)
    End Function
End Class
```

Now consider the following code, placed in a form module:

```
Dim c1 As New Class1()
Dim c2 As New Class1Derived()

Dim c1var As Class1

c1var = c1
c1var.IncSalary(10000)    ' Shows 11000, 11000

c1var = c2
c1var.IncSalary(10000)    ' Shows 12000, 11000
```

The first call to IncSalary is made using a variable of type Class1 that refers to an object of type Class1. In this case, both of the following calls:

```
Me.IncSalary
MyClass.IncSalary
```

return the same value, because they both call IncSalary in the base class Class1.

However, in the second case, the variable of type Class1 holds a reference to an object of the derived class, Class1Derived. In this case, **Me** refers to an object of type Class1Derived, whereas **MyClass** still refers to the base class Class1 wherein the keyword **MyClass** appears. Thus,

```
Me.IncSalary
```

returns 12000 whereas the following:

```
MyClass.IncSalary
```

returns 10000.

Shadowing

VB.NET has a feature referred to as *shadowing* that is similar to overriding, but with some very important differences. Shadowing can apply to element types associated with any of the following statements:

Class Statement
Constant Statement

Declare Statement
Delegate Statement
Dim Statement
Enum Statement
Event Statement
Function Statement
Interface Statement
Property Statement
Structure Statement
Sub Statement

The best way to illustrate shadowing and the differences between shadowing and overriding is with an example. Consider two classes, Class1 and Class2, where Class2 derives from Class1:

```
Public Class Class1

    Public x As Integer = 1

    Public Overridable Sub TestOverride()
        MsgBox("Class1 method to override")
    End Sub

    Public Sub TestShadow()
        MsgBox("Class1 method to shadow")
    End Sub

End Class

Public Class Class2
    ' Derived class
    Inherits Class1

    Public Shadows x As Integer = 2

    Public Overrides Sub TestOverride()
        MsgBox("Class2 method that overrides")
    End Sub

    Public Shadows Sub TestShadow()
        MsgBox("Class2 method that shadows")
    End Sub

End Class
```

Class1 has two methods, TestOverride and TestShadow. Note that TestOverride is declared with the Overridable keyword. Class2 also defines two methods with the names TestOverride and TestShadow. Note that TestOverride is declared with the Overrides keyword, and TestShadow is declared with the Shadows keyword. Finally, note the presence of a public instance field, x, in each class.

Now, consider the following test code:

```
Dim c2 As Class2 = New Class2()
c2.TestOverride()
```

```
c2.TestShadow()
MsgBox("x=" & c2.x)
```

Because the object reference c2 is to an object of Class2, the calls to the Test-Override and TestShadow methods, as well as the public variable x, all refer to code in Class2, so the output messages are as expected:

```
Class2 method that overrides
Class2 method that shadows
x = 2
```

Now consider the code:

```
Dim c1 As Class1 = New Class2()
c1.TestOverride()
c1.TestShadow()
MsgBox("x=" & c1.x)
```

Here, we have a variable of type Class1 that refers to an object of Class2. The output in this case is:

```
Class2 method that overrides
Class1 method that shadows
x = 1
```

To explain this, note that overriding works as follows: the method that is called is the version that is implemented not in the type (class) of the variable, but in the type (class) of the object to which that variable refers. This is a key feature of overriding and is generally referred to as a form of polymorphism. (The variable c1 takes on many forms, based on the type of object to which it refers, rather than its own type.)

On the other hand, shadowing is different from overriding: the process is not polymorphic, and so it is the type of the variable itself and not the referenced object that determines the implementation that is used. Since the variable has type Class1, the VB.NET compiler ignores the "extra goodies" that exists because c1 happens to point to a derived class object and looks only at the Class1 portion of the object, so to speak. There is no polymorphism here.

Note that member variables, such as x, can only be shadowed; they cannot be overridden.

One other difference between shadowing and overriding is that any element type in the preceding list can shadow any other element type. For instance, a method in the derived class can shadow a variable of the same name in the base class.

Unfortunately, the Microsoft documentation makes this point at the expense of the real issue, that of polymorphism. After all, it would seem to be bad programming practice to shadow elements of different types. But shadowing methods may make some sense.

Shadowing occurs in another context that is referred to as *shadowing by scope*. For example, if a module contains a Public variable declaration and one of the procedures within the module contains a variable declaration of the same name but perhaps a different data type, then within the procedure, the local variable will shadow the module-level variable.

Interfaces, Abstract Members, and Classes

We have alluded to the fact that a class may implement all, some, or none of the members of the interfaces that it defines. Any interface member that does not have an implementation is referred to as an *abstract member*. The purpose of an abstract member is to provide a member signature (a *template*, if you will) that can be implemented by one or more *derived classes*, generally in different ways.

Let us clarify this with an example. Recall from our discussion of inheritance that the CEmployee class defines and implements an IncSalary method that increments the salary of an employee. Recall also that the CExecutive and CSecretary derived classes override the implementation of the IncSalary method in the base class CEmployee.

Suppose that, in a more complete employee model, there is a derived class for every type of employee. Moreover, each of these derived classes overrides the implementation of the IncSalary method in the base class CEmployee. In this case, the implementation of IncSalary in the base class will never need to be called! So why bother to give the member an implementation that will never be used?

Instead, we can simply provide an empty IncSalary method, as shown here:

```
' Employee class
Public Class CEmployee


    . . .


    Public Overridable Sub IncSalary(ByVal sngPercent As Single)
    End Sub

End Class
```

Alternatively, if we want to *require* that all derived classes implement the IncSalary method, we can use the MustOverride keyword, as shown here:

```
' Employee class
Public MustInherit Class CEmployee


    . . .


    Public MustOverride Sub IncSalary(ByVal sngPercent As Single)

End Class
```

As mentioned earlier, when using MustOverride, there is no End Sub statement associated with the method. Note also that when using the MustOverride keyword, Microsoft requires that the class be declared with the MustInherit keyword. This specifies that we cannot create objects of type CEmployee.

In each of the previous cases, the IncSalary member of the base class CEmployee is an abstract member.

Any class that contains at least one abstract member is termed an *abstract class*. (Thus, the CEmployee class as defined earlier is an abstract class.) This terminology comes from the fact that it is not possible to create an object from an abstract class because at least one of the object's methods would not have an implementation.

There are also situations where we might want to define a class in which all members are abstract. In other words, this is a class that only *defines* an interface. We might refer to such a class as a *pure abstract* class, although this terminology is not standard.

For example, imagine a Shape class called CShape that is designed to model the general properties and actions of geometric shapes (ellipses, rectangles, trapezoids, etc.). All shapes need a Draw method, but the implementation of the method varies depending on the type of shape—circles are drawn quite differently than rectangles, for example. Similarly, we want to include methods called Rotate, Translate, and Reflect, but, as with the Draw method, each of these methods require a different implementation based on the type of shape.

Thus, we can define the CShape class in either of the following ways:

```
Public Class Class2

    Public Overridable Sub Draw()
    End Sub

    Public Overridable Sub Rotate(ByVal sngDegrees As Single)
    End Sub

    Public Overridable Sub Translate(ByVal x As Integer, _
                        ByVal y As Integer)
    End Sub

    Public Overridable Sub Reflect(ByVal iSlope As Integer, _
                        ByVal iIntercept As Integer)
    End Sub

End Class
```

or:

```
Public MustInherit Class CShape

    Public MustOverride Sub Draw()
    Public MustOverride Sub Rotate(ByVal sngDegrees As Single)
    Public MustOverride Sub Translate(ByVal x As Integer, _
                        ByVal y As Integer)
    Public MustOverride Sub Reflect(ByVal iSlope As Integer, _
                        ByVal iIntercept As Integer)

End Class
```

Now we can define derived classes such as CRectangle, CEllipse, and CPolygon. Each of these derived classes will (or must, in the latter case) implement the members of the base class CShape. (We won't go into the details of such an implementation here, since it is not relevant to our discussion.)

Interfaces Revisited

We have seen that interfaces can be defined in class modules. VB.NET also supports an additional method of defining an interface, using the `Interface` keyword. The following example defines the IShape interface:

```
Public Interface IShape
      Sub Draw()
      Sub Rotate(ByVal sngDegrees As Single)
      Sub Translate(ByVal x As Integer, ByVal y As Integer)
      Sub Reflect(ByVal iSlope As Integer, _
               ByVal iIntercept As Integer)
End Interface
```

Note that we cannot *implement* any of the members of an interface defined using the `Interface` keyword—that is, not within the module in which the interface is defined. However, we can implement the interface using an ordinary class module. Note the use of the `Implements` statement (which was also available in VB 6, but could be applied only to external interfaces):

```
Public Class CRectangle

' Implement the interface IShape
Implements IShape

Public Overridable Sub Draw() Implements IShape.Draw
    ' code to implement Draw for rectangles
End Sub

Public Overridable Sub Spin() Implements IShape.Rotate
    ' code to implement Rotate for rectangles
End Sub

End Class
```

Note also the use of the `Implements` keyword in each function that implements an interface member. This keyword allows us to give the implementing function any name—it does not need to match the name of the method (see the Spin method earlier in this section, which implements the `IShape` interface's Rotate method). However, it is probably less confusing (and better programming practice) to use the same name.

The main advantage of using the `Implements` keyword approach to defining an interface is that a single class can implement multiple interfaces, whereas VB.NET does not permit a single class to inherit directly from multiple base classes. On the other hand, the main disadvantage of the `Interface` keyword approach is that no implementation is possible in the module that defines the interface. Thus, *all* interface members must be implemented in *every* class that implements the interface. This can mean code repetition if an interface member has the same implementation in more than one implementing class.

Polymorphism and Overloading

Fortunately, we don't need to go into the details of polymorphism and overloading, which is just as well, because they tend to be both confusing and ambiguous. For instance, some computer scientists say that overloading is a form of polymorphism, whereas others say it is not. We will discuss only those issues that are directly relevant to the .NET Framework.

Overloading

Overloading refers to an item being used in more than one way. Operator names are often overloaded. For instance, the plus sign (+) refers to addition of integers, addition of singles, addition of doubles, and concatenation of strings. Thus, the plus symbol (+) is overloaded. It's a good thing, too; otherwise, we would need separate symbols for adding integers, singles, and doubles.

Function names can also be overloaded. For instance, the absolute value function, *Abs*, can take an integer parameter, a single parameter, or a double parameter. Because the name *Abs* represents several different functions, it is overloaded. In fact, if you look at the documentation for the Abs member of the Math class (in the System namespace of the Framework Class Library), you will find the following declarations, showing the different functions using the Abs name:

```
Overloads Public Shared Function Abs(Decimal) As Decimal
Overloads Public Shared Function Abs(Double) As Double
Overloads Public Shared Function Abs(Integer) As Short
Overloads Public Shared Function Abs(Integer) As Integer
Overloads Public Shared Function Abs(Long) As Long
Overloads Public Shared Function Abs(SByte) As SByte
Overloads Public Shared Function Abs(Single) As Single
```

Note the use of the Overloads keyword, which tells VB that this function is overloaded.

Specifically, a function name is overloaded when two defined functions use the same name but have different *argument signatures*. For instance, consider a function that retrieves a current account balance. The account could be identified either by the person's name or by the account number. Thus, we might define two functions, each called GetBalance:

```
Overloads Function GetBalance(sCustName As String) As Decimal
Overloads Function GetBalance(sAccountNumber As Long) As Decimal
```

Note also that VB.NET permits function overloading only because the argument signatures of the two functions are different, so that no ambiguity can arise. The function calls:

```
GetBalance("John Smith")
GetBalance(123456)
```

are resolved by the compiler without difficulty, based on the data type of the argument. This type of overloading is often referred to as overloading the function *GetBalance*. On the other hand, there are two different functions here, so it seems more appropriate to say that the function *name* is being overloaded. Overloading is very common and not exclusive to object-oriented programming.

Polymorphism

The term *polymorphism* means having or passing through many different forms. In the .NET Framework, polymorphism is tied directly to inheritance. Again, let us consider our Employee example. The function *IncSalary* is defined in three classes: the base class CEmployee and the derived classes CExecutive and CSecretary. Thus, the *IncSalary* function takes on three forms. This is polymorphism, VB. NET style.

In case you are interested, many computer scientists would not consider this to be polymorphism. They would argue that the function *IncSalary* takes on only one form. It is the implementation that differs, not the function. They would refer to the situation described here for *IncSalary* as function overloading. The main point here is that there is a lot of confusion as to how Microsoft and others use the terms overloading and polymorphism, so you should be on guard when reading documentation.

Accessibility in Class Modules

The notion of accessibility (or scope) in class modules is more involved than it is in standard modules. As far as local variables (block-level and procedure-level) are concerned, there is no difference—we have block scope and procedure-level scope.

However, members of a class module can be assigned one of the following access modifiers:

- Public
- Private
- Friend
- Protected
- Protected Friend

(For standard modules, only Public, Private, and Friend are allowed.)

Actually, we can dispense with the Protected Friend modifier in one statement: Protected Friend is equivalent to Protected or Friend. Put another way, if Protected sets a specific range of accessibility (or inheritance—see below) and Friend sets a different range, then Protected Friend sets accessibility to the *union* of those ranges—if a member falls into *either* range, it passes the accessibility (or inheritance) criterion.

Note that class modules themselves can be declared with any one of the three access modifiers: Public, Private, or Friend (Protected is not allowed). When a class module declaration specifies one of these access modifiers, this simply restricts all of its members to that level of access, unless a member's access is further restricted by the access modifier on the member declaration itself. For instance, if the class has Friend access, no member can have Public access. (Put another way, the Public access is overridden by the Friend class access.)

On the other hand, all four access modifiers apply to members of the class module—that is, to variable, constant, enum, and procedure declarations within the class module.

To avoid confusion in discussing the access modifiers, it helps to separate the issue of accessibility of members from that of inheritance of members.

Member Inheritance

Let us first address member inheritance. Suppose that a class named Class1 has a derived class named Class1Derived, as shown in the following:

```
Public Class Class1
    Public pub As Integer = 1
    Private priv As Integer = 1
    Protected p As Integer = 1
    Friend f As Integer = 1
    Protected Friend pf As Integer = 1
End Class

Public Class Class1Derived
    Inherits Class1
    Public Sub test()

        ' Not allowed - private members are not inherited
        Me.priv = 4

        ' Allowed only in derived classes in the same project as base
class
        Me.f = 4

        ' Allowed in all derived classes
        Me.pub = 4
        Me.p = 4
        Me.fp = 4

    End Sub
End Class
```

Note that the Me. syntax is optional, and we could write, for instance, simply:

```
pub = 4
p = 4
f = 4
fp = 4
```

The fact that the code:

```
Me.p = 4
```

is valid in Class1Derived means that this class has *inherited* the member p. In other words, an object of class Class1Derived has a member variable named p. The fact that:

```
Me.f
```

fails to work in Class1Derived if Class1Derived is in a different project than Class1 means that such classes do not inherit the member f.

Now, the rules of inheritance are:

- Private members are never inherited.

- Public members are inherited by all derived classes.

- Protected members are inherited by all derived classes (and therefore so are Protected Friend members).

- Friend members are inherited by all derived classes in the same project as the base class only.

Member Accessibility

Now we come to member accessibility. Unfortunately, the term accessibility is used quite loosely in most documentation, but to make absolutely clear sense of the issue, we must be specific. Many writers simply refer to a member's accessibility, but this is ambiguous. To illustrate, consider the code:

```
Public Class Class1
    Public x As Integer = 1
End Class

Public Class Class2
    Inherits Class1
End Class
```

Now, it makes sense to ask about the accessibility of the Public member x of Class1 or the (inherited) Public member x of Class2. It does not make sense to ask about the accessibility of the member x alone, without mention of the class involved. Indeed, we say that the Public member x of Class1 is accessible from a class Class3 if the following is legal:

```
Public Class Class3
    Public Sub Test()
        Dim c1 As new Class1()
        c1.x = 5
    End Sub
End Class
```

On the other hand, the Public member x of class Class2 is accessible from Class3 if we can write:

```
Public Class Class3
    Public Sub Test()
        Dim c2 As new Class2()
        c2.x = 5
    End Sub
End Class
```

With this in mind, we can describe the accessibility rules clearly:

Private
    If ClassA is a class with a Private member m, we cannot access the member m of ClassA from any other class.

Public

If ClassA is a class with a Public member m, we can access the member m of ClassA from any other class.

Friend

If ClassA is a class with a Friend member m, we can access the member m of ClassA from any other class that is in the same project as ClassA.

Protected

Let m be a Protected member of ClassA. Then from any subclass ClassB of ClassA, we can access the member m of ClassB or the member m of any subclass of ClassB. Another way to phrase this is as follows. Let m be declared as Protected in a class ClassA. Let Class B be a subclass of ClassA. Then the member m of ClassB is accessible in each class between ClassB and ClassA in the inheritance hierarchy.

Clearly, the definition of **Protected** needs clarification. To do so, consider a chain of derived classes (that is, ClassN+1 is derived from ClassN):

```
Class1
Class2
  .
  .
  .
ClassA
    ' This is the first appearance of the protected method MyMethod
    ' Thus, all classes below inherit MyMethod
    Protected Sub MyMethod()
  .

  .
ClassB
    ' ClassB can call MyMethod because it has been inherited
    ' This is accessibility of MyMethod for ClassB
    MyMethod()
    ' Note that this is equivalent to
    Me.MyMethod()
    ' Can access MyMethod for any Class at or below this class
    ' For example, the following are legal:
    Dim b As New ClassB
    b.MyMethod()
    Dim c As New ClassC
    c.MyMethod()
    ' But the following is not legal
    Dim a As New ClassA
    a.MyMethod()
  .

  .

  .
ClassC
    ' Can access MyMethod for any Class at or below this class
    ' For example, the following are legal:
    Me.MyMethod()
    Dim c As New ClassC
    c.MyMethod()
```

```
Dim d As New ClassD
d.MyMethod()
' But the following is not legal
Dim b As New ClassB
b.MyMethod()
    .
    .
    .
ClassD
    .
    .
    .
ClassN
```

As you can see, the rules for Protected mode access are a bit involved. Actually, Protected mode should be used with some care. For instance, declaring a member variable Protected violates one of the principal rules of good object-oriented programming, encapsulation, as does declaring the member Public. Thus, it should be done only if you are certain that derived classes will be well behaved (or are willing to accept the risk). The same applies to Protected methods.

CHAPTER 5

The .NET Framework: General Concepts

In this chapter, we discuss some of the main concepts in the .NET Framework. This is intended as a general overview, just to give you the "lay of the .NET land," so to speak. For more information, see Thuan Thai and Hoang Q. Lam's *.NET Framework Essentials* (O'Reilly, 2001).

Namespaces

The notion of a *namespace* plays a fundamental role in the .NET Framework. In general, a namespace is a logical grouping of types for the purpose of identification. For example, imagine that in a certain business there is an executive named John Smith, a secretary named John Smith, and a custodian named John Smith.

In this case, the name John Smith is ambiguous. When the paymaster stands on a table and calls out the names of people to receive their pay checks, the executive John Smith won't be happy if he rushes to the table when the paymaster calls out his name and the envelope contains the custodian John Smith's pay check.

To resolve the naming ambiguity, the business can simply define three namespaces: Executive, Secretarial, and Custodial. Now the three individuals can be unambiguously referred to by their fully qualified names:

* Executive.John Smith
* Secretarial.John Smith
* Custodial.John Smith

The .NET *Framework Class Library* (FCL), which we look at in more detail in Chapter 6, consists of several thousand classes and other types (such as interfaces, structures, and enumerations) that are divided into over 90 namespaces. These namespaces provide basic system services, such as:

* Basic and advanced data types and exception handling (the System namespace)
* Data access (the System.Data namespace)

- User-interface elements for standard Windows applications (the System.Windows.Forms namespace)

- User-interface elements for web applications (the System.Web.UI namespace)

In fact, the VB.NET language itself is implemented as a set of classes belonging to the Microsoft.VisualBasic namespace. (The C# and JScript languages are also implemented as a set of classes in corresponding namespaces.)

For information on accessing the members of a namespace, see the "Assemblies and VB.NET" section later in this chapter.

Namespaces are not necessarily unique to the Framework Class Library; you can also create your own namespaces by using the Namespace statement at the beginning of a code file.

Common Language Runtime (CLR), Managed Code, and Managed Data

The *Common Language Runtime* (CLR) is an environment that manages code execution and provides application-development services. Compilers such as VB.NET expose the CLR's functionality to enable developers to create applications. Code that is created under this environment is called *managed code*. Note that COM components are *not* managed code, although they (as well as other unmanaged code) can be used in applications that are built under the CLR.

The output of a compiler includes *metadata*, which is information that describes the objects that are part of an application, such as:

- Data types and their dependencies

- Objects and their members

- References to required components

- Information (including versioning information) about components and resources that were used to build the application

Metadata is used by the CLR to do such things as:

- Manage memory allocations

- Locate and load class instances

- Manage object references and perform garbage collection

- Resolve method invocations

- Generate native code

- Make sure that the application has the correct versions of necessary components and resources

- Enforce security

The metadata in a compiled software component makes the component self-describing. This implies that components, even those written in another language, can interact with the given component directly.

Objects that are managed by the CLR are referred to as *managed data*. (It is also possible to use unmanaged data in applications.)

Managed Execution

Managed execution is the name given for the process of creating applications under the .NET Framework. The steps involved are as follows:

1. Write code using one or more .NET compilers. Note that for software components to be useable by components that are written in other languages, these components must be written using only language features that are part of the Common Language Specification (CLS).

2. Compile the code. The compiler translates source code to Microsoft Intermediate Language (MSIL) and generates the necessary metadata for the application.

3. Run the code. When code is executed, the MSIL is compiled into native code (which is CPU-specific code that runs on the same computer architecture as the compiler) by a *Just In Time* (JIT) compiler. If required, the JIT checks the code for type safety. If the type-safety check fails, an exception is thrown.

Code that cannot access invalid memory addresses or perform other illegal operations that may result in an application crash is called *type-safe code*. Code that is verified to be type-safe by the JIT is called *verifiably type-safe code*. Due to limitations in the verification process, code can be type-safe and yet not be verifiably type-safe.

Assemblies

The purpose of an assembly is to specify a logical unit, or building block, for .NET applications that *encapsulate* certain properties.

The term *assembly* refers to both a logical construct and a set of physical files. To draw an analogy on the logical side, we might use the term neighborhood to refer to a zip code, a neighborhood name, and a list of street addresses. On the physical side, a neighborhood consists of the actual houses that are located at those addresses. Thus, we can speak of physically moving (i.e., deploying) the neighborhood.

A .NET application consists of one or more assemblies. Logically speaking, an assembly is just a set of specifications. In particular:

- An assembly specifies the (MSIL) code that is associated with the assembly. This code lies in a Portable Executable (PE) file. (PE files are the traditional file types for Microsoft's code, but the format is extended for .NET applications.)

- An assembly specifies security permissions for itself, if any.

- An assembly specifies a list of data types and provides scoping for those types. Every data type in a .NET application must specify the assembly to which it belongs. The scoping provided by an assembly means that different types may have the same name, as long as they belong to different assemblies and can therefore be distinguished by means of the assembly to which they belong. Microsoft refers to this by saying that an assembly provides a type boundary.

- An assembly specifies rules for resolving external types and external references, including references to other assemblies. In this way, assemblies form a reference scope boundary. Included in this information are any version dependencies for the external references.

- An assembly specifies which of its parts are exposed outside the assembly and which are private to the assembly itself.

In addition to these specifications listed, an assembly is an object (or logical unit) that possesses certain properties:

- An assembly has version properties. This includes a major and minor version number, as well as a revision and build number. Indeed, an assembly is the smallest unit that has versioning properties. Put another way, all elements of an assembly (types and resources) are versioned as a unit—they are assigned the version numbers of the assembly to which they belong. In other words, an assembly is a *versioning unit*.

- An assembly forms a *deployment unit*. More specifically, at any given time, a .NET application only needs access to the assemblies that specify the code *under execution*. Other assemblies that make up the application need not be present if the code they specify is not currently needed for execution. These assemblies can be retrieved upon demand, so that the downloading of applications can be more efficient.

Finally, we note that multiple versions of a single assembly can be run at the same time, on the same system, or even in the same process. This is referred to as *side-by-side execution*.

The specifications in an assembly are collectively referred to as the assembly's *manifest*. The data in the manifest is also called *metadata*. Specifically, the manifest contains:

- The name of the assembly

- Version information for the assembly

- Security information for the assembly

- A list of all files that are part of the assembly

- Type reference information for the types specified in the assembly

- A list of other assemblies that are referenced by the assembly

- Custom information, such as a user-friendly assembly title, description, and product information (company name, copyright information, and so on)

Physically, an assembly consists of one or more files—files that contain code, as well as resources, such as bitmaps. The assembly's manifest can be a separate file or part of another file in the assembly.

Assemblies and VB.NET

To a VB.NET programmer, an assembly is similar to a traditional DLL or EXE file, except that it contains additional information, such as reference and type information (which in COM was often contained in a separate OLB or TLB file, called a type library). When a VB.NET application is compiled, the compiler creates an assembly for the target EXE or DLL.

In the .NET environment, namespaces are part of assemblies. An assembly can contain many namespaces, and namespaces can be nested.

For instance, the System namespace is the fundamental namespace in the .NET environment. This is not the time to go into details, but one example will be useful. The System namespace identifies the Array class (Microsoft likes to say that the namespace *contains* classes.) One of the members of the Array class is the Copy method, which copies a portion of one array to another array. Thus, we can write code such as the following:

```
Imports System      ' Optional since System is always imported
Dim array1() As Integer = {1, 2, 3, 4}
Dim array2(3) As Integer
Array.Copy(array1, array2, 3)
```

To use an existing assembly in a VB.NET project, you must do two things:

* Add a reference to the assembly to your project. There are two exceptions to this rule, however. A reference to the assembly containing the System namespace (*mscorlib.dll*) is added automatically, as is a reference to the assembly containing the language being used (for VB.NET, this is *Microsoft.VisualBasic.dll*).

* Access the member or members of the namespace, as described later in this section.

To access a member of a namespace, you can use its fully qualified name. For example, to create an instance of the Timers class, which is found in the System.Timers namespace, you can use a code fragment like the following:

```
Dim oTimer As New System.Timers.Timer(2000)
```

Since using fully qualified names tends to be relatively cumbersome, you can include an **Imports** statement at the beginning of a code file, before any references to variables or classes. Its syntax is:

```
Imports [aliasname = ] namespace
```

where *aliasname* is an optional alias for the namespace, and *namespace* is its fully qualified name. For example, if you import the System.Timers namespace as follows:

```
Imports System.Timers
```

you do not have to qualify a reference to the Timer class, which can be instantiated as follows:

```
Dim oTimer As New Timer(2000)
```

In the event that there is a naming conflict (either two namespaces have identically named types, or a named type conflicts with a name in your project), you can specify an alias for the namespace, as follows:

```
Imports TI = System.Timers
```

and then instantiate a Timer object as follows:

```
Dim oTimer As New TI.Timer(2000)
```

If you're using the Visual Basic command-line compiler, you have to explicitly import the Microsoft.VisualBasic namespace, or your code will not compile. If you're using Visual Studio, VB's language elements are accessed automatically without your having to import the namespace.

CHAPTER 6

The .NET Framework Class Library

VB.NET is about classes, classes, and more classes. Even something as simple as a string is implemented in a class (the String class of the System namespace). As we mentioned in Chapter 5, the .NET Framework defines an extensive network of classes and namespaces called the *Framework Class Library* (FCL). This consists of a set of namespaces that provide basic system services (like the System namespace, whose classes define .NET data types, provide exception handling, and handle garbage collection, among other things). It also includes additional namespaces, such as System.Data, System.Windows.Forms, and System.Web.UI, which provide application services. In total, there are over 90 namespaces containing several thousand classes, interfaces, structures, enumerations, and other items (such as delegates) in the .NET Framework Class Library.

The System namespace is at the top of the namespace hierarchy, and the Object class is at the top of the object hierarchy. All types in the .NET Framework Class Library derive from the Object class.

The .NET Framework Class Library is sufficiently extensive to require an entire book for its description. In this chapter, we provide just a brief introduction and some examples. This should prepare you to dive into the Microsoft Class Library documentation. Note also that the reference portion of this book, Chapter 10, documents selected language elements from the Framework Class Library that seem particularly useful to VB programmers. For more on which classes are included in the reference section, see its introduction.

Before becoming intimidated by the size of the Framework Class Library, we should also keep in mind that VB.NET provides wrappers for some elements of the Framework Class Library, so we can often just call a VB function rather than resort to accessing the classes in the Framework Class Library directly. More generally, while the class library does have much to offer a VB programmer and should not be ignored, it can be studied and used on an "as needed" basis.

Let us illustrate a simple case in which the FCL has something to offer. We mentioned in Chapter 3 that the built-in VB data types are wrappers for a corresponding BCL class (for reference types) or structure (for value types). However, the Visual Basic language typically does not implement all of the members of the BCL class. For instance, if we want to verify that a user has entered a number that lies within the range of type Integer, we can use code such as the following:

```
Dim s As String
Dim i As Integer
s = InputBox("Enter an integer")
If IsNumeric(s)
    If (CDbl(s) >= i.MinValue) And (CDbl(s) <= i.MaxValue) Then
        i = CInt(s)
    Else
        Debug.WriteLine("Invalid number")
    End If
Else
    Debug.WriteLine("Non-numeric value")
End If
```

Because the VB Integer data type is a wrapper for the BCL's Int32 structure, the MinValue and MaxValue properties of the Int32 data type are accessible to the Integer variable i. Incidentally, because the MaxValue and MinValue members are shared, we could also have written:

```
If IsNumeric(s)
    If (CDbl(s) >= Integer.MinValue) _
        And (CDbl(s) <= Integer.MaxValue) Then
```

which, in my opinion, is more readable.

In order to prevent a compiler error when compiling this code with Option Strict On, we've converted the String s to a Double before comparing its value with the Integer class's MinValue and MaxValue properties. This is because a Double is the least restrictive numeric data type, and we want to be sure that the numeric equivalent of the String s is within the range of a more restrictive numeric (integer) data type.

The System Namespace

The System namespace contains classes for such broad ranging things as:

- Data types
- Data type conversions
- Method-parameter manipulation
- Events and event handlers
- Mathematics
- Program invocation
- Application-environment management

Data Type Conversion

To illustrate data type conversion, the System namespace defines a class called Convert. If you check the documentation, you'll find that one of the methods of the Convert class is ToBoolean. The documentation lists the following for ToBoolean:

```
Overloads Public Shared Function ToBoolean(String) As Boolean
Overloads Public Shared Function ToBoolean(Double) As Boolean
Overloads Public Shared Function ToBoolean(Single) As Boolean
Overloads Public Shared Function ToBoolean(Char) As Boolean
Overloads Public Shared Function ToBoolean(Byte) As Boolean
Overloads Public Shared Function ToBoolean(Object) As Boolean
Overloads Public Shared Function ToBoolean(Boolean) As Boolean
Overloads Public Shared Function ToBoolean(Long) As Boolean
Overloads Public Shared Function ToBoolean(Integer) As Boolean
```

As you can see, there are many ToBoolean functions—each one with a different argument signature—to take care of converting various data types to Boolean.

Now, just for exercise, we can write:

```
Dim s As String
Dim b As Boolean
s = "false"
b = System.Convert.ToBoolean(s)
msgbox(b)
```

Because the System namespace is always available (or if we are programming outside of Visual Studio, we can import it using the Imports statement), we can omit the System qualifier and write:

```
b = Convert.ToBoolean(s)
```

Of course, we can also use the built-in VB.NET function *CBool*.

The Convert class contains methods for converting data to the standard Visual Basic data types, as well as to the data types supported by the .NET Framework but not wrapped by Visual Basic, such as the unsigned-integer data types. The most important of these methods are shown in Table 6-1.

Table 6-1: Members of the System.Convert class

Method	Description
ToBoolean	Converts a value to a Boolean
ToByte	Converts a value to a Byte
ToChar	Converts a value to a Char
ToDateTime	Converts a value to DateTime (Date in Visual Basic)
ToDecimal	Converts a value to Decimal
ToDouble	Converts a value to Double
ToInt16	Converts a value to Int16 (Short in Visual Basic)
ToInt32	Converts a value to Int32 (Integer in Visual Basic)
ToInt64	Converts a value to Int64 (Long in Visual Basic)
ToSByte	Converts a value to SByte, the unsigned-byte data type in the BCL
ToSingle	Converts a value to Single

Table 6-1: Members of the System.Convert class (continued)

Method	Description
ToString	Converts a value to String
ToUInt16	Converts a value to UInt16, an unsigned 16-bit integer
ToUInt32	Converts a value to UInt32, an unsigned 32-bit integer
ToUInt64	Converts a value to UInt64, an unsigned 64-bit integer

The Array Class

The Array class contains useful methods for dealing with arrays. For instance, the Array object has a Sort method (at last) that sorts the elements of an array. Here is an example:

```
Sub sortArray()
Dim i As Integer
Dim intArray() As Integer = {9, 8, 12, 4, 5}
For i = 0 To 4
    console.WriteLine(CStr(intArray(i)))
Next
Array.Sort(intarray)
Console.WriteLine("Sorted:")
For i = 0 To 4
    console.WriteLine(intArray(i))
Next
End Sub
```

The output is:

```
9
8
12
4
5
Sorted:
4
5
8
9
12
```

Some of the more important methods of the Array class are shown in Table 6-2.

Table 6-2: Some members of the System.Array class

Method	Description
BinarySearch	Searches a sorted one-dimensional array for a value
IndexOf	Returns the first occurrence of a particular value in a one-dimensional array
LastIndexOf	Returns the last occurrence of a particular value in a one-dimensional array
Reverse	Reverses the order of the elements in a one-dimensional array or a portion of a one-dimensional array
Sort	Sorts a one-dimensional array

The Math Class

The Math class has a number of mathematical-function methods (such as trigono-metric functions), as well as some more useful methods, such as Max and Min. Therefore, we can just write:

```
MsgBox(Math.Max(4,7))
```

Table 6-3 shows the members of the Math class.

Table 6-3: The members of the Math class

Topic	Description
Abs function	Absolute value
Acos function	Arccosine
Asin function	Arcsine
Atan function	Arctangent; returns the angle whose tangent is a specified number
Atan2 function	Arctangent; returns the angle whose tangent is the quotient of two specified numbers
Ceiling function	Returns the smallest integer greater than or equal to the argument number
Cos function	Cosine
Cosh function	Hyperbolic cosine
E field	The natural number e
Exp function	Exponential function
Floor function	Returns the largest integer less than or equal to the argument number
IEEERemainder function	Returns the remainder after dividing x by y
Log function	Natural (base e) logarithm
Log10 function	Common (base 10) logarithm
Max function	Maximum
Min function	Minimum
Mod operator	Returns the modulus, that is, the remainder when number1 is divided by number2
Pi field	Pi, the ratio of the circumference of a circle to its diameter
Pow function	Generalized exponential function
Randomize statement	Initializes the random number generator
Rnd function	Returns a random number
Round function	Rounds a given number to a specified number of decimal places
Sign function	Determines the sign of a number
Sin function	Sine
Sinh function	Hyperbolic sine
Sqrt function	Square root
Tan function	Tangent
Tanh function	Hyperbolic tangent

.NET FCL

The String Class

The String class implements a collection of methods for string manipulation, including methods for locating substrings, concatenation, replacement, padding, trimming, and so on. One interesting method is Insert, which inserts a new string into an existing string.

The VB.NET String data type is equivalent to the System.String class, so we can apply the methods of System.String directly to VB strings, as in:

```
Dim s As String = "To be to be"
msgbox(s.Insert(6, "or not "))
```

This displays the message "To be or not to be." Table 6-4 shows the members of the String class.

Table 6-4: The members of the String class

Member	Description
Chars property	Returns the character at a specified character position in the string
Clone method	Returns a reference to an instance of the string
Compare method	A shared method that compares two string objects
CompareOrdinal method	A shared method that compares two string objects without considering localization
CompareTo method	Compares a string with a designated object
Concat method	Concatenates one or more instances of string
Copy method	A shared function that creates a new instance of a string with the same content as a designated string
CopyTo method	Copies a number of characters from a string to a specified position in an array of Unicode characters
Empty field	A read-only field that represents an empty string.
EndsWith method	Determines whether the end of a string matches a specified string
Equals method	Determines whether the string is equal to another string
Format method	Replaces a format specification with its textual equivalent
IndexOf method	Returns the position of the first occurrence of a substring within a string
IndexOfAny method	Returns the position of the first occurrence in a string of any of a set of characters
Insert method	Inserts a substring into a string
Join method	A shared method that concatenates a string separator and the elements of a string array
LastIndexOf method	Returns the position of the last occurrence of a substring within a string
LastIndexOfAny method	Returns the position of the last occurrence in a string of any of a set of characters
Length property	Returns the number of characters in the string
PadLeft method	Right aligns the characters in a string
PadRight method	Left aligns the characters in a string
Remove method	Deletes a specified number of characters from a string starting at a particular position

Table 6-4: The members of the String class (continued)

Member	Description
Replace method	Replaces all occurrences of a substring in a string with another substring
Split method	Splits a delimited string into a string array
StartsWith method	Determines whether the beginning of a string matches a particular substring
Substring method	Extracts a substring from a string
ToCharArray method	Copies the characters in a string to a character array
ToLower method	Converts a string to lowercase
ToUpper method	Converts a string to uppercase
Trim method	Removes all occurrences of a set of characters from the beginning and end of a string
TrimEnd method	Removes all occurrences of a set of characters from the end of a string
TrimStart method	Removes all occurrences of a set of characters from the beginning of a string

Other Namespaces

Nested just below the System namespace are a number of second-level namespaces, which contain such classes as:

System.CodeDOM
>   Contains classes representing the elements and structure of a source code document.

System.Collections
>   Contains interfaces and classes that define various collections of objects, such as lists, queues, arrays, hashtables, and dictionaries.

System.ComponentModel
>   Contains classes that are used to implement the runtime and design-time behavior of components and controls.

System.Configuration
>   Contains classes that allow the creation of custom installers for software components.

System.Data
>   Consists mostly of the classes that constitute the ADO.NET architecture and are used for database connectivity.

System.Diagnostics
>   Contains classes that allow debugging of applications and code tracing.

System.DirectoryServices
>   Contains classes that provide access to the Active Directory from managed code.

System.Drawing
>   Contains classes that provide access to GDI+ basic graphics functionality. (More advanced functionality is provided in the System.Drawing.Drawing2D, System.Drawing.Imaging, and System.Drawing.Text namespaces.)

.NET FCL

System.IO

Contains classes that allow synchronous and asynchronous reading from and writing to data streams and files.

System.Net

Contains classes that provide a simple programming interface to many of the common network protocols, such as FTP and HTTP. (The System.Net.Sockets namespace provides lower-level network access control.)

System.Reflection

Contains classes and interfaces that provide a managed view of loaded types, methods, and fields, with the ability to create and invoke types dynamically.

System.Resources

Contains classes for managing resources (culture-specific resources and resource files).

System.Security

Contains classes that provide access to the underlying structure of the .NET Framework security system.

System.ServiceProcess

Contains classes that allow us to install and run services. (Services are long-running executables that run without a user interface.)

System.Text

Contains classes representing ASCII, Unicode, UTF-7, and UTF-8 character encodings, as well as abstract base classes for converting blocks of characters to and from blocks of bytes, and more.

System.Text.RegularExpressions

Contains classes that provide access to the .NET Framework regular expression engine.

System.Threading

Provides classes and interfaces that enable multithreaded programming.

System.Timers

Contains classes that provide the Timer component, which allows you to raise an event on a specified interval.

System.Web and related namespaces

Contain classes and interfaces that enable browser/server communication and that allow you to develop ASP.NET applications and web services.

System.Windows.Forms

Contains classes for creating Windows-based applications that take full advantage of the rich user-interface features available in the Microsoft Windows operating system. In this namespace, you will find the Form class and many other controls that can be added to forms to create user interfaces.

System.Xml

Contains classes that provide standards-based support for processing XML.

Let's take a look at some of these other classes in the BCL.

System.Collections

This namespace contains classes for implementing a variety of collection types, such as stacks and queues. As you may know, a queue is a first-in, first-out data structure. The following code illustrates the use of the Queue class:

```
Dim s As String
Dim q As New Collections.Queue()
q.Enqueue("To")
q.Enqueue("be")
q.Enqueue("or")
q.Enqueue("not")

Do While q.Count > 0
    s = s & " " & CStr(q.Dequeue)
Loop
msgbox(s)
```

The output is "To be or not".

System.Data

System.Data and its nested namespaces, notably System.Data.OleDb and System. Data.SqlClient, provide data access using ADO.NET. The OleDb and SqlClient namespaces are responsible for defining data providers that can connect to a data source, retrieve data from a data source, write data back to a data source, and execute commands against the data source. The most important class in each of these namespaces is a data adapter class (in the OleDb namespace, it's the OleDb-DataAdapter class; in the SqlClient namespace, it's the SqlDataAdapter class) which is responsible for retrieving data from a data source and writing it to a dataset. A dataset in turn is a collection of related data that's disconnected from its original data source.

 ADO.NET is not the same thing as ADO, nor is ADO.NET a new version of ADO. Instead, ADO (or ActiveX Data Objects) is a COM-based object model for data access. ADO.NET is an entirely new model for data access that is based on the disconnected dataset.

System.IO

The System.IO namespace contains classes that provide a variety of input/output functionality, such as:

- Manipulating directories (Directory class) and files (File class)
- Monitoring changes in directories and files (FileSystemWatcher class)
- Reading and writing single bytes, mulitbyte blocks, or characters to and from streams
- Reading and writing characters to and from strings (StringReader and String-Writer)

- Writing and reading data types and objects to and from streams (BinaryWriter and BinaryReader)

- Providing random access to files (FileStream)

It appears that, for VB programmers, the System.IO namespace and its classes are intended to take the place of the FileSystemObject object model that is part of the Microsoft Scripting Runtime. The System.IO namespace is certainly much more extensive. The File and Directory classes duplicate the functionality of the File-SystemObject. For more on these classes, see their entries in this book's reference section.

System.Text.RegularExpressions

The System.Text.RegularExpressions namespace contains classes that provide access to the .NET Framework's regular expression engine. This is not the place to go into details about regular expressions, but we can make a few comments.

In its simplest form, a regular expression is a text string that represents a *pattern* that other strings may or may not match. In this way, regular expressions form a very powerful method of string matching. In more complicated forms, a regular expression is a kind of programming statement. For instance, the expression:

```
s/ab*c/def
```

says to match the given string against the regular expression ab*c (strings that start with ab and end with c). If a match exists, then replace the given string with the string def. Here are some simple regular expressions for pattern matching:

Single character
> This is matched only by itself.

Dot (.)
> This is matched by any character except the newline character.

[string of characters]
> This matches any single character that belongs to the string of characters. For example, [abc] matches the *single* character a, b, or c. A dash can also be used in the character list, for instance, [0-9] matches any single digit. We can also write [0-9a-z] to match any single digit or any single lowercase character, and [a-zA-Z] to match any single lower- or uppercase character.
>
> The ^ symbol can be used to negate the match. For instance, [^0-9] matches any character *except* a digit.

Special match abbreviations
> \d matches any single digit; \D matches any single nondigit.
>
> \w is equivalent to [a-zA-Z_], thus matching any letter or underscore; \W is the negation of \w.

*Asterisk (*)*
> The occurrence of an asterisk within a regular expression gives a match if and only if there are zero or more repeated instances of the single character preceding the asterisk. For example, the regular expression \da*\d is matched by any string beginning with a single digit, continuing with zero or more as and ending with a single digit, as with 01 or 0aaa1.

Plus sign (+)

The occurrence of a plus sign within a regular expression gives a match if and only if there are one or more repeated instances of the single character preceding the plus sign. For example, the regular expression \da+\d is matched by any string beginning with a single digit, continuing with one or more as and ending with a single digit, as with 0aaa1 (but not 01).

Question mark (?)

The occurrence of a question mark within a regular expression gives a match if and only if there are zero or one instances of the single character preceding the question mark. For example, the regular expression \da?\d is matched by any string beginning with a single digit, continuing with zero or one as and ending with a single digit, as with 01 and 0a1.

General multiplier

The occurrence of the substring {x,y}, where x and y are nonnegative integers within a regular expression, gives a match if and only if there are at least x but at most y instances of the single character preceding the opening bracket. For example, the regular expression \da{5,10}\d is matched by any string beginning with a single digit, continuing with at least 5 but at most 10 as and ending with a single digit, as with 0aaaaaa1.

Note that you can leave out one of x or y. Thus, {x,} means "at least x," and {,y} means "at most y."

The System.Text.RegularExpressions namespace has a Regex class, whose objects represent regular expressions. Here's a simple example of the use of the Regex class:

```
' Define a new Regex object with pattern \da{3,5}\d
Dim rx As New System.Text.RegularExpressions.Regex("\da{3,5}\d")


' Do some matching
MsgBox(rx.IsMatch("0a1"))        ' Displays False
MsgBox(rx.IsMatch("0aaa1"))      ' Displays True
```

The System.Text.RegularExpressions namespace contains classes for string replacement as well, but we do not go into these matters in this brief introduction.

System.Windows.Forms

This namespace is the mother of all namespaces for creating Windows applications. To quote the documentation:

The System.Windows.Forms namespace contains classes for creating Windows-based applications that take full advantage of the rich user interface features available in the Microsoft Windows operating system. In this namespace you will find the Form class and many other controls that can be added to forms to create user interfaces.

In fact, each new form added to a VB.NET project contains the line:

```
Imports System.Windows.Forms
```

Fortunately, Visual Studio provides the functionality of the System.Windows.Forms namespace to us as VB programmers, so we don't need to program directly against this namespace.

.NET FCL

CHAPTER 7

Delegates and Events

In this chapter, we discuss delegates and events, two additional .NET framework topics that are important to VB programmers.

Delegates

In a never-ending effort to deny VB programmers the right to use pointers, Microsoft has implemented a feature called delegates that, according to the documentation, provide a safe alternative to function pointers.

As you may know, a *pointer variable* (or *pointer*) is simply a variable whose value is interpreted by the compiler as a memory address. The address to which the pointer points is the *target* of the pointer, and we say that the pointer variable *points* to that target address. If the target address is a variable of data type Integer, for example, then we say that the pointer is of *type* Integer or is an Integer pointer. Thus, the type of a pointer is the type of the target variable. (We have seen that, as reference types, variables of type Object and String are both pointers; i.e., their values point to the address of the data in memory.)

A pointer can also point to a function, that is, contain the address of a function. Even though a function is not a variable, it does have a physical location in memory and so can be the target of a pointer. (Actually, it's reasonable to think of a function as a type of variable, but that is another story.) In this case, we have a *function pointer*.

Function pointers are very useful in certain situations for calling or specifying functions. This is commonly done in the C++ programming language, where function pointers are supported directly.

One area in which function pointers are used is in the context of *callback functions*. To illustrate, if we want to enumerate all of the fonts on a given system, the Windows API provides a function called *EnumFontFamiliesEx*, defined as follows:

```
Public Declare Function EnumFontFamiliesEx Lib "gdi32" _
    Alias "EnumFontFamiliesExA" ( _
    ByVal hdc As Long, _
    lpLogFont As LOGFONT, _
    ByVal lpEnumFontProc As Long, _
    ByVal lParam As Long, _
    ByVal dw As Long) _
As Long
```

The third parameter requires the address of a function we must declare, called a
callback function. The reason for this term is that Windows will call our callback
function for each font in the system, passing information about the font in the
parameters of the function. According to the documentation, the callback function
must have a particular form:

```
Public Function EnumFontFamExProc(ByVal lpelfe As Long, _
                                  ByVal lpntme As Long, _
                                  ByVal FontType As Long,
                                  ByRef lParam As Long) As Long
```

The point here is that to use *EnumFontFamiliesEx*, we need to pass the address of
a function as one of the parameters. As you may know, this is done in VB using
the AddressOf operator. In earlier versions of VB, this operator is described as
follows:

> A unary operator that causes the address of the procedure it precedes to be passed to
> an API procedure that expects a function pointer at that position in the argument list.

Put another way, the AddressOf operator is implemented in VB 6 for the express
purpose of passing function addresses to API functions.

In VB.NET, the AddressOf operator returns a delegate, which is, as the documentation states:

> A unary operator that creates a procedure delegate instance that references the
> specific procedure.

So let us discuss delegates. We begin with a rather unhelpful definition: a *delegate*
is an object of a class derived from either the Delegate class or the Multicast-
Delegate class. These two classes are abstract, so no objects of these classes can
be created. Nevertheless, other classes can be derived from these classes, and
objects can be created from these derived classes.

In VB.NET, delegates can be used to call methods of objects or to supply callback
functions. In addition, VB.NET uses delegates to bind event handlers to events.
Fortunately, VB.NET also supplies tools (such as the AddHandler method) to auto-
mate this process, so we don't need to use delegates directly for this purpose.

A delegate object inherits a number of properties and methods from the Delegate
or MulticastDelegate class. In particular, a delegate object has:

- A Target property that references the object or objects whose method or
  methods are to be called

- A Method property that returns a MethodInfo object that describes the method
  or methods associated with the delegate

- An Invoke method that invokes the target method or methods

By now you have probably guessed that there are two delegate classes because delegates derived from the Delegate class can only call a single method, whereas delegates derived from MulticastDelegate can call multiple methods.

Using a Delegate to Call a Method

To call a method using a delegate, we call the Invoke method of the delegate. To illustrate, consider the class module with a simple method:

```
Public Class Class1
    Public Sub AMethod(ByVal s As String)
        Msgbox(s)
    End Sub
End Class
```

Now, in a module with a Windows Form (referred to as a form module in earlier versions of VB), we declare a (single cast) delegate with the same parameters as the target method we wish to call:

```
Delegate Sub AMethodDelegate(ByVal s As String)
```

The following code then uses the delegate to call the AMethod of Class1:

```
Protected Sub Form1_Click(ByVal sender As Object, _
                          ByVal e As System.EventArgs) _
                          Handles MyBase.Click
    ' Object of type Class1 _
    Dim obj As New Class1()

    ' Declare a new delegate
    Dim delg As ADelegate

    ' Define the delegate, passing the address
    ' of the object's method
    delg = New ADelegate(AddressOf obj.AMethod)

    ' Now call the method using the delegate's Invoke method
    delg.Invoke("test")

End Sub
```

Note that the documentation describes the delegate constructor as taking two parameters, as in:

```
delg = New ADelegate(TargetObject, PointerToMethodOfObject)
```

However, Visual Basic is not capable of handling the second parameter, so VB supports the special syntax:

```
delg = New ADelegate(AddressOf obj.AMethod)
```

We point this out only to warn you about the documentation on the delegate class constructor.

Using a Delegate as a Function Pointer

The following example illustrates the use of a delegate in the context of a call-back function. In this example, we want to create a generic sort function for sorting integer arrays. The function uses the bubble sort algorithm for sorting, but it's generic in the sense that one of its parameters is a compare function that is used to do the comparison of adjacent integers. Thus, by varying the external comparison function, we can change the type of sorting (ascending, descending, or some other method) without changing the main sort function. The compare function is a callback function, since it is a function we supply that is called by the main sort function. (In this case, the callback function is not supplying us with information, as in the font enumeration case described earlier. Instead, it is called to help the sort function do its sorting.)

First, we declare a delegate. As part of the declaration of a delegate, we must specify the signature of the method that is associated with the delegate, which, in our case, is the compare function. Since the compare function should take two (adjacent) integers and return True if and only if we need to swap the integers in the bubble sort algorithm, we declare the delegate as follows:

```
' Returns True if need to swap
Delegate Function CompareFunc(ByVal x As Integer, _
                             ByVal y As Integer) _
                             As Boolean
```

Here are two alternative target methods for the delegate—one for an ascending sort and one for a descending sort:

```
Function SortAscending(ByVal x As Integer, ByVal y As Integer) As Boolean
    If y < x Then
        SortAscending = True
    End If
End Function

Function SortDescending(ByVal x As Integer, _
                        ByVal y As Integer) As Boolean
    If y > x Then
        SortDescending = True
    End If
End Function
```

Now we can define the sort routine. Note the call to the Invoke method of the delegate:

```
Sub BubbleSort(ByVal CompareMethod As CompareFunc, _
               ByVal IntArray() As Integer)
    Dim i, j, temp As Integer
    For i = 0 To Ubound(IntArray)
        For j = i + 1 To Ubound(IntArray)
            If CompareMethod.Invoke(IntArray(i), IntArray(j)) Then
                Temp = IntArray(j)
                IntArray(j) = IntArray(i)
                IntArray(i) = Temp
            End If
        Next j
```

```
        Next i
    End Sub
```

Here is some code to exercise this example:

```
Protected Sub Button1_Click(ByVal sender As Object, _
                            ByVal e As System.EventArgs)
    Dim i As Integer
    Dim iArray() As Integer = New Integer() {6, 2, 4, 9}
    BubbleSort(AddressOf SortAscending, iArray)
    For i = 0 To 3
        Debug.WriteLine(CStr(iArray(i)))
    Next
    Debug.WriteLine
    BubbleSort(AddressOf SortDescending, iArray)
    For i = 0 To 3
        Debug.WriteLine(CStr(iArray(i)))
    Next
End Sub
```

Alternatively, we can define delegate variables instead of using the **Addressof** operator directly:

```
Private Sub Button1_Click(ByVal sender As System.Object, ByVal e As
System.EventArgs) Handles Button1.Click

    Dim i As Integer
    ' Instances of the delegate type CompareFunc
    Dim dlgAsc As New CompareFunc(AddressOf SortAscending)
    Dim dlgDesc As New CompareFunc(AddressOf SortDescending)
    Dim iArray() As Integer = New Integer() {6, 2, 4, 9}
    BubbleSort(dlgAsc, iArray)
    For i = 0 To 3
        Debug.WriteLine(CStr(iArray(i)))
    Next
    Debug.WriteLine("")
    BubbleSort(dlgDesc, iArray)
    For i = 0 To 3
        Debug.WriteLine(CStr(iArray(i)))
    Next

End Sub
```

The output is, as you would expect:

```
2
4
6
9

9
6
4
2
```

Events and Event Binding

An *event* is an action that occurs. This action can take place on the part of the user of an application (such as when the user clicks a command button), on the part of application code (such as when a change is made to a record in a recordset), or on the part of the operating system (such as a timer event). When an event occurs, we say that the event is *raised*, or *fired*.

Each event has a *source*. This is the object to which the action is applied, such as the button that was clicked. The source is responsible for alerting the operating system that an event has occurred. It does so by sending an event notification message, generally to its parent or container window. For this reason, Microsoft refers to the event source as the *sender*.

An event often has an *event argument*, which is simply data that pertains to the event. For instance, the press of a keyboard key generates an event that includes event arguments describing the keycode of the key pressed and information on the state of modifier keys (the Shift, Alt, and Ctrl keys). The event arguments are part of the message sent by the event source.

An *event handler* is a procedure (or method) that is executed as a result of event notification. The process of declaring an event handler for an event is called *binding* the procedure to the event.

Control-Related Events

Most controls have a large number of *built-in events* associated with them. For instance, the textbox control has events associated with changing the text in the textbox, hitting a key while the textbox has the focus, clicking on the textbox with the mouse, dragging the mouse over the textbox, and more.

The VB IDE can be used to insert an empty event handler, complete with the proper event parameters, for any built-in control. The procedure is simply to select the control, then click the Events button in the Properties window. This displays a list of built-in events for the control. Selecting one of these events causes the VB IDE to insert an empty event handler for that event into the code editor window.

Note that each control has a *default event*. For instance, the default event for the command button is the Click event. As a shortcut, we can get the VB IDE to insert an empty event handler for the default event simply by double clicking the control. For instance, double clicking a command button produces the following code:

```
Private Sub button1_Click(ByVal sender As System.Object, _
                          ByVal e As System.EventArgs) _
        Handles button1.Click
End Sub
```

The sender variable is the source of the event. The second parameter is an object whose properties describe the event arguments.

Note the **Handles** clause, which tells the compiler that this procedure handles the button1.Click event. Using this clause, we can assign any procedure to handle this event. We will discuss this further when we talk about `AddHandler` later in this chapter.

As another example, double clicking a Windows form causes the VB IDE to insert the following empty event handler:

```
Protected Sub Form1_Click(ByVal sender As Object, _
                          ByVal e As System.EventArgs)

End Sub
```

WithEvents

To define a custom event in a class module, we can use the `WithEvents` keyword. To illustrate with a very simple example, suppose we create the class module shown here:

```
Public Class Class1

    ' Declare an event
    Public Event AnEvent(ByVal EventParam As Integer)

    ' Method to raise the event
    Public Sub RaiseTheEvent(ByVal iEventNumber As Integer)
        RaiseEvent AnEvent(iEventNumber)
    End Sub

End Class
```

In a class module with a Windows form, we declare a variable of type Class1 using the `WithEvents` keyword to hook the class' events:

```
Public WithEvents ev As Class1
```

This automatically causes the VB IDE to add the variable name *ev* to the left-hand drop-down list above the code window. When we select this variable, the right-hand drop-down list displays the events for this class. In this case, the list contains only the ev_AnEvent event. Selecting this event places an empty event shell in the code editor window (to which we have added a single line of code):

```
Public Sub ev_AnEvent(ByVal EventParam As System.Integer) _
    Handles ev.AnEvent
    MsgBox("Event raised: " & EventParam)
End Sub
```

Finally, in a button click event, we can place code to implement our simple example:

```
Protected Sub Button1_Click(ByVal sender As Object, _
                            ByVal e As System.EventArgs) _
                            Handles Button1.Click
    ' Define a new Class1 instance
    ev = New Class1()
    ' Raise the event
    ev.RaiseTheEvent(7)
End Sub
```

We should note that the `WithEvents` keyword approach to event handling has one slight drawback. Namely, we cannot use the `New` keyword with `WithEvents`, as in:

```
Public WithEvents ev As New Class1
```

Thus, the object must be instantiated separately from the variable declaration, as we did in the previous example.

AddHandler and RemoveHandler

The `AddHandler` statement can be used to bind an event handler to a built-in or custom event using code. This makes it possible to bind several event handlers to a single event. To illustrate, proceed as follows. Add the default event handler for a form's Click event:

```
Protected Sub Form1_Click(ByVal sender As Object, _
                          ByVal e As System.EventArgs) _
                          Handles MyBase.Click
    MsgBox("Default Click Event")
End Sub
```

Next, add another procedure with the same signature as the default event handler:

```
Protected Sub Form1Click(ByVal sender As Object, _
                         ByVal e As System.EventArgs)
    msgbox("Custom Click Event")
End Sub
```

Finally, we use the `AddHandler` statement, which must be executed in order to bind the custom Form1Click event handler to the Click event:

```
AddHandler Form1.Click, AddressOf Me.Form1Click
```

This is actually shorthand for:

```
AddHandler Form1.Click, New EventHandler(AddressOf Me.Form1Click)
```

In general, the `AddHandler` statement has the following syntax:

```
AddHandler NameOfEventSender, AddressOf NameOfEventHandler
```

Note that the binding can also be accomplished using the `Handles` keyword, as shown in the default event syntax. However, using `AddHandler` and `RemoveHandler` allows dynamic binding of event handlers to events.

The syntax for `RemoveHandler` is the same as that of `AddHandler`:

```
RemoveHandler NameOfEventSender, AddressOf NameOfEventHandler
```

CHAPTER 8

Attributes

Attributes are declarative tags that can be used to annotate types or class members, thereby modifying their meaning or customizing their behavior. This descriptive information provided by the attribute is stored as metadata in a .NET assembly and can be extracted either at design time or at runtime using reflection.

To see how attributes might be used, consider the <WebMethod> attribute, which might appear in code as follows:

```
<WebMethod(Description:="Indicates the number of visitors to a page")> _
        Public Function PageHitCount(strULR As String) As Integer
```

Ordinarily, public methods of a class can be invoked locally from an instance of that class; they are not treated as members of a web service. In contrast, the <WebMethod> attribute marks a method as a function callable over the Internet as part of a web service. This <WebMethod> attribute also includes a single property, Description, which provides the text that will appear in the page describing the web service.

You may wonder why attributes are used on the .NET platform and why they are not simply implemented as language elements. The answer comes from the fact that attributes are stored as metadata in an assembly, rather than as part of its executable code. As an item of metadata, the attribute describes the program element to which it applies and is available through reflection both at design time (if a graphical environment such as Visual Studio .NET is used), at compile time (when the compiler can use it to modify, customize, or extend the compiler's basic operation), and at runtime (when it can be used by the Common Language Runtime or by other executable code to modify the code's ordinary runtime behavior).

The behavior of interface objects (i.e., controls) in Visual Studio .NET illustrates the importance of attributes. Since Visual Studio offers drag-and-drop placement of controls on forms or web pages, it is necessary for controls to have a design time behavior in addition to their runtime behavior. For instance, when you double click on a control in a designer, you ordinarily want the code or the code template for its default event handler to be displayed. Note that the question posed here is *not* how the control should respond to a double-click event, since the Double-Click event occurs at runtime and, if an event handler is present, causes that event handler's executable code to be executed. Because we're concerned with the standard behavior of a control in its design time environment, an attribute provides an excellent solution. Indeed, the .NET Framework provides the <DefaultEvent> attribute, which allows you to define a control's default event. Since information on the attribute is stored in the assembly's metadata, Visual Studio can simply look to see whether a <DefaultEvent> attribute is attached to a particular control when it is double-clicked in a designer window.

The attribute-based system of programming implemented in .NET is extensible. In addition to the attributes predefined by Visual Basic or by the .NET Framework, you can define custom attributes that you apply to program elements. For an attribute to be meaningful, there must also be code that attempts to detect the presence of the attribute at design time, at compile time, or at runtime, and accordingly that performs an action dictated by the attribute's presence.

This chapter discusses the syntax and use of attributes, and then shows how to define and use custom attributes.

Syntax and Use

In Visual Basic, an attribute appears within angle brackets (a less-than (<) and a greater-than symbol (>)). The attribute name is followed by parentheses, which are used to enclose arguments that might be passed to the attribute. For example, the <Obsolete> attribute marks a type or type member as obsolete. We can apply <Obsolete> as a parameter-less attribute as follows:

```
<Obsolete()>
```

If no arguments are assigned to the attribute, we can omit the trailing parentheses:

```
<Obsolete>
```

If more than one attribute is applied to a single program element, the attributes are enclosed in a single set of angle brackets and delimited from one another by a comma. For example:

```
<Obsolete(), WebMethod()> Public Function PageCount( _
                strURL As String) As Integer
```

Each attribute corresponds to a class derived from System.Attribute. (In fact, the VB.NET compiler actually treats an attribute as an instance of the attribute's class.) By convention, we drop the trailing string "Attribute" from the class name to form the attribute name, although the attribute name can also be identical to the class name. Thus, for example, the <WebMethod> attribute corresponds to the WebMethodAttribute class in the System.Web.Services namespace, which in turn is found in *System.Web.Services.dll*. Alternately, you can also specify the attribute as <WebMethodAttribute>. If the namespace containing the attribute class is not automatically accessible to the Visual Basic compiler or to Visual Studio, the Imports directive should be used, and a reference should be added to the project either using the References dialog in Visual Studio or the /r switch in the command-line compiler.

If the shortened attribute name is a Visual Basic .NET keyword, use an attribute name that's identical to the attribute's class name to prevent a compiler error. For example, the following declaration produces an error because **ParamArray** is a VB.NET keyword:

```
<ParamArray()> lScores As Long
```

However, the following code compiles correctly:

```
<ParamArrayAttribute()> lScores As Long)
```

The attribute class constructor or constructors determine whether any arguments are required. For example, the `<VBFixedString>` attribute corresponds to the VBFixedStringAttribute class, which has the following constructor:

```
New(ByVal Size As Integer)
```

Hence, the `<VBFixedString>` attribute can be used as follows:

```
<VBFixedString(10)> Private sID As String
```

Attribute constructors can be overloaded. Any required arguments must correspond to those expected by one of the constructors in number and data type.

Required arguments must be supplied to the attribute as positional arguments *only*; named arguments are not accepted. A comma separates all arguments, whether named or positional.

Optional arguments correspond to class properties and can be supplied to the attribute as named arguments. For example, in addition to its constructor, which indicates to what language elements the attribute applies, the `<AttributeUsage>` attribute, which is used to define the language elements to which a custom attribute applies, has a Boolean property, Inherited, that indicates whether the attribute is inherited by derived classes and overridden members. Its default value is **True**. To set it to **False**, you could use the attribute as follows:

```
<AttributeUsage(AttributeTargets.Class, Inherited:=False)> _
Public Class MyCustomClass
```

Be sure to recognize that attributes are evaluated at compile time, when their data is written to the assembly's metadata. This means that only literal values can be passed as arguments to the attribute's constructor.

Unless it has a modifier, an attribute immediately precedes the language element to which it applies and must be on the same logical line as that language element. If they are on different lines, the Visual Basic .NET line continuation character (the underscore, or _) must be used. This syntax is valid for attributes applied to the following language elements:

Class
Constructor

Delegate
Enum
Event
Field
Interface
Method
Parameter
Property
Return Value
Structure

For example, the following **Class** statement illustrates this general usage of an attribute:

```
<AttributeUsage(AttributeTargets.All)> _
Public Class MyCustomAttrAttribute
```

The following statement indicates how attributes are used with parameter declarations:

```
Public Sub MyFunction(strName As String, _
                    <ParamArrayAttribute()> lValues As Long)
```

There are two exceptions to this rule. Some attributes must be prefaced with a modifier (either **Assembly:** or **Module:**) indicating the program element to which the attribute applies. In that case, the attribute must be placed at the top of the source file (i.e., immediately following any **Option** and **Imports** statements), along with any other attributes that require a modifier. This syntax is valid for an attribute applied to an assembly or a module only.

For example:

```
Option Strict On
Imports System.Data.SqlClient
<Assembly: AssemblyDescription("Supplementary data access library")>

Namespace SqlAccess
```

Defining a Custom Attribute

An attribute is merely a class that inherits from System.Attribute, which makes it very easy to implement a custom attribute. In this section, we'll build a custom attribute called <DeveloperNote>, which allows a developer to add assorted information (the developer's name, the date, a comment, and whether a code modification was a response to a bug) to code. The steps are as follows:

1. Define a public class that inherits from System.Attribute or another attribute class derived from System.Attribute. For example:

   ```
   Public Class DeveloperNoteAttribute
     Inherits System.Attribute
   ```

   Note that, by convention, the name of the class ends with the substring "Attribute".

2. Apply the `<AttributeUsage>` attribute, which defines the language elements to which the custom attribute can be applied, to the class (as shown in the following code fragment). The attribute's only required argument is one of the following members of the `AttributeTargets` enumeration:

```
All
Assembly
Class
Constructor
Delegate
Enum
Event
Field
Interface
Method
Module
Parameter
Property
ReturnValue
Struct
```

If an attribute applies to multiple programming elements, but not all elements, the relevant constants can be ORed together. In the case of our `<DeveloperNote>` attribute, we want the attribute to apply to all program elements. In addition, we want to make the `<DeveloperNote>` attribute extensible through inheritance, so we set the `<AttributeTarget>` attribute's *Inherited* argument to `True`. Finally, we want to allow the application of multiple attributes to the same program element; hence, we want to set the *AllowMultiple* argument to `True` as well. In view of this setting, our code should look as follows:

```
<AttributeUsage(AttributeTargets.All, _
 Inherited:=True, _
 AllowMultiple:=True)> _
Public Class DeveloperNoteAttribute
 Inherits System.Attribute
```

3. Create the class constructor (the *New* subroutine), which is called when the attribute is applied to a particular language element. The class constructor defines the attribute's required or positional arguments. At a minimum, we'll want a developer to record his or her name, a comment, and the date. Our constructor appears as follows:

```
Public Sub New(Name As String, Comment As String, _
 DateRecorded As String)
 MyBase.New()
 strName = Name
 strComment = Comment
 datDate = CDate(DateRecorded)
End Sub
```

Note that the date is passed to the constructor as a String type. There is some restriction on the data types that can be used as attribute parameters. Parameters can be any integral data type (Byte, Short, Integer, Long) or floating point data type (Single and Double), as well as Char, String, Boolean, an enumerated type, or System.Type. Thus, Date, Decimal, Object, and structured types cannot be used as parameters.

Each required parameter also corresponds to a class property or field. These parameters are added to the class in the next step.

4. Declare properties or fields. The attribute's public properties and fields correspond both to parameters required by the class constructor and to optional parameters supplied when the attribute is applied to a language element. In the case of our attribute, we'll want properties that correspond to each attribute, as well as an additional Bugs property that indicates whether or not the comment corresponds to a code modification that resulted from a bug. The code is:

```
Public Property Name As String
    Get
        Return strName
    End Get
    Set
        strName = Value
    End Set
End Property

Public Property Comment As String
    Get
        Return strComment
    End Get
    Set
        strComment = Value
    End Set
End Property

Public Property DateRecorded As Date
    Get
        Return datDate
    End Get
    Set
        datDate = Value
    End Set
End Property

Public Property Bug As Boolean
    Get
        Return blnBug
    End Get
    Set
        blnBug = Value
    End Set
End Property
```

The complete code for the attribute class is shown in Example 8-1.

Attributes

Example 8-1: The DeveloperNoteAttribute attribute class

```
Option Strict On
Imports System

Namespace Extensions.CustomAttributes

<AttributeUsage(AttributeTargets.All, _
                Inherited:=True, _
                AllowMultiple:=True)> _
Public Class DeveloperNoteAttribute
    Inherits System.Attribute

Protected strName, strComment As String
Protected blnBug As Boolean
Protected datDate As Date

Public Sub New(Name As String, Comment As String, DateRecorded As String)
    MyBase.New()
    strName = Name
    strComment = Comment
    datDate = CDate(DateRecorded)
End Sub

Public Property Name As String
    Get
        Return strName
    End Get
    Set
        strName = Value
    End Set
End Property

Public Property Comment As String
    Get
        Return strComment
    End Get
    Set
        strComment = Value
    End Set
End Property

Public Property DateRecorded As Date
    Get
        Return datDate
    End Get
    Set
        datDate = Value
    End Set
End Property

Public Property Bug As Boolean
    Get
        Return blnBug
```

Example 8-1: The DeveloperNoteAttribute attribute class (continued)

```
    End Get
    Set
       blnBug = Value
    End Set
End Property

End Class

End Namespace
```

Using a Custom Attribute

The Visual Basic compiler and .NET platform automatically recognize the meaning of the attributes based on attribute classes in the .NET Framework Class Library. This recognition isn't true, however, for custom attributes. Thus, not only must you define them, you must also develop a set of routines that will identify the presence of an attribute so your code can handle them.

NET assemblies are self-describing; when the compiler creates the .NET assembly, it writes metadata describing the assembly and its classes and methods to the assembly manifest. This metadata is then accessed programmatically at runtime by using the .NET Framework's reflection classes.

 An assembly's metadata is similar to a COM type library. In addition to their greater accessibility through .NET Framework APIs, assembly metadata is always stored along with the assembly. In contrast, although a type library can be stored in the EXE or DLL containing the COM object (as did previous versions of Visual Basic), it is most commonly stored in a file different from the file containing the COM objects it describes.

The .NET Framework provides support for reflection in the Type class (in the System namespace) and in the types found in the System.Reflection namespace. The following code creates a console mode application that uses the reflection classes to extract information about the <DeveloperNote> custom attribute and the program elements to which it is applied:

```
Option Strict On

Imports Microsoft.VisualBasic
Imports System
Imports System.Reflection
Imports System.Text
Imports Extensions.CustomAttributes

Module modComments

Public Sub Main()
```

```
      Dim strFile As String = Command()
      Dim sOutput As String

      If strFile = "" Then
         Console.WriteLine("Syntax is: " & vbCrLf & _
                           "    DevNotes <filename>")
         Exit Sub
      End If

      ' Load assembly
      Dim oAssem As System.Reflection.Assembly = _
                  System.Reflection.Assembly.LoadFrom(strFile)

      ' Get any assembly-level attributes
      Dim oAttribs() As Attribute = Attribute.GetCustomAttributes(oAssem)
      if UBound(oAttribs) >= 0 Then
         sOutput = DisplayDeveloperNotes(oAttribs)
         if sOutput <> "" Then
            Console.WriteLine(oAssem.GetName.Name & _
                              " Assembly Developer Notes:" & vbCrLf)
            Console.WriteLine(sOutput)
         End If
      End If

      ' Get any module-level attributes
      Dim oMod As System.Reflection.Module
      Dim oMods() As System.Reflection.Module = oAssem.GetModules()
      For Each oMod in oMods
         oAttribs = Attribute.GetCustomAttributes(oMod)
         If UBound(oAttribs) >= 0 Then
            sOutput = DisplayDeveloperNotes(oAttribs)
            If sOutput <> "" Then
               Console.WriteLine(oMod.Name & " Module Developer Notes: " _
                                 & vbCrLf)
               Console.WriteLine(sOutput)
            End If
         End If
      Next
      ' Enumerate types
      EnumerateTypes(oAssem)

   End Sub

   ' Show information about each attribute
   Public Function DisplayDeveloperNotes(oAttribs() As Object) As String

      Dim sMsg As New StringBuilder
      Dim oAttrib As Attribute
      Dim oNote As DeveloperNoteAttribute

      For Each oAttrib in oAttribs
         Try
            oNote = CType(oAttrib, DeveloperNoteAttribute)
            sMsg.Append("  Developer: " & oNote.Name & vbCrLf)
```

```vb
            sMsg.Append("   Comment: " & oNote.Comment & vbCrLf)
            sMsg.Append("   Date: " & oNote.DateRecorded & vbCrLf)
            sMsg.Append("   Bug: " & oNote.Bug & vbCrLf)
        Catch
            ' No need to do anything
        End Try
    Next
    Return sMsg.ToString
End Function

Private Sub EnumerateTypes(oObj As Object)
    Dim sOutput As String
    Dim oType, oTypes() As Type
    If oObj.GetType.ToString = "System.Reflection.Assembly" Then
        Dim oAssem As System.Reflection.Assembly = CType(oObj, _
                    System.Reflection.Assembly)
        oTypes = oAssem.GetTypes()
    Else
        oTypes.SetValue(oObj, 0)
    End If
    For each oType in oTypes
        Dim strType, strTypeAttr, strMeth As String
        If oType.IsClass Then
            strType = "Class"
        ElseIf oType.IsValueType Then
            strType = "Structure"
        ElseIf oType.IsInterface Then
            strType = "Interface"
        ElseIf oType.IsEnum Then
            strType = "Enum"
        End If
        sOutput = strType & " " & oType.Name & ":" & vbCrLf

        ' Get any type-level attributes
        Dim oCustAttribs() As Object = oType.GetCustomAttributes(False)
        If oCustAttribs.Length > 0 Then
            strTypeAttr = DisplayDeveloperNotes(oCustAttribs)
        End If

        strMeth = EnumerateTypeMembers(oType)

        ' Display Type and Member Info
        If strMeth <> "" Or strTypeAttr <> "" Then
            Console.WriteLine(sOutput)
            If strTypeAttr <> "" Then
                Console.WriteLine(strTypeAttr)
            End If
            If strMeth <> "" Then
                Console.WriteLine(strMeth & vbCrLf)
            End If
        End If
    Next
End Sub
```

```
Private Function EnumerateTypeMembers(oType As Type) As String
    Dim strMeth, strRetVal As String
    Dim oAttribs() As Object
    ' Get members of type
    Dim oMembersInfo(), oMemberInfo As MemberInfo
    oMembersInfo = oType.GetMembers
    For Each oMemberInfo in oMembersInfo
        ' Determine if attribute is present
        oAttribs = oMemberInfo.GetCustomAttributes(False)
        If oAttribs.Length > 0 Then
            ' determine member type
            Select Case oMemberInfo.MemberType
                Case MemberTypes.All
                    strMeth = " All "
                Case MemberTypes.Constructor
                    strMeth = " Constructor "
                Case MemberTypes.Custom
                    strMeth = " Custom method "
                Case MemberTypes.Event
                    strMeth = " Event "
                Case MemberTypes.Field
                    strMeth = " Field "
                Case MemberTypes.Method
                    strMeth = " Method "
                Case MemberTypes.NestedType
                    strMeth = " Nested type "
                Case MemberTypes.Property
                    strMeth = " Property"
                Case MemberTypes.TypeInfo
                    strMeth = " TypeInfo"
            End Select
            If oMemberInfo.Name = ".ctor" Then
                strMeth = "New " & strMeth
            Else
                strMeth = oMemberInfo.Name & strMeth
            End If
            strMeth = strMeth & vbCrLf & DisplayDeveloperNotes(oAttribs) _
                        & vbCrLf
            strRetVal = strRetVal & strMeth
        End If
    Next
    Return strRetVal
End Function

End Module
```

The program's entry point, the *Main* routine, first instantiates an Assembly object (in the System.Reflection namespace) representing the assembly by calling the LoadFrom method and passing it the filename containing the assembly. It then calls the Attribute class' shared GetCustomAttributes method, passing it a reference to an Assembly object, which returns an array of Attribute objects representing each custom attribute, if any exist. These attributes are then displayed by calling the DisplayDeveloperNotes method.

The shared GetCustomAttributes method of the Attribute class has several over-loads that allow you to retrieve custom attributes belonging to assemblies, modules, class members, and parameters. (Unfortunately, the method does not retrieve the custom attributes belonging to types.) Since derived classes call the base class implementation, you can also retrieve attributes of a specific custom type with the following code:

```
Dim oAttribs() As Attribute = _
    DeveloperNoteAttribute.GetCustomAttributes(oAssem)
```

After listing any DeveloperNoteAttributes applied to the assembly, the code retrieves the modules in the assembly by calling the Assembly object's GetModules method, which returns an array of Module objects. The code then iterates these modules and again calls the Attribute class' shared GetCustomAttributes method, this time passing it a Module object (to retrieve an array of custom Attribute objects belonging to that module). These objects are also displayed by calling the DisplayDeveloperNotes method.

Finally, *Main* calls the EnumerateTypes method, a generic routine that it uses to iterate the types in the Assembly object. (The routine could also be called from a type to extract information about custom attributes in its nested types.) This iteration casts the generic object passed as a parameter to an Assembly object, and then calls the Assembly object's GetTypes method to return an array of Type objects (defined in the System namespace) containing information about each type (such as a class, interface, delegate, structure, or num) in the assembly. Each Type object's GetCustomAttributes method is then called and its custom attributes are displayed.

While iterating the type objects, the EnumerateTypes method also calls the EnumerateTypeMembers method, which is responsible for iterating the members of each type and extracting their custom DeveloperNoteAttribute attributes. The EnumerateTypeMembers method first extracts an array of MemberInfo objects corresponding to each member by calling the GetMembers method of *oType*, the Type object passed to it as a parameter. GetMembers returns an array of Member-Info objects, each element of which corresponds to a member of the type. The method then calls the MemberInfo object's GetCustomAttributes method to extract information about any custom types. Instead, it could also have called the Attribute object's GetCustomAttributes method, passing it a MemberInfo object representing the member whose custom attribute information was to be retrieved.

The program can be easily extended by adding recursion (allowing it to retrieve information about custom attributes in a nested class and its members), as well as by retrieving information about custom attributes applied to parameters belonging to individual methods.

CHAPTER 9

Error Handling in VB.NET

In this chapter, we take a concise look at error-handling techniques in VB.NET. Note that the terms *exception* and *error* are used synonymously throughout the VB.NET documentation, and so we use them interchangeably in this chapter.

VB.NET supports the `On Error Goto` style of error handling, which is supported by earlier versions of Visual Basic (with some new wrinkles). This type of error handling is referred to as *unstructured error handling*. However, unlike earlier versions of Visual Basic, VB.NET also supports the *structured exception handling* technique familiar to C++ programmers, which is now the preferred method of error handling in VB.NET.

Error Detection and Error Handling

Let us begin by clarifying some terminology. We agree to say that handling an error means responding to a *detected* error. Thus, there is a clear distinction between *error detecting* and *error handling*. The reason for this distinction is that these processes can take place at different times and in different locations within the code of an application. We also agree to refer to the procedure (or module) in which an error occurs as the *offending procedure* (or module).

There are two types of errors that can occur in a running program. (We will not discuss compile-time or syntax errors.) A *runtime error* occurs when Visual Basic attempts to perform an operation that is impossible to perform, such as opening a file that does not exist or dividing by 0. Visual Basic automatically takes care of error *detection* for runtime errors because it has no other choice. On the other hand, proper error *handling* of runtime errors is up to the programmer, for otherwise Visual Basic itself handles the error by presenting an error message and terminating the application, which is not a good solution to the problem.

A *logical error* is often defined as the production of an unexpected result. It might be better to define it as the production of an unexpected and incorrect result (although even this is still somewhat ambiguous). For instance, consider a func-

128

tion that returns the IQ for an individual based on a set of IQ test scores. If the individual is very smart, we might expect an IQ in the range of 120 or more. A result of 100 might be unexpected, but it is not necessarily an error. On the other hand, if the function returns an IQ of −350, that is a logical error.

Visual Basic (or, for that matter, any other language) does not provide error detection for logical errors, because to Visual Basic, no error has occurred. However, a logical error may subsequently result in a runtime error, which Visual Basic will certainly recognize. For instance, code that is intended to retrieve a positive integer for later use in an integer variable may instead retrieve 0. This is a logical error. But if that integer is later used as a denominator in some other part of the application, we can surely expect a runtime error.

Thus, it is up to the programmer to anticipate logical errors and provide both error detection and error handling. From this perspective, logical errors are far more serious and much more difficult to deal with than runtime errors. After all, a runtime error won't be completely overlooked—at least Visual Basic will do something about it, even if that consists only of presenting an error message to the user and terminating the application.

The problem with an overlooked logical error is that it may give the user specious information (that is, invalid information that looks valid). This is no doubt the most insidious behavior a program can produce. If we are lucky, a logical error will generate a runtime error at some later time, but we may still have great difficulty determining the location of the logical error from the runtime error message.

Runtime Error Handling

As we have mentioned, VB currently supports both unstructured and structured error handling. Let us first look at unstructured error handling.

Unstructured Error Handling

Error-handling techniques that revolve around the various On Error... statements are referred to as *unstructured* error-handling techniques. These techniques generally use the Err object and the Visual Basic call stack.

The Err object

Visual Basic's built-in error object, called *Err*, is one of the main tools for unstructured error handling. This object has several properties and methods, as shown in Tables 9-1 and 9-2, respectively.

Table 9-1: Properties of the Err object

Property	Description
Description	A short string describing the error.
HelpContext	The context ID for a help topic associated with the error.
HelpFile	The fully qualified filename of the associated help file, if any.

Table 9-1: Properties of the Err object (continued)

Property	Description
LastDLLError	The return code from a call made to a function in an external DLL. Note, however, that this property may change value at any time, so it is wise to store the current value in a variable *immediately* upon return from the DLL call. Note also that even if the DLL call resulted in an error, this is not considered an error by VB. (VB has no way of knowing the meaning of return values from external functions, after all.)
Number	This is the error number of the error.
Source	A string that specifies the object that generated the error. When the error is generated within your application, the Source property is the project's name, which is more or less useless. (It would have been nice to get the name of the offending procedure.) However, when the error is generated by an external COM component, the Source property returns the *programmatic ID* of that component, which has the form `application.objectname`, as in `Excel.Application`, for example.

Table 9-2: Methods of the Err object

Method	Description
Clear	Clears the values of all properties of the Err object. Its syntax is: `Err().Clear()` Note that the Clear method is called implicitly when any of the following statements is executed: a `Resume` statement of any type; an `Exit Sub`, `Exit Function`, or `Exit Property` statement; or any `On Error` statement.
Raise	Causes Visual Basic to generate a runtime error and sets the properties of the Err object to the values given by the parameters of the Raise method. Its syntax is: `Err.Raise(Number, Source, Description, _` `                HelpFile, HelpContext)` where all but the first named argument is optional. Each parameter corresponds to the property of the same name.

Dealing with runtime errors

Visual Basic detects a runtime error as soon as it occurs, sets the properties of the Err object, and directs the flow of execution to a location that the programmer has specified by the most recent On Error... line. This location can be one of the following:

- The line of code immediately following the line that caused the error.

- Another location within the offending procedure.

- The procedure that called the offending procedure, if there is one. If not, VB issues an error message itself and terminates the application.

Let us take a closer look at each of these possibilities.

In-line error handling. Code execution will be "redirected" to the line following the offending line of code (that is, execution will continue immediately following the offending line) if the most recent preceding On Error statement is:

```
On Error Resume Next
```

This is referred to as *in-line error handling*. Here is an example that involves renaming a file. Note the typical use of a `Select Case` statement to handle the error based on the value of Err.Number. Incidentally, one way to obtain error numbers is to deliberately invoke a particular error and break execution (with a breakpoint) to examine Err.Number:

```
Dim sOldName, sNewName As String

On Error Resume Next

' Ask for an existing file name
sOldName = InputBox("Enter the file name to rename")

' Ask for new name
sNewName = InputBox("Enter the new file name")

' Rename file
Rename("c:\" & sOldName, "c:\" & sNewName)

' Deal with error
If Err().Number = 53 Then
    ' File not found error
    MsgBox("File " & sOldName & " not found")
    Exit Sub
Else
    ' All other errors
    MsgBox(Err().Number & ": " & Err().Description)
    Exit Sub
End If
```

Centralized error handling. While in-line error handling does have its uses, there is much to be said for centralizing error handling within a procedure. (This often improves readability and makes code maintenance easier.) We can direct code execution to a central error handler using the code:

```
On Error Goto label
```

This is outlined in the following code shell:

```
Sub Example()

On Error Goto ErrHandler

'' If run-time error occurs here
'' Visual Basic directs execution to ErrHandler

Exit Sub

ErrHandler:

'' Code can be placed here to handle errors
'' or pass them up the calls list.
'' We have knowledge of Err().Number, Err().Description,
```

```
'' and Err().Source.
```

```
End Sub
```

Once the `On Error Goto` *label* line is executed, we say that the error handler beginning at the label `ErrHandler` is *active*.

Once code execution is directed to the error handler, there are several possibilities for dealing with the error. The most common possibility is simply to handle the error in the active error handler, perhaps by displaying an error message asking the user to take corrective action.

Another common (and useful) approach is passing information about an error to the calling procedure with parameters or with the return value of the offending function. For instance, if a function is designed to rename a file, the function might return an integer error code indicating the success or failure of the operation. This is quite common among the Win32 API functions. In particular, the error code might be 0 for success, −1 if the file does not exist, −2 if the new filename is invalid, and so on.

A third possibility is to pass the error to the calling procedure by invoking the Err. Raise method within the active error handler, as in:

```
Err.Raise(Err.Number, Err.Source, Err.Description, _
          Err.HelpFile, Err.HelpContext)
```

This triggers the calling procedure's error handler (or more precisely, the next enabled error handler in the calls list). This process is called *regenerating* or *reraising* the error.

Note that it is possible to deactivate an active error handler using the line:

```
On Error Goto 0
```

If there is no active error handler, then VB reacts to errors just as though no error handler existed in the procedure. We describe this situation in the next section.

No enabled error-handler. If there is no enabled error handler in the offending procedure, either because there is no `On Error` statement in the procedure or because error handling has been disabled with an `On Error Goto 0` statement, then Visual Basic automatically sends the error to the *calling* procedure's error handler. If the calling procedure has no error handler, the error continues up the calls list until it reaches an enabled error handler. If none is found, then Visual Basic handles the error by displaying an error message and terminating the application.

Structured Exception Handling

Structured exception handling uses a `Try...Catch...Finally` structure to handle errors. As we will see, VB.NET's structured exception handling is a much more object-oriented approach, involving objects of the Exception class and its derived classes.

Try...Catch...Finally

The syntax of the `Try...Catch...Finally` construct is given here:

```
Try
    tryStatements

[Catch1 [exception [As type]] [When expression]
    catchStatements1
[Exit Try]

Catch2 [exception [As type]] [When expression]
    catchStatements2
[Exit Try]
. . .
Catchn [exception [As type]] [When expression]
    catchStatementsn]
[Exit Try]

[Finally
    finallyStatements]
End Try
```

The *tryStatements* (which are required) constitute the `Try` block and are the statements that are monitored for errors by VB. Within the `Try` block, we say that error handling is *active*.

The `Catch` blocks (of which there can be more than one) contain code that is executed in response to VB "catching" a particular type of error within the `Try` block. Thus, the `Catch` blocks consist of the error handlers for the `Try` block.

The phrases *exception* [As *type*] and [When *expression*] are referred to as *filters* in the VB.NET documentation. In the former case, *exception* is either a variable of type Exception, which is the base class that "catches" all exceptions, or a variable of one of Exception's derived classes.

(We provide a list of these classes a bit later.) For instance, the variable declared as:

```
Catch e As Exception
```

will catch (that is, handle) any exception. The variable declared as:

```
Catch e As ArgumentNullException
```

catches (handles) any exception of class ArgumentNullException. In short, *type* is the name of one of the exception classes.

The `When` filter is typically used with user-defined errors. For instance, the code in the following `Try` block raises an error if the user does not enter a number. The `Catch` block catches this error:

```
Try
    Dim sInput As String
    sInput = Inputbox("Enter a number.")
    If Not IsNumeric(sInput) Then
        Err.Raise(1)
    End If
Catch When Err.Number = 1
```

```
        Msgbox("Error1")
End Try
```

Note that code such as:

```
Dim x As Integer
Try
    x = 5
Catch When x = 5
    MsgBox(x)
End Try
```

does not work (that is, the Catch statements are never executed) because no error was generated.

The Exit Try statement is used to break out of any portion of a Try...Catch... Finally block. The optional *finallyStatements* code block is executed regardless of whether an error occurs (or is caught), unless an Exit Try statement is executed. This final code can be used for cleanup in the event of an error. (By placing an Exit Try at the end of the Try block, the *finallyStatements* are not executed if no error occurs.)

As with unstructured error handling, VB may pass an error up the call stack when using structured error handling. This happens in the following situations:

- If an error occurs within a Try block that is not handled by an existing Catch block

- If an error occurs outside any Try block (provided, of course, that no On Error–style error handlers are active).

Exception classes

The System namespace contains the Exception class, which is the base class for a substantial collection of derived exception classes, listed as follows. Note that the indentation indicates class inheritance. For example, EntryPointNotFoundException (the fifth from the last entry in the list) inherits from TypeLoadException.

```
Exception
            ApplicationException
            SystemException
                AccessException
                    FieldAccessException
                    MethodAccessException
                    MissingMemberException
                        MissingFieldException
                        MissingMethodException
                AppDomainUnloadedException
                AppDomainUnloadInProgressException
                ArgumentException
                    ArgumentNullException
                    ArgumentOutOfRangeException
                    DuplicateWaitObjectException
                ArithmeticException
```

DivideByZeroException
NotFiniteNumberException
OverflowException
ArrayTypeMismatchException
BadImageFormatException
CannotUnloadAppDomainException
ContextMarshalException
CoreException
    ExecutionEngineException
    IndexOutOfRangeException
    StackOverflowException
ExecutionEngineException
FormatException
InvalidCastException
InvalidOperationException
MulticastNotSupportedException
NotImplementedException
NotSupportedExccption
    PlatformNotSupportedException
NullReferenceException
OutOfMemoryException
RankException
ServicedComponentException
TypeInitializationException
TypeLoadException
    EntryPointNotFoundException
TypeUnloadedException
UnauthorizedAccessException
WeakReferenceException
URIFormatException

As Microsoft states: "Most of the exception classes that inherit from Exception do not implement additional members or provide additional functionality." Thus, it is simply the class name that distinguishes one type of exception from another. The properties and methods applied to an exception object are inherited from the Exception base class.

When writing `Catch` blocks, we always face the question of whether to simply trap the generic exception class, as in:

```
Sub test()
    Try
    ...
    Catch e As Exception
    ...
    End Try
End Sub
```

or whether to trap specific exception classes. Of course, the time to trap specific exception classes is when we want to handle errors differently based on their class. For instance, this may take the form of issuing different custom error messages for different exception types.

Also, there are occasions when we may want to take advantage of members of a particular exception class that are not implemented in the Exception base class. For instance, the ArgumentException class has a ParamName property that returns the name of the parameter that causes the exception. Now, if we simply trap the generic Exception class, as in the following code:

```
Sub test()
    Try
        Dim s, d As String
        s = "c:\temp.txt"
        ' Attempt to copy a file to a nonvalid target
        FileCopy(s, d)
    Catch e As Exception
        MsgBox(e.Message)
    End Try
End Sub
```

then we cannot take advantage of the ParamName property. On the other hand, if we specifically trap the ArgumentException class, as in the following code:

```
Sub test1()
    Try
        Dim s, d As String
        s = "c:\temp.txt"
        ' Attempt to copy a file to a nonvalid target
        FileCopy(s, d)
    Catch e As ArgumentException
        MsgBox(e.Message & " Parameter: " & e.ParamName)
    End Try
End Sub
```

then we can retrieve the name of the offending parameter.

Now let us take a look at some of the members of the Exception class:

Message property
    A string containing an error message.

Source property
    A string that describes the application or object that threw the exception.

StackTrace property
    A string that contains the stack trace immediately before the exception was thrown. We provide an example of this in a moment (although in this case its value is Nothing.

TargetSite property
    A string that gives the method that threw the exception.

ToString method
    A string that returns the fully qualified name of the exception, possibly the error message, the name of the inner exception, and the stack trace. Its syntax is simply:

```
ToString()
```

The best way to get a feel for these members is with an example. Consider the following code, which consists of three subroutines. The first subroutine,

Exception0, contains a `Try`...`Catch`... statement. In the `Try` code block, the subroutine *Exception0* calls the subroutine *Exception1*, which simply calls *Exception2*.

```
Sub Exception0()
    Dim s As String
    Try
        Exception1()
    Catch e As Exception
        s = "Message: " & e.Message
        s = s & ControlChars.CrLf & "Source: " & e.Source
        s = s & ControlChars.CrLf & "Stack: " & e.StackTrace
        s = s & ControlChars.CrLf & "Target: " & e.TargetSite.Name
        s = s & ControlChars.CrLf & "ToString: " & e.ToString
        debug.writeline(s)
    End Try

End Sub

Sub Exception1()
    Exception2()
End Sub

Sub Exception2()
    Throw New ArgumentNullException()
End Sub
```

In *Exception2*, there is a single line of code that executes the `Throw` statement, which throws an exception. This is similar to raising an error with the Err.Raise method. However, as you can see by the `New` keyword, the `Throw` statement actually creates an object of one of the exception types.

The output from the call to Exception0 is:

```
Message: argument can't be null
Source:
Stack: at WindowsApplication3.Form1.Exception2()
          in C:\VBNET\Form1.vb:line 68
       at WindowsApplication3.Form1.Exception1()
          in C:\VBNET\Form1.vb:line 66
       at WindowsApplication3.Form1.Exception0()
          in C:\VBNET\Form1.vb:line 53
Target: Exception2
ToString: System.ArgumentNullException: argument can't be null
   at WindowsApplication3.Form1.Exception2()
          in C:\VBNET\Form1.vb:line 68
   at WindowsApplication3.Form1.Exception1()
          in C:\VBNET\Form1.vb:line 66
   at WindowsApplication3.Form1.Exception0()
          in C:\VBNET\Form1.vb:line 53
```

Dealing with Logical Errors

Since Visual Basic makes the handling of runtime errors a relatively straightforward process, it seems reasonable to try to mimic this process for logical errors.

Detecting Logical Errors

To detect a logical error, we place error-detection code immediately following the potential offender. For instance, consider the following procedure shell for getting a sequence of positive integers from the user, starting with the number of integers:

```
Public Sub GetSomeData()
Dim DataCt As Integer
DataCt = CInt(InputBox("Enter number of items."))
' Code here to get the individual data values ...
End Sub
```

The proper place for error-detecting code is immediately following the *InputBox* function, where we can check for a nonpositive integer:

```
Public Sub GetSomeData()
Dim DataCt As Integer
DataCt = CInt(InputBox("Enter number of items."))
' Check for error
If DataCt < = 0 then
    ' something here
End If
' Code here to get the individual data values ...
End Sub
```

Note that the alternative to *immediate* detection of logical errors is to place the error-detecting code just prior to *using* the value of `DataCt`, but this is both dangerous and inefficient. It is dangerous since we might forget to place the code, and it is inefficient since we may use `DataCt` in a variety of locations in the program, each of which would require error-detecting code.

Where to Handle a Logical Error

Once a logical error is detected, we have three choices as to where to handle that error.

Handling the error on the spot

A logical error can be handled at the location where it was detected. Here is an example:

```
Public Sub GetSomeData()
TryAgain:
DataCt = CInt(InputBox("Enter number of items."))
' Check for error
If DataCt < = 0 then
    If MsgBox("Number must be a positive integer." & _
    " Try again or cancel.", vbQuestion+vbOKCancel) _
    = vbOK then
        Goto TryAgain
    Else
        Exit Sub
    End If
End If
'' Code here to get the individual data values ...
End Sub
```

Handling a logical error on the spot may be appropriate when the required code is short. It is also appropriate in Property procedures, which often amount to little more than a single line that sets a private instance variable, preceded by data validation, which is essentially logical-error detection.

Handling the error in the offending procedure's error handler

We can duplicate the procedure that Visual Basic uses for runtime errors simply by raising our own runtime error. Here is an example using structured exception handling:

```
Try
    Dim DataCt As Integer = CInt(InputBox("Enter number of items."))
    ' Check for error
    If DataCt <= 0 Then
        ' Throw an exception
        Throw New Exception("Must enter a positive number.")
    End If
Catch ex As Exception
    MsgBox(ex.Message)
End Try
```

Note that the Exception class constructor (in one of its overloaded forms) is:

```
Overloads Public Sub New(String)
```

where **String** is the error message to be associated with the error.

Here is an example of error raising using unstructured error handling:

```
Public Sub GetSomeData()

On Error Goto ErrGetSomeData

DataCt = CInt(InputBox("Enter number of items."))

' Check for error
If DataCt < = 0 then
    ' Raise an error
    Err().Raise Number:= ErrBadDataCt
End If
' Code here to get the individual data values ...
Exit Sub

' Error-handler
ErrGetSomeData:
Select Case Err().Number
    Case ErrBadDataCt
        '' Deal with this error by displaying
        '' message and getting help from user
    Case Else
        '' Deal with other errors
End Select
Exit Sub

End Sub
```

Passing the error to the calling procedure

As with runtime errors, passing the error to the calling procedure can be done in a parameter of the offending procedure or as the return value of the offending function. Also, the calling procedure's error handler can be called by throwing (or raising) an error.

Error Constants

To raise our own errors using the Err.Raise method, we need error numbers that do not conflict with those used by Visual Basic. The Visual Basic documentation says that error numbers in the range vbObjectError to vbObjectError + 65535, where *vbObjectError* is a built-in constant whose value is the signed integer –2147220991 (or &H80040000 as an unsigned hexadecimal integer), are designed to signal an error generated by an object.

It further says that error numbers below vbObjectError + 512 may conflict with values reserved for OLE, so these numbers are *verboten*. Thus, we are left with numbers in the range vbObjectError + 512 to vbObjectError + 65535, which should be plenty.

Many programmers like to assign symbolic constants to error numbers, since it tends to improve readability and cut down on the need for comments. For instance, we could add the line:

```
Public Const ErrBadDataCt = vbObjectError + 1024
```

in a standard module.

PART II

Reference

This section consists only of one very long chapter (Chapter 10, *The Language Reference*), which contains an alphabetic reference to VB.NET language elements. The chapter documents the following:

- Statements, such as `AddHandler` or Structure...End Structure.

- Procedures, such as `AppActivate` or `Rename`. These were statements in previous versions of Visual Basic, but now they are methods of one class or another within the Microsoft.VisualBasic namespace. The official documentation describes them as functions, but since they don't return a value, we've chosen to describe them as procedures.

- Functions, such as *Format* or *IsReference*.

- Compiler directives, such as `#Const` or `#If`.

- Visual Basic classes and their members. The two intrinsic objects available in Visual Basic are the `Collection` class and the `Err` object.

- Selected classes in the .NET Framework Class Library, along with their members. Documentation of the Framework Class Library, however, is highly selective; we've chosen classes and their members either because they replace language elements that were present in VB 6, or because they provide much needed functionality that supplements existing language elements.

- Attributes, such as `<AttributeUsage>` and `<VBFixedString>`. Of the approximately 100 attributes available in the .NET Framework, we've documented only those of greatest interest to the VB programmer.

When you're looking for a particular language element but don't quite remember what it's called, an alphabetic reference is of little value. For this reason, we've included Appendix B, *Language Elements by Category*.

Finally, two language elements are covered in the appendixes rather than in Part II. With a few exceptions (notably, `Like` and `Is`) that are documented in Part II, Visual Basic operators are covered in Appendix C, *Operators*. And Visual Basic constants and enumerations are listed in Appendix D, *Constants and Enumerations*.

CHAPTER 10

The Language Reference

This long chapter documents VB.NET language elements. To help you speed the process of finding the right element to perform a particular task, you can use Appendix B to determine what language elements are available for the purpose you require. If you're using Visual Studio .NET, you can also make use of its Object Browser to browse the Microsoft.VisualBasic namespace.

In documenting the VB.NET language, we've tried to provide a consistent and uniform treatment of particular types of language elements. These language elements are:

Functions
> The entry for each function provides the standard information that you'd expect for a function: its syntax, parameters (if it has any), return value, and description. In addition, we list rules for using the function (see the "Rules at a Glance" section), discuss tips and tricks related to the function (see the "Programming Tips and Gotchas" section), frequently provide examples, and list related language elements.

> In addition, each VB.NET function is in fact a method, since it is a member of a particular class in the Microsoft.VisualBasic namespace. In each case, we've listed the class to which the function belongs.

> For the first time, Visual Basic supports both named and positional arguments for all functions, procedures, and methods, with just a few exceptions. Functions, procedures, or methods that accept parameter arrays as arguments don't accept named arguments if the ParamArray parameter is present. And "functions" that are actually resolved by the compiler at compile time (the conversion functions fall into this category) do not accept named arguments.

To see how named arguments work, let's look at the syntax of the *Mid* function:

```
Mid(Str As String, Start As Integer, Length As Integer)
```

Using positional arguments, you might call the function as follows:

```
iPos = Mid(strName, 12, 10)
```

The same function call using named arguments might appear as follows:

```
iPos = Mid(start:=12, str:=strName, length:=10)
```

Since named arguments are nearly universally accepted, we only note when you can't use named arguments with a particular function. The name of each argument is provided in the function's syntax statement.

Finally, we've noted any differences between the operation of the function under previous versions of Visual Basic and under VB.NET.

Procedures

Procedures are really functions that don't return a value to the caller. Consequently, except for the absence of a return value, the same information is presented for procedures as for functions.

Procedures are interesting as a separate language category. Under previous versions of Visual Basic, they were statements. With the rationalization and streamlining of Visual Basic for its .NET version, they were moved into classes in the Microsoft.VisualBasic namespace and became procedures. The official documentation describes them as functions, although they do not return a value.

Statements

Visual Basic statements are not class members, don't support named arguments, and don't return a value. Aside from these three items, the same information is presented for statements as for procedures and functions.

Directives

Visual Basic directives are really statements that provide instructions to the VB.NET compiler or to a .NET development environment like Visual Studio. Like statements, they are not class members, don't support named arguments, and don't return a value. In general, the same information is presented for directives as for statements.

Classes and Objects

Entries for classes and objects identify the namespace to which the class belongs (something that is particularly important in the case of the Framework Class Library) and indicate whether the class is createable. If a class is createable, a new instance of that class can be created by using the New keyword, as in:

```
Dim colStates As New Collection()
```

In some cases, the entry for the class or object also includes a summary listing of the class' members, along with their syntax and a brief description.

Class Members (Properties, Methods, and Events)

When the members of a class seem to be particularly interesting or important, we've devoted separate entries to each. These contain the same items of information as functions.

Attributes

Attributes are classes derived from System.Attribute that allow us to store information with an assembly's metadata. We've included only the attributes that VB programmers are most likely to use. The standard format for presenting information about attributes include some standard information (Class, Description, etc.), as well as the class constructors (these define the attribute's required arguments) and properties (which define the attribute's optional arguments).

#Const Directive

Syntax

```
#Const constantname = expression
```

constantname   *required; String literal*
Name of the constant

expression   *required; literal*
Any combination of literal values, other conditional compilation constants defined with the #Const directive, and arithmetic or logical operators except Is

Description

Defines a conditional compiler constant.

By using compiler constants to create code blocks that are included in the compiled application only when a particular condition is met, you can create more than one version of the application using the same source code. This is a two-step process:

- Defining the conditional compiler constant. This step is optional; conditional compiler constants that are not explicitly defined by the #Const directive, but are referenced in code, default to a value of Nothing.

- Evaluating the constant in the conditional compiler #If...Then statement block.

A conditional compiler constant can be assigned any string, numeric, or logical value returned by an expression. However, the expression itself can only consist of literals, operators other than Is, and another conditional compiler constant.

When the constant is evaluated, the code within the conditional compiler #If... Then block is compiled as part of the application only when the expression using the conditional compiler constant evaluates to True.

Rules at a Glance

- Conditional compiler constants are evaluated by the conditional compiler #If... Then statement block.

- You can use any arithmetic or logical operator in the expression except Is.

- You cannot use other constants defined with the standard Const statement in the expression.

- You cannot use intrinsic functions or variables in *expression*.

- Constants defined with #Const can only be used in conditional code blocks.

- You can place the #Const directive anywhere within a source file. If placed outside of all modules, the defined constant is visible throughout the source file, but is not visible to any other source files in the project. If placed in a module, the scope of the constant is that module. If placed in a procedure, the scope is that procedure and all called procedures.

- The #Const directive must be the first statement on a line of code. It can be followed only by a comment. Note that the colon, which is used to combine two complete sets of statements onto a single line, cannot be used on lines that contain #Const.

Programming Tips and Gotchas

- Conditional compiler constants help you debug your code, as well as provide a way to create more than one version of your application. You can include code that only operates when run in debug mode. The code can be left in your final version and does not compile unless running in the debugger. Therefore, you don't need to keep adding and removing debugging code.

- Conditional compiler constants may be defined in terms of other conditional compiler constants. For example, the following code fragment works as expected:

  ```
  #Const Flag1 = 1
  #Const Flag2 = 1
  #Const Flags = Flag1 + Flag2
  ```

- A conditional compiler constant can be defined at the command line using the /define or /d switch.

  It is important to remember that the constant defined by #Const is evaluated at compile time and therefore does not return information about the system on which the application is running.

See Also

#If Then #Else Directive

#If . . . Then . . . #Else Directive

Syntax

```
#If expression Then
    statements
[#ElseIf furtherexpression Then
    [elseifstatements]]
[#Else
```

```
    [elsestatements]]
    #End If
```

expression   *required*
> An expression made up of literals, operators, and conditional compiler constants that will evaluate to True or False

statements   *required*
> One or more lines of code or compiler directives, which is executed if *expression* evaluates to True

furtherexpression   *optional*
> An expression made up of literals, operators, and conditional compiler constants that will evaluate to True or False. *furtherexpression* is only evaluated if the preceding expression evaluates to False

elseifstatements   *optional*
> One or more lines of code or compiler directives, which is executed if *furtherexpression* evaluates to True

elsestatements   *optional*
> One or more lines of code or compiler directives, which are executed if *expression* or *furtherexpression* evaluates to False

Description

Defines a block or blocks of code that are only included in the compiled application when a particular condition is met, allowing you to create more than one version of the application using the same source code.

Conditionally including a block of code is a two-step process:

* Use the #Const directive to assign a value to a conditional compiler constant.

* Evaluate the conditional compiler constant using the #If...Then...#End If statement block.

Only code blocks whose expressions evaluate to True are included in the executable. You can use the #Else statement to execute code when the #If...Then expression evaluates to False. You can also use an #ElseIf statement to evaluate more expressions if previous expressions in the same block have evaluated to False.

Some uses of conditional compilation code are:

* To provide blocks of debugging code that can be left within the source code and switched on and off using a conditional constant. Since debug statements such as Debug.Write have no effect in compiled executables, they do not need to be included in conditional compilation code for the purpose of removing them from the final executable.

* To provide blocks of code that can perform different functions based on the build required by the developer. For example, you may have a sample version of your application that offers less functionality than the full product. This can be achieved using the same source code and wrapping the code for menu options, etc., within conditional compiler directives.

- To provide blocks of code that reference different components depending upon the build criteria of the application.

Rules at a Glance

- Unlike the normal `If...Then` statement, you cannot use a single-line version of the `#If...Then` statement.

- All expressions are evaluated using `Option Compare Text`, regardless of the setting of `Option Compare`.

- If a conditional compiler constant is undefined, comparing it to `Nothing`, 0, `False`, or an empty string (`""`) returns `True`.

Example

```
#Const ccVersion = 2.5
Private oTest as Object

Sub GetCorrectObject()

#If ccVersion = 2.5 Then
    Set oTest = New MyObject.MyClass
#Else
    Set oTest = New MyOtherObject.MyClass
#End If

End Sub
```

Programming Tips and Gotchas

- You can negate the evaluation of the expression in the `#If...Then` or `#ElseIf...Then` statements by placing the `Not` operator before the expression. For example, `#If Not ccVersion = 5 Then` forces the code after this line to compile in all situations where `ccVersion` does not equal 5.

- Conditional compilation helps you debug your code, as well as provides a way to create more than one version of your application. You can include code that will only operate when run in debug mode. The code can be left in your final version and will not compile unless running in the debugger; therefore, you don't need to keep adding and removing code.

See Also

#Const Directive

#Region...#End Region Directive

Syntax

```
#Region "identifier_string"
' code goes here
#End Region
```

identifier_string   *required; String literal*
    The title of the code block (or region)

Description

Marks a block of code as an expandable and collapsible region or code block in the Visual Studio .NET editor

Rules at a Glance

- Code blocks delineated with the #Region...#End Region directive are collapsed by default.

- *identifier_string* serves as the title to identify the region when it is collapsed.

- Code blocks defined by other directives (such as #If) must be entirely contained within the #Region...#End Region block.

Abs Function

Class

System.Math

Syntax

```
Math.Abs(value)
```

value   *required; any valid numeric expression*
   A number whose absolute value is to be returned

Return Value

The absolute value of *value*. The data type is the same as that of the argument passed to the function.

Description

Returns the absolute value of *value*. If *value* is an uninitialized variable, the return value is 0

Rules at a Glance

- Only numeric values can be passed to the *Abs* function.

- This is a Shared member of the Math class, so it can be used without creating any objects.

Example

In this example, the *LineLength* function is used to determine the length of a line on the screen. If the line runs from left to right, *X1* is less than *X2*, and the expression *X2* − *X1* returns the length of the line. If, however, the line runs from right to left, *X1* is greater than *X2*, and a negative line length is returned. As you know, in most circumstances it does not matter which way a line is pointing; all you want to know is how long it is. Using the *Abs* function allows you to return the same figure whether the underlying figure is negative or positive:

```
Function LineLength(X2 as Integer) as Integer
```

```
    Dim X1 As Integer

    X1 = 100
    LineLength = Math.Abs(X2 - X1)

End Function
```

Programming Tips and Gotchas

Because the *Abs* function can only accept numeric values, you may want to check the value you pass to *Abs* using the *IsNumeric* function to avoid generating an error. This is illustrated in the following code snippet:

```
If IsNumeric(sExtent) Then
    Math.Abs(sExtent)
    ...
End If
```

VB.NET/VB 6 Differences

In VB 6, *Abs* is an intrinsic VB function. In the .NET platform, it is a member of the Math class in the **System** namespace, and so it is not part of the VB.NET language.

See Also

Sign Function

Acos Function

Class

System.Math

Syntax

```
    Math.Acos(d)
```

d   *required; Double or any valid numeric expression*
A cosine, which is a number greater than or equal to −1 and less than or equal to 1

Return Value

A Double between 0 and pi that is the arccosine of *d* in radians

Description

Returns the arccosine of *d* in radians

Rules at a Glance

- If *d* is out of range (less than −1 or greater than 1), *Acos* returns **NaN**.
- This is a Shared member, so it can be used without creating any objects.

Programming Tips and Gotchas

To convert from radians to degrees, multiply by 180/pi.

VB.NET/VB 6 Differences

The *Acos* function did not exist in VB 6.

See Also

Asin Function, Atan Function, Atan2 Function

AddHandler Statement

Syntax

```
AddHandler NameOfEventSender, AddressOf NameOfEventHandler
```

NameOfEventSender   *required; String literal*
   The name of a class or object instance and its event, such as Button1.Click

NameOfEventHandler   *required; String literal*
   The name of a subroutine that is to serve as the event handler for
   NameOfEventSender

Description

Binds an event handler to a built-in or custom event. This makes it possible to
bind several event handlers to a single event.

* NameOfEventSender takes the form class.event or object.event.
* You can stop handling events defined by the **AddHandler** statement by calling the **RemoveHandler** statement.

Example

For an illustration, see the AddHandler and RemoveHandler" section in Chapter 7.

Programming Tips and Gotchas

The **Handles** keyword can be used to receive event notification for the lifetime of
an object. In contrast, **AddHandler** and **RemoveHandler** can be used to dynamically add and remove event notification at runtime.

See Also

RemoveHandler Statement

AddressOf Operator

Syntax

```
AddressOf procedurename
```

procedurename   *required*
   The name of a procedure that is referenced by the procedure delegate

Description

The **AddressOf** operator returns a procedure delegate instance that references a
specific procedure.

The AddressOf operator is used in the following situations:

- If a parameter to a procedure (a VB procedure or a Win32 API function) requires a function pointer (the address of a function), then we can pass the expression:

  ```
  AddressOf functionname
  ```

  where *functionname* is the name of the function. This function is called a *callback function*.

- AddressOf is also used to create delegate objects, as in:

  ```
  delg = New ADelegate(AddressOf obj.AMethod)
  ```

- AddressOf is used to bind event handlers to events through the AddHandler statement:

  ```
  AddHandler Form1.Click, AddressOf Me.Form1Click
  ```

Examples of all three applications of AddressOf can be found in the Delegates" section in Chapter 7.

VB.NET/VB 6 Differences

In VB 6, the AddressOf operator can only be used in a call to a Windows API function. Moreover, the argument passed to AddressOf must be the name of a procedure in a standard code module. However, in VB.NET these restrictions no longer apply.

AppActivate Procedure

Class

Microsoft.VisualBasic.Interaction

Syntax

```
[Interaction.]AppActivate(title)
```

title   *required; String or Integer*
    The name of the application as currently shown in the application window title bar. This can also be the task ID returned from the *Shell* function.

Description

Activates a window based on its caption

Rules at a Glance

- AppActivate performs a case-insensitive search on all top-level windows for a window caption that matches *title*. If an exact match is found, the window is activated. If no match is found, then the window captions are searched for a prefix match (*title* matches the beginning of the window caption). For example, the *title* "Microsoft Word" matches "Microsoft Word – MyDocument.doc". If a prefix match is found, the window is activated. Note that if multiple prefix matches are found, there is no way to predict which matching window will be activated.

- The window state (Maximized, Minimized, or Normal) of the activated application is not affected by **AppActivate**.

- If a matching application cannot be found, an exception of type System. ArgumentException is raised, and runtime error 5, "Invalid procedure call or argument," is generated.

Example

```
Private Sub Button2_Click(ByVal sender As System.Object, _
                          ByVal e As System.EventArgs) _
                          Handles Button2.Click

    Dim bVoid As Boolean
    bVoid = ActivateAnApp("Microsoft Excel")

End Sub

Function ActivateAnApp(vAppTitle As String) As Boolean

    On Error GoTo Activate_Err

    ActivateAnApp = False
    AppActivate(vAppTitle)
    ActivateAnApp = True

    Exit Function

Activate_Err:
    MsgBox ("Application " & vAppTitle &
            " could not be activated")

End Function
```

Programming Tips and Gotchas

- **AppActivate** searches only top-level windows.

- You can also use the task ID returned by the *Shell* function with the **AppActivate** statement, as this simple example demonstrates:

```
Option Explicit
Private vAppID

Private Sub Button1_Click(ByVal sender As System.Object, _
                          ByVal e As System.EventArgs) _
                          Handles Button1.Click
    vAppID = Shell("C:\Program Files\Internet Explorer\IEXPLORE.EXE")
End Sub
Private Sub Button2_Click(ByVal sender As System.Object, _
                          ByVal e As System.EventArgs) _
                          Handles Button2.Click
    AppActivate vAppID
End Sub
```

- **AppActivate** is very difficult to use with applications whose application titles change to reflect the state or context of the application. Microsoft Outlook illustrates an excellent example of this problem. If the user has Outlook in the Calendar section, the title bar reads "Calendar – Microsoft Outlook," whereas if in the Inbox section, the title bar reads "Inbox – Microsoft Outlook." In situations such as this, we must resort to other techniques, such as using Win32 API methods, to enumerate all windows and check the captions directly.

- **AppActivate** is often used to give the focus to a particular window before keystrokes are sent to it using the **SendKeys** statement, which sends keystrokes to the active window only.

VB.NET/VB 6 Differences

In VB 6, **AppActivate** has a second optional parameter, *wait*, a Boolean that determines whether the application calling **AppActivate** must have the focus for the window indicated by *title* to be activated. In VB.NET, *wait* is not supported.

See Also

Shell Function

Application Class

Namespace

System.Windows.Forms

Createable

No

Description

The Application object provides a diverse range of functionality, including support for multithreaded programming, access to the system registry, and support for subclassing (intercepting messages sent to application windows). It also includes a variety of informational functions, such as properties to retrieve the company name, to retrieve the application's executable path, and to retrieve the application's name and version.

Application objects can be created as follows:

```
Dim obj As Application
```

However, because all of the Application object's members are shared, you do not need to instantiate the Application object to access its properties and methods. Hence, you can retrieve the executable path of your application, for instance, with the code fragment:

```
Dim sPath As String = Application.ExecutablePath
```

Application class members marked with a plus sign (+) are discussed in detail in their own entries.

Public Properties

AllowQuit
CommonAppDataPath
CommonAppDataRegistry
CompanyName +
CurrentCulture
CurrentInputLanguage
ExecutablePath +
LocalUserAppDataPath
MessageLoop
ProductName +
ProductVersion +
SafeTopLevelCaptionFormat
StartupPath
UserAppDataPath
UserAppDataRegistry

Public Shared Methods

AddMessageFilter
DoEvents +
Exit
ExitThread
OleRequired
OnThreadException
RemoveMessageFilter
Run

Public Shared Events

ApplicationExit
Idle
ThreadException
ThreadExit

See Also

Application.CompanyName Property, Application.DoEvents Method, Application.
ExecutablePath Property, Application.ProductName Property, Application.Product-
Version Property

Application.CompanyName Property

Class

System.Windows.Forms.Application

Syntax

```
Application.CompanyName()
```

Return Value

A String containing the company name for the application

Description

Gets the company name for the application. This is a read-only property.

The value of the CompanyName property can be defined by including the `<AssemblyCompany>` attribute in the AssemblyInfo file for the application. Its syntax is:

```
<Assembly: AssemblyCompany("sCompany")>
```

where *sCompany* is a string literal containing the company name.

See Also

Application Class, Application.ProductName Property, Application.ProductVersion Property

---

Application.DoEvents Method

Class

System.Windows.Forms.Application

Syntax

```
Application.DoEvents()
```

Description

Allows the operating system to process events and messages waiting in the message queue.

For example, you can allow a user to click a Cancel button while a processor-intensive operation is executing. In this case, without DoEvents, the click event is not processed until after the operation had completed. With DoEvents, Windows allocates time for the Cancel button's Click event to fire and the event handler to execute.

Example

The following example uses a form with two command buttons to illustrate DoEvents. Suppose the user clicks CommandButton1. Then the `Do` loop in the click event executes indefinitely. However, if the user clicks CommandButton2, its click event is processed when the `DoEvents` statement in CommandButton1_Click is executed. This sets the Boolean flag to `False`, which terminates the `Do` loop.

```
Option Explicit
Private lngCtr As Long
Private blnFlag As Boolean

Private Sub Button1_Click(ByVal sender As System.Object, _
                          ByVal e As System.EventArgs) _
                          Handles Button1.Click

    blnFlag = True

    Do While blnFlag
```

```
        lngCtr = lngCtr + 1
        DoEvents()
    Loop
    MsgBox("Loop interrupted after " & lngCtr & _
        " iterations.")
End Sub

Private Sub CommandButton2_Click()

    blnFlag = False

End Sub
```

Programming Tips and Gotchas

- While DoEvents can be indispensable for increasing the responsiveness of your application, it should at the same time be used judiciously, since it entails an enormous performance penalty. For example, the following table compares the number of seconds required for a simple For...Next loop to iterate one million times when DoEvents isn't called, on the one hand, and when it's called on each iteration of the loop, on the other.

Without DoEvents	0.01 seconds
With DoEvents	49.26 seconds

- If most of a procedure's processing occurs inside of a loop, one way to avoid too many calls to DoEvents is to call it conditionally every ten, hundred, or thousand iterations of the loop. For example, the following code calls DoEvents every thousand iterations:

```
Dim lCtr As Long
For lCtr = 0 To 1000000
    If (lCtr Mod 1000) = 0 Then
        DoEvents
    End If
Next
```

- DoEvents should not be used in any event procedure or callback routine that is invoked automatically by the operating system. Doing so causes re-entrance problems. (The event or routine may be called again during the processing of the DoEvents method.) For the same reason, DoEvents should not be used in in-process COM objects created with Visual Basic.

See Also

Application Class

Application.ExecutablePath Property

Class

System.Windows.Forms.Application

Syntax

```
Application.ExecutablePath()
```

Return Value

A String containing the complete path of the executable file for the application

Description

Gets the complete path of the executable file for the application. This is a read-only property.

VB.NET/VB 6 Differences

The ExecutablePath property in the .NET Framework corresponds to the App.Path property in VB 6.

See Also

Application Class

Application.ProductName Property

Class

System.Windows.Forms.Application

Syntax

```
Application.ProductName()
```

Return Value

A String containing the product name of the application

Description

Gets the product name of the application. This is a read-only property.

The value of the ProductName property can be defined by including the <AssemblyProduct> attribute in the application's AssemblyInfo file. Its syntax is:

```
<Assembly: AssemblyProduct("sProduct")>
```

where *sProduct* is a string literal containing the product name.

VB.NET/VB 6 Differences

The ProductName property in the .NET Framework corresponds to the App. ProductName property in VB 6.

See Also

Application Class, Application.CompanyName Property, Application.Product-Version Property

Application.ProductVersion Property

Class

System.Windows.Forms.Application

Syntax

```
Application.ProductVersion()
```

Return Value

A String containing the product version of the application

Description

Gets the product version of the application.

This is a read-only property. The product version typically has the form:

```
MajorVersionNumber.MinorVersionNumber.BuildNumber.PrivatePartNumber
```

Its default value is "1.0.*", which indicates that Visual Studio maintains default build and revision numbers.

The value of the ProductVersion property can be defined by including the <AssemblyVersion> attribute in the application's AssemblyInfo file. Its syntax is:

```
<Assembly: AssemblyVersion("maj.min.bld.rev")>
```

where *maj* is the major version number, *min* is the minor version number, *bld* is the build number, and *rev* is the revision number.

VB.NET/VB 6 Differences

The ProductVersion property in the .NET Framework corresponds to the App. Major, App.Minor, and App.Revision properties in VB 6.

See Also

Application.Class, Application.CompanyName Property, Application.ProductName Property

Array Class

Namespace

System

Createable

Yes

Description

An Array object (that is, an instance of the Array class) that represents an array.

Arrays defined in VB.NET are Array objects, so they support the members of the Array class. Array class members marked with a plus sign (+) are discussed in detail in their own entries.

Public Instance Properties

IsFixedSize
IsReadOnly
IsSynchronized
Length
Rank
SyncRoot

Public Shared Methods

BinarySearch +
Clear
Copy +
CreateInstance
IndexOf +
LastIndexOf +
Reverse +
Sort +

Public Instance Methods

Clone
CopyTo
Equals
GetEnumerator
GetHashCode
GetLength
GetLowerBound
GetType
GetUpperBound
GetValue
Initialize
SetValue
ToString

Array.BinarySearch Method

Class

System.Array

Syntax

```
Array.BinarySearch(array, value, [comparer])
Array.BinarySearch(array, index, length, value, [comparer])
```

array   *required; any array*
  The one-dimensional array to be searched

---

value   *required in first overloaded function; any*
    The value to search for in *array*

index   *required in second overloaded version; Integer*
    The array element at which the search is to start

length   *required in second overloaded version; Integer*
    The number of array elements to be searched

comparer   *optional;* IComparer
    A BCL or user-defined class implementing the IComparer interface that deter-
    mines how two items are compared for equality.

Return Value

An Integer representing the zero-based ordinal position of the element matching
value

Description

This method provides a quick way to search for a value in a *sorted* one-dimensional
array, returning the smallest index whose element is that value. It uses a binary
search algorithm, which tends to take $\log^2(n)$ comparisons to find an item in an
array of length n. For example, if n = 100,000, the number of comparisons is on the
order of 17.

To illustrate, if **arr** is an array of names in alphabetical order, then the code:

```
Array.BinarySearch(arr, "steve")
```

returns the smallest index with element "steve." If no such element exists, Binary-
Search returns the negative number whose bitwise complement is the index of the
first element that is larger than "steve."

Rules at a Glance

- The array must be a one-dimensional array sorted in *ascending* order.

- If *value* is not found in the array, the method returns a negative number,
  which is the bitwise complement of the index of the first element that is larger
  than *value*. To extract this value, you can use the Not operator, as in the
  following code fragment:

  ```
  iResult = Array.BinarySearch(lArr, lSearch)
  if iResult >= 0 Then
      MsgBox(iResult)
  Else
      MsgBox(iResult & vbcrlf & Not iResult)
  End If
  ```

- By default, the System.Collections.Comparer class is used to compare *value*
  with the members of *array*. This means that string comparisons are case
  sensitive.

Programming Tips and Gotchas

- If an array contains Boolean values, the method fails to correctly identify the
  position of the first **False** value in the array.

- In addition to the Comparer class, you can also pass an instance of the System.Collections.CaseInsensitiveComparer class as the *comparer* argument. It provides for case-insensitive comparisons. For example:

```
Dim sArr() As String = {"Alaska", "ALASKA", "Michigan", "MICHIGAN", _
                        "New York", "NEW YORK"}
Dim sSearch As String
Dim lResult As Long
Dim oComp As New CaseInsensitiveComparer

sSearch = "MICHIGAN"
iResult = Array.BinarySearch(sArr, sSearch, oComp)
```

In this case, because of the case-insensitive comparison, the value of lResult is 2.

See Also

Array.IndexOf, ArrayLastIndexOf Methods, Array.Sort Method

Array.Copy Method

Class

System.Array

Syntax

```
Array.Copy(sourceArray, destinationArray, length)

Array.Copy(sourceArray, sourceIndex, destinationArray, _
           destinationIndex, length)
```

sourceArray   *required; any array*
   The array to be copied

sourceIndex   *required in second overloaded version; integer*
   The index in *sourceArray* at which copying begins

destinationArray   *required; any array*
   The target array

destinationIndex   *required in second overloaded version; Integer*
   The index in *destinationArray* where the first element is to be copied

length   *required; Integer*
   The number of elements to copy

Return Value

None

Description

Makes a copy of all or part of an array.

Since arrays are reference types, when we set one array variable equal to another, we are just assigning a new reference to the same array. For instance, consider the following code:

```
Dim a() As Integer = {1, 2, 3}
Dim b() As Integer
' Array assignment
b = a
' Change b
b(0) = 10
' Check a
MsgBox(a(0))     'Displays 10
```

The fact that changing b(0) also changes a(0) shows that a and b point to the same array.

Rules at a Glance

- Using the first syntax, you can copy a range of values from the beginning of *sourceArray* to the beginning of *destinationArray*. Using the second syntax, you can copy a range of values from anywhere in *destinationArray* to anywhere in *targetArray*.

- *sourceArray* and *destinationArray* must have the same number of dimensions.

- *length* is the total number of elements to be copied. If sArr1 is a two-dimensional array, for example, the statement:

    ```
    Array.Copy(sArr1, 0, sArr2, 0, 3)
    ```

    copies the values from sArr(0,0), sArr(0,1), and sArr(1,0) to sArr2.

- To copy all elements, you can supply UBound(`sourceArray`) + 1 as an argument to *length*.

- If *sourceArray* and *destinationArray* are the same, and *destinationIndex* lies within the range of values being copied (that is, if the source and target ranges overlap), no data will be lost. The method behaves as if it copies *length* elements from *sourceArray* to a temporary buffer, then copies from the temporary buffer to *destinationArray*.

Example

```
Dim a() As Integer = {1, 2, 3}
Dim c() As Integer
' Array copy
ReDim c(UBound(a) + 1)
Array.Copy(a, c, UBound(a) + 1)
'Change c
c(0) = 20
'Check a
MsgBox(a(0))     'Displays 1
```

VB.NET/VB 6 Differences

Since arrays were not a reference type in VB 6, you could simply create a copy of an existing array through assignment, thus eliminating the need for a Copy method.

Array.IndexOf Method

Class

System.Array

Syntax

```
Array.IndexOf(Array, Value[, startIndex[, count]])
```

`Array`   *required; any array*
   The array to be searched

`Value`   *required; any*
   The object that is searched for

`startIndex`   *optional; Integer*
   The index at which to start the search

`count`   *optional; Integer*
   The number of items to search

Return Value

The index of the first occurrence of `Value` in `Array`, or –1

Description

Returns an Integer representing the index of the first occurrence of `value` in `Array`

Rules at a Glance

- `Array` must be a one-dimensional array.

- By default, the IndexOf method searches for `Value` from the beginning to the end of `Array`.

- If `startIndex` is provided without `count`, IndexOf searches from `startIndex` to the last element of `Array`.

- If both `startIndex` and `count` are provided, the method searches `count` elements starting at `startIndex`. In other words, it searches from `array(startIndex)` to `array(startIndex + count - 1)`.

- If `startIndex` is present and is outside of the range of the elements in `Array`, the method returns –1.

- If `count` is present and `startIndex + count - 1` exceeds the total number of elements in `Array`, the method call generates an ArgumentOutOfRange-Exception exception.

Example

The following code searches for a value in an Integer array:

```
Dim i As Integer
Dim a(99999) As Integer
For i = 0 To 99999
    a(i) = CInt(Rnd() * 100000)
```

```
Next
MsgBox(Array.IndexOf(a, 36500))
```

You can also specify the starting index for the search, as well as the number of elements to search. For example:

```
Array.IndexOf(array:=a, value:=136500, startIndex:=100, _
              count:=1000)
```

Array.LastIndexOf Method

Class

System.Array

Syntax

```
Array.LastIndexOf(Array, Value[, startIndex, count])
```

Array   *required; any array*
    The array to be searched

Value   *required; any*
    The object that is searched for

startIndex   *optional; Integer*
    The index at which to start the search

count   *optional; Integer*
    The number of elements to search

Return Value

An Integer containing the index of the last occurrence of *Object* in *Array*

Description

Returns the index of the last occurrence of *Object* in *Array*

Rules at a Glance

- *Array* must be a one-dimensional array.

- The LastIndexOf method has the same syntax as the IndexOf method and works the same way as IndexOf, except that it searches from the end of the array and returns the largest index of a matching element.

- By default, the LastIndexOf method searches for *Value* from the end to the beginning of *Array*.

- If *startIndex* is provided without *count*, LastIndexOf searches from *startIndex* to the first element of *Array*.

- If both *startIndex* and *count* are provided, the method searches *count* elements backward starting at *startIndex*. In other words, it searches from `array(startIndex)` to `array(startIndex - count + 1)`.

- If *startIndex* is present and is outside of the range of the elements in *array*, the method returns –1.

- If *count* is present and `startIndex` < `count` − 1, the method call generates an ArgumentOutOfRangeException exception.

Example

The following code searches for a value in an Integer array:

```
Dim i As Integer
Dim a(100000) As Integer
For i = 0 To 99999
    a(i) = CInt(Rnd() * 100000)
Next
MsgBox(Array.LastIndexOf(a, 36500))
```

You can also specify the starting index for the search, as well as the number of elements to search. For example:

```
Array.LastIndexOf(array:=a, value:=136500, startIndex:=100, _
                  count:=50)
```

See Also

Array.IndexOf Method

Array.Reverse Method

Class

System.Array

Syntax

```
Array.Reverse(array[, startindex, endindex])
```

array   *required; any array*
    The array to be reversed

startIndex   *optional; Integer*
    The index at which to start the reversal process

endIndex   *optional; Integer*
    The index at which to end the reversal process

Return Value

None

Description

Reverses a portion of or all of the elements of an array

Example

```
Dim a() As Integer = {1, 2, 3, 4, 5}
Dim i As Integer
array.Reverse(a, 1, 3)
For i = 0 To 4
    debug.Write(a(i))
Next
```

This code prints the sequence 14325, which is the original array 12345 with the middle section from index 1 to index 3 reversed.

Array.Sort Method

Class

System.Array

Syntax

```
Array.Sort(array)
Array.Sort(array, comparer)
Array.Sort(array, index, length)
Array.Sort(array, index, length, comparer)

Array.Sort(keys, items)
Array.Sort(keys, items, comparer)
Array.Sort(keys, items, index, length)
Array.Sort(keys, items, index, length, comparer)
```

array   *required; any array*
    The array of objects to be sorted.

keys   *required; any array*
    The array of keys to use for sorting. This array is also sorted.

items   *required; any array*
    A parallel array of values to be sorted in the order of *keys*, their corresponding keys.

index   *required; Integer*
    The index at which to start the sort.

length   *required; Integer*
    The index at which to end the reversal process.

comparer   *required;* IComparer *interface*
    An object implementing the IComparer interface to be used for sorting. If Nothing, then the IComparable implementation of each element (in the case of arrays of keys) or value type (in the case of arrays).

Return Value

None

Description

Sorts a portion of, or sorts an entire one-dimensional array, with an optionally specified key array and an optionally specified IComparer interface

Example

```
Sub sortArray()
Dim i As Integer
Dim intArray() As Integer = {9, 8, 12, 4, 5}
For i = 0 To 4
    console.WriteLine(CStr(intArray(i)))
```

```
    Next
    System.Array.Sort(intarray)
    Console.WriteLine("Sorted:")
    For i = 0 To 4
        console.WriteLine(CStr(intArray(i)))
    Next
    End Sub
```

The output is:

```
9
8
12
4
5
Sorted:
4
5
8
9
12
```

Asc, AscW Functions

Class

Microsoft.VisualBasic.Strings

Syntax

```
Asc(string)
AscW(str)
```

string, str   *required; String or Char*
    Any expression that evaluates to a *nonempty* string

Return Value

An Integer that represents the character code of the first character of the string. The range for the returned value is 0 – 255 on nonDBCS systems, and −32768 to 32767 on DBCS systems.

Description

Returns an Integer representing the character code for the first character of the string passed to it. All other characters in the string are ignored

Rules at a Glance

* The string expression passed to the function must contain at least one character or a runtime error is generated.

* Only the first character of the string is evaluated by *Asc* or *AscW.*

Example

```
Dim sChars As String
Dim iCharCode As Integer
```

```
sChars = TextBox1.Text
If Len(sChars) > 0 Then
    iCharCode = Asc(sChars)
    If iCharCode >= 97 And iChar <= 122 Then
        MsgBox "The first character must be uppercase"
    End If
End If
```

Programming Tips and Gotchas

- Check that the string you are passing to the function contains at least one character using the *Len* function, as the following example shows:

```
If Len(sMyString) > 0 Then
    iCharCode = Asc(sMyString)
Else
    MsgBox("Cannot process a zero-length string")
End If
```

- Use *Asc* within your data-validation routines to determine such conditions as whether the first character is upper- or lowercase and whether it is alphabetic or numeric, as the following example demonstrates:

```
Private Sub Button1_Click(ByVal sender As System.Object, _
                          ByVal e As System.EventArgs) _
                          Handles Button1.Click

    Dim sTest As String
    Dim iChar As Integer

    sTest = TextBox1.Text

    If Len(sTest) > 0 Then
        iChar = Asc(sTest)
        If iChar >= 65 And iChar <= 90 Then
            MsgBox "The first character is UPPERCASE"
        ElseIf iChar >= 97 And iChar <= 122 Then
            MsgBox "The first character is lowercase"
        Else
            MsgBox "The first character isn't alphabetical"
        End If
    Else
        MsgBox "Please enter something in the text box"
    End If

End Sub
```

- Use the *Asc* function and the related *Chr* function to create rudimentary encryption methods. Once you have obtained the character code for a particular character, you can perform calculations on this code to come up with a different number and then convert this to a character using the *Chr* function. To decrypt your string, simply reverse the calculation. You may want to avoid character codes less than 20, however, since these can be interpreted as special nonprinting characters and cause undesirable effects if displayed or printed.

```
Private Sub CommandButton2_Click()

Dim MyEncryptedString, MyDecryptedString As String
Dim MyName As String = "Paul Lomax"
Dim i As Integer

For i = 1 To Len(MyName)
   MyEncryptedString = MyEncryptedString & _
                       Chr(Asc(Mid(MyName, i, 1)) + 25)
Next i

MsgBox("Hello, my name is " & MyEncryptedString)

For i = 1 To Len(MyName)
   MyDecryptedString &= Chr(Asc(Mid(MyEncryptedString, i, 1)) - 25)
Next i

MsgBox("Hello, my name is " & MyDecryptedString)
End Sub
```

See Also

Chr, ChrW Functions

AssemblyVersion Attribute

Class

System.Reflection.AssemblyVersionAttribute

Applies To

Assembly

Description

Specifies the version of the assembly. The version is represented as a four-part number, as follows:

<major_version>.<minor_version>.<build_number>.<revision>

Ordinarily, the .NET runtime considers a difference in any one of these four-part numbers to indicate a different version.

A wildcard indicates that an assembly can be used with clients requesting any value for the wildcard elements. For example, if the version is set to 1.0.*, the assembly can be used for clients requesting version 1.0.1681.0, 1.0.1723.0, and 1.0.1723.2.

 In Visual Studio .NET, the <AssemblyVersion> attribute is automatically added to the AssemblyInfo.vb file and its value is set to 1.0.*.

Constructor
    New(version)

version   *String*
    The version of the assembly

Properties

Version   *String*
    Read-only. The version of the assembly. Its value is set by the required
    version parameter of the attribute's class constructor.

Asin Function

Class

System.Math

Syntax
    Math.Asin(d)

d   *required; Double or any valid numeric expression*
    A number representing a sine, which can range from –1 to 1

Return Value

A Double between –pi/2 and pi/2 that is the arcsine of *d* in radians

Description

Returns the arcsine of *d*, in radians

Rules at a Glance

- If *d* is out of range, the function returns NaN.
- This is a Shared member, so it can be used without creating any objects.

Programming Tips and Gotchas

To convert from radians to degrees, multiply by 180/pi.

VB.NET/VB 6 Differences

The *Asin* function did not exist in VB 6.

See Also

Acos Function, Atan Function, Atan2 Function

Atan Function

Class

System.Math

Syntax

```
Math.Atan(d)
```

d   *required; Double or any valid numeric expression*
A number representing a tangent

Return Value

A Double that is the arctangent in radians of *d*, in the range –pi/2 to pi/2

Description

Takes the ratio of two sides of a right triangle (*d*) and returns the corresponding angle in radians. The ratio is the length of the side opposite the angle divided by the length of the side adjacent to the angle.

Rules at a Glance

- If *d* is out of range, the function returns NaN.

- This is a Shared member, so it can be used without creating any objects.

Example

```
Private Sub Main()

    Dim dblSideAdj As Double
    Dim dblSideOpp As Double
    Dim dblRatio As Double
    Dim dblAtangent As Double

    dblSideAdj = 50.25
    dblSideOpp = 75.5

    dblRatio = dblSideOpp / dblSideAdj
    dblAtangent = Math.Atan(dblRatio)
    'convert from radians to degrees
    dblDegrees = dblAtangent * (180 / 3.142)
    MsgBox dblDegrees & " Degrees"

End Sub
```

Programming Tips and Gotchas

- To convert radians to degrees, multiply radians by 180/pi.

- Do not confuse *Atan* with the cotangent. *Atan* is the inverse *trigonometric* function of *Tan*, whereas the cotangent is the reciprocal of the tangent.

VB.NET/VB 6 Differences

The *Atan* function corresponds to the VB 6 *Atn* intrinsic function.

See Also

Acos Function, Asin Function, Atan2 Function

Atan2 Function

Class

System.Math

Syntax

```
Math.Atan2(y, x)
```

x   *required; Double*
   The x coordinate of a point

y   *required; Double*
   The y coordinate of a point

Return Value

A Double that is the arctangent of the *ratio* x/y, in radians

Description

Returns the angle in the Cartesian plane formed by the x-axis and a vector starting from the origin (0,0) and terminating at the point (x, y). More specifically, the return value *q* satisfies the following:

- For (x, y) in quadrant 1, 0 < q < pi/2.
- For (x, y) in quadrant 2, pi /2 < q < pi.
- For (x, y) in quadrant 3, −pi < q < −pi /2.
- For (x, y) in quadrant 4, −pi /2 < q < 0.

Rules at a Glance

This is a Shared member, so it can be used without creating any objects.

VB.NET/VB 6 Differences

The *Atan2* function does not exist in VB 6.

See Also

Acos Function, Asin Function, Atan Function

AttributeUsage Attribute

Class

System.AttributeUsageAttribute

Applies to

Class

Description

Defines the program elements to which a custom attribute can be applied. Its use is required when defining a custom attribute.

Constructor

```
New(validOn)
```

validOn   `System.AttributeTargets`
Indicates the program elements to which a custom attribute can be applied. Possible values are `All`, `Assembly`, `Class`, `Constructor`, `Delegate`, `Enum`, `Event`, `Field`, `Interface`, `Struct`, `Method`, `Module`, `Parameter`, `Property`, and `ReturnValue`.

Properties

AllowMultiple   *Boolean*
Indicates whether the attribute can be used more than once on a single program element. Its default value is `False`.

Inherited   *Boolean*
Indicates whether attribute is automatically inherited by derived classes and overridden members. Its default value is `True`.

ValidOn   `AttributeTargets` *enumeration*
Read-only. Indicates the program elements to which the attribute can be applied. Its value is set by the required *validOn* parameter of the class constructor.

Example

See Defining a Custom Attribute" in Chapter 8 for more details and an example.

Beep Procedure

Class

Microsoft.VisualBasic.Interaction

Syntax

```
Beep
```

Description

Sounds a tone through the computer's speaker

Example

```
Private Sub Main()

    iVoid = DoSomeLongFunction()
    Beep
    MsgBox "Finished!"

End Sub
```

Programming Tips and Gotchas

- We have found the `Beep` statement to be completely unreliable, and therefore we never use it in applications intended for distribution.

- If you do decide to use the `Beep` statement, please remember that its overuse will not endear you to your users!

- The frequency and duration of the tone depends on the computer's hardware. Bear in mind that on some systems, a mouse click is louder than the beep!

- Since the successful operation of the `Beep` statement does not require the presence of any multimedia hardware (such as a sound card, for example), it can be used when a system is not configured to support sound. For example, if the following is defined in the declarations section of a code module:

```
Declare Function waveOutGetNumDevs Lib "winmm.dll" () As Long
Declare Function PlaySound Lib "winmm.dll" _
        Alias "PlaySoundA" (ByVal lpszName As String, _
        ByVal hModule As Long, ByVal dwFlags As Long) _
        As Long


Public Const SND_APPLICATION = &H80
Public Const SND_ASYNC = &H1
Public Const SND_FILENAME = &H20000
Public Const SND_NODEFAULT = &H2


Public HasSound As Boolean

Public Function IsSoundSupported() As Boolean
    If (waveOutGetNumDevs > 0) Then _
        IsSoundSupported = True
End Function
```

then the following procedure takes advantage of any existing sound hardware to play a wave file or simply beeps the built-in PC speaker if no sound hardware is found.

```
Private Sub Form_Load(ByVal sender As System.Object, _
                ByVal e As System.EventArgs) _
                Handles MyBase.Load
    Dim intCtr As Integer
    HasSound = IsSoundSupported()
    If HasSound Then
        Call PlaySound("c:\windows\media\tada.wav", 0, _
                SND_FILENAME Or SND_NODEFAULT)
    Else
        For intCtr = 0 To 3
            Beep
        Next
    End If
End Sub
```

Call Statement

Syntax

```
[Call] procedurename[(argumentlist)]
```

procedurename   *required; n/a*
    The name of the subroutine being called

argumentlist   *optional; any*
    A comma-delimited list of arguments to pass to the subroutine being called

Description

Passes execution control to a procedure, function, or dynamic-link library (DLL) procedure or function

Rules at a Glance

* Use of the `Call` keyword is optional.

* Regardless of whether the `Call` keyword is used, *argumentlist*, if it is present, must be enclosed in *parentheses*.

* If you use `Call` to call a function, the function's return value is discarded.

Example

```
Call myProcedure(True, iMyInt)

Sub myProcedure(blnFlag as Boolean, iNumber as Integer)
...
End Sub
```

Programming Tips and Gotchas

* To pass a whole array to a procedure, use the array name followed by empty parentheses.

* Some programmers suggest that code is more readable when the `Call` keyword is used to call subroutines.

VB.NET/VB 6 Differences

* In VB 6, parentheses had to be omitted if the `Call` keyword was omitted and *procedurename* had more than one argument. In VB.NET, parentheses are required whenever arguments are present.

* In VB 6, if *argumentlist* consisted of a single argument, enclosing it in parentheses and omitting the `Call` statement reversed the method by which the argument was passed to the called function. Thus, an argument ordinarily called by value would be called by reference, and vice versa. In VB.NET, this confusing behavior is not supported.

* In VB 6, when calling an external routine defined using the `Declare` statement, you can override the default method of passing an argument by specifying the `ByVal` or `ByRef` keywords before the argument. In VB.NET you cannot change whether an argument is passed by value or by reference in the call to the routine.

See Also

CallByName Function

CallByName Function

Class

Microsoft.VisualBasic.Interaction

Named Arguments

Yes, if *Args*() is omitted

Syntax

```
CallByName(Object, ProcName, UseCallType, Args())
```

`Object`   *required; Object*
A reference to the object containing the procedure being called.

`ProcName`   *required; String*
The name of the procedure to call.

`UseCallType`   *required;* `CallType` *constant*
A constant of the type `CallType` indicating what type of procedure is being
called. `CallType` constants are listed in the following table.

Constant	Value	Description
Method	1	The called procedure is a method.
Get	2	The called procedure retrieves a property value.
Let	4	The called procedure sets the value of a property.

`Args`   *optional; any*
A ParamArray argument representing the arguments required by the procedure being called.

Return Value

Depends on the return value (if any) of the called procedure

Description

Provides a method for calling a class member by name.

Since *ProcName* is a string expression, rather than the literal name of a routine, it
is possible to call routines dynamically at runtime using a string variable to hold
the various procedure names.

Rules at a Glance

- The return type of *CallByName* is the return type of the called procedure.

- *ProcName* is not case sensitive.

- *UseCallType* can either be a numeric value or a constant of the `CallType`
  enumeration. In the latter case, the enumeration name must be specified
  along with the constant name, as in CallType.Method.

- *Args()* must be a parameter array. A parameter array is an array used to contain function, procedure, or property arguments that can have a variable number of elements.

Programming Tips and Gotchas

- Since the member to be called is not known at compile time, the performance of *CallByName* is inferior to calling members directly by literal name.

- Using *CallByName* does not necessarily require that `Option Strict` be set Off.

Example

The following example uses a parameter array to call the Multiply method of a class named Math:

```
Imports Microsoft.VisualBasic
Imports System

Module modMain

Public Sub Main()

Dim oMath As New Math
Dim dArr() As Double = {1,2,3}

' Call using ParamArray
MsgBox(CallByName(oMath, "Multiply", CallType.Method, dArr))

End Sub

End Module

Public Class Math

Public Function Multiply(a() As Double) As Double

Dim result as double = 1.0
Dim intCtr As Integer
Dim intIndex As Integer = 0

for intIndex = 0 to ubound(a)
    result = result * a(intIndex)
next

Multiply = result

End Function

End Class
```

VB.NET/VB 6 Differences

In VB 6, you don't have to specify VbCallType as the name of the enumeration to access its constants. In VB.NET, you must specify CallType as the name of the enumeration to access its constants.

See Also

Call Statement

CBool Function

Named Arguments

No

Syntax

```
CBool(expression)
```

expression   *required; String or Numeric*
    Any numeric expression or a string representation of a numeric value

Return Value

expression converted to Boolean data type (True or False)

Description

Casts *expression* as a Boolean data type

Rules at a Glance

When a numeric value is converted to Boolean, any nonzero value is converted to True, and zero is converted to False.

If the expression to be converted is a string, the string must be capable of being evaluated as a number, or it must be "True" or "False". Any other string generates a runtime error. For example, CBool("one") results in a type mismatch error, whereas CBool("1") is converted to True, and CBool("True") is converted to True.

Programming Tips and Gotchas

- You can check the validity of the expression prior to using the *CBool* function by using the *IsNumeric* function.

- Like most of the conversion functions, *CBool* is not actually a function in the Microsoft.VisualBasic namespace. Instead, it is similar to a Visual C++ macro; the compiler translates the function call into inline code.

CByte Function

Named Arguments

No

Syntax

```
CByte(expression)
```

expression   *required; String or Numeric*
A string or numeric expression that evaluates to a number between 0 and 255

Return Value

expression converted to Byte data type

Description

Converts *expression* to a Byte data type

Rules at a Glance

- If the expression to be converted is a string, the string must be capable of conversion to a numeric expression; this can be checked using the *IsNumeric* function.

- If *expression* evaluates to less than 0 or more than 255, a runtime error is generated.

- If the value of *expression* is not a whole number, *CByte* rounds the number prior to conversion.

Example

```
If IsNumeric(sMyNumber) Then
    If val(sMyNumber) >= 0 and val(sMyNumber) <= 255 Then
        BytMyNumber = CByte(sMyNumber)
    End If
End If
```

Programming Tips and Gotchas

- Check that the value you pass to *CByte* is neither negative nor greater than 255.

- Use *IsNumeric* to ensure that the value passed to *CByte* can be converted to a numeric expression.

- When using *CByte* to convert floating point numbers, fractional values up to but not including .5 are rounded down, while values above but not including .5 are rounded up. Values whose fractional component is exactly equal to .5 are rounded up if their integral component is odd and down if their integral component is even.

- The *CByte* function converts an expression to an unsigned byte data type. To convert *expression* to a signed byte data type, create an instance of the SByte class and call its Parse method.

- Like most of the conversion functions, *CByte* is not actually a function in the Microsoft.VisualBasic namespace. Instead, it is similar to a Visual C++ macro; the compiler translates the function call into inline code.

CChar Function

Named Arguments

No

Syntax

```
CChar(expression)
```

expression   *required; String*
    Any string expression

Return Value

A value of type Char

Description

Converts the first character in a string *expression* to a Char data type

Rules at a Glance

CChar extracts the first character of expression and converts it to a Char data type.

Example

```
MsgBox(CChar("abc"))      ' Displays a
MsgBox(CChar("56"))       ' Displays 5
```

Programming Tips and Gotchas

- If you wish to convert a numeric code to its corresponding Char data type, use the *ChrW* function.

- Like most of the conversion functions, *CChar* is not actually a function in the Microsoft.VisualBasic namespace. Instead, it is similar to a Visual C++ macro; the compiler translates the function call into inline code.

See Also

Chr, ChrW Functions

CDate Function

Named Arguments

No

Syntax

```
CDate(expression)
```

expression   *required; String or Numeric*
    Any valid representation of a date and time

Return Value

expression converted into a Date data type

Description

Converts *expression* to a Date data type.

The format of *expression*—the order of day, month, and year—is determined by the locale setting of the local computer. To be certain a date is recognized correctly by *CDate*, the month, day, and year elements of *expression* must be in the same sequence as the local computer's regional settings; otherwise, the *CDate* function has no idea, for example, that 4 was supposed to be the fourth day of the month, not the month of April.

Rules at a Glance

*   You can use any of the date delimiters specified in your computer's regional settings; for most systems, this includes `,`, `/`, `-`, and `.`

*   The earliest date that can be handled by the Date data type is 01/01/100. The latest date that can be handled by the Date data type is 12/31/9999.

Programming Tips and Gotchas

*   Use the *IsDate* function to determine if *expression* can be converted to a date or time.

*   If you pass an empty string to *CDate*, an error is generated.

*   A modicum of intelligence has been built into the *CDate* function. It can determine the day and month from a string, regardless of their position in the string; this applies only where the day number is larger than 12, which automatically distinguishes it from the number of the month. For example, if the string "30/12/97" is passed into the *CDate* function on a system expecting a date format of mm/dd/yy, *CDate* sees that 30 is too large to represent a month and thus treats it as the day. This can lead to problems because if we accidentally pass a string such as "30/12/97" instead of the intended "3/12/ 97," then VB does not issue an error message!

*   If we pass a string whose year specification is less than three characters in length, then VB interprets the year as belonging to the twenty-first century. For instance, the string "1/1/1" is interpreted as "1/1/2001."

*   If you do not specify a year, the *CDate* function uses the year from the current date on your computer.

*   Like most conversion functions, *CDate* is not actually a function in the Microsoft. VisualBasic namespace. Instead, it is similar to a Visual C++ macro; the compiler translates the function call into inline code.

CDbl Function

Named Arguments

No

Syntax

```
CDbl(expression)
```

expression   *required; Numeric or String*
    −1.79769313486232E308 to −4.94065645841247E-324 for negative values, and
    4.94065645841247E-324 to 1.79769313486232E308 for positive values

Return Value

expression cast as a Double data type

Description

Converts *expression* to a Double data type

Rules at a Glance

- If the value of *expression* is outside the range of the double data type, an overflow error is generated.

- *expression* must evaluate to a numeric value; otherwise, a type-mismatch error is generated.

Example

```
Dim dblMyNumber as Double
If IsNumeric(sMyNumber) then
    dblMyNumber = CDbl(sMyNumber)
End If
```

Programming Tips and Gotchas

- When converting a string representation of a number to a numeric value, the data type conversion functions, such as *CDbl*, are preferable to the older function, *Val*. This is because the data type conversion functions take account of the system's regional settings, whereas *Val* recognizes only the period as a decimal separator. For example, if a user inputs a value of 6,231,532.11, *CDbl* correctly converts it to a double with a value of 6231532.11, while *Val* returns a value of 6.

- Use *IsNumeric* to test whether *expression* evaluates to a number.

- Like most conversion functions, *CDbl* is not actually a function in the Microsoft. VisualBasic namespace. Instead, it is similar to a Visual C++ macro; the compiler translates the function call into inline code.

See Also

CSng Function

CDec Function

Named Arguments

No

Syntax

```
CDec(expression)
```

expression   *required; Numeric or String*

The range is +/–79,228,162,514,264,337,593,543,950,335 for numbers with no
decimal places. The range is +/–7.9228162514264337593543950335 for
numbers with up to 28 decimal places. The smallest possible nonzero number
is 0.0000000000000000000000000001.

Return Value

expression cast as a Decimal type

Description

This function casts *expression* as a Decimal value.

Rules at a Glance

- If the value of *expression* is outside the range of the Decimal data type, an
  overflow error is generated.

- *expression* must evaluate to a numeric value; otherwise a type-mismatch
  error is generated. To prevent this, it can be tested beforehand with the *IsNumeric* function.

Example

```
Dim decMyNumber As Decimal
If IsNumeric(sMyNumber) then
    decMyNumber = CDec(sMyNumber)
End If
```

Programming Tips and Gotchas

- The Decimal data type replaces the VB 6 Currency data type and is appropriate for very large, very small, or very high precision numbers.

- Use *IsNumeric* to test whether *expression* evaluates to a number.

- When converting a string representation of a number to a numeric, you
  should use the data type conversion functions—such as *CDec*—instead of *Val*,
  because the data type conversion functions take account of the system's
  regional settings. In particular, the *CDec* function recognizes the thousands
  separator if it is encountered in the string representation of a number. For
  example, if the user inputs the value 1,827,209.6654, *CDec* converts it to the
  decimal value 1827209.6654, while *Val* converts it to a Double value of 1.

- Like most of the conversion functions, *CDec* is not actually a function in the
  Microsoft.VisualBasic namespace. Instead, it is similar to a Visual C++ macro;
  the compiler translates the function call into inline code.

Ceiling Function

Class

System.Math

Syntax

```
Math.Ceiling(a)
```

Reference A-C

Return Value

A Double containing the smallest integer greater than or equal to the argument *a*

Description

Returns the smallest integer greater than or equal to the argument *a*

Example

```
Console.WriteLine(Math.Ceiling(12.1))     ' Returns 13
Console.WriteLine(Math.Ceiling(12.5))     ' Returns 13
Console.WriteLine(Math.Ceiling(-12.5))    ' Returns -12
Console.WriteLine(Math.Ceiling(-12.8))    ' Returns -12
```

Rules at a Glance

- Because this function can accept only numeric values, you may want to check the value you pass using the *IsNumeric* function to prevent generating an error.

- This is a Shared member, so it can be used without creating any objects.

VB.NET/VB 6 Differences

The Ceiling function is new to the .NET Framework.

See Also

Floor Function

ChDir Procedure

Class

Microsoft.VisualBasic.FileSystem

Syntax

```
ChDir(path)
```

path   *required; String*
The path of the directory to set as the new default directory

Description

Changes the current working (default) directory.

Rules at a Glance

- *path* can be an absolute or relative reference.

- Changing the default directory does not change the default drive; it only changes a particular drive's default directory.

Example

```
ChDir("c:\program files\my folder\")
ChDir("..") 'c:\program files is now the default directory.
```

Programming Tips and Gotchas

- The single dot (" . ") represents the current directory and the double dot (" . . ") represents the parent of the current directory. If the root directory is the current directory, the statement:

    ```
    ChDir("..")
    ```

    does not change the current directory and does not produce a syntax error.

- If *path* is not found, or a FileNotFoundExeception exception, 76, "Path not found," is generated. However, if *path* refers to another machine on the network, error 75, "Path/File access error," is generated.

- Although you can use a network path such as *NTSERV1**d$*\\*TestDir*\ to change the current directory on the network admin share \\*NTSERV1*\\*d$*, you can't access this drive using *ChDrive* without having the drive mapped to a drive letter, which makes using network paths with *ChDir* a little pointless!

- Use *CurDir* to determine the current directory for a particular drive.

VB.NET/VB 6 Differences

In VB.NET, *ChDir* is implemented as a procedure (a method of the FileSystem class). In VB 6, it is implemented as a statement. As a result, the VB.NET version requires parentheses around the *path* argument.

See Also

ChDrive Procedure, CurDir Function

ChDrive Procedure

Class

Microsoft.VisualBasic.FileSystem

Syntax

```
ChDrive(drive)
```

drive   *required; String or Char*
  The letter of the drive (A–Z) to set as the new default drive

Description

Changes the current working (default) disk drive

Rules at a Glance

- If a zero-length string is supplied, the drive is not changed.

- If *driveletter* consists of more than one character, only the first character is used to determine the drive.

Example

The following example demonstrates a utility function that uses *ChDrive* to determine if a given drive is available. By centralizing the test, this reduces the amount of coding required each time you need to use *ChDrive*.

```
Private Function IsAvailableDrive(sDrive As String) _
                As Boolean

    'if an error occurs goto to the next line of code
    On Error Resume Next

    Dim sCurDrv As String

    'get the letter of the current drive
    sCurDrv = Left$(CurDir, 1)

    'attempt to change the drive
    ChDrive(sDrive)

    'did an error occur?
    If Err.Number = 0 Then
        'no - this drive is OK to use
        IsAvailableDrive = True
    Else
        'yes - don't use this drive
        IsAvailableDrive = False
    End If
    'set the drive back to what it was
    ChDrive(sCurDrv)

End Function
```

The following code snippet shows how this function could be implemented within your application:

```
If IsAvailableDrive(sDrv) Then
    ChDrive(sDrv)
Else
    MsgBox ("Cannot use Drive " & sDrv & ":\")
End If
```

Programming Tips and Gotchas

- The current directory is unaffected by the *ChDrive* procedure.

- Since *ChDrive* only processes the first letter of the **drive** string, it's not possible to supply a piped name as a network drive name (for example, *NTServer*\). Instead, the machine on which your program runs must have a drive letter mapped to the network resource using Explorer or other network commands. If **drive** is specified as a UNC path, the function raises error number 5, "Invalid procedure call or argument," or generates an ArgumentException exception.

- If **drive** is invalid, the function returns error number 68, "Device unavailable," or generates an IOException exception.

- To determine which drive is current, call the *CurDir* function with no arguments. Then use the *Left* function to extract its first character, as the following code fragment illustrates:

```
Dim sDrive As String = Left(CurDir(), 1)
```

VB.NET/VB 6 Differences

In VB.NET, *ChDrive* is implemented as a procedure (a method of the FileSystem class). In VB 6, it is implemented as a statement. As a result, the VB.NET version requires parentheses around the *drive* argument.

See Also

ChDir Procedure, CurDir Function

Choose Function

Class

Microsoft.VisualBasic.Interaction

Named Arguments

No

Syntax

```
Choose(index, item_1[,item_2, ...[, item_n]])
```

index   *required; Single*
> An expression that evaluates to the (1-based) index of the object to choose from the list

item_1-item_n   *required; any*
> A comma-delimited list of values from which to choose, or a ParamArray containing values from which to choose

Return Value

The object chosen from the list.

Description

Programmatically selects an object from a predefined list of objects (which are passed as parameters to the function) based on its ordinal position in the list. Using *Choose* is a simpler alternative to populating an array with fixed values.

Rules at a Glance

- The list of items is based from 1, rather than the more usual VB default base of 0.

- Because the list consists of objects, you can mix data types within the list; you are not forced to use the same data type for each item in the list. For example, *item_1* can be a string, while *item_2* can be a long integer, and *item_3* can be a floating point number.

- If the rounded value of *index* does not correspond to an item in the list, the function returns a null string.

Programming Tips and Gotchas

- If *index* is not a whole number, it is rounded before being used.

- It is important to note that all items in the list are evaluated. Thus, if we use functions or expressions as parameters, all of the functions are called or all of the expressions are evaluated.

- By providing *item_1* through *item_n* in the form of a ParamArray, the list of values can be expanded or contracted programmatically at runtime.

- You can save memory and create more efficient and self-documenting code by using the *Choose* function instead of creating an array and populating it with fixed values each time the program executes. As the following example illustrates, you can turn several lines of code into one:

```
Dim vMyArray(3)
vMyArray(1) = "This"
vMyarray(2) = "That"
vMyArray(3) = "The Other"
...
Sub chooseFromArray(iIndex as Integer)
    vResult = vMyArray(iIndex)
End Sub

Sub chooseFromChoose(sglIndex as Single)
    vResult = Choose(sglIndex, "This", "That", "The Other")
End Sub
```

VB.NET/VB 6 Differences

- In VB 6, *item_1* through *item_n* must only take the form of a comma-delimited list. In VB.NET, these arguments can also take the form of an array. This allows the list of choices to be modified dynamically at runtime.

- In VB 6, *idx* must be greater than .5 and less than .5 plus the number of items in the list, or a runtime error results. In VB.NET, if *idx* is out of range, the function returns a null string.

See Also

Switch Function

Chr, ChrW Functions

Class

Microsoft.VisualBasic.Strings

Syntax

```
Chr(charcode)
ChrW(charcode)
```

charcode   *required; Integer*
An expression that evaluates to a Unicode character code

Return Value

A Char that contains the character represented by *charcode*

Description

Returns the character represented by the *charcode*

Programming Tips and Gotchas

- Use Chr(34) to embed quotation marks inside a string, as shown in the following example:

```
sSQL = "SELECT * FROM myTable _
        where myColumn = " & Chr(34) & sValue & Chr(34)
```

- The following table lists some of the more commonly used character codes that are supplied in the call to the *Chr* function:

Code	Constant	Description
0	vbNullChar	For C/C++ string functions, the null character required to terminate standard strings
8	vbBack	A backspace character
9	vbTab	A tab character
10	vbLf	A linefeed character
13	vbCr	A carriage return character
34	ControlChars.Quote	A quotation mark

VB.NET/VB 6 Differences

- The *ChrB* function is no longer supported.

- The VB 6 version of the *Chr* function returns a String; the VB.NET version returns a Char.

See Also

Asc, AscW Functions

CInt Function

Named Arguments

No

Syntax

```
CInt(expression)
```

expression   *required; Numeric or String*
The range of *expression* is −2,147,483,648 to 2,147,483,647; fractions are rounded.

Return Value

expression cast as an Integer

Description

Converts *expression* to an Integer; any fractional portion of *expression* is rounded.

Rules at a Glance

- *expression* must evaluate to a numeric value; otherwise, a type-mismatch error is generated.

- If the value of *expression* is outside the range of the Integer data type, an overflow error is generated.

- When the fractional part of *expression* is exactly .5, *CInt* always rounds it to the nearest even number. For example, .5 rounds to 0, and 1.5 rounds to 2.

Example

```
Dim iMyNumber as Integer
If IsNumeric(sMyNumber) then
    iMyNumber = CInt(sMyNumber)
End If
```

Programming Tips and Gotchas

- When converting a string representation of a number to a numeric data type, you should use the data type conversion functions—such as *CInt*—instead of *Val*, because the data type conversion functions take into account the system's regional settings. In particular, *CInt* recognizes the thousands separator if it's present in *expression*, whereas *Val* does not. For example, if *expression* is 1,234, then *CInt* successfully converts it to the integer value 1234, while *Val* converts it to 1.

- Use *IsNumeric* to test whether *expression* evaluates to a number before performing the conversion.

- *CInt* differs from the *Fix* and *Int* functions, which truncate, rather than round, the fractional part of a number. Also, *Fix* and *Int* always return the same type of value as was passed in.

- *CInt* converts an expression to a signed 32-bit integer. To convert an expression to an unsigned 32-bit integer, create an instance of the UInt32 structure, and call its Parse method.

- Like most of the conversion functions, *CInt* is not actually a function in the Microsoft.VisualBasic namespace. Instead, it is similar to a Visual C++ macro; the compiler translates the function call into inline code.

VB.NET/VB 6 Differences

The VB.NET *CInt* function actually corresponds to the VB 6 *CLng* function, since both return 32-bit integers.

See Also

CLng Function, CShort Function

Class Statement

Syntax

```
[accessmodifier] [Shadows] [inheritability] Class Name
    statements
End Class
```

---

accessmodifier   *optional; Keyword*

> The possible values of *accessmodifier* are Public, Private, and Friend. For more information, see the section entitled Accessibility in Class Modules" in Chapter 4.

Shadows   *optional; Keyword*

> Indicates that the *Name* class shadows any element of this same name in a base class.

inheritability   *optional; Keyword*

> One of the keywords, MustInherit or NotInheritable, must be used. MustInherit specifies that objects of this class cannot be created, but that objects of derived classes can be created. NotInheritable specifies that this class cannot be used as a base class.

Name   *required; String literal*

> The name of the class.

Description

Defines a class and delimits the statements that define that class' variables, properties, and methods. For a detailed discussion with examples, see Chapter 4.

Rules at a Glance

- If the Inherits or Implements statements appear in a class module, they must appear before any other statements in the module. Moreover, the Inherits keyword must appear before the Implements keyword.

- *Name* follows standard Visual Basic variable-naming conventions.

- Within a class code block, members are declared as Public, Private, Protected, Friend, or Protected Friend. The Dim keyword is equivalent to Private when used in class modules (but it is equivalent to Public in structures). Property declarations are automatically Public.

- The Class...End Class construct can include the following elements:

  Private variable or procedure declarations
  > These items are accessible within the class, but do not have scope outside of the class.

  Public variable or procedure declarations
  > Public variables are public properties of the class; Public procedures are public methods of the class.

  Property declarations
  > These are the public properties of the class. Default properties can be declared by using the Default keyword.

- To define a custom constructor within a class module, define a subroutine called *New*. Note that the *New* subroutine (like any other procedure) can be overloaded.

- To define a destructor within a class module, define a function called *Destruct*. Destructors cannot be overloaded.

- To create an object of a class, use syntax such as:

```
Dim oObj As CClass
oObj = New CClass(arguments_for_constructor)
or:
Dim oObj = New CClass(arguments_for_constructor)
or:
Dim oObj As CClass = New CClass(arguments_for_constructor)
```

- The Shadows keyword has the following meaning: If this class is derived from a base class and if *Name* is used in the base class as the name of any element type (property, method, constant, enum, etc.), then any use of *Name* in classes derived from the class *Name* refers to the *Name* class rather than the *Name* element in the base class. For more on shadowing, see Chapter 4.

Programming Tips and Gotchas

- A property defined as a simple public variable cannot be designated the class' default member.

- According to accepted object-oriented programming practices, public properties should be defined using the Property statement, since this allows the value of a property to be modified in a controlled and predictable way. It allows you to validate data and allows your program to know when a property value is being changed. Because this is not possible using simple public variables, defining a public variable that is accessible outside of the class is considered poor programming practice.

- The Me or MyClass keywords can be used within the Class...End Class construct to reference the class.

VB.NET/VB 6 Differences

The Class...End Class construct is new to VB.NET. In VB 6, each class was defined in its own class module, which corresponded to a separate CLS file.

See Also

Property Statement, Structure...End Structure Statement

Clipboard Class

Namespace

System.Windows.Forms

Createable

No

Description

The Clipboard object represents the Windows Clipboard, an object that allows data to be shared across processes. The members of the Clipboard class allow data to be placed in and retrieved from the Clipboard.

The Clipboard object can be created as follows:

```
Dim obj As Clipboard
```

However, because the Clipboard object's members are shared, you do not need to instantiate the Clipboard object to access its properties and methods. Hence, you can place data on the Clipboard, for instance, with the following code fragment:

```
Clipboard.SetDataObject(strData)
```

Application class members marked with a plus sign (+) are discussed in detail in their own entries.

Public Shared Methods

GetDataObject +
SetDataObject +

See Also

Clipboard.GetDataObject Method, Clipboard.SetDataObject Method

---

Clipboard.GetDataObject Method

Class

System.Windows.Forms.Clipboard

Syntax

```
Clipboard.GetDataObject()
```

Return value

An IDataObject object that represents the data currently on the clipboard

Description

Retrieves data from the Clipboard

Rules at a Glance

- If the Clipboard contains no data, the GetDataObject method returns Nothing.

- Once you have an IDataObject object, you can use the members of the IDataObject class to get information about the Clipboard data, as shown in the following example. The relevant IDataObject members for Clipboard manipulation in VB are GetData, GetDataPresent, and GetFormats.

Example

The following example extracts the text that is currently on the Clipboard:

```
' Declare IDataObject variable and get clipboard IDataObject
Dim di As IDataObject = Clipboard.GetDataObject

Dim obj As Object

' Fire GetData method of IDataObject object to get clipboard data
obj = di.GetData(DataFormats.Text, False)
```

```
' Show the text, if any
If obj Is Nothing Then
    MsgBox("No text on clipboard.")
Else
    MsgBox(CStr(obj))
End If
```

VB.NET/VB 6 Differences

While the .NET Base Class Library uses the GetDataObject method to retrieve all data from the Clipboard, the Clipboard object in VB 6 included the GetFormat, GetData, and GetText methods to retrieve Clipboard data.

See Also

Clipboard Class, Clipboard.SetDataObject Method, IDataObject Interface

---

Clipboard.SetDataObject Method

Class

System.Windows.Forms.Clipboard

Syntax

```
SetDataObject(data)
```

data   *required; any*
    Data to place on the Clipboard

Description

Places data on the Clipboard

Example

The following example places text on the clipboard:

```
Dim s As String = "donna"
clipboard.SetDataObject(s)
```

VB.NET/VB 6 Differences

While the .NET Base Class Library uses the SetDataObject method to place all data on the Clipboard, the Clipboard object in VB 6 includes two methods, SetData and SetText, depending on the format of the data to be placed on the Clipboard.

See Also

Clipboard Class, Clipboard.GetDataObject Method, IDataObject Interface

---

CLng Function

Named Arguments

No

Syntax

```
CLng(expression)
```

expression   *required; Numeric or String*
Ranges from −9,223,372,036,854,775,808 to 9,223,372,036,854,775,807; fractions are rounded.

Return Value

expression cast as a Long data type

Description

Converts *expression* to a long integer; any fractional element of *expression* is rounded.

Rules at a Glance

- *expression* must evaluate to a numeric value; otherwise, a type-mismatch error is generated.

- If the value of *expression* is outside the range of the Long data type, an overflow error is generated.

- When the fractional part is exactly .5, *CLng* always rounds it to the nearest even number. For example, .5 rounds to 0, and 1.5 rounds to 2.

Example

```
Dim lngMyNumber as Long
If IsNumeric(sMyNumber) then
    lngMyNumber = CLng(sMyNumber)
End If
```

Programming Tips and Gotchas

- When converting a string representation of a number to a numeric, you should use the data type conversion functions—such as *CLng*—instead of *Val*, because the data type conversion function takes into account the system's regional settings. In particular, *CLng* is able to recognize the thousands separator if it's included in *expression*, while *Val* cannot. For example, if a user enters a value of 1,098,234 into a textbox, *CLng* converts it to the long integer 1098234, but *Val* converts it to a value of 1.

- Use *IsNumeric* to test whether *expression* evaluates to a number.

- *CLng* differs from the *Fix* and *Int* functions, which truncate, rather than round, the fractional part of a number. Also, *Fix* and *Int* always return the same type of value as was passed in.

- *CLng* converts an expression to a signed long integer. To convert an expression to an unsigned long integer, create an instance of the UInt64 structure and call its Parse method.

- Like most of the conversion functions, *CLng* is not actually a function in the Microsoft.VisualBasic namespace. Instead, it is similar to a Visual C++ macro; the compiler translates the function call into inline code.

VB.NET/VB 6 Differences

The VB.NET *CLng* function returns a 64-bit integer, whereas the VB 6 *CLng* function returns a 32-bit integer.

See Also

CInt Function, CShort Function

CLSCompliant Attribute

Class

System.CLSCompliantAttribute

Applies to

All

Description

Indicates whether the program element compiles with the Common Language Specification. If the `CLSCompliant` attribute is not present, the VB.NET compiler does not enforce CLS compliance. This can prevent other languages from successfully accessing components written in VB.NET.

If a particular program element is marked as CLS-compliant, it is assumed that all contained program elements are CLS-compliant as well unless they are explicitly marked otherwise.

By default, Visual Studio adds the `<CLSCompliant>` attribute to the AssemblyInfo. vb file and sets its value to `True`.

Constructor

```
New(isCompliant)
```

isCompliant   *Boolean*
Indicates whether the program element must be CLS-compliant

Property

IsCompliant   *Boolean*
Read-only. Indicates whether the program element must be CLS-compliant. Its value is set by the required *isCompliant* parameter of the class constructor.

CObj Function

Named Arguments

No

Syntax

```
CObj(expression)
```

expression   *required; any*

Return Value

expression cast as an Object data type

Description

Converts any expression that can be interpreted as an object to Object

Rules at a Glance

expression can be any data type, including a strongly typed object, as the following code fragment illustrates:

```
Dim oSomeClass As New CSomeClass
Dim oObj As Object
oObj = CObj(oSomeClass)
```

Example

The following code:

```
Dim obj As Object
obj = CObj("test")
```

casts the string `"test"` to type Object and places it in the Object variable *obj*.

Programming Tips and Gotchas

- The operation of the *CObj* function is possible because all VB.NET data types are either structures or objects.

- Once a data type is converted to type Object, you can display its value by calling its ToString method, as in the following code fragment:

```
Dim bFlag As Boolean = True

oObj = CObj(bFlag)
MsgBox(oObj.ToString)
```

- Instead of using the *CObj* function to convert a strongly typed object to a generic Object data type, you can also use simple assignment, as the following code fragment illustrates:

```
Dim oSomeClass As New CSomeClass
Dim oObj As Object
oObj = oSomeClass
```

- Like most of the conversion functions, *CObj* is not actually a function in the Microsoft.VisualBasic namespace. Instead, it is similar to a Visual C++ macro; the compiler translates the function call into inline code.

VB.NET/VB 6 Differences

The *CObj* function is new to VB.NET. The closest equivalent in VB 6 is *CVar*, which converts a data type to a Variant.

Collection Class

Namespace

Microsoft.VisualBasic

Createable

Yes

Syntax

```
Dim objectvariable As [New] Collection
```

objectvariable   *required; Collection*
    The name of the Collection object

Description

A Collection object allows you to store members of any data type, including object data types or even other collection objects, and to retrieve them using a unique key.

Collection objects allow us to create a form of associative array, which is an array whose members are indexed by something more meaningful than an integer. The real power of a collection comes by using collections with class objects. The Collection object is discussed in more detail in Chapter 3.

Collection objects are created in exactly the same way as other objects, as in:

```
Dim obj As New Collection
```

or:

```
Dim obj As Collection
obj = New Collection
```

In the former syntax, the Collection object is created at the time that the *obj* variable is declared, which may be sooner than you actually need the Collection object. The latter syntax gives you more control over the creation process.

Rules at a Glance

- You can use a Collection object to store data of any data type, including object types and even other Collection objects.

- The Add method of the Collection object is used to add items to the collection (see the Collection.Add entry).

- Members of a collection can be accessed using either their ordinal number or their key, assuming that one was assigned at the time that the member was added to the collection (see the Collection.Item entry).

- The first member in a collection is stored at ordinal position 1 (not at 0, as with arrays).

- The Count method returns the number of members in the collection (see the Collection.Count entry).

- The Remove method removes items from a collection (see the Collection. Remove entry).

Example

This example shows how you can nest one collection within another collection. We create 10 instances of colSubCollection, each containing two integer values. These colSubCollection objects are stored in the collection named colMainCollection. The code also shows how to read the values of colMainCollection and colSubCollection:

```
Sub testCollection()
    'declare objects for the main and sub collections
    'creating a new instance of the main collection
    'in the process
    Dim colMainCollection As New Collection
    Dim colSubCollection As Collection
    Dim i As Integer

    For i = 1 To 10
        'create a new instance of the sub collection object
        colSubCollection = New Collection
        'populate the sub collection with two integer values
        colSubCollection.Add(Item:=i + 6, _
                            Key:="MySixPlusVal")
        colSubCollection.Add(Item:=i + 3, _
                            Key:="MyThreePlusVal")
        'now add the sub collection to the main collection
        'using the count converted to a string as the key
        colMainCollection.Add(Item:=colSubCollection, _
                            Key:=CStr(i))
        'destroy the reference the sub collection
        colSubCollection = Nothing
    Next i

    MsgBox(colMainCollection.Count)

    For i = 1 To colMainCollection.Count
        'use the Item method to obtain a reference to the
        'subcollection
        colSubCollection = _
                            colMainCollection.Item(CStr(i))
        'display the values held in the sub collection.
        Console.WriteLine("6 + " & i & " = " & _
                colSubCollection.Item("MySixPlusVal"))
        Console.WriteLine("3 + " & i & " = " & _
                colSubCollection.Item("MyThreePlusVal"))
        'destroy the reference to the sub collection
        colSubCollection = Nothing
    Next i
End Sub
```

Programming Tips and Gotchas

- A highly efficient method of enumerating the members of a collection is to use the For Each...Next loop, as the following example shows:

```
Dim colMyCollection As New Collection
Dim colSubCollection As Collection

For i = 1 To 10
    Set colSubCollection = New Collection
    colSubCollection.Add Item:=i + 6, _
                    Key:="MySixPlusVal"
    colSubCollection.Add Item:=i + 3, _
                    Key:="MyThreePlusVal"
    colMyCollection.Add Item:=colSubCollection, _
                    Key:=CStr(i)
    Set colSubCollection = Nothing
Next i

For Each colSubCollection In colMyCollection
    MsgBox colSubCollection.Item("MySixPlusVal")
Next
```

- Interestingly, although most Visual Basic data types are merely wrappers for data types in the Base Class Library, the Collection object is a "native" VB data type that's derived from System.Object and implements the ICollection, IEnumerable, and IList interfaces. This can be seen from the following code fragment:

```
Dim oColl As New Collection
Dim oType As Type, oInt As Type

oType = oColl.GetType()
Console.WriteLine("Type: " & oType.ToString)
Console.WriteLine("Base Type: " & oType.BaseType.ToString)
Dim oTypes() As Type = oType.GetInterfaces
For Each oInt in oTypes
    Console.WriteLine("Interface: " & oInt.ToString)
Next
```

See Also

Collection.Add Method, Collection.Count Property, Collection.Item Method, Collection.Remove Method, Hashtable Class, Queue Class, Stack Class

---

Collection.Add Method

Class

Microsoft.VisualBasic.Collection

Syntax

```
objectvariable.Add item [, key, before, after]
```

objectvariable   *required; Collection Object*
   The name of the Collection object to which an item is to be added

item   *required; Object*
   An object of any type that specifies the member to add to the collection

key   *optional; String*
   A unique string expression that specifies a key string that can be used, instead
   of a positional index, to access a member of the collection

before   *optional; Object*
   The member to be added placed in the collection before the member identified by the *before* argument (more on this in the "Rules at a Glance" section)

after   *optional; Object*
   The member to be added placed in the collection after the member identified
   by the *after* argument (more on this in the "Rules at a Glance" section)

Description

Adds an object to a collection

Rules at a Glance

- If you do not specify a *before* or *after* value, the member is appended to
  the end of the collection (in index order).

- If you do not specify a *key* value, you cannot access this member using a
  key, but instead must access it either by using its ordinal number or by
  enumerating all the members of the collection with the For Each...Next
  construct. Thus, keys are highly recommended.

- The *before* or *after* argument can refer to an index or a key. For instance,
  consider the following code:

  ```
  Dim c As New Collection()
  c.Add("donna", "111")
  c.Add("steve", "222")
  'c.Add("bill", "333", "222")
  'c.Add("bill", "333", 2)
  MsgBox(c.Item(2))
  ```

  Both of the commented lines of code adds the item "bill" between "donna"
  and "steve." The first line uses the key to specify the *before* object, and the
  second line specifies the ordinal position of the *before* object.

- Key values must be unique or an error (runtime error 457, "This key is already
  associated with an element of this collection") is generated.

- You can specify a *before* or *after* position, but not both.

Example

```
colComposers.Add(Item:="Ludwig von Beethoven" _
                 Key:="Beethoven")
```

Programming Tips and Gotchas

- Using named parameters helps to self-document your code:

```
colMyCollection.Add Item:="VB.NET Language in a Nutshell" _
                 Key:="Title"
```

- If your *key* parameter is a value being brought in from outside your program, you must ensure that each value is always unique. One method for doing this is illustrated in the entry for the Collection.Item Method.

See Also

Collection Class, Collection.Count Property, Collection.Item Method, Collection. Remove Method

Collection.Count Property

Class

Microsoft.VisualBasic.Collection

Syntax

```
objectvariable.Count
```

objectvariable   *required; Collection Object*
    Object variable referring to a Collection object

Description

Returns an Integer containing the number of members in the collection

Rules at a Glance

Collections are 1-based; that is, the index of the first element of a collection is 1. In contrast, arrays are 0-based; the index of the first element of an array is 0.

Example

```
For i = 1 To colMyCollection.Count
    Set colSubCollection = colMyCollection.Item(CStr(i))
    MsgBox colSubCollection.Item("Name")
    Set colSubCollection = Nothing
Next i
```

Programming Tips and Gotchas

Because collections are 1-based, you can iterate the members of a collection by using index values ranging from 1 to the value of *objectvariable*.Count.

See Also

Collection Class, Collection.Add Method, Collection.Item Method, Collection. Remove Method

Collection.Item Method

Class

Microsoft.VisualBasic.Collection

Syntax

```
objectvariable.Item(index)
```

objectvariable   *required; Collection Object*
An object variable of type Collection

index   *required; Integer or String*
Either the index (the ordinal position) of the object in the collection, or the
unique key name belonging to the object

Description

Returns the member of the collection for the specified key or ordinal position

Programming Tips and Gotchas

- When writing wrapper classes for collections, you can make your object
  model more readable by making the name of the property that wraps the
  Item method the same as the name of the object obtained from the collection. For example, if your collection class is called Employees and is a collection of Employee records, your object model reads much better to have an
  Employee Property procedure, as follows:

  ```
  Public Property Employee(vKey as Object) As Boolean
     Get
         Employee = mcolEmployees.Item(vKey)
     End Get
     . . .
  End Property
  ```

  Note that in the previous Property procedure, the parameter is passed as an
  object so that the argument can be either a string (the item's key) or an integer (the item's ordinal position).

- There is no Exists method in the Collection object, so you cannot find out in
  advance if a particular key exists within the collection. However, you can create an *Exists* function by calling the Item method with a given key and returning an appropriate value based on whether an error occurred, as the
  following code shows:

  ```
  Public Function Exists(ByVal oKey As Object) As Boolean
      Try
          moValue = mCollection.Item(oKey)
          Exists = True
      Catch e As NullReferenceException
          Exists = False
      End Try
  End Function
  ```

- The Item method is the default member of the Collection object, and since it
  is parameterized, we do not need to include an explicit call to the Item
  method. The following two statements, for example, are identical to one
  another:

  ```
  set objMember = objCollection.Item(6)
  set objMember = objCollection(6)
  ```

See Also

Collection Class, Collection.Add Method, Collection.Count Property, Collection. Remove Method

Collection.Remove Method

Class

Microsoft.VisualBasic.Collection

Syntax

```
objectvariable.Remove (index)
```

or:

```
objectvariable.Remove (key)
```

objectvariable   *required; Collection Object*
An object variable of the Collection type

index   *required; Integer*
The ordinal position of the item to remove

key   *required; String*
The key of the item to remove

Description

Removes a member from a collection

Example

```
colMyCollection.Remove ("Name")
```

Programming Tips and Gotchas

- Members of the collection that follow the removed member are automatically moved downward by one ordinal position; therefore, no gaps are left in the collection.

- Because the collection is reindexed after each deletion, you should be sure not to delete a member of the collection based on a stored numeric value of *index*, since this value could change. Instead, you should either delete the member by key or retrieve the index value just before calling the Remove method.

- If you are deleting multiple members of a collection by numeric index value, you should delete them backwards—from highest index value to lowest—because the collection is reindexed after each deletion.

- If you are using a collection as the basis for a class module, or if you are using functions in your application to wrap and enhance the limited functionality of a collection, you can include a Clear method to remove all the members in your collection. The method should be written to remove the member in position 1 until no members are left, as the following code demonstrates:

```
Public Sub Clear()
```

```
Dim i As Integer

For i = 1 To mcolMyCollection.Count
    mcolMyCollection.Remove(1)
Next i

End Sub
```

Alternately, you could do the same thing by working from the end of the collection forward, as the following code illustrates:

```
Dim intCtr As Integer

For intCtr = objCollec.Count To 1 Step -1
    objCollec.Remove(intCtr)
Next
```

- When using named arguments, providing an index value with the key:= keyword or providing a key name with the index:= keyword generates a runtime error.

See Also

Collection Class, Collection.Add Method, Collection.Count Property, Collection. Item Method

---

ColorDialog Class

Namespace

System.Windows.Forms

Createable

Yes

Description

Represents a common dialog box for selecting a color.

The ColorDialog object has properties for setting the initial appearance and functionality of the color dialog box, a property for returning the color selected by the user, and a method for showing the dialog box.

Selected ColorDialog Members

The following provides a brief description of the more important members of the ColorDialog class:

AllowFullOpen property
Returns or sets a Boolean value indicating whether the user can use the dialog box to define custom colors. The default is True.

AnyColor property
Returns or sets a Boolean value indicating whether the dialog box displays all available colors, although in Beta 2 of VB.NET, this property seems to have no effect. The default is False.

Color property

Returns an instance of a Color structure, which contains information about the color selected by the user. The Color structure, which is a type belonging to the System.Drawing namespace, has a number of members, including:

- Over 140 named color properties, from Red, Green, and Blue, to Papaya-Whip, MistyRose, and MediumSeagreen. These properties return a Color structure.

- The Name property, which returns the name of the color, or its ARGB value for custom colors. (The A component is the alpha component of the color, which determines the color's opacity.)

- The R property, G property, and B property, which return a byte specifying the red, green, or blue color component of the RGB color value, respectively.

- The IsKnownColor, IsNamedColor, and IsSystemColor properties, which give information about the color.

CustomColors property

Represents an array of Integers used to set or return the set of custom colors that will be shown in the ColorDialog dialog box.

FullOpen property

Represents a Boolean property that sets or retrieves the value indicating whether the dialog box is opened with the controls used to create custom visible controls. (The default is **False**, but the user can always click the Custom Colors button to display the custom colors controls.)

Reset method

Resets the dialog box by setting all options and custom colors to their default values and setting the selected color to black.

SolidColorOnly property

For systems displaying 256 colors or less, if this property is set to **True**, restricts the dialog box to solid colors only, that is, to colors that are not composites of other colors.

VB.NET/VB 6 Differences

While the ColorDialog class is implemented in the .NET Base Class Library, VB 6 offered the CommonDialog custom control. Although the two offer similar functionality, their public interfaces are almost completely different.

Example

The following code asks the user for a color and displays that color:

```
Dim cd As New ColorDialog()
Dim c As New Color()
If cd.ShowDialog() = DialogResult.OK Then
    Console.WriteLine(cd.Color.ToString)
    Console.WriteLine(cd.Color.Name)
Else
    Console.WriteLine("No color chosen")
End If
```

Note the use of the `DialogResult` enumeration to check user action on the dialog box. Here is the precise output if red is selected:

```
Color [Alpha=255, Red=255, Green=0, Blue=0]
ffff0000
```

COMClass Attribute

Class

Microsoft.VisualBasic.COMClassAttribute

Applies to

Class

Description

Adds metadata that allows a .NET class to be exposed as a COM object. You can supply the attribute with a class identifier, an interface identifier, and an event identifier. All are globally unique identifiers (GUIDs) that can be generated either by using the *guidgen.exe* utility or automatically by using the COM Class Wizard. They ensure that the COM component retains the same GUIDs when it is recompiled.

Constructor

```
New([[[classID], interfaceID], eventID])
```

classID   *String*
    The class identifier (CLSID) that will uniquely identify the COM class

interfaceID   *String*
    The interface identifier (IID) that uniquely identifies the class' default COM interface

eventID   *String*
    The event identifier that uniquely identifies an event

Properties

ClassID   *String*
    Read-only. Provides the class identifier (CLSID) that uniquely identifies a COM class. Its value is set by the *classID* parameter of the class constructor.

EventID   *String*
    Read-only. Provides the GUID that uniquely identifies an event. Its value is set by the *eventID* parameter of the class constructor.

InterfaceID   *String*
    Read-only. Provides the interface identifier (IID) that uniquely identifies a COM interface. Its value is set by the *interfaceID* parameter of the class constructor.

InterfaceShadows   *Boolean*
    Indicates whether the COM interface name is the same as the name of another member of the class or the base class. Its default value is `False`.

Example

The example defines a simple class named CContact that includes the `<ComClass>` attribute. Note that the GUIDs are in standard registry format except for the beginning and closing brace.

```
<ComClass(CContact.ClassID, CContact.InterfaceID, CContact.EventID), _
Description("COM Contact Class")> Public Class CContact

Friend Const ClassID As String = _
          "C7BA6669-DCFB-43d6-9A74-B1BCC6EE467B"
Friend Const InterfaceID As String = _
          "72663B50-6A44-46e7-83B6-F1A4F149FF5F"
Friend Const EventID As String = _
          "BD2C0D5E-C0D7-4e1e-A9E8-AD29C8003D4B"

Private sName As String
Private sCity, sState, sZip As String

Public Property Name() As String
Get
    Return sName
End Get
Set(ByVal Value As String)
    sName = Value
End Set
End Property

Public Sub New()
    MyBase.New()
End Sub

End Class
```

Command Function

Class

Microsoft.VisualBasic.Interaction

Syntax

```
Command()
```

Return Value

A String containing the command-line arguments

Description

Returns the arguments used when launching VB or an application created with VB

Rules at a Glance

- For applications created with VB and compiled into an EXE, *Command* returns a string containing everything entered after the executable filename.

- If the executable has been launched with no command-line arguments, *Command* returns a null string.

Programming Tips and Gotchas

- Once you've used the *Command* function to retrieve the command-line arguments, you still have to parse the string it returns. This should be as simple as a call to the *Split* function, as shown in the following code fragment:

```
Dim sCmdLineStr, sCmdLine() As String
sCmdLineStr = Command()
If Not sCmdLineStr = "" Then
    sCmdLine = Split(Command, " ")
End If
```

- Instead of calling the *Command* function, you may find it easier to use the shared GetCommandLineArgs method of the System.Environment class. It returns a string array whose first element is the program name and whose remaining elements are the command-line arguments. The following code fragment determines whether any command-line arguments are present:

```
Dim sArgs() As String = System.Environment.GetCommandLineArgs()
If sArgs.Length > 1 Then
    ' handle the command line arguments
End If
```

Example

The following example demonstrates how to parse command-line arguments to set up a series of options in your executable. This example (which is bereft of all error handling) looks for a hyphen or a forward slash in the command-line arguments and assumes that the character following it is a command-line switch. Given the command-line arguments:

```
-d:50 -f -g -k
```

the program displays the following in the Immediate window:

```
Got option d
Option d Parameter = 50
Got option f
Got option g
Got option k
```

The source code is as follows:

```
Private Sub ParseCommandLine()

    Dim i As Integer
    Dim s, sChar, sParam As String
    Dim sPattern As String = "[-/]"

    For i = 1 To Len(Command)
        sChar = mid(Command, i, 1)
        If sChar = "-" or sChar = "/" Then
            s = Mid(Command, i + 1, 1)
            Select Case s
                Case "d"
```

```
                Console.WriteLine("Got option d")
                sParam = Mid(Command, i + 3, 2)
                Console.WriteLine("Option d Parameter = " & _
                        sParam)
            Case "f"
                Console.WriteLine("Got option f")
            Case "g"
                Console.WriteLine("Got option g")
            Case "k"
                Console.WriteLine("Got option k")
            Case "l"
                Console.WriteLine("Got option l")
            End Select
        End If
    Next I

End Sub
```

Programming Tips and Gotchas

- During the development phase, you can pass arguments to your program using the Command Line Arguments textbox, which can be found on the Property Pages dialog box for the project (right-click the project name in the Solution Explorer window). In particular, the textbox is found under Start Options in the Debugging subnode of the Configuration Properties node.

- To handle command-line arguments, you must write a routine similar to the one shown earlier to parse the string returned by *Command*, since the function only returns a single string containing all input after the name of the executable file.

- Command-line arguments are ideal for specifying various options on unattended applications.

Const Statement

Syntax

    [accessmodifier] Const constantname [As type] = constantvalue

`accessmodifier`   *optional; Keyword*
One of the keywords Public, Private, Protected, Friend, or Protected Friend. For more information, see the section entitled Accessibility in Class Modules" in Chapter 4.

`constantname`   *required; String Literal*
The name of the constant.

`type`   *optional; Keyword*
The data type; it can be Byte, Boolean, Char, Short, Integer, Long, Single, Double, Decimal, Date, or String, as well as any of the data types defined in the Base Class Library.

`constantvalue`   *required; Numeric or String*
A literal, constant, or any combination of literals and constants that includes arithmetic or logical operators, except Is.

Description

Associates a constant value with a name. This feature is provided to make code more readable. The name is referred to as a *symbolic constant*.

Rules at a Glance

- The rules for *constantname* are the same for those of any variable: the name can be up to 255 characters in length and can contain any alphanumeric character, although it must start with an alphabetic character. In addition, the name can include almost any other character except a period or any of the data type definition characters ($, &, %, !).

- The *constantvalue* expression cannot include any of the built-in functions or objects, although it can be a combination of absolute values and operators. The expression can also include previously defined constants. For example:

```
Private Const CONST_ONE = 1
Private Const CONST_TWO = 2
Private Const CONST_THREE = CONST_ONE + CONST_TWO
```

- Scoping rules are the same as for variables. For more on scope, see Chapter 4.

- If Option Strict is on, the data type of the constant must be defined by using the As *type* clause.

Example

```
Private Const  MY_CONSTANT = 3.1417
```

Programming Tips and Gotchas

- Your code may be more readable if you take advantage of the fact that VB allows lengthy constant (and variable) names. This allows you to choose these names in a more meaningful way.

- If you are building a large application with many different modules, you may find your code easier to maintain if you create a single separate code module to hold your Public constants.

- If two or more constants are related, you should define them as members of an enumeration using the Enum statement.

See Also

Enum Statement

Cos Function

Class

System.Math

Syntax

```
Math.Cos(d)
```

d   *required; Double or numeric expression*
    An angle in radians

Return Value

A Double data type denoting the cosine of an angle

Description

Takes an angle specified in radians and returns a ratio representing the length of the side adjacent to the angle divided by the length of the hypotenuse

Rules at a Glance

- The cosine returned by the function is between −1 and 1.
- This is a Shared member, so it can be used without creating any objects.

Example

```
Dim dblCosine as Double
dblCosine = Math.Cos(dblRadians)
```

Programming Tips and Gotchas

- To convert degrees to radians, multiply degrees by pi/180.
- To convert radians to degrees, multiply radians by 180/pi.

VB.NET/VB 6 Differences

In VB 6, *Cos* was an intrinsic VB function. In the .NET platform, it is a member of the Math class in the System namespace, and so it is not part of the VB.NET language.

See Also

Cosh Function, Sin Function, Tan Function

Cosh Function

Class

System.Math

Syntax

```
Math.Cosh(value)
```

value   *required; Double or numeric expression*
An angle in radians

Return Value

A Double denoting the hyperbolic cosine of the angle

Description

Returns the hyperbolic cosine of an angle

Rules at a Glance

This is a Shared member, so it can be used without creating any objects.

The *Cosh* function is new to the .NET platform; it did not exist in VB 6.

See Also

Cos Function, Sinh Function, Tanh Function

CreateObject Function

Class

Microsoft.VisualBasic.Interaction

Named Arguments

No

Syntax

```
objectvariable = CreateObject(progid [, servername])
```

objectvariable   *required; Object*
> A variable to hold the reference to the instantiated object

progid   *required; String*
> The programmatic identifier (or ProgID) of the class of the object to create

servername   *optional; String*
> The name of the server on which the object resides

Return Value

A reference to a COM or ActiveX object

Description

Creates an instance of an OLE Automation (ActiveX) object.

Prior to calling the methods, functions, or properties of a COM or ActiveX object, you are required to create an instance of that object. Once an object is created, reference it in code using the object variable you defined.

Rules at a Glance

- If your project does not include a reference to the object, you must declare the object variable type as Object; this allows the variable to reference any type of object.

- If an instance of the ActiveX object is already running, *CreateObject* may start a new instance when it creates an object of the required type.

- *CreateObject* can only be used to create instances of COM (or ActiveX) objects; it cannot be used to instantiate .NET components.

Example

The following routine defines a generic Object variable, as well as an Excel application object. It then uses the *Timer* function to compare the performance of the code fragment that uses late binding to instantiate the Excel application object

---

with the one that uses early binding. (For a discussion of late and early binding, see the second item under the "Programming Tips and Gotchas" section.)

```
Private Sub TestBinding()

Dim dblTime As Double
Dim strMsg As String

' Calculate time for late binding
dblTime = Timer()
Dim objExcelLate As Object
objExcelLate = CreateObject("excel.application")
objExcelLate = Nothing
strMsg &= "Late Bound: " & Timer() - dblTime
strMsg &= vbCrLf

' Calculate time for early binding
dblTime = Timer()
Dim objExcelEarly As Excel.Application
objExcelEarly = Excel.Application
objExcelEarly = Nothing
strMsg &= "Early Bound: " & Timer() - dblTime

MsgBox (strMsg, vbOKOnly, "Late and Early Binding")

End Sub
```

Programming Tips and Gotchas

- The ProgID is defined in the system registry and usually takes the form *library.class* or *application.class*.

- The Object data type is the most generic of Visual Basic objects. When an object variable has been defined as type Object, *CreateObject* performs what is termed *late binding*. This means that, because the precise object type is unknown at compile time, the object cannot be bound into your program when it is compiled. Instead, this binding occurs only at runtime, when the program is run on the target system and the *CreateObject* function is executed. This need to determine the object type by referencing the relevant interfaces at runtime is time-consuming and results in poor performance. You can vastly improve this performance by utilizing *early binding*. Early binding necessitates adding a reference to the required object to your project.

- The *servername* parameter permits the specification of the name of the server on which the ActiveX object is registered. This means that you could even specify different servers depending upon prevailing circumstances, as this short example demonstrates:

```
Dim sMainServer As String
Dim sBackUpServer As String

sMainServer = "NTPROD1"
sBackUpServer = "NTPROD2"

If IsOnline(sMainServer) Then
```

```
        CreateObject("Sales.Customer",sMainServer)
    Else
        CreateObject("Sales.Customer",sBackUpServer)
    End If
```

- To use a current instance of an already running ActiveX object, use the *Get-Object* function.

- If an object is registered as a single-instance object—i.e., an out-of-process ActiveX EXE—only one instance of the object can be created. Regardless of the number of times *CreateObject* is executed, you will obtain a reference to the same instance of the object.

- It is considered good programming practice (and often a necessary one) to tidy up after you have finished using an object by setting `objectvariable` to Nothing. This has the effect of freeing the memory taken up by the instance of the object, and, if there are no other "live" references to the object, shutting it down. For example:

```
    objectvariable = Nothing
```

See Also

GetObject Function

CShort Function

Named Arguments

No

Syntax

```
    CShort(expression)
```

`expression`   *required; Numeric or String*
    The range of `expression` is –32,768 to 32,767; fractions are rounded.

Return Value

`expression` cast as a Short

Description

Converts `expression` to a Short value; any fractional portion of `expression` is rounded.

Rules at a Glance

- `expression` must evaluate to a numeric value; otherwise, a type-mismatch error is generated.

- If the value of `expression` is outside the range of the Short data type, an overflow error is generated.

- When the fractional part of `expression` is exactly .5, *CShort* always rounds it to the nearest even number. For example, .5 rounds to 0, and 1.5 rounds to 2.

Example

```
Dim iMyNumber as Short
If IsNumeric(sMyNumber) then
    iMyNumber = CShort(sMyNumber)
End If
```

Programming Tips and Gotchas

- When converting a string representation of a number to a numeric, you should use the data type conversion functions—such as *CShort*—instead of *Val*, because the data type conversion functions take into account the system's regional settings. In particular, *CShort* recognizes the thousands separator if it's present in **expression**, whereas *Val* does not. For example, if **expression** is 1,234, *CShort* successfully converts it to the integer value 1234, while *Val* converts it to 1.

- Use *IsNumeric* to test whether **expression** evaluates to a number before performing the conversion.

- *CShort* differs from the *Fix* and *Int* functions, which truncate, rather than round, the fractional part of a number. Also, *Fix* and *Int* always return the same type value as was passed in.

- Like most of the conversion functions, *CShort* is not actually a function in the Microsoft.VisualBasic namespace. Instead, it is similar to a Visual C++ macro; the compiler translates the function call into inline code.

VB.NET/VB 6 Differences

The *CShort* function is new to VB.NET. However, it corresponds directly to the VB 6 *CInt* function, since both return 16-bit integers.

See Also

CInt Function, CLng Function

CSng Function

Named Arguments

No

Syntax

```
CSng(expression)
```

expression   *required; Numeric or String*
The range of **expression** is −3.402823E38 to −1.401298E-45 for negative values, and 1.401298E-45 to 3.402823E38 for positive values.

Return Value

expression cast as a Single data type

Description

Returns a single-precision number

Rules at a Glance

- *expression* must evaluate to a numeric value; otherwise, a type-mismatch error is generated.

- If the value of *expression* is outside the range of the Double data type, an overflow error is generated.

Example

```
Dim sngMyNumber As Single
If IsNumeric(sMyNumber) Then
    sngMyNumber = CSng(sMyNumber)
End If
```

Programming Tips and Gotchas

- You can use *IsNumeric* to test an expression before passing it to *CSng*.

- When converting a string representation of a number to a numeric, you should use the data type conversion functions—such as *CSng*—instead of *Val*, because the data type conversion functions take into account the computer's regional settings. The thousands separator is the most important of these regional settings. For example, if the value of *expression* is the string 1,234. 987, *CSng* converts it to 1234.987, while *Val* incorrectly converts it to 1.

- Like most of the conversion functions, *CSng* is not actually a function in the Microsoft.VisualBasic namespace. Instead, it is similar to a Visual C++ macro; the compiler translates the function call into inline code.

See Also

CDbl Function

CStr Function

Named Arguments

No

Syntax

```
CStr(expression)
```

expression   *required; any*
   Any numeric, date, string, or Boolean expression

Return Value

expression converted to a string

Description

Returns a string representation of *expression*

Rules at a Glance

If *expression* is Boolean, the function returns one of the strings `"True"` or `"False"`. For an expression that can be interpreted as a date, the return value is a

---

string representation of that date, in the short date format of the host computer. For a numeric expression, the return is a string representing the number.

Example

```
Dim sMyString as String
sMyString = CStr(100)
```

Programming Tips and Gotchas

- The string representation of Boolean values is either "True" or "False", as opposed to their underlying values of 0 and –1.

- Uninitialized numeric data types passed to *CStr* return "0."

- An uninitialized date variable passed to *CStr* returns "12:00:00AM."

- Like most of the conversion functions, *CStr* is not actually a function in the Microsoft.VisualBasic namespace. Instead, it is similar to a Visual C++ macro; the compiler translates the function call into inline code.

See Also

Str Function

CType Function

Named Arguments

No

Syntax

```
CType(expression, typename)
```

expression   *required; any*
   The data item to be converted

typename   *required; Keyword*
   The data type, object type, structure, or interface to which *expression* is to be converted

Return Value

expression cast as a *typename* interface, object, structure, or data type

Description

Converts an expression to the specified data type if possible; otherwise, returns an error.

Rules at a Glance

- *expression* can be any data, object, structure, or interface type.

- *typename* can be any data type (such as Boolean, Byte, Decimal, Long, Short, String, etc.), structure type, object type, or interface that can be used with the As clause in a Dim statement.

- If the function fails, or if the converted value of *expression* is outside the range allowed by *typename*, an InvalidCastException exception occurs.

- When Option Strict is set to On, then implicit data type conversions can only be widening; that is, implicit data type conversion only occurs from smaller data types to "wider" data types, such as from Integer to Long. In this case, to perform a narrowing type conversion, we can use *CType*. For instance, if Option Strict is On, the following code produces an error:

```
Dim iInteger As Integer = 1
Dim lLong As Long = 2
iInteger = lLong
On the other hand, the following code is fine:
Dim iInteger As Integer = 1
Dim lLong As Long = 2
iInteger = Ctype(lLong, Integer)
```

Example

```
Option Strict On
Imports Microsoft.VisualBasic
Imports System

Interface IEmployee
    Property Name() As String
    Property Salary() As Decimal
End Interface

Public Class CSalaried
Implements IEmployee

Dim sName As String
Dim decSalary AS DEcimal

Public Property Name() As String     Implements IEmployee.Name
    Get
        Name = sName
    End Get
    Set
        sName = Value
    End Set
End Property

Public Property Salary() As Decimal Implements IEmployee.Salary
    Get
        Salary = decSalary
    End Get
    Set
        decSalary = Value
    End Set
End Property

End Class
```

```
Module modMain

Public Sub Main()

Dim oSal As New CSalaried
Dim oSal2 As CSalaried
Dim oEmp As IEmployee

oSal.Name = "John Doe"
oSal.Salary = 30000
console.writeline(oSal.Name)

oEmp = CType(oSal, IEmployee)
console.writeline(oEmp.Name)

oSal2 = CType(oEmp, CSalaried)
console.writeline(oSal2.name)

End Sub

End Module
```

Programming Tips and Gotchas

- *CType* can perform the same conversions as the individual conversion functions and raises a runtime error if it is asked to perform a conversion that an individual conversion function cannot perform. For example, in the function call:

    ```
    bVal = CType(Var1, Boolean)
    ```

    Var1 can be any numeric value, any numeric string, or a string whose value is either **"True"** or **"False"**.

- Like most of the conversion functions, *CType* is not actually a function in the Microsoft.VisualBasic namespace. Instead, it is similar to a Visual C++ macro; the compiler translates the function call into inline code.

- In part, *CType* is a "convenience function" that provides the functionality of the entire set of conversion functions in a single function. Its real significance, however, comes when you want to convert a derived object to the type of its base class, or when you want to convert an object to the type of its virtual base class (that is, its interface).

- Upcasting a derived object to its parent object type can be done implicitly. However, downcasting back from the base class type to the derived object type cannot be done implicitly if **Option Strict** is On. Instead, *CType* can be used to perform this conversion. This is illustrated in the example.

VB.NET/VB 6 Differences

The *CType* function is new to VB.NET.

See Also

See Also

CBool Function, CByte Function, CChar Function, CDate Function, CDbl Function, CDec Function, CInt Function, CLng Function, CObj Function, CShort Function, CSng Function, CStr Function

CurDir Function

Class

Microsoft.VisualBasic.FileSystem

Syntax

```
CurDir[(drive)]
```

drive   *optional; String or Char*
The name of the drive

Return Value

A String containing the current path

Description

Returns the current directory of a particular drive or the default drive

Rules at a Glance

- If no drive is specified or if *drive* is a zero-length string (""), *CurDir* returns the path for the current drive.
- *drive* can be the single-letter drive name with or without a colon (i.e., both "C" and "C:" are valid values for *drive*).
- If *drive* is invalid, the function will generate runtime error 68, "Device unavailable."
- Because *CurDir* can only accept a single-character string, you cannot use network drive names, share names, or UNC drive names.

Example

```
Sub TestCurDir()
    MsgBox CurDir("C")
End Sub
```

See Also

ChDir Procedure, ChDrive Procedure, MkDir Procedure, RmDir Procedure

DateAdd Function

Class

Microsoft.VisualBasic.DateAndTime

Syntax

```
DateAdd(interval, number, datevalue)
```

interval   *required; String or* `DateInterval` *enum*

A String expression (see the first item in the "Rules at a Glance" section) or a member of the `DateInterval` enumeration (see the second item in the "Rules at a Glance" section) that specifies the interval of time to add

number   *required; Double*

An expression denoting the number of time intervals you want to add (it can be positive or negative)

datevalue   *required; Date, or an expression capable of conversion to a date*

Date representing the starting date to which the interval is to be added

Return Value

A past or future Date that reflects the result of the addition

Description

Returns a Date representing the result of adding (or subtracting, if *number* is negative) a given number of time periods to or from a given date. For instance, you can calculate the date 178 months before today's date, or the date and time 12,789 minutes from now.

Rules at a Glance

- *interval* can be one of the following literal strings:

String	Description
yyyy	Year
q	Quarter
m	Month
y	Day of year
d	Day
w	Weekday
ww	Week
h	Hour
n	Minute
s	Second

- *interval* can also be a member of the `DateInterval` enum:

```
Enum DateInterval
    Day
    DayOfYear
    Hour
    Minute
    Month
    Quarter
    Second
```

```
        Week
        Weekday
        WeekOfYear
    End Enum
```

- If *number* is positive, the result will be in the future; if *number* is negative, the result will be in the past. (The meaning of "future" and "past" here is relative to *datevalue*.)

- The *DateAdd* function has a built-in calendar algorithm to prevent it from returning an invalid date. For example, you can add 10 minutes to 31 December 1999 23:55, and *DateAdd* automatically recalculates all elements of the date to return a valid date, in this case 1 January 2000 00:05. This includes leap years; the calendar algorithm takes the presence of 29 February into account for leap years.

Example

```
DateAdd(DateInterval.Day, 120, #3/3/2001#)    ' Returns 7/1/2001
```

Programming Tips and Gotchas

- You can check that a date is valid using the *IsDate* function prior to passing it as a parameter to the function.

- To add a number of days to *datevalue*, use either the day of the year ("y" or `DateInterval.DayOfYear`), the day ("d" or `DateInterval.Day`), or the weekday ("w" or `DateInterval.Weekday`).

- *DateAdd* generates an error if the result does not lie in the range of dates of the Date data type.

- If *number* contains a fractional value, it is rounded to the nearest whole number before being used in the calculation.

- You can also use the members of the `DateTime` structure of the BCL to manipulate dates and times.

VB.NET/VB 6 Differences

VB 6 lacks the `DateInterval` enumeration and therefore only accepts a string as the *interval* argument.

See Also

DateDiff Function

DateDiff Function

Class

Microsoft.VisualBasic.DateAndTime

Syntax

```
DateDiff(interval, date1, date2[, dayofweek[, weekofyear]])
```

interval   *required; String or* `DateInterval` *enum*

    A String expression (see the first item in the "Rules at a Glance" section) or a
    member of the `DateInterval` enumeration (see the second item in the
    "Rules at a Glance" section) that specifies the units of time used to express the
    difference between *date1* and *date2*

date1, date2   *required; Date or a literal date*

    The starting and ending dates, whose difference is computed as *date2-*
    date1

dayofweek   *optional;* `FirstDayOfWeek` *enum*

    A member of the `FirstDayOfWeek` enum

weekofyear   *optional;* `FirstWeekOfYear` *enum*

    A member of the `FirstWeekOfYear` enum

Return Value

A Long specifying the number of time intervals between the two dates

Description

Calculates the number of time intervals between two dates. For example, you can
use the function to determine how many days there are between 1 January 1980
and 31 May 1998.

Rules at a Glance

- *interval* can be one of the following literal strings:

String	Description
yyyy	Year
q	Quarter
m	Month
y	Day of year
d	Day
w	Weekday
ww	Week
h	Hour
n	Minute
s	Second

- *interval* can also be a member of the `DateInterval` enum:

```
Enum DateInterval
    Day
    DayOfYear
    Hour
    Minute
    Month
    Quarter
    Second
    Week
```

```
        Weekday
        WeekOfYear
    End Enum
```

- To calculate the number of days between *date1* and *date2*, you can use either of the DateInterval constants, DayOfYear or Day, or the string literals "y" or "d".

- When *interval* is Weekday or "w", *DateDiff* returns the number of weeks between the two dates. If *date1* falls on a Monday, *DateDiff* counts the number of Mondays until *date2*. It counts *date2*, but not *date1*. If *interval* is Week or "ww", however, *DateDiff* returns the number of calendar weeks between the two dates. It counts the number of Sundays between *date1* and *date2*. *DateDiff* counts *date2* if it falls on a Sunday, but it doesn't count *date1*, even if it does fall on a Sunday.

- The *DayOfWeek* argument affects calculations that use the Week or "w" and Weekday or "ww" *interval* settings only.

Example

```
DateDiff(DateInterval.Day, #1/1/1945#, #3/3/2001#, _
        FirstDayOfWeek.System, FirstWeekOfYear.System)
```

Programming Tips and Gotchas

- When working with dates, always check that a date is valid using the *IsDate* function prior to passing it as a function parameter.

- If *date1* or *date2* is enclosed in double quotation marks (" ") and you omit the year, the current year is inserted in your code each time the *date1* or *date2* expression is evaluated. This makes it possible to write code that can be used in different years.

- When comparing December 31 to January 1 of the immediately succeeding year, *DateDiff* with *interval* set equal to Year, or "yyyy", returns 1 even though only a day has elapsed.

- *DateDiff* considers the four quarters of the year to be January 1–March 31, April 1–June 30, July 1–September 30, and October 1–December 31. Consequently, when determining the number of quarters between March 31 and April 1 of the same year, for example, *DateDiff* returns 1, even though the latter date is only one day after the former.

- If *interval* is Month or "m", *DateDiff* simply counts the difference in the months in which the respective dates fall. For example, when determining the number of months between January 31 and February 1 of the same year, *DateDiff* returns 1, even though the latter date is only one day after the former.

- In calculating the number of hours, minutes, or seconds between two dates, if an explicit time is not specified, *DateDiff* provides a default value of midnight (00:00:00).

VB.NET/VB 6 Differences

VB 6 lacks the DateInterval enumeration and therefore only accepts a string as the *interval* argument.

DateAdd Function

DatePart Function

Class

Microsoft.VisualBasic.DateAndTime

Syntax

```
DatePart(interval, datevalue[, firstdayofweekvalue[, _
    firstweekofyearvalue]])
```

interval   *required; String or a member of the* DateInterval *enum*
     A String literal (see the second item in the "Rules at a Glance" section) or a constant of the DateInterval enum (see the third item in the "Rules at a Glance" section) that defines the part of the date/time to extract from *datevalue*

datevalue   *required; Date, literal date, or an expression*
                               capable of conversion to a date
     The Date value to evaluate

firstdayofweekvalue   *optional;* FirstDayOfWeek *enum*
     A member of the FirstDayOfWeek enum

firstweekofyearvalue   *optional;* FirstWeekOfYear *enum*
     A member of the FirstWeekOfYear enum

Return Value

An Integer containing the specified part

Description

Extracts an individual component of the date or time (like the month or the second) from a date/time value

Rules at a Glance

- The *DatePart* function returns an Integer containing the specified portion of the given date. *DatePart* is a single function encapsulating the individual *Year*, *Month*, *Day*, *Hour*, *Minute*, and *Second* functions.

- *interval* can be one of the following literal strings:

String	Description
yyyy	Year
q	Quarter
m	Month
y	Day of year
d	Day
w	Weekday

String	Description
ww	Week
h	Hour
n	Minute
s	Second

- *interval* can also be a member of the **DateInterval** enum:

  ```
  Enum DateInterval
      Day
      DayOfYear
      Hour
      Minute
      Month
      Quarter
      Second
      Week
      Weekday
      WeekOfYear
  End Enum
  ```

- The *firstdayofweekvalue* argument can be any of the following members of the **FirstDayOfWeek** enumeration:

  ```
  Enum FirstDayOfWeek
      System      'uses first day of week setting on local system
      Sunday
      Monday
      Tuesday
      Wednesday
      Thursday
      Friday
      Saturday
  End Enum
  ```

- The *firstdayofweekvalue* argument affects only calculations that use either the **Week** (or **"w"**) or **Weekday** (or **"ww"**) *interval* values.

- The *firstweekofyearvalue* argument can be any of the following members of the **FirstWeekOfYear** enumeration:

FirstWeekOfYear constant	Value	Description
System	0	Uses the local system setting
Jan1	1	Starts with the week in which January 1 occurs (the default value)
FirstFourDays	2	Starts with the first week that has at least four days in the new year
FirstFullWeek	3	Starts with the first full week of the year

Example

```
MsgBox("Current hour: " & DatePart(DateInterval.Hour, Now))
```

Programming Tips and Gotchas

- When working with dates, always check that a date is valid using the *IsDate* function prior to passing it as a function parameter.

- If you attempt to extract the hours, minutes, or seconds, but *datevalue* does not contain the necessary time element, the function assumes a time of midnight (0:00:00).

- If you specify *datevalue* within quotation marks (" ") and omit the year, the year is assumed to be the current year taken from the computer's date. For example:

  ```
  Console.WriteLine(DatePart(DateInterval.Year, cDate("01/03")))
  ```

VB.NET/VB 6 Differences

- VB 6 lacks the `DateInterval` enumeration and therefore only accepts a string as the *interval* argument.

- VB 6 supports a number of constants beginning with **vb**... as values for the *firstdayofweekvalue* and *firstweekofyearvalue* arguments. While these are still supported in VB.NET, VB.NET has also added the `FirstDayOfWeek` and `FirstWeekOfYear` enumerations.

See Also

DateSerial Function, DateString Property, DateValue Function

DateSerial Function

Class

Microsoft.VisualBasic.DateAndTime

Syntax

```
DateSerial(year, month, day)
```

year   *required; Integer*
Number between 100 and 9999, inclusive, or a numeric expression

month   *required; Integer*
Any numeric expression to express the month between 1 and 12

day   *required; Integer*
Any numeric expression to express the day between 1 and 31

Return Value

A Date representing the date specified by the arguments

Description

Returns a Date whose value is specified by the three date components (year, month, and day).

For the function to succeed, all three components must be present, and all must be numeric values. The value returned by the function takes the short date format defined by the Regional Settings applet in the Control Panel of the client machine.

Rules at a Glance

- If the value of a particular element exceeds its normal limits, *DateSerial* adjusts the date accordingly. For example, if you tried `Date-Serial(96,2,31)`—February 31, 1996—*DateSerial* returns March 2, 1996.

- You can specify expressions or formulas that evaluate to individual date components as parameters to *DateSerial*. For example, `DateSerial(98,10+9,23)` returns 23 March 1999. This makes it easier to use *DateSerial* to form dates whose individual elements are unknown at design time or that are created on the fly as a result of user input.

Example

```
Dim iYear As Integer = 1987
Dim iMonth As Integer = 3 + 11
Dim iday As Integer = 16

MsgBox(DateSerial(iYear, iMonth, iday))
```

Programming Tips and Gotchas

- If any of the parameters exceed the range of the Integer data type (−32,768 to 32,767), an error (runtime error 6, "Overflow") is generated.

- *DateSerial* handles two-digit years in the same way as other Visual Basic date functions. A year argument between 0 and 29 is taken to be in the 21st century (2000 to 2029); year arguments between 30 and 99 are taken to be in the 20th century (1930 to 1999). Of course, the safest way to specify a year is to use the full four digits.

See Also

DatePart Function, DateString Property, DateValue Function

DateString Property

Class

Microsoft.VisualBasic.DateAndTime

Syntax

```
DateString()
```

Return Value

A String representing the current system date

Description

Returns or sets a string representing the current system date in the format "mm-dd-yyyy"

Rules at a Glance

The allowed formats for setting the date are "m-d-yyyy," "m-d-y," "m/d/yyyy," and "m/d/y."

Programming Tips and Gotchas

- To get or set the current system time as a String, use the TimeString property.
- To access the current system date as a Date, use the Today property.

VB.NET/VB 6 Differences

The DateString property is new to VB.NET. It is a replacement for the VB 6 Date statement, which sets the system date, and the *Date* and *Date$* functions, which retrieve the system date.

See Also

Now Property, TimeString Property, Today Property

DateValue Function

Class

Microsoft.VisualBasic.DateAndTime

Syntax

```
DateValue(stringdate)
```

stringdate   *required; String*
A string containing any of the date formats recognized by *IsDate*

Return Value

A Date that represents the date specified by the **stringdate** argument

Description

Returns a Date containing the date represented by **stringdate**.

The date value is formatted according to the short date setting defined by the Regional Settings applet in the Control Panel. *DateValue* can successfully recognize a **stringdate** in any of the date formats recognized by *IsDate*. *DateValue* does not return time values in a date/time string; they are simply dropped. However, if **stringdate** includes a valid date value but an invalid time value, a runtime error results.

Rules at a Glance

- The order of the day, month, and year within **stringdate** must be the same as the sequence defined by the computer's regional settings.
- Only those date separators recognized by *IsDate* can be used.
- If you don't specify a year in your date expression, *DateValue* uses the current year from the computer's system date.

Example

```
Dim sDateExpression As String

sDateExpression = 10 & "/" & "March" & "/" & 1998

If IsDate(sDateExpression) Then
    Console.WriteLine(DateValue(sDateExpression))
Else
    Console.WriteLine("invalid date")
End If
```

Programming Tips and Gotchas

- When working with dates, always check that a date is valid using the *IsDate* function prior to passing it as a function argument.

- If *stringdate* includes time information as well as date information, the time information is ignored; however, if only time information is passed to *DateValue*, an error is generated.

- *DateValue* handles two-digit years in the following manner: `Year` arguments between 0 and 29 are taken to be in the 21st century (2000 to 2029), while year arguments between 30 and 99 are taken to be in the 20th century (1930 to 1999). Of course, the safest way to specify a year is to use the full four digits.

- On Windows NT/2000 systems, the date formats are held as string values in the following registry keys:

  Date Separator
  HKEY_CURRENT_USER\Control Panel\International, sDate value entry

  Long Date
  HKEY_CURRENT_USER\Control Panel\International, sLongDate value entry

  Short Date
  HKEY_CURRENT_USER\Control Panel\International, sShortDate value entry

- The more common approach to date conversion is to use the *CDate* function. Microsoft also recommends using the C… conversion functions due to their enhanced capabilities and their locale awareness.

See Also

DatePart Function, DateSerial Function, DateString Property

Day Function

Class

Microsoft.VisualBasic.DateAndTime

Syntax

```
Day(datevalue)
```

datevalue   *required; Date or literal date*

Return Value

An Integer from 1 to 31, representing the day of the month

Description

Returns an Integer ranging from 1 to 31, representing the day of the month of datevalue

Rules at a Glance

The range of *datevalue* is 1/1/1 to 12/31/9999.

Programming Tips and Gotchas

- When working with dates, always check that a date is valid using the *IsDate* function prior to passing it as a function parameter.

- With Option Strict On, you must first convert *datevalue* to a Date data type before passing it to the *Day* function. You can use the *CDate* function for this purpose.

- If the day portion of *datevalue* is outside of its valid range, the function regenerates runtime error 13, "Type mismatch." This is also true if the day and month portion of *datevalue* is 2/29 for a non-leap year.

- To return the day of the week, use the *WeekDay* function.

See Also

DatePart Function, WeekdayName Function

DDB Function

Class

Microsoft.VisualBasic.Financial

Syntax

```
DDB(cost, salvage, life, period[, factor])
```

cost   *required; Double*
    The initial cost of the asset.

salvage   *required; Double*
    The value of the asset at the end of *life*.

life   *required; Double*
    Length of life of the asset.

period   *required; Double*
    Period for which the depreciation is to be calculated.

factor   *optional; Double*
    The rate at which the asset balance declines. If omitted, 2 (double-declining method) is assumed. However, the documentation doesn't mention what other values are supported or what they mean.

Return Value

Double representing the depreciation of an asset

Description

Returns a Double representing the depreciation of an asset for a specific time period. This is done using the double-declining balance method or another method that you specify using the *factor* argument.

The double-declining balance calculates depreciation at a differential rate, which varies inversely with the age of the asset. Depreciation is highest at the beginning of an asset's life and declines over time.

Rules at a Glance

- *life* and *period* must be specified in the same time units. In other words, both must be expressed in units of months, or both must be years.

- All arguments must be positive numbers.

Example

```
Dim dblInitialCost As Double = 2000
Dim dblSalvageValue As Double = 50
Dim dblUsefulLife As Double = 12
Dim dblTotDepreciation As Double = 0
Dim dblPeriod, dblThisPeriodDepr As Double

For dblPeriod = 1 To 12
    dblThisPeriodDepr = DDB(dblInitialCost, _
                dblSalvageValue, dblUsefulLife, dblPeriod)
    dblTotDepreciation = dblTotDepreciation + _
                dblThisPeriodDepr
    Console.WriteLine("Month " & dblPeriod & ": " & _
                dblThisPeriodDepr)
Next dblPeriod

Console.WriteLine("TOTAL: " & dblTotDepreciation)
```

Programming Tips and Gotchas

- The double-declining balance depreciation method calculates depreciation at a higher rate in the initial period and a decreasing rate in subsequent periods.

- The *DDB* function uses the following formula to calculate depreciation for a given period:

```
Depreciation / period = ((cost - salvage) * factor) / life
```

Debug Class

Namespace

System.Diagnostics

Createable

No

Description

The Debug object is used to send messages to the Output window (formerly called the Immediate window). The Debug object can also send output to other targets, such as text files, referred to as *listeners*. See the "Debug.Listeners Property" entry. The Debug class also allows you to check program logic with assertions.

Because the Debug class' members are shared, you do not need to instantiate the Debug object before accessing its members. The following code fragment, for instance, illustrates a call to the Debug object's WriteLine method:

```
Debug.WriteLine(intCount & " iteration through the loop")
```

Debug class members marked with an plus sign (+) are discussed in detail in their own entries.

Public Shared Properties

AutoFlush +
IndentLevel +
IndentSize +
Listeners +

Public Shared Methods

Assert +
Close +
Fail
Flush +
Indent +
Unindent +
Write +
WriteIf +
WriteLine +
WriteLineIf +

VB.NET/VB 6 Differences

The VB 6 Debug object has only two methods, Assert and Print. The VB.NET Assert method is similar to the VB 6 method, except that the latter displays a message if an expression is False, while the former suspends program execution. In VB.NET, the VB 6 Print method is gone, replaced by the Write, WriteIf, Write-Line, and WriteLineIf methods.

See Also

Debug.Assert Method, Debug.Write Method, Debug.WriteLine Method

---

Debug.Assert Method

Class

System.Diagnostics.Debug

Syntax

```
Debug.Assert(booleanexpression[[, string1], string2])
```

booleanexpression   *required; Boolean*
   Expression that evaluates to a Boolean value.

string1   *required; String*
   String to output if **booleanexpression** is **False**.

string2   *required; String*
   Detailed string to output. If **booleanexpression** is **False**, **string2** is
   output to Output window.

Return Value

None

Description

Outputs messages to the Output window if the condition is **False**

Rules at a Glance

booleanexpression must evaluate to a Boolean value.

Programming Tips and Gotchas

* Assert is typically used when debugging to test an expression that should
  evaluate to **True**.

* Debug.Assert executes only when an application is run in the design-time
  environment; the statement has no effect in a compiled application. This
  means that Debug.Assert will never produce a runtime error if the call to it is
  inappropriate, nor will it suspend program execution outside of the VB IDE.
  Because of this, you do not have to remove Debug.Assert statements from finished code or separate them with conditional **#If...Then** statements.

Debug.AutoFlush Property

Class

System.Diagnostics.Debug

Syntax

```
Debug.AutoFlush
```

Return Value

Boolean

Description

Sets or returns a Boolean value indicating whether each Write should be automatically followed by a Flush operation. By default, its value is **False**.

See Also

Debug.Flush Method

Debug.Close Method

Class

System.Diagnostics.Debug

Syntax

```
Debug.Close()
```

Return Value

None

Description

Flushes the output buffer and closes the listeners (except for the default Output window)

Debug.Flush Method

Class

System.Diagnostics.Debug

Syntax

```
Debug.Flush()
```

Return Value

None

Description

Flushes the output buffer, which causes all pending data to be written to the listeners

Debug.Indent Method

Class

System.Diagnostics.Debug

Syntax

```
Debug.Indent()
```

Description

Increases the current IndentLevel by 1. The property is useful for improving the readability of output sent to the Output window.

See Also

Debug.IndentLevel Property, Debug.IndentSize Property, Debug.Unindent Method

Debug.IndentLevel Property

Class

System.Diagnostics.Debug

Syntax

```
Debug.IndentLevel()
```

Return Value

An Integer specifying the indent level. The default is 0.

Description

Sets or retrieves the current indent level for the Debug object. The property is useful for improving the readability of output sent to the Output window.

See Also

Debug.IndentSize Property, Debug.Unindent Method

Debug.IndentSize Property

Class

System.Diagnostics.Debug

Syntax

```
Debug.IndentSize
```

Return Value

An Integer specifying the number of spaces per indent level. The default is 4.

Description

Sets or retrieves the current indent-size setting, which is the number of spaces per indent level. The property is useful for improving the readability of output sent to the Output window.

See Also

Debug.IndentLevel Property, Debug.Unindent Method

Debug.Listeners Property

Class

System.Diagnostics.Debug

Syntax

```
Debug.Listeners
```

Description

Retrieves the TraceListenerCollection collection of all TraceListener objects that monitor the debug output.

Example

The following code adds a text file to the listeners collection. As a result, all Debug.Write... methods will not only send the output to the Output window (the default listener) but also to the text file:

```
' Define a new TextWriterTraceListener
Dim trace As New TextWriterTraceListener()

' Define a new FileStream object
Dim fs As FileStream = New FileStream("c:\log.txt", FileMode.Append, _
                                    FileAccess.Write)

' Set the Writer property to a new StreamWriter for this FileStream
trace.Writer = New StreamWriter(fs)

' Add listener
Debug.Listeners.Add(trace)

' Output
Debug.WriteLine("xxxxx")
Debug.WriteLine("yyyyy")

' Close up
Debug.Close()
fs.Close()

' Remove listener
Debug.Listeners.Remove(trace)

' This goes only to Output window
Debug.WriteLine("zzzzz")
```

Debug.Unindent Method

Class

System.Diagnostics.Debug

Syntax

```
Debug.Unindent()
```

Description

Decreases the current IndentLevel by 1. The property is useful for improving the readability of output sent to the Output window.

See Also

Debug.Indent Method, Debug.IndentLevel Property

Debug.Write Method

Class

System.Diagnostics.Debug

Syntax

```
Debug.Write(Output[, Category])
```

Output   *required; String or Object*
  The string to be sent to the Output window, or the object whose name is to be sent to the Output window

Category   *optional; String*
  A category name used to group output messages

Description

Prints text in the Output window in the design-time environment

Rules at a Glance

- If *Output* is a string, the string is printed to the Output window.

- If *Output* is a nonstring object, the ToString property of the **Object** object is invoked. This just outputs a string version of the name of the object.

- Supplying a *Category* argument is useful when you want to organize the output from several **Debug.Write** statements by category. Output from the method then takes the form:

      ```
      Category: Output
      ```

  if *Output* is a string, and:

      ```
      Category: Output.ToString
      ```

  if *Output* is a nonstring object.

Programming Tips and Gotchas

In Visual Basic applications, Debug.Write executes only when an application is run in the design-time environment; the statement has no effect in a compiled application.

See Also

Debug.WriteIf Method, Debug.WriteLine Method, Debug.WriteLineIf Method

---

Debug.WriteIf Method

Class

System.Diagnostics.Debug

Syntax

```
Debug.WriteIf(condition, message[, Category])
```

or:

```
Debug.WriteIf(condition, value[, Category])
```

condition   *required; Boolean*
    Condition required for output to proceed

message   *required; String*
    The string to be sent to the Output window, or the object whose name is to
    be sent to the Output window

value   *required; Any*
    An object whose name is to be sent to the Output window

Category   *optional; String*
    A category name used to group output messages

Description

Prints text in the Output window in the design-time environment, provided that
condition is True

Rules at a Glance

This method behaves identically to Debug.Write, with the exception that nothing
is output unless *condition* is True.

See Also

Debug.Write Method, Debug.WriteLine Method, Debug.WriteLineIf Method

---

Debug.WriteLine Method

Class

System.Diagnostics.Debug

Syntax

```
Debug.WriteLine(Output[, Category])
```

Output   *required; String or Object*
    The string to be sent to the Output window, or the object whose name is to
    be sent to the Output window

Category   *optional; String*
    A category name used to group output messages

Description

Prints text, followed by a newline command, in the Output window in the design-
time environment

Rules at a Glance

This method is identical to Debug.Write except that a newline command is sent to
the Output window after any text is written.

Debug.Write Method, Debug.WriteIf Method, Debug.WriteLineIf Method

---

Debug.WriteLineIf Method

Class

System.Diagnostics.Debug

Syntax

```
Debug.WriteLineIf(booleanexpression, Output[, Category])
```

`booleanexpression`   *required; Boolean*
  Condition required for output to be produced

`Output`   *required; String or Object*
  The string to be sent to the Output window, or the object whose name is to
  be sent to the Output window

`Category`   *optional; String*
  A category name used to group output messages

Description

Prints text followed by a newline character in the Output window in the design-
time environment, provided that *booleanexpression* is `True`

Rules at a Glance

This method behaves identically to Debug.WriteLine, except that nothing is output
unless *booleanexpression* is `True`.

See Also

Debug.Write Method, Debug.WriteIf Method, Debug.WriteLine Method

---

Declare Statement

Syntax

Syntax for subroutines:

```
[accessmodifier] Declare [Ansi|Unicode|Auto] Sub name Lib "libname" _
    [Alias "aliasname"] [([arglist])]
```

Syntax for functions:

```
[accessmodifier] Declare [Ansi|Unicode|Auto] Function name _
    Lib "libname" [Alias "aliasname"] [([arglist])] [As type]
```

`accessmodifier`   *optional; Keyword*
  accessmodifier can be any one of the following: `Public`, `Private`,
  `Protected`, `Friend`, or `Protected Friend`. The following table describes

the effects of the various access modifiers. Note that *Direct Access* refers to accessing the member without any qualification, as in:

```
classvariable = 100
```

and *Class/Object Access* refers to accessing the member through qualification, either with the class name or the name of an object of that class.

	Direct Access scope	Class/Object Access scope
Private	Declaring class	Declaring class
Protected	All derived classes	Declaring class
Friend	Derived in-project classes	Declaring project
Protected Friend	All derived classes	Declaring project
Public	All derived classes	All projects

For more information, see the section entitled Accessibility in Class Modules" in Chapter 4.

Ansi   *optional; Keyword*
Converts all strings to ANSI values.

Unicode   *optional; Keyword*
Converts all strings to Unicode values.

Auto   *optional; Keyword*
Converts the strings according to .NET rules based on the name of the method (or the alias name, if specified). If no modifier is specified, Auto is the default.

name   *required; String literal*
Any valid procedure name. Note that DLL entry points are case sensitive. If the *aliasname* argument is used, *name* represents the name by which the function or procedure is referenced in your code, while *aliasname* represents the name of the routine as found in the DLL.

Lib   *required; Keyword*
Indicates that a DLL or code resource contains the procedure being declared.

libname   *required; String literal*
Name of the DLL or code resource that contains the declared procedure.

Alias   *optional; Keyword*
Indicates that the procedure being called has another name in the DLL. This is useful when the external procedure name is the same as a keyword. You can also use Alias when a DLL procedure has the same name as a public variable, constant, or any other procedure in the same scope. Alias is also useful if any characters in the DLL procedure name aren't allowed by VB.NET naming conventions.

aliasname   *optional; String literal*
Name of the procedure in the DLL or code resource. If the first character is not a number sign (#), *aliasname* is the name of the procedure's entry point in the DLL. If # is the first character, all characters that follow must indicate the ordinal number of the procedure's entry point.

arglist *optional*
> List of variables representing arguments that are passed to the procedure when it is called.

type *optional; Keyword*
> Data type of the value returned by a Function procedure; may be `Byte`, `Boolean`, `Char`, `Short`, `Integer`, `Long`, `Single`, `Double`, `Decimal`, `Date`, `String`, `Object`, or any user-defined type. Arrays of any type cannot be returned, but an Object containing an array can.

Description

Used at module level to declare references to external procedures in a dynamic-link library (DLL)

Rules at a Glance

* *arglist* is optional and has the following syntax:

  ```
  [ByVal | ByRef] varname[( )] [As type]
  ```

  `ByVal` *optional; Keyword*
  > The argument is passed by value; that is, a local copy of the variable is assigned the value of the argument. ByVal is the default method of passing arguments.

  `ByRef` *optional; Keyword*
  > The argument is passed by reference; that is, the local variable is simply a reference to the argument being passed. All changes made to the local variable are reflected in the calling argument.

  `varname` *required; String literal*
  > The name of the local variable containing either the reference or value of the argument.

  type *optional; Keyword*
  > The data type of the argument. Can be Byte, Boolean, Char, Short, Integer, Long, Single, Double, Decimal, Date, String, Object, or any user-defined type, object type, or data type defined in the BCL.

* The number and type of arguments included in *arglist* are checked each time the procedure is called.

* The data type you use in the `As` clause following *arglist* must match that returned by the function.

Example

The following example retrieves the handle of a window from its title bar caption. This is done using the *FindWindow* API function.

```
Declare Function FindWindow Lib "user32" Alias "FindWindowA" ( _
        ByVal lpClassName As String, _
        ByVal lpWindowName As String _
    ) As Integer

Private Sub GetWindowHandle()
    MsgBox(FindWindow(vbNullString, "Document - WordPad"))
End Sub
```

Programming Tips and Gotchas

- Using an *Alias* is useful when the name of an external procedure conflicts with a Visual Basic keyword or with the name of a procedure within your project, or when the name of the procedure in the code library is not allowed by Visual Basic naming conventions. In addition, *aliasname* is frequently used with functions in the Win32 API that have string parameters, where the "official" documented name of the function is used in code to call either of two "real" functions—one an ANSI and the other a Unicode version. For example:

```
Declare Function ExpandEnvironmentStrings _
    Lib "kernel32" Alias "ExpandEnvironmentStringsA" _
    (ByVal lpSrc As String, ByVal lpDst As String, _
    ByVal nSize As Long) As Long
```

defines the documented Win32 function *ExpandEnvironmentStrings* to a VB application. However, although calls to the function take the form:

```
lngBytes = ExpandEnvironmentStrings(strOriginal, _
    strCopy, len(strCopy))
```

the actual name of the function as it exists in *Kernel32.dll* is *Expand-EnvironmentStringsA*. (Windows API functions ending in "A" are the ANSI string versions, and those ending in "W" (for Wide) are the Unicode string versions.)

- You can use the # symbol at the beginning of *aliasname* to denote that *aliasname* is in fact the ordinal number of a procedure within the DLL or code library. In this case, all characters following the # sign and composing the *aliasname* argument must be numeric. For example:

```
Declare Function GetForegroundWindow Lib "user32" _
    Alias "#237" () As Long
```

- Remember that DLL entry points are case sensitive. In other words, either *name* or *aliasname* (if it is present and does not represent a routine's ordinal position) must correspond in case exactly to the routine as it is defined in the external DLL. Otherwise, VB displays runtime error 453, "Specified DLL function not found." If you aren't sure how the routine name appears in the DLL, use the *DumpBin.exe* utility to view its export table. For instance, the following command displays the export table of *advapi32.dll*, one of the Windows system files:

```
dumpbin /exports c:\windows\system32\advapi32.dll
```

- *libname* can include an optional path that identifies precisely where the external library is located. If the path is not included along with the library name, VB by default searches the current directory, the Windows directory, the Windows system directory, and the directories in the path, in that order.

- If the external library is one of the major Windows system DLLs (such as *Kernel32. dll* or *Advapi32.dll*), *libname* can consist of only the root filename, rather than the complete filename and extension.

- One of the most common uses of the `Declare` statement is to make routines in the Win32 API accessible to your programs. For more on this topic, see *Win32 API Programming with Visual Basic* by Steven Roman (O'Reilly 1999).

- In addition to the standard VB data types, you can also include BCL data types that are not wrapped by VB in `arglist`. Most useful are the unsigned integers, UShort, UInt16, and UInt32.

- In many cases, you can use routines available in the .NET Base Class Library or Framework Class Library instead of calling the Win32 API.

VB.NET/VB 6 Differences

- In VB 6, it is possible to declare the data type of an argument as `Any`, which suspends typechecking by the VB runtime engine. In VB.NET, this usage is not supported.

- In VB 6, if `ByVal` or `ByRef` is not specified, an argument is passed to the calling procedure by reference. In VB.NET, arguments are passed by value by default.

- In VB 6, it is possible to override the method in which an argument is passed to an external function within the call itself by specifying either `ByVal` or `ByRef` before the argument. In VB.NET, this usage is not permitted.

- The size of the integer data types in VB 6 and VB.NET are different, making it necessary to rewrite any `arglist` that has a data type of Integer or Long in VB 6. The VB 6 Integer data type is equivalent to the VB.NET Short data type. The VB 6 Long data type is equivalent to the VB.NET Integer data type.

- VB 6 lacks a signed 8-bit integer data type and unsigned data types to correspond to the Integer and Long types. In the .NET platform, unsigned data types are available for 16-bit integers (UInt16), 32-bit integers (UInt32), and 64-bit integers (UInt64). A signed byte data type (SByte) is also available. All are BCL classes not wrapped by VB.NET.

DefaultMember Attribute

Class

System.Reflection.DefaultMemberAttribute

Applies to

Class, Struct, or Interface

Description

Defines the default member of a structure, class, or interface. The *default member* is the member executed by the Type object's InvokeMember method when a null string is supplied as the method's *name* argument.

The Visual Basic .NET `Default` keyword is ultimately translated by the Visual Basic .NET compiler into the `<DefaultMember>` attribute. Visual Basic, however, requires that default members be parameterized. The use of the default member then allows you to specify a particular array element without having to explicitly reference the member. For instance, if the Items property is the default member of NewObject1, the statement

```
NewObject1.Items(10) = "Sleeping bag"
```

is functionally identical to

```
NewObject(10) = "Sleeping bag"
```

This works in VB.NET because the latter code statement is translated by the compiler into a call to the InvokeMember method that looks something like the following:

```
Dim t As Type = GetType(NewClass1)
Dim iFlags As BindingFlags = BindingFlags.Public Or _
                             BindingFlags.Instance Or _
                             BindingFlags.SetProperty
Dim arr() As Object = { 10, "Sleeping bag" }
t.InvokeMember("", iFlags, Nothing, NewObject, arr)
```

Because the <DefaultMember> attribute, unlike the Default keyword, does not have to refer to a parameterized property, you can use the <DefaultMember> attribute to define default members that are not parameterized. However, this does not allow you to omit a reference to that member in code. For instance, if the default member of the oCounter object is a member named Value, you cannot reference it implicitly as follows:

```
oCounter = 10
```

You can, however, invoke that member using the InvokeMember method of the Type class without explicitly naming it.

The <DefaultMember> attribute and Default keyword are incompatible in one other important respect. If you use <DefaultMember> rather than Default to define a parameterized property as the default member of a class, at runtime Visual Basic will be unable to resolve implicit references to the member. Hence, the sole capability that the <DefaultMember> attribute affords you is the ability to *explicitly* invoke a default member using the InvokeMember method of the Type class.

Note that if you use both the Default keyword and the <DefaultMember> attribute in the same class definition, even if both reference the same member, an ExecutionEngineException exception results.

 If *memberName* is not a member of the class, structure, or interface, the <DefaultMember> attribute is ignored, and no error is raised.

Constructor

```
New(memberName)
```

memberName   *String*
    The name of the default member

Properties

MemberName   *String*

> Read-only. The name of the default member. Its value is set by the constructor's *memberName* parameter.

Example

```
Option Strict

Imports System
Imports System.Reflection

<DefaultMember("GetName")> Public Class CContact

Private sName As String
Private sCity As String
Private sComments() As String

Public Sub New()
   Me.New("John Doe", "Anywhere, U.S.A.")
End Sub

Public Sub New(strName As String, strCity As String)
   MyBase.New()
   sName = strName
   sCity = strCity
End Sub

Public Property Name As String
   Get
       Return sName
   End Get
   Set
       sName = Value
   End Set
End Property

Public Property Comments(index As Integer) As String
   Get
       Return sComments(index)
   End Get
   Set
       sComments(index) = Value
   End Set
End Property

Public Function GetName() As String
   Return sName
End Function

Public Function GetCity() As String
   Return sCity
End Function
```

```
End Class

Module modMain

    Public Sub Main

        Dim oContact As New CContact
        Dim t As Type = GetType(CContact)
        Dim iFlags As BindingFlags = BindingFlags.Instance Or _
                            BindingFlags.Public Or _
                        BindingFlags.InvokeMethod

        Console.WriteLine(t.InvokeMember("", iFlags, Nothing, oContact, _
                        Nothing))
        Console.WriteLIne(t.InvokeMember("GetName", iFlags, Nothing, _
                        oContact, Nothing))
        Console.WriteLine(t.InvokeMember("GetCity", iFlags, Nothing, _
                        oContact, Nothing))
    End Sub

End Module
```

Delegate Statement

Syntax

```
[AccessModifier] Delegate Sub name [([arglist])])
[AccessModifier] Delegate Function name [([arglist])]) As type
```

AccessModifier   *optional; Keyword*

Specifies scope/accessibility the same as when declaring a subroutine or function. Can be one of Public, Private, Protected, Friend, Protected Friend, or Shadows.

name   *required; String literal*

The name of the delegate class.

arglist   *optional*

The argument list; it has the same syntax as when defining a subroutine or function.

Description

Declares the parameters and return type of a delegate class. Note that the syntax is the same as that used when declaring a subroutine or function, with the addition of the keyword Delegate.

Rules at a Glance

- Any procedure whose argument list and return type matches that of a declared delegate class can be used to create an instance of this delegate class, as the upcoming example illustrates.

- For more information on delegates, see the Delegates" section in Chapter 7.

Example

Consider the following method:

```
Public Class Class1
    Public Sub AMethod(ByVal s As String)
        Msgbox(s)
    End Sub
End Class
```

Consider the following delegate declaration:

```
Delegate Sub ADelegate(ByVal s As String)
```

The following code uses the delegate to call the AMethod of Class1:

```
Protected Sub Form1_Click(ByVal sender As Object, _
                          ByVal e As System.EventArgs) _
                          Handles MyBase.Click

    ' Object of type Class1
    Dim obj As New Class1()

    ' Declare a new delegate
    Dim delg As ADelegate

    ' Define the delegate, passing the address of the object's method
    delg = New ADelegate(AddressOf obj.AMethod)

    ' Call the method using the Invoke method of the delegate
    delg.Invoke("test")

End Sub
```

DeleteSetting Procedure

Class

Microsoft.VisualBasic.Interaction

Syntax

```
DeleteSetting(appname[, section[, key]])
```

appname   *required; String*
> The name of the application. This must be a subkey of the HKEY_CURRENT_
> USER\Software\VB and VBA Program Settings registry key.

section   *optional; String*
> The name of the application key's subkey that is to be deleted. *section* can
> be a single key or a registry path separated with backslashes.

key   *optional; String*
> The name of the value entry to delete.

Description

Deletes a complete application key, one of its subkeys, or a single value entry from the Windows registry

Rules at a Glance

- *section* can contain a relative path (similar to that used to describe the folders on a hard drive) to navigate from the application key to the subkey to be deleted. For example, to delete the value entry named TestKey in the registry key HKEY_CURRENT_USER\Software\VB and VBA Program Settings\ RegTester\BranchOne\BranchTwo, you would use:

  ```
  DeleteSetting "RegTester", "BranchOne\BranchTwo", _
            "TestKey"
  ```

- You cannot use DeleteSetting to delete entries from registry keys that are not subkeys of HKEY_CURRENT_USER\Software\VB and VBA Program Settings.

- If *key* is supplied, only the value entry named *key* and its associated value are deleted.

- If *key* is omitted, the subkey named *section* is deleted.

- If *section* is omitted, the entire application key named *appname* is deleted.

Example

```
Sub TestTheReg()
    SaveSetting("MyRealGoodApp", _
        "TestBranch\SomeSection\AnotherSection", _
        "TestKey", 10 )
    MsgBox("Now look in RegEdit")
End Sub

Sub TestDelete()

    If GetSetting("MyRealGoodApp", _
            "TestBranch\SomeSection\AnotherSection", _
            "TestKey") <> "" Then

    DeleteSetting("MyRealGoodApp", _
    "TestBranch\SomeSection\AnotherSection", _
    "TestKey")

    MsgBox("Look again!")
    End If
End Sub
```

Programming Tips and Gotchas

- DeleteSetting was designed to operate on initialization files in 16-bit platforms and on the registry in 32-bit platforms. But the terminology used to describe the statement in the official documentation is based on initialization files, rather than on the registry. In particular, what is described as a *key* is a named key in an initialization file and a value entry in the registry.

- The behavior of the DeleteSetting statement differs under Windows 95 and Windows NT when it is used to remove a key from the registry. Under Windows 95, if the statement is used to delete either *appname* or *section*, all subkeys belonging to the key to be deleted will also be deleted. Under Windows NT, on the other hand, the keys *appname* and *section* are only deleted if they don't contain subkeys.

- DeleteSetting cannot be used to delete the default value (i.e., the unnamed value entry) belonging to any key. If you're using only the VB registry functions, though, this isn't a serious limitation, since SaveSetting does not allow you to create a default value.

- Unless you are quite sure about what you're doing, you should only delete registry settings that have been placed in the registry by your own code. Inadvertently deleting the wrong entries can have disastrous consequences. However, because this statement only gives you access to the subkeys of HKEY_CURRENT_USER\Software\VB and VBA Program Settings, the potential damage is minimized.

- Never assume that the key you want to delete is necessarily present in the registry. DeleteSetting deletes a user key (that is, a subkey of HKEY_CURRENT_USER); except on Windows 95 systems that are not configured to support multiple users, the user key is formed from a file that reflects only the present user's settings. This means that when one user runs an application, user settings are stored in his registry key. But when a second user runs the application for the first time, settings for that user are not likely to be present. Attempting to delete a nonexistent key produces runtime error 5, "Invalid procedure call or argument." To prevent the error, you should first test for the presence of the registry key, as shown in the earlier example.

- Rather than rely on the relatively underpowered registry-access functionality available in Visual Basic, we highly recommend that you instead use the Registry and RegistryKey classes available in the BCL's Microsoft.Win32 namespace.

See Also

GetAllSettings Function, GetSetting Function, SaveSetting Procedure

---

Dim Statement

Syntax

```
[accessmodifier] [Shared] [Shadows] [readonly] Dim [WithEvents] _
varname[([subscripts])] _
            [As [New] type] [= initexpr]
```

accessmodifier   *optional; Keyword*
    Can be one of Public, Protected, Friend, Protected Friend, Private, or Static. If one of these is included, the Dim keyword can be omitted.

Shared   *optional; Keyword*

    Indicates the the variable is not associated with any particular class instance but is accessible directly using the class name and is therefore "shared" by all class instances.

Shadows   *optional; Keyword*

    Indicates that the variable shadows any programming elements (variables, procedures, enums, constants, etc.) of the same name in a base class.

WithEvents   *optional; Keyword*

    In an object variable definition, indicates that the object will receive event notification

varname   *required*

    The name of the variable

subscripts   *optional*

    Dimensions of an array variable

New   *optional; Keyword*

    Keyword that creates an instance of an object

type   *optional unless* Option Strict *is* On

    The data type of *varname*

initexpr   *optional*

    Any expression that provides the initial value to assign to the variable; cannot be used if an **As New** clause is used

Description

Declares and allocates storage space in memory for variables. The Dim statement is used either at the start of a procedure or the start of a module to declare a variable of a particular data type.

Rules at a Glance

- Public, Friend, Shared, Shadows, and ReadOnly can only be used at the module, namespace, or file level, not at the procedure level.

- Protected and Protected Friend can appear only at the class level.

- Private can appear only at the module level.

- Static can be used only at the procedure level.

- Static and Shared cannot appear in the same Dim statement.

- Static cannot appear with either Shared or Shadows.

- If you use WithEvents, the variable type cannot be of type Object.

- Object is the default data type created when no data type is explicitly declared.

- The declaration of a nonobject variable actually creates the variable. For an object variable, the variable is not created unless the optional New statement is used. If not, then the object variable is set to Nothing and must be assigned a reference to an existing object at some later point in the code.

- When multiple variables are declared on the same line, if a variable is not declared with an explicit type declaration, then its type is that of the next variable with an explicit type declaration. Thus, in the line:

  ```
  Dim x As Long, i, j, k As Integer, s As String
  ```

  the variables i, j, and k have type Integer. (In VB 6, the variables i and j have type Variant.)

- VB.NET permits the initialization of variables in the same line as their declaration (at long last!). Thus, we may write:

  ```
  Dim x As Integer = 5
  ```

  to declare an Integer variable and initialize it to 5. Similarly, we can declare and initialize more than one variable on a single line:

  ```
  Dim x As Integer = 6, y As Integer = 9
  ```

- Variables that are not explicitly initialized by the `Dim` statement have the following default values:

Data type	Initial value
All numeric types	0
Boolean	False
Date	01/01/0001 12:00:00 AM
Decimal	0
Object	Nothing
String	Nothing

- Local variables can have *procedure-level scope* or *block-level scope*. A variable that is declared using the `Dim` keyword within a Visual Basic procedure but not within a code block has procedure-level scope; that is, its scope consists of the procedure in which it is declared. On the other hand, if a variable is declared inside a *code block* (i.e., a set of statements that is terminated by an `End...`, a `Loop`, or a `Next` statement), then the variable has block-level scope; that is, it is visible only within that block.

- A variable cannot be declared using the `Dim` statement with `WithEvents` within a method, function, or procedure, since this creates a local variable with procedure-level scope only.

- In VB.NET, all arrays have a lower bound of 0. This is a change from earlier versions of VB, where we could choose the lower bound of an array.

- To declare a one-dimensional array variable, use one of the following example syntaxes:

  ```
  'Implicit constructor: No initial size & no initialization
  Dim Arrayname() As Integer

  'Explicit constructor: No initial size & no initialization
  Dim Arrayname() As Integer = New Integer() {}

  'Implicit constructor: Initial size but no initialization
  ```

```
Dim Arrayname(6) As Integer

'Explicit constructor: Initial size but no initialization
Dim Arrayname() As Integer = New Integer(6) {}

'Implicit constructor: Initial size implied by initialization
Dim Arrayname() As Integer = {1, 2, 3, 4, 5, 6, 7}

'Explicit constructor, Initial size and initialization
Dim Arrayname() As Integer = New Integer(6) {1, 2, 3, 4, 5, 6, 7}
```

- To declare a multidimensional array, use one of the following example syntaxes:

```
' Two-dimensional array of unknown size
Dim arrayname(,) As Integer

' Two-dimensional array of unknown size
Dim arrayname(,) As Integer = New Integer(,) {}

' Two-dimensional array of size 3 by 2
Dim arrayname(3, 2) As Integer

' Two-dimensional array of size 3 by 2
Dim arrayname(,) As Integer = New Integer(3, 2) {}

' Two-dimensional array of size 3 by 2, initialized
Dim arrayname(,) As Integer = {{1, 4}, {2, 5}, {3, 6}}

' Two-dimensional array of size 3 by 2, initialized
Dim arrayname(,) As Integer = New Integer(3, 2) {{1, 4},
                                         {2, 5}, {3, 6}}
```

- The WithEvents keyword cannot be used when declaring an array.

- You can set or change the number of elements of an array using the ReDim statement.

- The maximum allowed dimensions for an array are 60.

Programming Tips and Gotchas

- When you declare an object reference as WithEvents, that object's events can be handled within your application. Object variables must be declared WithEvents at the module level to allow you to provide an error handler.

  When you declare an object variable as WithEvents in the declarations section of the module, the name of the object variable appears in the Object drop-down list at the top left of your code window. Select this and note that the events exposed by the object are available in the Procedure drop-down list at the top right of the code window. You can then add code to these event procedures in the normal way, as shown here:

```
Private WithEvents oEmp As Employee

Private Sub oEmp_CanDataChange(EmployeeCode As String, _
                     Cancel As Boolean)
    'event handling code goes here
```

```
End Sub

Private Sub oEmp_DataChanged(EmployeeCode As String)
    'event handling code goes here
End Sub
```

For a fuller description and discussion of the uses of **WithEvents**, **Event**, and **RaiseEvent**, see the Event, RaiseEvent, and WithEvents entries.

- One word of warning when using the **WithEvents** keyword: if you are building a client-server system using a **WithEvents** object reference, you must ensure that the client machine gives permission for the server machine to create processes on it. Otherwise, even though the client can create instances of the object on the server, the server will not be able to call back to the client with event notifications. In fact, your application will not even launch before a "Permission Denied" or similar error is generated. You can alter the permissions on the client using the DCOM Config utility.

- The way in which you declare an Object variable with the **Dim** statement dictates whether your application uses early binding or late binding. Early binding allows object references to be resolved at compile time. Late binding resolves an object reference at runtime, which has a negative impact on runtime efficiency. To optimize the performance, you should use early binding whenever possible. For more information on this, see the discussion of binding in Chapter 3.

- When you declare an array without dimensioning it, you risk an ArgumentNullException exception if you attempt to iterate the array, as in the following code fragment:

```
Dim aInts(), iCtr As Integer

For iCtr = 0 To UBound(aInts)
    Console.WriteLine(aInts(iCtr))     ' Raises exception
Next
One workaround is to declare an empty array as having -1 element, as
the following code fragment illustrates:
Dim aInts(-1) As Integer
For iCtr = 0 to UBound(aInts)     ' For loop never executed
    Console.WriteLine(aInts(iCtr))
Next
```

VB.NET/VB 6 Differences

- In VB 6, all variables declared using **Dim** without specifying a specific data type are created as Variants. In VB.NET, all variables whose data type is not specified are Objects.

- When multiple variables are declared on a single line of code in VB 6, variables not explicitly assigned a data type are cast as variants. For example, in the statement:

```
Dim Var1, Var2, Var3 As String
```

both *Var1* and *Var2* are variants rather than strings. In VB.NET, the type declaration applies to all undeclared variables since the last explicit type declaration. So the previous statement in VB.NET would cast *Var1*, *Var2*, and *Var3* as strings.

- In VB 6, variables cannot be initialized at the same time they are declared. In VB . NET, variables can be assigned an initial value when they are declared.

- In VB 6, all variables defined within a procedure using the `Dim` keyword have procedure-level scope. In VB.NET, variables defined using `Dim` in code blocks (such as loops) have block-level scope and are not accessible throughout the procedure. Hence, code such as the following works under VB6 but may fail to compile under VB.NET:

```
Dim iCtr As Integer

'Nested loop
For iCtr = 0 To 10000
    Dim iCtr2 As Integer
    For iCtr2 = 0 To 10000
    Next
Next

' Reinitialize iCtr2
iCtr2 = 0

End Sub
```

- VB 6 supports fixed-length strings, but they are not supported in VB.NET.

- In VB 6, if an object is instantiated using the `New` keyword as part of a `Dim` statement, testing for the validity of the object reference with a statement such as:

```
If obj Is Nothing Then
```

always fails, since the statement itself reinstantiates the object if it is Nothing. In VB.NET, this undesirable behavior has been changed, and setting the object to Nothing destroyes the object.

- In VB 6, you could instantiate an object instantiated using the `New` keyword as part of a `Dim` statement, release the object reference by setting it to nothing, then reinstantiate the object by referencing it or its members. In VB.NET, setting the object reference to Nothing destroys the object; subsequent attempts to reference the object generate a NullReferenceException exception.

- In VB 6, arrays could be either fixed length or dynamic; in VB.NET, all arrays are dynamic.

- VB 6 allows you to define the lower bound of an array when it is initialized. In VB.NET, all arrays have a lower bound of 0. For example, the VB 6 syntax:

```
Dim array(1 To 20) As String
```

is not supported in VB.NET.

- In VB.NET, an array cannot be declared using the `New` keyword. Practically, this means that you cannot create an array of creatable objects, and must instead use a collection. VB 6, in contrast, allows arrays of objects.

See Also

Private Statement, Public Statement, ReDim Statement, Static Statement, WithEvents Keyword

Dir Function

Class

Microsoft.VisualBasic.FileSystem

Syntax

```
Dir[(pathname[, attributes])]
```

pathname   *optional; String*
A string expression that defines a path, which may contain a drive name, a folder name, and a filename

attributes   *optional; Numeric or Constant of the* FileAttribute *enumeration*
A FileAttribute enumeration constant or numeric expression specifying the file attributes to be matched

Return Value

String

Description

Returns the name of a single file or folder matching the pattern and attribute passed to the function

Rules at a Glance

- A zero-length string ("") is returned if a matching file is not found.

- Possible values for *attributes* are:

FileAttribute enumeration	Value	Description
Normal	0	Normal (not hidden and not a system file)
ReadOnly	1	Read-only file
Hidden	2	Hidden
System	4	System file
Volume	8	Volume label; if specified, all other attributes are ignored
Directory	16	Directory or folder
Archive	32	Archive
Alias	64	Alias or link

- The *attributes* constants can be Ored together to create combinations of attributes to match; e.g., FileAttribute.Hidden Or FileAttribute. Directory will match hidden directories.

- If *attributes* is not specified, files matching *pathname* are returned regardless of *attributes*.

- You can use the wildcard characters * and ? within *pathname* to return multiple files.

- Although *pathname* is optional, the first call you make to *Dir* must include it. *pathname* must also be specified if you are specifying `attributes`. In addition, once *Dir* returns a zero-length string, subsequent calls to *Dir* must specify pathname, or runtime error 5, "Invalid procedure call or argument," results.

- A call to *Dir* with no arguments continues the search for a file matching the last used *pathname* argument (and `attribute` argument, if it was supplied).

Example

```
Private Sub Button1_Click(ByVal sender As System.Object, _
                          ByVal e As System.EventArgs) _
        Handles Button1.Click

    Dim sFileName As String
    Dim sPath As String = "c:\windows\*.txt"

    sFileName = Dir(sPath)

    Do While sFileName > ""
        ListBox1.Items.Add(sFileName)
        sFileName = Dir()
    Loop

End Sub
```

Programming Tips and Gotchas

- *Dir* can only return one filename at a time. To create a list of more than one file that matches *pathname*, you must first call the function using the required parameters, then make subsequent calls using no parameters. When there are no more files matching the initial specification, a zero-length string is returned. Once *Dir* has returned a zero-length string, you must specify a *pathname* in the next call, or an error is generated.

- In previous versions of Visual Basic, the *Dir* function was commonly employed to determine whether a particular file existed. Although it can still be used for this purpose, the use of the BCL System.IO namespace's File.Exists method is more straightforward. Since Exists is a shared public member of the File class, it can be called as follows:

```
If File.Exists("c:\windows\network.txt")
```

- The *Dir* function returns filenames in the order in which they appear in the file-allocation table. If you need the files in a particular order, you should first store the names in an array before sorting. Note that an array can be easily sorted using the Array object's Sort method; the Array class is part of the BCL's System namespace.

- The *Dir* function saves its state between invocations. This means that the function cannot be called recursively. For example, if the function returns the name of the directory, you cannot then call the *Dir* function to iterate the files in that directory and then return to the original directory.

- If you are calling the *Dir* function to return the names of one or more files, you must provide an explicit file specification. In other words, if you want to retrieve the names of all files in the *Windows* directory, for instance, the function call:

```
strFile = Dir("C:\Windows", FileAttribute.Normal)
```

necessarily fails. Instead, the *Dir* function must be called with *pathname* defined as follows:

```
strFile = Dir("C:\Windows\*.*", FileAttribute.Normal)
```

- A major limitation of *Dir* is that it returns only the filename; it does not provide other information, such as the size, date, and timestamp, or attributes of a file.

- Many difficulties with the *Dir* function result from not fully understanding how various *attributes* constants affect the file or files returned by the function. By default, *Dir* returns a "normal" file (i.e., a file whose hidden or system attributes are not set). Hidden returns a normal file or a hidden file, but not a system file and not a system file that is hidden. System returns a normal file or a system file, but not a hidden file, including a system file that is hidden. FileAttribute.System Or FileAttribute.Hidden returns any file, regardless of whether it is normal, hidden, system, or system and hidden.

DirectCast Function

Named Arguments

No

Syntax

```
DirectCast(expression, typename)
```

expression   *required; Any*
     The data item to be converted

typename   *required; Keyword*
     The data type, object type, structure, or interface to which expression is to be converted

Return Value

expression cast as a *typename* interface or object

Description

Converts an expression to its runtime data type, if possible; otherwise, returns an error.

Rules at a Glance

- *expression* must be a reference type, typically a variable of type Object..

- *typename* can be any data type (such as Boolean, Byte, Decimal, Long, Short, String, etc.), structure type, object type, or interface.

- If the function fails, an InvalidCastException exception occurs.

Programming Tips and Gotchas

- In contrast to the *CType* function, *DirectCast* converts a reference type (i.e., an object) to its runtime type. For instance,

```
Option Strict On

Imports System

Public Module modMain
    Public Sub Main
        Dim oVal As Object = "a"c
        Dim chVal As Char = DirectCast(oVal, Char)
        Console.WriteLine(chVal)
    End Sub
End Module
```

- *DirectCast* can also be used to convert an object of a derived type to its base type. For example:

```
Option Strict On

Imports System

Public Class Person
    ' Implementation of Person
End Class

Public Class Worker
    Inherits Person

    ' Implementation of Worker
End Class

Public Module modMain
    Public Sub Main
        ' Conversion of a derived to a base type
        Dim oWorker As New Worker()
        Dim oPerson As Person = oWorker
        Dim oPerson As Person = DirectCast(oWorker, Person)
    End Sub
End Module
```

- Like most of the conversion functions, *DirectCast* is not actually a function in the Microsoft.VisualBasic namespace. Instead, it is similar to a Visual C++ macro; the compiler translates the function call into inline code.

VB .NET/VB 6 Differences

The *DirectCast* function is new to VB .NET.

See Also

CType Function

Directory Class

Namespace

System.IO

Createable

No

Description

The Directory class represents a directory or folder. (It appears that Microsoft is retreating from the term *folder*, in favor of the legacy term *directory*.) The Directory class has a number of methods that allow you to retrieve information about the directory's system properties, to move and delete a directory, and to create a new directory. (Unfortunately, however, the Directory class lacks a Copy method.)

All of the members of the Directory class are shared methods, so they can be called without instantiating any objects. For example, you can call the CreateDirectory method as follows:

```
Directory.CreateDirectory("C:\projects\project1")
```

This syntax may seem a bit awkward, especially to those familiar with earlier version of VB. Rather than the Directory object itself representing a directory, as it does in the case of a Folder object in the VB 6 FileSystemObject object model, the Directory class is simply a means to access a set of directory-related functions.

Directory class members marked with a plus sign (+) are discussed in further detail in their own entries.

Public Shared Methods

CreateDirectory +
Delete +
Exists +
GetCreationTime +
GetCurrentDirectory
GetDirectories +
GetDirectoryRoot +
GetFiles +
GetFileSystemEntries +
GetLastAccessTime
GetLastWriteTime
GetLogicalDrives +
GetParent +
Move +
SetCreationTime
SetCurrentDirectory
SetLastAccessTime
SetLastWriteTime

VB.NET/VB 6 Differences

The `Directory` object loosely corresponds to the `Folder` object in the File-SystemObject object model. (The `FileSystemObject` object and its child objects are implemented in the Microsoft Scripting Runtime Library in the file *scrun.dll.*) There is, however, a significant difference in the members of each class, and in some cases, methods with similar functionality have different names.

See Also

File Class

Directory.CreateDirectory Method

Class

System.IO.Directory

Syntax

```
Directory.CreateDirectory(path)
```

path   *required; String*
> The path of the new directory

Return Value

None

Description

Creates a new directory

Rules at a Glance

- *path* must represent a legal path.
- *path* can be an absolute or a relative path. For cxample:

    ```
    Directory.CreateDirectory("C:\Temp")
    ```

    specifies an absolute path (it begins with a drive's root directory), while:

    ```
    Directory.CreateDirectory("..\Chapter2")
    ```

    is a relative path that begins from the current directory. Relative paths can make use of the "." and ".." characters, which represent the current directory and the parent of the current directory, respectively.

- The CreateDirectory method creates all directories required to create a specified path. For example, the code:

    ```
    Directory.CreateDirectory("c:\NewDirectory\NewSubDirectory")
    ```

    will create the *NewDirectory* folder if it does not exist and then the *newSubDirectory* folder if it does not exist.

- *path* can be either a path on the local system, the path of a mapped network drive, or a UNC path.

Programming Tips and Gotchas

The CreateDirectory method does not raise an error if the directory to be created already exists.

Directory.Delete Method

Class

System.IO.Directory

Syntax

```
Directory.Delete(path [,recursive])
```

`path`   *required; String*
　　The path of the folder to delete.

`recursive`   *optional; Boolean*
　　Indicates whether the folder and its contents are to be deleted if the folder is not empty. Its default value is `False`.

Return Value

None

Description

Removes or deletes an existing directory

Rules at a Glance

- If `path` does not exist, the method generates a runtime error.
- If `recursive` is set to `False` (its default value), the directory must be empty to be successfully deleted; otherwise, a runtime error will be generated.
- If `recursive` is set to `True`, the method will delete not only the final directory in `path`, but also of its files and all of its subdirectories, as well as all nested subdirectories and nested files.
- `path` can be either an absolute path (a complete path from the root directory to the directory whose existence is to be confirmed) or a relative path (starting from the current directory to the path whose existence is to be confirmed).
- `path` can be either a path on the local system, the path of a mapped network drive, or a UNC path.
- `path` cannot contain wildcard characters.

Programming Tips and Gotchas

- The Delete method permanently deletes directories and their contents. It doesn't move them to the Recycle Bin.
- Care must be taken when setting `recursive` to `True` due to the danger of accidentally removing files, especially since the method does not prompt whether it should delete any folders or files.

- If the user has adequate rights, the source or destination can be a network path or share name. For example:

```
Directory.Delete("\\NTSERV1\d$\RootTwo")
Directory.Delete("\\RootTest")
```

Directory.Exists Method

Class

System.IO.Directory

Syntax

```
Directory.Exists(path)
```

path   *required; String*
    The path of the directory whose existence is to be determined

Return Value

True if the specified path exists; **False** otherwise

Description

Determines whether a given directory exists

Rules at a Glance

- *path* can be either an absolute path (a complete path from the root directory to the directory whose existence is to be confirmed) or a relative path (starting from the current directory to the path whose existence is to be confirmed).

- *path* can be either a path on the local system, the path of a mapped network drive, or a UNC path.

- *path* cannot contain wildcard characters.

Directory.GetCreationTime Method

Class

System.IO.Directory

Syntax

```
Directory.GetCreationTime(path)
```

path   *required; String*
    A valid path

Return Value

A Date value indicating the creation date and time of the directory

Description

Indicates when a given directory was created

Rules at a Glance

- *path* can be either an absolute path (a complete path from the root directory to the directory whose creation time is to be retrieved) or a relative path (starting from the current directory to the directory whose creation time and existence is to be retrieved).

- *path* can be either a path on the local system, the path of a mapped network drive, or a UNC path.

- *path* cannot contain wildcard characters.

Directory.GetDirectories Method

Class

System.IO.Directory

Syntax

```
Directory.GetDirectories(path [, searchpattern])
```

path   *required; String*
  A valid path to a directory

searchpattern   *optional; String*
  A directory specification, including wildcard characters

Return Value

An array of strings, each element of which is the name of a subdirectory

Description

Returns the names of the subdirectories in a particular directory

Rules at a Glance

- *path* can be either an absolute path (a complete path from the root directory to the directory whose subdirectories are to be retrieved) or a relative path (starting from the current directory to the directory whose subdirectories are to be retrieved).

- *path* can be either a path on the local system, the path of a mapped network drive, or a UNC path.

- *path* cannot contain wildcard characters.

- If *searchpattern* is specified, the method returns only those directories whose names match the string, which can contain wildcard characters. Otherwise, *searchpattern* returns the names of all the subdirectories in the target directory specified by *path*.

- If the directory specified by *path* has no subdirectories, or if no directories match *searchpattern*, an empty array is returned.

Example

The following code displays all subdirectories of *c:* whose names start with the letter P:

```
Dim sDirs() As String
Dim i As Integer
sDirs = Directory.GetDirectories("c:\", "P*")
For i = 0 To UBound(sDirs)
    Console.WriteLine(sDirs(i))
Next
```

Programming Tips and Gotchas

Since GetDirectories can return an empty array, you can prevent an array access error in either of two ways: you can iterate the returned array using the For Each...Next construct, or you can retrieve the value of the *UBound* function, which is −1 in the case of an uninitialized array.

See Also

Directory.GetFiles Method, Directory.GetFileSystemEntries Method

---

Directory.GetDirectoryRoot Method

Class

System.IO.Directory

Syntax

```
Directory.GetDirectoryRoot(path)
```

path   *required; String*
    A valid path to a directory

Return Value

A String containing the name of the root directory of **path**

Description

Returns the name of the root directory of the drive on which **path** resides (assuming that **path** is valid). For example, the code:

```
Directory.GetDirectoryRoot("c:\program files\accessories")
```

returns the string C:\ as the root directory.

Rules at a Glance

- **path** can be either an absolute path (a complete path from the root directory to the target directory) or a relative path (starting from the current directory to the target directory).

- **path** can be either a path on the local system, the path of a mapped network drive, or a UNC path. For example, the code:

```
Directory.GetDirectoryRoot("\\Pentium\C\AFolder")
```

returns \\Pentium\C, and if the folder *Pentium\C\AFolder* maps to the network drive Z, then:

```
Directory.GetDirectoryRoot("Z:\temp")
```

returns Z:\.

- *path* cannot contain wildcard characters.

See Also

Directory.GetParent Method

Directory.GetFiles Method

Class

System.IO.Directory

Syntax

```
Directory.GetFiles(path [, searchpattern])
```

path   *required; String*
   A valid path to a directory

searchpattern   *optional; String*
   A file specification, including the wildcard characters * and ?

Return Value

An array of strings, each element of which contains the name of a file

Description

Returns the names of the files in a specified directory

Rules at a Glance

- *path* can be either an absolute path (a complete path from the root directory to the directory whose filenames are to be retrieved) or a relative path (starting from the current directory to the directory whose filenames are to be retrieved).
- *path* can be either a path on the local system, the path of a mapped network drive, or a UNC path.
- *path* cannot contain wildcard characters.
- If *searchpattern* is specified, the method returns only those files whose names match the string, which can contain wildcard characters. Otherwise, the function returns the names of all the files in the *path* directory.
- If the directory specified by *path* has no files, or if no files match *searchpattern*, an empty array is returned.

Example

The following code displays all files in *c:* that have the extension .txt:

```
Dim sFiles() As String
Dim i As Integer
```

```
sFiles = Directory.GetFiles("c:\", "*.txt")
For i = 0 To UBound(sFiles)
    Console.WriteLine(sFiles(i))
Next
```

Programming Tips and Gotchas

Since GetFiles can return an empty array, you can prevent an array-access error in either of two ways: you can iterate the returned array using the For Each... Next construct, or you can retrieve the value of the *UBound* function, which is −1 in the case of an uninitialized array.

See Also

Directory.GetDirectories Method, Directory.GetFileSystemEntries Method

Directory.GetFileSystemEntries Method

Class

System.IO.Directory

Syntax

```
Directory.GetFileSystemEntries(path [, searchpattern])
```

path   *required; String*
    A valid path to a directory

searchpattern   *optional; String*
    A file specification, including wildcard characters

Return Value

An array of strings, each element of which contains the name of a filesystem entry (that is, a file or directory) in the **path** directory

Description

Returns the names of the filesystem entries (that is, of files and directories) in a specified directory

Rules at a Glance

- **path** can be either an absolute path (a complete path from the root directory to the directory whose entries are to be retrieved) or a relative path (starting from the current directory to the directory whose entries are to be retrieved).

- **path** can be either a path on the local system, the path of a mapped network drive, or a UNC path.

- **path** cannot contain wildcard characters.

- If **searchpattern** is specified, the method returns only those filesystem entries whose names match the string, which can contain wildcard characters. Otherwise, the function returns the names of all the filesystem entries in the target directory specified by **path**.

- If the directory specified by *path* has no filesystem entries, or if no filesystem entries match *searchpattern*, an empty array is returned.

Example

The following code displays all filesystem entries in *c:*:

```
Dim sEntries() As String
Dim i As Integer
sEntries = Directory.GetFileSystemEntries("c:\")
For i = 0 To UBound(sEntries)
    Console.WriteLine(sEntries (i))
Next
```

Programming Tips and Gotchas

- The GetFileSystemEntries method combines the functionality of the Get-Directories and GetFiles methods.
- Since GetFileSystemEntries can return an empty array, you can prevent an array-access error in either of two ways: you can iterate the returned array using the For Each...Next construct, or you can retrieve the value of the *UBound* function, which is –1 in the case of an uninitialized array.

See Also

Directory.GetDirectories Method, Directory.GetFiles Method

Directory.GetLogicalDrives Method

Class

System.IO.Directory

Syntax

```
Directory.GetLogicalDrives()
```

Return Value

An array of strings, each element of which contains the name of the root directory on each logical drive on a system

Description

Retrieves the names of all logical drives and root directories on a system

Rules at a Glance

In the case of a mapped network drive, GetLogicalDrives returns the letter to which the drive is mapped. For instance, if the folder *\\Pentium\C\AFolder* is mapped to the Z drive, then GetLogicalDrives will return Z:\ for this logical drive.

Example

```
Dim sDrives() As String
Dim i As Integer
sDrives = Directory.GetLogicalDrives()
```

```
For i = 0 To UBound(sDrives)
    Console.WriteLine(sDrives(i))
Next
```

On my system, this code displays the following:

```
A:\
C:\
D:\
E:\
F:\
G:\
```

Directory.GetParent Method

Class

System.IO.Directory

Syntax

```
GetParent(path)
```

path   *required; String*
    A valid path to a directory

Return Value

A DirectoryInfo object representing the parent directory of *path* (assuming that *path* is valid).

Rules at a Glance

- *path* can be either an absolute path (a complete path from the root directory to the directory whose filenames are to be retrieved) or a relative path (starting from the current directory to the directory whose filenames are to be retrieved).

- *path* can be either a path on the local system, the path of a mapped network drive, or a UNC path.

- *path* cannot contain wildcard characters.

Programming Tips and Gotchas

The DirectoryInfo object has properties Name and ToString (among others). The Name property returns only the name of the directory, while the ToString property returns its absolute path. Thus, the following code displays the string program files:

```
MsgBox(Directory.GetParent("c:\program files\accessories").Name)
```

whereas the following code displays the string c:\program files:

```
MsgBox(Directory.GetParent("c:\program files\accessories").ToString)
```

See Also

Directory.GetDirectoryRoot Method

Directory.Move Method

Class

System.IO.Directory

Syntax

```
Directory.Move(sourcedirname, destdirname)
```

sourcedirname   *required; String*
> The name of the directory to be moved

destdirname   *required; String*
> The location to which the source drive and its contents are to be moved

Return Value

None

Description

Moves a directory and all its contents, including nested subdirectories and their files, to a new location

Rules at a Glance

- *sourcedirname* can be either an absolute path (a fully qualified path from the root directory to the directory to be moved) or a relative path (starting from the current directory to the directory to be moved).

- *sourcedirname* and *destdirname* can be either a path on the local system, the path of a mapped network drive, or a UNC path.

- Neither *sourcedirname* nor *destdirname* can contain wildcard characters.

- *destdirname* must be either a fully qualified path or a relative path.

- *destdirname* can also be an absolute path or a relative path, except that it must include the name to be assigned to the moved directory. This allows you to rename the directory at the same time as you move it.

- If the directory indicated by *destdirname* already exists, an error occurs.

Example

Suppose that the C drive contains the following folders:

```
c:\docs\letters
c:\Documents and Settings
```

Moving the *letters* folder to make it a subdirectory of *c:\Documents and Settings* is done by the following code:

```
Directory.Move("c:\docs\letters", _
               "c:\Documents and Settings\letters")
```

Thus, the first argument is the fully qualified name of the folder to move. The second argument is the path that results *after the move is made*, whereas one might have expected this argument to be the target folder for letters, which is *c:\Documents and Settings*.

Do...Loop Statement

Syntax

```
Do [{While | Until} condition]
   [statements]
[Exit Do]
   [statements]
Loop
```

or:

```
Do
   [statements]
[Exit Do]
   [statements]
Loop [{While | Until} condition]
```

`condition`   *optional; Boolean expression*

An expression that evaluates to **True** or **False**

`statements`   *optional*

Program statements that are repeatedly executed while, or until, `condition` is **True**

Description

Repeatedly executes a block of code while or until a condition becomes **True**

Rules at a Glance

- On its own, Do...Loop infinitely executes the code that is contained within its boundaries. You therefore need to specify within the code under what conditions the loop is to stop repeating. In addition, if the loop executes more than once, the variable controlling loop execution must be modified inside of the loop. For example:

  ```
  Do
      intCtr = intCtr + 1    ' Modify loop control variable
      MsgBox("Iteration " & intCtr & " of the Do loop...")
      ' Compare to upper limit
      If intCtr = 10  Then Exit Sub
  Loop
  ```

  Failure to do this results in the creation of an endless loop.

- Adding the Until keyword after Do instructs your program to Do something Until the condition is **True**. Its syntax is:

  ```
  Do Until condition
      'code to execute
  Loop
  ```

  If `condition` is **True** before your code gets to the Do statement, the code within the Do...Loop is ignored.

- Adding the While keyword after Do repeats the code while a particular condition is True. When the condition becomes False, the loop is automatically exited. The syntax of the Do While statement is:

```
Do While condition
  'code to execute
Loop
```

Again, the code within the Do...Loop construct is ignored if *condition* is False when the program arrives at the loop.

- In some cases, you may need to execute the loop at least once. You might, for example, evaluate the values held within an array and terminate the loop if a particular value is found. In that case, you would need to execute the loop at least once. To accomplish this, you can place the Until or the While keyword along with the condition *after* the Loop statement. Do...Loop Until always executes the code in the loop at least once, and continues to loop until the condition is True. Likewise, Do...Loop While always executes the code at least once, and continues to loop while the condition is True. The syntax of these two statements is as follows:

```
Do
  'code to execute
Loop Until condition
```

```
Do
  'code to execute
Loop While condition
```

- A Null *condition* is treated as False.
- Your code can exit the loop at any point by executing the Exit Do statement.

Programming Tips and Gotchas

You'll also encounter situations in which you intend to execute the loop continually while or until a condition is True, except in a particular case. This type of exception is handled using the Exit Do statement. You can place as many Exit Do statements within a Do...Loop structure as you require. As with any exit from a Do...Loop, whether it is exceptional or normal, the program continues execution on the line directly following the Loop statement. The following code fragment illustrates the use of Exit Do:

```
Do Until condition1
  'code to execute
  If condition2 Then
    Exit Do
  End if
  'more code to execute - only if condition2 is false
Loop
```

See Also

While...End While Statement

E Field

Class

System.Math

Syntax

```
Math.E
```

Description

This field returns the approximate value of the irrational number e, which is the base of the natural logarithm and the base of the natural exponential function. In particular:

```
Math.E = 2.71828182845905
```

Rules at a Glance

This is a Shared member, so it can be used without creating any objects.

VB.NET/VB 6 Differences

The E Field is new to VB.NET.

See Also

Pi Field

End... Statement

Syntax

```
End
End Class
End Enum
End Function
End Get
End If
End Interface
End Module
End Namespace
End Property
End Select
End Set
End Structure
End Sub
End SyncLock
End Try
End With
End While
```

Description

Ends a procedure or a block of code

Rules at a Glance

The End statement is used as follows:

Statement	Description
End	Terminates program execution
End Class	Marks the end of a class definition
End Enum	Marks the end of a series of enumerated constants
End Function	Marks the end of a Function procedure
End Get	Marks the end of a Property Get definition
End If	Marks the end of an If...Then...Else statement
End Interface	Marks the end of an interface definition
End Module	Marks the end of a code module
End Namespace	Markes the end of a namespace definition
End Property	Marks the end of a Property Let, PropertyGet, or Property Set procedure
End Select	Marks the end of a Select Case statement
End Set	Marks the end of a Property Set definition
End Structure	Ends the definition of a structure or user-defined type
End Sub	Marks the end of a Sub procedure
End SyncLock	Terminates synchronization code
End Try	Marks the end of a Try...Catch statement
End With	Marks the end of a With statement
End While	Marks the end of a While statement

Programming Tips and Gotchas

When used alone, the End statement wraps calls to the private FileSystem.Close-AllFiles function, as well as to the System.Environment object's Exit method, making it relatively safe to call to terminate an application. However, it does not release resources not automatically handled by the garbage collector, and does not automatically call the Finalize destructor.

VB.NET/VB 6 Differences

- In VB 6, the End statement used by itself was to be avoided, since it terminated program execution abruptly without performing normal cleanup operations. In VB.NET, End is much safer, and is not to be avoided.

- A number of the End... statements are new to VB.NET. These include End Class (classes are defined in separate CLS files in VB 6), End Get (Property Get statements are terminated with an End Property statement in VB 6), End Interface (interfaces are implemented as virtual base classes in VB 6), End Module (code modules are defined in separate BAS files in VB 6), End Namespace (namespaces do not exist in VB 6), End Set (Property Set and Property Let statements are terminated with an End Property statement in VB 6), End Try (VB 6 does not support structured exception handling), and End While (VB 6 supports the Wend statement to terminate a While loop).

Enum Statement

Syntax

```
accessmodifier Enum name [As type]
    membername [= constantexpression]
    membername [= constantexpression]
    . . .
End Enum
```

accessmodifier   *optional; Keyword*
> The possible values of *accessmodifier* are Public, Private, Friend, Protected, or Protected Friend. For more information, see the section entitled Accessibility in Class Modules," in Chapter 4.

name   *required; String literal*
> The name of the enumerated data type.

membername   *required; String literal*
> The name of a member of the enumerated data type.

constantexpression   *optional; Long*
> The value to be assigned to *membername*.

type   *optional; Keyword*
> The data type of the enumeration. All enumerated members must be integers; possible values are Byte, Short, Integer, and Long.

Description

Defines an enumerated data type. All of the values of the data type are defined by the instances of *membername*.

Rules at a Glance

- The Enum statement can only appear at module level, in the declarations section of a form, code module, or class module.

- Access rules for Enums are the same as for variables and constants. In particular, the optional *accessmodifier* can be any one of the following: Public, Private, Protected, Friend, or Protected Friend. The following table describes the effects of the various access modifiers:

	Direct access scope	*Class/object access scope*
Private	Declaring class	Declaring class
Protected	All derived classes	Declaring class
Friend	Derived in-project classes	Declaring project
Protected Friend	All derived classes	Declaring project
Public	All derived classes	All projects

- *constantexpression* can be either a negative or a positive number. It can also be another member of an enumerated data type or an expression that includes integers and enumerated data types.

- If you assign a floating point value to *constantexpression*, it is automatically rounded and converted to an integer only if Option Strict is off; otherwise, it generates a compiler error.

- If you do not specify *type*, it defaults to Integer.

- If *constantexpression* is omitted, the value assigned to *membername* is 0 if it is the first expression in the enumeration. Otherwise, its value is 1 greater than the value of the preceding *membername*.

- The values assigned to *membername* cannot be modified at runtime.

Programming Tips and Gotchas

- Once you define an enumerated type, you can use *name* as the return value of a function. For example, given the enumeration:

```
Public Enum enQuarter
    enQ1 = 1
    enQ2 = 2
    enQ3 = 3
    enQ4 = 4
End Enum
```

you can use it as the return value of a function, as illustrated by the following function declaration:

```
Public Function QuarterFromDate(datVar as Date) _
        As enQuarter
```

You can also use it in a procedure's parameter list when defining a parameter's data type, as in the following code fragment:

```
Public Function GetQuarterlySales(intQ As enQuarter) _
        As Double
```

- Although you can declare an enumerated type as the argument to a procedure or the return value of a function, VB.NET does not provide type safety in these cases. That is, if the value of the argument or the return value of the function is outside of the range of the enumerated type, VB.NET does not generate an error. In cases such as these, you should rely on validation routines to make sure that an input value is in fact within the range of an enumerated type.

- Individual values of an enumerated type can be used in your program just like normal constants, except that they must be prefaced with the name of the enumeration.

- Enumerated types provide the advantage of allowing you to replace numeric values with more mnemonic labels and of allowing you to select values using the Auto List Members feature in the Visual Studio IDE.

- If you want to retrieve or display the name of an enumerated member rather than its value, you can use the member's ToString method. For example:

```
Public Module modMain

Public Enum WorkDayTypes
    Weekday = 0
    Weekend = 1
    Holiday = 2
    Floating = 3
    Personal = 4
    Vacation = 5
End Enum

Public Sub Main
    Dim enDay As WorkDayTypes = WorkDayTypes.Vacation
    Console.WriteLine(enDay.ToString())    ' Displays
                                           '"Vacation"
End Sub

End Module
```

VB.NET/VB 6 Differences

- In VB 6, members of an enumeration can be accessed without having to qualify them with the name of the enumeration to which they belong. In VB.NET, this behavior is not permitted; all members of an enumeration can only be accessed by referring to the name of their enumeration.

- In VB 6, all enumerated members are Longs. In contrast, VB.NET allows you to define the integer data type of the enumeration's members.

- In VB 6, members of a public enumeration can be hidden from the Object Browser by adding a leading underscore to the member name. For example, in the enumeration:

```
Public Enum Primes
    [_x0] = 0
    x1 = 1
    x2 = 3
End Enum
```

the constant _x0 is hidden in Intellisense and the Object Browser unless the Object Browser's Show Hidden Members option is selected. In Visual Studio .NET, a leading underscore does not hide a member.

See Also

Const Statement

Environ Function

Class

Microsoft.VisualBasic.Interaction

Syntax

```
Environ(expression)
```

expression   *required; String, or a numeric expression*

> If *expression* is a string, it must be the name of the required environment variable; if *expression* is numeric, it must be the 1-based ordinal number of the environment variable within the environment table.

Return Value

A String containing the text assigned to *expression*

Description

Returns the value assigned to an operating-system environment variable

Rules at a Glance

- A zero-length string ("") is returned if *expression* does not exist in the operating system's environment-string table or if there is no environment string in the position specified by *expression*.

- *expression* can be either a string or a numeric expression; that is, you can specify one or the other, but not both.

Example

```
Public Module modMain

Public Structure env
    Dim strVarName As String
    Dim strValue As String
End Structure

Public Sub Main()

Dim intCtr, intPos As Integer
Dim strRetVal As String
Dim udtEnv As env

intCtr = 1
Do
    strRetVal = Environ(intCtr)
    If strRetVal <> "" Then
        intPos = InStr(1, strRetVal, "=")
        udtEnv.strVarName = Left(strRetVal, intPos - 1)
        udtEnv.strValue = Mid(strRetVal, intPos + 1)
        Console.Writeline(udtEnv.strVarName & ": " & udtEnv.strValue)
    Else
        Exit Do
    End If
    intCtr = intCtr + 1
Loop

End Sub
End Module
```

Programming Tips and Gotchas

- If *expression* is numeric, both the name and the value of the variable are returned. An equal sign (=) is used to separate them. For example, the function call *Environ(1)* might return the string TEMP=C:\WINDOWS\TEMP.

- If you retrieve environment variables and their values by ordinal position, the first variable is in position 1, not position 0.

- Due to the flexibility offered, it is now accepted and recommended practice to use the registry for variables needed by your application, rather than the environment-string table.

- Environment variables can be defined in a variety of ways, including by the *AUTOEXEC.BAT* and *MSDOS.SYS* files, as well as by the HKEY_LOCAL_MACHINE\System\CurrentControlSet\Control\SessionManager\Environment and HKEY_CURRENT_USER\Environment keys in the registry.

VB.NET/VB 6 Differences

- In VB 6, the *Environ* function retrieved environmental variables and their values only from the environment-string table. In VB.NET, the function retrieves values both from the environment-string table and the system registry.

- In VB 6, the function could be called using either the *envstring* named argument (if the argument was the name of an environment variable) or the *number* named argument (if the number represented the ordinal position of the variable in the environment table). VB.NET replaces these with a single named argument, *expression*.

EOF Function

Class

Microsoft.VisualBasic.FileSystem

Syntax

EOF(*filenumber*)

filenumber   *required; Integer*
    Any valid file number

Return Value

A Boolean indicating when the end of the file has been reached

Description

Returns a Boolean indicating when the end of the file has been reached. Applies to files opened for binary, random, or sequential input.

Rules at a Glance

- *filenumber* must be an Integer that specifies a valid file number.

- If a file is opened for binary access, you cannot use *EOF* with the Input procedure. Instead, use *LOF* and *Loc*. If you want to use *EOF*, you must use

---

FileGet rather than Input. In this case, *EOF* returns `False` until the previous *FileGet* procedure is unable to read an entire record.

Example

```
Dim fr As Integer = FreeFile()
Dim sLine As String
FileOpen(fr, "c:\data.txt", OpenMode.Input, OpenAccess.Read, _
        OpenShare.Default, -1)
Do While Not EOF(fr)
   sLine = LineInput(fr)
   Console.WriteLine(sLine)
Loop
```

Programming Tips and Gotchas

- *EOF* allows you to test whether the end of a file has been reached without generating an error.

- Because you always write data to sequential files at the end of the file, the file marker is always at the end of the file, and *EOF* will therefore always return True when testing files opened with their modes set equal to either Input or Append.

See Also

LOF Function

Erase Statement

Syntax

```
Erase arraylist
```

arraylist   *required; String literal*
   A list of array variables to clear

Description

Releases an array object. This is equivalent to setting the array variable to Nothing.

Rules at a Glance

- Specify more than one array to be erased by using commas to delimit *arraylist*.

- The Erase statement causes all memory allocated to arrays to be released.

Programming Tips and Gotchas

Once you use Erase to clear an array, it must be redimensioned with ReDim before being used again. This is because Erase releases the memory storage used by the array.

See Also

Dim Statement, ReDim Statement

Erl Property

Class

Microsoft.VisualBasic.Information

Syntax

```
Erl
```

Return Value

An Integer containing the line number

Description

Indicates the line number on which an error occurred

Rules at a Glance

- *Erl* returns the line number only if one has been provided in the source code.
- If the error occurs on a line that does not have a line number, *Erl* returns 0.

Programming Tips and Gotchas

- *Erl* is not affected by compiler settings. Compiling with the /debug- switch does not prevent *Erl* from accurately reporting the line number.
- Line numbers are rarely used in modern VB code. In VB.NET, line numbers are labels that must be followed by a colon.
- Although programmers have been requesting an error-handling function that reports the line number on which an error occurred, *Erl* has one major limitation: namely, it requires that the developer assign a line number to source code lines in advance.
- *Erl* is not new to VB.NET. It was an undocumented and little known function in previous versions of Visual Basic (and of QBasic as well).

VB.NET/VB 6 Differences

In VB 6, line numbers are distinct from labels, and do not require that any symbol (other than white space) separate them from their lines' source code. In VB.NET, line numbers are labels that must be followed by a colon.

Err Object

Class

Microsoft.VisualBasic.ErrObject

Createable

No

Description

The Err object contains properties and methods that allow you to obtain information about a single runtime error in a Visual Basic program. The Err object also lets you generate errors and reset the error object. Because the Err object is an intrinsic object with global scope (which means that it is part of every VB project you create), you do not need to create an instance of it within your code.

When an error is generated in your application—whether it is handled or not—the properties of the Err object are assigned values that you can then access to gain information about the error that occurred. You can even generate your own errors explicitly using the Err.Raise method. You can also define your own errors to unify the error-handling process.

When your program reaches an **Exit Function**, **Exit Sub**, **Exit Property**, **Resume**, or **On Error** statement, the Err object is cleared and its properties reinitialized. This can also be done explicitly using the Err.Clear method.

Public Instance Properties

Property name	Description
Description	The string associated with the given error number
HelpContext	A context ID within a Visual Basic Help file
HelpFile	The path to a Visual Basic Help file
LastDLLError	The last error code generated by a DLL; available only on 32-bit Windows systems
Number	A long integer used to describe an error (i.e., an error code)
Source	Either the name of the current project or the class name of the application that generated the error

Public Instance Methods

Method name	Description
Clear	Resets all the properties of the Err object
Raise	Forces an error of a given number to be generated

Programming Tips and Gotchas

- The Visual Basic Err object is not a collection; it contains information about the last error only, if one occurred. You could, however, implement your own error collection class to store a number of errors by copying error information from the Err object into an application-defined error collection object.

- An Err object cannot be passed back from a class module to a standard code module.

- VB also supports structured error-handling through the **Try...Catch... Finally** statement.

- For a full description of error handling, see Chapter 9.

Err.Description Property, Err.HelpContext Property, Err.HelpFile Property, Err. Number Property, Err.Source Property

---

Err.Clear Method

Class

Microsoft.VisualBasic.ErrObject

Syntax

```
Err.Clear()
```

Description

Explicitly resets all the properties of the Err object after an error has been handled

Rules at a Glance

You need to clear the Err object only if you need to reference its properties for another error within the same subroutine, or before another On Error statement within the same subroutine.

Example

```
On Error Resume Next

i = oObjectOne.MyFunction(iVar)

If Err.Number <> 0 Then
    MsgBox ("The Error : " & Err.Description & vbCrLf _
        & " was generated in " & Err.Source)
    Err.Clear
End If

j = oObjectTwo.YourFunction(iVar)

If Err.Number <> 0 Then
    MsgBox ("The Error : " & Err.Description & vbCrLf _
        & " was generated in " & Err.Source)
    Err.Clear
End If
```

Programming Tips and Gotchas

- Resetting the Err object explicitly using the Clear method is necessary in situations where you are using On Error Resume Next and are testing the value of Err.Number repeatedly. Unless you reset the Err object, you run the very real risk of catching the previously handled error, the details of which are still lurking in the Err object's properties.

- The Err object is automatically reset when either a Resume, Exit Sub, Exit Function, Exit Property, or On Error statement is executed.

- You can achieve the same results by setting the Err.Number property to 0; however, your code will be more readable if you use the Clear method.

- VB also supports structured error-handling through the `Try...Catch... Finally` statement.

- Internally, in VB.NET the Err object is an instance of the Microsoft.VisualBasic. ErrObject class. It is returned by the Err property of the Microsoft.VisualBasic. Information class.

See Also

Err.Raise Method

Err.Description Property

Class

Microsoft.VisualBasic.ErrObject

Syntax

To set the property:

```
Err.Description = string
```

To return the property value:

```
string = Err.Description
```

string   *required; String*
   Any string expression

Description

A read/write property containing a short string describing a runtime error

Rules at a Glance

- When a runtime error occurs, the Description property is automatically assigned the standard description of the error.

- For application-defined errors, you must assign a string expression to the Description property, or the error will not have an accompanying textual message.

- You can override the standard description by assigning your own description to the Err object for both VB errors and application-defined errors.

Programming Tips and Gotchas

- If an error occurs within a class module, an ActiveX DLL, or an EXE—regardless of whether it is running in or out of your application's process space—no error information from the component will be available to your application unless you explicitly pass back an error code as part of the error-handling routine within the component. This is done using the Err.Raise method, which allows you to raise an error on the client, passing custom arguments for Number, Source, and Description.

- If you raise an error with the Err.Raise method and do not set the Description property, the Description property will be automatically set to "Application-efined or Object-Defined Error."

- You can also pass the Err.Description to a logging device, such as a log file in Windows 95 or the application log in Windows NT, by using the App. LogEvent method, as the following code fragment demonstrates:

```
EmployeesAdd_Err:
App.LogEvent "EmployeesAdd" & "; " & _
            Err.Description, vbLogEventTypeError
```

- The best way to set the Description property for your own application-defined errors is to use the named-description argument with the Raise method, as the following code shows:

```
Sub TestErr()

On Error GoTo TestErr_Err

    Err.Raise 65444, _
            Description="Meaningful Error Description"

TestErr Exit:
    Exit Sub

TestErr_Err:
    MsgBox (Err.Description)
    Resume TestErr_Exit

End Sub
```

- VB also supports structured error-handling through the `Try...Catch... Finally` statement.

See Also

Err.HelpContext Property, Err.HelpFile Property, Err.Number Property, Err.Source Property

---

Err.GetException Method

Class

Microsoft.VisualBasic.ErrObject

Syntax

```
Err.GetException()
```

Return Value

A System.Exception object or an object inherited from it containing the current exception

Description

Returns the Exception object associated with the current exception

Rules at a Glance

- The GetException method can be called at any time in a program.
- If there is no exception, the method returns an uninitialized exception object (i.e., an object whose value is Nothing).

Example

The following code renames a file:

```
Private Sub RenameFile()
Dim sOldName, sNewName As String
Try
    sOldName = InputBox("Enter the file name to rename")
    sNewName = InputBox("Enter the new file name")
    Rename("c:\" & sOldName, "c:\" & sNewName)
Catch ex As Exception
    MsgBox(Err.GetException().ToString)
    Exit Sub
End Try
End Sub
```

If the user inputs an invalid filename in the first input box, the result is the following message that displays information about the error:

```
System.IO.FileNotFoundException: File not found at
Microsoft.VisualBasic.FileSystem.Rename(String OldPath, String NewPath)
at WindowsApplication2.Form1.RenameFile() in
C:\Documents and Settings\sr\My Documents\Visual Studio Projects\
ClipboardSave2\WindowsApplication2\Form1.vb:line 59
```

Programming Tips and Gotchas

- The Err.GetException method can be used with the unstructured On Error Resume Next statement as well as with the Try...Catch...End Try structure.
- Since GetException is a member of the Err object, its major application is to provide access to error information stored to an instance of the Exception class from code that relies on unstructured exception handling.

VB.NET/VB6 Differences

The GetException method is new to VB.NET.

See Also

Exception Class

Err.HelpContext Property

Class

Microsoft.VisualBasic.ErrObject

Syntax

```
Err.HelpContext
```

Description

A read/write property that either sets or returns an Integer value containing the context ID of the appropriate topic within a Help file.

Rules at a Glance

- The Err object sets the HelpContext property automatically when an error is raised if Err.Number is a standard VB.NET error.

- If the error is user-defined and you don't explicitly set the HelpContext property yourself, the Err object will set the value to 1000095, which corresponds to the "Application-defined or object-defined error" help topic in the VB Help file. (The HelpContext property is set by the fifth parameter to the Err.Raise method.)

- HelpContext IDs are decided upon when writing and creating a Windows Help file. Once the Help file has been compiled, the IDs cannot be changed. Each ID points to a separate Help topic.

Example

```
Sub TestErr()

On Error GoTo TestErr_Err

    Dim i
    i = 8

    MsgBox(i / 0)

TestErr_Exit:
    Exit Sub

TestErr_Err:
    MsgBox(Err.Description, vbMsgBoxHelpButton, "ErrorVille", _
        Err.HelpFile, Err.HelpContext)
    Resume TestErr_Exit

End Sub
```

Programming Tips and Gotchas

- You can display a topic from the Visual Basic Help file by using the *MsgBox* function with the **vbMsgBoxHelpButton** constant and passing **Err.HelpContext** as the **HelpContext** argument (as shown in the previous example). While this is a simple and very effective way to add much more functionality to your applications, bear in mind that some of your users could find the explanations within the VB Help file somewhat confusing. If time and budget allow, the best method is to create your own help file (for which you will need the Help compiler and other Help file resources from the full version of VB) and to pass both the HelpContext and HelpFileName to *MsgBox*.

- Some objects that you may use within your application have their own help files, which you can access using HelpContext to display highly focused help to your users.

See Also

Err.HelpFile Property, Err.Number Property, Err.Source Property

---

Err.HelpFile Property

Class

Microsoft.VisualBasic.ErrObject

Syntax

```
Err.HelpFile
```

Description

A read/write String property that contains the fully qualified path of a Windows Help file.

Rules at a Glance

The HelpFile property is automatically set by the Err object when an error is raised.

Example

See Err.HelpContext.

Programming Tips and Gotchas

- You can display a topic from the Visual Basic Help file by using the *MsgBox* function with the vbMsgBoxHelpButton constant and passing Err.HelpFile as the HelpFile argument (as shown in the example for the Err.HelpContext property). While this is a simple and very effective way to add more functionality to your applications, bear in mind that some of your users could find the explanations within the VB Help file somewhat confusing. If time and budget allow, the best method is to create your own help file (for which you will need the Help compiler and other Help file resources from the full version of VB) and to pass both the HelpContext and HelpFileName to *MsgBox*.

- Some objects that you may use within your application have their own help files, which you can access using HelpFile to display highly focused help to your users.

- Remember that once the program encounters an Exit... statement or an On Error statement, all the properties of the Err object are reset; this includes the Help file. You must therefore set the Err.HelpFile property each time that your application needs to access the help file.

See Also

Err.HelpContext Property, Err.Number Property

Err.LastDLLError Property

Class

Microsoft.VisualBasic.ErrObject

Syntax

```
Err.LastDLLError
```

Description

A read-only property containing a system error code representing a system error produced within a DLL called from a VB program.

Rules at a Glance

- Only direct calls to a Windows system DLL from VB code will assign a value to LastDLLError.

- The value of the LastDLLError property depends upon the particular DLL being called. Your code must be able to handle the various codes that can be returned by the DLL you are calling.

- Don't forget that a failed DLL call does not itself raise an error within your VB program. As a result, the Err object's Number, Description, and Source properties are not filled.

Programming Tips and Gotchas

- The LastDLLError property can be changed by VB at any time, so it is important to save the value in an independent variable as soon as possible.

- The LastDLLError property is only used by system DLLs, such as *kernel32.dll*. Therefore, errors that occur within DLLs you may have created will not cause an error code to be assigned to the property.

- Obtaining accurate documentation about the return values of system DLLs can be a challenging experience! Most useful information can be found by studying the API documentation for Visual C++. However, you can use the Win32 API *FormatMessage* function to return the actual Windows error message string from within *Kernel32.DLL*, which incidentally will also be in the correct language. The following is a brief example that you can use in your applications to display the actual Windows error description:

```
Module modMain

Declare Function FormatMessage Lib "kernel32" _
        Alias "FormatMessageA" ( _
        ByVal dwFlags as Integer, ByRef lpSource As Integer, _
        ByVal dwMessageId As Integer, _
        ByVal dwLanguageId As Integer, _
        ByVal lpBuffer As String, ByVal nSize As Integer, _
        By Ref Arguments As Integer) As Integer

Public Const FORMAT_MESSAGE_FROM_SYSTEM As Integer = &H1000
Public Const FORMAT_MESSAGE_IGNORE_INSERTS As Integer = &H200
```

```
Function apiErrDesc (iErrCode As Integer) As String
    Dim sErrDesc As String = Space(256)
    Dim iReturnLen, lpNotUsed As Integer

    iReturnLen = FormatMessage(FORMAT_MESSAGE_FROM_SYSTEM _
                 Or FORMAT_MESSAGE_IGNORE_INSERTS, _
                 lpNotUsed, iErrCode, 0&, sErrDesc, _
                 Len(sErrDesc), lpNotUsed)
    if iReturnLen > 0 Then
        apiErrDesc = Left(sErrDesc, iReturnLen)
    End If
End Function

End Module
```

Here's a snippet demonstrating how you can use this utility function:

```
lReturn = SomeAPICall(someparams)
If lReturn <> 0 then
    Err.Raise(Err.LastDLLError & vbObjectError, _
            "MyApp:Kernel32.DLL", _
                apiErrDesc(Err.LastDLLError))
End If
```

- Note that some API calls return 0 to denote a successful function call, and others return 0 to denote an unsuccessful call. You should also note that some API functions do not appear to set the LastDLLError property. In most cases, these are functions that return an error code. You could therefore modify the previous snippet to handle these cases:

```
lReturn = SomeAPICall(someparams)
If lReturn <> 0 then
    If Err.LastDLLError <> 0 Then
        Err.Raise(Err.LastDLLError & vbObjectError, _
                "MyApp:Kernel32.DLL", _
                apiErrDesc(Err.LastDLLError))
    Else
        Err.Raise(lReturn & vbObjectError, _
                "MyApp:Kernel32.DLL", _
                apiErrDesc(lReturn))
    End If
End If
```

See Also

Err Object

Err.Number Property

Class

Microsoft.VisualBasic.ErrObject

Syntax

```
Err.Number
```

Description

A read/write property containing a numeric value that represents the error code for the last error generated

Rules at a Glance

- When a runtime error is generated within the program, the error code is automatically assigned to Err.Number.

- The Number property is updated with an application-defined error whose code is passed as an argument to the Err.Raise method.

- When using the Err.Raise method in normal code, your user-defined error codes cannot be greater than 65536 nor less that 0. (For an explanation, see the final note in the "Programming Tips and Gotchas" section of the "Err.Raise Method" entry.)

- VB reserves error numbers in the range of 1–1000 for its own trappable errors. In addition, error numbers from 31001 to 31037 are also used for VB trappable errors. In implementing a series of application-defined errors, your error handlers should either translate application errors into VB trappable errors or, preferably, assign a unique range to application-defined errors.

- When using the Err.Raise method in ActiveX objects, add the **vbObjectError** constant (−2147221504) to your user-defined error code to distinguish OLE errors from local-application errors.

- When control returns to the local application after an error has been raised by the OLE server, the application can determine that the error originated in the OLE server and extract the error number with a line of code like the following:

```
Dim lError as Long
If (Err.Number And vbObjectError) > 0 Then
    lError = Err.Number - ObjectError
End If
```

Programming Tips and Gotchas

- An error code is a useful method of alerting your program that a function within an ActiveX or class object has failed. By returning a number based on the **vbObjectError** constant, you can easily determine that an error has occurred. (**vbObjectError** is a constant that is defined in the Microsoft. VisualBasic.Constants class.) By then subtracting **vbObjectError** from the value returned by the object's function, you can determine the actual error code:

```
If Err.Number < 0 then
    Err.Number = Err.Number - ObjectError
End If
```

- You can create a sophisticated multiresult error-handling routine by using the Err.Number property as the **Case** statement within a **Select Case** block, taking a different course of action for different errors, as this snippet demonstrates:

```
Select Case Err.Number
    Case < 0
```

```
            'OLE Object Error
            Set oObject = Nothing
            Resume DisplayErrorAndExit
        Case 5
            'increment the retry counter and try again
            iTries = iTries + 1
            If iTries < 5 Then
               Resume RetryFunctionCall
            Else
               Resume DisplayErrorAndExit
            End If
        Case 20
            'we almost expected this one!
            Resume Next
        Case Else
            Resume DisplayErrorAndExit
    End Select
```

- Directly assigning a Visual Basic–defined error code to the Number property does not automatically update the Description or other properties of the Err object.

See Also

Err.HelpContext Property, Err.HelpFile Property, Err.Source Property

---

Err.Raise Method

Class

Microsoft.VisualBasic.ErrObject

Syntax

```
Err.Raise(number, source, description, _
           helpfile, helpcontext)
```

number   *required; Long integer*
    A numeric identifier of the particular error

source   *optional; String*
    The name of the object or application responsible for generating the error

description   *optional; String*
    A useful description of the error

helpfile   *optional; String*
    The fully qualified path of a Microsoft Windows Help file containing help or reference material about the error

helpcontext   *optional; Long*
    The context ID within *helpfile*

Description

Generates a runtime error

Rules at a Glance

- To use the Err.Raise method, you must specify an error number.

- If you supply any of the *number, source, description, helpfile*, and *helpcontext* arguments when you call the Err.Raise method, they are supplied as values to the Number, Source, Description, HelpFile, and HelpContext properties, respectively. Refer to the entries for the individual properties for full descriptions of and rules for each property.

- The *number* argument is a Long integer that identifies the nature of the error. Visual Basic errors (both Visual Basic–defined and user-defined errors) are in the range 0–65535. The range 0–512 is reserved for system errors; the range 513–65535 is available for user-defined errors. When setting the Number property to your own error code in a class module, you add your error-code number to the **vbObjectError** constant.

Programming Tips and Gotchas

- The Err.Raise method replaces the older **Error** statement, which should not be used in new code.

- The Raise method does not reinitialize the Err object prior to assigning the values you pass in as arguments. This can mean that if you Raise an error against an Err object that has not been cleared since the last error, any properties for which you don't specify values will still contain the values from the last error.

- As well as using Raise in a runtime scenario, you can put it to good use in the development stages of your program to test the viability of your error-handling routines under various circumstances.

- The fact that Err.Number only accepts numbers in the range 0–65536 may appear to be strange at first because the data type of the Error Number parameter in the Raise event is a Long. However, deep in the recesses of the Err object, the error code must be declared as an unsigned integer—a data type not supported by VB.

See Also

Err.Clear Method

Err.Source Property

Class

Microsoft.VisualBasic.ErrObject

Syntax

```
Err.Source
```

Description

A read/write string property containing the name of the application or the object that has generated the error.

Rules at a Glance

- When a runtime error occurs in your code, the Source property is automatically assigned the project name (that is, the string that is assigned to the project's Name property). Note that this is not necessarily the filename of the project file.

- For clarity of your error messages, when you raise an error in a class module, the format of the source parameter should be *project.class*.

Programming Tips and Gotchas

Knowing what type of error has occurred within a program without knowing where the error was generated is often of little use to the programmer. However, if you enhance the standard Source by adding the name of the procedure, you can cut your debugging time dramatically.

See Also

Err.HelpContext Property, Err.HelpFile Property, Err.Number Property

---

Error Statement

Syntax

```
Error [errornumber]
```

errornumber   *optional; Long*
  Any valid error code

Description

Raises an error

Rules at a glance

The **Error** statement is included only for backward compatibility; instead, if you're using standard Visual Basic error handling, you should use the Err.Raise method and the **Err** object. Otherwise, you should use structured exception handling with the **Try...Catch** construct.

Programming Tips and Gotchas

The **Error** statement has been a "compatibility" statement for several versions of Visual Basic. Interestingly, it managed to survive the general purge of outdated language elements. Despite its persistence, we still recommend that its use be strictly avoided.

See Also

Err.Raise Method, Try...Catch...Finally Statement

ErrorToString Function

Class

Microsoft.VisualBasic.Conversion

Syntax

```
ErrorToString([errornumber])
```

errornumber   *optional; Long*
A numeric error code

Return Value

A String containing an error message

Description

Returns the error message or error description corresponding to a particular error code

Rules at a Glance

- If *errornumber* is present, the function returns the text of the error message corresponding to that error code.

- If no arguments are passed to the function, it returns the text of the error message corresponding to the Description property of the Err Object.

See Also

Err.Description Property

Event Statement

Syntax

```
[accessmodifier] [Shadows] Event eventName [(arglist)]
[Implements interfacename.interfaceeventname]
```

accessmodifier   *optional; Keyword*
Can be one of **Public**, **Private**, **Protected**, **Friend**, and **Protected Friend**

Shadows   *optional; Keyword*
Indicates that the event shadows any programming elements of the same name in a base class

eventName   *required; String literal*
The name of the event

arglist is optional and has the following syntax:

```
[ByVal | ByRef] varname[( )] [As type]
```

ByVal   *optional; Keyword*
The argument is passed by value; that is, a local copy of the variable is assigned the value of the argument.

ByRef   *optional; Keyword*
The argument is passed by reference; that is, the local variable is simply a reference to the argument being passed. All changes made to the local variable are reflected in the calling argument. **ByRef** is the default method of passing variables.

varname   *required; String literal*
>   The name of the local variable containing either the reference or value of
>   the argument.

type   *optional; Keyword*
>   The data type of the argument. It can be Byte, Boolean, Char, Short,
>   Integer, Long, Single, Double, Decimal, Date, String, Object, or any user-
>   defined type, object type, or data type defined in the BCL.

Implements *interfacename.interfaceeventname*   *optional*
>   Indicates that the event implements a particular event named *interface-*
>   *eventname* in the interface named *interfacename*.

Description

Defines a custom event that the object can raise at any time using the `RaiseEvent`
statement.

Rules at a Glance

- The event declaration must be `Public` so that it is visible outside the object
  module; it cannot be declared as `Friend` or `Private`. However, the `Public`
  keyword can be omitted from the declaration, since it is `Public` by default.

- An `Event` statement can only appear in the Declarations section of an object
  module, that is, in a form or class module.

Example

The following code snippet demonstrates how you can use an event to communicate a status message back to the client application. To take advantage of this
functionality, the client must declare a reference to this class using the `WithEvents`
keyword.

```
Public Event Status(Message As String)

Private Function UpdateRecords() as Boolean
...
    RaiseEvent Status("Opening the database...")
...
    RaiseEvent Status("Executing the query...")
...
    RaiseEvent Status("Records were updated...")
...
End Function
```

Programming Tips and Gotchas

- To allow the client application to handle the event being fired, the object variable must be declared using the `WithEvents` keyword.

- VB custom events do not return a value; however, you can use a `ByRef` argument in *arglist* to simulate a return value. For more details, see the `Raise-`
  `Event` statement.

- Unlike parameter lists used with other procedures, `Event` parameters lists
  cannot include `Optional` or `ParamArray` arguments or default values.

- If you use the **Event** statement in a standard interface class (i.e., a class in which only properties and methods are defined, but no code is included in the procedures) for use with the **Implements** statement, the **Implements** statement does not recognize the "outgoing interfaces" used by events, and therefore the event will be ignored.

- For more information about implementing your own custom events, see the Events and Event Binding" section in Chapter 7.

See Also

RaiseEvent Statement, Throw Statement

Exception Class

Namespace

System

Createable

Yes

Description

The Exception class and its inherited (child) classes represent runtime exceptions.

Selected Exception Class Members

The following provides a brief description of the more important members of the Exception class:

HelpFile property
> Sets or retrieves a link to the help file associated with the exception. Its value is a Uniform Resource Name (URN) or Uniform Resource Locator (URL).

InnerException property
> Returns a reference to the inner Exception object in the case of nested exceptions.

Message property
> Returns the text of the error message.

Source property
> Returns or sets a string containing the name of the application or the object that causes the error.

StackTrace property
> Returns a string (the stack trace) consisting of a list of all methods that are currently in the stack. The following shows a stack trace when the procedure *DoArithmetic* calls the procedure *Arithmetic*, which generates an exception that is thrown up to *DoArithmetic* (the string has been formatted to fit the margins of the page):

```
at WindowsApplication6.Form1.Arithmetic(String Action, Double x,
Double y) in C:\Projects\WindowsApplication6\Form1.vb:line 68
```

```
at WindowsApplication6.Form1.DoArithmetic() in
C:\Projects\WindowsApplication6\Form1.vb:line 87
```

TargetSite property

Returns a MethodBase object representing the method that throws the exception. For example, if e is the exception whose stack trace is shown in the discussion of the StackTrace property, then the code.

```
e.TargetSite.Name
```

will return the string Arithmetic.

GetBaseException Method

This method returns the exception object for the innermost exception. For instance, in the previous example (see the discussion of the StackTrace property) the code:

```
e.GetBaseException.ToString
```

returns the string:

```
System.ArithmeticException: There was an overflow or
underflow in the arithmetic operation.
    at WindowsApplication6.Form1.Arithmetic(String Action,
Double x, Double y) in
C:\Projects\WindowsApplication6\Form1.vb:line 68
    at WindowsApplication6.Form1.DoArithmetic() in
C:\Projects\WindowsApplication6\Form1.vb:line 87///
```

ToString Method

Returns the fully qualified name of the exception and possibly the error message, the name of the inner exception, and the stack trace.

Children of the Exception Class

The System namespace contains the Exception class, which is the base class for a substantial collection of derived exception classes, listed as follows. Note that the indentation indicates class inheritance. For example, EntryPointNotFoundException (the fifth from the last entry in the list) inherits from TypeLoadException.

```
Exception
    ApplicationException
    SystemException
        AccessException
            FieldAccessException
            MethodAccessException
            MissingMemberException
                MissingFieldException
                MissingMethodException
        AppDomainUnloadedException
        AppDomainUnloadInProgressException
        ArgumentException
            ArgumentNullException
            ArgumentOutOfRangeException
            DuplicateWaitObjectException
        ArithmeticException
            DivideByZeroException
```

NotFiniteNumberException
OverflowException
ArrayTypeMismatchException
BadImageFormatException
CannotUnloadAppDomainException
ContextMarshalException
CoreException
   ExecutionEngineException
   IndexOutOfRangeException
   StackOverflowException
ExecutionEngineException
FormatException
InvalidCastException
InvalidOperationException
MulticastNotSupportedException
NotImplementedException
NotSupportedException
   PlatformNotSupportedException
NullReferenceException
OutOfMemoryException
RankException
ServicedComponentException
TypeInitializationException
TypeLoadException
   EntryPointNotFoundException
TypeUnloadedException
UnauthorizedAccessException
WeakReferenceException
URIFormatException

Programming Tips and Gotchas

- As Microsoft states: "Most of the exception classes that inherit from Exception do not implement additional members or provide additional functionality." Thus, it is simply the class name that distinguishes one type of exception from another. The properties and methods applied to an exception object are inherited from the Exception base class.

- You can trap the generic Exception object, or you can trap a specific exception object. There are two circumstances in particular when you may want to trap a specific exception, rather than the more general Exception object:

  — You want to handle errors differently based on their class. For instance, you may want to issue different custom error messages for different exception types.

  — You want to take advantage of members of a particular exception class that are not implemented in the Exception base class. For instance, the ArgumentException class has a ParamName property that returns the name of the parameter that causes the exception. If you trap the Exception class rather than the ArgumentException class, this member is unavailable.

VB.NET/VB 6 Differences

The Exception class, along with Structured Exception Handling (SEH), is new to the .NET platform.

Exit Statement

Syntax

```
Exit Do
Exit For
Exit Function
Exit Property
Exit Select
Exit Sub
Exit Try
Exit While
```

Description

Prematurely exits a block of code

Rules at a Glance

Exit Do

Exits a Do...Loop statement. If the current Do...Loop is within a nested Do...Loop, execution continues with the next Loop statement wrapped around the current one. If, however, the Do...Loop is standalone, program execution continues with the first line of code after the Loop statement.

Exit For

Exits a For...Next loop or a For Each...Next statement. If the current For...Next is within a nested For...Next loop, execution continues with the next Next statement wrapped around the current one. If, however, the For...Next loop is standalone, program execution continues with the first line of code after the Next statement.

Exit Function

Exits the current function. Program execution is passed to the line following the call to the function.

Exit Property

Exits the current property procedure. Program execution is passed to the line following the call to the property.

Exit Select

Immediately exits a Select Case construct. Execution continues with the statement immediately following the End Select statement.

Exit Sub

Exits the current sub procedure. Program execution is passed to the line following the call to the procedure.

Exit Try

> Immediately exits a `Try...Catch` block. Program execution proceeds with the `Finally` block, if it is present, or with the statement following the `End Try` statement.

Exit While

> Immediately exits a `While` loop. Program execution proceeds with the code following the `End While` statement. If `Exit While` is within a nested `While` loop, it terminates the loop at the level of nesting in which `Exit While` occurs.

Programming Tips and Gotchas

Using `Exit Sub` can save having to wrap lengthy code within an `If...Then` statement. Here is an example with `Exit Sub`:

```
Sub MyTestSub(iNumber As Integer)
    If iNumber = 10 Then
        Exit Sub
    End If
    . . .'code
End Sub
```

and without `Exit Sub`:

```
Sub MyTestSub(iNumber As Integer)
    If iNumber <> 10 Then
        . . . 'code
    End If
End Sub
```

See Also

End… Statement

Exp Function

Class

System.Math

Syntax

```
Math.Exp(d)
```

d   *required; Numeric*
> Any valid numeric expression

Return Value

Double

Description

A Double representing the natural number e raised to the power *d*. Note that the irrational number e is *approximately* 2.7182818.

Rules at a Glance

- The maximum value for *d* is 709.782712893.

- *Exp* is the inverse of the *Log* function.

- Because this function can accept numeric values only, you may want to check the value you pass using the *IsNumeric* function to prevent generating an error.

- This is a Shared member, so it can be used without creating any objects.

VB.NET/VB 6 Differences

- In VB 6, *Exp* was an intrinsic VB function. In VB.NET, it is a member of the Math class in the System namespace. Hence, in VB.NET, calls to *Exp* must be prefaced with the Math class name.

See Also

Log Function, Log10 Function, E Field, Pow Function

File Class

Namespace

System.IO

Createable

No

Description

A File object represents a file. The members of the File class are listed in the "Public Static Methods" section.

The Microsoft.VisualBasic.FileSystem class has members that duplicate much of the functionality of the File class. One significant omission from the FileSystem class is that there is no Exists method. Consequently, the File.Exists method is documented in its own entry.

All of the methods of the File class are shared. Consequently, you don't need to instantiate a `File` object to access File class methods; you can simply reference the File class itself.

Public Static Methods

AppendText
Copy
Create
CreateText
Delete
Exists
GetAttributes
GetCreationTime

GetLastAccessTime
GetLastWriteTime
Move
Open
OpenRead
OpenText
OpenWrite
SetAttributes
SetCreationTime
SetLastAccessTime
SetLastWriteTime

See Also

Directory Class

File.Exists Method

Class

System.IO.File

Syntax

```
File.Exists(path)
```

path   *required; String*
The file path

Return Value

A Boolean indicating whether the file exists

Description

Indicates whether a file exists

Rules at a Glance

* *path* is a fully qualified filename or a relative path (which is interpreted as starting in the current directory).

* The Exists method returns True only if the specified file exists; otherwise, it returns False. Note that Exists returns False if *path* describes a directory instead of a folder.

Programming Tips and Gotchas

Since the File class is shared, you don't have to instantiate any objects before calling the File.Exists method.

See Also

Directory.Exists Method

FileAttr Function

Class

Microsoft.VisualBasic.FileSystem

Syntax

```
FileAttr(filenumber)
```

filenumber   *required; Integer*
    Any valid file number

Return Value

An `OpenMode` constant, as shown in the following table:

Mode	Value
Input	1
Output	2
Random	4
Append	8
Binary	32

Description

Returns the file-access mode for a file opened using the *FileOpen* procedure

VB.NET/VB 6 Differences

In VB 6, *FileAttr* includes a superfluous **returntype** parameter that must be set to 1 or an error results. In VB.NET, the parameter has been eliminated.

See Also

FileOpen Procedure

FileClose Procedure

Class

Microsoft.VisualBasic.FileSystem

Syntax

```
FileClose([filenumber][, filenumber][,...])
```

filenumber   *optional; Integer*
    The file number (or numbers) of an open file (or files), opened using the *File-Open* procedure

Description

Closes one or more files opened with the *FileOpen* procedure

Rules at a Glance

- If *filenumber* is omitted, all open files are closed.

- If the file you are closing was opened for Output or Append, the remaining data in the I/O buffer is written to the file. The memory buffer is then reclaimed.

- When the *FileClose* procedure is executed, the file number used is freed for further use.

- *filenumber* can either be a literal number, a numeric constant, or a numeric variable.

Programming Tips and Gotchas

- With the *FileClose* procedure, you can close more than one file at once by specifying the file numbers as a comma-delimited list, as shown here:

  ```
  FileClose(1, 3, 4)
  ```

- The *FileClose* procedure does not check first to see if there is a file associated with the given file number. Therefore, no error occurs if you use the *FileClose* procedure with a nonexistent file number. The drawback to this is that you may inadvertently think you have closed a file, when in fact you haven't.

VB.NET/VB 6 Differences

FileClose is new to VB.NET. It replaces the Close statement in VB 6.

See Also

FileOpen Procedure, Reset Procedure

FileCopy Procedure

Class

Microsoft.VisualBasic.FileSystem

Syntax

```
FileCopy(source, destination)
```

source   *required; String*
    The name of the source file to be copied

destination   *required; String*
    The name and location of the file when copied

Return Value

None

Description

Copies a file

Rules at a Glance

- The *source* and *destination* arguments may contain a drive name and a folder name, but they must *always* contain the filename.

- You cannot copy a file that is currently open.

Programming Tips and Gotchas

- If you don't specify a drive or folder in either the *source* or *destination*, the file is assumed to be in the current drive or folder.

- Unlike copying a file from one folder to another from outside VB, when using the *FileCopy* procedure, it is not sufficient to simply enter a path for *destination*. You must supply a filename, even if it's the same as the *source*; otherwise, runtime error 75, "Path/File access error," results.

- *FileCopy* is a procedure and not a function; there is no return value. You therefore have to assume that, if there are no errors generated from calling the *FileCopy* procedure, the file has been successfully copied. So be sure to wrap *FileCopy* in robust error handling.

- Be aware that if the *destination* file already exists, it will be overwritten without warning.

- A number of functions allow you to use the copy operation to rename a file. (Typically, this is done by specifying the same path in the destination as in the source, along with a different filename.) The *FileCopy* procedure, however, does not work in this way.

- For the copy operation to succeed, *source* must not be open by another application; if it is, runtime error 70, "Permission denied," is generated. If *source* has already been opened by the application, the copy operation will still succeed if the file is not locked (i.e., has been opened with the Shared keyword) or has been opened with a write lock only. If *source* has already been opened with either a read lock or a read-write lock, the *FileCopy* operation will generate runtime error 70, "Permission denied."

- *destination* must not be open if the copy operation is to succeed. If it has been opened by another application, runtime error 70, "Permission denied," is generated. If it has already been opened by the application itself, runtime error 55, "File already open," is generated.

FileDateTime Function

Class

Microsoft.VisualBasic.FileSystem

Syntax

```
FileDateTime(pathname)
```

pathname   *required; String*
    The filename, along with an optional drive and path

Return Value

A Date containing the date and time at which the specified file was created or last modified (whichever is later)

Description

Obtains the date and time at which a particular file was created or last modified (whichever is later)

Rules at a Glance

If you don't specify a drive or folder with *pathname*, the file is assumed to be in the current drive or folder.

Programming Tips and Gotchas

- Use the File.Exists method (in the System.IO namespace) to determine that the file exists before calling *FileDateTime*. If *pathname* does not exist, your application generates runtime error 53, "File not found."

- If a file has not been modified, its creation date and last modified date will be identical. However, if the file has been modified since its creation, the *FileDateTime* function returns only the last modified date. To obtain the file's creation date, you have to resort to using the Window's API. The *GetFileTime* API call returns not only the date last modified, but the file's creation date and last access date as well.

- You can also use *FileDateTime* on hidden files.

See Also

File.Exists Method

FileGet, FileGetObject Procedures

Class

Microsoft.VisualBasic.FileSystem

Syntax

```
FileGet(FileNumber, Value, RecordNumber)

FileGetObject(FileNumber, Value, RecordNumber)
```

FileNumber   *required; Integer*
   Any valid file number

Value   *required; any (see the first two items in "Rules at a Glance")*
   Variable in which to place file contents

RecordNumber   *optional; Integer*
   The location at which reading begins

Description

Copies data from a file on disk into a variable

Rules at a Glance

- For the *FileGet* procedure, the variable can have one of the following data types:

  > Array
  > Boolean
  > Byte
  > Char
  > Date
  > Decimal
  > Double
  > Integer
  > Long
  > Short
  > Single
  > String

- For the *FileGetObject* procedure, the variable must be of type Object.

- For files opened in Random mode, *RecordNumber* refers to the record number in the file.

- For files opened in Binary mode, *RecordNumber* refers to the byte number within the file.

- The number of bytes read by the *FileGet* procedure is governed by the data type of *Value*. The following is the number of bytes read by each data type:

Data type	Bytes read
Boolean	2
Byte	1
Char	1
Date	8
Decimal	8
Double	16
Integer	4
Long	8
Short	2
Single	8
String	Len(*string*)

Note that the number of bytes read by a String variable depends on the length of the string. Hence, a string must be initialized to the desired size before calling the *FileGet* procedure.

- The position of the first record or byte within a file is always 1.

- When a record or a number of bytes is read from a file using *FileGet*, the file pointer automatically moves to the record or byte following the one just read. You can therefore read all data sequentially from a Random or Binary file by omitting *RecordNumber*, as this snippet shows:

```
Dim fr As Integer = FreeFile()
Dim sChar As Char

FileOpen(fr, "c:\data.txt", OpenMode.Binary, OpenAccess.Read)
FileGet(fr, sChar, 1)
do while loc(fr) <> LOF(fr)
   FileGet(fr, sChar)
   ' do something with sChar. . .
Loop
FileClose(fr)
```

- *FileGet* is most commonly used to read data from files written with the *FilePut* function.

Example

This example illustrates the use of the Char data type to read and output each byte of a file:

```
Public Sub Main

Dim fr As Integer = FreeFile()
Dim sFile As String = Space(FileLen("C:\data.txt"))

FileOpen(fr, "c:\data.txt", OpenMode.Binary, OpenAccess.Read)
FileGet(fr, sFile)
Console.WriteLine(sFile)         ' Displays entire file

FileClose(fr)

End Sub
```

Programming Tips and Gotchas

With the increase in the power, flexibility, and ease of use of modern DBMSs, the use of external standalone data files has fallen dramatically, which means that statements such as *FileGet* and *FileOpen* are becoming much less important.

VB.NET/VB 6 Differences

The *FileGet* and *FileGetObject* procedures are new to VB.NET. They are replacements for the Get statement in VB 6, whose syntax is similar to that of *FileGet*.

See Also

FileOpen Procedure, FilePut, FilePutObject Procedures

FileLen Function

Class

Microsoft.VisualBasic.FileSystem

Syntax

```
FileLen(pathname)
```

pathname   *required; String*

The filename, along with its path and drive name (optionally)

Return Value

A Long containing the length of the specified file in bytes

Description

Specifies the length of a file on disk

Rules at a Glance

If you don't specify a drive or folder with *pathname*, the file is assumed to be in the current drive or folder.

Programming Tips and Gotchas

- Use the File.Exists method in the System.IO namespace to determine that the file exists before calling *FileLen*. If the file does not exist, *FileLen* generates runtime error 53, "File not found."

- Because *FileLen* returns the length of a file based on the file allocation table, the value returned by *FileLen* will reflect the size of the file before it was opened. In the case of open files, you should instead use the *LOF* function to determine the open file's current length.

See Also

LOF Function

FileOpen Procedure

Class

Microsoft.VisualBasic.FileSystem

Syntax

```
FileOpen(filenumber, filename, mode, access, share, recordlength)
```

filenumber   *required; Integer*
An available file number.

filename   *required; String*
The name of the file to open, along with an optional path.

mode   *optional;* `OpenMode` *enum*
The file-access mode. Options are: OpenMode.Append, OpenMode. Binary, OpenMode.Input, OpenMode.Output, or OpenMode.Random (the default value).

access   *optional;* `OpenAccess` *enum*
Specifies the allowable operations by the current process. Options are: `Open-Access.Default`, `OpenAccess.Read`, `OpenAccess.ReadWrite` (the default value), or `OpenAccess.Write`.

share   *optional;* OpenShare *enum*

Specifies the allowable operations by other processes. Options are: Open-Share.Shared (the default value), OpenShare.LockRead, OpenShare. LockWrite, or OpenShare.LockreadWrite.

recordlength   *optional; Integer (at most, 32767)*

The length of the record (for random access) or of the I/O buffer (for sequential access).

Description

Opens a disk file for reading and/or writing

Rules at a Glance

- There are three modes of file access: sequential, binary, and random. The Input, Output, and Append access modes are sequential access modes. *Sequential access* is designed for text files consisting of individual Unicode characters (and control codes). Most of the file-manipulation functions (*LineInput, Print, PrintLine,* and so on) apply to files opened for sequential access. *Random access* is designed to be used with files that have a structure—more specifically, files that consist of records, each of which is made up of the same set of fields. For instance, a record might contain name, address, and social security number fields. The *binary access* mode is for binary access, where each byte in the file is accessible independently.

- *filename* may include the directory or folder and drive; if these are omitted, the file is assumed to reside in the current working directory. If *filename* does include drive and path information, this may take the form of a path relative to the local system or a UNC path.

- The default mode for opening a disk file (when *mode* is not specified) is OpenMode.Random.

- If the specified file does not exist when opening in Input mode, an error occurs.

- A new file is created if the specified file does not exist when opening in Append, Binary, Output, or Random mode.

- *access* allows you to restrict the actions that can be taken against the file in the current process, by specifying Read, Write, or ReadWrite. The default is OpenAccess.ReadWrite.

- The *share* argument allows you to restrict the operations performed on the open file by other processes, and accepts one of the following members of the OpenShare enumeration:

Lock type	Description
Shared	Other processes can open the file for both read and write operations.
LockRead	Other processes can only write to the file.
LockWrite	Other processes can only read from the file.
LockReadWrite	Other processes cannot open the file.

- The *recordlength* argument is treated differently, depending upon the open mode, as the following table shows:

Open mode	Meaning of Len=
Random	Length in bytes of each record
Binary	Ignored
Append/Input/Output	The number of characters to buffer

Example

The following example opens a random access data file, adds two records, and then retrieves the second record:

```
Module modMain

Structure Person
    <vbFixedString(10)> Public Name As String
    Public Age As Short
End Structure

Public Sub Main

Dim APerson As New Person()
Dim fr As Integer = FreeFile()

FileOpen(fr, "c:\data.txt", OpenMode.Random, _
         OpenAccess.ReadWrite, OpenShare.Default, len(APerson))

APerson.Name = "Donna"
APerson.Age = 20
FilePut(fr, APerson, 1)

APerson.Name = "Steve"
APerson.Age = 30
FilePut(fr, APerson, 2)

FileGet(fr, APerson, 2)
MsgBox(APerson.Age)
FileClose(fr)

End Sub

End Module
```

Since random access files require a fixed record length, note the use of the `<vbFixedString(length)>` attribute to ensure that the Name field is a constant size.

Programming Tips and Gotchas

- To avoid using the file number of an already open file and generating an error, use the *FreeFile* function to allocate the next available file number.

- You can open an already opened file using a different file number in Binary, Input, and Random modes. However, you must close a file opened using Append or Output before you can open it with a different file number.

VB.NET/VB 6 Differences

The *FileOpen* procedure is new to VB.NET. It is a more or less direct replacement for the VB 6 Open statement.

See Also

FileClose Procedure, FileGet, FileGetObject Procedures, FilePut, FilePutObject Procedures

---

FilePut, FilePutObject Procedures

Class

Microsoft.VisualBasic.FileSystem

Syntax

```
FilePut(filenumber, value, [recordnumber])

FilePutObject(filenumber, value, [recordnumber])
```

filenumber   *required; Integer*
  Any valid file number

value   *required; any (see the first item in "Rules at a Glance")*
  The name of the variable containing the data to be written to the file

recordnumber   *optional; Integer*
  Record number (for random access) or byte number (for binary access) at which to begin the write operation

Description

Writes data from a program variable to a disk file

Rules at a Glance

- The *value* argument of the *FilePut* procedure can be any data type except Object. The *value* argument of the *FilePutObject* procedure must be of type Object.

- If *filenumber* is opened in random access mode, *recordnumber* refers to the record number; if the file is opened in binary access mode, *recordnumber* refers to a byte number.

- Both bytes and records in a file are numbered starting with 1.

- If *recordnumber* is omitted, the next byte or record to be written will be placed at the position immediately after the position pointed to by the last *FileGet* or *FilePut* procedure, or by the last *Seek* function.

- If you have opened the file in Random mode, it is important to ensure that the record length specified in the *recordNumber* argument of the *FileOpen* procedure matches the actual length of the data being written. If the length of the data being written is less than that specified by the *recordNumber* argument, the space up to the end of the record will be padded with the current contents of the file buffer—whatever that may be. If, on the other hand, the actual data length is more than that specified, an error occurs.

- The *FilePut* procedure cannot be used to write objects to disk. The *FilePutObject* procedure is used for this purpose.

- If you open the file in Binary mode, the *RecordNumber* argument has no effect. When you use *FilePut* to write data to the disk, the data is written contiguously, and no padding is placed between records.

Example

The following code writes the letters A–Z to a file:

```
Dim fr As Integer = FreeFile()
Dim sChar As Char
Dim i As Integer
FileOpen(fr, "c:\data2.txt", OpenMode.Binary)

For i = Asc("A") To Asc("Z")
    sChar = Chr(i)
    FilePut(fr, sChar)
  Next

FileClose(fr)
```

Programming Tips and Gotchas

- Because of the structured format of data written with the *FilePut* procedure, it is customary to read the data back from the file using the *FileGet* procedure.

- The *FilePutObject* procedure can be used to write data of type Object whose subtype is one of the standard datatypes (Boolean, Byte, Char, etc.). It cannot be used to write object data defined by the **Class...End Class** construct (including classes residing in .NET libraries), nor can it be used to write data from COM objects to disk. The following is a rewritten version of the example code that uses *FilePutObject*:

```
Dim fr As Integer = FreeFile()
Dim oChar As Object
Dim i As Integer
FileOpen(fr, "c:\data2.txt", OpenMode.Binary)

For i = Asc("A") To Asc("D")
    oChar = Chr(i)
    FilePutObject(fr, oChar)
Next
FileClose(fr)
```

- If you use the *FilePut* procedure to write data, you can use the *FileGet* procedure to read it. Similarly, if you use the *FilePutObject* procedure, you should should the *FileGetObject* procedure.

VB.NET/VB 6 Differences

The *FilePut* and *FilePutObject* procedures are new to VB.NET. They are almost direct replacements for the VB 6 Put statement.

See Also

FileClose Procedure, FileGet, FileGetObject Procedures, FileOpen Procedure

---

FileWidth Procedure

Class

Microsoft.VisualBasic.FileSystem

Syntax

```
FileWidth(filenumber, recordwidth)
```

filenumber   *required; Integer*
  Any valid file number

recordwidth   *required; Numeric*
  A number between 0 and 255

Description

Specifies a virtual file width when working with files opened with the *FileOpen* function

Rules at a Glance

- *recordwidth* defines the number of characters that can be placed on a single output line.

- The default *recordwidth* of 0 denotes that there is no limit to the number of characters that can be placed on a single output line.

VB.NET/VB 6 Differences

The *FileWidth* procedure is new to VB.NET.

See Also

FileOpen Procedure

Filter Function

Class

Microsoft.VisualBasic.Strings

Syntax

```
Filter(Source, Match[, Include[, Compare]])
```

Source   *required; String or Object*
  An array containing values to be filtered.

Match   *required; String*
  The substring of characters to find in the elements of the source array.

Include   *optional; Boolean*
  A Boolean (`True` or `False`) value. If `True` (the default value), *Filter* includes
  all matching values in the returned array; if `False`, *Filter* excludes all
  matching values (or, to put it another way, includes all nonmatching values).

Compare   *optional;* `CompareMethod` *enumeration*
  A constant whose value can be `CompareMethod.Text` or `CompareMethod.`
  `Binary` (the default).

Return Value

A 0-based String array of the elements filtered from *Source*

Description

The *Filter* function produces an array of matching values from an array of source
values that either match or do not match a given filter string.

Put another way, individual elements are copied from a source array to a target
array if they either match (*Include* is `True`) or do not match (*Include* is `False`)
a filter string. A match occurs for an array element if *Match* is a substring of the
array element.

Rules at a Glance

- The default *Include* value is `True`.

- The default *Compare* value is CompareMethod.Binary.

- `CompareMethod.Binary` is case sensitive; that is, *Filter* matches both character and case. In contrast, `CompareMethod.Text` is case insensitive, matching
  only character regardless of case.

- If no matches are found, *Filter* returns an empty array.

Programming Tips and Gotchas

- Although the *Filter* function is primarily a string function, you can also filter
  numeric values. To do this, specify a *Source* of type Object and populate this
  array with numeric values. Then assign the string representation of the
  numeric value you wish to filter on to the *Match* parameter. Note, though,
  that the returned string contains string representations of the filtered numbers. For example:

```
Dim oArray() As Object = _
          {123,222,444,139,1,12,98,908,845,22,3,9,11}

Dim sResult() As String = Filter(oArray, "1")
```

  In this case, the resulting array contains five elements: 123, 139, 1, 12, and 11.

Example

```
Dim sKeys() As String = {"Microsoft Corp.", "AnyMicro Inc.", _
                    "Landbor Data", "Micron Co."}
Dim sMatch As String = "micro"
```

```
Dim blnInclude As Boolean = True
Dim sFiltered() As String = Filter(sKeys, sMatch, blnInclude, _
                            CompareMethod.Text)
Dim sElement As String

For Each sElement In sFiltered
   Console.WriteLine(sElement)
Next
```

Fix Function

Class

Microsoft.VisualBasic.Conversion

Syntax

```
Fix(number)
```

number   *required; Double or any numeric expression*
   A number whose integer portion is to be returned

Return Value

A number of the same data type as *number* whose value is the integer portion of *number*

Description

For nonnegative numbers, *Fix* returns the floor of the number (the largest integer less than or equal to *number*).

For negative numbers, *Fix* returns the ceiling of the number (the smallest integer greater than or equal to *number*).

Rules at a Glance

* If *number* is Nothing, *Fix* returns Nothing.
* The operation of *Int* and *Fix* are identical when dealing with positive numbers: numbers are rounded down to the next lowest whole number. For example, both Int(3.14) and Fix(3.14) return 3.
* If *number* is negative, *Fix* removes its fractional part, thereby returning the next greater whole number. For example, Fix(-3.667) returns –3. This contrasts with *Int*, which returns the negative integer less than or equal to number (or –4, in the case of our example).
* The function returns the same data type as was passed to it.

Example

```
Sub TestFix()

   Dim dblTest As Double
   Dim objTest  As Object
```

```
dblTest = -100.9353
objTest = Fix(dblTest)
' returns -100
Console.WriteLine(objTest & " " & TypeName(objTest))

dblTest = 100.9353
objTest = Fix(dblTest)
'returns 100
Console.WriteLine(objTest & " " & TypeName(objTest))
```

    End Sub

Programming Tips and Gotchas

Fix does not round *number* to the nearest whole number; it simply removes the fractional part of *number*. Therefore, the integer returned by *Fix* will be the nearest whole number less than (or greater than, if the number is negative) the number passed to the function.

See Also

Int Function, Round Function

Flags Attribute

Class

System.Flags

Applies to

Enum

Description

Indicates that an enumerated type should be treated as a set of flags that can be added together, rather than as a set of mutually exclusive values.

Constructor

    New()

Properties

None

Floor Function

Class

System.Math

Syntax

    Math.Floor(d)

Return Value

Returns a Double containing the largest integer less than or equal to the argument *d*

Description

Returns the largest integer less than or equal to the argument *d*

Example

```
Math.Floor(12.9)      ' Returns 12
Math.Floor(-12.1)     ' Returns -13
```

Rules at a Glance

- Because this function can accept numeric values only, you may want to check the value you pass using the *IsNumeric* function to prevent generating an error.

- This is a Shared member, so it can be used without creating any objects.

VB.NET/VB 6 Differences

The *Floor* function is new to the .NET Framework.

See Also

Ceiling Function

FontDialog Class

Namespace

System.Windows.Forms

Createable

Yes

Description

Represents a common dialog box for selecting or saving a font.

The FontDialog object has properties for setting the initial appearance and functionality of the dialog box, a property for returning the font selected by the user, as well as a method for showing the dialog box.

Selected FontDialog Members

The following provides a brief description of the more important members of the FontDialog class:

Color property

Sets or retrieves the color of the font. The return value is an instance of the Color structure. The Color structure has a number of members, among which are:

- Over 140 named color properties, from Red, Green, and Blue, to Papaya-Whip, MistyRose, and MediumSeagreen. These properties return a `Color` structure.

- A Name property, which returns the name of the color or its ARGB value for custom colors. (The A component is the alpha component of the color, which determines the color's opacity.)

- The R property, G property, and B property, which return a byte specifying the red, green, or blue color component of the RGB color value, respectively.

- The IsKnownColor, IsNamedColor, and IsSystemColor properties, which give information about the color. Please see the documentation for more information on these properties.

Font property

Sets or retrieves the font chosen by the user. The return value is an instance of the Font class in the System.Drawing namespace. The Font class has a number of members, among which are:

Bold, Italic, Strikout, Underline properties

Boolean properties used to set or retrieve the corresponding attribute of the font.

FontFamily property

Returns a `FontFamily` object associated with the font. Use the Name property to get the name of the font family.

Name property

Returns the face name of the font as a String.

SizeInPoints

Returns the size of the font, in points, as a Single.

Style

Returns a `FontStyle` constant that contains information about the style of the font. The `FontStyle` constants are Bold, Italic, Regular, Strikeout, and Underline, and they can be combined using bitwise operations.

MaxSize, MinSize properties

These are properties of type Integer that specify the maximum and minimum sizes that can be entered into the Font dialog box.

Show... properties

The FontDialog has properties that specify the features of the dialog box. These include:

ShowApply

Indicates whether the dialog box has an Apply button. (The default is `False`.)

ShowColor

Indicates whether the dialog box shows the font color choice controls. (The default is `False`.)

ShowEffects
> Indicates whether the dialog box shows the strikethrough and underline options. (The default is `True`.)

Example

The following code displays the Font dialog box and then displays the user's choice of font family:

```
Imports Microsoft.VisualBasic
Imports System
Imports System.Windows.Forms
Imports System.Drawing

Module modMain

Public Sub Main

Dim fn As New FontDialog()
fn.ShowEffects = True
fn.ShowDialog()
MsgBox(fn.Font.FontFamily.Name)

End Sub

End Module
```

VB.NET/VB 6 Differences

While the FontDialog class is implemented in the .NET Base Class Library, VB 6 offers the CommonDialog custom control. Although the two offer similar functionality, their public interfaces are almost completely different.

For...Next Statement

Syntax

```
For counter = initial_value To maximum_value _
          [Step stepcounter]
   'code to execute on each iteration
   [Exit For]
Next [counter]
```

counter   required (optional with *Next* statement); any valid numeric variable
> A variable that serves as the loop counter

initial_value   required; any valid numeric expression
> The starting value of *counter* for the first iteration of the loop

maximum_value   required; any valid numeric expression
> The value of *counter* during the last iteration of the loop

stepcounter   optional (required if *Step* is used); any valid numeric expression
> The amount by which *counter* is to be incremented or decremented on each iteration of the loop

Description

Defines a loop that executes a given number of times, as determined by a loop counter.

To use the `For...Next` loop, you must assign a numeric value to a counter variable. This counter is either incremented or decremented automatically with each iteration of the loop. In the `For` statement, you specify the value that is to be assigned to the counter initially and the maximum value the counter will reach for the block of code to be executed. The `Next` statement marks the end of the block of code that is to execute repeatedly, and it also serves as a kind of flag that indicates that the counter variable is to be modified.

Rules at a Glance

- If *maximum_value* is greater than *initial_value* and no `Step` keyword is used or the step counter is positive, the `For...Next` loop is ignored and execution commences with the first line of code immediately following the `Next` statement.

- If *initial_value* and *maximum_value* are equal and *stepcounter* is 1, the loop will execute once.

- *counter* cannot be a Boolean variable or an array element.

- *counter* is incremented by one with each iteration unless the `Step` keyword is used.

- The `For...Next` loop can contain any number of `Exit For` statements. When the `Exit For` statement is executed, program execution commences with the first line of code immediately following the `Next` statement.

- If the `Step` keyword is used, *stepcounter* specifies the amount *counter* is incremented (if *stepcounter* is positive) or decremented (if it is negative).

Example

The following example demonstrates the use of a `For...Next` statement to iterate through the items in a combo box until an item in the combo box list matches a particular value entered in a text box:

```
Dim sSought As String = txtSeek.Text
Dim i As Integer
Dim iCount As Integer = cboCombo.Items.Count
For i = 0 To iCount - 1
    If cboCombo.Items(i) = sSought Then
        cboCombo.SelectedIndex = i
        Exit For
    End If
Next i
```

The following example demonstrates how to iterate from the end to the start of an array of values:

```
For i = UBound(sArray) to LBound(sArray) Step - 1
    Console.WriteLine(sArray(i))
Next i
```

The following example demonstrates how to select only every other value from an array of values:

```
For i = LBound(sArray) to UBound(sArray) Step 2
    Console.WriteLine(sArray(i))
Next i
```

Programming Tips and Gotchas

- You can also nest For...Next loops, as shown here:

```
For iDay = 1 to 365
    For iHour = 1 to 23
        For iMinute = 1 to 59
            ...
        Next iMinute
    Next iHour
Next iDay
```

- Although the counter following the Next keyword is optional, you will find your code is much easier to read if you use it, especially when nesting For... Next loops.

- You can increment the loop by a non-integral value by supplying a Single, Double, or Decimal value in the Step clause. This also requires that *counter* be a Single, Double, or Decimal data type. If *counter* is a Single or Double, what should be the final iteration of the loop may be skipped because of rounding error. To prevent this half the value of *stepcounter* can be added to *maximum_value*. For example:

```
Dim sngCtr As Single
For sngCtr = 1 to 2.05 step .1
```

- You should avoid changing the value of *counter* in the code within the loop. Not only can this lead to unexpected results; it makes for code that's incredibly difficult to read and to understand.

- Once the loop has finished executing, the value of *counter* is officially undefined. That is, you should not make any assumptions about its value outside of the For...Next loop, and you should not use it unless you first reinitialize it.

See Also

For Each...Next Statement

For Each...Next Statement

Syntax

```
For Each element In group
[statements]
[Exit For]
[statements]
Next [element]
```

element   *required; Object or any user-defined object type*
    An object variable to which the current element from the group is assigned

group   *required*
    An object collection or array

statements   *optional*
    A line or lines of program code to execute within the loop

Description

Loops through the items of a collection or the elements of an array

Rules at a Glance

- The For Each...Next code block is executed only if *group* contains at least one element. If *group* is an empty collection or an array that has not yet been dimensioned, an error (runtime errors 92, "For loop not initialized," and 424, "Object required," respectively, or a NullReferenceException exception) results.

- All *statements* are executed for each *element* in *group* in turn until either there are no more elements in *group* or the loop is exited prematurely using the Exit For statement. Program execution then continues with the line of code following Next.

- For Each...Next loops can be nested, but each *element* must be unique. For example:

```
For Each myObj In AnObject
    For Each subObject In myObj
        SName = subObject.NameProperty
    Next
Next
```

uses a nested For Each...Next loop, but two different variables, *myObj* and *subObject*, represent *element*.

- Any number of Exit For statements can be placed within the For Each... Next loop to allow for premature, conditional exit of the loop. Once the loop is exited, execution of the program continues with the line immediately following the Next statement. For example, the following loop terminates once the program finds a name in the *myObj* collection that has fewer than ten characters:

```
For Each subObject In myObj
    SName = subObject.NameProperty
    If Len(Sname) < 10 then
        Exit For
    End if
Next
```

Programming Tips and Gotchas

- Because the elements of an array are assigned to *element* by value, *element* is a "local" copy of the array element and not a reference to the array element itself. This means that you cannot make changes to the array elements, as the following example demonstrates:

```
Dim sArray(2) As String
Dim ele As String

sArray (0) = "aa"
sArray (1) = "bb"

For Each ele In sArray
    ele = "xx"
    Console.WriteLine(ele)
Next

For Each ele In sArray
    Console.WriteLine(ele)
Next
```

The output is:

```
xx
xx
aa
bb
```

which shows that the original array has not been changed.

VB.NET/VB 6 Differences

In VB 6, *element* had to be a variable of type Variant. VB.NET removes this restriction; *element* can be a strongly typed data type, as well as a variable of type Object, VB.NET's "universal" data type.

See Also

For...Next Statement

Format Function

Class

Microsoft.VisualBasic.Strings

Syntax

```
Format(expression[, style[, dayofweek[, _
    weekofyear]]])
```

expression   *required; String/Numeric*
    Any valid string or numeric expression

style   *optional; String*
    A valid named or user-defined format expression

dayofweek   *optional;* FirstDayOfWeek *enumeration*
    A constant that specifies the first day of the week

weekofyear   *optional;* FirstWeekOfYear *enumeration*
    A constant that specifies the first week of the year

First Day of Week Constants

Constant	Value	Description
System	0	NLS API setting
Sunday	1	Sunday (default)
Monday	2	Monday
Tuesday	3	Tuesday
Wednesday	4	Wednesday
Thursday	5	Thursday
Friday	6	Friday
Saturday	7	Saturday

First Week of Year Constants

Constant	Value	Description
UseSystemDayOfWeek	0	Use the NLS API setting.
FirstJan1	1	Start with the week in which January 1 occurs (default).
FirstFourDays	2	Start with the first week that has at least four days in the new year.
FirstFullWeek	3	Start with first full week of the year.

Return Value

A string containing the formatted expression

Description

Allows you to use either predefined or user-defined formats to output string, numeric, and date/time data

Rules at a Glance

- *style* can be either a predefined or user-defined format.

- User-defined formats for numeric values are created with up to four sections, delimited by semicolons. Each section is used for a different type of numeric value. The four possible sections are shown in the following table:

Section	Applies to
1	All values if used alone; positive values if used with more than one section
2	Negative values
3	Zero values
4	Nothing value

- It is not necessary to include all four sections in the *style* clause. However, the number of sections present determines what types of numeric values each section defines, as the following table shows:

Number of sections	Applies to
1	All numeric values
2	Positive and zero values; negative values
3	Positive values; negative values; zero values
4	As shown in previous table

- If you leave a section blank, it will use the same format as that defined for positive values. For example, the format string:

  ```
  "#.00;;#,##"
  ```

  means that negative values will appear in the same format as positive values.

- Only one section is allowed where one of the named formats is used.

- User-defined formats for string values can have two sections. The first is for all values; the second applies only to Null values or zero-length strings.

- The predefined date and time formats are:

Format	Example	Returns
General Date	Format("01/06/98","General Date")	1/6/98
Long Date	Format("01/06/98","Long Date")	Tuesday, January 06, 1998
Medium Date	Format("01/06/98","Medium Date")	06-Jan-98
Short Date	Format("01/06/98","Short Date")	1/6/98
Long Time	Format("17:08:06","Long Time")	5:08:06 PM
Medium Time	Format("17:08:06","Medium Time")	05.00 PM
Short Time	Format("17:08:06","Short Time")	17:08

- The predefined numeric formats are:

Format	Examples	Returns
General Number	Format(562486.2356, "General Number")	562486.2356
Currency	Format(562486.2356, "Currency")	$562,486.24
Fixed	Format(0.2, "Fixed")	0.20
Standard	Format(562486.2356, "Standard")	562,486.24
Percent	Format(.7521, "Percent")	75.21%
Scientific	Format(562486.2356, "Scientific")	5.62E+05
Yes/No	Format(0,"Yes/No")	No
	Format(23,"Yes/No")	Yes
True/False	Format(0,"True/False")	False
	Format(23,"True/False")	True
On/Off	Format(0,"On/Off")	Off
	Format(23,"On/Off")	On

- Characters used to create user-defined date and time formats are:

Char	Element Used In	Display As	Example	Returns
c	Date	A date and/or time based on the short-date and short-time international settings of the current Windows system	`Format("01/06/98 17:08:06", "c")`	1/6/98 5:08:06 PM
dddddd	Date	A complete date based on the long-date international setting of the current Windows system	`Format("01/06/98", "dddddd")`	Tuesday, January 06, 1998
(/)	Date separator	A date delimited with the specified character	`Format("01/06/98", "mm-dd-yyyy")`	01-06-1998
d	Day	A number (1–31) without a leading zero	`Format("01/06/98", "d")`	6
dd	Day	A number (01–31) with a leading zero	`Format("01/06/98", "dd")`	06
ddd	Day	An abbreviation (Sun–Sat)	`Format("01/06/98", "ddd")`	Tue
dddd	Day	A full name (Sunday–Saturday)	`Format("01/06/98", "dddd")`	Tuesday
ddddd	Date	A date based on the short date section in the computer's Windows international settings	`Format("01/06/98", "ddddd")`	1/6/98
h	Hour	A number (0–23) without leading zeros	`Format("05:08:06", "h")`	5
hh	Hour	A number (00–23) with leading zeros	`Format("05:08:06", "hh")`	05
n	Minute	A number (0–59) without leading zeros	`Format("05:08:06", "n")`	8
nn	Minute	A number (00–59) with leading zeros	`Format("05:08:06", "nn")`	08
m	Month	A number (1–12) without a leading zero	`Format("01/06/98", "m")`	1
mm	Month	A number (01–12) with a leading zero	`Format("01/06/98", "mm")`	01
mmm	Month	An abbreviation (Jan–Dec)	`Format("01/06/98", "mmm")`	Jan
mmmm	Month	A full month name (January–December)	`Format("01/06/98", "mmmm")`	January
q	Quarter	A number (1–4)	`Format("01/06/98", "q")`	1

Char	Element Used In	Display As	Example	Returns
s	Second	A number (0–59) without leading zeros	Format("05:08:06", "s")	6
ss	Second	A number (00–59) with leading zeros	Format("05:08:06", "ss")	06
ttttt	Time	A time based on the 12-hour clock, using the time separator and leading zeros specified in Windows locale settings	Format("05:08:06", "ttttt")	5:08:06 AM
AM/PM	Time	A 12-hour clock format using uppercase AM and PM	Format("17:08:06", "hh:mm:ss AM/PM")	05:08:06 PM
am/pm	Time	A 12-hour clock format using lowercase am and pm	Format("17:08:06", "hh:mm:ss am/pm")	05:08:06 pm
A/P	Time	A 12-hour clock format using an uppercase "A" for AM and "P" for PM	Format("17:08:06", "hh:mm:ss A/P")	05:08:06 P
a/p	Time	A 12-hour clock format using a lowercase "a" for AM and "p" for PM	Format("17:08:06", "hh:mm:ss a/p")	05:08:06 p
(:)	Time separator	A time format using a nonstandard character	Format("17:08:06", "hh::mm::ss")	17::08::06
ww	Week	A number (1 – 54)	Format("01/06/98", "ww")	2
w	Weekday	A number (1 for Sunday through 7 for Saturday)	Format("01/06/98", "w")	3
y	Day of Year	A number (1 – 366)	Format("01/06/98", "y")	6
yy	Year	A 2-digit number (00 – 99)	Format("01/06/98", "yy")	98
yyyy	Year	A 4-digit number (100 – 9999)	Format("01/06/98", "yyyy")	1998

- Characters used to create user-defined number formats are as follows:

Char	Description	Examples
(0)	Digit placeholder. If *expression* contains a digit in the appropriate position, the digit is displayed; otherwise, a 0 will be displayed. The format definition dictates the number of digits after the decimal point, forcing the number held within an expression to be rounded to the given number of decimal places. It does not, however, affect the number of digits shown to the left of the decimal point.	Format(23.675, "00.0000") returns 23.6750 Format(23.675, "00.00") returns 23.68 Format(2658, "00000") returns 02658 Format(2658, "00.00") returns 2658.00

Char	Description	Examples
(#)	Digit placeholder. If *expression* contains a digit in the appropriate position, the digit is displayed; otherwise, nothing will be displayed.	`Format(23.675, "##.##")` returns 23.68 `Format(23.675, "##.####")` returns 23.675 `Format(12345.25, "#,###.##")` returns 12,345.25
(.)	Decimal placeholder. The actual character displayed as a decimal placeholder depends on the international settings of the local Windows system.	
(%)	Percentage placeholder. Displays *expression* as a percentage by first multiplying the value of *expression* by 100.	`Format(0.25, "##.00%")` returns 25.00%
(,)	Thousands separator. The actual character displayed as a thousands separator depends on the international settings of the local Windows system. You only need to show one thousands separator in your definition.	`Format(1000000, "#,###")` returns 1,000,000
(E- E+ e- e+)	Scientific format. If the format expression contains at least one digit placeholder (0 or #) to the right of E-, E+, e-, or e+, the number is displayed in scientific format, and the letter E or e that was used in the *format* expression is inserted between the number and its exponent. The number of digit placeholders to the right determines the number of digits displayed in the exponent. Use E- or e- to place a minus sign next to negative exponents. Use E+ or e+ to place a minus sign next to negative exponents and a plus sign next to positive exponents.	
- + $ ( )	Displays a literal character.	`Format(2345.25, "$#,###.##")` returns $2,345.25
(\)	The character following the backslash will be displayed as a literal character. Use the backslash to display a special formatting character as a literal.	`Format(0.25, "##.00\%")` returns .25% Note the difference between the result of this example and the result of the % formatting character.

Programming Tips and Gotchas

- A little known and very important use of the *Format* function is to prevent an "Invalid Use of Null" error from occurring when assigning values from a recordset to a variable within your program. For example, if a field within either a DAO or RDO recordset created from either an Access or SQL Server database contains a Null value, you could trap this and change its value to "" as follows:

```
If IsNull(rsMyRecordSet!myValue) Then
    sMyString = ""
```

```
Else
    sMyString = rsMyRecordSet!myValue
End If
```

However, assigning the value returned by the *Format* function that has been passed the recordset field can do away with this long and tedious coding, as the following line of code illustrates:

```
sMyString = Format(rsMyRecordSet!myValue)
```

- If you are passing a date to SQL Server, what date format should you use? By default, SQL Server expects an American date format, mmddyy, but it is possible for the database to have been altered to accept other date formats, or you could be passing data to a stored procedure that begins with a date-time conversion statement (SET DATEFORMAT *dateformat*). The only sure way of passing a date into SQL Server is by using the ANSI standard date format 'yyyymmdd' (including the single quotation marks).

- When passing a date to a Jet (Access) database, you should surround the date with hash characters (#); for example, #12/31/1999#.

- Formatting numbers using *Format* without a format definition is also preferable to simply using the *Str* function. Unlike *Str*, the *Format* function removes the leading space normally reserved for the sign from positive numbers.

- You can also use the *Format* function to scale numbers by 1000. This is achieved by placing a thousands separator to the immediate left of the decimal point for each 1000 you wish the number to be scaled by. Thus:

```
'one separator divides the expression by 1000 = 1000
Format(1000000, "##0,.")
'two separators divides the expression by 1,000,000 = 1
Format(1000000, "##0,,.")
```

VB.NET/VB 6 Differences

The VB 6 version of the *Format* function defined five special symbols (@, &, <, >, and !) for creating user-defined string formats. In VB.NET, these symbols are treated as literal characters.

See Also

FormatCurrency, FormatNumber, FormatPercent Functions, FormatDateTime Function

---

FormatCurrency, FormatNumber, FormatPercent Functions

Class

Microsoft.VisualBasic.Strings

Syntax

```
FormatCurrency(expression[,NumDigitsAfterDecimal][, _
    IncludeLeadingDigit[,UseParensForNegativeNumbers[, _
```

```
            GroupDigits]]]])

    FormatNumber(expression[,NumDigitsAfterDecimal][, _
        IncludeLeadingDigit[,UseParensForNegativeNumbers[, _
        GroupDigits]]]])

    FormatPercent(expression[,NumDigitsAfterDecimal][, _
        IncludeLeadingDigit[,UseParensForNegativeNumbers[, _
        GroupDigits]]]])
```

expression   *required; Object*
> The number or numeric expression to be formatted.

NumDigitsAfterDecimal   *optional; Long*
> The number of digits the formatted string should contain after the decimal
> point.

IncludeLeadingDigit   *optional;* TriState *constant*
> Indicates whether the formatted string is to have a 0 before floating point
> numbers between 1 and –1.

UseParensForNegativeNumbers   *optional;* TriState *constant*
> Specifies whether parentheses should be placed around negative numbers.

GroupDigits   *optional;* TriState *constant*
> Determines whether digits in the returned string should be grouped using the
> delimiter specified in the computer's regional settings. For example, on
> English language systems, the value 1000000 is returned as 1,000,000 if
> *GroupDigits* is True.

Return Value

String

Description

Functions used to format currency, numbers, and percentages.

The three functions are almost identical. They all take identical arguments. The
only difference is that *FormatCurrency* returns a formatted number beginning with
the currency symbol specified in the computer's regional settings, *FormatNumber*
returns just the formatted number, and *FormatPercent* returns the formatted
number followed by a percentage sign (%).

Rules at a Glance

- If *NumDigitsAfterDecimal* is not specified, its default value is –1, which
  means that the value in the computer's regional settings is used.

- The TriState constant values are True, False, and UseDefault.

- When optional arguments are omitted, their values are defined by the computer's regional settings.

- In the *FormatCurrency* function, the position of the currency symbol in relation to the currency value is defined by the computer's regional settings.

Programming Tips and Gotchas

These three functions first appeared in VBScript Version 2 as "light" alternatives to the *Format* function, which had originally been left out of VBScript due to its size. They are quick and easy to use and make your code more self-documenting; you can instantly see what format is being applied to a number without having to decipher the format string.

See Also

Format Function, FormatDateTime Function

FormatDateTime Function

Class

Microsoft.VisualBasic.Strings

Syntax

```
FormatDateTime(expression[,dateformat])
```

expression   *required; Date*
    Date variable or literal date

dateformat   *optional;* DateFormat *enum*
    Defines the format of the date to return

Return Value

String representing the formatted date or time

Description

Formats a date or time expression based on the computer's regional settings

Rules at a Glance

- The Dateformat enum is:

DateFormat.GeneralDate   *Value: 0*
    Displays a date and/or time. If there is a date part, displays it as a short date. If there is a time part, displays it as a long time. If present, both parts are displayed.

DateFormat.LongDate   *Value: 1*
    Uses the long-date format specified in the client computer's regional settings.

DateFormat.ShortDate   *Value: 2*
    Uses the short-date format specified in the client computer's regional settings.

DateFormat.LongTime   *Value: 3*
    Uses the time format specified in the computer's regional settings.

DateFormat.ShortTime   *Value: 4*
    Uses a 24-hour format (hh:mm).

- The default date format is GeneralDate.

Programming Tips and Gotchas

- Remember that date and time formats obtained from the client computer are based upon the client computer's regional settings. It is not uncommon for a single application to be used internationally, so date formats can vary widely. Not only that, but you can never be sure that a user has not modified the regional settings on her computer. In short, never take a date coming in from a client machine for granted; ideally, you should always verify that it is in the format you need prior to using it.

- There is no appreciable difference in either coding or performance between these two statements:

```
sDate = FormatDateTime(dDate, LongDate)
sDate = Format(dDate, "Long Date")
```

See Also

Format Function, FormatCurrency, FormatNumber, FormatPercent Functions

FreeFile Function

Class

Microsoft.VisualBasic.FileSystem

Syntax

```
FreeFile()
```

Return Value

An integer representing the next available file number

Description

Returns the next available file number for use in a *FileOpen* function

Programming Tips and Gotchas

- It is good programming practice to *always* use *FreeFile* to obtain a file number to use in the *FileOpen* procedure.

- You should call *FreeFile* and store the returned file number to a variable rather than passing the *FreeFile* function directly as the `filenumber` argument of the *FileOpen* procedure. In this way, you save the file handle for a subsequent call to the *FileClose* procedure.

- After using the *FreeFile* function to retrieve a file handle, you should immediately call the *FileOpen* procedure, particularly if your file access code resides in a multithreaded application or component. Failure to do so may cause the same handle to be assigned to two different variables, so that one of the calls to *FileOpen* fails.

- The names of function parameters become the function's named arguments. Because of this, it is best to use meaningful names for parameters, and to avoid the use of Hungarian notation.

Friend Keyword

Description

The Friend keyword is used to declare classes, module-level variables (but not local variables), constants, enumerations, properties, methods, functions, and subroutines.

When the Friend keyword is used, the item being declared has direct access scope inside of the class module in which the item is declared, as well as in all derived classes in the same project. However, if the item is declared using Protected Friend, then the scope is all derived classes, including those that are in other projects.

For more information on access modifiers, including Friend, see the following topics, as well as Chapter 4:

Class Statement
Const Statement
Enum Statement
Function Statement
Property Statement
Sub Statement

Function Statement

Syntax

```
[ClassBehavior][AccessModifier] Function name _
        [(arglist)] [As type][()]
   [statements]
   [name = expression]
   [statements]
End Function
```

ClassBehavior   optional; Keyword
   One of the following keywords:

   Overloads
      Indicates that more than one declaration of this function exists (with different argument signatures). For more detail, see Chapter 4.

   Overrides
      For derived classes, indicates that the function overrides the function by the same name (and argument signature) in the base class. For more detail, see Chapter 4.

   Overridable
      Indicates that the function can be overridden in a derived class. For more detail, see Chapter 4.

   NotOverridable
      Indicates that the function cannot be overridden in a derived class. For more detail, see Chapter 4.

MustOverride

Indicates that the function must be overridden in a derived class. For more detail, see Chapter 4.

Shadows

In a derived class definition, indicates that this element shadows any elements of the same name in the base class.

Shared

A shared function is callable without creating an object of the class. It is, in this strange sense, shared by all objects of the class. These are also called static functions.

AccessModifier   *optional; Keyword*

One of the following keywords: Public, Private, Protected, Friend, Protected Friend. The following table describes the effects of the various access modifiers. Note that direct access refers to accessing the member without any qualification, as in:

    classvariable = 100

and class/object access refers to accessing the member through qualification, either with the class name or the name of an object of that class:

	Direct access scope	*Class/object access scope*
Private	Declaring class	Declaring class
Protected	All derived classes	Declaring class
Friend	Derived in-project classes	Declaring project
Protected Friend	All derived classes	Declaring project
Public	All derived classes	All projects

For more information, see Accessibility in Class Modules" in Chapter 4.

name   *required; String literal*

The name of the function.

arglist   *optional*

A comma-delimited list of variables to be passed to the function as arguments from the calling procedure.

arglist uses the following syntax and parts:

    [Optional] [ByVal | ByRef] [ParamArray] varname[( )] [As type] _
        [= defaultvalue]

Optional   *optional; Keyword*

An optional argument is one that need not be supplied when calling the function. However, all arguments following an optional one must also be optional. A ParamArray argument cannot be optional.

ByVal   *optional; Keyword*

The argument is passed by value; that is, the local copy of the variable is assigned the value of the argument.

ByRef   *optional; Keyword*

 The argument is passed by reference; that is, the local variable is simply a
 reference to the argument being passed. All changes made to the local
 variable will be also reflected in the calling argument. `ByVal` is the
 default method of passing variables.

ParamArray   *optional; Keyword*

 Indicates that the argument is an optional array of Objects (or a strongly
 typed array, if `Option Strict` is on) containing an arbitrary number of
 elements. It can only be used as the last element of the argument list and
 cannot be used with the `ByRef` or `Optional` keywords.

varname   *required; String literal*

 The name of the local variable containing either the reference or value of
 the argument.

type   *optional; Keyword*

 The data type of the argument.

defaultvalue   *optional; String literal*

 For optional arguments, you must specify a default value.

type   *optional; Keyword*

 The return data type of the function.

statements   *optional*

 Program code to be executed within the function.

expression   *optional*

 The value to return from the function to the calling procedure.

Description

Defines a function procedure

Rules at a Glance

- `Overloads` and `Shadows` cannot be used in the same declaration.

- Functions cannot be nested; that is, you cannot define one function inside
  another function. (This applies to all procedures.)

- If you do not include one of the access keywords, a function will be `Public`
  by default.

- Any number of `Exit Function` statements can be placed within the function. Execution will continue with the line of code immediately following the
  call to the function. If a value has not been assigned to the function when the
  `Exit Function` statement executes, the function will return the default initialization value of the data type specified for the return value of the function. If the data type of the function was an object reference, the exited
  function will return `Nothing`.

- The return value of a function is passed back to the calling procedure by
  either assigning a value to the function name or by using the `Return` statement. However, the `Return` statement also exits the function, whereas assigning the return value to the function name does not exit the function.

- To return arrays of any type from a procedure, you must use parentheses after the data type in the return value of the function declaration, as in:

```
Public Function Test() As Integer()
```

- If you specify an optional parameter in your function declaration, you must also provide a default value for that parameter. For example:

```
Private Function ShowMessage(Optional sMsg _
                        As String = "Not given")
```

Programming Tips and Gotchas

- There is often confusion between using the ByRef and ByVal methods to assign arguments to a function. ByRef assigns a reference of the variable in the calling procedure to the variable in the function; any changes made to the variable from within the function are in reality made to the variable in the calling procedure. On the other hand, ByVal assigns the value of the variable in the calling procedure to the variable in the function. Changes made to the variable in the function have no effect on the variable in the calling procedure. In general, ByRef arguments within class modules take longer to perform, since marshaling back and forth between function and calling module must take place; so unless you explicitly need to modify a variable's value within a function, it's best to pass parameters by value.

- Since a variable passed to a function by reference is actually modified by the function, you can use such variables to "return" multiple values from the function.

VB.NET/VB 6 Differences

- If a parameter array is used in VB 6, it is a comma-delimited list of values in the calling procedure that is treated as an array of variants in the called function. In VB.NET, the arguments can be any data type, and they can be either a comma-delimited list of scalar values or an array.

- In VB 6, the elements in parameter arrays are passed by reference; in VB.NET, they are passed by value.

- If you do not specify whether an individual element in *arglist* is passed ByVal or ByRef, it is passed by reference in VB 6. In VB.NET, it is passed by value.

- In VB 6, you can call a function that has arguments in a number of ways:

```
x = SomeFunction(arg1, arg2)
Call SomeFunction(arg1, arg2)
SomeFunction arg1, arg2
```

In VB.NET, parentheses are required in the function call:

```
x = SomeFunc(arg1, arg2)
Call SomeFunc(arg1, arg2)
SomeFunc(arg1, arg2)
```

- In VB 6, optional arguments do not require that you specify a default value. Instead, the *IsMissing* function is used to determine whether the optional argument is supplied (although in some cases it is unreliable). In VB.NET, you must assign a default value to an optional argument.

See Also

Sub Statement

FV Function

Class

Microsoft.VisualBasic.Financial

Syntax

```
FV(rate, nper, pmt[, pv [, due]])
```

rate   *required; Double*
> The interest rate per period

nper   *required; Integer*
> The number of payment periods in the annuity

pmt   *required; Double*
> The payment made in each period

pv   *optional; Variant*
> The present value of the loan or annuity

due   *optional; Constant of the* `DueDate` *enumeration*
> Specifies whether payments are due at the start or the end of the period. The value can be `DueDate.BegOfPeriod` or `DueDate.EndOfPeriod` (the default).

Return Value

A Double specifying the future value of an annuity

Description

Calculates the future value of an annuity (either an investment or loan) based on a regular number of payments of a fixed value and a static interest rate over the period of the annuity.

Rules at a Glance

- The time units used for the number of payment periods, the rate of interest, and the payment amount must be the same. In other words, if you state the payment period in months, you must also express the interest rate as a monthly rate and the amount paid per month.

- The rate per period is stated as a fraction of 100. For example, 10% is stated as .10. If you are calculating using monthly periods, you must also divide the rate per period by 12. Therefore, 10% per annum, for example, equates to a rate per period of .00833.

- The *pv* argument is most commonly used as the initial value of a loan. The default is 0.

- Payments made against a loan or added to the value of savings are expressed as negative numbers.

- The default value for the *due* argument is `DueDate.EndOfPeriod`.

See Also

IPmt Function, NPer Function, NPV Function, PPmt Function, PV Function, Rate Function

---

Get Statement

Syntax

```
Get()
    [ statements ]
End Get
```

statements   *optional*
Program code to be executed when the Property Get procedure is called

Description

Defines a Property Get procedure that returns a property value to the caller

Rules at a Glance

- The `Get` statement can only be used within a `Property...End Property` construct.

- The property value can be returned either by using the `Return` statement or by assigning the value to a variable whose name is the same as the property. For example:

```
Public Property MyProp As String

    Private sSomeVar as String

    Property Get()
        Return sSomeVar
    End Get
    ...
    End Property
```

or:

```
Public Property MyProp As String

    Private sSomeVar as String

    Property Get()
        MyProp = sSomeVar
    End Get
    ...
    End Property
```

- The value returned by a property is usually the value of a Private variable. This adheres to accepted object-oriented techniques by protecting the property value from accidental modification.

VB.NET/VB 6 Differences

The `Property Get` statement in VB 6 corresponds to the `Get` statement in VB.NET. Though the purpose and basic operation of the two constructs is identical, the syntax of the VB.NET construct is vastly simplified and more intuitive.

See Also

Property Statement, Set Statement

GetAllSettings Function

Class

Microsoft.VisualBasic.Interaction

Syntax

    GetAllSettings(appname, section)

appname   *required; String*
    Name of the application

section   *required; String*
    Relative path from *appname* to the key containing the settings to retrieve

Return Value

An object containing a two-dimensional array of strings

Description

Returns the registry value entries and their corresponding values for the application

Rules at a Glance

- *GetAllSettings* works exclusively with the subkeys of `HKEY_CURRENT_USER\`
  `Software\VB and VBA Program Settings`.

- The elements in the first dimension of the array returned by *GetAllSettings* contain the value entry names.

- The elements in the second dimension of the array returned by *GetAllSettings* contain the values for the respective value entries.

- The two-dimensional array returned by *GetAllSettings* is based at 0 (as are all arrays) so the first value entry name is referenced using (0,0).

- A call to *GetAllSettings* will return only the value entry names and data belonging to the final registry key specified by the *section* argument. If that key itself has one or more subkeys, their data will not be retrieved by the function.

- If either *appname* or *section* do not exist, *GetAllSettings* will return an uninitialized Object.

Programming Tips and Gotchas

- *GetAllSettings* is a function that was developed to retrieve data from initialization files in 16-bit environments and to retrieve data from the registry under Windows 9x and Windows NT. The language of the documentation, however, reflects the language of initialization files. The arguments labeled *appname* and *section* are in fact registry keys; the argument labeled *key* is in fact a registry value entry.

- The built-in registry-manipulation functions allow you to create professional 32-bit applications that use the registry for holding application-specific data, in the same way that .INI files were used in the 16-bit environment. You can, for example, store information about the user's desktop settings (i.e., the size and position for forms) the last time the program was run.

- Because the built-in registry functions in VB only create string-type registry keys, *GetSetting* and *GetAllSettings* return string values. Therefore, before you use numeric values returned from the registry, you should explicitly convert the value to a numeric data type.

- *GetAllSettings*, *SaveSettings*, and *GetSetting* allow you direct access to only a limited section of the windows registry, that being a special branch created for your application (`HKEY_CURRENT_USER\Software\VB and VBA Program Settings`). You cannot access or change other registry settings without using the Win32 API.

- Use the code Application.ExecutablePath to pass your application's name to the *GetAllSetting* function.

- Only those settings that were created using either the Win32 API or the *SaveSetting* function will be returned. In other words, a VB application does not have a registry entry unless you have created one explicitly.

- If the key read by *GetAllSettings* has a default value, that value will not be retrieved by the function. If you want to store and retrieve default values, you must call the Win32 API directly.

- Because *GetAllSettings* returns an uninitialized Object when either *appname* or *section* do not exist, if you subsequently try to perform a *UBound* or *LBound* function on the object, a "Type Mismatch" error will be generated. You can test the validity of the returned value, as follows:

```
Dim MySettings(,) As String
Dim intSettings As Integer
' Place some settings in the registry.
SaveSetting("WindowsApplication6", "Startup", "Top", "75")
SaveSetting("WindowsApplication6", "Startup", "Left", "50")
' Retrieve the settings.
MySettings = GetAllSettings(appname:="WindowsApplication6", _
    section:="Startup")
If Not (MySettings Is Nothing) Then
    For intSettings = 0 To UBound(MySettings, 1)
        Console.WriteLine(MySettings(intSettings, 0))
        Console.WriteLine(MySettings(intSettings, 1))
```

```
        Next intSettings
        DeleteSetting("WindowsApplication6", "Startup")
    else
        MsgBox("No settings")
    End If
```

- Because *GetAllSetting* retrieves data from the user branch of the registry, and the physical file that forms the user branch of the registry may change (depending, of course, on who the user is and, in the case of Windows 9x systems, whether the system is configured to support multiple users), never assume that an application has already written data to the registry. In other words, even if you're sure that your application's installation routine or the application itself has successfully stored values in the registry, never assume that a particular value entry exists, and always be prepared to substitute a default value if it does not.

- Rather than rely on the relatively underpowered registry-access functionality available in Visual Basic, we highly recommend that you instead use the Registry and RegistryKey classes available in the BCL's Microsoft.Win32 namespace.

See Also

DeleteSetting Procedure, GetSetting Function, SaveSetting Procedure

GetAttr Function

Class

Microsoft.VisualBasic.FileSystem

Yes

Syntax

```
GetAttr(pathname)
```

pathname   *required; String*
    Filename and an optional pathname

Return Value

An integer representing the sum of the following constants or members of the `FileAttribute` enumeration, which reflect the attributes set for the file:

FileAttribute Enum	Constant	Value	Description
Normal	VbNormal	0	Normal
ReadOnly	VbReadOnly	1	Read-only
Hidden	VbHidden	2	Hidden
System	VbSystem	4	System
Directory	VbDirectory	16	Directory or folder
Archive	VbArchive	32	File has changed since last backup

Description

Determines which attributes have been set for a file or directory

Rules at a Glance

- *pathname* may optionally include a directory name and a drive letter, including a network drive. *pathname* can also follow the UNC format of *//machine_name/drive*.

- You can check if a particular attribute has been set by performing a bitwise comparison of the *GetAttr* return value and the value of the attribute constant using the And operator. A nonzero result means that the particular attribute has been set; conversely, a zero value indicates that the attribute has not been set. For example:

```
If (GetAttr(myfile.txt) And VbReadOnly) = 0 then
    Msgbox "The file is Read-Write"
Else
    MsgBox "The file is Read-Only"
End If
```

Programming Tips and Gotchas

If *pathname* is invalid, a FileNotFoundException exception is generated.

GetChar Function

Class

Microsoft.VisualBasic.Strings

Syntax

```
GetChar(str, index)
```

str   *required; String*
     The string from which to extract a character

index   *required; Integer*
     Position of character (1-based)

Return Value

A Char containing the character at position *index*

Description

Returns the character that is at position *index* within a given string

Rules at a Glance

- The first character in *str* is at index 1.

- If *index* exceeds the number of character positions in *str*, an error is generated.

VB.NET/VB 6 Differences

The *GetChar* function is new to VB.NET.

See Also

InStr Function, Left Function, Mid Function, Right Function

GetObject Function

Class

Microsoft.VisualBasic.Interaction

Syntax

```
GetObject([pathname] [, class])
```

pathname   *optional; String*
    The full path and name of the file containing the COM (or ActiveX) object.

class   *optional; String*
    The class of the object. The *class* argument has these parts:

    Appname   *required; String*
        The name of the application.

    Objecttype   *required; String*
        The class of object to create, delimited from *Appname* by using a point (.). For example, `Appname.Objecttype`.

Return Value

Returns a reference to an ActiveX object

Description

Accesses an ActiveX server held within a specified file

Rules at a Glance

* Although both *pathname* and *class* are optional, at least one parameter must be supplied.

* In situations where you cannot create a project-level reference to an ActiveX object, you can use the *GetObject* function to assign an object reference from an external ActiveX object to an object variable.

* *GetObject* is used when there is a current instance of the ActiveX object; to create the instance, use the *CreateObject* function.

* If you specify *pathname* as a zero-length string, *GetObject* will return a new instance of the object—unless the object is registered as single instance, in which case the current instance will be returned.

* If you omit the pathname, the current instance of the object will be returned.

* An error is generated if *pathname* is not specified and no current instance of the object can be found.

* The object variable you will use within your program to hold a reference to the ActiveX object is dimensioned as type Object. This causes the object to be

late bound; that is, your program knows nothing of the type of object nor its interface until the object has been instantiated within your program:

```
Dim myObject As Object
myObject = GetObject("C:\OtherApp\Library.lib")
```

- The details of how you create different objects and classes are determined by how the server has been written, and you'll need to read the documentation available for the server to determine what you need to do to reference a particular part of the object. There are basically three ways in which you can access an ActiveX object:

  1. The overall object library. This is the highest level and will give you access to all public sections of the library and all its public classes:

     ```
     GetObject("C:\OtherApp\Library.lib")
     ```

  2. A section of the object library. To access a particular section of the library, use an exclamation mark (!) after the filename, followed by the name of the section:

     ```
     GetObject("C:\OtherApp\Library.lib!Section")
     ```

  3. A class within the object library. To access a class within the library, use the optional **Class** parameter:

     ```
     GetObject("C:\OtherApp\Library.lib", "App.Class")
     ```

Programming Tips and Gotchas

- Pay special attention to objects registered as single instance. As their type suggests, there can only ever be one instance of the object created at any one time. Calling *CreateObject* against a single-instance object more than once has no effect; you will still be returning a reference to the same object. The same is true of using *GetObject* with a pathname of ""; rather than returning a reference to a new instance, you will be obtaining a reference to the original instance of the object. In addition, you must use a pathname argument with single-instance objects (even if this is ""); otherwise an error will be generated.

- You can't use *GetObject* to obtain a reference to a class created with Visual Basic.

- When possible, you should use early binding in your code. For more details on early and late binding, see Chapter 3. You can use *GetObject* in early binding with COM objects, as in:

  ```
  Dim objExcel As Excel.Application
  objExcel = GetObject(, "Excel.Application")
  ```

- The following table shows when to use *GetObject* and when to use *CreateObject*:

Task	Use
Create a new instance of an OLE server	*CreateObject*
Create a subsequent instance of an already instantiated server (if the server is not registered as single instance)	*CreateObject*
Obtain another reference to an already instantiated server without launching a subsequent instance	*GetObject*

Task	Use
Launch an OLE server application and load an instance of a subobject	*GetObject*
Instantiate a class created with VB	*CreateObject*
Instantiate a class registered on a remote machine	*CreateObject*

See Also

CreateObject Function

GetSetting Function

Class

Microsoft.VisualBasic.Interaction

Syntax

```
GetSetting(appname, section, key[, default])
```

appname   *required; String*
    The name of the application

section   *required; String*
    The path from the application key to the key containing the value entries

key   *required; String*
    The name of the value entry whose value is to be returned

default   *optional; String*
    The value to return if no value can be found

Return Value

A string containing the value of the specified *key*; *default* if *key*, *section*, or *appname* were not found.

Description

Returns a single value from a specified section of your application's entry in the HKEY_CURRENT_USER\Software\VB and VBA Program Settings\ branch of the registry.

Rules at a Glance

- If at least one of *appname*, *section*, or *key* is not found in the registry, *GetSetting* returns *default*.

- If *default* is omitted, it is assumed to be a zero-length string ("").

- The function retrieves a value from a subkey of the KEY_CURRENT_USER\Software\VB and VBA Program Settings key of the registry.

- *section* need not be an immediate subkey of *appname*; instead, *section* can be a fully qualified path to a nested subkey, with each subkey separated from its parent by a backslash. For example, a value of Settings\Coordinates for the *section* argument indicates that the value is to be retrieved from

HKEY_CURRENT_USER\Software\VB and VBA Program Settings\ appname\Settings\Coordinates.

Programming Tips and Gotchas

- *GetSetting* is a function that was developed to retrieve data from initialization files in 16-bit environments and to retrieve data from the registry under Windows 9x and Windows NT. The language of the official documentation, however, reflects the language of initialization files. The arguments labeled *appname* and *section* are in fact registry keys; the argument labeled *key* is in fact a registry value entry.

- Because the built-in registry functions in VB create only string-type registry-value entries, *GetSetting* and *GetAllSettings* return string values. Therefore, before you use numeric values returned from the registry, you should explicitly convert the value to a numeric data type by using the appropriate conversion function.

- Use the Application.ExecutablePath property to pass your application's name to the *GetSetting* function as the value of the *appname* parameter, both when reading and writing registry data.

- The built-in registry-manipulation functions allow you to create professional 32-bit applications that use the registry for holding application-specific data, in the same way that .INI files were used in the 16-bit environment. You can, for example, store information about the user's desktop settings (i.e., the size and position of forms) the last time the program was run.

- *GetSetting*, *GetAllSettings*, and *SaveSettings* allow you direct access to only a limited section of the windows registry, that being a special branch created for your application (HKEY_CURRENT_USER\Software\VB and VBA Program Settings*yourappname*). You cannot access or change other registry settings without resorting to the Windows API.

- *GetSetting* does not allow you to retrieve the default value of a registry key. Attempting to do so produces runtime error 5, "Invalid procedure call or argument." This is not as great a limitation as it may appear, since *SaveSetting* also cannot write a default value to a registry key.

- Because *GetSetting* retrieves data from the user branch of the registry, and the physical file that forms the user branch of the registry may change (depending, of course, on who the user is and, in the case of Windows 9x systems, whether the system is configured to support multiple users), never assume that an application has already written data to the registry. In other words, even if you're sure that your application's installation routine or the application itself has successfully stored values in the registry, always supply a meaningful value for the *default* argument.

- Only those settings that were created using either the Windows API or the *SaveSetting* function will be returned. In other words, a VB application does not have a registry entry unless you have created one explicitly.

- Although *GetSetting* writes only string data to the registry, you can use a variable of almost any data type to retrieve it. The *GetSetting* function automatically handles the conversion of string data to the data type of the variable to which the return value of *GetSetting* is assigned. The only exceptions are user-defined data types and arrays of byte data.

- Rather than rely on the relatively underpowered registry-access functionality available in Visual Basic, we highly recommend that you instead use the Registry and RegistryKey classes available in the BCL's Microsoft.Win32 namespace.

See Also

DeleteSetting Procedure, GetAllSettings Function, SaveSetting Procedure

GetTimer Function

Class

Microsoft.VisualBasic.VBMath

Syntax

```
GetTimer()
```

Return Value

A Double indicating the number of seconds

Description

Returns the number of seconds since midnight

Programming Tips and Gotchas

- You can use the *GetTimer* function as an easy method of passing a seed number to the *Randomize* procedure, as follows:

```
Randomize GetTimer()
```

- The *GetTimer* function is ideal for measuring the time taken to execute a procedure or block of code, as the following snippet shows:

```
Dim dblStartTime As Double
Dim i As Integer

dblStartTime = Timer()
For I = 1 to 100
    Console.WriteLine("Hello")
Next
Console.WriteLine("Time Taken = " & GetTimer() - _
                  dblStartTime & " Seconds")
```

VB.NET/VB 6 Differences

- The *GetTimer* function is new to VB.NET. However, it is functionally identical to the VB 6 *Timer* function (and VB.NET Timer property), which continues to be supported.

- In contrast to the VB 6 *Timer* function, which returned a Single, the VB.NET *GetTimer* function and Timer property return a Double.

See Also

Timer Property

GetType Operator

Syntax

```
GetType(typename)
```

typename   *required; n/a*
   The name of a type

Return Value

A Type object containing information about **typename**

Description

Returns type information about a particular type, such as a class, interface, enumeration, delegate, or structure.

Rules at a Glance

- **typename** must be the name of a valid type.

- Passing an instance variable to **typename** generates a compiler error.

Programming Tips and Gotchas

If you don't know the name of the type about which you'd like to get information, but you do have an object instance of that type, you can instead retrieve a Type object using the Type.GetType method.

VB.NET/VB 6 Differences

The GetType operator is new to VB.NET

GoTo Statement

Syntax

```
GoTo label
```

label   *required*
   Type: String literal
   A subroutine name

Description

Passes execution to a specified line within a procedure

Rules at a Glance

label must be a line label

Programming Tips and Gotchas

- GoTo can branch only to lines within the procedure where it appears.

- It is not permitted to branch from outside a `Try...Catch...Finally` block to a point inside the `Catch` or `Finally` block.

- It is also not permitted to branch from within the `Catch` or `Finally` block to a label outside the block.

- The `GoTo` statement is most commonly used with the `On Error` statement to direct control to an error-handling routine.

- `GoTo` is frequently used to control program flow within a procedure, a technique that often produces highly unreadable "spaghetti code." Accordingly, great care should be taken when using the `GoTo` statement.

VB.NET/VB 6 Differences

In VB 6, *label* could be either a line number or a label. In VB.NET, *label* can be only a label.

See Also

On Error Statement

Guid Attribute

Class

System.Runtime.InteropServices.GuidAttribute

Applies to

Assembly, Class, Delegate, Enum, Interface, Struct

Description

Assigns an explicit Globally Unique Identifier (GUID) to a program element when an automatically generated GUID is undesirable. The `<Guid>` attribute is used for COM interop. A GUID can be generated by a utility named *guidgen.exe*.

The major reason for explicitly assigning a GUID to a program element, rather than allowing Visual Studio to do it automatically, is to ensure that it remains constant over successive recompilations of the source code. Because COM uses GUIDs to identify program elements, inadvertently changing a GUID typically causes COM to fail to recognize a component. For example, Visual Studio automatically adds the `<Guid>` attribute to each *AssemblyInfo.vb* file to ensure that, should a type library be generated for a particular project, its library identifier (or LibID) will remain unchanged when the project is recompiled.

Constructor

New(*guid*)

guid   *String*
> The GUID to be assigned to the program element.

Properties

Value   *String*
> Read-only. Returns the GUID of the program element.

Handles Keyword

Syntax

```
Handles name.event
```

name   *required; String literal*
    The name of the class or object whose event the subroutine is handling

event   *required; String literal*
    The name of the event that the subroutine is handling

Description

Defines a procedure as the event handler for a particular event

Rules at a Glance

- The `Handler` keyword is used to define event handlers for events trapped by an object defined with the `WithEvents` keyword.

- The `Handles` keyword can only be used with a procedure declaration, since an event handler must be a procedure rather than a function.

- The `Handles` keyword must be placed on the same line as, and at the end of, a procedure declaration.

Example

In a Windows application, the following definition appears in the declarations section of the Form1 class module:

```
Public WithEvents Button1 As Button
```

The Button1 object is then instantiated with a line of code like the following in the *New* subroutine or another initialization routine:

```
Me.Button1 = New Button
```

The Button1 object's Click event can then be handled with a event handler like the following:

```
Private Sub Button1_Click(ByVal sender As System.Object, _
                    ByVal e As System.EventArgs) _
            Handles Button1.Click
    MsgBox("Hello, World!")
End Sub
```

Programming Tips and Gotchas

- The `WithEvents` and `Handles` are designed to define event handlers at compile time. If you want to define event handlers dynamically at runtime, use the `AddHandler` and `RemoveHandler` statements.

- By convention, event handlers take the form *objectname_eventname*. For example, the Click event of an object named Button1 could be trapped by an event handler named Button1_Click. Although this convention is highly recommended, it is not obligatory.

VB.NET/VB 6 Differences

The `Handles` keyword is new to VB.NET. In VB 6, the link between an object and its event handler was handled automatically and transparently by Visual Basic.

See Also

WithEvents Keyword

Hashtable Class

Namespace

System.Collections

Createable

Yes

Description

A Hashtable object represents a collection of *values* (of type Object) that are indexed by objects called *keys* (also of type Object). We can also think of a hash table as containing key/value pairs.

Identification of the location of elements in a hash table is done using a *hashing function*. Simply put, a hashing function is a function that assigns a location in the hash table to each element, based on the element's value. This is not the place to go into any detail about hashing. It is worth mentioning that hash tables can be very efficient structures for storing and retrieving elements. However, there is no "best approach" to defining hashing functions, and so only experimentation can determine whether this particular implementation of a hash table is efficient in any given case.

Note that the Hashtable class is more flexible than the Collection class of the Microsoft.VisualBasic namespace.

Hashtable class members marked with a plus sign (+) are discussed in detail in their own entries.

Public Shared Method

Synchronized

Public Instance Properties

Count +
IsFixedSize
IsReadOnly
IsSynchronized
Item +
Keys +
SyncRoot
Values +

Public Instance Methods

    Add +
    Clear +
    Clone
    Contains
    ContainsKey +
    ContainsValue +
    CopyTo +
    Equals
    GetEnumerator
    GetHashCode
    GetObjectData
    GetType
    OnDeserialization
    Remove +
    ToString

Example

The following example illustrates most of the members that we will discuss:

```
Private Sub DoHashtable()
    Dim i As Integer
    Dim s() As DictionaryEntry
    Dim obj() As Object
    Dim icKeys As ICollection

    ' Define a new hash table
    Dim h As New Hashtable()

    ' Add some elements to the hash table
    h.Add("Be", "Beethoven")
    h.Add("Ch", "Chopin")
    h.Add("Mo", "Mozart")
    h.Add("Sc", "Schubert")

    ' Copy elements to an array of DictionaryEntry objects and display
    ReDim s(h.Count)
    h.CopyTo(s, 0)
    For i = 0 To h.Count - 1
        Console.WriteLine(s(i).Value)
    Next

    ' Show the keys
    icKeys = h.Keys
    ReDim obj(h.Count)
    icKeys.CopyTo(obj, 0)
    For i = 0 To h.Count - 1
        Console.WriteLine(CStr(obj(i)))
    Next

    ' Does the hash table contain the value "Beethoven"
    MsgBox("Beethoven: " & CStr(h.ContainsValue("Beethoven")))
```

```
    ' Clear the hash table
    h.Clear()
End Sub
```

VB.NET/VB 6 Differences   .

The Hashtable object is new to the .NET platform.

See Also

Collection Class, Queue Class, Stack Class

Hashtable.Add Method

Class

System.Collections.Hashtable

Syntax

```
hashtablevariable.Add(Key, Value)
```

Key   *required; Object*
    The hash table entry's key

Value   *required; Object*
    The hash table entry's value

Return Value

None

Description

Adds a key/value pair to the hash table

Rules at a Glance

- *Key* must be unique or a runtime error occurs.

- Keys are immutable. Once added, a particular key value cannot be changed during the lifetime of the hash table except by removing it through the Remove or Clear method and then adding it once again.

- *Value* need not be unique.

Programming Tips and Gotchas

- According to the documentation, it is better to build a key from a `String` object than the Base Class Library's `StringBuilder` object.

- The Item property can also be used to add new members to the hash table.

- To ensure that key is unique when calling the Add method, you can call the ContainsKey method beforehand.

See Also

Hashtable.ContainsKey Method, Hashtable.Item Property

Hashtable.Clear Method

Class

System.Collections.Hashtable

Syntax

```
hashtablevariable.Clear()
```

Return Value

None

Description

Removes all entries from the hash table

Rules at a Glance

- The Clear method removes all items from the collection, leaving the `Hashtable` object uninitialized. It does not set the object to `Nothing`.
- The Clear method sets the `Hashtable` object's Count property to 0.

Hashtable.ContainsKey Method

Class

System.Collections.Hashtable

Syntax

```
hashtablevariable.ContainsKey(Key)
```

Key   *required; Object*
    The key to search for among the hash table entries

Return Value

A Boolean indicating whether the key exists (`True`) or not (`False`)

Description

Indicates whether a given key is contained in the hash table

Hashtable.ContainsValue Method

Class

System.Collections.Hashtable

Syntax

```
hashtablevariable.ContainsValue(Value)
```

Value   *required; Object*
    The value to search for among the hash table entries

Return Value

A Boolean indicating whether the value exists (`True`) or not (`False`)

Description

Indicates whether a given value is contained in the hash table

Programming Tips and Gotchas

ContainsValue is intended to determine whether a value exists in the hash table; it is not designed to indicate the key belonging to a particular value or to determine whether multiple occurrences of a particular value exist.

Hashtable.CopyTo Method

Class

System.Collections.Hashtable

Syntax

```
hashtablevariable.CopyTo(array, arrayindex)
```

array   *required; Array of* `DictionaryEntry` *structures*
The destination of the items copied from the hash table

arrayindex   *required; Integer*
The first index that is to receive an element of the hash table

Return Value

None

Description

Copies the hash table values into an array of `DictionaryEntry` structures. A `DictionaryEntry` structure is a key/value pair. Note that the array must be sized to accommodate the elements of the hash table prior to calling the CopyTo method.

Rules at a Glance

- *array* must be a one-dimensional array.

- Elements are copied from the hash table to *array* in the same order in which the hash table is iterated.

- The CopyTo method copies each key/value pair in the hash table to a `DictionaryEntry` structure.

- *array*, the array of `DictionaryEntry` structures, must be sized before calling the CopyTo method. This is illustrated in the example.

Example

```
Dim hshStates As New Hashtable
Dim aDE() As DictionaryEntry
```

```
Dim oDE As DictionaryEntry

hshStates.Add("NY", "New York")
hshStates.Add("MI", "Michigan")
hshStates.Add("CA", "California")
hshStates.Add("WI", "Wisconsin")
hshStates.Add("VT", "Vermont")
hshStates.Item("WA") = "Washington"

Redim aDE(hshStates.Count - 1)
hshStates.CopyTo(aDE, 0)
For each oDE in aDE
    Console.WriteLine(oDE.Key & ": " & oDE.Value)
Next
```

See Also

Hashtable.Keys Property

Hashtable.Count Property

Class

System.Collections.Hashtable

Syntax

> *hashtablevariable*.Count()

hashtablevariable   *required;* Hashtable *object*
    A reference to a **Hashtable** object

Return Value

An Integer indicating the number of elements in the hash table

Description

This read-only property returns an Integer specifying the number of elements in the hash table.

Hashtable.Item Property

Class

System.Collections.Hashtable

Syntax

> *hashtablevariable*.Item(*key*)

hashtablevariable   *required; Hashtable object*
    A reference to a Hashtable object

key   *required; Object*
    The key whose value is to be retrieved

Return Value

An Object representing the value associated with *key*

Description

Returns an Object that is the value associated with a particular key/value pair.

Rules at a Glance

- Item is the default property of the `Hashtable` object, and since it is parameterized, we can write:

  hashtablevariable(key)

- Item is a read/write property. In other words, you can use the Item property to retrieve the value belonging to a particular key, as well as to modify the value belonging to a particular key.

- If *key* does not exist in the hash table when you attempt to retrieve a value, the Item property returns `Nothing`.

- If *key* does not exist in the hash table when you attempt to modify a value, the key and its associated value are added to the hash table, as a sort of implicit add. For example, if the key `"AK"` does not exist in a hash table, the code fragment:

  ```
  hshStates.Item("AK") = "Alaska"
  ```

  adds the key `"AK"` and its associated value, `"Alaska"`.

Programming Tips and Gotchas

- To guard against inadvertently adding a member to the hash table when you intend to modify an existing value, call the ContainsKey method beforehand.

- You can also retrieve individual members of the `Hashtable` object by iterating it using the `For Each...Next` statement. Each iteration of the loop returns a `DictionaryEntry` object containing a single key/value pair. For information on the `DictionaryEntry` object, see the entry for the Hashtable. CopyTo method.

Hashtable.Keys Property

Class

System.Collections.Hashtable

Syntax

```
hashtablevariable.Keys()
```

hashtablevariable   *required; Hashtable object*
    A reference to a Hashtable object

Return Value

An `ICollection` interface containing the keys in the hash table

Description

Returns an `ICollection` interface that contains the keys in the hash table. There is not much we can do with an `ICollection` object except copy it to an array of Objects using its CopyTo method, as the following example illustrates.

Example

```
Dim hshStates As New Hashtable
Dim iColl As ICollection
Dim aKeys(), sKey As String

hshStates.Add("NY", "New York")
hshStates.Add("MI", "Michigan")
hshStates.Add("CA", "California")
hshStates.Add("WI", "Wisconsin")
hshStates.Add("VT", "Vermont")
hshStates.Item("WA") = "Washington"
hshStates.Item("AK") = "Alaska"

Redim aKeys(hshStates.Count - 1)
iColl = hshStates.Keys
iColl.CopyTo(aKeys, 0)
for each sKey in aKeys
    Console.WriteLine(hshStates.Item(sKey))
Next
```

Programming Tips and Gotchas

You can work around the inconvenience of calling the `ICollection` object's CopyTo method to convert the interface to another object by defining a class that inherits from or implements `ICollection`.

See Also

Hashtable.Values Property

Hashtable.Remove Method

Class

System.Collections.Hashtable

Syntax

hashtablevariable.Remove(*key*)

hashtablevariable   *required; Hashtable object*
    A reference to a Hashtable object

key   *required; Object*
    The key whose key/value pair is to be removed

Return Value

None

Description

Removes an element from a hash table

Rules at a Glance

- If *key* is found in the hash table, the member is removed, and the Count property is decreased by one.

- If *key* is not found in the hash table, the hash table remains unchanged, and no exception is thrown.

Programming Tips and Gotchas

For cases in which you need to know whether the call to the Remove method has actually removed a key, you can call the ContainsKey method beforehand to make sure that the key you want to remove actually exists.

Hashtable.Values Property

Class

System.Collections.Hashtable

Syntax

```
hashtablevariable.Values()
```

hashtablevariable   *required; Object*
   A reference to a Hashtable object

Return Value

An `ICollection` object containing the values in the hash table

Description

Returns an `ICollection` object that contains the values in the hash table. There is not much we can do with an `ICollection` object except copy it to an array of objects.

See Also

Hashtable.Keys Property

Hex Function

Class

Microsoft.VisualBasic.Conversion

Syntax

```
Hex(number)
```

number   *required; Numeric or String*
   A valid numeric or string expression

Return Value

String representing the hexadecimal value of *number*

Description

Returns a string that represents the hexadecimal value of *number*

Rules at a Glance

- If *number* contains a fractional part, it will be automatically rounded to the nearest whole number before the *Hex* function is evaluated.

- *number* must evaluate to a numeric expression that ranges from –2,147,483,648 to 2,147,483,647. If the argument is outside of this range, runtime error 6, "Overflow," results.

- The return value of *Hex* is dependent upon the value and type of *number*:

number	Return value
Nothing	Zero (0)
Any other number	Up to eight hexadecimal characters

Programming Tips and Gotchas

If the value of *number* is known beforehand and is not the result of an expression, you can represent the number as a hexadecimal by simply affixing &H to *number*. Each of the following two statements assigns a hexadecimal value to a variable, for instance:

```
lngHexValue1 = &HFF                       ' Assigns 255
lngHexValue2 = "&H" & Len(dblNumber)      ' Assigns 8
```

See Also

Oct Function

Hour Function

Class

Microsoft.VisualBasic.DateAndTime

Syntax

```
Hour(timevalue)
```

timevalue   *required; Date*
    Date variable or literal date

Return Value

An Integer from 0 to 23, specifying the hour of the day

Description

Extracts the hour element from a time expression

Example

The line:

```
MsgBox(Hour(#1:33:00 PM#))
```

displays the number 13.

Rules at a Glance

- Regardless of the time format passed to *Hour*, the return value will be a whole number between 0 and 23, representing the hour of a 24-hour clock.

- If *time* contains Nothing, 0 is returned, so be careful here to check for Nothing.

- You can also use the *DatePart* function.

See Also

Minute Function, Second Function

IDataObject Interface

Namespace

System.Windows.Forms

Createable

No

Description

The IDataObject interface is used by the Clipboard for data-transfer operations. It is also used for drag-and-drop operations. An instance of the IDataObject interface is returned by the Clipboard object's GetData method.

Public Instance Methods

Those methods marked with a plus sign (+) are covered in more detail in their own entries:

```
GetData +
GetDataPresent +
GetFormats +
SetData
```

VB.NET/VB 6 Differences

The IDataObject interface is new to VB.NET.

See Also

Clipboard Class

IDataObject.GetData Method

Class

System.Windows.Forms.IDataObject

Syntax

```
GetData(format [,autoconvert])
```

format   *required; String or Type object*
Field member of the DataFormats class (see later for more information on this) or a Type object representing the format of the data

autoconvert   *optional; Boolean*
True to convert the data to the specified format

Return value

An Object that contains Clipboard data in the specified format

Description

Retrieves the data of the given format, optionally converting the data format

Rules at a Glance

- The *format* argument can be one of the following string values:

    DataFormats.Bitmap
    DataFormats.CommaSeparatedValue
    DataFormats.Dib
    DataFormats.Dif
    DataFormats.EnhancedMetafile
    DataFormats.FileDrop
    DataFormats.Html
    DataFormats.Locale
    DataFormats.MetafilePict
    DataFormats.OemText
    DataFormats.Palette
    DataFormats.PenData
    DataFormats.Riff
    DataFormats.Rtf
    DataFormats.Serializable (a format that encapsulates any type of Windows Forms object)
    DataFormats.StringFormat
    DataFormats.SymbolicLink
    DataFormats.Text
    DataFormats.Tiff
    DataFormats.UnicodeText
    DataFormats.WaveAudio

- If *format* is a string, the *autoconvert* argument can be supplied in the method call.

- If the GetData method cannot find data in *format*, it attempts to convert the data to *format*. If the data cannot be converted to the *format*, or if the data was stored with *autoconvert* set to `False`, the method returns `Nothing`.

Example

The following example extracts the text that is currently on the Clipboard:

```
' Declare IDataObject variable and get clipboard IDataObject
Dim di As IDataObject = Clipboard.GetDataObject

Dim obj As Object

' Call GetData method of IDataObject object to get clipboard data
obj = di.GetData(DataFormats.Text, False)

' Show the text, if any
If obj Is Nothing Then
    MsgBox("No text on clipboard.")
Else
    MsgBox(CStr(obj))
End If
```

See Also

IDataObject.GetDataPresent Method, IDataObject.GetFormats Method

---

IDataObject.GetDataPresent Method

Class

System.Windows.Forms.IDataObject

Syntax

```
GetDataPresent(format [,autoconvert])
```

format   *required; String or Type object*
   Field member of the DataFormats class (see later for more information on this) or a Type object representing the format of the data for which to search

autoconvert   *optional; Boolean*
   True to convert the data to the specified format

Return value

Boolean value indicating whether the Clipboard holds data of the specified format or of a format that can be converted to *format*

Description

Returns a Boolean value indicating whether the Clipboard holds data of the specified format or of a format that the present data can be converted to

Rules at a Glance

- The *format* argument can be one of the following string values:

    DataFormats.Bitmap
    DataFormats.CommaSeparatedValue
    DataFormats.Dib
    DataFormats.Dif
    DataFormats.EnhancedMetafile
    DataFormats.FileDrop
    DataFormats.Html
    DataFormats.Locale
    DataFormats.MetafilePict
    DataFormats.OemText
    DataFormats.Palette
    DataFormats.PenData
    DataFormats.Riff
    DataFormats.Rtf
    DataFormats.Serializable (a format that encapsulates any type of Windows Forms object)
    DataFormats.StringFormat
    DataFormats.SymbolicLink
    DataFormats.Text
    DataFormats.Tiff
    DataFormats.UnicodeText
    DataFormats.WaveAudio

- If *format* is a string, the *autoconvert* argument can be supplied in the method call. A value of **False** indicates that the function should determine whether the data stored by the **IDataObject** instance is in the format defined by *format*; a value of **True** indicates that the function should determine whether the data stored by the **IDataObject** instance is in or is capable of being converted to the format defined by *format*.

Example

The following code will inform us whether the Clipboard contains a bitmap:

```
Dim di As IDataObject
di = clipboard.GetDataObject
MsgBox(di.GetDataPresent(Dataformats.Bitmap))
```

See Also

IDataObject.GetData Method, IDataObject.GetFormats Method

IDataObject.GetFormats Method

Class

System.Windows.Forms.IDataObject

Syntax

```
GetDataFormats([autoconvert])
```

autoconvert   *optional; Boolean*

    `True` to retrieve all formats that the Clipboard data is associated with or can be converted to; `False` to retrieve only native data formats

Return Value

A String array containing a list of all supported formats

Description

Retrieves a list of all the formats that the Clipboard data is associated with or can be converted to

Rules at a Glance

The elements in the array returned by the method can take any of the following values:

    DataFormats.Bitmap
    DataFormats.CommaSeparatedValue
    DataFormats.Dib
    DataFormats.Dif
    DataFormats.EnhancedMetafile
    DataFormats.FileDrop
    DataFormats.Html
    DataFormats.Locale
    DataFormats.MetafilePict
    DataFormats.OemText
    DataFormats.Palette
    DataFormats.PenData
    DataFormats.Riff
    DataFormats.Rtf
    DataFormats.Serializable (a format that encapsulates any type of Windows Forms object)
    DataFormats.StringFormat
    DataFormats.SymbolicLink
    DataFormats.Text
    DataFormats.Tiff
    DataFormats.UnicodeText
    DataFormats.WaveAudio

See Also

IDataObject.GetData Method, IDataObject.GetDataPresent Method

---

IEEERemainder Function

Class

System.Math

Syntax

```
Math.IEEERemainder(x, y)
```

x and *y*   *required; Double*

Return Value

Returns the remainder after dividing *x* by *y*

Description

Returns a Double whose value is the remainder after dividing *x* by *y*

Example

```
Math.IEEEremainder(4, 3)          ' Returns 1
```

Rules at a Glance

- VB has a built-in Mod operator that also returns the remainder upon division.

- The *IEEERemainder* function complies with the remainder operation as defined in Section 5.1 of ANSI/IEEE Std 754-1985; IEEE Standard for Binary Floating-Point Arithmetic; Institute of Electrical and Electronics Engineers, Inc; 1985.

Programming Tips and Gotchas

This is a Shared member, so it can be used without creating any objects.

VB.NET/VB 6 Differences

The IEEERemainder function is new to the .NET Framework.

If...Then...Else Statement

Syntax

```
If condition Then
    [statements]
[ElseIf condition-n Then
    [elseifstatements] ...
[Else
    [elsestatements]]
End If
```

Or, you can use the single line syntax:

```
If condition Then [statements] [Else elsestatements]
```

`condition`   *required; Boolean*
An expression returning either True or False or an object type

`statements`   *optional*
Program code to be executed if `condition` is true

`condition-n`   *optional*
Same as condition

elseifstatements *optional*

Program code to be executed if the corresponding *condition-n* is True

elsestatements *optional*

Program code to be executed if the corresponding *condition* or *condition-n* is False

Description

Executes a statement or block of statements based on the Boolean (True or False) value of an expression

Rules at a Glance

- If *condition* is True, the statements following the If are executed.

- If *condition* is False and no Else or ElseIf statement is present, execution continues with the corresponding End If statement. If *condition* is False and ElseIf statements are present, the condition of the next ElseIf is tested. If *condition* is False and an Else is present, the statements following the Else are executed.

- In the block form, each If statement must have a corresponding End If statement. ElseIf statements do not have their own End If. For example:

  ```
  If condition Then
      statements
  ElseIf condition Then
      statements
  End If
  ```

- ElseIf and Else are optional, and any number of ElseIf and Else statements can appear in the block form. However, no ElseIf statements can appear after an Else.

- *condition* can be any statement that evaluates to True or False.

- If *condition* returns Null, it will be treated as False.

- You can also use the If statement to determine object types by using the TypeOf and Is keywords, as follows:

  ```
  If TypeOf objectname Is objecttype Then
  ```

- *statements* are only optional in the block form of If. However, *statements* are required when using the single-line form of If in which there is no Else clause.

Programming Tips and Gotchas

- You can use the single-line form of the If statement to execute multiple statements, which you can specify by delimiting the statements using colons. However, single-line If statements are hard to read and maintain and should be avoided for all but the simplest of situations.

- In situations where you have many possible values to test, you will find the Select Case statement much more flexible, manageable, and readable than a bunch of nested If statements.

- You will come across situations in which very large blocks of code have to be executed based one or more conditions. In these—and in all situations—you should try to make your code as readable as possible, not only for other programmers, but for yourself, since you will probably need to revisit the code several months down the line. For example, consider a scenario in which, at the beginning of a procedure, a check is made to see if the procedure should be executed under a given set of circumstances. You have the choice of surrounding the whole code with an If...Then...End If construct, like this:

  ```
  If iSuccess Then
      ...
      ...
      ...
  End If
  ```

  Or you can instead check for a False condition and, if found, exit the subroutine:

  ```
  If Not iSuccess Then
      Exit Sub
  End If
  ...
  ...
  ...
  ```

  The latter alternative can be much easier to read.

- Indentation is important for the readability of If, and especially nested If, statements. The set of statements within each new If...Else...EndIf block should be indented. When using the Visual Studio IDE, you can simply select a block of code and press the tab key to indent the complete selected block. The following example shows correctly indented code:

  ```
  If x = y Then
      DoSomethingHere
      If y < z Then
          DoSomethingElseToo
      Else
          DoAnotherThing
          If z - 1 = 100 Then
              DoAThing
          End If
      End If
  Else
      DoAlternative
  End If
  ```

- You may often run into code such as:

  ```
  If iSuccess Then ...
  ```

  where iSuccess is an Integer variable. The statement works because Visual Basic interprets all non-zero values as equal to Boolean True and all zero values as equal to Boolean False. However, if Option Strict is on, statements such as these will generate a compiler error, since VB.NET will not automatically convert the *iSuccess* integer to the Boolean required by the If statement.

- Logical comparison operators can be included in the *condition* expression, allowing you to make decisions based on the outcome of more than one individual element. The most common of these is `And` and `Or`. You can create conditions like:

```
If (x = 0) Or (1/x = 2) Then
```

  Note the use of parentheses to improve readability.

- VB.NET has introduced the `AndAlso` and `OrElse` operators, which work exactly like the `And` and `Or` operators, respectively, except that they evaluate the statement parts from left to right *only* until enough information is obtained to determine the truth value of the whole statement. For example, consider the statement

```
If (X AndAlso Y) Then
```

  If X is `False`, then Y is not evaluated because the entire statement is `False` regardless of the truth value of Y. This is referred to as *short-circuiting*. It provides a significant advantage in case evaluation of Y would produce an error. For example, we want to employ short-circuiting in the following case

```
If (x <> 0) AndAlso (1/x > 10) Then . . .
```

  because in this case if **x** = 0, then the statement 1/x>10 will produce an error if it is evaluated.

- The `If` statement is also used with objects to determine if an object variable is `Nothing`. This is done using the `Is` operator:

```
If Not (objectvar Is Nothing) Then
```

See Also

IIf Function

IIf Function

Class

Microsoft.VisualBasic.Interaction

Syntax

```
IIf(expression, truepart, falsepart)
```

expression   *required; Boolean*
    Expression to be evaluated

truepart   *required; any value or expression*
    Expression or value to return if *expression* is `True`

falsepart   *required; any value or expression*
    Expression or value to return if *expression* is `False`

Return Value

The value or result of the expression indicated by *truepart* or *falsepart*

Description

Returns one of two results, depending on whether *expression* evaluates to True or False

Rules at a Glance

- *IIf* will evaluate only one of *truepart* or *falsepart*, depending on the value of *expression*.

- The *IIf* function is the equivalent of:

```
If testexpression Then
    Return truepart
Else
    Return falsepart
End If
```

- *truepart* and *falsepart* can be a variable, constant, literal, expression, or the return value of a function call.

Programming Tips and Gotchas

- The *IIf* function is ideal for very simple tests resulting in single expressions. If you really feel the need, *IIf* function calls can be nested; however, your code can very quickly become difficult to read. The following code fragment illustrates the use of a nested *IIf* function:

```
Dim x As Integer
x = CInt(Text1.Text)
MsgBox(IIf(x < 10, "Less than ten", IIf(x < 20, _
        "Less than 20", "Greater than 20")))
```

- In previous versions of VB, developers tended to avoid the *IIf* function in favor of the If statement for all but the most simple uses because of its poor performance. In VB.NET, the performance of *IIf* has been improved significantly, although it remains significantly slower than an If statement. The average number of seconds required to call the *IIf* function a million times and to execute an If...ElseIf...Else...End If statement a million times under the two VB versions showed the following differences:

	IIf function	If statement
VB 6	11.09	0.52
VB.NET	6.12	0.02

In other words, the performance of *IIf* from VB 6 to VB.NET has improved by 100%. At the same time, the function is over 300 times slower than an If statement under VB.NET!

See Also

If...Then...Else Statement

Implements Keyword

Syntax

```
Implements interfacename.interfacemember [, ...]
```

`interfacename`   *required; String literal*
 The name of the interface being implemented by a class

`interfacemember`   *required; String literal*
 The name of the interface property, function, procedure, or event that is
 being implemented by a class

Description

Indicates that a class member provides the implementation of a member defined in
an interface

Rules at a Glance

- The `Implements` keyword can only be used in a class module in which the
  `Implements` statement has been used to define an abstract base class that the
  class is to implement.

- The `Implements` keyword follows the property, function, procedure, or event
  definition, and must be on the same line.

- The class member implementing the interface member must be of the same
  type (property, function, procedure, or event) as the interface member, and its
  argument list and, in the case of functions and properties, return type must
  also be identical to that of the interface member.

- Class members must implement all of the members declared in the interface.

Example

See the example in the Implements Statement" entry.

VB.NET/VB 6 Differences

- The `Implements` keyword is new to VB.NET. Its addition means that the
  implementation of a property, function, procedure, or event does not have to
  use the name defined by the interface. This modifies the VB 6 practice, which
  requires that class members that implement an interface definition have the
  form `interfacename_membername`.

- VB 6 does not allow derived classes to implement events defined in interfaces. VB.NET removes this restriction.

See Also

Implements Statement, Interface Statement

Implements Statement

Syntax

```
Implements InterfaceName [, InterfaceName][, ...]
```

InterfaceName   *required; String literal*
   The name of the interface that a class implements

Description

The **Implements** statement specifies that you will *implement* an interface within
the class in which the **Implements** statement appears.

Rules at a Glance

* Implementing an interface or class means that the implementing class will
  provide code to implement every Public member of the implemented interface or class. If you fail to implement even a single Public member, an error
  will result.

* The **Implements** statement cannot be used in a standard module; it is used
  only in class modules.

* By convention, interface names begin with a capital I, as in **IMyInterface**.

* For more information on this topic, see Chapter 4.

Example

```
Friend Interface IAnimal

    ReadOnly Property Name() As String
    Function Eat() As String
    Function SoundNoise() As String
End Interface

Public Class CWolf
    Implements IAnimal

    Public ReadOnly Property Name() As String _
                        Implements IAnimal.Name
      Get
         Return "Wolf"
      End Get
    End Property

    Public Function Eat() As String Implements IAnimal.Eat
        Eat = "caribou, salmon, other fish"
    End Function

    Public Function Sound() As String Implements IAnimal.SoundNoise
        Sound = "howl"
    End Function
End Class

Module modMain

Public Sub Main
    Dim oWolf As New CWolf
    Console.WriteLine(oWolf.Sound)
```

```
    oWolf = Nothing
End Sub

End Module
```

Programming Tips and Gotchas

- If you do not wish to support a procedure from the implemented class, you must still create a procedure declaration for the implemented procedure. However, you can simply raise an error using the special error constant `Const E_ NOTIMPL = &H80004001` so a user will know that the member is not implemented in any meaningful way. Alternately, you can also raise a NotImplementedException exception.

- Interfaces, or abstract base classes, allow for greater coherence when developing in teams. For example, all developers could use a set of interfaces to produce controls and objects of a particular type without being constrained by implementation. That is, each developer would be free to implement a particular property or method in the way that he saw fit.

- Maintaining compatibility across multiple versions dictates that interfaces should not change once they have been written and distributed. Any additional functionality required should be provided by defining additional interfaces.

- VB.NET provides only single inheritance using the `Inherits` statement. However, by using interface-based inheritance with the `Implements` statement, you can in effect implement multiple inheritance.

VB.NET/VB 6 Differences

- In VB 6, the `Implements` statement does not support events; any events publicly declared in an interface are ignored. VB.NET, on the other hand, allows derived classes to trap the events defined in interfaces.

See Also

Implements Statement, Interface Statement

Reference I-K

Imports Statement

Syntax

```
Imports [aliasname = ] namespace [.element]
```

aliasname   *optional; String literal*
    The name by which the namespace will be referenced in the module

namespace   *required; String literal*
    The name of the namespace being imported

element   *optional*
    The name of an element in the namespace

Description

Imports namespaces or parts of namespaces, making their members available to the current module

Rules at a Glance

- A single `Imports` statement can import one namespace.

- A module can have have as many `Imports` statements as needed.

- `Imports` statements are used to import names from other projects and assemblies, as well as from namespaces in the current project.

- `Imports` statements must be placed in a module before references to any identifiers (e.g., variables, classes, procedures, functions, etc.).

- *namespace* must be a fully qualified namespace name, even if you use the /rootnamespace compiler option or supply a value for the "Root namespace" text box in the General tab of a project's Properties dialog in Visual Studio.

- If *aliasname* is absent from an `Imports` statement, types in that namespace can be referenced without qualification.

- If *aliasname* is present in an `Imports` statement, types in that namespace must be qualified with *aliasname* in order to be accessible.

- The name *aliasname* must not be assigned to any other member within the module.

- If *element* is specified, it can be the name of an enumeration, structure, class, or module within the namespace. If specified, this restricts importation to members of that element only.

Programming Tips and Gotchas

- In ASP.NET, a number of namespaces are imported automatically. These include System.Web and its child namespaces.

- You do not use the `Imports` statement to import namespaces into an ASP.NET application. Instead, you can import a namespace into an ASP.NET application in a number of ways:

  — By creating an `<add namespace>` directive in a *web.config* configuration file. For example:

    ```
    <compilation>
       <namespaces>
          <add namespace="System.IO" />
          ...
       </namespaces>
    ```

    imports the System.IO namespace within the scope defined in the *web.config* file.

  — By adding an `@ Import` directive to *global.asax*. For example:

    ```
    <%@ Import namespace="System.IO" %>
    ```

    imports the System.IO namespace for the ASP.NET application.

  — By adding an `@ Import` page directive. This has the same form as the *global.asax* directive, and must appear at the beginning of the page.

See Also

Namespace Statement

Inherits Statement

Syntax

```
Inherits classname
```

<code>classname</code>   *required; String literal*
    The name of the inherited (base) class

Description

Specifies the name of the class that is being inherited, that is, the base class. The statement can appear immediately after the `Class` statement or the `Interface` statement.

Rules at a Glance

- The `Inherits` statement must be the first line of code in the class module. It can be preceeded only by blank lines or comments. For example:

```
Public Class CDerivedClass
    Inherits CBaseClass
    ...
```

- VB.NET supports single code-based inheritance only. That is, there can be only a single `Inherits` statement in any class module.

- If the `Inherits` statement is used to define the interfaces inherited by an interface, multiple interfaces can be listed, with a comma used to delimit them. For example:

```
Interface IPerson
    Property Name As String
End Interface

Interface IEmployee
    Property SSN As String
End Interface

Interface ISalaried
    Inherits IPerson, IEmployee

    Property Salaried As Boolean
    Property Salary As Decimal
End Interface
```

Programming Tips and Gotchas

The `Inherits` statement implements code inheritance. You can also use the `Implements` statement to implement interface inheritance. In that case, a class can be derived from more than one virtual base class. (In other words, you can effectively implement multiple inheritance through interface inheritance using the `Implements` statement.)

See Also

Class Statement, Interface Statement

Input Procedure

Class

Microsoft.VisualBasic.FileSystem

Syntax

    Input(filenumber, value)

`filenumber`   *required; Integer*
    Any valid file number

`value`   *required; any*
    Data to read from file

Description

Reads delimited data from a file into variables. This statement is used to read files that were created using the *Write* procedure, in which case the items are comma delimited with quotation marks around strings.

Rules at a Glance

- Data read by *Input* has usually been written using the *Write* procedure.

- Use this statement with files that have been opened in Input or Binary mode only.

- If `value` is numeric and the *Input* procedure encounters non-numeric data, an InvalidCastException exception occurs.

- The *Input* procedure strips off the quotation marks that it finds around strings.

- After the *Input* procedure reads `value`, it advances the file pointer to the next unread variable or, if the file contains no additional delimited data, to the end of the file.

- If the end of the file is reached during the operation of the *Input* procedure, an error is generated.

- The *Input* procedure assigns string or numeric data to `value` without modification. However, other types of data can be modified as shown in the following table:

Data	Value assigned to variable
Delimiting comma or blank line	"" (empty string)
#TRUE# or #FALSE#	True or False
#yyyy-mm-dd hh:mm:ss#	Date and/or time

Note that `#TRUE#` and `#FALSE#` are case sensitive.

Example

If the file *c:\data.txt* contains the following data:

    "one", "two", "three"

then the following code will print each string on a separate line in the Output window:

```
Dim fr As Integer = FreeFile()
Dim sLine As String

FileOpen(fr, "c:\data.txt", OpenMode.Input)

Do While Not EOF(fr)
    Input(fr, sLine)
    Console.WriteLine(sLine)
Loop

FileClose(fr)
```

Programming Tips and Gotchas

- Use the *EOF* function to determine whether the end of the file has been reached.

- Use the *Write* procedure to write data to a file, since *Write* delimits data fields correctly. This ensures that the data can be read correctly with the *Input* procedure.

VB.NET/VB 6 Differences

The VB.NET *Input* procedure corresponds to the VB 6 *Input* procedure, with a number of significant differences:

- The # symbol, which optionally preceded `filenumber` in VB 6, is not supported in VB.NET.

- In VB 6, the `value` argument could be a comma-delimited list of variables. In VB.NET, it must be a single variable of any type.

- In VB 6, if `value` is numeric and the data read from the file is not numeric, `value` is initialized to the default value for that type. In VB.NET, this generates an exception.

- In addition to the standard data types, VB 6 also recognizes Empty, Null, and Error types. In VB.NET, these are not supported.

See Also

Write Procedure

InputBox Function

Class

Microsoft.VisualBasic.Interaction

Syntax

```
InputBox(prompt[, title] [, defaultresponse] [, xpos] _
        [, ypos])
```

prompt *required; String*

The message in the dialog box

title *optional; String*

The title bar of the dialog box

defaultresponse *optional; String*

String to be displayed in the text box on loading

xpos *optional; Numeric*

The distance in twips from the left-hand side of the screen to the left-hand side of the dialog box

ypos *optional; Numeric*

The distance in twips from the top of the screen to the top of the dialog box

Return Value

A String containing the contents of the text box from the *InputBox* dialog box

Description

Displays a dialog box containing a prompt for the user, a text box for entering data, and an OK, a Cancel, and (optionally) a Help button. When the user clicks OK, the function returns the contents of the text box.

Rules at a Glance

- If the user clicks Cancel, a zero-length string ("") is returned. Thus, once again, Microsoft has apparently made it impossible for us to distinguish when the user enters the empty string and when the user hits the Cancel button.

- *prompt* can contain approximately 1,000 characters, including nonprinting characters like the intrinsic **vbCrLf** constant.

- If the *title* argument is omitted, the name of the current application or project is displayed in the title bar.

- If you don't use the *default* parameter to specify a default entry for the text box, the text box is shown as empty, and a zero-length string is returned when the user does not enter anything in the text box prior to clicking OK.

- *xpos* and *ypos* are specified in twips.

- If the *xpos* parameter is omitted, the dialog box is centered horizontally.

- If the *ypos* parameter is omitted, the top of the dialog box is positioned approximately one-third of the way down the screen.

Programming Tips and Gotchas

- If you are omitting one or more of the optional arguments and are using subsequent arguments, you must use a comma to signify the missing parameter. For example, the following code fragment will display a prompt, a default string in the text box, and the Help button, but default values will be used for the title and positioning.

```
Dim sString As String = InputBox("Enter it now", , _
                                 "Something")
```

- Note that *InputBox* returns a string. Your code is responsible for converting it to the required data type before using it.

See Also

MsgBox Function

InputString Function

Class

Microsoft.VisualBasic.FileSystem

Syntax

```
InputString(filenumber, charcount)
```

filenumber   *required; Integer*
    Any valid file number

charcount   *required; Integer*
    Number of characters to read from file

Return Value

A String containing *charcount* characters

Description

Reads data from a file into a string variable

Rules at a Glance

- *InputString* should only be used with files opened in input (OpenMode. Input) or binary mode (OpenMode.Binary).
- *InputString* begins reading from the current position of the file pointer.
- *InputString* returns all the characters it reads, regardless of their type. This include spaces, carriage returns, linefeeds, commas, end-of-file markers, unprintable characters, etc.
- Once the function finishes reading *charcount* characters, it also advances the file pointer *charcount* characters.

Example

If the file *c:\data.txt* contains the data:

```
abcdefghijklmnopq
```

the following code reads the characters, three at a time:

```
Dim fr As Integer = FreeFile()
Dim sLine As String
Dim i As Long
FileOpen(fr, "c:\data2.txt", OpenMode.Input)

For i = 1 To LOF(fr) \ 3
    sLine = InputString(fr, 3)
```

```
        Console.WriteLine(sLine)
    Next

    FileClose(fr)
```

Programming Tips and Gotchas

- *InputString* reads data written to a file using the *Print*, *PrintLine*, or *FilePut* functions.

- *InputString* always attempts to precisely read **charcount** characters from the file. If there are no **charcount** characters from the position of the file pointer to the end of the file, *InputString* attempts to read beyond the end of the file, thereby generating an exception. To prevent this, you should use the *LOF* function after opening the file to ensure that you don't attempt to read past the end-of-file marker.

VB.NET/VB 6 Differences

- Though a new function in VB.NET, *InputString* directly corresponds to the *Input*, *Input$*, *InputB*, and *InputB$* functions in VB 6.

- The order of parameters is reversed in VB.NET and VB 6. In VB 6, the first parameter is **charcount**, and the second is **filenumber**.

- The # symbol, which optionally preceded **filenumber** in VB 6, is not supported in VB.NET.

See Also

FilePut, FilePutObject Procedures, Print, PrintLine Procedures

---

InStr Function

Class

Microsoft.VisualBasic.Strings

Syntax

```
    InStr(start, string1, string2[, compare])
```

or:

```
    InStr(string1, string2[, compare])
```

start   *required in first syntax; Numeric*
    The starting position for the search

string1   *required; String*
    The string being searched

string2   *required; String*
    The string being sought

compare   *optional;* CompareMethod *enumeration*
    The type of string comparison

Return Value

An Integer indicating the position of the first occurrence of *string2* in *string1*

Description

Finds the starting position of one string within another

Rules at a Glance

- The return value of *InStr* is influenced by the values of *string1* and *string2*, as the following table details:

Condition	InStr return value
string1 is zero-length or Nothing	0
string2 is zero-length or Nothing	start
string2 not found	0
string2 found within *string1*	Position at which the start of *string2* is found
start > len(string2)	0

- In the second syntax, *InStr* commences the search with the first character of *string1*.
- If the *start* argument is 0 or Nothing, an error occurs.
- The *compare* argument can be one of CompareMethod.Binary (a case-sensitive comparison) or CompareMethod.Text (a case-insensitive comparison). If *comparemode* is omitted, the type of comparison is determined by the Option Compare setting.

See Also

InstrRev Function

InStrRev Function

Class

Microsoft.VisualBasic.Strings

Syntax

```
InstrRev(stringcheck, stringmatch[, start[, compare]])
```

stringcheck   *required; String*
    The string to be searched.

stringmatch   *required; String*
    The substring to be found within *stringcheck*.

start   *optional; Numeric*
    The starting position of the search. If no value is specified, *start* defaults to 1.

compare   *optional;* CompareMethod *enumeration*
A constant indicating how *stringcheck* and *stringmatch* should be compared.

Return Value

Long

Description

Determines the starting position of a substring within a string by searching from the end of the string to its beginning

Rules at a Glance

- While *InStr* searches a string from left to right, *InStrRev* searches a string from right to left.

- The *compare* argument can be one of CompareMethod.Binary (for a case-sensitive search) or CompareMethod.Text (for a case-insensitive search). If *compare* is omitted, the type of comparison is binary. Note that Option Compare is not used, unlike with the *InStr* function.

- *start* designates the starting point of the search as counted from the start of *stringcheck*. To start the search at the end of *stringcheck*, either omit the *start* argument or set it to −1.

- If *stringmatch* is not found, *InStrRev* returns 0.

- If *stringmatch* is found within *stringcheck*, the value returned by *InStrRev* is the position of *stringcheck* from the start of the string.

Example

This example uses both *InStr* and *InStrRev* to highlight the different results produced by each. Using a *stringcheck* of "I like the functionality that InStrRev gives", *InStr* finds the first occurrence of "th" at character 8, while *InStrRev* finds the first occurrence of "th" at character 26.

```
Dim myString, sSearch As String

myString = "I like the functionality that InsStrRev gives"
sSearch = "th"

Console.WriteLine(InStr(myString, sSearch))
Console.WriteLine(InStrRev(myString, sSearch))
```

See Also

InStr Function

Int Function

Class

Microsoft.VisualBasic.Conversion

Syntax

```
Int(number)
```

number   *required; any valid numeric data type*
    The number to be processed

Return Value

Returns a value of the data type passed to it

Description

Returns the integer portion of a number

Rules at a Glance

- The fractional part of *number* is removed, and the resulting integer value is returned. *Int* does not round *number* to the nearest whole number. For example, Int(100.9) returns 100.

- If *number* is negative, *Int* returns the first negative integer less than or equal to *number*. For example, Int(-10.1) returns –11.

Programming Tips and Gotchas

- *Int* and *Fix* work identically with positive numbers. However, for negative numbers, *Fix* returns the first negative integer greater than *number*, while *Int* returns the first negative integer less than *number*. For example, Fix(-10. 1) returns –10, while Int(-10.1) returns -11.

- Don't confuse the *Int* function with *CInt*. *CInt* casts the number passed to it as an Integer data type, whereas *Int* returns the same data type that was passed to it.

See Also

CInt Function, Fix Function, Round Function

Interface Statement

Syntax

```
[ accessmodifier ] [Shadows] Interface name
...statements
End Interface
```

accessmodifier   *optional; Keyword*
    One of the following keywords, which determines the visibility of the interface:

Public   *optional; Keyword*
    Indicates that the interface is publicly accessible anywhere both inside and outside of the project.

Private   *optional; Keyword*
    Indicates that the interface is accessible to any nested types, as well as to the type (if any) in which it is defined.

Protected   *optional; Keyword*

> Indicates that the interface is accessible only to derived classes; a protected interface can only be declared inside of a class.

Friend   *optional; Keyword*

> Indicates that the interface is accessible only within the project that contains the interface definition.

Protected Friend   *optional; Keyword*

> Indicates that the interface is declard inside of a class and that it is accessible throughout the project that contains the interface definition, as well as to derived classes.

Shadows   *optional; Keyword*

> Indicates that the interface shadows an identically named element in a base class.

name   *required; String literal*

> The name of the interface

statements   *required*

> Code that defines the interface members that derived classes must implement

Description

Defines a virtual base class along with its public members. The interface can then be implemented by derived classes using the `Implements` statement.

Rules at a Glance

- The standard naming conventions for *name* apply. However, by convention, interface names generally begin with the letter I.

- If *accessmodifier* is omitted, the interface is `Public` by default.

- The interface definition (*statements*) may contain the following elements:

  Inherits statement

  > Indicates that *name* inherits its properties and methods from another interface. Its syntax is:

  ```
  Inherits interfacename[, interfacename...]
  ```

  > where *interfacename* is the name(s) of the interface(s) from which *name* inherits.

  Property definitions

  > Property definitions take the form:

  ```
  [ Default ] Property procname([arglist]) As type
  ```

  > where *procname* is the name of the property, `Default` indicates that *procname* is a property array (whose argument list is defined by *arglist*) that is the interface's default property, and *type* indicates the data type of the property. The `ReadOnly` and `WriteOnly` keywords can also be used.

  Function definitions

  > Functions are defined as follows:

  ```
  Function membername([arglist]) As type
  ```

where *membername* is the name of the function, `arglist` defines the number and type of arguments that can be passed to the procedure, and `type` indicates the function's return value.

Procedure definitions

Procedures are defined as follows:

```
Sub membername[(arglist)]
```

where *membername* is the name of the procedure, and `arglist` specifies the number and type of arguments that can be passed to the procedure.

Event definitions

Events are defined as follows:

```
Event membername[(arglist)]
```

where *membername* is the name of the event, and `arglist` defines the number and type of arguments that are passed back to an event handler whenever the event is fired.

In each case, the syntax of the statement is different from the "standard" VB. NET syntax. Access modifiers, for instance, are not permitted as a part of interface member definitions, nor are **End...** statements, such as **End Function, End Sub**, or **End Property**.

- The *name* interface cannot inherit from an interface whose access type is more restrictive than its own. For example, if *name* is a Public interface, it cannot inherit from a Friend interface.

- Classes that implement the interface must implement each of its methods, which must have the same argument list and, in the case of functions and properties, return a value of the same data type as specified by the interface definition.

Rules at a Glance

- An interface can only inherit from another interface that has equal or wider accessability. Thus, for instance, a Public interface cannot inherit from a Private interface, but the reverse is allowed.

Programming Tips and Gotchas

An interface can have only one default property. This includes properties defined in base interfaces, as well as in the interface itself.

VB.NET/VB 6 Differences

The **Interface...End Interface** construct is new to VB.NET. In VB 6, an interface is defined by creating a class module whose members have no implementation.

See Also

Implements Keyword, Implements Statement

IPmt Function

Class

Microsoft.VisualBasic.Financial

Syntax

```
IPmt(rate, per, nper, pv[, fv[, due]])
```

rate   *required; Double*
> The interest rate per period.

per   *required; Double*
> The period for which a payment is to be computed.

nper   *required; Double*
> The total number of payment periods.

pv   *required; Double*
> The present value of a series of future payments.

fv   *optional; Double*
> The future value or cash balance after the final payment. If omitted, the default value is 0.

due   *optional;* DueDate *enumeration*
> A value indicating when payments are due. DueDate.EndOfPeriod (or 0) indicates that payments are due at the end of the payment period; DueDate. BegOfPeriod (or 1) indicates that payments are due at the beginning of the period. If omitted, the default value is DueDate.EndOfPeriod.

Return Value

A Double representing the interest payment

Description

Computes the interest payment for a given period of an annuity based on periodic, fixed payments and a fixed interest rate. An annuity is a series of fixed cash payments made over a period of time. It can be either a loan payment or an investment.

Rules at a Glance

* The value of *per* can range from 1 to *nper*.

* If *pv* and *fv* represent liabilities, their value is negative; if they represent assets, their value is positive.

Example

The *ComputeSchedule* function accepts a loan amount, an annual percentage rate, and a number of payment periods. It uses the *Pmt* function to calculate the payment per period, then returns a two-dimensional array in which each subarray contains the number of the period, the interest paid for that period, and the principal paid for that period.

```
Private Function ComputeSchedule(dblAmount As Double, _
                  dblRate As Double, dblNPer As Double) _
                  As Object(,)

    Dim dblIPmt, dblPmt, dblPrincipal As Double
    Dim intPer As Integer
    Dim strFmt As String
    Dim objArray(,) As Object
    ReDim objArray(CInt(dblNPer), 2)

    strFmt = "###,###,##0.00"
    dblPmt = Pmt(dblRate / 12, dblNPer, -dblAmount, 0, 0)

    For intPer = 1 To CInt(dblNPer)
        dblIPmt = IPmt(dblRate / 12, intPer, dblNPer, -dblAmount)
        dblPrincipal = PPmt(dblRate / 12, intPer, dblNPer, _
                       -dblAmount)
        dblAmount = dblAmount - dblPrincipal
        objArray(intPer, 0) = intPer & "."
        objArray(intPer, 1) = Format(dblIPmt, strFmt)
        objArray(intPer, 2) = Format(dblPrincipal, strFmt)
    Next

    ComputeSchedule = objArray

    End Function
```

Programming Tips and Gotchas

- *rate* and *nper* must be expressed in the same time unit. That is, if *nper* reflects the number of monthly payments, *rate* must be the monthly interest rate.

- The interest rate is a percentage expressed as a decimal. For example, if *nper* is the total number of monthly payments, an annual percentage rate (APR) of 12% is equivalent to a monthly percentage rate of 1%. The value of *rate* is therefore .01.

See Also

FV Function, NPer Function, NPV Function, Pmt Function, PPmt Function, PV Function, Rate Function

---

IRR Function

Class

Microsoft.VisualBasic.Financial

Syntax

```
IRR(valuearray()[, guess])
```

valuearray()   *required; array of Double*
    An array of cash flow values

guess   *optional; Double*
   Estimated value to be returned by the function

Return Value

A Double representing the internal rate of return

Description

Calculates the internal rate of return for a series of periodic cash flows (payments and receipts).

The internal rate of return is the interest rate generated by an investment consisting of payments and receipts that occur at regular intervals. It is generally compared to a "hurdle rate," or a minimum return, to determine whether a particular investment should be made.

Rules at a Glance

*   *valuearray* must be a one-dimensional array that contains at least one negative value (a payment) and one positive value (a receipt).

*   Individual members of *valuearray* are interpreted sequentially. That is, *valuearray(0)* is the first cash flow, *valuearray(1)* is the second, etc.

*   If *guess* is omitted, the default value of 0.1 is used.

*   *IRR* begins with *guess* and uses iteration to derive an internal rate of return that is accurate to within 0.00001 percent. If *IRR* cannot do this within 20 iterations, the function fails.

Programming Tips and Gotchas

*   Each element of *valuearray* represents a payment or a receipt that occurs at a regular time interval. If this is not the case, *IRR* will return erroneous results.

*   If the function fails because it could not calculate an accurate result in 20 iterations, try a different value for *guess*.

See Also

MIRR Function

Is Operator

Syntax

    object1 Is object2

object1   *required; Object or any reference type*
object2   *required; Object or any reference type*

Return Value

Boolean

Description

Compares two object variables or reference variables to determine whether they reference the same object

Rules at a Glance

- Both *object1* and *object2* must be reference-type variables. This includes string variables, object variables, and array variables, for instance.

- The operation returns a result of **True** if the references are identical and **False** if they are not.

- It is also possible to determine whether an object contains a valid reference by replacing *object2* with the special **Nothing** keyword. For example:

      If oDrive Is Nothing Then

  returns **True** if *oDrive* does not refer to an object and **False** if it does. This is the only method that should be used to test for an uninitialized object reference.

Programming Tips and Gotchas

- You can call the *IsReference* function to ensure that both *object1* and *object2* are reference types.

- You may wonder why there is a special **Is** operator for reference types. When you perform a comparison of scalar variables, you want to know if their values are the same. But in the case of objects, you want to know if two references point to a single object. (Since many objects have identical property values, a test for equal values is meaningless.) Hence, the **Is** operator is used for this purpose.

- Typically, the **Is** operator is used in an **If...Then...Else** construct to take some action if two reference-type variables are the same or if a reference type variable does not point to a valid object.

- The **Is** operator also can be used with the **TypeOf** operator and the **If... Then...** construct to determine the type of an object variable. For example:

      If TypeOf(sName) Is String Then

  If the variable passed to the **TypeOf** operator is a reference type, it must hold a valid object reference in order for the type comparison to be **True**.

- The **Is** operator reports that uninitialized reference types are equal. For instance, the **Is** operator reports that all of the following are equal:

      Dim obj1 As Object
      Dim obj2 As Object
      If obj1 Is obj2 Then   ' Evaluates to True

      Dim arrSt1() As String
      Dim arrSt2() As String
      If arrSt1 Is arrSt2 Then   ' Evaluates to True

      Dim str1 As String
      Dim str2 As String
      If str1 Is str2 Then   ' Evaluates to True

VB.NET/VB 6 Differences

In VB.NET, strings and arrays are reference types. In VB 6, strings and arrays are not reference types and, therefore, cannot be used with the **Is** operator.

IsArray Function

Class

Microsoft.VisualBasic.Information

Syntax

```
IsArray(varname)
```

varname   *required; any variable*
     A variable that may be an array

Return Value

Boolean (**True** or **False**)

Description

Tests whether an object variable points to an array

Rules at a Glance

If the variable passed to *IsArray* is an array or contains an array, **True** is returned; otherwise, *IsArray* returns **False**.

Example

The following code displays **True**:

```
Dim s() As Integer = {1, 2}
Dim t As Object
t = s
MsgBox(IsArray(t))
```

Programming Tips and Gotchas

- Due to the nature of Objects, it is not always obvious if an Object variable contains an array, especially if you have passed the variable to a function and the function may or may not have attached an array to the variable. Calling the array function *UBound* or trying to access an element in an array that does not exist will generate an error. In these situations, you should first use the *IsArray* function to determine if you can safely process the array.

- An uninitialized array returns **False**. For example:

```
Dim strArr() As String
Console.WriteLine(IsArray(strArr))      ' Returns False
```

- Array-like data structures, such as the **Collection** object, return **False** when passed to the *IsArray* function.

VB.NET/VB 6 Differences

In VB 6, the *IsArray* function returns `True` when passed an uninitialized array. In VB.NET, it returns `False`.

IsDate Function

Class

Microsoft.VisualBasic.Information

Syntax

```
IsDate(expression)
```

expression   *required; any*
   Expression containing a date or time

Return Value

Boolean indicating whether the expression can be converted to a Date

Description

Determines if an expression is of type Date or can be converted to type Date

Rules at a Glance

*   Returns `True` if and only if *expression* is of type Date or can be converted to type Date.

*   Uninitialized date variables also return `True`.

Programming Tips and Gotchas

*   *IsDate* uses the locale settings of the current Windows system to determine if the value held within the variable is recognizable as a date. Therefore, what is a legal date format on one machine may fail on another.

*   *IsDate* is particularly useful for validating data input. However, don't use *IsDate* in the VB text box control's Change event. The Change event is fired with every keystroke, which means that when the user starts to enter the date, chances are that the date will be invalid until the point at which the user has completed the data entry.

IsDBNull Function

Class

Microsoft.VisualBasic.Information

Syntax

```
IsDBNull(expression)
```

expression *required; any expression*

Return Value

Boolean

Description

Determines whether *expression* evaluates to DbNull (that is, is equal to System. DbNull.Value).

Rules at a Glance

- DbNull is not the same as Nothing or an empty string. DbNull is used to denote the fact that a variable contains a missing or nonexistent value, and it is used primarily in the context of database field values.

- Since any expression that contains DbNull evaluates to DbNull, an expression such as:

  ```
  If var = DbNull Then
  ```

  will always fail. The only way to test for a DbNull value is to use *IsDbNull*.

VB.NET/VB 6 Differences

The *IsDBNull* function is new to VB.NET.

IsError Function

Class

Microsoft.VisualBasic.Information

Syntax

```
IsError(expression)
```

expression *required; Object*
An object variable that may be an Exception object

Return Value

Boolean (True if *expression* is an Exception object, False otherwise)

Description

Indicates whether an object is an instance of the Exception class or one of its derived classes

Example

```
Module modMain

Public Sub Main

Dim oUnk As Object = "This is an object of subtype String."
'Dim oUnk As Object = 10
Dim oResult As Object = Increment(oUnk)
If Not IsError(oResult) Then
```

```
      Console.WriteLine(oResult)
   Else
      Console.WriteLine(oResult.Message)
   End If

   End Sub

   Public Function Increment(o As Object) As Object
      If IsNumeric(o) Then
         o += 1
         Return o
      Else
         Dim e As New System.InvalidOperationException
         Return e
      End If
   End Function

   End Module
```

VB.NET/VB 6 Differences

In VB 6, the *IsError* function takes a variant argument and determines if its subtype is **vbError**. Most commonly, it is used with the *CVErr* function to determine if the value returned from a function is an error. In VB.NET, the *IsError* function is used to test whether an object is an instance of the Exception class or its derived classes.

See Also

Exception Class

IsNothing Function

Class

Microsoft.VisualBasic.Information

Syntax

```
IsNothing(expression)
```

expression   *required; any*

Return Value

Boolean

Description

Determines whether **expression** evaluates to Nothing. The line:

```
If IsNothing(obj) Then
```

is equivalent to:

```
If obj Is Nothing Then
```

VB.NET/VB 6 Differences

The *IsNothing* function is new to VB.NET.

IsNumeric Function

Class

Microsoft.VisualBasic.Information

Syntax

```
IsNumeric(expression)
```

expression   *required; any expression*

Return Value

Boolean

Description

Determines whether **expression** can be evaluated as a number

Rules at a Glance

If the expression passed to *IsNumeric* evaluates to a number, **True** is returned; otherwise, *IsNumeric* returns **False**.

Programming Tips and Gotchas

If **expression** is a date or time, *IsNumeric* evaluates to **False**.

IsReference Function

Class

Microsoft.VisualBasic.Information

Syntax

```
IsReference(expression)
```

expression   *required; any*

Return Value

Boolean

Description

Returns **True** if **expression** contains reference type data, as opposed to value type data

Rules at a Glance

- *IsReference* returns **False** if **expression** is one of the value data types (Byte, Short, Integer, Long, Single, Double, Boolean, Date, or Char).

- *IsReference* returns `True` if *expression* is a reference data type (String or Object), including an object of a specific type, such as a `Collection` object.

- *IsReference* returns `True` if *expression* is an array, since an array is a reference type.

- *IsReference* returns `False` if *expression* is a structure, since a structure is a value type.

Example

```
Private Class CEmployee
...
End Class

' The following message will display
Dim obj As Object
If IsReference(obj) Then
    MsgBox("obj is reference type, but is Nothing")
End If

' The following message will display
' (CEmployee is a class module)
Dim c As New CEmployee()
If IsReference(c) Then
    MsgBox("c is reference type")
End If

' The following message does NOT display
Dim i As Integer = 4
If IsReference(1) Then
    MsgBox("Integer is reference type")
End If
```

Programming Tips and Gotchas

Just because a variable has been declared to be of type Object does not mean that the *IsReference* function will return `True` when that variable is passed to it as an argument. Consider the following code:

```
Dim oObj As Object
Console.WriteLine(IsReference(oObj))        'Returns True

oObj = New CEmployee
Console.WriteLine(IsReference(oObj))        'Returns True

oObj = 3
Console.WriteLine(IsReference(oObj))        'Returns False

oObj = "This is a string"
Console.WriteLine(IsReference(oObj))        'Returns True
```

In other words, the *IsReference* function returns `True` only if a variable of type Object is `Nothing` or if its data subtype is one of the reference types (that is, an instance of a class or a string). If its data subtype is a value type, the function returns `False`.

The *IsReference* function is new to VB.NET.

Join Function

Class

Microsoft.VisualBasic.Strings

Syntax

```
result = Join(sourcearray, [delimiter])
```

sourcearray   *required; String or Object array*
    Array whose elements are to be concatenated

delimiter   *optional; String*
    Character used to delimit the individual values in the string

Return Value

String

Description

Concatenates an array of values into a delimited string using a specified delimiter

Rules at a Glance

- If no delimiter is specified, the space character is used as a delimiter.

- If you want to concatenate numeric or other nonstring values in *sourcearray*, use an Object array. If, for example, you specify a numeric data type for *sourcearray*, the function will generate a compiler error.

Programming Tips and Gotchas

The *Join* function is ideal for quickly and efficiently writing out a comma-delimited text file from an array of values.

Kill Procedure

Class

    Microsoft.VisualBasic.FileSystem

Syntax

```
Kill(pathname)
```

pathname   *required; String*
    The file or files to be deleted

Description

Deletes a file from disk

Rules at a Glance

- If *pathname* does not include a drive letter, the folder and file are assumed to be on the current drive.

- If *pathname* does not include a folder name, the file is assumed to be in the current folder.

- You can use the multiple-character (*) and single-character (?) wildcards to specify multiple files to delete.

- If the file is open or is set to read only, an error will be generated.

Programming Tips and Gotchas

- Note that the deleted file is not placed in the Recycle Bin. However, the following code demonstrates how to use the *FileOperation* API found in *Shell32. DLL* to move a file to the Windows Recycle Bin:

```
Option Explicit

'declare the file operation structure
Type SHFILEOPSTRUCT
    hWnd As Long
    wFunction As Long
    pFrom As String
    pTo As String
    fFlags As Integer
    fAborted As Boolean
    hNameMaps As Long
    sProgress As String
End Type

'declare two constants needed for the delete operation
Private Const FO_DELETE = &H3
Private Const FO_FLAG_ALLOWUNDO = &H40

'declare the API call function
Declare Function SHFileOperation Lib "shell32.dll" _
        Alias "SHFileOperationA" _
        (lpFileOp As SHFILEOPSTRUCT) As Long

Public Function WinDelete(sFileName As String) As Long
    'create a copy of the file operation structure
    Dim SHFileOp As SHFILEOPSTRUCT

    'need a Null terminated string
    sFileName = sFileName & vbNullChar

    'assign relevant values to structure
    With SHFileOp
        .wFunction = FO_DELETE
        .pFrom = sFileName
        .fFlags = FO_FLAG_ALLOWUNDO
    End With
```

```
                'pass the structure to the API function
            WinDelete = SHFileOperation(SHFileOp)

        End Function
```

- Use the *RmDir* procedure to delete folders.

See Also

RmDir Procedure

LBound Function

Class

Microsoft.VisualBasic.Information

Syntax

```
    LBound(array[, rank])
```

`array`   *required; any array*
    An array whose lower bound is to be determined

`rank`   *optional; Integer*
    The dimension whose lower bound is desired

Return Value

An Integer whose value is 0

Description

Determines the lower boundary of a specified dimension of an array. The lower
boundary is the smallest subscript you can access within the specified array.

Rules at a Glance

- Unless it is passed an invalid argument, the *LBound* function always returns 0.

- If `array` is uninitialized, it generates an ArgumentNullException error when
  passed to the *LBound* function. You can prevent this by comparing `array` to
  Nothing, as in the following code fragment:

  ```
      If Not oArray Is Nothing Then
  ```

- To determine the lower limit of the first dimension of an array, set `rank` to 1,
  set it to 2 for the second, and so on.

- If `rank` isn't specified, 1 is assumed.

Programming Tips and Gotchas

Since VB.NET does not allow you to change the lower bound of an array, the
LBound function would appear to be superfluous except for reasons of backward
compatibility. Its continued use may be a good idea, though, in the event that a
future version of VB.NET allows you to set the lower boundary of an array.

VB.NET/VB 6 Differences

Since VB 6 offers a number of ways to set the lower bound of all arrays or a specific array, the *LBound* function is particularly useful when iterating the elements of an array. In VB.NET, its use is a matter of choice.

See Also

UBound Function

LCase Function

Class

Microsoft.VisualBasic.Strings

Syntax

```
LCase(value)
```

`value`   *required; String or Char*
    A valid string expression or a character

Return Value

String or Char

Description

Converts a string to lowercase

Rules at a Glance

- *LCase* only affects uppercase letters; all other characters in `value` are unaffected.
- *LCase* returns Nothing if `value` contains a Nothing.
- *LCase* returns the same data type as `value`.

See Also

UCase Function

Left Function

Class

Microsoft.VisualBasic.Strings

Syntax

```
Left(str, length)
```

`str`   *required; String*
    The string to be processed

`length`   *required; Long*
    The number of characters to return from the left of the string

Return Value

String

Description

Returns a string containing the leftmost *length* characters of *str*

Rules at a Glance

- If *length* is 0, a zero-length string ("") is returned.
- If *length* is greater than the length of *str*, *str* is returned.
- If *str* is Nothing, *Left* returns Nothing.

Programming Tips and Gotchas

- Use the *Len* function to determine the overall length of *str*.
- The *Left* function corresponds to the BCL System.String class' Substring method. For example, the following two assignments to the *sCity* variable are functionally identical:

```
Dim sCity As String
Dim sLocation As String = "New York, New York"
sCity = Left(sLocation, 8)
sCity = sLocation.Substring(0, 8)
```

Note that the Substring method uses a zero-based index to determine the starting position of the substring.

See Also

Mid Function, Right Function

Len Function

Class

Microsoft.VisualBasic.Strings

Syntax

```
Len(expression)
```

expression   *required; any*
    Any valid variable name or expression

Return Value

Integer

Description

Counts the number of characters within a string or the size of a given variable

Rules at a Glance

- If *expression* contains Nothing, *Len* returns 0.

- For a string or String variable, *Len* returns the number of characters in the string.

- For a nonobject and nonstructure variable, *Len* returns the number of bytes required to store the variable in memory.

- For a variable of type Object, *Len* returns the length of its data subtype. If the object is uninitialized, its length is 0. However, if the object contains a strongly typed class instance, an InvalidCastException exception is thrown.

- For a structure, *Len* returns the number of bytes required to store the structure as a file. (But see the comment in the "Programming Tips and Gotchas" section.)

- For a strongly typed object variable, such as one defined by the **Class... End Class** construct, *Len* generates an InvalidCastException exception.

- If *varname* is an array, you must also specify a valid subscript. In other words, *Len* cannot be used to determine the total number of elements in or the total size of an array.

Programming Tips and Gotchas

- *Len* cannot accurately report the number of bytes required to store structures that contain variable-length strings. If you need to know how many bytes of storage space will be required by a structure that includes string members, you can fix the length of the strings by using the `<vbFixedString(length)>` attribute in the **Structure** statement. For details, see the "Structure...End Structure Statement " entry.

- *Len* is functionally similar to the BCL's System.String.Length public instance method. One significant difference is that *Len* retuns a 0 in the case of an uninitialized String variable, whereas the Length method raises a NullReference-Exception exception. In addition, of course, the Length method can be used only on strings, whereas *Len* can be used on all data types other than strongly typed objects.

Like Operator

Syntax

```
result = string Like pattern
```

string   *required; String*
   The string to be tested against *pattern*

pattern   *required; String*
   A series of characters used by the **Like** operator to determine if *string* and *pattern* match

Return Type

Boolean

Description

If *string* matches *pattern*, *result* is True; otherwise, *result* is False.

Rules at a Glance

- If either *string* or *pattern* is Nothing, then *result* will be Nothing.

- The default comparison method for the Like operator is Binary. This can be overridden using the Option Compare statement.

- Binary comparison is based on comparing the internal binary number representing each character; this produces a case-sensitive comparison.

- Text comparison, the alternative to binary comparison, is case insensitive; therefore, A = a.

- The sort order is based on the code page currently being used, as determined by the Windows regional settings.

- The following table describes the special characters to use when creating a pattern; all other characters match themselves.

Character	Meaning
?	Any single character
*	Zero or more characters
#	Any single digit (0–9)
[list]	Any single character in *list*
[!list]	Any single character not in *list*
[]	A zero-length string ("")

- *list* is used to match a group of characters in *pattern* to a single character in *string* and can contain almost all available characters, including digits.

- Use a hyphen (-) in *list* to create a range of characters to match a character in *string*. For example, [A-D] will match A, B, C, or D in that character position in *string*.

- Multiple ranges of characters can be included in *list* without the use of a delimiter. For example, [A-D J-L].

- Ranges of characters should appear in sort order. For example, [c-k].

- Use the hyphen at the start or end of *list* to match to itself. For example, [- A-G] matches a hyphen or any character from A to G.

- The exclamation point in pattern matching is like the negation operator in C. Use an exclamation point before a character or range of characters in *list* to match all but that character. For example, [!A-G] matches all characters apart from the characters from A to G.

- The exclamation point outside of the bracket matches itself.

- To use any special character as a matching character, you should enclose the special character in brackets. For example, to match to a question mark, use [?].

Example

The following example will display OK if the text entered into Text1 starts with either V or A, followed by any characters, and ends with "in a Nutshell." Therefore,

"Paul in a Nutshell" returns Wrong, whereas either "ASP in a Nutshell" or "VB.NET Language in a Nutshell" returns OK.

```
Private Sub Button1_Click(ByVal sender As System.Object, _
                          ByVal e As System.EventArgs) _
           Handles Button1.Click
    Dim sTitle As String = "in a Nutshell"
    Dim sPattern As String = "[V A]* " & sTitle
    If TextBox1.Text Like sPattern Then
        MsgBox("OK")
    Else
        MsgBox("Wrong")
    End If
End Sub
```

Programming Tips and Gotchas

- Different languages place different priority on particular characters with relation to sort order. Therefore, the same program using the same data may yield different results when run on machines in different parts of the world, depending upon the locale settings of the systems.

- Regular expressions provide an even more powerful method for searching and comparing strings. You can use regular expressions through the .NET Framework's System.Text.RegularExpressions.RegEx class.

LineInput Function

Class

Microsoft.VisualBasic.FileSystem

Syntax

```
LineInput(filenumber)
```

filenumber   *required; Integer*
    Any valid file number

Return Value

A String containing the line read from the file

Description

Assigns a single line from a sequential file opened in Input mode to a string variable

Rules at a Glance

- Data is read into a buffer one character at a time until a line feed or carriage-return sequence (either Chr(13) or Chr(13)+Chr(10)) is encountered. When this happens, all the characters in the buffer are returned as a string, without the carriage-return sequence, and the buffer is cleared.

- After reading a line, the file pointer advances to the first character after the end of the line or to the end-of-file marker.

Example

The following code reads all of the lines in a text file and sends them to the Output window:

```
Dim fr As Integer = FreeFile()
Dim sLine As String
FileOpen(fr, "c:\data.txt", OpenMode.Input, OpenAccess.Read)
Do While Not EOF(fr)
    Console.WriteLine(LineInput(fr))
Loop
FileClose(fr)
```

Programming Tips and Gotchas

You use the *LineInput* function to read data from text files. To write data back to this type of file, use the *PrintLine* function.

VB.NET/VB 6 Differences

The VB.NET *LineInput* function corresponds directly to the VB 6 `LineInput` statement, with the following differences:

- The VB 6 `LineInput` statement has a second argument, **varname**, which is the variable to receive the line read by the function. It is not supported by the VB.NET *LineInput* function, since the line read is the return value of the function.

- The first argument of the VB 6 `LineInput` statement, *filenumber*, could be preceded by the # symbol. In VB.NET, this format is not supported.

Loc Function

Class

Microsoft.VisualBasic.FileSystem

Syntax

```
Loc(filenumber)
```

filenumber   *required; Integer*
   Any valid file number

Return Value

A Long indicating the current position of the read/write pointer in a file

Description

Determines the current position of the file read/write pointer

Rules at a Glance

- If you have opened the file in Random mode, *Loc* returns the record number of the last record read or written.

- If you have opened the file in Input or Output modes (sequential), *Loc* returns the current byte position in the file divided by 128.

- If you have opened the file in Binary mode, *Loc* returns the position of the last byte read or written.

Example

```
Dim fr As Integer = FreeFile()
Dim sChar As Char
FileOpen(fr, "c:\data.txt", OpenMode.Binary, OpenAccess.Read)

Do While Loc(fr) < LOF(fr)
    FileGet(fr, sChar)
    Debug.Write(Loc(fr) & ": ")
    Console.WriteLine(sChar)
Loop
```

Programming Tips and Gotchas

- For sequential files, the return value of *Loc* is not required and should not be used.

- Note that you cannot set the position of the file pointer using *Loc*.

See Also

FileOpen Procedure, LOF Function

Lock Procedure

Class

Microsoft.VisualBasic.FileSystem

Syntax

```
Lock(filenumber[, record])
```

or:

```
Lock(filenumber[, fromrecord, torecord]
```

filenumber	*required; Integer*
Any valid file number	
record	*optional; Long*
The record or byte number at which to commence the lock	
fromrecord	*optional; Long*
The first record or byte number to lock	
torecord	*optional; Long*
The last record or byte number to lock	

Description

The *Lock* procedure prevents another process from accessing a record, section, or whole file until it is unlocked by the *Unlock* function.

Use the *Lock* procedure in situations where multiple programs or more than one instance of your program may need read and write access to the same data file.

Rules at a Glance

- Use the *Lock* procedure with only the *filenumber* argument to lock the whole file.

- *record* is interpreted as a record number in the case of random files and a byte number in the case of binary files. Records and bytes in a file are always numbered sequentially from 1 onward.

- To lock a particular record, specify its record number as *record*, and only that record will be locked.

- The *Lock* procedure locks an entire file opened in Input or Output (sequential) mode, regardless of the *record* argument.

- If you omit the *start* argument, *Lock* will lock all records from the start of the file to record or byte number *end*.

- Attempting to access a locked file or portion of a file returns runtime error 70, "Permission denied."

Programming Tips and Gotchas

- You must take care to remove all file locks with the *Unlock* procedure before either closing a file or ending the application; otherwise, you can leave the file in an unstable state. This of course means that, where appropriate, your error-handling routines must be made aware of any locks you currently have in place so that they may be removed if necessary.

- You use the *Lock* and *Unlock* procedures in pairs, and the argument lists of both statements must match exactly.

- The *Lock* procedure does not guarantee under all circumstances that the locked file will be protected from access by other processes. There are two major circumstances under which an apparent access violation can occur:

  — The file has already been opened but has not been locked by a process when the current process locks it. However, the first process will not be able to perform operations on the file once the second file successfully locks it.

  — The block of code responsible for opening the file and then locking it is interrupted by the scheduling policy of the operating system before the file can be locked. If a second process then opens and locks the file, it— and not the first process—will have sole use of the file.

  Because of this, the *Lock* procedure should immediately follow the *File-Open* procedure in code. This reduces, but does not eliminate, the problems that result from the fact that opening and locking a file is not an automatic operation.

VB.NET/VB 6 Differences

In the VB 6 Lock statement, you can separate the *fromrecord* and *torecord* arguments with the To keyword. In the VB.NET *Lock* procedure, this syntax is not supported.

LOF Function

Class

Microsoft.VisualBasic.FileSystem

Syntax

```
LOF(filenumber)
```

filenumber   *required; Integer*
    Any valid file number

Return Value

Long Integer

Description

Returns the size of an open file in bytes

Rules at a Glance

filenumber must be the number of a file opened using the *FileOpen* function.

Example

The following example shows how to use the *LOF* function to prevent reading past the end of a file in binary mode:

```
Dim fr As Integer = FreeFile()
Dim sChar As Char
FileOpen(fr, "c:\data.txt", OpenMode.Binary, OpenAccess.Read)

Do While Loc(fr) < LOF(fr)
    FileGet(fr, sChar)
    Debug.Write(Loc(fr) & ": ")
    Console.WriteLine(sChar)
Loop
```

Programming Tips and Gotchas

LOF works only on an open file; if you need to know the size of a file that isn't open, use the *FileLen* function.

See Also

FileLen Function, FileOpen Procedure

Log Function

Class

System.Math

Syntax

```
Math.Log(d)
```

or:

```
Math.Log(a, newbase)
```

d or a   *required; Double*
A numeric expression greater than zero

newbase   *required; Double*
The base of the logarithm

Return Value

Double

Description

Returns the natural (base e) logarithm of a given number (the first syntax) or the logarithm of a given number in a specified base (the second syntax)

Rules at a Glance

- The natural logarithm is the logarithm base e, a constant whose value is approximately 2.718282. The natural logarithm satisfies the equation:

    ```
    e^Log(x) = x
    ```

    In other words, the natural logarithm function is the inverse function of the exponential function.

- *d* or *a*, the value whose natural logarithm the function is to return, must be a positive real number. If number is negative or zero, the function generates runtime error 5, "Invalid procedure call or argument."

- This is a Shared member, so it can be used without creating any objects.

Programming Tips and Gotchas

- You can calculate base-*n* logarithms for any number, *x*, by dividing the natural logarithm of *x* by the natural logarithm of *n*, as the following expression illustrates:

    ```
    Logn(x) = Log(x) / Log(n)
    ```

    For example, the Log10 function shows the source code for a custom function that calculates base-10 logarithms:

    ```
    Static Function Log10(X)
        Log10 = Log(X) / Log(10#)
    End Function
    ```

- The inverse trigonometric functions, which are not intrinsic to VB, can be computed using the value returned by the *Log* function. The functions and their formulas are:

    Inverse hyperbolic sine
    ```
    HArcsin(X) = Log(X + Sqr(X * X + 1))
    ```

Inverse hyperbolic cosine
```
HArccos(X) = Log(X + Sqr(X * X - 1))
```

Inverse hyperbolic tangent
```
HArctan(X) = Log((1 + X) / (1 - X)) / 2
```

Inverse hyperbolic secant
```
HArcsec(X) = Log((Sqr(-X * X + 1) + 1) / X)
```

Inverse hyperbolic cosecant
```
HArccosec(X) = Log((Sgn(X) * Sqr(X * X + 1) +1) / X)
```

Inverse hyperbolic cotangent
```
HArccotan(X) = Log((X + 1) / (X - 1)) / 2
```

See Also

Exp Function, Log10 Function

Log10 Function

Class

System.Math

Syntax

```
Math.Log10(d)
```

d   *required; Double*
    A numeric expression greater than zero

Return Value

Double

Description

Returns the common (base-10) logarithm of a given number

Rules at a Glance

- The common logarithm is the logarithm base-10. The common logarithm satisfies the equation:

    ```
    10^Log10(x) = x
    ```

- *d*, the value whose common logarithm the function is to return, must be a positive real number. If number is negative or zero, the function generates runtime error 5, "Invalid procedure call or argument."

- This is a Shared member, so it can be used without creating any objects.

VB.NET/VB 6 Differences

The *Log10* function is new to the .NET platform.

See Also

Exp Function, Log Function

LSet Function

Class

Microsoft.VisualBasic.Strings

Syntax

```
LSet(Source, Length)
```

Source   *required; String*
    The string to be left aligned

Length   *required; Integer*
    The length of the returned string

Return Value

String

Description

Left aligns a string

Rules at a Glance

- If the length of *Source* is greater than or equal to *Length*, the function returns only the leftmost *Length* characters.

- If the length of *Source* is less than *Length*, spaces are added to the right of the returned string so that its length becomes *Length*.

VB.NET/VB 6 Differences

- In VB 6, LSet was implemented as a kind of assignment statement. Because it is implemented as a function in VB.NET, its syntax is completely different.

- In VB 6, LSet could be used only with fixed-length strings. In VB.NET, *LSet* works with all CTS String data.

See Also

RSet Function

LTrim Function

Class

Microsoft.VisualBasic.Strings

Syntax

```
LTrim(str)
```

str   *required; String*
    A valid string expression

Return Value

String

Description

Removes any leading spaces from *str*

Rules at a Glance

- If *str* has no leading spaces, the function returns *str* unmodified.

- If *str* is Nothing, *LTrim* returns Nothing.

Programming Tips and Gotchas

It is unwise to create data relationships that rely on leading spaces, especially since most string-based data types in relational database-management systems (like SQL Server and Access) automatically remove leading spaces.

See Also

RTrim Function, Trim Function

MarshalAs Attribute

Class

System.Runtime.InteropServices.MarshalAsAttribute

Applies to

Field, Parameter, ReturnValue

Description

Defines the correct type conversion between managed and unmanaged code. Unmanaged types are defined by the UnmanagedType enumeration, which is shown in the following table:

UnmanagedType	Value	Description
AnsiBStr	35	An ANSI BSTR (a character string whose first byte indicates the string length).
AsAny	40	Dynamic type determination at runtime.
Bool	2	4-byte Boolean (True <> 0, False = 0).
BStr	19	A Unicode BSTR (a character string whose first 2 bytes indicates the string length).
ByValArray	30	An array passed by value. An array that is a field in a structure must have this attribute. The SixeConst field must be set to the number of array elements, and the ArraySubType field can optionally be set to the unmanaged data type of the array.
ByValTStr	23	An inline fixed-length character array within a structure. The character type is determined by the *CharSet* argument of the containing structure's <StructLayout> attribute.
Currency	15	A COM Currency data type. Used on the VB.NET and .NET Decimal data type.

UnmanagedType	Value	Description
Custom-Marshaler	44	A custom marshaler class. The class is defined by the MarshalType or MarshelTypeRef field. Additional information can be passed to the custom marshaler by the MarshalCookie field.
Error	45	An HRESULT. The native .NET type should be a 4-byte signed or unsigned integer.
FunctionPtr	38	A function pointer.
I1	3	A 1-byte signed integer.
I2	5	A 2-byte signed integer.
I4	7	A 4-byte signed integer.
I8	9	An 8-byte signed integer.
IDispatch	26	A COM IDispatch pointer.
Interface	28	A COM interface pointer.
IUnknown	25	A COM IUnknown pointer.
LPArray	42	A C-style array. Its length is indicated by the SizeConst and SizeParamIndex fields. Optionally, the ArraySubType field can indicate the unmanaged type of string elements within the array.
LPStr	20	An ANSI (single-byte) character string.
LPStruct	43	A pointer to a structure.
LPTStr	32	A platform-dependent character string (ANSI on WIndows 9x, Unicode on WIndows NT/2000/XP). LPTStr is supported only for platform invoke, and not for COM interop.
LPWStr	21	A Unicode (double-byte) character string.
R4	11	A 4-byte floating point number.
R8	12	An 8-byte floating point number.
SafeArray	29	A SafeArray (a self-describing array that includes information on its type, dimension, and bounds).
Struct	27	A C-style structure used to marshal .NET formatted classes and value types.
SysInt	31	A platform-dependent integer (4 bytes on 32-bit Windows, 8 bytes on 64-bit Windows).
SysUInt	32	The hardware's natural sized unsigned integer.
TBStr	36	A length-prefixed, platform-dependent character string (ANSI in Windows 9x, Unicode on Windows NT/2000/XP).
U1	4	A 1-byte unsigned integer.
U2	6	A 2-byte unsigned integer.
U4	8	A 4-byte unsigned integer.
U8	10	An 8-byte unsigned integer.
VariantBool	37	A 2-byte OLE-defined Boolean value (True = -1, False = 0).
VBByRefStr	34	Allows Visual Basic to change a string in unmanaged code and reflect the changed skin in managed code.

Constructor

New(unmanagedType)

unmanagedType   *Short or* UnmanagedType *enumeration*
Indicates the COM (unmanaged) data type to which the data is to be converted. unmanagedType can either be a constant of the UnmanagedType enumeration or its corresponding Short value, as shown in the previous table.

Properties

Value   UnmanagedType *enumeration*
The COM (unmanaged) data type that the .NET (managed) data is to be marshaled as.

Fields

ArraySubType   UnmanagedType *enumeration*
The subtype of an array of type ByValArray or LPArray. It is used when an array contains strings so that the runtime knows how to marshal a string array to COM.

MarshalCookie   *String*
An undefined field that can be used to pass user-defined data to a custom marshaler. The value of the MarshalCookie field as passed to the custom marshaler's GetInstance method.

MarshalType   *String*
The fully qualified name of a custom marshaler. It is required if the Value property is CustomMarshaler.

MarshalTypeRef   *Type*
Implements the MarshalType value as a Type, rather than a string.

SafeArraySubType   VarEnum *enumeration*
The data type of a SafeArray. Possible values are the members of the VarEnum enumeration, which is shown in the following table:

Constant	Description
VT_ARRAY	A SAFEARRAY pointer
VT_BLOB	A length-prefixed collection of bytes
VT_BLOB_OBJECT	A VT_BLOB containing an object
VT_BOOL	A Boolean value
VT_BSTR	A string of type BSTR
VT_BYREF	A value passed by reference
VT_CARRAY	A C-style array
VT_CF	Clipboard format
VT_CLSID	A class identifier (CLSID)
VT_CY	A currency value
VT_DATE	A date value
VT_DECIMAL	A decimal value
VT_DISPATCH	An IDispatch pointer
VT_EMPTY	A value was not specified
VT_ERROR	An SCODE
VT_FILETIME	A FILETIME value
VT_HRESULT	An HRESULT

Constant	Description
VT_I1	A char value
VT_I2	A short (two-byte) integer
VT_I4	A long (4-byte) integer
VT_I8	A 64-bit integer
VT_INT	An integer value
VT_LPSTR	A null-terminated string
VT_LPWSTR	A null-terminated Unicode string
VT_NULL	A null reference (Nothing)
VT_PTR	A pointer
VT_R4	A floating-point value
VT_R8	A double value
VT_RECORD	A user-defined type
VT_SAFEARRAY	A SAFEARRAY
VT_STORAGE	A named storage
VT_STORED_OBJECT	Storage containing an object
VT_STREAM	A named stream
VT_STREAMED_OBJECT	A Stream containing an object
VT_UI1	An unsigned byte
VT_UI2	An unsigned (2-byte) short
VT_UI4	An unsigned (4-byte) long
VT_UI8	A 64-bit unsigned integer
VT_UINT	An unsigned integer
VT_UNKNOWN	An IUnknown pointer
VT_USERDEFINED	A user-defined type
VT_VARIANT	A VARIANT far pointer
VT_VECTOR	A simple counted array
VT_VOID	A C-style void

SafeArrayUserDefinedSubType   *Type object*

The user-defined type of the SAFEARRAY. This field is used only if the value of the SafeArraySubType field is VT_UNKNOWN, VT_DISPATCH, or VT_RECORD.

SizeConst   *Integer*

The number of elements in a fixed-length array

SizeParamIndex   *Short*

Indicates which zero-based parameter contains a count of array elements

Max Function

Class

System.Math

Syntax

```
Math.Max(val1, val2)
```

val1, val2   *required; any*

A numeric data type or expression

Return Value

Returns the maximum of *val1* and *val2*, in the widest datatype of the two numbers

Description

Returns the maximum of *val1* and *val2*

Rules at a Glance

- If the two arguments do not have the same data type, then the narrower data type is cast to the wider type. For instance, the line:

```
Dim x As Integer = 5
Dim y As Double = 454.8
MsgBox(Math.Max(x, y))
```

    displays 454.8.

- This is a Shared member, so it can be used without creating any objects.

VB.NET/VB 6 Differences

The *Max* function is new to the .NET Framework.

See Also

Min Function

Me Operator

Syntax

```
Me
```

Description

Represents a reference to the current class from within the class

Rules at a Glance

- Me is an explicit reference to the current object as defined by the Class... End Class construct.

- Me corresponds to the C++ this operator.

Example

In this example, a class passes an instance of itself to a function outside the class by using the Me operator.

```
Private Class CCounter

Private lCtr As Long = 1

Public ReadOnly Property Value
```

```
    Get
        Value = lCtr
    End Get
End Property

Public Sub Increment()
    lCtr += 1
End Sub

Public Function ShowCount() As Long
    ShowCount = ShowObjectValue(Me)
End Function

End Class

Module modMain

Public Sub Main
    Dim oCtr = New CCounter
    oCtr.Increment
    oCtr.Increment
    MsgBox("Count: " & oCtr.ShowCount)
End Sub

Public Function ShowObjectValue(oObj As Object) AS Object
    ShowObjectValue = oObj.Value
End Function

End Module
```

Programming Tips and Gotchas

- The **Me** operator can't be used on the left side of an expression.

- **Me** is particularly useful when passing an instance of the current class as a parameter to a routine outside the class.

See Also

MyClass Keyword

Mid Function

Class

Microsoft.VisualBasic.Strings

Syntax

```
Mid(str, start[, length])
```

str   *required; String*
>   The expression from which to return a substring

start   *required; Long*
>   The starting position of the substring

---

length   *optional; Long*
    The length of the substring

Return Value

String

Description

Returns a substring of a specified length from a given string

Rules at a Glance

- If *str* contains Nothing, *Mid* returns Nothing.

- If *start* is greater than the length of *str*, a zero-length string is returned.

- If *start* is less than zero, runtime error 5, "Invalid procedure call or argument," is generated.

- If *length* is omitted or *length* is greater than the length of *str*, all characters from *start* to the end of *str* are returned.

Example

The following example parses the contents of a text box control (named txtString) and writes each word to a list box (named lstWord). Note the use of the *InStr* function to determine the position of either a space or a carriage return/line feed character combination—the two characters that can terminate a word in this case:

```
Private Sub btnParse_Click(ByVal sender As System.Object, _
                           ByVal e As System.EventArgs) _
        Handles btnParse.Click

    Dim strString, strWord As String
    Dim intStart, intEnd, intStrLen, intCrLf As Integer
    Dim blnLines As Boolean

    lstWords.Items.Clear()
    intStart = 1
    strString = Trim(txtString.Text)
    intStrLen = Len(strString)
    intCrLf = InStr(1, strString, vbCrLf)
    If intCrLf Then blnLines = True

    lstWords.BeginUpdate()

    Do While intStart > 0
        intEnd = InStr(intStart, strString, " ") - 1
        If intEnd <= 0 Then intEnd = intStrLen
        If blnLines And (intCrLf < intEnd) Then
            intEnd = intCrLf - 1
            intCrLf = InStr(intEnd + 2, strString, vbCrLf)
            If intCrLf = 0 Then blnLines = False
            lstWords.Items.Add(Mid(strString, intStart, _
                                intEnd - intStart + 1))
```

```
        intStart = intEnd + 3
    Else
        lstWords.Items.Add(Mid(strString, intStart, _
                             intEnd - intStart + 1))
        intStart = intEnd + 2
    End If
    If intStart > intStrLen Then intStart = 0
Loop

lstWords.EndUpdate()

End Sub
```

Programming Tips and Gotchas

- Use the *Len* function to determine the total length of `str`.

- Use *InStr* to determine the starting point of a given substring within another string.

See Also

Left Function, Mid Function, Right Function

Mid Statement

Syntax

```
Mid(target, start[, length]) = string
```

`target`   *required; String*
> The name of the string variable to be modified

`start`   *required; Long*
> The position within `stringvar` at which the replacement commences

`length`   *optional; Long*
> The number of characters in `stringvar` to replace

`string`   *required; String*
> The string used to replace characters within `stringvar`

Description

Replaces a section of a string with characters from another string

Rules at a Glance

- If you omit `length`, as many characters of `string` as can fit into `stringvar` are used.

- If `start + length` is greater then the length of `stringvar`, `string` is truncated to fit in the same space as `stringvar`. This means that the length of `stringvar` is not altered by the Mid statement.

- If `start` is less than 0, runtime error 5, "Invalid procedure call or argument," occurs.

Programming Tips and Gotchas

- If *string* is Nothing, a runtime error occurs.

- VB includes the *Replace* function, which enhances the functionality of the Mid statement by allowing you to specify the number of times the replacement is carried out in the same string.

- Because it is a statement, this version of Mid does not accept named arguments.

- As a statement, Mid is implemented by the compiler, rather than by the Microsoft.VisualBasic.Strings class.

See Also

Mid Function

Min Function

Class

System.Math

Syntax

```
Math.Min(val1, val2)
```

val1, val2   *required; any numeric*
    A numeric data type or expression

Return Value

Returns the minimum of *val1* and *val2* in the widest data type of the two numbers

Description

Returns the minimum of *val1* and *val2*, in the same data type as the numbers. See "Rules at a Glance" for more detail.

Rules at a Glance

- If the two arguments do not have the same data type, then the narrower data type is cast to the wider type. For instance, the code fragment:

```
Dim x As Integer = 5
Dim y As Double = 454.8
MsgBox(Math.Min(x, y))
```

displays 454.8 without error. The datatype returned by the function in this instance is a Double.

- This is a Shared member, so it can be used without creating any objects.

VB.NET/VB 6 Differences

The *Min* function is new to the .NET Framework.

See Also

Max Function

Minute Function

Class

Microsoft.VisualBasic.DateAndTime

Syntax

    Minute(TimeValue)

`TimeValue`   *required; Date*
    Date variable or literal date

Return Value

An Integer between 0 and 59, representing the minute of the hour

Description

Extracts the minute component from a given date/time expression

Rules at a Glance

- If *TimeValue* is not a valid date/time expression, the function generates run-time error 13, "Type mismatch." To prevent this, use the *IsDate* function to check the argument before calling the *Minute* function.

- If *TimeValue* contains Nothing, 0 is returned, so be careful here to check for Nothing.

- You can also use the *DatePart* function.

See Also

Hour Function, Second Function

MIRR Function

Class

Microsoft.VisualBasic.Financial

Syntax

    MIRR(valuearray(), financerate, reinvestrate)

`valuearray()`   *required; Array of Double*
    An array of cash flow values

`financerate`   *required; Double*
    The interest rate paid as the cost of financing

`reinvestrate`   *required; Double*
    The interest rate received on gains from cash investment

Return Value

A Double representing the modified internal rate of return

Description

Calculates the modified internal rate of return, which is the internal rate of return when payments and receipts are financed at different rates

Rules at a Glance

- *valuearray* must be a one-dimensional array that contains at least one negative value (a payment) and one positive value (a receipt). The order of elements within the array should reflect the order in which payments and receipts occur.

- *financerate* and *reinvestrate* are percentages expressed as decimal values. For example, 10% is expressed as 0.10.

Programming Tips and Gotchas

Each element of *valuearray* represents a payment or a receipt that occurs at a regular time interval. If this is not the case, *MIRR* will return erroneous results.

See Also

IRR Function

MkDir Procedure

Class

Microsoft.VisualBasic.FileSystem

Syntax

```
MkDir(path)
```

path   *required; String*
  The name of the folder to be created

Description

Creates a new folder

Rules at a Glance

- If you omit the drive from *path*, a new folder will be created on the current drive.

- You can specify the drive by using either its local drive letter or its UNC name.

- *path* can either be a fully qualified path (i.e., a path from the drive's root directory to the directory to be created) or a relative path (i.e., a path from the current directory).

- If the directory to be created by the *MkDir* procedure already exists, an IOException exception is raised.

Programming Tips and Gotchas

- If your program is running on Windows NT, ensure that the logged-in user has the right to create a folder on the specified drive prior to calling the *MkDir* procedure.

- VB does not automatically make the new folder the current folder after a call to *MkDir*. You will need to call the *ChDir* procedure to do this.

- To remove a folder, use the *RmDir* procedure.

- Use *CurDir* to determine the current drive.

See Also

RmDir Procedure

Mod Operator

Syntax

```
result = number1 Mod number2
```

number1, number2   *required; any*
    A numeric expression

Return Value

Returns the modulus

Description

Returns the modulus, that is, the remainder when *number1* is divided by *number2*. This return value is a non-negative integral data type.

Rules at a Glance

- Floating point numbers are rounded to integers before the division.

- If *number1* or *number2* is Nothing, then an error occurs.

- The Mod operator returns the data type of *number1* and *number2* if they are the same type, or the widest data type of *number1* and *number2* if they are different.

Example

```
MsgBox(10 Mod 3)    ' returns 1
```

Module...End Module Statement

Syntax

```
accessmodifier Module modulename
    ' statements
End Module
```

accessmodifier   *optional*
    Type: Keyword

One of the following keywords determine the visibility of the module:

Public
> Makes the module visible to all applications

Friend
> Makes the module visible throughout the project

modulename   *required*
> Type: String literal

> The name of the code module

Description

Defines a code block as a code module

Rules at a Glance

- If *accessmodifier* is omitted, the module is Public by default.

- *modulename* follows standard Visual Basic naming conventions and must be unique within its assembly.

- *statements* can consist of the following:

    — Constant and variable definitions

    — Function and procedure definitions

Programming Tips and Gotchas

- Code modules are similar to classes in which the public variables are treated as static fields and the public functions and procedures are treated as static (shared) methods. This means that, particularly in the event of a naming conflict (where two routines in different code modules have the same name), you can qualify the function or procedure with the name of the module in which it resides. For example, if the *SayHello* procedure is found in a module named modLibrary, it can be called as follows:

    ```
    modLibrary.SayHello()
    ```

- Although modules are similar to classes, there are some important differences. The members of a module have scope equal to the module's containing namespace, rather than just to the module itself. Also, modules cannot be instantiated, do not support inheritance, and cannot implement interfaces.

- If a code module is to contain a routine that serves as a program entry point, that routine must be named Sub Main. It must also have Public scope.

VB.NET/VB 6 Differences

The statement is new to VB.NET. VB 6 placed each code module in a separate BAS file, which rendered beginning and ending statements unnecessary. A single VB.NET file, on the other hand, can contain multiple code modules and classes, thus necessitating the use of beginning and ending statements.

See Also

Class Statement

Month Function

Class

Microsoft.VisualBasic.DateAndTime

Syntax

```
Month(datevalue)
```

datevalue   *required; Date*
    Date variable or literal date

Return Value

An Integer between 1 and 12

Description

Returns an integer representing the month of the year of a given date expression

Rules at a Glance

If *datevalue* contains Nothing, *Month* returns Nothing.

Programming Tips and Gotchas

- The validity of the date expression, as well as the position of the month element within the date expression, is initially determined by the locale settings of the current Windows system. However, some intelligence has been built into the *Month* function that surpasses the usual comparison of a date expression to the current locale settings. For example, on a Windows machine set to US date format (mm/dd/yyyy), the date "13/12/1998" would technically be illegal. However, the *Month* function returns 12 when passed this date. The basic rule for the *Month* function is that if the system-defined month element is outside legal bounds (i.e., greater than 12), the system-defined day element is assumed to be the month and is returned by the function.

- Since the *IsDate* function adheres to the same rules and assumptions as *Month*, it can be used to determine whether a date is valid before passing it to the *Month* function.

- Visual Basic also has a new *MonthName* function for returning the name of the month.

- You can also use the *DatePart* function.

See Also

Day Function, Year Function

MonthName Function

Class

Microsoft.VisualBasic.DateAndTime

Syntax

```
MonthName(month [, abbreviate])
```

month   *required; Integer*
    The ordinal number of the month, from 1 to 12

abbreviate   *optional; Boolean*
    A flag to indicate if an abbreviated month name should be returned

Return Value

String containing the name of the specified month

Description

Returns the month name of a given month. For example, a *month* of 1 returns January or (if *abbreviate* is True) Jan.

Rules at a Glance

The default value for *abbreviate* is False.

Example

```
Public Function GetMonthName(dat As Date) As String

Dim iMonth As Integer = Month(dat)
GetMonthName = MonthName(iMonth)

End Function
```

Programming Tips and Gotchas

- *month* must be an integer; it cannot be a date. Use DatePart("m", *dateval*) to obtain a month number from a date.

- If *month* has a fractional portion, it is rounded before calling the *MonthName* function.

- *MonthName* with *abbreviate* set to False is the equivalent of Format(dateval, "mmmm").

- *MonthName* with *abbreviate* set to True is the equivalent of Format(dateval, "mmm").

See Also

WeekdayName Function

MsgBox Function

Class

Microsoft.VisualBasic.Interaction

Syntax

```
MsgBox(prompt[, buttons][, title])
```

prompt   *required; String*

    The text of the message to display in the message box dialog box

buttons   *optional;* MsgBoxStyle *enumeration*

    The sum of the Button, Icon, Default Button, and Modality constant values

title   *optional; String*

    The title displayed in the title bar of the message box dialog box

Return Value

A MsgBoxResult enumeration constant indicating the button clicked by the user to close the message box

Description

Displays a dialog box containing a message, buttons, and optional icon to the user. The action taken by the user is returned by the function in the form of an enumerated constant.

Rules at a Glance

- *prompt* can contain approximately 1,000 characters, including carriage return characters such as the built-in vbCrLf constant.

- If the *title* parameter is omitted, the name of the current application or project is displayed in the title bar.

- If you omit the *buttons* argument, the default value is 0; that is, VB opens an application modal dialog box containing only an OK button.

- The constants of the MsgBoxStyle enumeration can be added together to form a complete *buttons* argument. The constants can be divided into the following groups:

    Button Display Constants
    Icon Display Constants
    Default Button Constants
    Modality Constants

    Only one constant from each group can be used to make up the overall *buttons* value.

Button Display Constants

Constant	Value	Buttons to display
MsgBoxStyle.OKOnly	0	OK only
MsgBoxStyle.OKCancel	1	OK and Cancel
MsgBoxStyle.AbortRetryIgnore	2	Abort, Retry, and Ignore
MsgBoxStyle.YesNoCancel	3	Yes, No, and Cancel
MsgBoxStyle.YesNo	4	Yes and No
MsgBoxStyle.RetryCancel	5	Retry and Cancel

Icon Display Constants

Constant	Value	Icon to display
MsgBoxStyle.Critical	16	Critical Message
MsgBoxStyle.Question	32	Warning Query
MsgBoxStyle.Exclamation	48	Warning Message
MsgBoxStyle.Information	64	Information Message

Default Button Constants

Constant	Value	Default button
MsgBoxStyle.DefaultButton1	0	First button
MsgBoxStyle.DefaultButton2	256	Second button
MsgBoxStyle.DefaultButton3	512	Third button
MsgBoxStyle.DefaultButton4	768	Fourth button

Modality Constants

Constant	Value	Modality
MsgBoxStyle.ApplicationModal	0	Application
MsgBoxStyle.SystemModal	4096	System

Return Values

The following intrinsic constants can be used to determine the action taken by the user and represent the value returned by the *MsgBox* function:

Constant	Value	Button clicked
MsgBoxResult.OK	1	OK
MsgBoxResult.Cancel	2	Cancel (or Esc key pressed)
MsgBoxResult.Abort	3	Abort
MsgBoxResult.Retry	4	Retry
MsgBoxResult.Ignore	5	Ignore
MsgBoxResult.Yes	6	Yes
MsgBoxResult.No	7	No

If the *MsgBox* contains a Cancel button, the user can press the Esc key and the function's return value will be that of the Cancel button.

Programming Tips and Gotchas

- *Application modality* means that the user cannot access other parts of the application until a response to the message box has been given. In other words, the appearance of the message box prevents the application from performing other tasks or from interacting with the user other than through the message box.

- *System modality* used to mean that all applications were suspended until the message box was closed. However, with multitasking operating systems, such as Windows 95 and Windows NT, this is not the case. Basically, the message box is defined to be a "Topmost" window that is set to "Stay on Top," which means that the user can switch to another application and use it without responding to the message box. But because the message box is the topmost window, it will be positioned on top of all other running applications.

- Unlike its *InputBox* counterpart, *MsgBox* cannot be positioned on the screen. It is always displayed in the center of the screen.

- If your application is to run out-of-process on a remote machine, you should remove all *MsgBox* functions since they will not be displayed to the user, but instead will appear on the monitor of the remote server!

- *MsgBox* should never be used in ASP.NET applications.

VB.NET/VB 6 Differences

In VB 6, the *MsgBox* function has five parameters. The last two, `helpfile` (which specified the path to a help file containing information about the error message) and `context` (which specified the help context ID within `helpfile`), are optional. In VB.NET, these two parameters are not supported.

See Also

InputBox Function

MTAThread Attribute

Class

System.MTAThreadAttribute

Applies to

Method

Description

Specifies that the class or application to which the program element belongs is to use the *multithreaded apartment* model for COM interop. If COM components are not called from the class or application, the attribute has no effect. The <MTAThread> attribute should be used only on the class or application's *Main* method or subroutine.

The <MTAThread> attribute is similar to setting a Thread object's ApartmentState property to `ApartmentState.MTA`. The difference is that the <MTAThread> attribute creates a multithreaded apartment from startup, whereas setting the property does it only from the point that the property is set.

Constructor

```
New()
```

Properties

None

MyBase Keyword

Syntax

```
MyBase
```

Description

Provides a reference to the base class from within a derived class. If you want to call a member of the base class from within a derived class, you can use the syntax:

```
MyBase.MemberName
```

where *MemberName* is the name of the member. This will resolve any ambiguity if the derived class also has a member of the same name.

Rules at a Glance

- MyBase will call through the chain of inherited classes until it finds a callable implementation. For example, in the code:

  ```
  Public Class CTestClass
  ...
  End Class

  Public Class CTestClass2
     Inherits CTestClass

     Public Function ShowType() As Type
        Return Mybase.GetType
     End Function
  End Class
  ```

  the call to ShowType is eventually resolved as a call to Object.GetType, since all classes are ultimately derived from the Object class.

- MyBase cannot be used to call **Private** class members.

- MyBase cannot be used to call base class members marked as **MustOverride**.

Programming Tips and Gotchas

- MyBase is commonly used to call back into the overridden member from the member that overrides it in the derived class.

- The MyBase keyword can be used to call the constructor of the base class to instantiate a member of that class, as in:

  ```
  MyBase.New(...)
  ```

VB.NET/VB 6 Differences

The MyBase keyword is new to VB.NET.

MyClass Keyword

Syntax

```
MyClass
```

Description

MyClass is a reference to the class in which the keyword is used.

Rules at a Glance

- When using MyClass (as opposed to Me) to qualify a method invocation, as in:

  ```
  MyClass.IncSalary()
  ```

  the method is treated as if it was declared using the NotOverridable keyword. Thus, regardless of the type of the object at runtime, the method called is the one declared in the class containing this statement (and not in any derived classes). The upcoming example illustrates this difference between MyClass and Me.

- MyClass cannot be used with shared members.

Example

The following code defines a class, Class1, and a derived class, Class1Derived, each of which has an IncSalary method.

```
Public Class Class1

    Public Overridable Function IncSalary(ByVal sSalary As Single) _
                                    As Single
        IncSalary = sSalary * CSng(1.1)
    End Function

    Public Sub ShowIncSalary(ByVal sSalary As Single)
        MsgBox(Me.IncSalary(sSalary))
        MsgBox(MyClass.IncSalary(sSalary))
    End Sub

End Class

Public Class Class1Derived
    Inherits Class1
    Public Overrides Function IncSalary(ByVal sSalary As Single) As Single
        IncSalary = sSalary * CSng(1.2)
    End Function
End Class
```

Now consider the following code, placed in a form module:

```
Dim c1 As New Class1()
Dim c2 As New Class1Derived()

Dim c1var As Class1
```

```
clvar = c1
clvar.ShowIncSalary(10000)   ' Shows 11000, 11000

clvar = c2
clvar.ShowIncSalary(10000)   ' Shows 12000, 11000
```

The first call to ShowIncSalary is made using a variable of type Class1 that refers to an object of type Class1. In this case, both calls:

```
Me.ShowIncSalary
MyClass.ShowIncSalary
```

return the same value, because they both call IncSalary in the base class Class1.

However, in the second case, the variable of type Class1 holds a reference to an object of the derived class Class1Derived. In this case, Me refers to an object of type Class1Derived, whereas MyClass still refers to the base class Class1 wherein the keyword MyClass appears. Thus:

```
Me.ShowIncSalary
```

returns 12000, whereas:

```
MyClass.ShowIncSalary
```

returns 10000.

VB.NET/VB 6 Differences

The MyBase keyword is new to VB.NET.

See Also

Me Operator

Namespace Statement

Syntax

```
Namespace name
    component types
End Namespace
```

name   *required; String literal*
  The name of the namespace

component types   *required*
  The elements that are being declared as part of the namespace, including Enums, Structures, Interfaces, Classes, Delegates, Modules, and other namespaces

Description

Declares a namespace and specifies the items in the namespace

Rules at a Glance

- Namespaces are used in the .NET Framework as an organized method of exposing program components to other programs and applications.

- Namespaces are always `Public`. However, the elements within a namespace can be `Public`, `Friend`, or `Private`. Private members are available only within the namespace declaration.

- *name*, the namespace name, must be unique.

Now Property

Class

Microsoft.VisualBasic.DateAndTime

Syntax

```
Now()
```

Return Value

A Date containing the current system date and time

Description

Returns the current date and time based on the system setting

Rules at a Glance

- The date returned by Now takes the Windows General Date format based on the locale settings of the local computer. The U.S. setting for General Date is `mm/dd/yy hh:mm:ss`.

- The Now property is read-only.

Example

The following example returns the date 10 days from today:

```
MsgBox(DateAdd(DateInterval.Day, 10, Now()))
```

Programming Tips and Gotchas

- It is often overlooked that workstations in a modern Windows environment are at the mercy of the user! If your application relies on an accurate date and time setting, you should consider including a line in the workstation's logon script to synchronize the time with one of the servers. Many so-called bugs have been traced to a workstation that has had its date or time incorrectly altered by the user. The following line of code, when added to the logon script of an Windows NT 4.0 machine, will synchronize the machine's clock with that of a server called **NTSERV1**:

  ```
  net time \\NTSERV1 /set
  ```

- The Now property is often used to generate timestamps. However, for short-term timing and intra-day timestamps, the *Timer* property, which returns the number of milliseconds elapsed since midnight, affords greater accuracy.

- The Now property wraps the BCL's System.DateTime.Now shared property. As a result, calls to the System.DateTime.Now property offer a slight performance improvement (about 20%) over calls to the VB.NET Now property.

See Also

Today Property

NPer Function

Class

Microsoft.VisualBasic.Financial

Syntax

```
NPer(rate, pmt, pv [, fv [, due]])
```

rate   *required; Double*
The interest rate per period.

pmt   *required; Double*
The payment to be made each period.

pv   *required; Double*
The present value of the series of future payments or receipts.

fv   *optional; Double*
The future value of the series of payments or receipts. If omitted, the default value is 0.

due   *optional;* DueDate *enumeration*
A value indicating when payments are due. DueDate.EndOfPeriod (0) indicates that payments are due at the end of the payment period, and DueDate.BegOfPeriod (1) indicates that payments are due at the beginning of the period. If omitted, the default value is 0.

Return Value

A Double indicating the number of payments

Description

Determines the number of payment periods for an annuity based on fixed periodic payments and a fixed interest rate

Rules at a Glance

- *rate* is a percentage expressed as a decimal. For example, a monthly interest rate of 1% is expressed as 0.01.

- For *pv* and *fv*, cash paid out is represented by negative numbers; cash received is represented by positive numbers.

Example

Typically, the amount of time required to repay credit-card debt is never explicitly stated. The following program uses the *NPer* function to determine how much time is required to repay credit-card debt:

```
Private Sub HowLongToPay()

Try
```

```
Dim dblRate, dblPV, dblPmt As Double
Dim lngNPer As Long

dblPV = InputBox("Enter the Credit Card balance: ")
dblPmt = InputBox("Enter the monthly payment: ")
dblRate = InputBox("Enter the monthly interest rate (.xxxx): ")

lngNPer = NPer(dblRate, -dblPmt, dblPV, 0, 1)

MsgBox("Your credit card balance will be paid in " & _
       lngNPer & " months." & vbCrLf & "That's " & _
       Int(lngNPer / 12) & " years and " & _
       Math.Round(lngNPer Mod 12, 2) & " months.")

Catch e As System.Exception

    MsgBox("Unable to compute period because of error " & e.Message)

End Try

End Sub
```

Programming Tips and Gotchas

- Both *rate* and *pmt* must be expressed in the same time unit. That is, if *pmt* reflects the monthly payment amount, *rate* must be the monthly interest rate.

- *NPer* is useful in calculating the number of payment periods required to repay a loan when the monthly loan payment is fixed or when an approximate amount of a monthly payment is known. In this case, *pv* reflects the amount of the loan, and *fv* is usually 0, reflecting the fact that the loan is to be entirely repaid.

- *NPer* is useful in determining the length of time required to meet some future financial goal. In this case, *pv* represents the current level of savings, and *fv* represents the desired level of savings.

See Also

FV Function, IPmt Function, NPV Function, Pmt Function, PPmt Function, PV Function, Rate Function

---

NPV Function

Class

Microsoft.VisualBasic.Financial

Syntax

```
NPV(rate, valuearray() )
```

rate   *required; Double*
    The discount rate over the period, expressed as a decimal

```
valuearray()                                                    required; Double
```
    An array of cash flow values

Return Value

A Double specifying the net present value

Description

Calculates the net present value of an investment based on a series of periodic variable cash flows (payments and receipts) and a discount rate

The *net present value* is the value today of a series of future cash flows discounted at some rate back to the first day of the investment period.

Rules at a Glance

* *rate* must be a percentage expressed as a decimal. For example, 10% is expressed as 0.10.

* *values* is a one-dimensional array that must contain at least one negative value (a payment) and one positive value (a receipt).

* The *NPV* investment begins one period before the date of the first cash flow value and ends with the last cash flow value in the array.

* *NPV* requires future cash flows. If the first cash flow occurs at the beginning of the first period, the first value must be added to the value returned by *NPV* and must not be included in *values*.

Programming Tips and Gotchas

* *rate* and the individual elements of *values* must reflect the same time period. For example, if *values* reflects annual cash flows, *rate* must be the annual discount rate.

* Individual members of *values* are interpreted sequentially. That is, *values(0)* is the first cash flow, *values(1)* is the second, etc.

* *NPV* is like the *PV* function, except that *PV* allows cash flows to begin either at the beginning or the end of a period and requires that cash flows be fixed throughout the investment.

See Also

FV Function, IPmt Function, NPer Function, Pmt Function, PPmt Function, PV Function, Rate Function

---

Obsolete Attribute

Class

System.ObsoleteAttribute

Applies to

Class, Struct, Enum, Constructor, Method, Property, Field, Event, Interface, and Delegate (i.e., all program elements except parameters and return values)

Description

Indicates that the program element is obsolete and either is deprecated or no longer supported

Constructors

```
New([[message], error])
```

message   *String*
   Provides a message that can contain workarounds or alternate program elements

error   *Boolean*
   Indicates whether the compiler generates an error if the program element is used

Properties

IsError   *Boolean*
   Read-only. Indicates whether the compiler generates an error if the program element is used. Default value is **False**.

Message   *String*
   Read-only. A message to be displayed to the programmer that indicates workarounds or alternate program elements.

Oct Function

Class

Microsoft.VisualBasic.Conversion

Syntax

```
Oct(number)
```

number   *required; Numeric or string capable of conversion to a number*
   A valid numeric or string expression

Return Value

String

Description

Returns the octal value of a given number

Rules at a Glance

* If *number* is not already a whole number, it is rounded to the nearest whole number before being evaluated.
* If *number* is Nothing, an error occurs.
* *Oct* returns up to 11 octal characters.

Programming Tips and Gotchas

You can also use literals in your code to represent octal numbers by appending &O to the relevant octal value. For example, 100 decimal has the octal representation &O144. The following two statements assign an octal value to a variable:

```
lngOctValue1 = &H200                 ' Assigns 128

lngOctValue2 = "&O" & Len(dblNumber)  ' Assigns 8
```

See Also

Hex Function

On Error Statement

Syntax 1

```
On Error GoTo label|0|-1
```

label   *Either* **label**, *0, or* –1 *is required*
    A valid label within the subroutine

Syntax 2

```
On Error Resume Next
```

Description

Enables or disables error handling within a procedure.

If you don't use an On Error statement or a Try...Catch block in your procedure, or if you have explicitly switched off error handling, the Visual Basic runtime engine will automatically handle the error. First, it will display a dialog box containing the standard text of the error message, something that many users are likely to find incomprehensible. Second, it will terminate the application. So any error that occurs in the procedure will produce a fatal runtime error.

Rules at a Glance

Syntax 1

- The 0 argument disables error handling within the procedure until the next On Error statement is executed.

- The –1 argument disables an enabled exception in the current procedure. (It resets the exception to Nothing.)

- The *label* argument specifies the label that defines an error-handling routine within the current procedure. Should an error occur, the procedure will be branched to this error-handling routine.

- A label must be suffixed with a colon. In addition, you cannot use a VB reserved word for a subroutine label name. For example:

```
someroutine:
```

- *label* must be in the same procedure as the On Error statement.

Syntax 2

When a runtime error occurs, program execution continues with the program line following the line that generated the error.

Programming Tips and Gotchas

- If you have no error handling in your procedure or if error handling is disabled, the VB runtime engine will trace back through the call stack until a procedure is reached where error handling is enabled. In that case, the error will be handled by that procedure. However, if no error handler can be found in the call stack, a runtime error occurs, and program execution is halted.

- `On Error Resume Next` is useful in situations either where you are certain that errors will occur or where the errors that could occur are minor. The following example shows how you can quickly cycle through the controls on a form and set the Text property to an empty string without checking what type of control you're dealing with. Of course, you are aware that many of the controls don't have a text property, so that the attempt to access their Text property will generate an error. By using the `On Error Resume Next` statement, you force your program to ignore this error and carry on with the next control.

```
On Error Resume Next
For Each Control In Me.Controls
    Control.Text = ""
Next
```

- Use of the `On Error Resume Next` statement should be kept to a minimum, since errors are basically ignored and their occurrence is silent to the user. This means that, should an *unexpected* error (that is, an error that you were not intending to handle when you chose to ignore errors) occur or should your application behave unexpectedly, the job of finding and correcting the cause of the error becomes almost impossible.

- The following is a template for error handling within your procedures using the `On Error` statement:

```
Sub/Function/Property Name ()
    On Error Goto Name_Err
    ... 'procedure code

Name_Exit:
    ... 'tidying up code - such as Set Object = Nothing
    Exit Sub/Function/Property

Name_Err:
    ... 'error handling code e.g. a MsgBox to inform the user
    Resume Name_Exit

End Sub/Function/Property
```

If cleanup code isn't required within the procedure, you can simplify the template by removing the `Name_Exit` label and removing the `Resume Name_Exit` statement.

- If you are writing an error-handling routine for use within a class module or a DLL, you should use the following template, which raises an error back to the client, thereby notifying the client of the error and allowing the client to handle it:

```
Sub/Function/Property Name ()
    On Error Goto Name_Err
    ... 'procedure code

    ... 'tidying up code - such as Set Object = Nothing
    Exit Sub/Function/Property

Name_Err:
    ... 'error handling and tidying up code
    Err.Raise etc...

End Sub/Function/Property
```

- Errors that occur within an error handler are passed up the call chain. To illustrate this, consider the following code:

```
Public Function Test() As Integer
    On Error Goto Err_Test
    Dim iTest() As Integer - {1, 2}
    Test = iTest(3) ' error
    Exit Function
Err_Test:
    MsgBox(iTest(4))  ' error
End Function

Sub Test2()
    On Error Goto Err_Test2
    Test()
    Exit Sub
Err_Test2:
    MsgBox("Error handled")
End Sub
```

When Test2 is run, the message "Error handled" is displayed. This indicates that the error that occurs in the error handler of Test is passed to Test2.

- For more on both unstructured and structured error handling, see Chapter 9.

VB.NET/VB 6 Differences

In VB 6, the *label* in `On Error GoTo` *label* can be either a label or a line number. In VB.NET, the use of line numbers is not supported.

See Also

Err Object

OpenFileDialog Class

Namespace

System.Windows.Forms

Createable

Yes

Description

Represents a common dialog box for selecting or opening a file.

The OpenFileDialog class has properties for setting the initial appearance and functionality of the file dialog box, a property for returning the filename or names selected by the user, as well as a method for showing the dialog box. An instance of the OpenFileDialog class does not itself open the file, but instead provides the information that allows your code to do this programmatically.

Under VB, the most common use for this dialog box is to get the name of a file from the user, after which we can use VB's functions to open that file.

An OpenFileDialog object can be instantiated as follows:

```
Dim oOpenDlg As New OpenFileDialog
```

Selected OpenFileDialog Members

The following is a brief description of some of the more important members of the OpenFileDialog class:

AddExtension property
> Gets or sets a Boolean value that determines whether the default file extension is automatically added to the Filename property if the user fails to enter an extension. Its default value is `True`.

CheckFileExists property
> Sets or retrieves a Boolean value indicating whether a warning message should be displayed if the user enters the name of a file that does not exist. The default value is `True`.

DefaultExt property
> Gets or sets a String that defines the default file extension. The string should consist of the file extension only without a period.

FileName property
> Returns a string that contains the fully qualified name (that is, complete path and filename) of the file selected by the user. If no file is selected, the property returns an empty string.

FileNames property
> Returns a String array that contains the fully qualified names (that is, complete paths and filenames) of the files selected by the user. If no file is selected, the property returns an empty array. Note that this property returns a single-element array if the Multiselect property is `False` and the user selects a file.

Filter property

Gets or sets a String containing the current filter, which determines the items that appear in the "Files of type" drop-down listbox. A single item consists of a file description, a vertical bar, and the file extension (usually "*." plus the file extension). If there are multiple extensions in a single item, they are separated by semicolons. If there are multiple items, they are separated by vertical bars. For example, the following code fragment assigns a filter string to a String variable:

```
sFilter = oFS.Filter="Text files (*.txt; *.vb)|*.txt;*.vb|" & _
          "Visual Basic files (*.vb)|*.vb|" & _
          "All files (*.*)|*.*"
```

FilterIndex property

Gets or sets an Integer value that determines which of the items defined by the Filter property are selected. The index is one-based, rather than zero-based. When the dialog is first displayed and no FilterIndex value is specified, it defaults to 1. When the method returns, its value indicates which filter item was selected by the user.

InitialDirectory property

Gets or sets a String that defines the directory initially displayed by the Open-FileDialog dialog

Multiselect property

Sets or retrieves a Boolean value indicating whether the user is allowed to select more than one file.

OpenFile method

Opens the file selected by the user, returning a Stream object. The file is opened in read-only mode. As Microsoft puts it: "The OpenFile method is used to provide a facility to quickly open a file from the dialog box. The file is opened in read-only mode for security purposes. To open a file in a read/write mode, you must use another call . . . "

ReadOnlyChecked property

Sets or retrieves a Boolean value indicating whether the read-only checkbox is selected on the dialog box.

RestoreDirectory property

Gets or sets a Boolean value indicating whether the current directory is restored before the dialog closes. Its default value is **False**.

ShowDialog method

The OpenFileDialog class inherits from the FileDialog class, which in turn inherits from the CommonDialog class. This class has a ShowDialog method that shows the dialog box. Once the user has dismissed the dialog box, the FileDialog's FileName and FileNames properties can be used to get the user's choice(s).

ShowReadOnly property

Sets or retrieves a Boolean value indicating whether the dialog box contains a read-only checkbox.

Title property

Gets or sets a String value containing the title of the Open dialog box.

Example

The following code asks the user for one or more files and displays the filenames in the Output window:

```
Dim fd As New OpenFileDialog()
Dim i As Integer
fd.Multiselect = True
If fd.ShowDialog() = DialogResult.OK Then
    For i = 0 To UBound(fd.FileNames)
        Console.WriteLine(fd.FileNames(i))
    Next
End If
```

VB.NET/VB 6 Differences

Whereas the OpenFileDialog class is implemented in the .NET Base Class Library, VB 6 offered the CommonDialog custom control. Although the two offer similar functionality, their public interfaces are almost completely different.

Option Compare Statement

Syntax

```
Option Compare {Binary | Text}
```

Description

Used to set the default method for comparing string data

Rules at a Glance

- When Option Compare is not used in a module, the default comparison method is Binary.

- When Option Compare is used, it must appear at the start of the module's declarations section, before any procedures.

- *Binary comparison*—the default text comparison method in Visual Basic— uses the internal binary code of each character to determine the sort order of the characters. For example, "A" < "a".

- *Text comparison* uses the locale settings of the current system to determine the sort order of the characters. Text comparison is case insensitive. For example, "A" = "a".

Option Explicit Statement

Syntax

```
Option Explicit [On | Off]
```

Description

Use Option Explicit to generate a compile-time error whenever a variable that has not been declared is encountered.

Rules at a Glance

- The Option Explicit statement must appear in the declarations section of a module before any procedures.

- In modules where the Option Explicit statement is not used, any undeclared variables are automatically cast as Objects.

- The default is Option Explicit On. In other words, the statement:

  ```
  Option Explicit
  ```

  is equivalent to:

  ```
  Option Explicit On
  ```

Programming Tips and Gotchas

- It is considered good programming practice to always use the Option Explicit statement. The following example shows why:

  ```
  1:   Dim iVariable As Integer

  2:   iVariable = 100
  3:   iVariable = iVarable + 50
  4:   MsgBox iVariable
  ```

  In this code snippet, an integer variable, *iVariable*, has been declared. However, because the name of the variable has been mistyped in line 3, the message box shows its value as only 50 instead of 150. This is because *iVarable* is assumed to be an undeclared variable whose value is 0. If the Option Explicit statement had been used, the code would not have compiled, and *iVarable* would have been highlighted as the cause.

- For an ASP.NET page, you use the @ PAGE directive rather than Option Explicit to require variable declaration. Its syntax is:

  ```
  <%@ Page Language="VB" Explicit=true|false %>
  ```

  By default, Explicit is true in ASP.NET pages.

  You can also use the <system.web> section of the WEB.Config file to require variable declaration for an entire virtual directory or ASP.NET application by adding an explicit attribute to the compliation section. Its syntax is:

  ```
  <compliation strict="true|false">
  ```

  In both cases, true corresponds to Option Explicit On, and false corresponds to Option Explicit Off.

Option Strict Statement

Syntax

```
Option Strict [On | Off]
```

Description

`Option Strict` prevents VB from making any *implicit* data type conversions that are *narrowing* since narrowing conversions may involve data loss. For example:

```
Dim lNum As Long = 2455622
Dim iNum As Integer = lNum
```

converts a Long (whose value can range from −9,223,372,036,854,775,808 to 9,223,372,036,854,775,807) to an Integer (whose value can range from 2,147,483,648 to 2,147,483,647). In this case, even though no data loss would result from the narrowing, `Option Strict On` would still not allow the conversion and would instead generate a compiler error. The reasoning here is that, although particular narrowing operations may not lose data, there is always the potential for data loss when working with variables—that is, with symbolic representations of numbers whose values are allowed to vary.

Rules at a Glance

- If the `Option Strict` statement is not present in a module, `Option Strict` is `Off`.

- The default is `Option Strict On`. In other words, the statement:

   ```
   Option Strict On
   ```

   is equivalent to the statement:

   ```
   Option Strict
   ```

- The `Option Strict` statement must appear in the declarations section of a module before any code.

- `Option Strict On` disallows all implicit narrowing conversions.

- `Option Strict On` also causes errors to be generated for late binding, as well as for any undeclared variables, since `Option Strict On` implies `Option Explicit On`.

- Conversions can be narrowing or widening. The widening conversions are conversions from a type to itself or any of the following:

   — Byte → Short, Integer, Long, Decimal, Single, Double

   — Short → Integer, Long, Decimal, Single, Double

   — Integer → Long, Decimal, Single, Double

   — Long → Decimal, Single, Double

   — Decimal → Single, Double

   — Single → Double

   — Any enumerated type → Integer type or wider

   — Char → String

   — Any type → Object

   — Any derived type → Any type from which it is derived

- — Any type → Any interface it implements
- — Nothing → Any type
- Narrowing conversions are:
  - — The reverse conversions of the widening conversions listed above
  - — Conversions between Boolean and any numeric type
  - — Any numeric type → any enumerated type
  - — Conversions between a Char array and a String
  - — Conversions between String and any numeric, Boolean, or Date type

Programming Tips and Gotchas

- Although the setting of Option Strict has no effect on BCL data types, BCL data types disallow implicit narrowing conversions.

- Explicit narrowing conversions are not affected by Option Strict. However, if data loss does occur as a result of an explicit conversion, an OverflowException exception is generated.

- One of the most commonly overlooked narrowing conversions is the use of "wider" arguments in function, procedure, and method calls. Passing a Long to an Integer parameter, for example, is an implicit narrowing conversion that Option Strict does not allow.

- In many cases, Option Strict On disallows seemingly "safe" conversions because it interprets literal values in unexpected ways. For example, the statement:

```
Dim decNum As Decimal = 10.32
```

generates a compiler error because 10.32 is interpreted as a Double, and implicit conversions from Double to Decimal are not allowed. You can correct this compiler error with a statement like:

```
Dim decNum As Decimal = 10.32D
```

- Setting Option Strict On is highly recommended.

- For an ASP.NET page, you use the @ Page directive rather than Option Strict to control strict type checking. Its syntax is:

```
<%@ Page Language="VB" Strict=true|false %>
```

By default, Strict is false in ASP.NET pages.

You can also use the <system.web> section of the WEB.Config file to control strict type checking for an entire virtual directory or ASP.NET application by adding a strict attribute to the compilation section. Its syntax is:

```
<compilation strict="true|false">
```

In both cases, true corresponds to Option Explicit On, and false corresponds to Option Explicit Off.

VB.NET/VB 6 Differences

The Option Strict setting is new to VB.NET.

Option Explicit Statement

Out Attribute

Class

System.Runtime.InteropServices.OutAttribute

Applies to

Parameter

Description

Defines the parameter to which it applies as an out parameter. An out parameter is a variation on a parameter passed by reference using the `ByRef` keyword. In the case of a parameter passed by reference, the caller of the method is responsible for allocating memory and passing its address to the caller, which can then modify the parameter value. In the case of an out parameter, memory for the parameter is allocated by the called method and only its value is returned to the caller. This makes out parameters rather than reference parameters far more efficient in remoting (i.e., calls across machines) and in web method calls.

Although you can define an out parameter using the <Out> attribute, the VB.NET compiler does not enforce it. That is, if you fail to assign a value to the out parameter, or if you indicate that the parameter is to be passed by value rather than by reference, the compiler does not generate an error. Because of this, be especially careful to make sure that all parameters marked with the <Out> attribute are passed using the `ByRef` keyword, and that you've explicitly assigned a value to the out parameter in the method.

Constructor

```
New()
```

Properties

None

Example

```
Imports System
Imports System.Runtime.InteropServices

Public Class CPerson

    Private iAge, iHeight, iWeight As Integer
    Private sName As String

    Public Sub New(strName As String)
```

```
            'Here we'd ordinarily perform a database lookup
            ' and assign values to the instance fields
            sName = strName
            iAge = 26
            iHeight = 73
            iWeight = 185
        End Sub

        Public Sub GetStats(<Out> ByRef intAge As Integer, _
                            <Out> ByRef intHt As Integer, _
                            <Out> ByRef intWt As Integer)
            intAge = iAge
            intHt = iHeight
            intWt = iWeight
        End Sub
    End Class

    Module modMain
        Public Sub Main()
            Dim oPerson As New CPerson("John Doe")
            Dim iAge As Integer, iHeight As Integer, iWeight As Integer
            oPerson.GetStats(iAge, iHeight, iWeight)
            Console.WriteLine("John Doe is " & iHeight & " inches tall.")
        End Sub
    End Module
```

ParamArray Attribute

Class

System.ParamArrayAttribute

Applies to

Parameter

Description

Indicates that the parameter represents a parameter array—i.e., a variable number of arguments.

The same effect is achieved by using the `ParamArray` keyword in a function or subroutine declaration. In fact, the `ParamArray` keyword is compiled into the `ParamArray` attribute.

If you do use the attribute, it must appear as `<ParamArrayAttribute>` rather than `<ParamArray>`, since `ParamArray` is a Visual Basic keyword.

Constructor

```
New()
```

Properties

None

Partition Function

Class

Microsoft.VisualBasic.Interaction

Syntax

```
Partition(number, start, stop, interval)
```

number   *required; Long*
    Number to evaluate against the intervals.

start   *required; Long*
    Start of the range. Must be non-negative.

stop   *required; Long*
    End of the range. Must be greater than *start*.

interval   *required; Long*
    Size of each interval into which the range is partitioned.

Return Value

A String containing the range within which *number* falls

Description

Returns a string that describes which interval contains the number

Rules at a Glance

- *start* must be greater than or equal to 0.

- *stop* cannot be less than or equal to *start*.

- *Partition* returns a range formatted with enough leading spaces so that there are the same number of characters to the left and right of the colon as there are characters in *stop*, plus one. This ensures that the interval text will be handled properly during any sort operations.

- If *number* is outside of the range of *start*, the range reported is:

  ```
  : (start - 1)
  ```

  If *number* is outside the range of *end*, the range reported is:

  ```
  (last_end_range + 1):
  ```

- If *interval* is 1, the range is *number:number*, regardless of the *start* and *stop* arguments. For example, if *interval* is 1, *number* is 100, and *stop* is 1000, *Partition* returns 100: 100.

- If any of its arguments are Null, *Partition* returns a Null.

Example

The code:

```
Dim i As Integer
For i = -1 To 110 \ 5
    Console.WriteLine(CStr(i * 5) & " is in interval " & _
```

```
                    Partition(i * 5, 0, 100, 10))
    Next
```

produces the following output:

```
-5 is in interval    :  -1
0 is in interval   0:  9
5 is in interval   0:  9
10 is in interval  10: 19
15 is in interval  10: 19
20 is in interval  20: 29
25 is in interval  20: 29
30 is in interval  30: 39
35 is in interval  30: 39
40 is in interval  40: 49
45 is in interval  40: 49
50 is in interval  50: 59
55 is in interval  50: 59
60 is in interval  60: 69
65 is in interval  60: 69
70 is in interval  70: 79
75 is in interval  70: 79
80 is in interval  80: 89
85 is in interval  80: 89
90 is in interval  90: 99
95 is in interval  90: 99
100 is in interval 100:100
105 is in interval 101:
110 is in interval 101:
```

Programming Tips and Gotchas

- The *Partition* function is useful in creating histograms, which give the number of integers from a collection that fall into various ranges.

VB.NET/VB 6 Differences

- The *Partition* function is new to VB.NET.

Pi Field

Class

System.Math

Syntax

```
Math.PI
```

Return Value

A Double containing the approximate value of the irrational number pi

Description

This field returns the approximate value of the irrational number pi. In particular:

```
Math.PI = 3.14159265358979
```

Rules at a Glance

This is a Shared member, so it can be used without creating any objects.

VB.NET/VB 6 Differences

The Pi field is new to VB.NET.

See Also

E Field

Pmt Function

Class

Microsoft.VisualBasic.Financial

Syntax

```
Pmt(rate, nper, pv[, fv[, due]])
```

rate   *required; Double*
    The interest rate per period.

nper   *required; Double*
    The total number of payment periods.

pv   *required; Double*
    The present value of the series of future payments.

fv   *optional; Double*
    The future value or cash balance after the final payment.

due   *optional;* `DueDate` *enumeration*
    A value indicating when payments are due. `EndOfPeriod` (0) indicates that payments are due at the end of the payment period; `BegOfPeriod` (1) indicates that payments are due at the beginning of the period. If omitted, the default value is 0.

Return Value

A Double representing the monthly payment

Description

Calculates the payment for an annuity based on periodic, fixed payments and a fixed interest rate. An annuity can be either a loan or an investment.

Rules at a Glance

- *rate* is a percentage expressed as a decimal. For example, an interest rate of 1% per month is expressed as 0.01.

- If *fv* is omitted, the default value of 0 (reflecting the complete repayment of a loan) is used.

- For *pv* and *fv*, cash paid out is represented by negative numbers; cash received is represented by positive numbers.

- If *due* is omitted, the default value of 0 (reflecting payments at the beginning of each period) is used.

Example

See the example for the IPmt Function" entry.

Programming Tips and Gotchas

- *rate* and *nper* must be calculated using payment periods expressed in the same units. For example, if *nper* reflects the total number of monthly payments, *rate* must be the monthly interest rate.

See Also

FV Function, IPmt Function, NPer Function, NPV Function, PPmt Function, PV Function, Rate Function

---

Pow Function

Class

System.Math

Syntax

```
result = Math.Pow(x, y)
```

x, y   *required; Double*

Return Value

A Double that is *x* (the base) raised to the power *y* (the exponent)

Description

This is a generalized exponential function; it returns the result of a number raised to a specified power.

Rules at a Glance

This is a Shared member, so it can be used without creating any objects.

VB.NET/VB 6 Differences

The *Pow* function is new to the .NET Framework.

See Also

Exp Function

PPmt Function

Class

Microsoft.VisualBasic.Financial

Syntax

```
PPmt(rate, per, nper, pv[, fv[, due]])
```

rate   *required; Double*
> The interest rate per period.

per   *required; Double*
> The period for which a payment is to be computed.

nper   *required; Double*
> The total number of payment periods.

pv   *required; Double*
> The present value of a series of future payments.

fv   *optional; Object*
> The future value or cash balance after the final payment. If omitted, the default value is 0.

due   *optional;* DueDate *enumeration*
> A value indicating when payments are due. It can be either DueDate.
> EndOfPeriod (or 0), for payments due at the end of the period, or DueDate.
> BegOfPeriod (or 1), for payments due at the beginning of the period. The
> default value is DueDate.EndOfPeriod.

Return Value

A Double representing the principal paid in a given payment

Description

Computes the payment of principal for a given period of an annuity, based on periodic, fixed payments and a fixed interest rate. An annuity is a series of fixed cash payments made over a period of time. It can be either a loan payment or an investment.

Rules at a Glance

- The value of *per* can range from 1 to *nper*.

- If *pv* and *fv* represent liabilities, their value is negative; if they represent assets, their value is positive.

- If *fv* is omitted, its default value of 0 is used.

- If *due* is omitted, the default value of 0 (reflecting payments at the beginning of each period) is used.

Example

See the example for the IPmt Function" entry.

Programming Tips and Gotchas

- *rate* and *nper* must be expressed in the same time unit. That is, if *nper* reflects the number of monthly payments, *rate* must be the monthly interest rate.

- The interest rate is a percentage expressed as a decimal. For example, if *nper* is the total number of monthly payments, an annual percentage rate (APR) of

12% is equivalent to a monthly percentage rate of 1%. The value of *rate* is therefore .01.

See Also

FV Function, IPmt Function, NPer Function, NPV Function, Pmt Function, PV Function, Rate Function

---

Print, PrintLine Procedures

Class

Microsoft.VisualBasic.FileSystem

Syntax

```
Print(filenumber, [outputlist()])

PrintLine(filenumber, [outputlist()])
```

filenumber   *required; Integer*
Any valid file number.

outputlist   *optional; Parameter Array*
A comma-separated list of expressions to output to a file.

outputlist can be either a scalar variable, a list of comma-delimited expressions, or a parameter array. Its comma-delimited expressions or parameter array can include the following:

Spc(n)   *optional*
Insert *n* space characters before expression.

Tab(n)   *optional*
Position the insertion point either at the next print zone (by omitting *n*) or at column number (*n*).

expression   *optional; any*
The data expression to output.

Description

Outputs formatted data to a disk file opened for Append or Output

Rules at a Glance

- *Print* and *PrintLine* are identical, except that *PrintLine* advances to the next line after printing.

- The Tab(*n*) argument does not actually insert any tab characters (Chr(9)); instead, it fills the space from the end of the last expression to column *n* (or to the start of the next print zone) with space characters.

- The *Print* procedure uses the locale settings of the current system to format dates, times, and numbers, using the correct separators.

- *outputlist* can be either a comma-separated list of expressions or a parameter array.

Example

The following code shows how to use the *Print* procedure to write to a file using both a comma-separated list of arguments and a parameter array:

```
Dim sInput As String
Dim iFile As Integer = FreeFile()
Dim iNum As Integer
Dim oOutput(1) As Object
FileOpen(iFile, "C:\dataprex.txt", openmode.append)
Do
    sInput = InputBox("Enter name: ")
    if sInput = "" Then Exit Do
    Print(iFile, sInput)

    iNum = Len(sInput)
    sInput = InputBox("Enter street address: ")
    oOutput(0) = spc(25 - iNum)
    oOutput(1) = sInput
    Print(iFile, oOutput)

    iNum += Len(sInput)
    sInput = InputBox("Enter city: ")
    PrintLine(iFile, spc(40 - iNum), sInput)
Loop While Not sInput = ""

FileClose(iFile)
```

Programming Tips and Gotchas

You may find that sequential data files written using the *Print* procedure are misinterpreted by the *Input* function. For heavily structured sequential data, you may get better results with the *Write* procedure, which ensures that all fields are correctly delimited.

VB.NET/VB 6 Differences

- In VB 6, the Print statement requires a # symbol in front of *filenumber*. In VB.NET, this usage is not supported.

- In VB 6, the final argument in *outputlist*, *charpos*, allows you to specify the starting character position of the next output. In VB.NET, however, this argument is not supported.

See Also

FileOpen Procedure

Private Statement

Syntax

```
Private [WithEvents] varname[([subscripts])] [As [New] _
        type] [, [WithEvents] varname[([subscripts])] _
        [As [New] type]] . . .
```

WithEvents *optional; Keyword*
> A keyword that denotes the object variable, *varname*, can respond to events triggered from within the object to which it refers

varname *required; any*
> The name of the variable, following Visual Basic naming conventions

subscripts *optional; Integer or Long*
> Denotes *varname* as an array and specifies the number and extent of array dimensions

New *optional; Keyword*
> Used to automatically create an instance of the object referred to by the object variable, *varname*

type *optional; Keyword*
> Data type of the variable *varname*

Description

Used at module level to declare a private variable and allocate the relevant storage space in memory. Private can also be used with procedures and class modules.

Rules at a Glance

- A `Private` variable's scope is limited to the module in which it is created.

- `WithEvents` is only valid when used to declare an object variable. The `WithEvents` keyword informs VB that the object being referenced exposes events. When you declare an object variable using `WithEvents`, an entry for the object variable is placed in the code window's Object List, and a list of the events available to the object variable is placed in its Procedures List. You can then write code in the object variable's event handlers in the same way you write other more common event handlers.

- There is no limit to the number of object variables that can refer to the same object using the `WithEvents` keyword; they will all respond to that object's events.

- You cannot create an array variable that uses the `WithEvents` keyword.

- The `New` keyword cannot be used in the same object-variable declaration as `WithEvents`. This is because `WithEvents` is designed to trap event notifications that would ordinarily be inaccessible to a Visual Basic program. Consequently, `WithEvents` can only be used when defining an instance of an existing object.

- The *subscripts* argument has the following syntax:

    ```
    upperbound [, upperbound]
    ```

    For example:

    ```
    Private strNames(10, 15)
    ```

    defines a two-dimensional array with 11 elements in the first coordinate and 16 elements in the second coordinate. Thus, the first element is str-Names(0,0), and the last element is strNames(10,15).

- Using the *subscripts* argument, you can declare up to 60 multiple dimensions for the array.

- To declare an array with no specified size, use commas with no integers between them, as in:

```
Private sNames()
Private sThings(,)
```

You can set or change the number of elements of an array using the ReDim statement.

- The New keyword is used only when declaring an object variable. For example:

```
Private oEmployee As Employee
oEmployee = New Employee
```

or:

```
Private oEmployee As New Employee
```

- The New keyword can only be used with early-bound objects.

- *datatype* may be Boolean, Byte, Char, Date, Decimal, Double, Integer, Long, Object, Short, Single, String, a user-defined type, or an object type.

Programming Tips and Gotchas

- All variables created at procedure level are Private by default. That is, they do not have scope outside of the procedure in which they are created.

- A new type of scope was introduced in Visual Basic 5.0. The Friend scope is halfway between Public and Private. It is useful in situations where Private is too restricting and Public is too open. For more information, refer to the Friend Keyword" entry.

- You should note that when you use the New keyword to declare an object variable, its class constructor is fired when the object variable is declared.

- The WithEvents keyword cannot be used with local variables whose scope is limited to a function or procedure.

VB.NET/VB 6 Differences

- In VB 6, the *subscripts* argument takes the form:

```
[lowerbound To] upperbound [, [lowerbound To] upperbound]
```

VB.NET, however, does not allow you to set the lower bound of an array.

- In VB 6, an array whose number of elements are declared in advance is a fixed array; it cannot be redimensioned. In VB.NET, all arrays are dynamic and can be redimensioned.

- In VB.NET, variables declared with the New keyword on the same line as the Private statement are no longer created when their first reference is encountered. Hence, whereas in VB 6, declaring an object variable using a statement such as:

```
Private oObj As New MyApp.SomeObject
```

could interfere with object destruction, in VB.NET this is not the case.

- In VB 6, the *type* argument can be Currency. The Currency data type, how-ever, is not supported by VB.NET.

See Also

Friend Keyword, Protected Keyword, Public Statement

Property Statement

Syntax

```
[Default] [accessmodifier] [ReadOnly| WriteOnly] _
    [ClassBehavior] Property name _
    [(arglist)] [As type] [Implements interfacemember]
Get
    [statements]
End Get
Set
    [statements]
End Set
End Property
```

Default   *optional; Keyword*

Specifies that the property is the default property. Must have both a Get and a Set block.

accessmodifier   *optional; Keyword*

One of the keywords Public, Private, Protected, Friend, or Protected Friend. For more information, see the section entitled Accessibility in Class Modules" in Chapter 4.

ReadOnly   *optional; Keyword*

Indicates that the property is read-only. Must have only a Get block. (If you try to write a Set block, VB will generate a syntax error.)

WriteOnly   *optional; Keyword*

Indicates that the property is write-only. Must have only a Set block. (If you try to write a Get block, VB will generate a syntax error.)

ClassBehavior   *optional; Keyword*

One of the following keywords:

Overloads

Indicates that more than one declaration of this function exists (with different argument signatures). For more detail, see Chapter 4.

Overrides

For derived classes, indicates that the function overrides the function by the same name (and argument signature) in the base class. For more detail, see Chapter 4.

Overridable

Indicates that the function can be overridden in a derived class. For more detail, see Chapter 4.

NotOverridable

Indicates that the function cannot be overridden in a derived class. For more detail, see Chapter 4.

MustOverride

Indicates that the function must be overridden in a derived class. For more detail, see Chapter 4.

Shadows   *optional; Keyword*

Indicates that the property shadows any element of this same name in a base class.

Shared

A shared function is callable without creating an object of the class. It is, in this strange sense, shared by all objects of the class. These are also called static functions.

name   *required; String literal*

The name of the property.

arglist   *optional; any*

A comma-delimited list of variables to be passed to the property as arguments from the calling procedure.

type   *optional*

The return data type of the property. The default is Object.

Implements *interfacename*   *optional*

Indicates that the property implements a property by the same name in the interface named *interfacename*.

Description

Declares a class property

Rules at a Glance

- Overloads and Shadows cannot be used in the same property declaration.

- Property procedures are Public by default.

- The Friend keyword is only valid within class modules. Friend procedures are accessible to all procedures in all modules and classes within a project, but are not listed in the class library for that project. Therefore, they cannot be accessed from projects or applications outside the defining application.

- Properties and procedures defined using the Friend keyword cannot be late bound.

- The Default keyword can be used only in the case of parameterized properties. Typically, these are properties that either return collection objects or are implemented as property arrays.

- By default, arguments are passed to the property procedures by *value* (ByVal).

- *type* defines not only the data type returned by the property, but also the data type of the value to be assigned to the property.

- A **Property Get** procedure is very similar to a function: the value returned by the property is indicated by assigning that value to a variable whose name is the same as the property.

- In a **Property Set** procedure, the value being assigned to the property is represented by the keyword **Value**. Its data type is represented by the **As** *type* clause.

- If an **Exit Property** statement is executed, the **Property** procedure exits and program execution immediately continues with the statement following the call to the property. Any number of **Exit Property** statements can appear in a **Property** procedure.

Programming Tips and Gotchas

- You should protect the values of properties by defining a **Private** variable to hold the internal property value and to control the updating of the property by outside applications through the **Property** statement, as the following template describes:

```
' Salary property is read/write
Private mdecSalary As Decimal
Property Salary() As Decimal
    Get
        Salary = mdecSalary
    End Get
    Set
        mdecSalary = Value
    End Set
End Property
```

Otherwise, if the variable used to store a property value is public, its value can be modified arbitrarily by any application that accesses the class module containing the property.

- Typically, *arglist* need be specified only in the case of property arrays. For example:

```
Public Class CEmployee

Private sPhone(2) As String

Property Phone(idx As Integer) As String
    Get
        Phone = sPhone(idx)
    End Get

    Set
        sPhone(idx) = Value
    End Set
End Property

End Class
```

- The class constructor is typically used to initialize property values to their default settings.

VB.NET/VB 6 Differences

The syntax for declaring properties in VB.NET is significantly different from the syntax in VB 6. Some of the differences include:

- VB 6 includes individual `Property Get` (to retrieve a property value), `Property Let` (to assign a property value), and `Property Set` (to assign a reference to a property value) statements. VB.NET replaces this with a single `Property...End Property` construct.

- In VB 6, all values—including the property values themselves—passed to property statements are expressed as parameters. In VB.NET, the value to be assigned to a property is represented by the `Value` keyword, rather than by a formal parameter.

- In VB 6, because `Property Set`, `Property Let`, and `Property Get` procedures are separate, standalone constructs, it is possible to expose property procedures with mixed visibility (a private `Property Let` procedure, for example, and a public `Property Get` procedure). In VB.NET, because the `Property` statement defines the visibility of the property as a whole, mixed visibility is not supported.

See Also

Get Statement, Set Statement

Protected Keyword

Description

Used to declare classes and their members.

When the `Protected` keyword is used to modify a member declaration, the member being declared has direct access scope to the class module in which the member is declared, as well as to all derived classes in all projects. However, as far as object access is concerned, the member is considered `Private`; that is, it can only be accessed within the declaring class. (See the upcoming example.)

Declaring a class module as `Protected` limits all of the class' members to Protected access (or stronger if the member has further specific access restrictions).

Example

Suppose we declare the following variable in a class module named Class1:

```
Protected sProtectedVar As String
```

Then within Class1 or any of its derived classes in any project, we can use the variable directly, as in:

```
Public Class Class2
    Inherits Class1

    Public Sub Test()
        MsgBox sProtectedVar
```

```
    End Sub

End Class
```

On the other hand, the following code, located in a form module, is illegal:

```
Dim c as New Class1
c.sProtectedVar = "Donna"
```

VB.NET/VB 6 Differences

The Protected keyword is new to VB.NET.

See Also

Friend Keyword

Public Statement

Syntax

```
[Overrides] [Shadows] Public [WithEvents] varname[([subscripts])] _
    [As [New] type] [, [WithEvents] _
    varname[([subscripts])] [As [New] type]] ...
```

Overrides   *optional; Keyword*
    In a derived class definition, indicates that a variable overrides a similar variable in a base class

Shadows   *optional; Keyword*
    In a derived class definition, indicates that calls to derived class members that are made through a base class ignore the shadowed implementation

WithEvents   *optional, Keyword*
    A keyword that denotes the object variable, **varname**, can respond to events triggered from within the object to which it refers

varname   *required; String literal*
    The name of the variable, which must follow Visual Basic naming conventions

subscripts   *optional; Numeric constant or literal*
    Denotes **varname** as an array and specifies the dimensions and number of elements of the array

New   *optional; Keyword*
    Used to automatically create an instance of the object referred to by the object variable, **varname**

type   *optional*
    Data type of the variable **varname**

Description

Used at module level to declare a public variable and allocate the relevant storage space in memory.

A Public variable has both project-level scope—that is, it can be used by all procedures in all modules in the project—and, when used in a Class module, it can have scope outside the project.

The `Public` keyword also applies to procedures and class modules.

Rules at a Glance

- The behavior of a Public variable depends on where it is declared, as the following table shows:

Variable declared in...	Scope
A procedure	Illegal—this generates a compile-time error.
Code module declarations section	Variable is available to all modules within the project.
Class module declarations section	Variable is available as a property of the class to all modules within the project and to all other projects referencing the class.
Form module declarations section	Variable is available as a property of the form to all modules within the project.

- `WithEvents` is only valid when used to declare an object variable.

- There is no limit to the number of variables that can refer to the same object using the `WithEvents` keyword; they will all respond to that object's events.

- You cannot create an array variable that uses the `WithEvents` keyword.

- The `New` keyword cannot be used in the same object-variable declaration as `WithEvents`.

- The *subscripts* argument has the following syntax:

      upperbound [, upperbound]

- Using the *subscripts* argument, you can declare up to 60 dimensions for the array.

- To declare an array with no specified size, use commas with no integers between them, as in:

      Public sNames()
      Public sThings(,)

  You can set or change a number of elements of an array using the `ReDim` statement.

- The `New` keyword denotes that a new instance of the object will be created when the first reference to the object is made. Use of the `New` keyword therefore negates the need to use the `Set` statement.

- You cannot use the `New` keyword to declare any of the following: variables of any intrinsic data type (the `New` keyword is for use with object variables only); instances of dependent objects (a dependant object is one that can only be created from a method or property in another object; a dependent object is not publicly createable); or a variable that uses the `WithEvents` argument.

Programming Tips and Gotchas

- Instead of declaring a variable as `Public` within either a form or class module, proper object-oriented programming techniques dictate that you should create a `Property` procedure that assigns and retrieves the value of a Private variable.

- Always use `Option Explicit` at the beginning of a module to prevent mis-named variables from causing hard to find errors.

VB.NET/VB 6 Differences

- In VB 6, the *subscripts* argument takes the form:

  `[lowerbound To] upperbound [, [lowerbound To] upperbound]`

  VB.NET, however, does not allow you to set the lower bound of an array.

- In VB 6, an array whose number of elements are declared in advance is a fixed array; it cannot be redimensioned. In VB.NET, all arrays are dynamic and can be redimensioned.

- In VB.NET, variables declared with the `New` keyword on the same line as the `Public` statement are no longer created when their first reference is encountered. Hence, whereas in VB 6, declaring an object variable using a statement such as:

  `Public oObj As New MyApp.SomeObject`

  could interfere with object destruction, in VB.NET this is not the case.

- In VB 6, the *type* argument can be `Currency`. The Currency data type, however, is not supported by VB.NET.

See Also

Friend Keyword, Protected Keyword, Public Statement

PV Function

Class

Microsoft.VisualBasic.Financial

Syntax

`PV(rate, nper, pmt[, fv [, due]])`

rate   *required; Double*
    The interest rate per period

nper   *required; Integer*
    The number of payment periods in the annuity

pmt   *required; Double*
    The payment made in each period

fv   *optional; Double*
    The future value of the loan or annuity

due   *optional; DueDate*
    Either `DueDate.BegOfPeriod` or `DueDate.EndOfPeriod`

Return Value

A Double specifying the present value of an annuity

Description

Calculates the present value of an annuity (either an investment or loan) based on a regular number of future payments of a fixed value and a fixed interest rate.

The *present value* is the current value of a future stream of equal cash flows discounted at some fixed interest rate.

Rules at a Glance

- The time units used for the number of payment periods, the rate of interest, and the payment amount must be the same. In other words, if you state the payment period in months, you must also express the interest rate as a monthly rate and the amount paid per month.

- The rate per period is stated as a fraction of 100. For example, 10% is stated as .10. If you are calculating using monthly periods, you must also divide the rate per period by 12. For example, 10% per annum equates to a rate per period of .00833.

- The *fv* argument indicates the future value or cash balance after the last payment. The default is 0, since that reflects the value of a loan after the final payment.

- Payments made against a loan or added to the value of savings are expressed as negative numbers.

- The *due* argument states whether the payment is made at the start of a period or at the end (the default value).

Programming Tips and Gotchas

Make sure that *nper*, *rate*, and *pmt* all reflect values for an identical time period. For example, if *pmt* represents a monthly payment, *rate* should represent the monthly interest rate, rather than an annual interest rate.

See Also

FV Function, IPmt Function, NPer Function, NPV Function, Pmt Function, PPmt Function, Rate Function

---

QBColor Function

Class

Microsoft.VisualBasic.Information

Syntax

```
QBColor(color)
```

color   *required; Integer*
    A whole number between 0–15

Return Value

Long

Description

Returns a Long integer representing the RGB system color code

Rules at a Glance

color can have any of the following values:

Number	Color
0	Black
1	Blue
2	Green
3	Cyan
4	Red
5	Magenta
6	Yellow
7	White
8	Gray
9	Light Blue
10	Light Green
11	Light Cyan
12	Light Red
13	Light Magenta
14	Light Yellow
15	Bright White

Programming Tips and Gotchas

- The *RGB* function allows much more flexibility than the older *QBColor* function, which is a remnant of QBasic.

- Visual Basic now contains a wide range of intrinsic color constants that can be used to assign colors directly to color properties of objects.

See Also

RGB Function

Queue Class

Namespace

System.Collections

Createable

Yes

Syntax

```
Dim queuevariable As [New] Queue
```

queuevariable   *required;* Queue *object*
> The name of the Queue object

Description

A Queue object is a model of a queue. Succinctly put, a *queue* is a first-in, first-out data structure. (This is often abbreviated FIFO.) Put another way, a queue is a data structure that models a line of items. There is a method for inserting items at the end of the line (*enqueueing*), as well as a method for removing the item that is currently at the front of the line (*dequeueing*). Under this scenario, the next item to be dequeued is the item that was placed in line first—hence the term first-in, first-out.

Note that the elements in a Queue object are of type Object.

Queue class members marked with a plus sign (+) are discussed in detail in their own entries.

Public Shared Method
> Synchronized

Public Instance Properties
> Count +
> IsReadOnly
> IsSynchronized
> SyncRoot

Public Instance Methods
> Clone
> Contains +
> CopyTo +
> Dequeue +
> Enqueue +
> Equals
> GetEnumerator
> GetHashCode
> GetType
> Peek +
> ToArray +
> ToString

Example

Here is a bit of code to illustrate the members of the Queue class:

```
' Define a new queue
Dim q As New Queue()
' Queue up some items
q.Enqueue("Chopin")
q.Enqueue("Mozart")
q.Enqueue("Beethoven")
' Is an item in the queue?
MsgBox("Beethoven in queue: " & CStr(q.Contains("Beethoven")))
```

```
' Peek at the first item
MsgBox("First item in queue is: " & q.Peek.ToString)
' Send queue to an array and display all items
Dim s() As Object = q.ToArray()
Dim i As Integer
For i = 0 To UBound(s)
    Console.WriteLine(CStr(s(i)))
Next
' Clear queue
q.Clear()
```

VB.NET/VB 6 Differences

The Queue object is new to the .NET Framework.

See Also

Collection Class, HashTable Class, Stack Class

Queue.Clear Method

Class

System.Collections.Queue

Syntax

```
queuevariable.Clear()
```

Return Value

None

Description

Removes all entries from the queue

See Also

Queue.Dequeue Method

Queue.Contains Method

Class

System.Collections.Queue

Syntax

```
queuevariable.Contains(obj)
```

obj   *required; any*
The value to search for on the queue

Return Value

Boolean (**True** or **False**) indicating whether *obj* is found in the queue

Description

Returns a Boolean indicating whether a given element whose value is *obj* is somewhere in the queue

Rules at a Glance

- *obj* must correspond exactly to an item in the queue for the method to return `True`.

- The method searches the queue sequentially. In other words, its performance is inversely proportional to the number of items in the queue.

Programming Tips and Gotchas

In comparing objects in the queue with *obj*, the Contains method in turn calls the BCL's Object.Equals method to perform the comparison. The Equals method returns `True` if two object instances are the same instance.

Queue.CopyTo Method

Class

System.Collections.Queue

Syntax

```
queuevariable.CopyTo(array, index)
```

array   *required; Array of Objects*
    Array to which to copy the queue's objects

index   *required; Integer*
    The index of the first array element to receive an element of the queue

Return Value

None

Description

Copies the queue elements into an array, starting at a specified array index

Rules at a Glance

- The array can be of any data type that is compatible with the queue elements. Thus, for instance, we cannot use an Integer array to hold queue elements that are strings (that is, Objects whose subtype is String).

- The array must be sized to accommodate the elements of the queue prior to calling the CopyTo method.

Example

```
' Define a new queue
Dim q As New Queue()
Dim aQueue(), oItem As Object

' Queue up some items
```

```
q.Enqueue("Chopin")
q.Enqueue("Mozart")
q.Enqueue("Beethoven")

' Size the array and copy to it
Redim aQueue(q.Count - 1)
q.CopyTo(aQueue,0)

For Each oItem in aQueue
   Console.WriteLine(oItem)
Next
```

See Also

Queue.ToArray Method

Queue.Count Property

Class

System.Collections.Queue

Syntax

```
queuevariable.Count()
```

Return Value

Integer

Description

This read-only property returns an Integer specifying the number of elements in the queue.

Queue.Dequeue Method

Class

System.Collections.Queue

Syntax

```
queuevariable.Dequeue()
```

Return Value

Object

Description

Removes the first item from the queue and returns it as an Object

Rules at a Glance

- Dequeue removes the item at the beginning of the queue and decrements the Count property by one.

- The Dequeue method generates an error if applied to an empty queue. Thus, it may be advisable to check for an empty queue using the Count property before attempting to dequeue.

Programming Tips and Gotchas

Dequeue is similar to the Peek method. The Peek method returns a reference to the object at the beginning of the queue, but unlike the Dequeue method, does not remove it from the queue.

See Also

Queue.Peek Method

Queue.Enqueue Method

Class

System.Collections.Queue

Syntax

```
queuevariable.Enqueue(obj)
```

obj   *required; Object*
    The item to place in the queue

Return Value

None

Description

Places an object at the end of the queue

Rules at a Glance

Enqueue adds an item to the end of the queue and increases the Count property by 1.

Queue.Peek Method

Class

System.Collections.Queue

Syntax

```
queuevariable.Peek()
```

Return Value

Object

Description

Returns the first item in the queue as an Object, but does not remove it from the queue

Programming Tips and Gotchas

The Peek method is similar to the Queue object's Dequeue method, except that it leaves the queue intact.

See Also

Queue.Dequeue Method

Queue.ToArray Method

Class

System.Collections.Queue

Syntax

```
queuevariable.ToArray()
```

Return Value

An Array of type Object

Description

This method creates an array of type Object, copies the elements of the queue—in order—to that array, and then returns the array.

Programming Tips and Gotchas

Unlike the CopyTo method, we do not need to define an array in advance. However, we cannot specify the starting array index for the copy procedure using ToArray.

RaiseEvent Statement

Syntax

```
RaiseEvent eventName([arglist])
```

eventName   *required; String literal*
    The name of the event

arglist   *optional; any (defined by the Event statement)*
    A comma-delimited list of arguments

Description

Generates a predefined, custom event within any procedure of an object module

Rules at a Glance

- *eventName* must already be defined in the Declarations section of the module using the Event statement.

- *arglist* must match the number and data type of parameters defined in the Event statement and must be surrounded by parentheses.

- The `RaiseEvent` and `Event` statements can only be used in class modules and not in standard modules.

Example

The following code snippet demonstrates how you can use an event to communicate a status message back to the client application and, at the same time, use a `ByRef` argument to trap a user response in the client application. This gets around the fact that events can't return values. To take advantage of this functionality, the client must declare a reference to this class using the `WithEvents` keyword:

```
Public Class CTransact

Public Event Status(Message As String, _
                    ByRef Cancel As Boolean)

Public Function UpdateRecords(iVal As Integer) as Boolean
    Dim blnCancel As Boolean = False

    If iVal > 1000 Then
        RaiseEvent Status("Is value too high?", blnCancel)
        If blnCancel Then
            Console.WriteLine("Abandoning operation...")
            Exit Function
        Else
            iVal = 1000
        End If
    End If
    console.writeline(iVal)
  End Function

End Class

Module modMain

    Public WithEvents oTran As New CTransact

    Public Sub Main
        otran.updaterecords(1100)
    End Sub

    Private Sub UpdateProb(sMsg As String, _
                        byref blnCancel as Boolean) _
                Handles oTran.Status

        If MsgBoxResult.Yes = MsgBox(sMsg, MsgBoxStyle.YesNo _
                            Or MsgBoxStyle.Question) Then
            blnCancel = True
        End If
    End Sub
End Module
```

Programming Tips and Gotchas

- To allow the client application to handle the event being fired, the client object variable must be declared using the WithEvents keyword.

- VB custom events do not return a value; however, you can use a ByRef argument in *arglist* to simulate a return value, as shown in the previous example.

- RaiseEvent is *not* asynchronous. In other words, when you call the Raise-Event statement in your class code, your class code will not continue executing until the event has been either handled by the client or ignored (if the client is not handling the events raised by the class). This can have undesirable side effects, and you should bear it mind when planning your application. For example, you may have a recordset open or a transaction pending and have to wait for the user to respond to a message dialog box at the client. This could easily turn into a bottleneck, adversely affecting the scalability of your application.

- For more information about implementing your own custom events, see Chapter 7.

See Also

Event Statement

Randomize Procedure

Class

Microsoft.VisualBasic.VBMath

Syntax

```
Randomize([number])
```

number   *optional; Object or any valid numeric expression*
   A number used to initialize the random-number generator

Description

Initializes the random-number generator

Rules at a Glance

- *Randomize* uses *number* as a new seed value to initialize the random-number generator used by the *Rnd* function. The seed value is an initial value that is used to generate a sequence of pseudorandom numbers.

- If you do not pass *number* to the *Randomize* procedure, the value of the system timer will be used as the new seed value.

- Repeatedly passing the same number to *Randomize* does not cause *Rnd* to repeat the same sequence of random numbers.

Programming Tips and Gotchas

If you need to repeat a sequence of random numbers, you should call the *Rnd* function with a negative number as an argument immediately prior to using *Randomize* with any numeric argument.

See Also

Rnd Function

Rate Function

Class

Microsoft.VisualBasic.Financial

Syntax

```
Rate(nper, pmt, pv[, fv[, due[, guess]]])
```

nper   *required; Double*
> The total number of periods in the annuity.

pmt   *required; Double*
> The payment amount per period.

pv   *required; Double*
> The present value of the payments or future receipts.

fv   *optional; Double*
> The future value or cash balance after the final payment. If omitted, its value defaults to 0.

due   *optional;* DueDate *enumeration*
> A flag indicating whether payments are due at the beginning of the payment period (a value of DueDate.BegOfPeriod) or at the end of the payment period (a value of DueDate.EndOfPeriod, the default).

guess   *optional; Double*
> An estimate of the value to be returned by the function. If omitted, its value defaults to .1 (10%).

Return Value

A Double representing the interest rate per period

Description

Calculates the interest rate for an annuity (a loan or an investment) that consists of fixed payments over a known duration

Rules at a Glance

- For *pv* and *fv*, cash paid out is expressed as a negative number; cash received is expressed as a positive number.

- The function works using iteration. Starting with *guess*, *Rate* cycles through the calculation until the result is accurate to within 0.00001 percent. If a result can't be found after 20 tries, the function fails.

Programming Tips and Gotchas

- In the case of a loan, *pv* is the loan amount. In the case of an investment, *pv* is the beginning balance.

- In the case of a loan, *fv* is typically 0, reflecting that the entire loan has been paid. In the case of an investment, *fv* is the value of the investment with interest at the end of the investment period.

- If the function fails because it could not calculate an accurate interest rate in 20 iterations, try a different value for *guess*.

- The value returned by the function rate is the interest rate for the same time period as payments were made. Typically, this is one month, in which case you must multiply by 12 to derive the annual percentage rate.

See Also

FV Function, IPmt Function, NPer Function, NPV Function, Pmt Function, PPmt Function, PV Function

---

ReDim Statement

Syntax

```
ReDim [Preserve] varname(subscripts) _
              [, varname(subscripts)  ...
```

Preserve *optional; Keyword*
Preserves the data within an array when changing the only or last dimension

varname *required; String literal*
Name of the variable

subscripts *required; Numeric*
Number of elements and dimensions of the array, using the syntax:

```
upper [, upper] ...
```

The number of upper bounds specified is the number of dimensions. Each upper bound specifies the size of the corresponding coordinate.

Description

Used within a procedure to resize and reallocate storage space for an array

Rules at a Glance

- Arrays can be sized or resized using the ReDim statement. There is no limit to the number of times you can redimension a dynamic array.

- The dimension cannot be changed, nor can the data type of the array be changed.

- If you do not use the Preserve keyword in redimensioning the array, you can resize any of the coordinates of the array.

- Use of the Preserve keyword allows you to retain the current values within the array, but it also allows you to resize only the last coordinate of an array.

- You can redimension an array in a called procedure if you pass the array to the procedure by reference. For example:

```
Public Sub Main

Dim lArr() AS Object = {1,2,3,4,5,6,7,8,9,10}
Dim lNum As Long

ResizeArray(lArr)

for each lNum in lARr
    Console.WriteLine(lNum)
Next

End Sub

Public Sub ResizeArray(ByRef arr() As Object)

ReDim Preserve arr(15)

arr(10) = 20
arr(11) = 50
arr(12) = 80
arr(13) = 90
arr(14) = 100
arr(15) = 200

End Sub
```

Note that this is contrary to the documentation, which indicates that arrays passed to called procedures by reference will return unmodified.

Programming Tips and Gotchas

- If the ReDim Preserve statement is used to reduce the number of array elements, the data in the discarded elements is lost. And although this can be interpreted as a "narrowing" operation, it is unaffected by the state of the Option Strict setting.

- Redimensioning an array, and particularly a large string array, can be expensive in terms of an application's performance. Consequently, frequent redimensioning, such as in the code fragment:

```
ReDim Preserve aNames(aNames(UBound)+1)
```

is not a good idea. Instead, it's best to allocate a "pool" of array elements by creating an array larger than needed, then using a counter to keep track of how many elements remain to be filled. For example:

```
If intCtr = UBound(aNames)) Then
    ReDim Preserve aNames(aNames(Ubound)+50)
    ...
```

VB.NET/VB 6 Differences

- In VB 6, it is possible (though not recommended) to declare a dynamic array using the ReDim statement, then use the ReDim statement again to redimension it. In VB.NET with `Option Explicit Off`, using the `ReDim` statement to declare an array is not permitted and generates a compiler error.

- In VB 6, only arrays declared without an explicit number of elements, such as:

  ```
  Dim arr() As Variant
  ```

  were dynamic arrays and could be redimensioned using `ReDim`. In VB.NET, all arrays are dynamic.

- VB 6 allows you to redimension both the upper and lower bounds of an array. Since VB.NET does not allow you to configure an array's lower bound, you can modify the array's upper bound only.

- In VB 6, it is possible to change the number of dimensions of an array as long as the `Preserve` keyword isn't used. VB.NET, on the other hand, does not allow you to change the number of dimensions of an array.

- Although neither VB 6 nor VB.NET permit you to change the data type of an array, the `ReDim` statement in VB 6 nevertheless supports an `As type` clause that allows you to declare the redimensioned array's data type. As long as `type` is the same as the originally declared type, `ReDim` won't generate a compiler error. In VB.NET, the use of the `As type` clause is not supported.

See Also

Dim Statement

Rem Statement

Syntax

```
Rem comment
' comment
```

`comment`   *optional*
   A textual comment to place within the code

Description

Use the `Rem` statement or an apostrophe (`'`) to place remarks within the code.

Rules at a Glance

- Text or code commented out using either the `Rem` statement or an apostrophe is not compiled into the final program and, therefore, does not add to the size of the executable.

- If you use the `Rem` statement on the same line as program code, a colon is required after the program code and before the `Rem` statement. For example:

  ```
  Set objDoc = MyApp.MyObj : Rem Define the object
                             Rem reference
  ```

  This is not necessary when using the much more common apostrophe:

  ```
  Set objDoc = MyApp.MyObj    ' Define the object reference
  ```

- Apostrophes held within quotation marks are not treated as comment markers, as this code snippet shows:

```
myVar = "'Something'"
```

Programming Tips and Gotchas

- The Visual Studio development environment contains block-comment and block-uncomment buttons on the Text Editor toolbar, which allow you to comment out or uncomment a selection of many rows of code at once.
- You cannot use the line-continuation character ("_") with comments.

VB.NET/VB 6 Differences

In VB 6, if a line containing a comment ends in an underscore (the line continuation character), the following line is interpreted as a comment as well. In VB.NET, line continuation characters are ignored at the end of a comment line; each comment line must be prefaced with the Rem statement or the ' symbol.

RemoveHandler Statement

Syntax

```
RemoveHandler NameOfEventSender, AddressOf NameOfEventHandler
```

NameOfEventSender   *required; String literal*
    The name of a class or object instance and its event, such as Button1.Click

NameOfEventHandler   *required; String literal*
    The name of a subroutine to remove as event handler for *NameOfEventSender*

Description

Removes a previous binding of an event handler to a built-in or custom event

Example

For an illustration, see the "AddHandler and RemoveHandlerr" section in Chapter 7.

Programming Tips and Gotchas

The Handles keyword can be used to receive event notification for the lifetime of an object. In contrast, AddHandler and RemoveHandler can be used to dynamically add and remove event notification at runtime.

See Also

AddHandler Statement

Rename Procedure

Class

Microsoft.VisualBasic.FileSystem

Syntax

```
Rename(oldpath, newpath)
```

oldpath   *required; String*
    The current filename and optional path

newpath   *required; String*
    The new filename and optional path

Description

Renames a disk file or folder

Rules at a Glance

- *newpath* must not already exist, or an error will be generated.

- *oldpath* must exist; the *Rename* procedure isn't able to create a new file or directory.

- When renaming a file or folder, both *newpath* and *oldpath* should include a path to the same folder, or the function will move the file or directory. For instance, the statement:

  ```
  Rename("c:\Temp\Graphics", "Images")
  ```

  renames the *Graphics* folder to *Images* and moves it so that it becomes a subdirectory of the current directory.

- Path information included in *newpath* and *oldpath* can take the form of the local system's path or the UNC path. The local system path can be either a fully qualified path or a relative path from the current directory.

- *newpath* and *oldpath* can be on different drives, but if they are, *Rename* cannot both move the files and rename them.

- *newpath* and *oldpath* cannot include the wildcard characters ? and *.

- You cannot use the *Rename* procedure with a file that is already open.

Programming Tips and Gotchas

The *Rename* procedure can be used to move a file from one folder to another and, optionally, to change the file's name at the same time. If the folder specified in *newname* exists and is different from that stated in *oldname*, the file will be moved to the folder specified in *newname*. If the filename in *newname* is also different, the file will be renamed at the same time.

VB.NET/VB 6 Differences

The *Rename* procedure is new to VB.NET.

Replace Function

Class

Microsoft.VisualBasic.Strings

Syntax

```
Replace(expression, find, replace [, _
        start[, count[, compare]]])
```

expression   *required; String*
    The complete string containing the substring to be replaced

find   *required; String*
    The substring to be found by the function

replace   *required; String*
    The new substring to replace *find* in **expression**

start   *optional; Long*
    The character position in **expression** at which the search for *find* begins

count   *optional; Long*
    The number of instances of *find* to replace

compare   *optional;* CompareMethod *constant*
    The method used to compare *find* with **expression**; its value can be
    CompareMethod.Binary (for case-sensitive comparison) or CompareMethod.
    Text (for case-insensitive comparison)

Return Value

The return value from *Replace* depends on the parameters you specify in the argument list, as the following table shows:

If	Return value
expression = ""	Zero-length string ("")
find = ""	Copy of *expression*
replace = ""	Copy of *expression* with all instances of *find* removed
start > Len(*expression*)	Zero-length string ("")
count = 0	Copy of *expression*

Description

Replaces a given number of instances of a specified substring in another string

Rules at a Glance

- If *start* is omitted, the search begins at the start of the string.

- If *count* is omitted, all instances of the substring after *start* are replaced.

- CompareMethod.BinaryCompare is case sensitive; that is, *Replace* matches both character and case, whereas CompareMethod.Text is case insensitive, matching only character regardless of case.

- The default value for *compare* is CompareMethod.Binary.

- *start* not only specifies where the search for *stringToReplace* begins, but also where the new string returned by the *Replace* function will commence.

Programming Tips and Gotchas

- If *count* is not used, be careful when replacing short strings that may form parts of unrelated words. For example, consider the following:

```
Dim sString
sString = "You have to be careful when you do this " _
          & "or you could ruin your string"
Console.WriteLine(Replace(sString, "you", "we"))
```

  Because we don't specify a value for *count*, the call to *Replace* replaces every occurrence of "you" in the original string with "we". But the fourth occurrence of "you" is part of the word "your", which is modified to become "wer".

- You must also be aware that if *start* is greater than 1, the returned string starts at that character and not at the first character of the original string, as you might expect. For example, given the statements:

```
sOld = "This string checks the Replace function"
sNew = Replace(sOld, "check", "test", 5, _
CompareMethod.Text)
```

  sNew will contain the value:

```
"string tests the Replace function"
```

- You can use the *Mid* function on the left side of an argument to replace part of string, but to replace more than one instance of a substring requires a complicated Do While loop that constantly checks for the position of any remaining instances of the substring to be replaced.

- The BCL's System.String class also has a public instance Replace method, which replaces all occurrences of a character or string with another. Its syntax is:

```
sString.Replace(oldValue, newValue)
```

  where *oldValue* is a String or Char value containing the text to be replaced and *newValue* is a String or Char value containing the replacement text.

See Also

InStr Function, InStrRev Function, Mid Statement

Reset Procedure

Class

Microsoft.VisualBasic.FileSystem

Syntax

```
Reset()
```

Description

Closes all files that have been opened using the *FileOpen* procedure

Rules at a Glance

The contents of any current file buffers are written to disk by the *Reset* procedure immediately prior to *Reset* closing the respective files.

Programming Tips and Gotchas

The *Reset* procedure is generally used as a last resort, cleaning up if your program is terminating abnormally. Normally, you should write code to close each open file using the *FileClose* procedure.

See Also

FileClose Procedure, FileOpen Procedure

Resume Statement

Syntax

```
Resume [0]
Resume Next
Resume label
```

Description

Used to continue program execution when an error-handling routine is complete

Rules at a Glance

Resume can take any of the forms shown in the following table:

Statement	Description
Resume	If the error-handling routine is in the same procedure as the statement that caused the error, program execution continues with the statement that caused the error.
	If the error occurred in an external procedure called by the procedure containing the error handler, program execution continues with the statement in the procedure containing the error handler that last called the external procedure.
Resume Next	If the error-handling routine is in the same procedure as the statement that caused the error, program execution continues with the statement following the statement that caused the error.
	If the error occurred in an external procedure called by the procedure containing the error handler, program execution continues with the statement containing the error handler immediately following the statement that last called the external procedure.
Resume label	label must be in the same procedure as the error handler.
	Program execution continues at the specified label.

Programming Tips and Gotchas

- You can only use the Resume statement in an error-handling routine; otherwise, a runtime error will be generated.

- An error-handling routine does not necessarily have to contain a Resume statement. If the error-handling routine is at the end of the procedure and the result of the error handling would be to exit the procedure, you can simply

---

allow the program to execute the **End Sub** or **End Function** statement. This has the effect of both resetting the **Err** object and exiting the procedure. This is shown in the following simple code snippet:

```
Private Sub DoSomething()

    On Error GoTo DoSomething_Err
    ...
DoSomething_Err:
    MsgBox(Err.Description)

End Sub
```

See Also

On Error Statement, Err Object

Return Statement

Syntax

In a subroutine:

```
Return
```

In a function:

```
Return ReturnValue
```

ReturnValue   *required; any*
    The return value of the function

Description

Returns to the calling program from a subroutine or function

Rules at a Glance

- If the **Return** statement appears in a function, it must specify a return value for the function.

- **Return** causes program flow to leave the function or subroutine and return to the calling program; any statements in the function or subroutine that follow **Return** are not executed.

Example

```
Public Sub Main

Dim d As Double = GetNumbers()
Console.WriteLine("The sum of values is " & d)

End Sub

Public Function GetNumbers As Double

Dim iCtr As Integer = 1
Dim sInput As String
```

```
    Dim dblNums(9), dblSum, dblTemp As Double

    Do
        sInput = InputBox("Enter number " & iCtr & ": ", "Sum")
        If sInput = "" Then
           if iCtr = 1 Then Return 0
             Exit Do
        End If
        If IsNumeric(sInput) Then
            dblNums(iCtr - 1) = CDbl(sInput)
            iCtr = iCtr + 1
        End If
    Loop While iCtr <= 9

    ' Sum array elements
    for each dblTemp in dblNums
        dblSum += dblTemp
    next

    return dblSum

    End Function
```

Programming Tips and Gotchas

Return is identical in operation to the Exit Sub statement: it prematurely transfers control from a procedure to the calling routine. It is also similar to the Exit
Function statement; while it prematurely transfers control out of the function, it
also allows a particular value to be returned by the function.

VB.NET/VB 6 Differences

In VB 6, Return is a legacy statement that returns control after GoSub has invoked
a subroutine within a procedure. In VB.NET, however, Return returns control
from a called function or procedure and optionally allows the function's return
value to be defined.

See Also

Exit Statement

RGB Function

Class

Microsoft.VisualBasic.Information

Syntax

```
RGB(red, green, blue)
```

red   *required; Integer*
    A number between 0 and 255, inclusive

green   *required; Integer*
    A number between 0 and 255, inclusive

---

blue *required*

Data type: Integer

A number between 0 and 255, inclusive

Return Value

An Integer representing the RGB color value

Description

Returns a system color code that can be assigned to object color properties

Rules at a Glance

- The RGB color value represents the relative intensity of the red, green, and blue components of a pixel that produces a specific color on the display.

- The *RGB* function assumes any argument greater than 255 to be 255.

- The following table demonstrates how the individual color values combine to create certain colors:

Color	Red	Green	Blue
Black	0	0	0
Blue	0	0	255
Green	0	255	0
Red	255	0	0
White	255	255	255

Programming Tips and Gotchas

- The RGB value is actually derived using the following formula:

```
RGB = red + (green * 256) + (blue * 65536)
```

In other words, the individual color components are stored in the opposite order than you would expect. VB stores the red color component in the low-order byte of the integer's low-order word, the green color in the high-order byte of the low-order word, and the blue color in the low-order byte of the high-order word.

- Visual Basic now contains a wide range of intrinsic color constants that can be used to assign color values directly to color properties of objects.

See Also

QBColor Function

Right Function

Class

Microsoft.VisualBasic.Strings

Syntax

```
Right(string, length)
```

string   *required; String*
    The string to be processed

length   *required; Integer*
    The number of characters to return from the right of the string

Return Value

String

Description

Returns a string containing the rightmost **length** characters of **string**

Rules at a Glance

*   If **length** is 0, a zero-length string ("") is returned.
*   If **length** is greater than the length of **string**, **string** is returned.
*   If **length** is less than zero or is Nothing, an error is generated.
*   If **string** contains a Nothing, *Right* returns Nothing.

Example

The following function assumes that it is passed either a filename or a complete path and filename, and it returns the filename from the end of the string:

```
Private Function ParseFileName(strFullPath As String) As String
    Dim intPos, intStart As Integer
    Dim strFilename As String

    intStart = 1
    Do
       intPos = InStr(intStart, strFullPath, "\")
       If intPos = 0 Then
          strFilename = Right(strFullPath, _
                 Len(strFullPath) - inStart + 1)
        Else
          intStart = intPos + 1
       End If
    Loop While intPos > 0

    ParseFileName = strFilename
End Function
```

Programming Tips and Gotchas

Use the *Len* function to determine the total length of **string**.

See Also

Left Function, Mid Function

RmDir Procedure

Class

Microsoft.VisualBasic.FileSystem

Syntax

```
RmDir(path)
```

path   *required; String*

    The path of the folder to be removed

Description

Removes a folder

Rules at a Glance

- You may include a drive letter in *path*; if you don't specify a drive letter, the folder is assumed to be on the current drive.

- *path* can be a fully qualified, relative, or UNC pathname.

- If the folder contains files or other folders, *RmDir* will generate runtime error 75, "Path/File access error."

Example

The following subroutine deletes all the files in a folder and removes its subfolders. If those contain files or folders, it deletes those too by recursively calling itself until all child folders and their files are removed.

```
Private Sub RemoveFolder(ByVal strFolder As String)

    Static blnLowerLevel As Boolean     ' A recursive call - no
    '                                     need to prompt user
    Dim blnRepeated As Boolean    ' Use Dir state info on
    '                               repeated calls
    Dim strFile As String        ' File/Directory contained in
    '                              strFolder

    ' Delete all files
    Do
        strFile = Dir(strFolder & "\*.*", _
            VbNormal Or VbHidden Or VbSystem)
        If strFile <> "" Then
            If Not blnLowerLevel Then
                If MsgBox("Delete files in directory " & _
                strFolder & "?", vbQuestion Or vbOKCancel, _
                "Confirm File Deletion") _
                = vbCancel Then Exit Sub
            End If
            strFile = strFolder & "\" & strFile
            Kill(strFile)
        End If
    Loop While strFile <> ""
    ' Delete all directories
```

```
        Do
            If Not blnRepeated Then
                strFile = Dir(strFolder & "\*.*", VbDirectory)
                blnRepeated = True
            Else
                strFile = Dir()
            End If
            If strFile <> "" And _
                strFile <> "." And strFile <> ".." Then
                If Not blnLowerLevel Then
                    blnLowerLevel = True
                    If MsgBox("Delete subdirectories of " & _
                    strFolder & "?", _
                    vbQuestion BitOr vbOKCancel, _
                    "Confirm Directory Deletion") _
                    = vbCancel Then Exit Sub
                End If
                RemoveFolder(strFolder & "\" & strFile)
                blnRepeated = False
            End If
        Loop While strFile <> ""

        RmDir(strFolder)

    End Sub
```

Programming Tips and Gotchas

*   Use the *Kill* procedure to delete any remaining files from the folder prior to removing the folder.

*   The effects of using *Kill* and *RmDir* are irreversible, since these statements do not move deleted files to the Recycle Bin.

See Also

MkDir Procedure

Rnd Function

Class

Microsoft.VisualBasic.VBMath

Syntax

```
Rnd[(number)]
```

number   *optional; Single*
    Any valid numeric expression that serves as a seed value

Return Value

A Single data type random number

Description

Returns a random number

Rules at a Glance

- The behavior of the *Rnd* function is determined by *number*, as described in the following table:

Number	Rnd generates
< 0	The same number each time, using *seed* as the seed number
> 0	The next random number in the current sequence
0	The most recently generated number
Not supplied	The next random number in the current sequence

- The *Rnd* function always returns a value between 0 and 1.

- If number is not supplied, the *Rnd* function will use the last number generated as the seed for the next generated number. This means that given an initial seed (seed), the same sequence will be generated if number is not supplied on subsequent calls.

Example

The following example uses the *Randomize* procedure along with the *Rnd* function to fill 100 cells of an Excel worksheet with random numbers. It requires that a reference to the Microsoft Excel Object Library be added to the project. It also leaves the instance of Excel running once the code has finished execution.

```
Public Sub GenerateRandomNumbers()

    Dim oApp As New Excel.Application()
    Dim objSheet As Excel.Worksheet
    Dim intRow, intCol As Integer

    oApp.Visible = True
    objSheet = oApp.Workbooks.Add.Worksheets(1)
    Randomize()

    ' Set the color of the input text to blue
    objSheet.Cells.Font.ColorIndex = 5

    ' Loop through first 10 rows & columns,
    ' filling them with random numbers
    For intRow = 1 To 10
      For intCol = 1 To 10
        objSheet.Cells(intRow, intCol).Value = Rnd()
      Next
    Next

    ' Resize columns to accommodate random numbers
    objSheet.Columns("A:C").AutoFit()
    objSheet = Nothing

End Sub
```

Programming Tips and Gotchas

- Before calling the *Rnd* function, you should use the *Randomize* procedure to initialize the random-number generator.

- The standard formula for producing numbers in a given range is as follows:

      Int((*highest* - *lowest* + 1) * Rnd + *lowest*)

  where *lowest* is the lowest required number in the range and *highest* is the highest.

See Also

Randomize Procedure

Round Function

Class

System.Math

Syntax

    Math.Round(*value*[,*digits*])

value   *required; Numeric expression*
    Any numeric expression

digits   *optional; Integer*
    The number of places to include after the decimal point

Return Value

The same data type as *value*

Description

Rounds a given number to a specified number of decimal places

Rules at a Glance

- *digits* can be any whole number between 0 and 16.

- *Round* follows standard rules for rounding. If the digit in the position to the right of *digits* is 5 or greater, the digit in the *digits* position is incremented by one; otherwise, the digits to the right of *digits* are dropped.

- This is a Shared member, so it can be used without creating any objects.

Programming Tips and Gotchas

- *Round* with *digits* set to 2 is the equivalent of Format (expression, "#.##").

- If *value* is a string representation of a numeric value, *Round* will convert it to a numeric value before rounding. However, if expression is not a string representation of a number, *Round* generates runtime error 13, "Type mismatch." The *IsNumeric* function can be used to ensure that expression is a proper numeric representation before calling *Round*.

- If *value* contains fewer decimal places than *digits*, *Round* does not pad the return value with trailing zeroes.

VB.NET/VB 6 Differences

The named parameters of the *Round* function differ in VB 6 and in the .NET Framework. In VB 6, the named arguments are *number* and *numdigitsafterdecimal*. In VB.NET, they're *value* and *digits*.

See Also

Fix Function, Int Function

RSet Function

Class

Microsoft.VisualBasic.Strings

Syntax

```
RSet(Source, Length)
```

Source   *required; String*
    The string to be right aligned

Length   *required; Integer*
    The length of the returned string

Return Value

String

Description

Right aligns a string

Rules at a Glance

- If the length of *Source* is greater than or equal to *Length*, the function returns only the leftmost *Length* characters.

- If the length of *Source* is less than *Length*, spaces are added to the left of the returned string so that its length becomes *Length*.

VB.NET/VB 6 Differences

- In VB 6, RSet was implemented as a kind of assignment statement. Because it is implemented as a function in VB.NET, its syntax is completely different.

- In VB 6, RSet could be used only with fixed-length strings. In VB.NET, *RSet* works with all CTS String data.

See Also

LSet Function

RTrim Function

Class

Microsoft.VisualBasic.Strings

Syntax

```
RTrim(string)
```

string   required; String
    A valid string expression

Return Value

String

Description

Removes any trailing spaces from string

Rules at a Glance

If string contains a Nothing, RTrim returns Nothing.

See Also

LTrim Function, Trim Function

SaveFileDialog Class

Namespace

System.Windows.Forms

Createable

Yes

Description

Represents a common dialog box for selecting or saving a file. The most common use of this dialog box is to ask the user for the name of a file, after which we can use VB's functions to save an existing file under that name, since the dialog box itself does not handle the process of saving a file.

The SaveFileDialog object has properties for setting the initial appearance and functionality of the dialog box, a property for returning the filename selected by the user, as well as a method for showing the dialog box. The object does not itself save the file, but instead provides the information that allows your code to do this programmatically.

A SaveFileDialog object can be instantiated as follows:

```
Dim oSaveDlg As New SaveFileDialog
```

Selected SaveFileDialog Members

The following is a brief list of some of the more important members of the Save-FileDialog class:

AddExtension property

Gets or sets a Boolean value that determines whether the default file extension is automatically added to the FileName property if the user fails to enter an extension. Its default value is `True`.

DefaultExt property

Gets or sets a String that defines the default file extension. The string should consist of the file extension only, without a period.

FileName property

Gets or sets a String containing the name that the user selected or entered in the dialog box.

Filter property

Gets or sets a String containing the current filter, which determines the items that appear in the "Save as type" drop-down listbox. A single item consists of a file description, a vertical bar, and the file extension (usually "*." plus the file extension). If there are multiple extensions in a single item, they are separated by semicolons. If there are multiple items, they are separated by vertical bars. For example, the following code fragment assigns a filter string to a String variable:

```
sFilter = "Text files (*.txt; *.vb)|*.txt;*.vb|" & _
          "Visual Basic files (*.vb)|*.vb|" & _
          "All files (*.*)|*.*"
```

FilterIndex property

Gets or sets an Integer value that determines which of the items defined by the Filter property is selected. The index is one-based, rather than zero-based. When the dialog box is first displayed and no FilterIndex value is specified, it defaults to 1. When the method returns, its value indicates which filter item was selected by the user.

InitialDirectory property

Gets or sets a String that defines the directory initially displayed by the Save-FileDialog dialog box.

OverwritePrompt property

Gets or sets a Boolean value that determines whether a confirmation message is displayed when the user enters or selects an existing file.

RestoreDirectory

Gets or sets a Boolean value indicating whether the current directory is restored before the dialog box closes. Its default value is `False`.

ShowDialog method

Opens the SaveFileDialog dialog box. Its syntax is:

```
oSaveDlg.ShowDialog()
```

It returns `DialogResult.OK` if the user clicks the OK button and `DialogResult.Cancel` if the user clicks the Cancel button to close the dialog box.

Example

```
Dim fd As New SaveFileDialog()
fd.OverwritePrompt = True
If fd.ShowDialog() = DialogResult().OK Then
    Console.WriteLine(fd.FileName)
End If
```

VB.NET/VB 6 Differences

Whereas the SaveFileDialog class is implemented in the .NET Base Class Library, VB 6 offered the CommonDialog custom control. Although the two offer similar functionality, their public interfaces are almost completely different.

See Also

OpenFileDialog Class

SaveSetting Procedure

Class

Microsoft.VisualBasic.Interaction

Syntax

```
SaveSetting(appname, section, key, setting)
```

appname   *required; String*
  The name of the application

section   *required; String*
  The name of the registry key

key   *required; String*
  The name of the value entry whose value is to be saved

setting   *required; String or numeric*
  The value to save

Description

Creates or saves an entry for a VB application in the Windows registry

Rules at a Glance

- If either the *appname* or *section* subkeys are not found in the registry, they are automatically created.

- The function writes a value to a subkey of the KEY_CURRENT_USER\ Software\ VB and VBA Program Settings key of the registry.

- *section* need not be an immediate subkey of *appname*; instead, *section* can be a fully qualified path to a nested subkey, with each subkey separated from its parent by a backslash. For example, a value of `Settings\Coordinates` for the *section* argument indicates that the value is to be retrieved from `HKEY_CURRENT_USER\Software\VB` and `VBA Program Settings\ appname\Settings\Coordinates`.

- Visual Basic writes *setting* to the registry as a string (`REG_SZ`) value. If *setting* is not a string, VB attempts to coerce it into a string in order to write it.

- If the setting cannot be saved, a runtime error will be generated.

Programming Tips and Gotchas

- The built-in registry-manipulation functions allow you to create professional 32-bit applications that use the registry for holding application-specific data, in the same way that .INI files were used in the 16-bit environment. You can, for example, store information about the user's desktop settings (i.e., the size and position of forms) the last time the program was run.

- Since it writes to the current user's registry key, *SaveSetting* should be used exclusively for storing user settings; it should not be used to store nonuser information (i.e., hardware information, system-level information, or application information that is independent of the user).

- *GetSetting*, *GetAllSettings*, and *SaveSetting* allow you direct access to only a limited section of the Windows registry, that being a special branch created for your application (`HKEY_CURRENT_USER\Software\VB and VBA Program Settings\yourappname`).

- *SaveSetting* does not allow you to write to the default value of a registry key. Attempting to do so produces runtime error 5, "Invalid procedure call or argument." This is not as great a limitation as it may appear, since *GetSetting* also cannot retrieve a default value from a registry key.

- This may seem obvious, but it has been often overlooked: if a user hasn't run the application before and your application's initialization doesn't set up the registry structure for the application, the key values won't be there.

- The previous point is particularly applicable when running your application on Windows in a multiuser environment since Microsoft chose to use the `HKEY_CURRENT_USER` branch of the registry to store entries for VB applications. This means that your application can be running swimmingly for one user, but when another user logs onto the machine, the registry settings are not available.

- Rather than rely on the relatively underpowered registry-access functionality available in Visual Basic, we highly recommend that you instead use the Registry and RegistryKey classes available in the BCL's Microsoft.Win32 namespace.

See Also

DeleteSetting Procedure, GetAllSettings Function, GetSetting Function

ScriptEngine Property

Class

Microsoft.VisualBasic.Globals

Syntax

```
ScriptEngine
```

Return Value

A String containing the value "VB"

Description

Indicates the programming language currently in use

Rules at a Glance

ScriptEngine is a read-only property.

Programming Tips and Gotchas

- A number of scripting engines support a *ScriptEngine* property or function, which allows you to determine the programming language used for a particular block of code. These languages, and the strings they return, are shown in the following table:

Language	String
Microsoft Jscript	JScript
VB.NET	VB
VBScript	VBScript

- The ScriptEngine property can be most useful when calling legacy code. On the .NET platform, the need to know the current scripting engine is substantially lessened by the existence of a unified type system.

VB.NET/VB 6 Differences

The property is new to VB.NET and is not supported in VB 6.

See Also

ScriptEngineMinorVersion Property, ScriptEngineMajorVersion Property, ScriptEngineBuildVersion Property

---

ScriptEngineBuildVersion Property

Class

Microsoft.VisualBasic.Globals

Syntax

```
ScriptEngineBuildVersion()
```

Return Value

An Integer containing the build number

Description

Returns the build number of the VB.NET language engine

Programming Tips and Gotchas

This property is implemented as a function in the JScript scripting engine.

VB.NET/VB 6 Differences

This property is new to VB.NET.

See Also

ScriptEngineMinorVersion Property, ScriptEngineMajorVersion Property, ScriptEngine Property

---

ScriptEngineMajorVersion Property

Class

Microsoft.VisualBasic.Globals

Syntax

```
ScriptEngineMajorVersion
```

Return Value

An Integer containing the major version number

Description

Indicates the major version (1, 2, etc.) of the programming language currently in use

Rules at a Glance

The initial version of VB.NET returns "7" as its major version number.

Programming Tips and Gotchas

- This property is implemented as a function in the JScript scripting engine.
- If your script requires some functionality available in a baseline version, ordinarily you want to make sure that the script is running on that version or a later version. You do not want to test for equality, since that may leave your code unable to run on later versions of the language engine.

VB.NET/VB 6 Differences

This property is new to VB.NET.

See Also

ScriptEngine Property, ScriptEngineBuildVersion Property, ScriptEngineMinorVersion Property

ScriptEngineMinorVersion Property

Class

Microsoft.VisualBasic.Globals

Syntax

```
ScriptEngineMinorVersion
```

Return Value

An Integer containing the minor version number

Description

Indicates the minor version (the number to the right of the decimal point) of the programming language currently in use

Programming Tips and Gotchas

- This property is implemented as a function in the JScript scripting engine.

- If your script requires some functionality available in a baseline minor version, ordinarily you would want to make sure that the script is running on that version or a later version. Test for a minor version with a code fragment like:

```
Dim iMajor As Integer = ScriptEngineMajorVersion()
Dim iMinor As Integer = ScriptEngineMinorVersion()
If (lMajor = x And lMinor >= y) Or (lMajor > x) Then
    . . .
```

VB.NET/VB 6 Differences

This property is new to VB.NET.

See Also

ScriptEngine Property, ScriptEngineBuildVersion Property, ScriptEngineMajorVersion Property

---

Second Function

Class

Microsoft.VisualBasic.DateAndTime

Syntax

```
Second(timevalue)
```

timevalue   required; Date
    Date variable or literal date

Return Value

An Integer in the range 0 to 59, specifying the second in timevalue

Description

Extracts the seconds from a given time expression

Rules at a Glance

If the time expression time is Nothing, the *Second* function returns 0.

See Also

Minute Function, Hour Function

Seek Function

Class

Microsoft.VisualBasic.FileSystem

Syntax

    Seek(*filenumber*)

filenumber   *required; Integer*
    Any valid file number

Return Value

A Long indicating the current read/write position

Description

Returns the current position of the read/write marker in the open file *filenumber*

Rules at a Glance

* The *Seek* function returns a whole number in the range 1 to 2,147,483,647.

* If *filenumber* was opened in Random mode, the number returned by the *Seek* function refers to the next record to be written or read.

* In all other file open modes (Append, Binary, Input, and Output), the number returned by the *Seek* function is the byte position at which the next read or write operation will occur.

See Also

Seek Procedure

Seek Procedure

Class

Microsoft.VisualBasic.FileSystem

Syntax

    Seek(*filenumber*, *position*)

filenumber   *required; Integer*
    Any valid file number

position   *required; Long*
  Any whole number between 1 and 2,147,483,647

Description

Places the read/write marker at a given position where the next read/write operation should occur

Rules at a Glance

- If the file has been opened in Random mode, *position* refers to the next record number that should be read or written.

- In all other file open modes (Append, Binary, Input, and Output), *position* is the byte where the next read or write operation will start.

- The use of a record number in any subsequent *FileGet* or *FilePut* procedure overrides the position set by the *Seek* procedure.

- The size of a file can be increased as the result of a write operation that is performed after a call to the *Seek* procedure in which *position* is beyond the end of the file.

- If *position* is 0 or negative, a runtime error will be generated.

Programming Tips and Gotchas

Unused records in a random-access data file are not necessarily blank. For example, if you open a brand new data file, then perform a seek operation to record number 10 and write a new record, the preceding 9 records will be filled with binary data that was present on the section of the disk used by the new file prior to its creation.

See Also

Seek Function

Select Case Statement

Syntax

```
Select Case testexpression
    [Case expressionlist-n
        [statements-n]] ...
    [Case Else
        [elsestatements]]
End Select
```

testexpression   *required; any*
  Any numeric or string expression whose value determines which block of code is executed

expressionlist-n   *required; any*
  Comma-delimited list of expressions to compare values with *testexpression*

---

statements-n   *optional*
   Program statements to execute if a match is found between any section of
   expressionlist and *testexpression*

elsestatements   *optional*
   Program statements to execute if a match between *testexpression* and any
   expressionlist cannot be found

expressionlist can use any (or a combination of any) of the following:

expressionlist syntax	Examples
expression	iVar - iAnotherVar
	iVar
expression To expression	5 To 10
	8 To 11, 13 to 15
	"A" To "D"
Is comparisonoperator expression	Is = 10

Description

Allows for conditional execution of a block of code, typically out of three or more
code blocks, based on some condition. Use the `Select Case` statement as an
alternative to complex nested `If...Then...Else` statements.

Rules at a Glance

- Any number of `Case` clauses can be included in the `Select Case` statement.

- If a match between *testexpression* and any part of *expressionlist* is
  found, the program statements following the matched *expressionlist* will
  be executed. When program execution encounters the next `Case` clause or
  the `End Select` clause, execution will continue with the statement immediately following the `End Select` clause.

- If multiple `Case` statements are `True`, only the statements belonging to the
  first true `Case` statement are executed.

- If used, the `Case Else` clause must be the last `Case` clause. Program execution will only encounter the `Case Else` clause—and thereby execute the
  elsestatements—if all other *expressionlist* comparisons have failed.

- Use the `To` keyword to specify a range of values. The lower value must precede the `To` clause, and the higher value follow it. Failure to do this does not
  generate a syntax error. Instead, it causes the comparison of the expression
  with *testexpression* to always fail, so that program execution falls through
  to the `Case Else` code block, if one is present.

- The `Is` keyword is used to precede any comparison operators. For example:

  ```
  Case Is >= 100
  ```

- `Select Case` statements can also be nested.

Example

The following example uses Select Case to act based on the response to a *MsgBox* function:

```
Select Case MsgBox("Backup file before changing.", vbYesNoCancel)
    Case vbYes
        ' do something
    Case vbNo
        ' do something
    Case vbCancel
        ' do something
End Select
```

Programming Tips and Gotchas

- The Select Case statement is the VB equivalent of the Switch construct found in C and C++.

- The Case Else clause is optional. However, as with If...Then...Else statements, it is often good practice to provide a Case Else to catch the exceptional instance when—perhaps unexpectedly—a match cannot be found in any of the *expressionlists* you have provided.

- The To clause can be used to specify ranges of character strings. However, it is often difficult to predict the thousands of possible combinations of valid characters between two words that will be successfully matched by Select Case.

- The Is keyword used in the Select Case statement is not the same as the Is comparison operator.

- Multiple conditions in a single Case statement are evaluated separately, not together; that is, they are connected with a logical OR, not a logical AND. For example, the statement:

```
Case Is > 20, Is < 40
```

will evaluate to True whenever the value of *testexpression* is greater than 20. In this case, the second comparison is never evaluated; it is evaluated only when *testexpression* is under 20. This suggests that if you use anything other than the most straightforward conditions, you should test them thoroughly.

See Also

If...Then...Else Statement

Send, SendWait Methods

Class

System.Windows.Forms.SendKeys

Syntax

```
SendKeys.Send(keys)

SendKeys.SendWait(keys)
```

String describing keys to send to the active window

Description

Sends keystrokes to the active window of the foreground application. For Send-Keys.Send, further execution continues without waiting for the keys to be processed. For SendKeys.SendWait, further execution is suspended until the keystrokes have been processed.

Rules at a Glance

- To send normal alphabetical or numeric characters, simply use the character or characters enclosed in quotation marks. For example, `"SOME Text 123"`.

- The following characters represent special keys or have special meaning within the *Keys* string:

Character	Special key representation
+	SHIFT
^	CTRL
%	ALT
~ or {ENTER}	ENTER

  To use these characters literally, you must surround the character with braces. For example, to specify the percentage key, use {%}.

- Preceding a string with the special characters described in the previous table allows you to send a keystroke combination beginning with Shift, Ctrl, or Alt. For example, to specify Ctrl followed by "M," use ^M.

- If you need to specify that the Shift, Ctrl, or Alt key is held down while another key is pressed, you should enclose the key or keys in parentheses and precede the parentheses with the special character code. For example, to specify the M key being pressed while holding down the Alt key, use %(M).

- The following table describes how to specify nondisplaying (action) characters in the *Keys* string:

Key	Code
Backspace	{BACKSPACE}, {BS}, or {BKSP}
Break	{BREAK}
Caps Lock	{CAPSLOCK}
Del or Delete	{DELETE} or {DEL}
Down Arrow	{DOWN}
End	{END}
Enter	{ENTER} or ~
Esc	{ESC}
Help	{HELP}
Home	{HOME}
Ins or Insert	{INSERT} or {INS}

Key	Code
Left Arrow	{LEFT}
Num Lock	{NUMLOCK}
Page Down	{PGDN}
Page Up	{PGUP}
Right Arrow	{RIGHT}
Scroll Lock	{SCROLLLOCK}
Tab	{TAB}
Up Arrow	{UP}
F1	{F1}
F2	{F2}
F3	{F3}
F4	{F4}
F5	{F5}
F6	{F6}
F7	{F7}
F8	{F8}
F9	{F9}
F10	{F10}
F11	{F11}
F12	{F12}
F13	{F13}
F14	{F14}
F15	{F15}
F16	{F16}

- Special formatting syntax allows you to specify a key being repeatedly pressed. The syntax is:

  {key numberoftimes}

  For example, {M 3} represents pressing the M key three times.

Example

The following program launches Notepad, loads a text file whose name is passed as a parameter, gives the focus to Notepad, then uses its File Exit menu option to close the application:

```
Private Sub LaunchNotepad(strFN As String)

Dim intTaskID As Integer
Dim strCmdLine As String

strCmdLine = "C:\windows\notepad.exe " & strFN
intTaskID = Shell(strCmdLine, vbNormalNoFocus)

' timing delay
```

```
DelayLoop(200000)

' Activate notepad by task ID
AppActivate(intTaskID)

' timing delay
DelayLoop(200000)

SendKeys.SendWait("%Fx")

End Sub

Private Sub DelayLoop(n As Integer)

Dim iCtr As Integer

For iCtr = 1 to iCtr
    if iCtr/10 = iCtr \ 10 Then
        Application.DoEvents
      End If
Next

End Sub
```

Programming Tips and Gotchas

- Send and SendWait will only work directly with applications designed to run in Microsoft Windows.

- You may find that some keys or key combinations cannot be sent successfully. For example, you cannot use Send and SendWait to send the Print Screen key to any application. You also cannot send the Alt and Tab keys (`"%{Tab}"`).

- Typically, Send or SendWait is used as a "convenience" feature to send an occasional keystroke to its application or to another application. It can also be used to add a keystroke-macro capability to an application. In some cases, it is even used for remotely controlling an application. In this latter case, Send or SendWait is often combined with the *Shell* function (to start an instance of another application) or the *AppActivate* procedure (to give it the focus before Send or SendWait is used). The example program illustrates this.

- It's worthwhile mentioning the difficulties of using Send or SendWait as a method for controlling a program remotely. Windows is an event-driven operating system. Consequently, the order of events is controlled primarily by the user, and the precise order of events is difficult or even impossible to anticipate. Remote control of an application using Send or SendWait, however, typically makes a number of assumptions about that application, the most basic of which is that it has the focus when Send or SendWait is called. Given that Send and SendWait do not offer close control over a remote application in the same way as OLE automation does, the event-driven character of Windows can easily intervene to invalidate those assumptions. This makes Send and SendWait less than optimal choices as tools for remote control of an application.

Set Statement

Syntax

```
Set
   [ statements ]
   [ variable = Value ]
End Set
```

statements   *optional*
    Program code to be executed when the Property Set procedure is called

variable   *optional; any (the data type of the property)*
    Typically, a Private variable to hold the property value

Value   *optional; Keyword*
    A keyword representing the value to be assigned to the property

Description

Defines a Set property procedure that sets a property value

Rules at a Glance

* The `Set` statement can only be used within a `Property...End Property` construct.

* The value assigned to the property is usually stored to a variable that's Private to the class. This protects the property value from modification other than by calling the Property Set procedure.

* The `Value` keyword represents the value to be assigned to the property. This value must be of the same data type as the property.

Example

The example code illustrates a class that has a simple property and a property array. The syntax documented above, rather than the "official" syntax (see the note in the "Programming Tips and Gotchas" section), is used, since in our opinion it is much clearer and intuitive.

```
Public Enum WageConstants
    Rate = 0
    Overtime = 1
    Differential = 2
End Enum

Public Class CEmployee

Dim strName As String
Dim decWage(2) As Decimal

Public Property Name() As String
    Set(sName As String)
        strName = sName
    End Set
    Get
```

```
            Return strName
        End Get
    End Property

    Public Property Wage(iType As WageConstants) As Decimal
        Get
            Wage = decWage(iType)
        End Get
        Set
            decWage(iType) = Value
        End Set
    End Property

End Class

Module modMain

Public Sub Main

Dim oEmp As New CEmployee
oEmp.Name = "Bill"
oEmp.Wage(WageConstants.Rate) = CDec(15.00)
oEmp.Wage(WageConstants.Overtime) = CDec(15.00 * 1.5)
oEmp.Wage(WageConstants.Differential) = CDec(15.00 * .1)

Console.WriteLine(oEmp.Name)
Console.Writeline(oEmp.Wage(WageConstants.Rate))

oEmp = Nothing

End Sub

End Module
```

Programming Tips and Gotchas

An alternative syntax for the Set statement (though it happens to be the officially documented one, as well as the one used by Visual Studio) is:

```
Set([ByVal] var As Type)
    [ statements ]
    [ variable = var ]
End Set
```

Here var is a variable representing the value to be assigned to the property, and Type is the data type of var. Type must be the same as the data type of the Property statement.

VB.NET/VB 6 Differences

The Property Let and Property Set statements in VB 6 correspond to the Set statement in VB.NET. Though the purpose and basic operation of these constructs are identical, the syntax of the VB.NET construct is vastly simplified and more intuitive.

See Also

Get Statement, Property Statement

SetAttr Procedure

Class

Microsoft.VisualBasic.FileSystem

Syntax

```
SetAttr(pathname, attributes)
```

pathname   *required; String*
>   The name of the file or directory whose attributes are to be set

attributes   *required;* `FileAttribute` *enumeration*
>   Numeric expression, `FileAttribute` enumerated constant, or global VB
>   constant specifying the attributes

Description

Changes the attribute properties of a file

Rules at a Glance

- You can use any sum of the following constants to set the attributes of a file:

Constant	Value	Description
VbNormal	0	Normal
VbReadOnly	1	Read-only
VbHidden	2	Hidden
VbSystem	4	System
VbArchive	32	File has changed since last backup

    Each global constant has a corresponding constant in the `FileAttribute` enu-
    meration. For example, `vbNormal` is identical to `FileAttribute.Normal`.
    The file-attribute constants `vbDirectory`, `vbAlias`, and `vbVolume` cannot be
    used when assigning attributes.

- File-attributes constants can be `Ored` to set more than one attribute at the
  same time. For example:

```
SetAttr "SysFile.Dat", FileAttribute.System Or FileAttribute.Hidden
```

- *pathname* can include a drive letter. If a drive letter is not included in *pathname*, the current drive is assumed. The file path can be either a fully qualified path or a relative path from the current directory.

- *pathname* can include a folder name. If the folder name is not included in
  pathname, the current folder is assumed.

- Attempting to set the attributes of an open file will generate a runtime error.

Example

```
Private Sub AddAttributes(strFN As String, _
                        intNewAttrib As Integer)

Dim intAttrib As Integer

intAttrib = GetAttr(strFN)
intAttrib = intAttrib Or intNewAttrib
SetAttr(strFN, intAttrib )

End Sub
```

Programming Tips and Gotchas

- Setting file attributes simultaneously *clears* any attributes that are not set with the `SetAttr` procedure. For example, if *SysFile.Dat* is a read-only, hidden, system file, the statement:

  ```
  SetAttr "sysfile.dat", VbArchive
  ```

  sets the archive attribute but clears the read-only, hidden, and system attributes. Clearly, this can have disastrous implications. To retain a file's attributes while setting new ones, first retrieve its attributes using the *GetAttr* function, as the example program illustrates.

- Setting a file's attributes to `VbNormal` clears all file attributes.

- Not all attribute values can be assigned to a file; many are assigned only by the operating system. For example, `FileAttribute.Directory` cannot be assigned to an existing directory or a file. Thus, when setting the attribute value of a file or directory, you must mask out these (or any other) illegal values. For example, the following code fragment shows how to do this in the case of a directory:

  ```
  Private Sub AddAttributes(strFN As String, _
                          intNewAttrib As Integer)

  Dim intAttrib As Integer

  intAttrib = GetAttr(strFN)

  ' If directory, mask out directory flag
  If intAttrib And FileAttribute.Directory Then
      intAttrib = intAttrib And &HFFFFFFEF
  End If

  intAttrib = intAttrib Or intNewAttrib
  SetAttr(strFN, intAttrib Or intNewAttrib)

  End Sub
  ```

See Also

GetAttr Function

Shadows Keyword

Syntax

```
Shadows
```

Description

When a member of a derived class has the same name as a member of the same type in the base class, and the keywords *Overridable* and *Overrides* are used appropriately, then the derived class member overrides the base class member. That is, any reference to the member using a derived class object refers to the implementation in the derived class.

Shadowing works in a similar way but allows any member type to "override" any other member type. Thus, for example, a method can "override" a property. For a complete discussion of shadowing (with an example), see the Shadowing section in Chapter 4.

VB.NET/VB 6 Differences

The Shadows keyword is new to VB.NET.

Shell Function

Class

Microsoft.VisualBasic.Interaction

Syntax

```
Shell(pathname[,style][, Wait][, Timeout] )
```

pathname   *required; String*
Name of the program to execute

style   *optional;* AppWinStyle *enumeration*
The style of window and whether it receives the focus; see the "Rules at a Glance" section

Wait   *optional; Boolean*
Boolean indicating whether to wait for the *pathname* application to finish execution before continuing execution of subsequent code

Timeout   *optional; Integer*
If *Wait* is *True*, number of milliseconds to wait for the *pathname* application to terminate before the *Shell* function times out

Return Value

An Integer representing the Process ID, or 0

Description

Launches another application and, if successful, returns that application's task ID

Rules at a Glance

- *pathname* can include a drive letter. If a drive letter is not included in *pathname*, the current drive is assumed.

- *pathname* can include a folder name. You can use either a fully qualified path (i.e., starting from the root directory) or a relative path (i.e., starting from the current directory). If the folder name is not included in *pathname*, the current folder is assumed.

- *pathname* can include any command-line arguments and switches required by the application. For example:

```
Shell("notepad.exe c:\data.txt", AppWinStyle.NormalFocus)
```

launches Notepad, which loads the file *data.txt*.

- Visual Basic includes the following intrinsic constants for setting the *style* argument:

AppWinStyle.Hide   *Value: 0*
New application window is hidden

Focus: New application

AppWinStyle.NormalFocus   *Value: 1*
New application window is shown in its original position and size

Focus: New application

AppWinStyle.MinimizedFocus   *Value: 2*
New application window is displayed as an icon

Focus: New application

AppWinStyle.MaximizedFocus   *Value: 3*
New application window is maximized

Focus: New application

AppWinStyle.NormalNoFocus   *Value: 4*
New application window is shown in its original position and size

Focus: Current application

AppWinStyle.MinimizedNoFocus   *Value: 6*
New application window is displayed as an icon

Focus: Current application

- The default when no *style* is specified is AppWinStyle.MinimizedFocus (2).

- If the application named in *pathname* executes successfully, *Shell* returns the windows task ID of the program. (The task ID is better known as the process ID or PID, a unique 32-bit value used to identify each running process.) It can be used as a parameter to the *AppActivate* procedure to give the application the focus—and possibly to control it remotely using the Send and SendWait methods. The process ID is also required by a number of Win32 API calls.

- If the application named in *pathname* fails to execute, a runtime error is generated.

- The file launched by *Shell* must be executable. That is, it must be a file whose extension is .EXE or .COM (an executable file), .BAT (a batch file), or .PIF (a DOS shortcut file).

- `Wait` determines whether the *Shell* function operates synchronously (`True`) or asynchronously (`False`). The default is `False`; control returns to the application, and code continues executing as soon as the process ID is known. If `True`, the *Shell* function returns only when the ***pathname*** application is closed or, if `Timeout` is not –1, when the timeout period has expired.

- If `Wait` is `False`, the *Shell* function returns the application's process ID. If `Wait` is `True`, it returns either the process ID (if control returns to the application because `Timeout` has elapsed) or 0 (if control returns to the application because the ***pathname*** application has been closed). In this latter case, *Shell* returns a 0 because, since the ***pathname*** application has been closed, its process ID is no longer valid.

- `Timeout` applies only when `Wait` is `True`. It defines the number of milliseconds that the application will wait for the ***pathname*** application to end before the wait is abandoned and application code resumes execution. Its default value is –1, which means that there is no timeout value and control returns to the application only when the ***pathname*** application has terminated.

Programming Tips and Gotchas

- `Wait` is a long-needed addition to the *Shell* function that allows your application to know when the launched application has terminated.

- The *Shell* function does not use file associations. You cannot, for example, supply *MyReport.Doc* as the ***pathname*** in the hope that VB will load Microsoft Word, which in turn will load *MyReport.Doc*.

- Setting `Wait` to `True` and leaving `Timeout` at its default value of –1 creates the possibility that control will never return from the ***pathname*** application to the VB.NET application.

VB.NET/VB 6 Differences

The `Wait` and `Timeout` arguments are new to VB.NET. They are not supported by VB 6.

Sign Function

Class

System.Math

Syntax

```
Sign(value)
```

value   *required; any numeric type, including Decimal*
    A numeric expression

Return Value

Integer

Description

Determines the sign of a number

Rules at a Glance

The return value of the *Sign* function is determined by the sign of *value*, as follows:

If number is	Sign returns
Positive	1
Zero	0
Negative	−1

Programming Tips and Gotchas

- *Sign* is useful in cases in which the sign of a quantity defines the sign of an expression. For example:

  ```
  lngResult = lngQty * Sgn(lngValue)
  ```

- This is a Shared member, so it can be used without creating any objects.

- If you are using the *Sign* function to evaluate a result to **False** (0) or **True** (any nonzero value), you could use the *CBool* function instead.

- A major use for *Sign* is to determine the sign of an expression.

VB.NET/VB 6 Differences

The name of this function has changed. In VB 6, it is named *Sgn*. In VB.NET, it is named *Sign* and is a member of the Math class of the System namespace.

See Also

If...Then...Else Statement

Sin Function

Class

System.Math

Syntax

```
Sin(a)
```

a required; Numeric

An angle expressed in radians

Return Value

A Double containing the sine of an angle

Description

Returns the ratio of two sides of a right triangle in the range −1 to 1

Rules at a Glance

- The ratio is determined by dividing the length of the side opposite the angle by the length of the hypotenuse.

- This is a Shared member, so it can be used without creating any objects.

Programming Tips and Gotchas

- You can convert degrees to radians using the formula:

    ```
    radians = degrees * (pi/180)
    ```

- You can convert radians to degrees using the formula:

    ```
    degrees = radians * (180/pi)
    ```

See Also

Cos Function, Tan Function

Sinh Function

Class

System.Math

Syntax

```
Math.Sinh(value)
```

value   *required; Double or numeric expression*
    An angle in radians

Return Value

A Double denoting the hyperbolic sine of the angle

Description

Returns the hyperbolic sine of an angle

Rules at a Glance

This is a Shared member, so it can be used without creating any objects.

VB.NET/VB 6 Differences

The *Sinh* function is new to the .NET Framework.

See Also

Cosh Function, Tanh Function

SLN Function

Class

Microsoft.VisualBasic.Financial

Syntax

```
SLN(cost, salvage, life)
```

cost   *required; Double*
> The initial cost of the asset

salvage   *required; Double*
> The value of the asset at the end of its useful life

life   *required; Double*
> The length of the useful life of the asset

Return Value

A Double representing depreciation per period

Description

Computes the straight-line depreciation of an asset for a single period

Rules at a Glance

- The function uses a very simple formula to calculate depreciation:

  ```
  (cost - salvage) / life
  ```

- The depreciation period is determined by the time period of *life*.

- All arguments must be positive numeric values.

See Also

DDB Function, SYD Function

Space Function

Class

Microsoft.VisualBasic.Strings

Syntax

```
Space(number)
```

number   *required; Integer*
> An expression evaluating to the number of spaces required

Return Value

A String containing *number* spaces

Description

Creates a string containing *number* spaces

Rules at a Glance

While *number* can be zero (in which case the function returns the empty string), runtime error 5, "Invalid procedure call or argument," is generated if *number* is negative.

Programming Tips and Gotchas

The *Space* function is most useful for creating a string buffer, an area where an external function can write data to be returned to the calling program.

Spc Function

Class

Microsoft.VisualBasic.FileSystem

Syntax

```
Spc(n)
```

n   *required; Integer*

The number of spaces required

Return Value

A String containing *n* spaces

Description

Inserts spaces between expressions in a *Print* or *PrintLine* procedure

Rules at a Glance

- *Spc* can only be used with the *Print* or *PrintLine* procedure.
- If the width of the device being printed to is greater than *n*, the print position is set to immediately after the number of spaces printed by the *Spc* function.
- If the width of the device being printed to is less than *n*, the print position is set to the current position plus the result of the formula *n* Mod *devicewidth*.
- If *n* is greater than the difference between the current print position and the width of the device, *Spc* inserts a line break and then inserts spaces in accordance with the following formula:

  ```
  n - (devicewidth - currentposition)
  ```

- When using a proportional font, the *Spc* function uses the average width of all characters for that particular font to determine the width of the space character to print.

Programming Tips and Gotchas

- When the number of fixed-width columns is important, you should use either the *Space* or the *Tab* function, since there is not necessarily a relationship between the spaces provided by the *Spc* function and fixed-width columns.

See Also

Print, PrintLine Procedures, Tab Function

Split Function

Class

Microsoft.VisualBasic.Strings

Syntax

```
Split(expression, [delimiter[, limit[, compare]]])
```

expression   *required; String*

A string to be broken up into multiple strings.

delimiter   *optional; String*

The character used to delimit the substrings in *expression.*

limit   *optional; Integer*

The maximum number of strings to return.

compare   *optional;* CompareMethod *Constant*

The method of comparison. Possible values are CompareMethod.Binary (the default) or CompareMethod.Text.

Return Value

A String array containing the substrings of *expression* delimited by *delimiter*

Description

Parses a single string containing delimited values into an array

Rules at a Glance

- If *expression* is a zero-length string, *Split* returns an empty array.

- If *delimiter* is not found in *expression*, *Split* returns the entire string in element 0 of the returned array.

- If *delimiter* is omitted, a space character (" ") is used as the delimiter.

- If *limit* is omitted or its value is –1, all strings are returned.

- The default comparison method is CompareMethod.Binary.

- Once one less than *limit* has been reached, the remainder of the string is placed, unprocessed, into the next element of the returned array. This is important, because it can lead to unexpected results. For instance, the code:

```
Dim s() As String
s = Split("x y z", " ", 1, CompareMethod.Text)
Console.WriteLine(s(0))
```

prints:

```
x y z
```

because the *Split* function stuffs the remaining portion of the original string into the last array element. This leaves no array elements for the actual split operation. To split off the first substring, we need to set count to at least 2:

```
Dim s() As String
s = Split("x y z", " ", 2, CompareMethod.Text)
Console.WriteLine(s(0))
```

Programming Tips and Gotchas

- Strings are written to the returned array in the order in which they appear in *expression*.

- The setting of *compare* is important only if *delimiter* is an alphabetic character, in which case `CompareMethod.Binary` will perform a case-sensitive comparison, and `Compare.Method.Text` will perform a case insensitive one.

See Also

Join Function

Sqrt Function

Class

System.Math

Syntax

```
Sqr (d)
```

d   *required; Double*

    Any numeric expression greater than or equal to 0

Return Value

A Double containing the square root of *d*

Description

Calculates the square root of a given number

Rules at a Glance

- *d* must be equal to or greater than zero, or runtime error 5, "Invalid procedure call or argument," occurs.

- This is a Shared member, so it can be used without creating any objects.

VB.NET/VB 6 Differences

The square root function in VB 6 is named *Sqr*, and it is an intrinsic VB function. In the .NET Framework, it is named *Sqrt*, and it is a member of the Math class in the System namespace.

Stack Class

Namespace

System.Collections

Createable

Yes

Syntax

```
Dim stackvariable As [New] Stack
```

`stackvariable`   *required; Stack object*
   The name of the Stack object

Description

A Stack object is a model of a stack.

Succinctly put, a *stack* is a last-in, first-out data structure. (This is often abbreviated LIFO.) Put another way, a stack is a data structure that models a *stack* of items (like a stack of dinner plates). There is a method for inserting items at the top of the stack (*pushing*) as well as a method for removing the item that is currently at the top of the stack (*popping*). Under this scenario, the next item to be popped is the item that was placed in line last—hence the phrase, last-in, first-out.

Note that the elements in a Stack object are of type Object.

Stack class members marked with a plus sign (+) are discussed in detail in their own entries.

Public Shared Method
   Synchronized

Public Instance Properties
   Count +
   IsReadOnly
   IsSynchronized
   SyncRoot

Public Instance Methods
   Clear +
   Clone
   Contains +
   CopyTo +
   Equals
   GetEnumerator
   GetHashCode
   GetType
   Peek +
   Pop +
   Push +
   ToArray +
   ToString

Example

```
' Define a new stack
Dim s As New Stack()
' Push some items onto the stack
s.Push("Chopin")
s.Push ("Mozart")
s.Push ("Beethoven")
```

```
' Is an item in the stack?
MsgBox("Beethoven in stack: " & CStr(s.Contains("Beethoven")))
' Peek at the first (top) item on the stack
MsgBox("First item in stack is: " & s.Peek.ToString)
' Send stack to an array and display all items
Dim s() As Object = s.ToArray()
Dim i As Integer
For i = 0 To UBound(s)
    Console.WriteLine(CStr(s(i)))
Next
' Clear stack
s.Clear()
```

VB.NET/VB 6 Differences

The Stack object is new to the .NET Framework.

See Also

Collection Class, Hashtable Class, Queue Class

Stack.Clear Method

Class

System.Collections.Stack

Syntax

```
stackvariable.Clear()
```

Return Value

None

Description

Removes all entries from the stack

See Also

Stack.Pop Method

Stack.Contains Method

Class

System.Collections.Stack

Syntax

```
stackvariable.Contains(obj)
```

obj   *required; any*
    The value to search for in the stack

Return Value

Boolean (True or False) indicating whether *obj* is found in the stack

Description

Returns a Boolean indicating whether a given element (Object) is somewhere in the stack

Rules at a Glance

- *obj* must correspond exactly to an item in the stack for the method to return True.

- String comparison is case sensitive and is not affected by the setting of Option Compare.

- The Contains method searches the stack sequentially. In other words, its performance is inversely proportional to the number of items in the stack.

Programming Tips and Gotchas

- In comparing objects in the stack with *obj*, the Contains method in turn calls the BCL's Object.Equals method to perform the comparison. The Equals method returns True if two object instances are the same instance.

Stack.CopyTo Method

Class

System.Collections.Stack

Syntax

```
stackvariable.CopyTo(array, index)
```

array   *required; Array of Objects*
    Array to which to copy the stack's objects

index   *required; Integer*
    The index of the first array element to receive an element of the stack

Return Value

None

Description

Copies the stack elements into an array, starting at a specified array index

Rules at a Glance

- The array can be of any data type that is compatible with the stack elements. Thus, for instance, we cannot use an Integer array to hold stack elements that are strings (that is, Objects whose subtype is String).

- The array must be sized to accommodate the elements of the stack prior to calling the CopyTo method.

Example

```
Public Sub Main

    ' Define a new stack
    Dim s As New Stack()
    Dim aStack(), oItem As Object

    ' Push some items onto stack
    s.Push("Chopin")
    s.Push("Mozart")
    s.Push("Beethoven")

    ' Size the array and copy to it
    Redim aStack(s.Count - 1)
    s.CopyTo(aStack, 0)

    For Each oItem in aStack
        Console.WriteLine(oItem)
    Next

End Sub
```

See Also

Stack.ToArray Method

Stack.Count Property

Class

System.Collections.Stack

Syntax

```
stackvariable.Count()
```

Return Value

Integer

Description

This read-only property returns an Integer specifying the number of elements in the stack.

Stack.Peek Method

Class

System.Collections.Stack

Syntax

```
stackvariable.Peek()
```

Return Value

Object

Description

Returns the first item in the stack as an Object, but does not remove it from the stack

Programming Tips and Gotchas

The Peek method is similar to the Stack object's Pop method, except that it leaves the stack intact.

See Also

Stack.Pop Method

Stack.Pop Method

Class

System.Collections.Stack

Syntax

```
stackvariable.Pop()
```

Return Value

Object

Description

Removes the top item from the stack and returns it as an Object

Rules at a Glance

- Pop removes the top item from the stack and decrements the Count property by one.

- Pop generates an error if applied to an empty stack. Thus, it's advisable to determine when a stack is empty by using the Count property before popping the stack.

Programming Tips and Gotchas

The Peek method returns a reference to the object at the top of the stack, but unlike the Pop method, does not remove it from the stack.

See Also

Stack.Clear Method, Stack.Peek Method

Stack.Push Method

Class

System.Collections.Stack

Syntax

```
stackvariable.Push(obj)
```

obj   *required; Object*
 The item to place in the stack

Return Value

None

Description

Places an Object on the top of the stack

Rules at a Glance

The Push method adds an item to the top of the stack and increases the Count property by 1.

Stack.ToArray Method

Class

System.Collections.Stack

Syntax

```
stackvariable.ToArray()
```

Return Value

An array of type Object

Description

Creates an array of type Object, copies the elements of the stack in order, and then returns the array

Programming Tips and Gotchas

Unlike the CopyTo method, the ToArray method does not require that we define an array in advance. However, we cannot specify the starting array index for the copy procedure.

See Also

Stack.CopyTo Method

STAThread Attribute

Class

System.STAThreadAttribute

Applies to

Method

Description

Specifies that the class or application to which the program element belongs is to use the *single-threaded apartment* model for COM interop. If COM components are not called from the class or application, the attribute is ignored. The <STAThread> attribute should be used only on the class or application's *Main* method or subroutine.

The <STAThread> attribute is similar to setting a Thread object's ApartmentState property to ApartmentState.STA. The difference is that the <STAThread> attribute creates a single-threaded apartment from startup, whereas setting the property does it only from the point that the property is set.

Constructor

    New()

Properties

None

***

Static Statement

Syntax

    Static varname[([subscripts])] [As [New] type] _
        [,varname[([subscripts])]] [As [New] type]] . . .

varname   *required; any*
> The name of the variable, following Visual Basic naming conventions

subscripts   *optional; Integer*
> Denotes varname as an array and specifies the dimension and upper bounds of the array

New   *optional; Keyword*
> Used to automatically create an instance of the object referred to by the object variable, varname

type   *optional; Keyword*
> Data type of the variable varname

Description

Used at procedure level to declare a Static variable and to allocate the relevant storage space in memory. Static variables retain their value between calls to the procedure in which they are declared.

Rules at a Glance

- A Static variable's scope is limited to the procedure in which it is created.

- The *subscripts* argument has the following syntax:

  upperbound [, upperbound]

- Using the *subscripts* argument, you can declare up to 60 multiple dimensions for the array.

- The New keyword specifies that a new instance of the object will be created. Use of the New keyword in the Static statement therefore eliminates the subsequent need to instantiate the object.

- You cannot use the New keyword to declare variables of any intrinsic data type or to declare instances of dependent objects.

- If you don't use the New keyword with an object variable, you must use an assignment statement to assign an existing object to the variable before you can use the variable.

- *datatype* may be Boolean, Byte, Char, Date, Decimal, Double, Integer, Long, Object, Short, Single, String, a user-defined type, or an object type.

- If you don't specify *datatype*, the variable will be cast as an Object.

- When multiple variables are declared on the same line, if a variable is not declared with a explicit type declaration, then its type is that of the next variable with an explicit type declaration. Thus, in the line:

  Static x As Long, i, j, k As Integer, s As String

  the variables i, j, and k have type Integer. (In VB 6, the variables i and j would have type Variant.)

- When a static variable is initialized on the same line as its declaration, the initialization process is performed only the first time the declaration line is encountered. (Otherwise, the variable would not be static.)

- VB.NET permits the initialization of variables in the same line as their declaration (at long last!). Thus, we may write:

  Static x As Integer = 5

  to declare an Integer variable and initialize it to 5. Similarly, we can declare and initialize more than one variable on a single line:

  Static x As Integer = 6, y As Integer = 9

- Variables that are not explicitly initialized by the Static statement have the following default values:

Data type	Initial value
All numeric types	0
Boolean	False
Date	01/01/0001 12:00:00 AM
Decimal	0
Object	Nothing
String	Zero-length string ("")

- Static variables can have procedure-level scope or block-level scope. Static variables with procedure-level scope last the lifetime of the application, but they are accessible only within the procedure in which they are defined. Static variables with block-level scope last the lifetime of the application, but they are accessible only within the code block (such as a looping construct or an If statement) in which they are defined.

Programming Tips and Gotchas

- It is a recognized programming practice when using the Static statement in a procedure to put the Static statement at the beginning of that procedure.

- Although their value persists between calls to a procedure, Static variables do not have scope outside of the procedure in which they are created.

- For more on static variables, see Chapter 3.

VB.NET/VB 6 Differences

- When multiple variables are declared on a single line of code in VB 6, variables not explicitly assigned a data type are cast as variants. For example, in the statement:

```
Static Var1, Var2, Var3 As String
```

both Var1 and Var2 are variants rather than strings. In VB.NET, the type declaration applies to all undeclared variables since the last explicit type declaration. So the previous statement in VB.NET would cast Var1, Var2, and Var3 as strings.

- In VB 6, declaring and initializing variables are separate steps; aside from allowing VB to assign variables their default values, variables cannot be initialized at the same time they are declared. In VB.NET, variables can be assigned an initial value when they are declared.

- VB 6 allowes you to declare fixed-length strings; they are not supported, however, in VB.NET.

- VB 6 allows you to define the lower bound of an array when it is initialized. In VB.NET, all arrays have a lower bound of 0. Hence, the VB 6 syntax:

```
Static array(1 To 20) As String
```

is not supported in VB.NET.

- In VB 6, arrays are either fixed length or dynamic; in VB.NET, all arrays are dynamic.

- In VB 6, it is possible to define a procedure or a function as Static, meaning that all local variables defined in that routine are static. In VB.NET, the use of the Static keyword with the Function or Sub statements is not supported.

See Also

Dim Statement

Stop Statement

Syntax

```
Stop
```

Description

Suspends program execution

Rules at a Glance

- There is no limit to the number and position of Stop statements within procedures.

- The Stop statement acts like a breakpoint—placing the program in break mode and highlighting the current line in the development environment—allowing you to step through the code line by line.

Programming Tips and Gotchas

- Stop is intended primarily for use in the design-time environment, where it suspends program execution without terminating it. In the runtime environment, however, Stop will cause the debugger to be invoked.

- Unlike the End statement, Stop does not explicitly close any open files or clear any variables, except in a compiled executable.

See Also

End Statement

Str Function

Class

Microsoft.VisualBasic.Conversion

Syntax

```
Str(number)
```

number   *required; Numeric*
   Any valid numeric expression or expression capable of conversion to a number

Return Value

A String representation of *number*

Description

Converts *number* from a numeric to a string

Rules at a Glance

- If *number* cannot be converted to a string, an InvalidCastException error occurs. To prevent this, you can check the value of *number* by passing it to the *IsNumeric* function before calling *Str*.

- If *number* is not a numeric value or is not capable of conversion to a number (so that it can in turn be converted to a string), an InvalidCastException exception occurs.

- If the return value is positive, the *Str* function always includes a leading space in the returned string for the sign of *number*.

Programming Tips and Gotchas

- Use the *LTrim* function to remove the leading space that the *Str* function adds to the start of the returned string.

- Both the *CStr* and *Format* functions have now superceded the *Str* function. The *CStr* function does not add a leading space for the sign of a positive number. Both the *CStr* and the *Format* functions are internationally aware, able to recognize decimal delimiters other than the period (.).

See Also

CStr Function

StrComp Function

Class

Microsoft.VisualBasic.Strings

Syntax

```
StrComp(string1, string2[, compare])
```

string1   *required; String*
    Any string expression

string2   *required; String*
    Any string expression

compare   *optional;* CompareMethod *constant*
    Either CompareMethod.Binary or CompareMethod.Text

Return Value

Integer

Description

Determines whether two strings are equal and, if not, which of two strings has the greater value

Rules at a Glance

- The *compare* argument is one of CompareMethod.Binary or CompareMethod.Text. If no comparison is specified, VB uses the value of Option Compare.

- The following table describes the possible return values from the *StrComp* function:

Scenario	Return value
string1 < string2	-1
string1 = string2	0
string1 > string2	1
string1 or *string2* is Null	Null

Programming Tips and Gotchas

- Using the comparison operators <, <=, >, and >= to compare strings performs a character-by-character binary comparison.

- The *StrComp* function can provide a significant performance improvement (in the neighborhood of 30% to 70%) over the comparison operators.

See Also

StrConv Function, StrDup Function, StrReverse Function

StrConv Function

Class

Microsoft.VisualBasic.Strings

Syntax

```
StrConv(str, conversion[, localeID])
```

`str`   *required; String*
    The string expression to convert

`conversion`   *required; Constant of the* VbStrConv *enumeration*
    One of the constants listed in the "Rules at a Glance" section

`localeID`   *optional; Integer*
    The locale identifier to use for the conversion

Return Value

A String converted according to `conversion`

Description

Performs special conversions on a string

Rules at a Glance

- The following intrinsic conversion constants specify the type of conversion to perform:

Constant	Converts...
VbStrConv.UpperCase	The entire string to uppercase.
VbStrConv.LowerCase	The entire string to lowercase.

Constant	Converts...
VbStrConv.ProperCase	The first letter of every word in *str* to an uppercase character.
VbStrConv.Wide	Narrow (single-byte) characters in *str* to wide (double-byte) characters.
VbStrConv.Narrow	Wide (double-byte) characters in *str* to narrow (single-byte) characters.
VbStrConv.Katakana	Hiragana characters in *str* to Katakana characters.
VbStrConv.Hiragana	Katakana characters in *str* to Hiragana characters.
VbStrConv.Linguistic-Casing	Uses linguistic rules for casing. Can be used only with UpperCase and LowerCase.
VbStrConv.None	Performs no conversion on *str*.
VbStrConv.Simpli-fiedChinese	Traditional Chinese characters in *str* to Simplified Chinese.
VbStrConv.Traditional-Chinese	Simplified Chinese characters in *str* to Traditional Chinese.

- You can combine some of these constants by adding them together or using a logical OR. For example:

      VbStrConv.UpperCase + VbStrConv.Wide

  The only restriction is that the constants must be mutually exclusive. For example, specifying the value:

      VbStrConv.UpperCase Or VbStrConv.ProperCase   ' Error

  produces an error.

- VbStrConv.Katakana and VbStrConv.Hiragana only apply to locales in Japanese. Use of these constants on systems using other locales generates runtime error 5, "Invalid procedure call or argument."

- VbStrConv.Wide and VbStrConv.Narrow only apply to locales in the Far East. Use of these constants on systems using other locales will generate a runtime error.

- When determining the start of a new word to convert to proper case, *StrConv* recognizes the following characters as word separators:

  — Null—Chr$(0)

  — Horizontal Tab—*Chr$(9)*

  — Line-feed—*Chr$(10)*

  — Vertical Tab—*Chr$(11)*

  — Form Feed—*Chr$(12)*

  — Carriage Return—*Chr$(13)*

  — Space—Chr$(32)

Programming Tips and Gotchas

If you convert to proper case, *StrConv* converts the first letter of each word to uppercase regardless of whether that word is significant. Hence, "this is the time" becomes "This Is The Time," even though "the" ordinarily would not be capitalized.

VB.NET/VB 6 Differences

Two *conversion* values supported by VB 6, `VbUnicode` and `VbFromUnicode`, have no equivalent in the `VbStrConv` enumeration. As a result, the function can no longer be used to convert ASCII to Unicode or Unicode to ASCII.

See Also

StrComp Function, StrDup Function, StrReverse Function

StrDup Function

Class

Microsoft.VisualBasic.Strings

Syntax

```
StrDup(number,character)
```

number   *required; Integer*
    The number of times to duplicate the first character in string

character   *required; String, Char, or Object containing a String or Char*
    The String or Char whose first character is to be duplicated

Return Value

A String containing the character duplicated the specified number of times

Description

Returns a string that consists of the first character of *character* duplicated *number* times

Example

The line:

```
MsgBox(StrDup(Number:=5, Character:="ABC"))
```

displays `"AAAAA"`.

VB.NET/VB 6 Differences

The *StrDup* function is new to VB.NET. It appears in part to be a replacement for the VB 6 *String* function.

StrReverse Function

Class

Microsoft.VisualBasic.Strings

Syntax

```
StrReverse(expression)
```

expression   *required; String*
    The string whose characters are to be reversed

Return Value

String

Description

Returns a string that is the reverse of the string passed to it. For example, if the string *and* is passed to it as an argument, *StrReverse* returns the string *dna*.

Structure...End Structure Statement

Syntax

```
accessmodifier Structure StructureName
   [Implements interfacenames]
   variable declarations
   procedure declarations
End Structure
```

accessmodifier   *optional; Keyword*
    The possible values of *accessmodifier* are `Public`, `Private`, `Friend`, `Protected`, `Protected Friend`. For more information, see the section entitled "Accessibility in Class Modules" in Chapter 4.

`Implements` *interfacenames*   *optional*
    Indicates that the structure implements the members of one or more interfaces

Description

Used to declare user-defined types. Structures are similar to classes, but they are value types rather than reference types.

Rules at a Glance

- The members of a structure can be variables, properties, methods, or events. Note, however, that each member must be declared with an access modifier: `Public` (or `Dim`), `Private`, or `Friend`.

- You cannot assign a structure member an initial value at the same time as you declare it. As a result, the following `Structure` construct is illegal:

```
Structure Point
    Public x As Integer = 0      ' Illegal
    Public y As Integer = 0      ' Illegal
End Structure
```

- Structure members can be other structures or objects.

- If a structure member is an array, it cannot be explicitly dimensioned.

- Structures can be passed as arguments to functions or as the return type of a function.

- Although structures are similar to classes, the following class features are not supported in structures:

  — Structures cannot explicitly inherit, nor can they be inherited.

  — All constructors for a structure must be parameterized.

  — Structures cannot define destructors.

  — Member declarations cannot include initializers, nor can they use the **As New** syntax or specify an initial array size.

Example

The simplest and most common use of structures is to encapsulate related variables. For instance, we might define a structure as follows:

```
Structure strPerson
    Public Name As String
    Public Address As String
    Public City As String
    Public State As String
    Public Zip As String
    Public Age As Short
End Structure
```

To define a variable of type **strPerson**, we write (as usual):

```
Dim APerson As strPerson
```

To access a member of a structure, we use the dot syntax, as in:

```
APerson.Name = "Beethoven"
```

Programming Tips and Gotchas

- Related items of information are often stored in multiple arrays (or in a multidimensional array). However, it is often preferable to store related data in a single array of structures.

- The **Structure** statement is often used to define a data structure capable of retrieving, storing, and saving fixed-length records. However, this is complicated by the absence of support for explicitly declared fixed-length strings in VB.NET. One solution is to use the **<vbFixedString(*length*)>** attribute, where *length* is the fixed length of the string, when defining a member of type String. This instructs the VB.NET compiler to enforce a particular string length for the structure. For example:

```
Structure Person
    <vbFixedString(10)> Public FName As String
    <vbFixedString(2)>  Public MName As String
    <vbFixedString(10)> Public LName As String
    Public Age As Short
End Structure
```

VB.NET/VB 6 Differences

- The **Structure...End Structure** construct is new to VB.NET. It replaces the **Type...End Type** construct in VB 6.

- VB 6 user-defined types are different than VB.NET structures. A VB 6 user-defined type is simply a composite data type that combines multiple data types; it allows the user-defined type to be treated as a contiguous, word- or double-word aligned block of memory. A VB.NET structure is in some sense a hybrid object that combines data types and methods; ordinarily, no assumptions should be made about its layout in memory.

- In VB 6, the declaration of user-defined type members did not permit an access modifier. In VB.NET, it is required.

Sub Statement

Syntax

```
[ClassBehavior] [AccessModifier] Sub name [(arglist)]
    [statements]
    [Exit Sub]
    [statements]
End Sub
```

ClassBehavior   *optional; Keyword*

One of the keywords shown in the following table:

Keyword	Description
Overloads	Indicates that more than one declaration of this subroutine exists (with different argument signatures).
Overrides	For derived classes, indicates that the subroutine overrides the subroutine by the same name (and argument signature) in the base class.
Overridable	Indicates that the subroutine can be overridden in a derived class.
NotOverridable	Indicates that the subroutine cannot be overridden in a derived class.
MustOverride	Indicates that the subroutine must be overridden in a derived class.
Shadows	In a derived class definition, indicates that calls to derived class members that are made through a base class ignore the shadowed implementation.
Shared	Callable without creating an object of the class. It is, in this strange sense, shared by all objects of the class. These are also called *static subroutines*.

AccessModifier   *optional*

The possible values of *AccessModifier* are **Public**, **Private**, **Friend**, **Protected**, or **Protected Friend**. The following table describes the effects of the various access modifiers. Note that "direct access" refers to accessing the member without any qualification, as in:

```
classvariable = 100
```

and "class/object access" refers to accessing the member through qualification, either with the class name or the name of an object of that class. For more information, see the "Accessibility in Class Modules" section in Chapter 4.

	Direct access scope	*Class/object access scope*
Private	Declaring class	Declaring class
Protected	All derived classes	Declaring class
Friend	Derived in-project classes	Declaring project
Protected Friend	All derived classes	Declaring project
Public	All derived classes	All projects

name   *required; String literal*

The name of the Sub procedure.

arglist   *optional; any*

A comma-delimited list of variables to be passed to the sub procedure as
arguments from the calling procedure.

arglist uses the following syntax and parts:

```
[Optional] [ByVal | ByRef] [ParamArray] varname[( )] _
    [As type] [= defaultvalue]
```

Optional   *optional; Keyword*

An optional argument is one that need not be supplied when calling the
function. However, all arguments following an optional one must also be
optional. A **ParamArray** argument cannot be optional.

ByVal   *optional; Keyword*

The argument is passed by value; that is, the local copy of the variable is
assigned the value of the argument. **ByVal** is the default method of
passing variables.

ByRef   *optional; Keyword*

The argument is passed by reference; that is, the local variable is simply a
reference to the argument being passed. All changes made to the local
variable will be also reflected in the calling argument.

ParamArray   *optional; Keyword*

Indicates that the argument is an optional array containing an arbitrary
number of elements. It can only be used as the last element of the argument list, and cannot be modified by either the **ByRef** or **Optional**
keywords. If **Option Strict** is on, the array type must also be
specified.

varname   *required; String literal*

The name of the local variable containing either the reference or value of
the argument.

type   *optional; Keyword*

The data type of the argument. It can be Boolean, Byte, Char, Date,
Decimal, Double, Integer, Long, Object, Short, Single, String, a user-
defined type, or an object type.

defaultvalue   *optional; any*

For optional arguments, you must specify a default value.

statements   *optional*

Program code to be executed within the procedure.

Description

Defines a subroutine

Rules at a Glance

- Subroutines cannot be nested; that is, you cannot define one subroutine inside another subroutine. (This applies to all procedures.)

- If you do not include one of the *accessmodifier* keywords, a subroutine will be `Public` by default.

- Any number of `Exit Sub` statements can be placed within the subroutine. Execution will continue with the line of code immediately following the call to the subroutine.

- If you specify an optional parameter in your subroutine declaration, you must also provide a default value for that parameter. For example:

```
Private Sub ShowMessage(Optional sMsg _
                   As String = "Not given")
```

- A subroutine is called by using its name and enclosing any arguments in parentheses. For example, a routine named *SomeRoutine* might be called as follows:

```
x = 12
y = 12
SomeRoutine(x, y)
```

Note that because it does not return a value, a subroutine cannot be assigned to a variable. For example, the following is illegal:

```
z = SomeRoutine(x, y)
```

Programming Tips and Gotchas

- There is often confusion between using the `ByRef` and `ByVal` methods of assigning arguments to the `Sub` procedure. `ByRef` assigns the reference of the variable in the calling procedure to the variable in the `Sub` procedure; that is, it passes a pointer containing the address in memory of the variable in the calling procedure. As a result, any changes made to the variable from within the `Sub` procedure are in reality made to the variable in the calling procedure. On the other hand, `ByVal` assigns the value of the variable in the calling procedure to the variable in the `Sub` procedure; that is, it makes a separate copy of the variable in a separate memory location. Changes made to the variable in the `Sub` procedure have no effect on the variable in the calling procedure. In general, `ByRef` arguments within class modules take longer to handle, since marshaling back and forth between `Sub` procedure and calling module must take place. So unless you explicitly need to modify a variable's value within a `Sub` procedure, it's best to pass parameters by value.

- The names of procedure parameters become the procedure's named arguments. Because of this, it is best to use meaningful names for parameters, and to avoid the use of Hungarian notation.

- If you do not specify whether an individual element in **arglist** is passed **ByVal** or **ByRef**, it is passed by reference in VB 6. In VB.NET, it is passed by value.

- If a parameter array is used in VB 6, it is an array of variants. In VB.NET, since the Variant is no longer supported, it must be an array of objects or a strongly typed array.

- In VB 6, a **Sub** procedure was called either by using the **Call** statement and including procedure arguments in parentheses or by using the name of the procedure and including arguments without parentheses. VB.NET features a standard calling syntax in which arguments are always enclosed in parentheses.

See Also

Function Statement

Switch Function

Class

Microsoft.VisualBasic.Interaction

Syntax

```
Switch(expr-1, value-1[, expr-2, value-2 ... [, _
    expr-n,value-n]])
```

expr   *required; Object*
  A number of expressions to be evaluated

value   *required; Object*
  An expression or value to return if the associated expression evaluates to **True**

Return Value

An Object value or expression

Description

Evaluates a list of expressions and, on finding the first expression to evaluate to **True**, returns an associated value or expression

Rules at a Glance

- A minimum of two expression/value pairs is required; additional pairs are optional.

- Expressions are evaluated from left to right.

- If none of the expressions is **True**, the *Switch* function returns **Nothing**.

- If multiple expressions are **True**, *Switch* returns the value that corresponds to the first **True** expression.

- **value** can be a constant, variable, or expression.

Example

The *GetTextColor* function uses the *Switch* function to return an RGB color value that depends on the sign of the integer passed to it as a parameter. To access the Color structure, it imports the System.Drawing namespace of the Base Class Library.

```
Private Function GetTextColor(lValue As Integer) As Integer

Dim fColor As New Color
Dim iColor As Integer
fColor = Switch(lValue > 0, Color.Blue, _
                lValue = 0, Color.Black, _
                lValue < 0, Color.Red)

' Convert color name to RGB color and strip out
' high order byte of high-order word
iColor = fColor.ToArgb and &H00FFFFFF
GetTextColor = iColor

End Function
```

Programming Tips and Gotchas

The *Switch* function can prove to be an efficient alternative to `If...Then... Else` statements, but it can't be used in situations where multiple lines of code are required to be executed on finding the first `True` expression.

Programming Tips and Gotchas

Switch does not use short-circuiting. That is, even though it returns only the first `True` expression, it evaluates all expressions. As a result, *Switch* will generate a runtime error if any of these expressions are invalid.

See Also

Choose Function

SYD Function

Class

Microsoft.VisualBasic.Financial

Syntax

```
SYD(cost, salvage, life, period )
```

cost   *required; Double*
    The initial cost of the asset

salvage   *required; Double*
    The value of the asset at the end of its useful life

life   *required; Double*
    The length of the useful life of the asset

period *required; Double*

The period whose depreciation is to be calculated

Return Value

A Double giving the sum-of-years depreciation of an asset for a given period

Description

Computes the sum-of-years' digits depreciation of an asset for a specified period. The sum-of-years' digits method allocates a larger amount of the depreciation in the earlier years of the asset.

Rules at a Glance

- `life` and `period` must be expressed in the same time unit. For example, if `life` represents the life of the asset in years, `period` must be a particular year for which the depreciation amount is to be computed.

- All arguments must be positive numeric values.

- To calculate the depreciation for a given period, *SYD* uses the formula:

  ```
  (Cost-Salvage)*((Life-Period + 1)/(Life*(Life + 1)/2))
  ```

See Also

DDB Function, SLN Function

SyncLock Statement

Syntax

```
SyncLock expression
...[ code ]
End SyncLock
```

expression *required; any reference type (class, module, interface, array, or delegate)*

An expression yielding a single result that can be used to determine the accessibility of *code*

code *optional*

The code statements to which access is synchronized and that will be executed sequentially

Description

Prevents multiple threads of execution in the same process from accessing shared data or resources at the same time

Rules at a Glance

SyncLock blocks a thread's access only if that thread belongs to the same object instance.

Programming Tips and Gotchas

- The SyncLock statement wraps a call to the BCL's System.Threading.Monitor. Enter method.

- The BCL includes a number of other synchronization mechanisms, all of which are located in the System.Threading namespace.

VB.NET/VB 6 Differences

The SyncLock statement is new to VB.NET. VB 6 provided the developer with no direct means of controlling threads of execution in applications or components.

SystemTypeName Function

Class

Microsoft.VisualBasic.Information

Syntax

```
SystemTypeName(vbname)
```

vbname   *required; String*
    The name of a VB.NET data type

Return Value

A String indicating the name of a CTS data type

Description

Returns the fully qualified type name of the Common Type System (CTS) data type that corresponds to a particular Visual Basic data type

Rules at a Glance

- *vbname* must be the name of a valid VB.NET data type, such as Boolean, Byte, Char, Date. Decimal, Double, Integer, Long, Object, Short, Single, or String.

- If *vbname* is not a valid VB.NET data type, the function returns Nothing.

- If *vbname* does not directly correspond to a CTS data type, the function returns Nothing. For example, user-defined types created with the Structure construct and classes created with the Class construct both return Nothing if their data type names are passed to the function.

Example

```
Public Structure Point
    Dim x As Integer
    Dim y As Integer
End Structure

Public Class CEmployee

End Class
```

```
Module modMain

Public Sub Main

    ' Returns System.Int32
    Dim i As Integer = 100
    Console.WriteLine("Type of i: " & SystemTypeName(TypeName(i)))

    ' Returns Nothing
    Dim o As Object
    Console.WriteLine("Type of o: " & SystemTypeName(TypeName(o)))

    ' Returns Nothing
    Dim oEmp As New CEmployee
    Console.WriteLIne("Type of oEmp: " & SystemTypeName(TypeName(oEmp)))

    ' Returns Nothing
    Dim uPt As Point
    Console.Writeline("Type of uPt: " & SystemTypeName(TypeName(uPt)))

    ' Returns System.String
    Dim sName As String = "This is a string."
    Console.WriteLine("Type of sName: " & SystemTypeName(TypeName(sName)))

End Sub

End Module
```

Programming Tips and Gotchas

- To determine the CTS data type of a particular variable, pass the variable as an argument to the *TypeName* function, and pass its return value as an argument to the *SystemTypeName* function. For example:

  ```
  strType = SystemTypeName(TypeName(myVar))
  ```

- The existence of the *SystemTypeName* function clearly indicates that VB.NET data types are wrappers for CTS data types.

VB.NET/VB 6 Differences

The SystemTypeName function is new to VB.NET.

See Also

TypeName Function, VbTypeName Function

Tab Function

Class

Microsoft.VisualBasic.FileSystem

Syntax

```
Tab[(column)]
```

---

column *optional; Short*

A column number to which the insertion point will move before displaying or printing the next expression

Return Value

A TabInfo structure

Description

Moves the text-insertion point to a given column or to the start of the next print zone

Rules at a Glance

- If the *column* argument is omitted, the text-insertion point will be moved to the beginning of the next print zone.

- The value of *column* determines the behavior of the insertion point:

Value of column	Position of insertion point
Current column > *column*	Moves one line down to the *column* column.
column > Output Width	Uses the formula *column* Mod width. If the result is less than the current insertion point, the insertion point will move down one line; otherwise, the insertion point will remain on the same line.
< 1	Column 1

- The left hand column is always 1.

- When expressions are output to files using the Print or PrintLine statement, the width of the output is determined by the Width statement.

- When output surface is divided into columns, the width of each column is the average width of all characters in the current point size of the current font. This means that the number of columns for tabulation purposes does not necessarily relate to the number of characters that can be printed across the width of the output surface.

Programming Tips and Gotchas

The *Tab* function without a *column* argument is useful when outputting data to a file using the Print or PrintLine statement—especially in locales where the comma would be recognized as a decimal separator.

See Also

Spc Function

Tan Function

Class

System.Math

Syntax

Tan(a)

a   *required; Double*
   An angle in radians

Return Value

A Double containing the tangent of an angle

Description

Returns the ratio of two sides of a right angle triangle

Rules at a Glance

* The returned ratio is derived by dividing the length of the side opposite the angle by the length of the side adjacent to the angle.

* This is a Shared member, so it can be used without creating any objects.

Programming Tips and Gotchas

* You can convert degrees to radians using the following formula:

    ```
    radians = degrees * (pi/180)
    ```

* You can convert radians to degrees using the following formula:

    ```
    degrees = radians * (180/pi)
    ```

See Also

Cos Function, Sin Function

Tanh Function

Class

System.Math

Syntax

```
Math.Tanh(number)
```

number   *required; Double or numeric expression*
   An angle in radians

Return Value

A Double denoting the hyperbolic tangent of the angle

Description

Returns the hyperbolic tangent of an angle

Rules at a Glance

This is a Shared member, so it can be used without creating any objects.

Tanh is new to the .NET Framework.

See Also

Cosh Function, Sinh Function

ThreadStatic Attribute

Class

System.ThreadStaticAttribute

Valid On

Field

Description

Specifies that the value of a static field is not shared across threads (that is, each thread in the application has its own value). In the absence of the `<ThreadStatic>` attribute, a static field is shared across threads.

Constructor

```
New()
```

Properties

None

Example

The example illustrates the use of the `<ThreadStatic>` attribute by creating a second thread and having both threads increment a static field. With the `<ThreadStatic>` attribute, the variable's value is maintained on a per thread basis. If you remove the `<ThreadStatic>` attribute and recompile the source, you would find that it is maintained on a per application basis.

```
Option Strict On

Imports Microsoft.VisualBasic
Imports System
Imports System.Threading

Public Class CMain

    <ThreadStatic> Private Shared lCount As Integer

    Public Shared Sub Main
        Dim oThread As New Thread(AddressOf Thread2Proc)
        oThread.Start

        Console.WriteLine("First call to CallCount")
        CallCount()
        DelayLoop(2000)
```

```
            Console.WriteLine("Second call to CallCount")
            CallCount()
            DelayLoop(2000)
            Console.WriteLine("Third call to CallCount")
            CallCount()

        End Sub

        Private Shared Sub CallCount()
            lCount += 1
            Console.WriteLine(lCount)
        End Sub

        Private Shared Sub DelayLoop(millisecs As Integer)
            Dim oThread As Thread
            oThread = Thread.CurrentThread
            oThread.Sleep(millisecs)
        End Sub

        Private Shared Sub Thread2Proc
            Console.WriteLine("2nd thread call 1 to CallCount")
            CallCount()
            DelayLoop(2000)
            Console.WriteLine("2nd thread call 2 to CallCount")
            CallCount()
            DelayLoop(2000)
            Console.WriteLine("2nd thread call 3 to CallCount")
            CallCount()
        End Sub
    End Class
```

Throw Statement

Syntax

```
Throw exception
```

exception   *required; an Exception object or an object derived from Exception*
   An Exception object representing the exception being thrown

Description

Throws an exception that can be handled using either structured exception
handling (a `Try . . . Catch` block) or unstructured exception handling (the `On
Error` statement)

Example

```
Try
    ' Ask for a positive number
    Dim DataCt As Integer = CInt(InputBox("Enter number of items."))
    ' Check for error
    If DataCt <= 0 Then
        ' Throw an exception
        Throw New Exception("Must enter a positive number.")
    End If
```

```
Catch ex As Exception
    MsgBox(ex.Message)
End Try
```

VB.NET/VB 6 Differences

The **Throw** statement is new to VB.NET.

See Also

Exception Class, Try...Catch...Finally Statement

TimeOfDay Property

Class

Microsoft.VisualBasic.DateAndTime

Syntax

```
TimeOfDay
```

Return Value

Date value giving the current system time

Description

Sets or returns the current system time

Example

The code:

```
TimeOfDay() = #9:05:13 AM#
```

sets the system time, and the code:

```
MsgBox(TimeOfDay())
```

displays the current system time.

Rules at a Glance

The TimeOfDay property returns the time in the time format defined by the system's regional settings.

Programming Tips and Gotchas

- The TimeOfDay property includes an incorrect date, 01/01/0001, along with the time. It can be eliminated with the *Format* or *FormatDateTime* function as follows:

    ```
    Format(TimeOfDay(), "Long Time")
    FormatDateTime(TimeOfDay(), DateFormat.LongTime)
    ```

- When setting the TimeOfDay property, any date component is ignored.

See Also

Now Property

Timer Property

Class

Microsoft.VisualBasic.DateAndTime

Syntax

```
Timer
```

Return Value

Double representing the number of seconds that have elapsed since midnight

Description

Returns the number of seconds since midnight

Programming Tips and Gotchas

- Timer is classified as a function in VB 6 and as a read-only property in VB.NET.

- You can use the Timer property as an easy method of passing a seed number to the *Randomize* procedure, as follows:

  ```
  Randomize Timer()
  ```

- The Timer property is ideal for measuring the time taken to execute a procedure or program statement, as the following snippet shows:

  ```
  Dim sStartTime As Single
  Dim i As Integer

  sStartTime = Timer()
      For i = 1 To 100
          Console.WriteLine("Hello")
      Next i
  MsgBox("Time Taken = " & Timer() - sStartTime & " Seconds")
  ```

VB.NET/VB 6 Differences

While the Timer property returns a Double in VB.NET, the VB 6 *Timer* function returns a Single.

See Also

GetTimer Function

TimeSerial Function

Class

Microsoft.VisualBasic.DateAndTime

Syntax

```
TimeSerial(hour, minute, second)
```

hour	*required; Integer*

A number in the range 0 to 23

minute	*required; Integer*

Any valid integer

second	*required; Integer*

Any valid integer

Return Value

A Date representing the time specified by the arguments to the function

Description

Constructs a valid time given a number of hours, minutes, and seconds

Rules at a Glance

- Any of the arguments can be specified as relative values or expressions.

- The *hour* argument requires a 24-hour clock format; however, the returned time is determined by the system's regional settings.

- If any value is greater than the normal range for the time unit to which it relates, the next higher time unit is increased accordingly. For example, a second argument of 125 will be evaluated as 2 minutes, 5 seconds.

- If any value is less than zero, the next higher time unit is decreased accordingly. For example, `TimeSerial(2,-1,30)` returns 01:59:30.

Programming Tips and Gotchas

Because *TimeSerial* handles time units outside of their normal limits, it can be used for time calculations. However, because the *DateAdd* function is more flexible and is internationally aware, it should be used instead for this purpose.

See Also

TimeOfDay Property, TimeString Property, TimeValue Function

TimeString Property

Class

Microsoft.VisualBasic.DateAndTime

Syntax

```
TimeString()
```

Return Value

String representing the current system time

Description

Returns or sets the current system time

Rules at a Glance

- The TimeString property returns the time in the format determined by the system's regional settings.

- You can use any time format recognized by *IsDate* when setting the time using the TimeString property.

Programming Tips and Gotchas

- The string returned by the TimeString property also includes an invalid date, 01/01/0001. It can be eliminated with the *Format* or *FormatDateTime* function as follows:

```
Format(TimeOfDay(), "Long Time")
FormatDateTime(TimeOfDay(), DateFormat.LongTime)
```

- To get or set the current system date as a String, use the DateString property.

- To access the current system time as a Date, use the TimeOfDay property.

VB.NET/VB 6 Differences

The TimeString property is new to VB.NET.

See Also

TimeOfDay Property, TimeSerial Function, TimeValue Function

TimeValue Function

Class

Microsoft.VisualBasic.DateAndTime

Syntax

```
TimeValue(stringtime)
```

stringtime   required; String
  Any valid string representation of a time

Return Value

A Date containing the time specified by the string argument, with the date set to January 1 of the year 1

Description

Converts a string representation of a time to a Date data type

Rules at a Glance

- If *stringtime* is invalid, a runtime error is generated.

- If *stringtime* is Nothing, *TimeValue* generates an error.

- *stringtime* can be in any time format recognized by the *IsDate* function. Both 12- and 24-hour clock formats are valid.

- The Date value returned by time is formatted based on the system's regional settings.

Programming Tips and Gotchas

- A time literal can also be assigned to a Date variable by surrounding the date with hash characters (#), as the following snippet demonstrates:

```
Dim dMyTime As Date
dMyTime = #12:30:00 AM#
```

- The *CDate* function can also cast a time expression contained within a string as a Date variable, with the additional advantage of being internationally aware.

- The string returned by the TimeString property also includes an invalid date, 01/01/0001. It can be eliminated with the *Format* or *FormatDateTime* function as follows:

```
Format(TimeOfDay(), "Long Time")
FormatDateTime(TimeOfDay(), DateFormat.LongTime)
```

VB/NET/VB 6 Differences

In VB 6, *TimeValue* returns the time only. In VB.NET, the function also returns an invalid date, 01/01/0001, along with the time.

See Also

TimeOfDay Property, TimeSerial Function, TimeString Property

Today Property

Class

Microsoft.VisualBasic.DateAndTime

Syntax

```
Today()
```

Description

Sets or retrieves the current system date

Rules at a Glance

- If you are setting the system date with numbers, as opposed to spelling the month, the sequence of Day, Month, and Year must be in the same sequence as the computer's regional settings.

- If you are running Microsoft Windows 95, 98, or 2000, the earliest system date you can set is January 1, 1980; the latest system date you can set is December 31, 2099.

- The date is returned in the short date format defined by the system's regional settings.

Example

```
Today() = "January 1, 1998"
```

Programming Tips and Gotchas

- It is good programming practice to synchronize the dates across the machines in a multiuser environment, most commonly from the date on a server. This can be done at the operating-system level within the logon script or at application level using the Today property and *TimeOfDay* function.

- It is risky to take a date format for granted. Wherever possible, use the *Format* function to explicitly set the date format that you require, prior to using a date value.

- Modern Windows systems are more reliant on system date than ever before. A single machine can have literally hundreds of different applications installed, many of which will use dates in one way or another. You should respect the machine on which your application is running, and only in exceptional circumstances should you change the system date programmatically.

See Also

Now Property

Trim Function

Class

Microsoft.VisualBasic.Strings

Syntax

    Trim(str)

str   *required; String*
   Any string expression

Return Value

String

Description

Removes both leading and trailing spaces from a given string

Rules at a Glance

If string is Nothing, the *Trim* function returns Nothing.

Programming Tips and Gotchas

Trim is equivalent to calling both the *RTrim* and *LTrim* functions.

VB.NET/VB 6 Differences

In VB 6, the function's single named argument is *string*. In VB.NET, its single named argument is *str*.

See Also

LTrim Function, RTrim Function

Try...Catch...Finally Statement

Syntax

```
Try
    tryStatements
[Catch1 [exception [As type]] [When expression]
    catchStatements1
[Exit Try]

Catch2 [exception [As type]] [When expression]
    catchStatements2
[Exit Try]
. . .
Catchn [exception [As type]] [When expression]
    catchStatementsn]
[Exit Try]

[Finally
    finallyStatements]
End Try
```

exception   *optional; System.Exception or a derived type*

The exception to catch. If *exception* is omitted or if it is System.Exception, all exceptions will be caught. However, if *exception* is omitted, no information about the exception will be accessible within the Catch block.

type   *optional*

The data type of the exception to be handled by the Catch block. Its value can be System.Exception or any derived type. If omitted, its value defaults to System.Exception, and all exceptions will be handled.

expression   *optional; Boolean*

A logical expression that defines a condition under which the error is to be handled by the Catch block.

Description

Used to handle runtime errors

Rules at a Glance

- The *tryStatements*, which are required, constitute the Try block and are the statements that VB monitors for errors.

- The Catch blocks, of which there can be more than one, contain code that is executed in response to VB "catching" a particular type of error within the Try block. Thus, the Catch blocks consist of the error-handlers for the Try block.

- The phrases *exception* [As *type*] and [When *expression*] are referred to as *filters* in the VB.NET documentation. In the former case, *exception* is either a variable of type Exception, which is the base class that "catches" all exceptions, or a variable of one of Exception's derived classes. The When filter is typically used with user-defined errors. (See the upcoming example.)

- The Exit Try statement is used to break out of any portion of a Try... Catch...Finally block.

- The optional *finallyStatements* code block is executed regardless of whether an error occurs (or is caught), unless an Exit Try statement is executed.

- Multiple Catch statements can be used. However, only the first Catch statement to be true is executed. This means that multiple Catch statements should be ordered from most specific to most general, with a Catch block handling errors of type System.Exception occurring last.

Example

The code in the following Try block will raise an error if the user does not enter a number. The Catch block will catch this error.

```
Try
    Dim sInput As String
    sInput = Inputbox("Enter a number.")
    If Not IsNumeric(sInput) Then
        Err().Raise(1)
    End If
Catch When Err.Number = 1
    Msgbox("Error1")
End Try
```

Programming Tips and Gotchas

As with unstructured error handling, VB may pass an error up the call stack when using structured error handling. This happens in the following situations:

- If an error occurs within a Try block that is not handled by an existing Catch block.

- If an error occurs outside any Try block (provided, of course, that no On Error–style error handlers are active).

VB.NET/VB 6 Differences

Structured exception handling using the Try...Catch...Finally construct is new to VB.NET. It replaces unstructured error handling using the On Error statement, which continues to be supported in VB.NET.

TypeName Function

Class

Microsoft.VisualBasic.Information

Syntax

```
TypeName(varname)
```

varname   *required; String literal*
    Name of a variable

Return Value

String

Description

Returns a string giving data type information about **varname**. The possible return values are:

String returned	Variable contents
Boolean	8-bit True or False value type
Byte	8-bit binary value type
Char	16-bit character value type
Date	64-bit date and time value type
DBNull	Reference type indicating missing or nonexistent data
Decimal	96-bit fixed point numeric value type
Double	64-bit floating point numeric value type
Error	Error object
Integer	32-bit integer value type
Long	64-bit integer value type
Nothing	Object variable with no object currently assigned to it, uninitialized string, or undimensioned array
Object	Reference type pointing to an unspecialized object
Short	16-bit integer value type
Single	32-bit floating point numeric value type
String	Reference type pointing to a string of 16-bit characters
<objectclass>	Reference type pointing to a specialized object created from class <objectclass>
<structure>	A variable created from a structure or user-defined type named structure
<typename>( )	Dimensioned array

Rules at a Glance

- If **varname** is declared as type Object, it returns the data subtype that has been assigned to it.

- **varname** returns the data type name of all value types. It returns Nothing for uninitialized reference types and the data type name for all initialized reference types.

- If **varname** is an array that has been initialized or dimensioned, the returned string will be the entry in the previous table corresponding to the underlying data type of the array, but with empty parentheses appended to the end of the name. For example, if **varname** points to an array of integers, *TypeName* returns Integer( ).

- When *TypeName* returns the name of a reference type, such as a class, it only returns the simple name, not the qualified name. For example, if **varname** points to an object of class System.Drawing.Printing.PaperSource, *TypeName* returns PaperSource.

- If *varname* is of type Object, *TypeName* returns the data subtype stored to that object.

Example

```
Dim obj As Object
obj = New CEmployee()
MsgBox(TypeName(obj))        ' Displays: CEmployee
obj = 100
MsgBox(TypeName(obj))        ' Displays: Integer
obj = Nothing
MsgBox(TypeName(obj))        ' Displays: Nothing
```

Programming Tips and Gotchas

The *TypeName* function also works directly with members of the Foundation Class Library that aren't wrapped by Visual Basic. It reports the following data types:

String returned	Variable contents
UINT16	Unsigned 16-bit integer
UINT32	Unsigned 32-bit integer
UINT64	Unsigned 64-bit integer
SBYTE	Signed byte

VB.NET/VB 6 Differences

- In VB 6, the call to the *TypeName* function in the code fragment:

```
Dim strVar As String
Console.WriteLine(TypeName(strVar))
```

  returns a String. In VB.NET, the *TypeName* function in an equivalent code fragment returns Nothing. This is because in VB.NET, strings are reference types and reference types are implemented as objects.

- In VB 6, passing a user-defined type to the *TypeName* function generates a compile error. In VB.NET, it returns the name of the user-defined type or structure.

- In VB 6, passing an uninitialized array to the *TypeName* function returns the type name plus parentheses. In VB.NET, it returns Nothing.

- In VB 6, a variable whose type is not declared is reported as a Variant; in VB .NET, it is an object.

See Also

VarType Function

UBound Function

Class

Microsoft.VisualBasic.Information

Syntax

```
UBound(array[, rank])
```

array *required; Any*
    The name of the array

rank *optional; Integer*
    A number specifying the dimension of the array

Return Value

Integer

Description

Indicates the upper limit of a specified coordinate of an array. The upper boundary is the largest subscript you can use with that coordinate.

Rules at a Glance

- To determine the upper limit of the first coordinate of an array, set *rank* to 1, set it to 2 for the second coordinate, and so on.

- If *rank* is not specified, 1 is assumed.

- The function returns –1 if the array is uninitialized.

Programming Tips and Gotchas

- Note that *UBound* returns the actual subscript of the upper bound of a particular array dimension.

- The number of valid indices for the ith coordinate is equal to UBound(array, i) + 1.

- If **array** is an uninitialized array, passing it to the *UBound* function generates an ArgumentNullException exception. To prevent this, you can declare the array as follows:

```
Dim arrValues(-1) As String
```

UCase Function

Class

Microsoft.VisualBasic.Strings

Syntax

```
UCase(value)
```

value *required; String*
    A valid string expression

Return Value

String

Description

Converts a string to uppercase

Rules at a Glance

- *UCase* only affects lowercase alphabetical letters; all other characters within `value` remain unaffected.

- *UCase* returns Nothing if `value` is Nothing.

See Also

LCase Function, StrConv Function

Unlock Procedure

Class

Microsoft.VisualBasic.FileSystem

Syntax

```
Unlock(filenumber[, record)

Unlock(filenumber[, fromrecord[, torecord]])
```

`filenumber`	*required; Integer*

Any valid file number

`record`	*required; Long*

The record or byte number at which to commence the lock

`fromrecord`	*required; Long*

The first record or byte number to lock

`torecord`	*required; Long*

The last record or byte number to lock

Description

Use the *Unlock* procedure in situations where more than one part of your program may need read and write access to the same data file. The *Unlock* procedure removes a lock that the *Lock* procedure placed on a section of the file or the whole file.

Rules at a Glance

- Use the *Unlock* procedure only with the `filenumber` parameter to unlock the whole file.

- The *Unlock* procedure unlocks an entire file opened in Input or Output (sequential) mode, regardless of the `record`, `fromrecord`, or `torecord` arguments.

- Records and bytes in a file are always numbered sequentially from 1 up.

- To unlock a particular record, specify its record number as `record`, and only that record will be unlocked.

- To unlock a range of bytes (in a binary file) or of records (in a random file), indicate the starting position as `fromrecord` and the ending position as `torecord`.

Programming Tips and Gotchas

- You must take care to remove all file locks using the *Unlock* procedure before either closing a file or ending the application; otherwise, you can leave the file in an unstable state. This means that, where appropriate, your error-handling routines must be made aware of any locks you currently have in place so that they may be removed if necessary.

- You use the *Lock* and *Unlock* procedures in pairs, and the argument lists of both statements must match exactly.

VB.NET/VB 6 Differences

- In VB 6, it is possible to omit the *fromrecord* argument and provide only the *torecord* argument, in which case all records (in random mode) or bytes (in binary mode) from the beginning of the file to *torecord* would be unlocked. In VB.NET, this syntax is not allowed.

- VB 6 allows you to precede the *filenumber* argument with the # symbol. In VB.NET, this syntax is not permitted.

- When specifying starting and ending records in VB 6, you use the To keyword to separate them. In VB.NET, this syntax is not permitted, instead, you must use a comma to separate the two arguments.

See Also

Lock Procedure

Val Function

Class

Microsoft.VisualBasic.Conversion

Syntax

    Val(expression)

expression   *required; String or Char*
  Any string representation of a number

Return Value

A Double able to hold the number contained in *expression*

Description

Converts a string representation of a number into a Double

Rules at a Glance

- The *Val* function starts reading the string with the leftmost character and stops at the first character that it does not recognize as being part of a valid number. For example, the statement:

      iNumber = Val("1A1")

  returns 1.

- &O and &H (the octal and hexadecimal prefixes) are recognized by the *Val* function.

- Currency symbols, such as $ and £, and delimiters, such as commas, are not recognized as numbers by the *Val* function.

- The *Val* function only recognizes the period (.) as a decimal delimiter.

- Prior to processing *expression*, *Val* removes spaces, tabs, and line-feed characters.

Programming Tips and Gotchas

If you are developing an international application, you should use the more modern, internationally aware *CDbl* function to convert strings to numbers, since *CDbl* can recognize all decimal separators.

ValDec Function

Class

Microsoft.VisualBasic.Conversion

Syntax

```
ValDec(expression)
```

expression   *required; String or Char*
    Any string representation of a number

Return Value

A Decimal able to hold the number contained in *expression*

Description

Converts a string representation of a number into a Decimal

Rules at a Glance

- The *ValDec* function starts reading the string with the leftmost character and stops at the first character that it does not recognize as being part of a valid number. For example, the statement:

    ```
    iNumber = ValDec("1A1")
    ```

    returns 1.

- &O and &H (the octal and hexadecimal prefixes) are recognized by the *ValDec* function.

- Currency symbols, such as $ and £, and delimiters, such as commas, are not recognized as numbers by the *ValDec* function.

- The *ValDec* function only recognizes the period (.) as a decimal delimiter.

- Prior to processing *expression*, *ValDec* removes spaces, tabs, and line-feed characters.

Programming Tips and Gotchas

If you are developing an international application, you should use the *CDec* function to convert strings to numbers, since *CDec* can recognize all decimal separators.

VB.NET/VB 6 Differences

The *ValDec* function is new to VB.NET.

VarType Function

Class

Microsoft.VisualBasic.Information

Syntax

```
VarType(varname)
```

varname   *required; any*
    The name of a variable

Return Value

A member of the **Variant.Type** enumeration indicating the variable type

Description

Determines the data type of a variable

Rules at a Glance

- The possible values returned by the function include the following members of the **VariantType** enumeration:

Constant	Value	Description
Array	8192	Array
Boolean	11	Boolean data type
Byte	17	Byte data type
Char	18	Char data type
Date	7	Date data type
Decimal	14	Decimal data type
Double	5	Double data type
Integer	3	Integer data type
Long	20	Long data type
Object	9	Object, uninitialized string, uninitialized array, object of a specific type
Short	2	Short data type
Single	4	Single data type
String	8	String
UserDefined-Type	36	A structure

- If *varname* is a dimensioned array, the *VarType* function returns `VariantType.Array` (8192), plus the value of the array's data type. For example, an array of strings returns 8192 + 8 = 8200. You can test for an array with a code fragment such as the following:

    ```
    If VarType(myVar) And VariantType.Array Then
    ```

    You can extract the data type of the array with the following code fragment:

    ```
    vartype(myVar) and &HFFFFDFFF
    ```

- All object variables, whether late-bound or early-bound, return `VariantType.Object`.

- Data types that are members of the base class library but are not wrapped by VB data types (i.e., UINT16, UINT32 etc.) return `VariantType.UserDefined-Type`.

VB.NET/VB 6 Differences

- In VB 6, passing a user-defined type as an argument to the *VarType* function generated an error. VB.NET allows you to pass a structure as an argument to the function.

- In VB 6, the *Vartype* function indicates that the data type of an object is the data type of its default property. In VB.NET, all objects, including objects (like Collection objects) that have default properties, return `VariantType.Object`.

See Also

TypeName Function

VBFixedArray Attribute

Class

Microsoft.VisualBasic.VBFixedArrayAttribute

Applies to

Field

Description

Defines a fixed array. It can be used in defining fixed arrays within structures, particularly structures that are to be passed to Win32 API functions, and for defining fixed-length structures used by VB file input and output functions.

Constructor

```
New(size1[, size2])
```

size1   *required; Integer*
  The upper limit of the array's first dimension

size2   *optional; Integer*
  The upper limit of the array's second dimension

Properties

Bounds   *Array of Integer*

The upper bounds of a particular dimension of the array. The first dimension is represented by *VBFixedArrayAttribute.*Bounds(0). The upper boundary of the array can be retrieved by calling the *UBound* function.

Length   *Integer*

The total number of elements in all dimensions of the array.

VBFixedString Attribute

Class

Microsoft.VisualBasic.VBFixedStringAttribute

Applies to

Field

Description

Defines a fixed-length string. It is the rough equivalent of the VB 6 declaration:

```
Dim s As String * length
```

It can be used to define fixed-length strings within structures, particularly structures that are to be passed to Win32 API functions, as well as to define fixed length strings to be written to and read from random access files.

Constructor

```
New(length)
```

length   *Integer*

The length of the string

Properties

Length   *Integer*

Read-only. The length of the string. Its value is set by the *length* parameter in the class constructor.

Example

The example creates a random access file, which must contain fixed-length records, and uses the <VBFixedString> attribute to create a fixed-length string of 10 characters. This ensures that all records will be a uniform length. Without the <VBFixedString> attribute, the example an IOException exception because of bad record length.

```
Option Strict Off
Imports Microsoft.VisualBasic
Imports System

Module modMain

Structure Person
```

```
        <vbFixedString(10)> Public Name As String
           Public Age As Short
      End Structure

      Public Sub Main

      Dim APerson As New Person()
      Dim fr As Integer = FreeFile()

      FileOpen(fr, ".\person.txt", OpenMode.Random, OpenAccess.ReadWrite, _
               OpenShare.Default, len(aperson))

      APerson.Name = "John"
      APerson.Age = 31
      FilePut(fr, APerson, 1)

      APerson.Name = "Jane"
      APerson.Age = 27
      FilePut(fr, APerson, 2)

      FileGet(fr, APerson, 2)
      Console.WriteLine(Trim(APerson.Name) & " is " & APerson.Age)
      FileClose(fr)

      End Sub

      End Module
```

VbTypeName Function

Class

Microsoft.VisualBasic.Information

Syntax

```
      VbTypeName(urtname)
```

urtname   *required; String*
    The name of a CTS datatype

Return Value

A String containing the name of a VB.NET datatype

Description

Returns the name of the VB.NET datatype that corresponds to a particular Common Type System (CTS) datatype

Rules at a Glance

- *urtname* must be the name of a valid CTS datatype, such as Int32, UInt32, String, or DateTime.

- If *urtname* is not a valid CTS datatype, the function returns Nothing.

- If *urtname* is a valid CTS datatype that does not directly correspond to a VB. NET datatype, the function returns Nothing.

Example

```
Public Sub Main

    ' Displays Short
    Dim intNum As Int16 = 1234
    Console.WriteLine(VbTypeName(intNum.GetType().ToString))

    ' Displays ""
    Dim uintNum As UInt16 = Convert.ToUInt16(1234)
    Console.WriteLine(VbTypeName(uintNum.GetType().ToString))

    ' Displays Char
    Dim chLetter As System.Char = Convert.ToChar("a")
    Console.WriteLine(VbTypeName(chLetter.GetType().ToString))

    ' Displays ""
    Dim sbytNum As SByte = Convert.ToSByte(-3)
    Console.WriteLine(VbTypeName(sbytNum.GetType().ToString))

End Sub
```

Programming Tips and Gotchas

- To determine the VB.NET datatype of a particular variable, call the variable's GetType method to retrieve a Type object, then call the Type object's ToString method to retrieve its datatype name. This string can then be passed to the *VbTypeName* function. For example:

    ```
    strType = VbTypeName(myVar.GetType().ToString)
    ```

- If passed the name of a structure defined with the **Structure** construct or an instance of a class defined with the **Class** construct, the *VbTypeName* function returns Nothing.

- The existence of the *VbTypeName* function clearly indicates that VB.NET datatypes are wrappers for some CTS datatypes.

VB.NET/VB 6 Differences

The VbTypeName function is new to VB.NET.

See Also

SystemTypeName Function, TypeName Function

WebMethod Attribute

Class

System.Web.Services.WebMethodAttribute

Applies to

Method

Description

Marks a method within a web service as a web method callable from a web client. The method and the class to which it belongs must be public and must be part of an ASP.NET application.

Constructors

```
New([[[[enableSession], transactionOption], cacheDuration],
bufferResponse])
```

enableSession   *Boolean*
    Indicates whether session state is enabled for the web method call.

transactionOption   *System.EnterpriseServices.TransactionOption enumeration*
    Indicates whether the web method supports transactions. Possible values are **Disabled**, **NotSupported**, **Supported**, **Required**, and **RequiresNew**.

cacheDuration   *Integer*
    Indicates the number of seconds the response to the web method request should be stored in the cache.

bufferResponse   *Boolean*
    Indicates whether the response to the web method request is buffered.

Properties

BufferResponse   *Boolean*
    Indicates whether the response to the web method request is buffered. Its default value is **True**.

CacheDuration   *Integer*
    Defines the number of seconds the server caches the response to the web method request. Its default value is 0; responses to web methods are not cached.

Description   *String*
    Provides a description for the web service that is displayed in the service description and web service help page. Its default value is an empty string.

EnableSession   *Boolean*
    Read-only. Indicates whether session state is enabled for the web method call. Its default value is **False**.

MessageName   *String*
    Identifies the public name by which the web method is invoked by clients. Since web methods do not support overloading, the property provides a method for identifying overloaded methods that share the same name. Its default value is the name of the web method

TransactionOption   *System.EnterpriseServices.TransactionOption enumeration*
    Read-only. Indicates whether the web method supports transactions. Possible values are **Disabled**, **NotSupported**, **Supported**, **Required**, and

RequiresNew. A web method must participate as the root object of a transaction. Because of this, `Supported` and `NotSupported` are both equivalent to `NotSupported`, and `Required` and `RequiresNew` are both equivalent to RequiresNew. Its default value is `Disabled`.

WebService Attribute

Class

System.Web.Services.WebServiceAttribute

Applies To

Class

Description

An optional element of a web service definition (the ASP.NET @ `Webservice` directive is required), the `<WebService>` attribute can be used to assign the web service a namespace and description.

Constructor

```
New()
```

Properties

Description   *String*

A textual description of the web service. The description is displayed in the Service Description page and the Service help page.

Name   *String*

The name to be assigned to the web service. Ordinarily, the web service name corresponds to the name of the class However, the Name property of the `<WebService>` attribute is used instead of the class name as the name of the web service.

Namespace   *String*

The web service's namespace. During development, the namespace *http://tempuri.org/* is used by default. However, a unique namespace should be assigned to any production web service. Although the namespace for a web service resembles a URL, it need not point to any valid Internet resource.

Example

The example uses an .asmx file with the following contents:

```
<%@ WebService Language="VB" Class="HelloWebService" Codebehind="Hello.
asmx.vb" %>
```

It has the following codebehind file:

```
Option Strict

Imports System.Web.Services

<WebService(Name:="Hello", _
```

```
          Description:="Displays a friendly greeting to the user.", _
          Namespace:="http://www.oreilly.com/VbNet")> _
Public Class HelloWebService

<WebMethod()> Public Function SayHello(Name As String) As String
    Return "Hello, " & Name
End Function

End Class
```

See Also

WebMethod Attribute

Weekday Function

Class

Microsoft.VisualBasic.DateAndTime

Syntax

```
Weekday(datevalue, [dayofweek])
```

date   *required; Date or valid date expression*
  Any valid date expression

dayofweek   *optional; Constant of* FirstDayOfWeek *enumeration*
  A constant indicating the first day of the week

Return Value

Integer

Description

Determines the day of the week of a given date

Rules at a Glance

*   The default for *dayofweek* is FirstDayOfWeek.Sunday.

*   To determine the day of the week, think of the day specified by *dayofweek*
    as day 1, and the value returned by the function as indicating the day relative
    to day 1. Then, for example, if the return value of *WeekDay* is 2, this speci-
    fies the day following *dayofweek*. A return value of 1 specifies *dayofweek*. A
    return value of 7 specifies the day before *dayofweek*.

*   The members of the FirstDayOfWeek enumeration are:

Constant	Value	Description
Sunday	1	Sunday
Monday	2	Monday
Tuesday	3	Tuesday
Wednesday	3	Wednesday

Constant	Value	Description
Thursday	4	Thursday
Friday	5	Friday
Saturday	6	Saturday
Sunday	7	Sunday

- Passing a value of 0 as the *dayofweek* argument uses the system's locale settings to determine the first day of the week.

Example

Since the code:

```
Weekday(#3/26/2001#, FirstDayOfWeek.Sunday)
```

returns 2, the date 3/26/2001 is a Monday.

Programming Tips and Gotchas

If passing a date literal as *datevalue*, the *Weekday* function requires that all four digits of the year be present.

VB.NET/VB 6 Differences

The names of the named parameters of the function have changed from *date* and *firstdayofweek* in VB 6 to *datevalue* and *dayofweek* in VB.NET.

See Also

DatePart Function, Day Function, WeekdayName Function

WeekdayName Function

Class

Microsoft.VisualBasic.DateAndTime

Syntax

```
WeekdayName(Weekday, [abbreviate [, FirstDayOfWeekValue]])
```

Weekday   *required; Long*
    The ordinal number of the required weekday, from 1 to 7

abbreviate   *optional; Boolean*
    Specifies whether to return the full day name or an abbreviation

FirstDayOfWeekValue   *optional;* FirstDayOfWeek *constant*
    Member of the FirstDayOfWeek enum indicating the first day of the week

Return Value

A String

Description

Returns the name of the day

Rules at a Glance

- *Weekday* must be a number between 1 and 7, or the function generates an ArgumentException error.

- The default value of *abbreviate* is `False`.

- For a list of the members of the FirstDayOfWeek enumeration, see the "Weekday Function" entry.

- The default value of *FirstDayOfWeekValue* is FirstDayOfWeek.Monday.

Programming Tips and Gotchas

- Since *Weekday* is an integer, to determine the name of the day of a particular date, combine *WeekDayName* with a call to the *WeekDay* function, as the following code fragment shows:

```
sDay = WeekDayName(Weekday(dDate, iFirstDay), _
                bFullName, iFirstDay)
```

Note that the value of the *FirstDayOfWeek* argument must be the same in the calls to both functions for *WeekdayName* to return an accurate result.

- Unlike the *Weekday* function, the *WeekdayName* function behaves predictably. For example, if you ask for the name of the first day of the week when the week starts on Monday, the function returns `Mon` or `Monday`. If you ask for the fifth day of the week for a week that starts on Sunday, the function returns `Thu` or `Thursday`.

See Also

Weekday Function

While...End While Statement

Syntax

```
While condition
    [statements]
[Exit While]
    [statements]
End While
```

condition   *required; Numeric or String*
  An expression evaluating to `True` or `False`

statements   *optional*
  Program statements to execute while condition remains `True`

Exit While   *optional; Keyword*
  Exits the While loop

Description

Repeatedly executes program code while a given condition remains `True`

Rules at a Glance

- A Null condition is evaluated as False.

- If *condition* evaluates to True, the program code between the While and End While statements is executed. After the End While statement is executed, control is passed back up to the While statement where *condition* is evaluated again. When *condition* evaluates to False, program execution skips to the first statement following the End While statement.

- You can nest While...End While loops within each other.

Programming Tips and Gotchas

The While...End While statement remains in Visual Basic for backward compatibility only. In our opinion, it has been superceded by the much more flexible Do...Loop statement.

VB.NET/VB 6 Differences

In VB 6, the ending statement that accompanies the While construct is Wend; in VB.NET, it is End While.

See Also

Do...Loop Statement

With Statement

Syntax

```
With object
    [statements]
End With
```

object   *required; Object*
    A previously declared object variable or user-defined type

statements   *optional*
    Program code to execute against *object*

Description

This statement is used to execute a series of statements on an object without having to qualify each statement with the object name.

Rules at a Glance

- The single object referred to in the With statement remains the same throughout the code contained within the With...End With block. Therefore, only properties and methods of *object* can be used within the code block without explicitly referencing the object. All other object references within the With...End With statement must start with a fully qualified object reference.

- With statements can be nested, as long as the inner With statement refers to a subobject or a dependent object of the outer With statement.

- A member of *object* is referenced within a With block by omitting the object name and simply including a period and the member name.

Example

```
Public Structure Point
Dim x As Integer
 Dim y As Integer
End Structure

Public Sub Main
Dim udtPt As POINT
With udtPt
.x = 10
 .y = 100
End With
Console.Writeline(udtpt.x)
End Sub
```

Programming Tips and Gotchas

It is important that you do not include code within the With statement block that forces execution to branch out of the block. Similarly, do not write code that forces program flow to jump into a With block. Both the With and its associated End With statement must be executed, or you will generate unpredictable results.

WithEvents Keyword

Syntax

```
Dim|Private|Public WithEvents objVarName As objectType
```

objVarName   *required; String*
The name of any object variable that refers to an object that exposes events

objectType   *required; any object type other than the generic Object*
The ProgID of a referenced object

Description

The WithEvents keyword informs VB that the object being referenced exposes events for which you intend to provide event handlers.

When you declare an object variable using WithEvents, an entry for the object variable is placed in the code window's drop-down Object List, and a list of the events available to the object variable is placed in the code window's drop-down Procedures List. You can then write code event handlers for the object variable.

Rules at a Glance

- An object-variable declaration using the WithEvents keyword can only be used in an object or class module.

- An object-variable declaration using the WithEvents keyword should only be placed in the Declarations section of the object module.

- Any ActiveX object or class module that exposes events can be used with the WithEvents keyword. WithEvents is only valid when used to declare an object variable.

- You cannot use WithEvents when declaring a generic Object type

- Unlike other variable declarations, the As keyword is mandatory.

- There is no limit to the number of object variables that can refer to the same object using the WithEvents keyword; they will all respond to that object's events.

- You cannot create an array variable that uses the WithEvents keyword.

- You cannot use the WithEvents keyword in a local variable declaration.

- If *objectType* does not expose any events, the WithEvents statement generates a compiler error.

Example

The following example demonstrates how to trap and respond to the events within an ADO recordset. An object variable is declared using the WithEvents keyword in the declarations section of a form module. This allows you to write event-handling code for the ADO's built-in events, in this case the FetchProgress event. (The FetchProgress event allows you to implement a Progress Bar control that shows progress in populating the recordset.)

```
Private WithEvents oADo As ADODB.Recordset

Private Sub oADo_FetchProgress(ByVal Progress As Long, _
                 ByVal MaxProgress As Long, _
                 adStatus As ADODB.EventStatusEnum, _
                 ByVal pRecordset As ADODB.Recordset) _
        Handles oADO.FetchProgress

    ProgressBar1.Max = MaxProgress
    ProgressBar1.Value = Progress

End Sub
```

Programming Tips and Gotchas

- Placing the object-variable declaration that uses the WithEvents keyword in a procedure does not add the object variable name to the module's Object List. In other words, the events fired from the object would only have scope in the procedure and therefore cannot be handled.

- Even if you declare the object variable using the Public keyword, the events fired by the object only have scope in the module in which the object variable has been declared.

- Because you cannot use WithEvents to declare a generic Object type, WithEvents can only be used with early-bound object references. In other words, objects must have been added to the project using the References dialog box. Without this prior knowledge of the object's interface, VB has no chance of knowing how to handle events from the object.

- If the object you are referencing doesn't expose any public events, you will generate a compile-time error, "This object does not raise Events."

In VB 6, object variables in a code module couldn't be declared with WithEvents. In VB.NET, this restriction has been lifted.

See Also

Dim Statement, Public Statement

Write Procedure

Class

Microsoft.VisualBasic.FileSystem

Named Arguments

No

Syntax

```
Write(filenumber, output)
```

filenumber   *required; Integer*
    Any valid file number

output   *required; Object (Any)*
    A comma-delimited list of expressions or a ParamArray to be written to the file

Description

Writes data to a sequential file

Rules at a Glance

- *output* can contain multiple expressions delimited with either a comma, a semicolon, or a space.

- *output* can also be an Object array containing values to be written to the file indicated by *filenumber*.

- The following table describes how the Write procedure handles certain types of data, regardless of the locale, to allow files to be read universally:

Data type	Data written to file
Numeric	Decimal separator is always a period (.)
Boolean	#TRUE# or #FALSE#
Date	#yyyy-mm-dd hh:mm:ss# (hours specified in 24-hour format)
Null	#NULL#
Error	#ERROR errorcode#

- The *Write* procedure automatically does the following:
  - Delimits data fields with a comma
  - Places quotation marks around string data

Programming Tips and Gotchas

The structured data written to a file using the *Write* procedure is most suited to being read back from the file using the Input procedure.

VB.NET/VB 6 Differences

- The VB 6 Write statement requires that *output* be a comma-delimited list of literal values or variables. The VB.NET WriteLine procedure also allows *outputlist* to be a parameter array.

- Calling the VB 6 Write statement with a single comma in place of *outputlist* forces a blank line to be written to the file. VB.NET requires that you call the WriteLine procedure.

- The VB 6 Write statement allowed a # symbol to precede the *filenumber* argument. In the VB.NET Write procedure, this usage is not permitted.

See Also

WriteLine Procedure

WriteLine Procedure

Class

Microsoft.VisualBasic.FileSystem

Named Arguments

No

Syntax

```
WriteLine(filenumber, [output])
```

filenumber   *required; Integer*
Any valid file number

output   *optional; Object (Any)*
A comma-delimited list of expressions or a ParamArray to be written to the file

Description

Writes data to a sequential file and then adds a line-feed character combination

Rules at a Glance

- *output* can contain multiple expressions delimited with either a comma, a semicolon, or a space.

- *output* can also be an Object array containing values to be written to the file indicated by *filenumber*.

- The following table describes how the *WriteLine* procedure handles certain types of data, regardless of the locale, to allow files to be read universally.

Data type	Data written to file
Numeric	Decimal separator is always a period (.)
Boolean	#TRUE# or #FALSE#
Date	#yyyy-mm-dd hh:mm:ss# (hours specified in 24-hour format)
Null	#NULL#
Error	#ERROR errorcode#

- The *WriteLine* procedure automatically does the following:
  - Delimits data fields with a comma
  - Places quotation marks around string data
  - Inserts a new-line character (Chr(13) + Chr(10)) after the last item in *output* is written to the file
- If the *output* argument is omitted, *WriteLine* writes a blank line to the file designated by *filenumber*.

Programming Tips and Gotchas

The structured data written to a file using the *WriteLine* procedure is most suited to being read back from the file using the *Input* procedure.

VB.NET/VB 6 Differences

The *WriteLine* procedure is new to VB.NET as a partial replacement for the VB 6 *Write* procedure.

See Also

Write Procedure

Year Function

Class

Microsoft.VisualBasic.DateAndTime

Syntax

Year(*datevalue*)

datevalue   *required; Date or valid date expression*
    Any valid date expression

Return Value

Integer

Description

Returns an integer representing the year in a given date expression

Rules at a Glance

- If *datevalue* contains Nothing, *Year* returns 1. (This assumes that Option Strict is off.) For example:

```
Dim oDat As Object
Console.Writeline(Year(sDat))       ' Displays 1
```

- If *datevalue* is a date literal (a date delimited with the # symbol), the year must contain four digits.

Programming Tips and Gotchas

- The validity of the date expression—and the position of the year element within the given date expression—is initially determined by the locale settings of the Windows system. However, some extra intelligence relating to two-digit year values (see the next item in this list) has been built into the *Year* function, which surpasses the usual comparison of a date expression to the current locale settings.

- What happens when you pass a date over to the *Year* function containing a two-digit year? Quite simply, when the *Year* function sees a two-digit year, it assumes that all values equal to or greater than 30 are in the 20th century (i.e., 30 = 1930, 98 = 1998) and that all values less than 30 are in the 21st century (i.e., 29 = 2029, 5 = 2005). Of course, it is much better programming practice to use—and require your clients to use—four-digit years.

See Also

DatePart Function

PART III

Appendixes

Part III contains six appendixes that supplement the core reference material provided in Part II. These include:

- Appendix A, *What's New and Different in VB.NET*, which surveys the extensive changes the language has undergone with the release of the .NET platform.

- Appendix B, *Language Elements by Category*, which lists each language element from Part II in several different categories. You can use it to identify a particular language element so that you can then look up its detailed entry in Part II.

- Appendix C, *Operators*, which lists VB.NET operators, including a somewhat more detailed treatment of logical and bitwise operators.

- Appendix D, *Constants and Enumerations*, which lists VB.NET intrinsic constants, as well as VB.NET enumerations and their members.

- Appendix E, *The VB.NET Command-Line Compiler*, which documents the operation of the Visual Basic command-line compiler.

- Appendix F, *VB 6 Language Elements Not Supported by VB.NET*, which lists the elements that have dropped out of the Visual Basic language as a result of its transition to the .NET Framework.

APPENDIX A

What's New and Different in VB.NET

This appendix is for readers who are familiar with earlier versions of Visual Basic, specifically Version 6. In this appendix, we describe the basic changes to the VB language, both in syntax and in functionality. (Readers familiar only with Version 5 of Visual Basic will also benefit from this chapter, although we discuss only the changes since Version 6.)

We also touch upon other changes to VB, such as error handling and additional object-oriented programming support.

Language Changes for VB.NET

In this section, we outline the changes made to the Visual Basic language from Version 6 to Visual Basic .NET. These language changes were made to bring VB under the umbrella of the .NET Framework and allow a Common Language Runtime for all languages in Visual Studio .NET. In some sense, the changes made to the VB language were to bring the language component of VB (as opposed to the IDE component) more in line with the C# language (which is a derivative of C and C++).

Since we assume in this chapter that you are familiar with VB 6, we will not necessarily discuss how VB 6 handles a given language feature, unless the contrast is specifically helpful. You can assume that if a VB.NET language feature is described in this chapter, there has been a change in its behavior since VB 6.

Data Types

There have been fundamental changes to data types in VB.NET, which we outline in this section. The most important change is that all of the languages under the . NET umbrella (VB, C#, and Managed C++) now implement a subset of a *common set* of data types, defined in the .NET Framework's Base Class Library (BCL). We say *subset* because VB.NET does not implement all of these data types. In any case, each data type in the BCL is implemented either as a class or as a structure (which is similar to a class) and, as such, has members. The VB.NET data types are wrappers for the corresponding BCL data type. While this need not concern the VB programmer, it can be used in some cases to expose a bit more functionality from a data type. For more on data types, see Chapter 3.

Now let us consider the specifics.

Strings

As you may know, in VB 6, strings were implemented as a data type known as the BSTR. A BSTR is a pointer to a character array that is preceded by a 4-byte Long specifying the length of the array. In VB.NET, strings are implemented as objects of the String class, which is part of the .NET Framework's System namespace.

One consequence of this reimplementation of strings is that VB.NET does not have fixed-length strings, as does VB 6. Thus, the following code is illegal:

```
Dim Name As String * 30
```

Note, though, that strings in VB.NET are immutable. That is, although you do not have to declare a string's length in advance, once a value is assigned to a string, its length cannot change. If you change that string, the .NET Common Language Runtime actually gives you a reference to a new String object. (For more on this, see Chapter 3.)

Integer/Long data type changes

VB.NET defines the following signed-integer data types:

Short
> The 16-bit integer data type. It is the same as the Int16 data type in the Base Class Library.

Integer
> The 32-bit integer data type. It is the same as the Int32 data type in the Base Class Library.

Long
> The 64-bit integer data type. It is the same as the Int64 data type in the Base Class Library.

Thus, with respect to the changes from VB 6 to VB.NET, we can say:

- The VB 6 Integer data type has become the VB.NET Short data type.

- The VB 6 Long data type has become the VB.NET Integer data type.

Variant data type

VB.NET does not support the Variant data type. The Object data type is VB.NET's *universal data type*, meaning that it can hold data of any other data type. According to the documentation, all of the functionality of the Variant data type is supplied by the Object data type.

We cannot resist the temptation to add that there are several penalties associated with using a universal data type, including poor performance and poor program readability. Thus, while VB.NET still provides this opportunity through the Object data type, its use is not recommended whenever it can be avoided.

The *VarType* function, which was used in VB 6 to determine the type of data stored in a variant variable (that is, the variant's data *subtype*), now reports the data subtype of the Object type instead. In addition, the *TypeName* function, which can be used to return a string that indicates the data type of a variable of type Object, is still supported.

Other data type changes

Here are some additional changes in data types:

- The `Deftype` statements (`DefBool`, `DefByte`, etc.), which were used to define the default data type for variables whose names began with particular letters of the alphabet, are not supported in VB.NET.

- The Currency data type is not supported in VB.NET. However, in VB.NET, the Decimal data type can handle more digits on both sides of the decimal point, and so it's a superior replacement. In VB.NET, Decimal is a strong data type; in VB 6, it was a Variant subtype, and a variable could be cast as a Decimal only by calling the *CDec* conversion function.

- In VB 6, a date is stored in a Double format using four bytes. In VB.NET, the Date data type is an 8-byte integer data type whose range of values is from January 1, 1 to December 31, 9999.

Variables and Their Declaration

The changes in variable declarations and related issues are described here.

Variable declaration

The syntax used to declare variables has changed for VB.NET, making it more flexible. Indeed, these are long awaited changes.

In VB.NET, when multiple variables are declared on the same line, if a variable is not declared with a type explicitly, then its type is that of the next variable with an explicit type declaration. Thus, in the line:

```
Dim x As Long, i, j, k As Integer, s As String
```

the variables i, j, and k have type Integer. (In VB 6, the variables i and j would have type Variant, and only the variable k would have type Integer.)

When declaring external procedures using the `Declare` statement, VB.NET does not support the `As Any` type declaration. All parameters must have a specific type declaration.

Variable initialization

VB.NET permits the initialization of variables in the same line as their declaration (at long last). Thus, we may write:

```
Dim x As Integer = 5
```

to declare an Integer variable and initialize its value to 5. Similarly, we can declare and initialize more than one variable on a single line:

```
Dim x As Integer = 6, y As Integer = 9
```

Variable scope changes

In VB 6, a variable that is declared *anywhere* in a procedure has *procedure scope*; that is, the variable is visible to all code in the procedure.

In VB.NET, if a variable is defined inside a *code block* (a set of statements that is terminated by an **End...**, **Loop**, or **Next** statement), then the variable has *block-level scope*; that is, it is visible only within that block.

For example, consider the following VB.NET code:

```
Sub Test()
    If x <> 0 Then
        Dim rec As Integer
        rec = 1/x
    End If

    MsgBox CStr(rec)
End Sub
```

In this code, the variable *rec* is not recognized outside the block in which it is defined, so the final statement will produce an error.

It is important to note that the *lifetime* of a local variable is always that of the entire procedure, even if the variable's scope is block-level. This implies that if a block is entered more than once, a block-level variable will retain its value from the previous time the code block was executed.

Arrays and array declarations

VB 6 permitted you to define the lower bound of a specific array, as well as the default lower bound of arrays whose lower bound was not explicitly specified. In VB.NET, the lower bound of every array dimension is 0 and cannot be changed. The following examples show how to declare a one-dimensional array, with or without an explicit size and with or without initialization:

```
' Implicit constructor: No initial size and no initialization
Dim Days() As Integer

' Explicit constructor: No initial size and no initialization
Dim Days() As Integer = New Integer() {}

' Implicit constructor: Initial size but no initialization
Dim Days(6) As Integer

' Explicit constructor: Initial size but no initialization
Dim Days() As Integer = New Integer(6) {}

' Implicit constructor: Initial size implied by initialization
Dim Days() As Integer = {1, 2, 3, 4, 5, 6, 7}
```

```
' Explicit constructor, Initial size and initialization
Dim Days() As Integer = New Integer(6) {1, 2, 3, 4, 5, 6, 7}
```

Note that in the declaration:

```
Dim ArrayName(X) As ArrayType
```

the number X is the upper bound of the array. Thus, the array has size X+1.

Multidimensional arrays are declared similarly. For instance, the following example declares and initializes a two-dimensional array:

```
Dim X(,) As Integer = {{1, 2, 3}, {4, 5, 6}}
```

and the following code displays the contents of the array:

```
Debug.Write(X(0, 0))
Debug.Write(X(0, 1))
Debug.Writeline(X(0, 2))
Debug.Write(X(1, 0))
Debug.Write(X(1, 1))
Debug.Write(X(1, 2))

123
456
```

In VB.NET, all arrays are dynamic; there is no such thing as a fixed-size array. The declared size should be thought of simply as the initial size of the array, which is subject to change using the ReDim statement. Note, however, that the number of dimensions of an array cannot be changed.

Moreover, unlike VB 6, the ReDim statement cannot be used for array declaration, but only for array resizing. All arrays must be declared initially using a Dim (or equivalent) statement.

Structure/user-defined type declarations

In VB 6, a structure or user-defined type is declared using the Type...End Type structure.

In VB.NET, the Type statement isn't supported. Structures are declared using the Structure...End Structure construct. Also, each member of the structure must be assigned an access modifier, which can be Public, Protected, Friend, Protected Friend, or Private. (The Dim keyword is equivalent to Public in this context.)

For instance, the VB 6 user-defined type:

```
Type RECT
    Left As Long
    Top As Long
    Right As Long
    Bottom As Long
End Type
```

is defined in VB.NET as:

```
Structure RECT
    Public Left As Long
```

```
      Public Top As Long
      Public Right As Long
      Public Bottom As Long
   End Structure
```

Actually, the VB.NET Structure type is far more reaching than its VB 6 user-defined type predecessor. Indeed, structures have many properties in common with classes; for instance, structures can have members (properties and methods). We discuss structures in detail in Chapter 3.

Boolean and Bitwise Operators

Eqv and Imp, two infrequently used Boolean and bitwise operators that are present in VB 6, have been removed from VB.NET.

In VB 6, Eqv is the logical equivalence operator. As a Boolean operator, it returns True if both expressions are either True or False, but it returns False if one is True while the other is False. As a bitwise operator, it returns 1 if both bits are the same (that is, if both are 1 or both are 0), but it returns 0 if they are different. In VB.NET, Eqv can be replaced with the equals comparison operator for logical operations. However, for bitwise operations, you'll have to resort to a bit-by-bit comparison, as the following code fragment shows:

```
Public Function BitwiseEqv(x1 As Byte, X2 As Byte) _
                      As Long

Dim b1, b2, bRet As Byte
Dim iCtr as Integer

For iCtr = 0 to len(x1) * 8 - 1
    b1 = x1 and 2^iCtr
    b2 = x2 and 2^iCtr
    if b1 = b2 then bRet += 2^iCtr
next

BitwiseEqv = bRet

End Function
```

In VB 6, Imp is the logical implication operator. As a Boolean operator, it returns True unless its first expression is True while the second is False. As a bitwise operator, it returns 1 unless the bit in the first expression is 1 while the bit in the second expression is 0. In VB.NET, Imp can be replaced with a combination of the Not and Or operators for logical operations. For example, the code fragment:

```
bResult = (Not bFlag1) Or bFlag2
```

is equivalent to the VB 6 statement:

```
bResult = bFlag1 Imp bFlag2
```

For bitwise operations, a bit-by-bit comparison is again necessary, as the following code fragment shows:

```
Public Function BitwiseImp(x1 As Byte, X2 As Byte) As Long
```

```
Dim b1, b2, bRet As Byte
Dim iCtr as Integer

For iCtr = 0 to len(x1)*8 - 1
    b1 = Not(x1) and 2^iCtr
    b2 = x2 and 2^iCtr
    if b1 Or b2 then
        bRet += 2^iCtr
    end If
next

BitwiseImp = bRet

End Function
```

Unlike previous versions of Visual Basic, most programming languages use *short-circuiting* when evaluating `If` statements. That is, if an `If` statement contains multiple subexpressions joined by Boolean operators, expressions are evaluated from left to right, and once the truth or falsity of the expression is known, the remaining subexpressions are not evaluated. This applies in particular to subexpressions joined by a logical And (the expression is necessarily `False` if the first subexpression is `False`) and by a logical Or (the expression is necessarily `True` if the first subexpression is `True`).

VB.NET now supports short circuiting through the use of the `AndAlso` and `OrElse` logical operators. If these operators are used, once the value of an expression is known, any further subexpressions will not be evaluated. For example, consider the statement:

```
If (X AndAlso Y) Then
```

If X is `False`, then Y is not evaluated because the entire statement is `False` regardless of the truth value of Y.

VB.NET has introduced new operators to support short circuiting, rather than simply modify the behavior of `And` and `Or`, largely for reasons of compatibility. In most cases, short circuiting has no effect on a program's execution other than an improvement in performance and an increase in robustness (expressions that are not evaluated cannot raise errors). This isn't the case, however, if an expression calls a function that modifies the value of a variable. For example:

```
If Increment(x) AndAlso Increment(y) Then
    ' Do something
End If
...

Private Function Increment(ByRef n As Integer) As Boolean
    If n <> 10 Then
        n += 1
        Return True
    Else
        Return False
    End If
End Function
```

Here, we can never be certain whether the second call to the *Increment* function will occur and whether the value of *y* will be incremented. In this case, it's preferable to avoid short-circuiting with `AndAlso` in favor of the `And` operator.

Changes Related to Procedures

VB.NET features a number of changes to the way in which procedures are defined and called, most of which tend to make the language more streamlined and consistent.

Calling a procedure

In VB 6, parentheses are required around arguments when making function calls. When calling a subroutine, parentheses are required when using the `Call` statement and proscribed when not using the `Call` statement.

In VB.NET, parentheses are always required around a *nonempty* argument list in any procedure call—function or subroutine. (In subroutine calls, the `Call` statement is optional.) When calling a parameterless procedure, empty parentheses are optional.

Default method of passing arguments

In VB 6, if the parameters to a function or subroutine were not explicitly prefaced with the ByVal or ByRef keywords, arguments were passed to that routine by reference, and modifications made to the argument in the function or subroutine were reflected in the variable's value once control returned to the calling routine. In VB.NET, on the other hand, if the ByRef or ByVal keyword is not used in a parameter, the argument is passed to the routine by value, and modifications made to the argument in the function or subroutine are discarded once control returns to the calling program.

Optional arguments

In VB 6, a procedure parameter can be declared as `Optional` without specifying a default value. For optional Variant parameters, the *IsMissing* function can be used to determine whether the parameter is present.

In VB.NET, an optional parameter must declare a default value, which is passed to the procedure if the calling program does not supply an argument for that parameter. The *IsMissing* function is not supported. The following example shows an optional parameter declaration:

```
Sub Calculate(Optional ByVal Switch As Boolean = False)
```

Return statement

In VB.NET, the `Return` statement is used to return control to the calling program from a function or subroutine. The `GoSub` statement is not supported. Note that the `Return` statement is used to return a value from a function.

The following function illustrates the `Return` statement:

```
Public Function Test() As Integer
    If MsgBox("Return", MsgBoxStyle.YesNo) = MsgBoxResult.Yes Then
```

```
        Return 0
    Else
        MsgBox("Continue")
        Return 1
    End If
End Function
```

Passing property parameters in procedures

Consider passing a property to a procedure by reference, as in:

```
Sub ShrinkByHalf(ByRef lSize As Long)
    lSize = CLng(lSize/2)
End Sub


Call ShrinkByHalf(Text1.Height)
```

In VB 6, when passing the value of a property by reference, the property is *not* updated. In other words, passing a property by reference is equivalent to passing it by value. Hence, in the previous example, the property Text1.Height will not be changed.

In VB.NET, passing a property by reference does update the property, so in this case, the Text1.Height property will be changed. Note, however, that the value of the property is not changed immediately, but rather when the called procedure returns.

ParamArray parameters

In VB 6, if the `ParamArray` keyword is used on the last parameter of a procedure declaration, the parameter can accept an array of Variant parameters. In addition, `ParamAarray` parameters are always passed by reference.

In VB.NET, `ParamArray` parameters are always passed by value, and the parameters in the array may be of any data type.

Miscellaneous Language Changes

VB.NET includes several miscellaneous changes that include the format of line numbers, the lack of support for the `GoTo` and `GoSub` statements, and the replacement of the `Wend` keyword by `End While`.

Line numbers

Visual Basic .NET requires that every line number be followed immediately by a colon (:). A statement can optionally follow the colon. In VB 6, line labels, which were used in particular for error handling by the `On Error GoTo` statement, had to be followed immediately by a colon, but line numbers did not.

On GoTo

The `On...GoSub` and `On...GoTo` constructs are not supported. However, VB.NET still supports the `On Error GoTo` statement.

While

The `While...Wend` construction loops through code while a specified condition is `True`. VB.NET retains that construction, but replaces the `Wend` keyword with the `End While` statement. The `Wend` keyword is not supported.

GoSub and Return statements

In VB.NET, the `GoSub` statement is not supported.

As remarked earlier, in VB.NET, the `Return` statement is used to return control to the *calling program* from a function or subroutine. The VB 6 `Exit Sub` and `Exit Function` statements continue to be supported in VB.NET; however, the advantage of the `Return` statement is that it allows you to specify the function's return value as an argument to the `Return` statement.

Changes to Programming Elements

VB.NET has removed support for several programming elements because the underlying .NET Framework Class Library and the Common Language Runtime (CLR) contain equivalent functionality. Here are the victims and their replacements. (We discuss the class library and CLR in Chapters 4 and 5.)

Constants

The Microsoft.VisualBasic.Constants class in the Base Class Library defines a number of constants, such as the familiar `vbCrLf` constant, so these can be used as always. However, some constants, such as the color constants `vbRed` and `vbBlue`, are no longer directly supported. Indeed, the color constants are part of the System.Drawing namespace's `Color` structure, so they are accessed as follows:

```
Me.BackColor = System.Drawing.Color.BlanchedAlmond
```

In most cases, to access a particular constant that is not a field in the Microsoft. VisualBasic.Constants class, you must designate the enumeration (or structure) to which it belongs, along with the constant name. For example, the `vbYes` constant in VB 6 continues to exist as an intrinsic constant in VB.NET. However, it has a counterpart in the `MsgBoxResult` enumeration, which can be accessed as follows:

```
If MsgBoxResult.Yes = MsgBox("OK to proceed?", ...
```

For a list of all built-in constants and enums, see Appendix D.

String Functions

The *String* function has been removed from the language. In its place, we simply declare a string and initialize it, using syntax such as:

```
Dim str As New String("A"c, 5)
```

which will define a string containing five `A`s. Note the use of the modifier `c` in `"A"c` to define a character (data type Char), as opposed to a String of length 1. This is discussed in more detail in Chapter 2.

Emptiness

In VB 6, the `Empty` keyword indicates an uninitialized variable, and the `Null` keyword is used to indicate that a variable contains no valid data. VB.NET does not support either keyword, but uses the `Nothing` keyword in both of these cases.

According to the documentation: "`Null` is still a reserved word in Visual Basic .NET 7.0, even though it has no syntactical use. This helps avoid confusion with its former meanings." Whatever.

In addition, the *IsEmpty* function is not supported in VB.NET.

Graphical Functionality

The System.Drawing namespace contains classes that implement graphical methods. For instance, the Graphics class contains methods such as DrawEllipse and DrawLine. As a result, the VB 6 Circle and Line methods have been dropped.

Note that the VB 6 PSet and Scale methods are no longer supported and that there are no direct equivalents in the System.Drawing namespace.

Mathematical Functionality

Mathematical functions are implemented as members of the Math class of the System namespace. Thus, the VB 6 math functions, such as the trigonometric functions, have been dropped. Instead, we can use statements such as:

```
Math.Cos(1)
```

Note also that the *Round* function has been replaced by the Round method of the System.Math class.

Diagnostics

The System.Diagonstics namespace provides classes related to programming diagnostics. Most notably, the VB 6 Debug object is gone, but its functionality is implemented in the System.Diagnostics.Debug class, which has methods such as Write, WriteLine (replacing Print), WriteIf, and WriteLineIf.

Miscellaneous

Here are a few additional changes to consider:

- The VB 6 *DoEvents* function has been replaced by the DoEvents method of the Application class of the System.Windows.Forms namespace.

- The VB 6 *IsNull* and *IsObject* functions have been replaced by the IsDBNull and IsReference methods of the Information class of the Microsoft.VisualBasic namespace. Since this namespace is implicitly loaded by VB as part of the project template when a project is created in Visual Studio, no `Imports` statement is required, and the members of its classes can be accessed without qualification.

- Several VB 6 functions have two versions: a String version and a Variant version. An example is provided by the *Trim$* and *Trim* functions. In VB.NET, these functions are replaced by a single overloaded function. Thus, for instance, we can call *Trim* using either a String or Object argument.

Obsolete Programming Elements

The following list shows some of the programming elements that have been removed from Visual Basic .NET:

As Any
All parameters are required to have a declared data type.

Atn function
Replaced by System.Math.Atan.

Calendar property
Handled by classes in the System.Globalization namespace.

Circle *statement*
Use methods in the System.Drawing namespace.

Currency data type
Replaced by the Decimal data type.

Date function
Replaced by the Today property of the DateTime structure in the System namespace.

Date *statement*
Replaced by the Today statement.

Debug.Assert method
Replaced by the Assert method of the Debug class of the System.Diagonistics namespace.

Debug.Print method
Replaced by the Write and WriteLine methods of the Debug class of the System.Diagonistics namespace.

Deftype *statements*
Not supported.

DoEvents function
Replaced by the DoEvents method of the Application class in System.Windows.Forms namespace.

Empty *keyword*
Replaced by the Nothing keyword.

Eqv *operator*
Use the equal sign.

GoSub *statement*
Not supported.

Imp *operator*
A Imp B is logically equivalent to (Not A) Or B.

Initialize event
> Replaced by the constructor method.

Instancing property
> Use the constructor to specify instancing.

IsEmpty function
> Not supported because the `Empty` keyword is not supported.

IsMissing function
> Not supported because every optional parameter must declare a default value.

IsNull function
> Not supported. The `Null` keyword is replaced by `Nothing`.

IsObject function
> Replaced by the *IsReference* function.

`Let` *statement*
> Not supported.

`Line` *statement*
> Use the DrawLine method of the Graphics class in the System.Drawing namespace.

`Null` *keyword*
> Use Nothing.

`On...GoSub` *construction*
> Not supported. No direct replacement.

`On...GoTo` *construction*
> Not supported. No direct replacement. `On Error...` is still supported, however.

`Option Base` *statement*
> Not supported. All arrays have lower bound equal to 0.

Option Private Module statement
> Use access modifiers in each individual `Module` statement.

Property Get, Property Let, and Property Set statements
> Replaced by a new unified syntax for defining properties.

PSet method
> Not supported. No direct replacement. See the System.Drawing namespace.

Round function
> Use the Round method of the Math class of the System namespace.

Scale method
> Not supported. No direct replacement. See the System.Drawing namespace.

`Set` *statement*
> Not supported.

Sgn function
> Use Math.Sign.

Sqr function
>   Use Math.Sqrt.

String function
>   Use the String class constructor with parameters.

Terminate event
>   Use the Destroy method.

Time function and statement
>   Instead of the *Time* function, use the TimeOfDay method of the `DateTime` structure of the System namespace. Instead of the `Time` statement, use the `TimeOfDay` statement.

`Type` *statement*
>   Use the `Structure` statement.

Variant data type
>   Use the Object data type.

VarType function
>   Use the *TypeName* function or the GetType method of the Object class.

`Wend` *keyword*
>   Replaced by `End While`.

Structured Exception Handling

VB.NET has added a significant new technique for error handling. Along with the traditional unstructured error handling through `On Error Goto` statements, VB.NET adds *structured exception handling*, using the `Try`...`Catch`...`Finally` syntax supported by other languages, such as C++. We discuss this in detail in Chapter 9.

Changes in Object-Orientation

As you may know, Visual Basic has implemented some features of object-oriented programming since Version 4. However, in terms of object-orientation, the step from Version 6 to VB.NET is very significant. Indeed, some people did not consider VB 6 (or earlier versions) to be a truly object-oriented programming language. Whatever your thoughts may have been on this matter, it seems clear that VB.NET is an object-oriented programming language by any reasonable definition of that term.

Here are the main changes in the direction of object-orientation. We discuss these issues in detail in Chapter 4.

Inheritance

VB.NET supports object-oriented inheritance (but not multiple inheritance). This means that a class can derive from another (base) class, thereby inheriting all of the properties, methods, and events of the base class. Since forms are also classes, inheritance applies to forms as well. This allows new forms to be created based on existing forms. We discuss inheritance in detail in Chapter 4.

Overloading

VB.NET supports a language feature known as *function overloading*. The idea is simple and yet quite useful. We can use the same name for different functions (or subroutines), as long as the functions can be distinguished by their *argument signature*. The argument signature of a function (or subroutine) is the sequence of data types of the arguments of the function. Thus, in order for two functions to have the same argument signature, they must have the same number of arguments, and the corresponding arguments must have the same data type. For example, the following declarations are legal in the same code module because they have different argument signatures:

```
Overloads Sub OpenFile()
    ' Ask user for file to open and open it
End Sub

Overloads Sub OpenFile(ByVal sFile As String)
    ' Open file sFile
End Sub
```

Object Creation

VB 6 supports a form of object creation called *implicit object creation*. If an object variable is declared using the New keyword:

```
Dim obj As New SomeClass
```

then the object is created the first time it is used in code. More specifically, the object variable is initially given the value Nothing, and then every time the variable is encountered during code execution, VB checks to see if the variable is Nothing. If so, the object is created at that time.

VB.NET does not support implicit object creation. If an object variable contains Nothing when it is encountered, it is left unchanged, and no object is created.

In VB.NET, we can create an object in the same statement as the object-variable declaration, as the following code shows:

```
Dim obj As SomeClass = New SomeClass
```

As a shorthand, we can also write:

```
Dim obj As New SomeClass
```

If the object's class constructor takes parameters, then they can be included, as in the following example:

```
Dim obj As SomeClass = New SomeClass(argument1, argument2,...)
```

As a shorthand, we can also write:

```
Dim obj As New SomeClass(argument1, argument2,...)
```

For details on class constructors, see Chapter 3.

Properties

There have been a few changes in how VB handles properties, particularly with respect to default properties and property declarations.

Default properties

As you know, you can use default properties in VB 6. For instance, if txt is a textbox control, then:

```
txt = "To be or not to be"
```

assigns the string "To be or not to be" to the default Text property of the textbox txt.

However, there is a price to pay for default properties: ambiguity. For example, if txt1 and txt2 are object variables referencing two TextBox controls, what does:

```
txt1 = txt2
```

mean? Are we equating the default properties or the object variables? In VB 6, this is interpreted as equating the default properties:

```
txt1.Text = txt2.Text
```

and we require the Set statement for object assignment:

```
Set txt1 = txt2
```

In VB.NET, default properties are not supported *unless* the property takes one or more parameters, in which case there is no ambiguity.

As Microsoft points out, default properties occur most commonly with collection classes. For example, in ActiveX Data Objects (ADO), the Fields collection of the Recordset object has a default Item property that returns a particular Field object. Thus, we can write:

```
rs.Fields.Item(1).Value
```

or, since the default Item property is parameterized:

```
rs.Fields(1).Value
```

Although we may not be used to thinking of this line as using default properties, it does.

Thus, in VB.NET, the line:

```
txt1 = txt2
```

is an *object* assignment. To equate the Text properties, we must write:

```
txt2.Text = txt1.Text
```

Since it is no longer needed, the Set keyword is not supported under VB.NET, nor is the companion Let keyword.

This settles the issue of equating object variables. For object variable *comparison*, however, we must use the Is operator, rather than the equal sign, as in:

```
If txt1 Is txt2 Then
```

or:

```
If Not (txt1 Is txt2) Then
```

Property declarations

In VB 6, properties are defined using `Property Let`, `Property Set`, and `Property Get` procedures. However, VB.NET uses a single property-declaration syntax of the form shown in the following example. Note also that there is no longer a need to distinguish between `Property Let` and `Property Set` because of the changes in default property support.

```
Property Salary() As Decimal
    Get
        Salary = mdecSalary
    End Get
    Set
        mdecSalary = Value
    End Set
End Property
```

Note the use of the implicitly defined `Value` variable that holds the value being passed into the property procedure when it is being set.

Note also that VB.NET does not support `ByRef` property parameters. All property parameters are passed by value.

APPENDIX B

Language Elements by Category

This appendix lists by category all the directives, statements, functions, procedures, and classes available within the VB.NET language. We have also included those Foundation Class Library members that are documented in this book. The categories are:

Array Handling
Clipboard
Collection Objects
Common Dialogs
Conditional Compilation
Conversion: Data Type Conversion and Other Conversion
Date and Time
Error Handling
Filesystem
Financial
IDataObject Interface
Information
Input/Output
Interaction
Mathematics
Programming: Object Programming and Miscellaneous Programming
Program Structure and Flow
Registry
String Manipulation
Variable and Constant Declaration

Where necessary, individual keywords may appear in more than one category.

Array Handling

Element	Description
Array class	Represents an array
Array.BinarySearch method	Searches for a value in a sorted one-dimensional array
Array.Copy method	Copies all or part of an array
Array.IndexOf method	Searches for the first occurrence of a value in an unsorted one-dimensional array
Array.LastIndexOf method	Searches for the last occurrence of a value in an unsorted one-dimensional array
Erase statement	Resets an array to its uninitialized state
IsArray function	Indicates whether a variable is an array
Join function	Concatenates an array of values into a delimited string
LBound function	Returns the lower boundary of an array
ReDim statement	Redimensions an arrayxs
UBound function	Returns the upper boundary of an array
VBFixedArray attribute	Defines a fixed-length arrayXS

Clipboard

Element	Description
Clipboard.GetDataObject method	Places data on the Clipboard
Clipboard.SetDataObject method	Retrieves an `IDataObject` object representing data on the Clipboard

Collection Objects

Element	Description
Collection.Add method	Adds a member to a Collection object
Collection.Count method	Indicates the number of items stored to a Collection object
Collection.Item method	Retrieves a member from a Collection object based on its key value or its ordinal position
Collection.Remove method	Removes the member associated with a given key or ordinal position from a Collection object
Hashtable.Add method	Adds a key-value pair to a `HashTable` object
Hashtable.Clear method	Removes all entries from the hash table
Hashtable.ContainsKey method	Indicates whether a given key exists among the hash table's items
Hashtable.ContainsValue method	Indicates whether a given value exists among the hash table's items
Hashtable.CopyTo method	Copies hash table values into an array of DictionaryEntry structures

Element	Description
Hashtable.Count property	Indicates the total number of elements in the hash table
Hashtable.Item property	Retrieves the value of a hash table item given its key
Hashtable.Keys property	Returns an `ICollection` object that contains the keys in the hash table
Hashtable.Remove method	Removes a key/value pair from the hash table
Hashtable.Values property	Returns an `ICollection` object that contains the values in the hash table
Queue.Clear method	Clears all items in the queue
Queue.Contains method	Indicates whether the queue contains a particular object
Queue.CopyTo method	Copies the queue elements to an array
Queue.Count method	Indicates the total number of items in the queue
Queue.Dequeue method	Removes an item from the queue
Queue.Enqueue method	Places an item at the end of the queue
Queue.Peek method	Returns the first item in the queue
Queue.ToArray method	Copies the queue elements to an array
Stack.Clear method	Clears all items in the stack
Stack.Contains method	Indicates whether the stack contains a particular object
Stack.CopyTo method	Copies the items in the stack to an array
Stack.Count method	Indicates the total number of items in the stack
Stack.Peek method	Returns the item at the top of the stack
Stack.Pop method	Removes the topmost item from the stack
Stack.Push method	Places an item at the top of the stack
Stack.ToArray method	Copies the items on the stack to an array

Common Dialogs

Element	Description
ColorDialog class	Allows programmatic control of the Windows Common Color dialog box
FontDialog class	Allows programmatic control of the Windows Common Font dialog box
OpenFileDialog class	Allows programmatic control of the Windows File Open dialog box
SaveFileDialog class	Allows programmatic control of the Windows SaveAs dialog box

Conditional Compilation

Element	Description
#Const directive	Declares a conditional compiler constant
#If...Then...End If directive	Defines a block of code that will only be compiled into the program if the expression with the conditional constant evaluates to `True`

Conversion

Data Type Conversion

Element	Description
CBool function	Converts an expression to a Boolean data type
CByte function	Converts an expression to a Byte data type
CChar function	Converts a string expression to a Char data type
CDate function	Converts an expression to a Date data type
CDbl function	Converts an expression to a Double data type
CDec function	Converts an expression to a Decimal data type
CInt function	Converts an expression to an Integer data type
CLng function	Converts an expression to a Long data type
CObj function	Converts an expression to an Object data type
CSng function	Converts an expression to a Single data type
CStr function	Converts an expression to a String data type
CType function	Converts an expression to any valid data type, structure, object type, or interface
DateValue function	Converts the string representation of a date to a date
DirectCast function	Converts a variable to its runtime type
Option Strict statement	Determines whether narrowing operations are allowed
Str function	Converts a numeric value to a string
TimeValue function	Converts a string representation of time to a Date data type
Val function	Converts a numeric string to a number
ValDec function	Converts a numeric string to a Decimal data type

Other Conversion

Element	Description
ErrorToString method	Returns the descriptive error message corresponding to a particular error code
Fix function	Returns the integer portion of a number
Hex function	Converts a number to a string representing its hexadecimal equivalent
Int function	Returns the integer portion of a number
Oct function	Converts a number to a string representing its octal equivalent
QBColor function	Converts a QBasic color code to an RGB color value
RGB function	Returns a system color code that can be assigned to object color properties

Date and Time

Element	Description
DateAdd function	Returns the result of adding or subtracting a date or time
DateDiff function	Returns the difference between two dates

Element	Description
DatePart function	Returns the part (month, day, year) of the date requested
DateSerial function	Returns a date from an expression containing month, day, and year components
DateString property	Retrieves or sets the current system date
DateValue function	Converts the string representation of a date to a date
Day function	Returns a number representing the day of the month
GetTimer function	Returns the number of seconds since midnight
Hour function	Extracts the hour element from a time
Minute function	Extracts the minutes element from a time
Month function	Extracts the month element from a date
MonthName function	Returns the name of the month for a given date
Now property	Returns the current system date and time
Second function	Extracts the seconds element from a time
TimeOfDay property	Sets or retrieves the current system time
Timer property	Returns the number of seconds that have elapsed since midnight
TimeSerial function	Returns a time from its hour, minute, and second components
TimeString property	Sets or returns the current system time
TimeValue function	Converts a string representation of time to a Date data type
Today property	Sets or retrieves the current system date
Weekday function	Determines the day of the week of a given date
WeekdayName function	Returns the weekday name for a given weekday number
Year function	Returns the year element from a date

Debugging

Element	Description
Debug.Assert method	Outputs a message if an expression is `False`
Debug.AutoFlush property	Determines whether each write operation should be followed by a call to the Flush method
Debug.Close method	Flushes the output buffer and closes any listeners except the Output window
Debug.Flush method	Flushes the output buffer
Debug.Indent method	Increases the value of the IndentLevel property by 1
Debug.IndentLevel property	Determines the indent level for `Debug` object output
Debug.IndentSize property	Defines the current indent size, in number of spaces
Debug.Listeners property	Returns a collection of all `TraceListener` objects that are monitoring the `Debug` object's output
Debug.Unindent method	Decreases the value of the IndentLevel property by 1
Debug.Write method	Sends output to the Output window and other listeners
Debug.WriteIf method	Sends output to the Output window and other listeners if an expression is `True`

Element	Description
Debug.WriteLine method	Writes output along with a newline character to the Output window
Debug.WriteLineIf method	Writes output along with a newline character to the Output window if an expression is True

Declaration

Element	Description
Const statement	Declares a constant
Class...End Class statement	Defines a class
Declare statement	Defines a prototype for a call to an external DLL library function
Dim statement	Declares a variable
Enum statement	Defines a series of constants as an enumerated type
Function statement	Defines a function
Friend keyword	Makes a procedure in a class callable from outside the class but within the project in which the class is defined
Option Explicit statement	Requires declaration of all variables
Private statement	Declares a local variable
Property statement	Defines a property
Protected statement	Declares a protected class member
Public statement	Declares a public or global variable
Static statement	Declares a static variable
Structure...End Structure statement	Declares a structure or user-defined type
Sub statement	Declares a subroutine

Error Handling

Element	Description
Erl function	Indicates the line number at which an error occurred
Err.Clear method	Clears the Err object
Err.Description property	Provides a textual description of an error
Err.GetException method	Returns the Exception object associated with the current error
Err.HelpContext property	Returns or sets the help file ID for the current error
Err.HelpFile property	Returns or sets the name and path of the help file containing information about the current error
Err.LastDLLError property	Returns the error number from an error raised by a system API DLL
Err.Number property	Returns or sets the current error code
Err.Raise method	Generates a user-defined error
Err.Source property	Returns or sets the source of an error

Element	Description
ErrorToString function	Converts an error number to the corresponding error message
Exception class	Base class for all exceptions
IsError function	Determines whether an object is an exception type
On Error statement	Enables or disables an error handler
Resume statement	Transfers control from an error handler
Throw statement	Throws an exception
Try...Catch...Finally statement	Handles particular errors that may occur in a block of code through structured exception handling

Filesystem

Element	Description
ChDir procedure	Changes the current directory
ChDrive procedure	Changes the current drive
CurDir function	Returns the current directory of a drive
Dir function	Returns the name of a file or directory matching a file specification and having particular file attributes
Directory.CreateDirectory method	Creates a new directory
Directory.Delete method	Deletes a directory
Directory.Exists method	Indicates whether a particular directory exists
Directory.GetCreation-Time method	Retrieves the date and time the directory was created
Directory.GetDirectories method	Retrieves the names of the subdirectories of a given directory
Directory.GetDirectory-Root method	Retrieves the name of the root directory of a given directory
Directory.GetFiles	Retrieves the names of the files in a given directory
Directory.GetFileSystem-Entries method	Retrieves the names of filesystem objects (files and directories) in a given directory
Directory.GetParent method	Retrieves a `DirectoryInfo` object representing the parent of a specified directory
Directory.Move method	Moves a directory and its contents, including nested subdirectories, to a new location
File.Exists method	Indicates whether a specified file exists
FileCopy function	Copies a file
FileDateTime function	Returns the date and time of file creation or last access
GetAttr function	Returns the attributes of a given file or directory
Kill function	Deletes one or more files
MkDir function	Creates a new directory
Rename function	Renames a file or directory
RmDir function	Removes a directory
SetAttr procedure	Sets a file or directory's attributes

Financial

Element	Description
DDB function	Returns double-declining balance depreciation of an asset for a specific period
FV function	Calculates the future value of an annuity
IPmt function	Computes the interest payment for a given period of an annuity
IRR function	Calculates the internal rate of return for a series of periodic cash flows
MIRR function	Calculates the modified internal rate of return
NPer function	Determines the number of payment periods for an annuity, based on fixed periodic payments and a fixed interest rate
NPV function	Calculates the net present value of an investment
Pmt function	Calculates the payment for an annuity
PPmt function	Computes the payment of principal for a given period of an annuity
PV function	Calculates the present value of an annuity
Rate function	Returns the interest rate per period for an annuity
SLN method	Computes the straight-line depreciation of an asset
SYD function	Computes the sum-of-years' digits depreciation of an asset for a specified period

IDataObject Interface

Element	Description
GetData method	Retrieves data from the Clipboard in a given format
GetDataPresent method	Indicates whether the Clipboard holds data of a particular format
GetFormats method	Retrieves a list of all the formats with which the Clipboard data is associated or to which it can be converted

Information

Element	Description
Application.CompanyName property	Returns the name of the company that created the application
Application.ExecutablePath property	Returns the executable path to the application
Application.ProductName property	Returns the application's product name
Application.ProductVersion property	Returns the application's version number
Erl function	Indicates the line number at which an error occurred
IsArray function	Indicates whether a variable is an array
IsDate function	Indicates whether an argument is—or can be converted to—a date
IsDBNull function	Determines whether an expression evaluates to DbNull

Element	Description
IsError function	Determines whether an object is an exception type
IsNothing function	Determines if an object reference evaluates to Nothing
IsNumeric function	Determines if an expression is a number or can be converted to a number
IsReference function	Determines if an expression is a reference type rather than a value type
RGB function	Returns a system color code that can be assigned to object color properties
Rem statement	Indicates a remark or comment placed within the code
ScriptEngine function	Returns the name of the programming language
ScriptEngineBuildVersion function	Returns the build number
ScriptEngineMajor-Version function	Returns the major version
ScriptEngineMinor-Version function	Returns the minor version
SystemTypeName function	Returns the name of the CTS datatype corresponding to a VB.NET datatype
TypeName function	Returns the data type name of a variable
VarType function	Returns a constant indicating the data type of a variable
VbTypeName function	Returns the name of a VB.NET datatype that corresponds to a CTS datatype

Input/Output

Element	Description
EOF function	Returns a flag denoting the end of a file
FileAttr function	Returns the file-access mode for a file opened using the FileOpen statement
FileClose function	Closes one or more open files
FileGet, FileGetObject functions	Read from a file to a variable
FileLen function	Returns the size of an open file
FileOpen function	Opens a file
FilePut, FilePutObject functions	Writes from a variable to a file
FileWidth function	Sets the line width of a file opened using the FileOpen function
FreeFile function	Returns the number of the next available file
Input function	Reads delimited data from a sequential file
InputString function	Reads a designated number of characters from a file
LineInput function	Returns a string containing a line read from a file
Loc function	Returns the current position of the read/write pointer in a file
Lock function	Locks a file, section of a file, or record in a file to prevent access by another process
LOF function	Returns the size of an open file in bytes
Print function	Writes formatted data to a sequential file

Element	Description
PrintLine function	Writes formatted data followed by a linefeed to a sequential file
Reset function	Closes all open files
Seek function	Returns the position of the file pointer
Seek procedure	Sets the position of the file pointer
Spc function	Inserts spaces between expressions in output
Tab function	Moves the text-insertion point to a given column or the start of the next print zone

Integrated Development Environment

Element	Description
#Region...#End Region	Defines collapsible sections of code in VB source code files
Debug object	Provides debugging services for the Output window and other listeners

Interaction

Element	Description
AppActivate statement	Gives the focus to a window based on its title or task ID
AppActivateHelper statement	Gives the focus to a window based on its window handle
Beep statement	Sounds a note using the computer speaker
Choose function	Returns a value from a list based on its index
Command function	Returns the argument portion of the command line
Environ function	Retrieves the value of an environment variable
IIf function	Returns one of two values based on the evaluation of a Boolean expression
InputBox function	Returns user input from a simple dialog box
MsgBox function	Displays a message box with buttons, icon, and a message, and returns the button selected by the user
Shell function	Launches an external application
Switch function	Returns the first value or expression in a list that is True
Send, SendWait methods	Send keystrokes to the active window

Mathematics

Element	Description
Abs function	Returns the absolute value of a number
Acos function	Returns the arccosine in radians
Asin function	Returns the angle in radians of a sine
Atan function	Returns the arctangent in radians of a tangent
Atan2 function	Returns the angle in the Cartesian plane formed by the x-axis and a vector starting from the origin (0, 0) and terminating at a point (x, y)

Element	Description
Ceiling function	Returns the smallest integer that's greater than or equal to a number
Cos function	Returns the cosine of an angle
Cosh function	Returns the hyperbolic cosine of an angle
E Field	Returns the approximate value of the irrational number *e*
Exp function	Returns the base of a natural logarithm raised to a power
Fix function	Returns the integer portion of a number
Floor function	Returns the largest integer less than or equal to a number
IEEERemainder function	Returns the remainder resulting from division
Int function	Returns the integer portion of a number
Log function	Returns the natural (base *e*) logarithm of a given number
Log10 function	Returns the common (base 10) logarithm of a given number
Max function	Returns the larger of two numbers
Min function	Returns the smaller of two numbers
Mod operator	Returns the modulus (the remainder after division)
Partition function	A string indicating the range into which a number falls
Pi Field	Returns the approximate value of `pi`
Pow function	Returns the result of a number raised to a specified power
Randomize function	Initializes the random-number generator
Rnd function	Returns a random number
Round function	Rounds a number to a specified number of decimal places
Sign function	Determines the sign of a number
Sin function	Returns the sine of an angle
Sinh function	Returns the hyperbolic sine of an angle
Sqrt function	Calculates the square root of a number
Tan function	Returns the ratio of two sides of a right triangle
Tanh function	Returns the hyperbolic tangent of an angle

Program Structure and Flow

Element	Description
Call statement	Calls an intrinsic or user-defined procedure or function, a method, or a routine in a dynamic link library
CallByName statement	Dynamically executes a class method, property let, or property set
Do...Loop statement	Repeatedly executes a block of code while or until a condition is true
Exit statement	Prematurely exits a code block
End statement	Marks the end of a block of code
For...Next statement	Iterates through a section of code a given number of times
For Each...Next statement	Iterates through a collection or array of objects or values, returning a reference to each of the members
GoTo statement	Passes program flow to a portion of code marked by a label
If...Then...Else statement	Defines a conditional block or blocks of code

Element	Description
Return statement	Transfers control from a function or procedure and returns a value from a function
Select Case statement	Executes one out of a series of code blocks based on the value of an expression
Stop statement	Suspends program execution
While...End While statement	Executes a block of code until a condition becomes `False`

Programming

Object Programming

Element	Description
AddHandler statement	Dynamically binds an event handler to an event
AddressOf operator	Creates a procedure delegate instance that references a particular procedure
Class...End Class statement	Defines a class and its members
COMClass attribute	Allows a .NET component to be exposed as a COM object
CreateObject function	Creates a new instance of a COM (ActiveX) object
Event statement	Declares a custom event
Get statement	Defines a Property Get procedure that returns a property value to the caller
GetObject function	Returns a reference to a COM (ActiveX) object
Handles keyword	Indicates that the procedure serves as the handler for an event
Implements keyword	Indicates that a class member implements a property, function, procedure, or event of an abstract base class
Implements statement	Specifies one or more interfaces that are implemented by a class
Imports statement	Imports a namespace from a project or an assembly, making its types and their members accessible to the current project
Inherits statement	Indicates that a class is derived from a base class
Interface...End Interface statement	Defines an interface and its members
Is operator	Compares two object references for equality
Me operator	Represents the current class instance
MyBase keyword	Represents the base class from which an inherited class is derived
MyClass keyword	Represents the current class instance
Namespace statement	Declares the name of a namespace
Property statement	Defines a property
RaiseEvent statement	Raises a custom event
RemoveHandler statement	Disassociates an event from an event handler defined using the `AddHandler` statement
Shadows keyword	Indicates that a derived class member is hidden when calls to the derived class member are made through the base class
WithEvents statement	Receives notification of events raised by an object

Miscellaneous Programming

Element	Description
AddressOf operator	Creates a procedure-delegate instance that references a particular procedure
Application.DoEvents method	Allows the operating system to process events and messages waiting in the message queue
Declare statement	Defines a prototype for a call to an external DLL library function
Environ statement	Retrieves the value of an environment variable
Len function	Returns the size in bytes of a given variable
SyncLock statement	Prevents multiple threads of execution in the same process from accessing shared data or resources at the same time

Registry

Element	Description
DeleteSetting statement	Removes a complete application key, one of its subkeys, or a single value entry from the system registry
GetAllSettings function	Returns all values from an application key in the system registry
GetSetting function	Returns a specific value from an application key in the system registry
SaveSetting procedure	Creates or saves a value in the system registry

String Manipulation

Element	Description
Asc, AscW functions	Return the character code of the first character of a string
Chr, ChrW functions	Return a string containing a character based on its numeric code
Filter function	Returns an array of strings matching (or not matching) a specified value
Format function	Returns a string formatted to a given specification
FormatCurrency function	Returns a string formatted using the currency settings for the current locale
FormatDateTime function	Returns a string formatted using the date/time setting for the current locale
FormatNumber function	Returns a numeric value in a specified format
FormatPercent function	Returns a numeric value formatted using the "%" symbol
GetChar function	Returns a Char containing the character at a particular position in a string
InStr function	Finds the starting position of a substring within a string
InStrRev function	Returns the first occurrence of a string within another string by searching from the end of the string

Element	Description
Join function	Concatenates an array of values into a delimited string
LCase function	Converts a character or string to lowercase
Left function	Returns a string containing the leftmost *n* characters of a string
Len function	Counts the number of characters in a string
Like operator	Compares two strings
Mid function	Extracts a substring from a larger string
Mid statement	Replaces a substring in a larger string
Option Compare statement	Sets the default method for comparing string data
Replace function	Replaces one or more occurrences of a substring within a larger string
Right function	Returns a string containing the rightmost characters of another string
RTrim function	Removes any trailing spaces from a string
Str function	Converts a numeric value to a string
Spc function	Inserts spaces between expressions in output
Space function	Fills a string with a given number of spaces
Split function	Returns an array of strings from a single delimited string
StrComp function	Returns the result of comparing two strings
StrConv function	Returns the result of converting a string in a number of possible ways
StrDup function	Returns a string consisting of the first character of another string duplicated a given number of times
StrReverse function	Reverses the characters of the strings passed to it
Trim function	Removes leading and trailing spaces from a string
UCase function	Converts a string to uppercase
Val function	Converts a numeric string to a number
VBFixedString attribute	Defines a fixed-length string

APPENDIX C

Operators

There are four groups of operators in VB.NET: arithmetic, concatenation, comparison, and logical. We will look at each group of operators in turn before discussing the order of precedence VB.NET uses when it encounters more than one type of operator within an expression.

Arithmetic Operators

The arithmetic operators are:

+

The addition operator. Used to add numeric expressions, as well as to concatenate (join together) two string variables. However, it is preferable to use the concatenation operator with strings to eliminate ambiguity. For example:

```
result = expression1 + expression2
```

-

The subtraction operator. Used to find the difference between two numeric values or expressions, as well as to denote a negative value. Unlike the addition operator, it cannot be used with string variables. For example:

```
result = expression1 - expression2
```

/

The division operator. Returns a floating point number. For example:

```
result = expression1 / expression2
```

*

The multiplication operator. Used to multiply two numerical values. For example:

```
result = expression1 * expression2
```

\

The integer division operator. Performs division on two numeric expressions and returns an integer result (no remainder or decimal places). For example:

```
result = expression1 \ expression2
```

Note that regardless of what specific numeric data types *expression1* and *expression2* are, integer division returns only an integral data type (Byte, Short, Integer, or Long). After the division is performed, the result is truncated to an integer data type.

Mod

The modulo operator. Performs division on two numeric expressions and returns the modulus, that is, the remainder when one number is divided by another. If either of the two numbers are floating point numbers, they are rounded to integer values prior to the modulo operation. The return value is a non-negative integral data type. For instance, the expression:

```
10 Mod 3
```

evaluates to 1, because the remainder when dividing 10 by 3 is 1. For example:

```
result = expression1 Mod expression2
```

^

The exponentiation operator. Raises a number to the power of the exponent. For example:

```
result = number ^ exponent
```

Assignment Operators

Along with the equal operator, there is one assignment operator that corresponds to each arithmetic and concatenation operator. Its symbol is obtained by appending an equal sign to the arithmetic or concatenation symbol.

The arithmetic and concatenation operators work as follows. They all take the form:

```
expression1 <operator>= expression2
```

where *<operator>* is one of the arithmetic or concatenation operators. This is equivalent to:

```
expression1 = expression1 <operator> expression2
```

To illustrate, consider the addition assignment operator. The expression:

```
x += 1
```

is equivalent to:

```
x = x + 1
```

which simply adds 1 to x. Similarly, the expression:

```
s &= "end"
```

is equivalent to:

```
s = s & "end"
```

which concatenates the string `"end"` to the end of the string s.

All of the "shortcut" assignment operators—such as the addition assignment operator or the concatenation assignment operator—are new to VB.NET.

The assignment operators are:

=

The equal operator, which is both an assignment operator and a comparison operator. For example:

```
oVar1 = oVar2
```

Note that in VB.NET, the equal operator alone is used to assign all data types; in previous versions of VB, the Set statement had to be used along with the equal operator to assign an object reference.

+=

Addition assignment operator. For example:

```
lNumber += 1
```

adds 1 to the value of lNumber and assigns the result to lNumber.

-=

Subtraction assignment operator. For example:

```
lNumber -= 1
```

subtracts 1 from the value of lNumber and assigns the result to lNumber.

^=

Exponential assignment operator. For example:

```
lNumber ^= 2
```

squares lNumber and assigns the result to lNumber.

*=

Multiplication assignment operator. For example:

```
lNumber *= 3
```

triples lNumber and assigns the result to lNumber.

/=

Division assignment operator. For example:

```
lNumber /= 2
```

halves lNumber and assigns the result to lNumber.

\=

Integer division assignment operator. For example:

```
dblNumber \= 2
```

divides dblNumber by 2, discards any fractional part, and assigns the result to dblNumber.

&=

> Concatenation assignment operator. For example:
>
> ```
> strVal &= "."
> ```
>
> appends a period to the end of strVal.

 Unlike the comparison operators, in which the order of symbols is reversible (that is, >= is the same as =>), the order of the "shortcut" operator symbols is *not* reversible. For example, while:

```
x += 1
```
increments x by 1, the expression:

```
x =+ 1
```
simply assigns 1 to the variable x.

Concatenation Operators

VB.NET has two string concatenation operators:

&

> The ampersand symbol is the recommended concatenation operator. It is used to bind a number of string variables together, creating one string from two or more individual strings. Any nonstring variable or expression is converted to a string prior to concatenation (even if Option Strict is on) Its syntax is:
>
> ```
> result = expression1 & expression2...
> ```

+

> Although in principle the + sign is identical to the & concatenation operator, it also doubles as the addition operator. Hence, as Microsoft states:
>
> > When you use the + operator, you may not be able to determine whether addition or string concatenation will occur. Use the & operator for concatenation to eliminate ambiguity and provide self-documenting code.

Comparison Operators

There are three main comparison operators: < (less than), > (greater than), and = (equal to). They can be used individually, or any two operators can be combined with each other. Their general syntax is:

```
result = expression1 <operator> expression2
```

The resulting expression is True (-1), False (0), or Null. A Null results if and only if either *expression1* or *expression2* itself is Null.

What follows is a list of all the comparison operators supported by VB.NET, as well as an explanation of the condition required for the comparison to result in True:

>

> *expression1* is greater than and not equal to *expression2*.

<

expression1 is less than and not equal to expression2.

<>

expression1 is not equal to expression2 (less than or greater than).

>=

expression1 is greater than or equal to expression2.

<=

expression1 is less than or equal to expression2.

=

expression1 is equal to expression2.

Comparison operators can be used with both numeric and string variables. However, if one expression is numeric and the other is a string, the numeric expression will always be "less than" the string expression. If both *expression1* and *expression2* are strings, the "greatest" string is the one that is the longest. If the strings are of equal length, the comparison is based on the value of the Option Compare setting. If its value is Binary, the comparison is case sensitive. (Lowercase letters are "greater" than their uppercase counterparts.) If its value is Text, the comparison is not case sensitive.

The Is Operator

While not strictly a comparison operator, the Is operator determines whether two object reference variables refer to the same object. Thus, in some sense, it tests for the "equality" of two object references. Its syntax is:

```
result = object1 Is object2
```

If both *object1* and *object2* refer to the same object, the result is True; otherwise, the result is False. You can also use the Is operator to determine if an object variable refers to a valid object. This is done by comparing the object variable to the special Nothing data type:

```
If oVar Is Nothing Then
```

The result is True if the object variable does not hold a reference to an object.

The Like Operator

The Like operator is used to match strings. It compares a string variable or string literal with a pattern expression and determines whether they match (the result is True) or not (the result is False). For more on this operator, see the entry for the Like Operator in the reference section.

Logical and Bitwise Operators

Logical operators allow you to evaluate one or more expressions and return a Boolean value (True or False). VB.NET supports four logical operators: And, AndAlso, Or, OrElse, Not, and Xor. These operators also double as bitwise operators. A bitwise comparison examines the bit positions in both expressions and sets or clears the corresponding bit in the result, depending upon the operator used. The result of a bitwise operation is a numeric value.

In performing logical operations, VB.NET, unlike VB 6, uses conditional *short-circuiting*. This means that, in compound logical expressions, the individual expressions are evaluated only until the expression's overall value is known, unless one of the individual expressions involves a call to another function or subroutine. Short-circuiting can occur in logical And operations when the first operand evaluates to False, as well as in logical Or operations when the first operand evaluates to True.

The six logical and bitwise operators are:

And

> Performs logical conjunction; that is, it returns True if and only if both *expression1* and *expression2* evaluate to True. If either expression is False, then the result is False. If either expression is Null, then the result is Null. Its syntax is:
>
> ```
> result = expression1 And expression2
> ```
>
> For example:
>
> ```
> If (x = 5) And (y < 7) Then
> ```
>
> In this case, the code after the If statement will be executed only if the value of x is five and the value of y is less than seven.
>
> As a bitwise operator, And returns 1 if the compared bits in both expressions are 1, and returns 0 in all other cases, as shown in the following table:

Bit in expression1	Bit in expression2	Result
0	0	0
0	1	0
1	0	0
1	1	1

> For example, the result of 15 And 179 is 3, as the following binary representation shows:
>
> ```
> 00000011 = 00001111 And 10110011
> ```

AndAlso

> As a comparison operator, works exactly like the And operator, except that it performs short-circuiting; an If statement will be evaluated from left to right only until the truth or falsity of the statement can be determined (that is, until the first False condition is encountered). Unlike And, AndAlso does not double as a bitwise operator.

Or

> Performs logical disjunction; that is, it returns True if and only if at least one (that is, one or both) of *expression1* or *expression2* evaluates to True. If either expression is Null, then the result is also Null. The syntax for the Or operator is:
>
> ```
> result = expression1 Or expression2
> ```

Operators

For example:

```
If x = 5 Or y < 7 Then
```

In this case, the code after the If statement will be executed if the value of x is five or if the value of y is less than seven.

As a bitwise operator, Or is the converse of And. Or returns 0 if the compared bits in both expressions are 0, and returns 1 in all other cases, as shown in the following table:

Bit in expression1	Bit in expression2	Result
0	0	0
0	1	1
1	0	1
1	1	1

For example, the result of 15 Or 179 is 191, as the following binary representation shows:

```
10111111 = 00001111 Or 10110011
```

And/Or: Conditional Short-Circuiting

The documentation implies that And and Or do no short-circuiting; that is, that every subexpression is evaluated, even if the result of the expression is known. In fact, both And and Or perform short-circuiting if the result of the expression is known and unevaluated subexpressions do not include calls to functions.

OrElse

As a comparison operator, works exactly like the Or operator, except that it performs short-circuiting; an If statement will be evaluated from left to right only until the truth or falsity of the statement can be determined (that is, until the first True condition is encountered). Unlike Or, OrElse does not double as a bitwise operator.

Not

Performs logical negation on a single expression; that is, it returns True if and only if the expression is False. If the expression is Null, though, the result of using the Not operator is still a Null. Its syntax is:

```
result = Not expression1
```

For example:

```
If Not IsNumeric(x) Then
```

In this example, the code following the If statement will be executed if IsNumeric returns False, indicating that x is not a value capable of being represented by a number.

As a bitwise operator, Not simply reverses the value of the bit, as shown in the following table:

expression1	Result
0	1
1	0

For example, the result of Not 16 is 239, as the following binary representation shows:

```
Not 00010000 = 11101111
```

Xor

Performs logical exclusion; that is, Xor (an abbreviation for eXclusive OR) returns True if and only if the two expressions have different truth values. If either expression is Null, the result is also Null. Its syntax is:

```
result = expression1 Xor expression2
```

As a bitwise operator, Xor returns 1 if the bits being compared are different and returns 0 if they are the same, as shown in the following table:

Bit in expression1	Bit in expression2	Result
0	0	0
0	1	1
1	0	1
1	1	0

Eqv and Imp

Eqv and Imp, two logical and bitwise operators, present in VB 6, have been removed from VB.NET. Eqv can simply be replaced with the = comparison operator. Hence, the expression:

```
exp1 Eqv exp2
```

is the same as:

```
exp1 = exp2
```

Imp can be replaced with an expression using the Not and Or operators. For example:

```
exp1 Imp exp2
```

can also be expressed as:

```
(Not exp1) Or exp2
```

For example, the result of 15 Xor 179 is 188, as the following binary representation shows:

```
10111100 = 00001111 Imp 10110011
```

Operator Precedence

If you include more than one operator in a single line of code, you need to know the order in which VB.NET will evaluate them. Otherwise, the results may be completely different from what you intended. The rules that define the order in which a language handles operators is known as the *order of precedence*. If the order of precedence results in operations being evaluated in an order other than the intended one, you can explicitly override the order of precedence through the use of parentheses. Indeed, we strongly recommend the use of sufficient parentheses to avoid any possible misinterpretation. Put another way, we recommend using enough parentheses so that operator precedence is no longer relevant!

When a single line of code includes operators from more than one category, they are evaluated in the following order:

> Arithmetic operators
> Concatenation operators
> Comparison operators
> Logical operators

Within each category of operators, except for the single concatenation operator, there is also an order of precedence. If multiple comparison operators appear in a single line of code, they are simply evaluated from left to right. The order of precedence of arithmetic operators is as follows:

> Exponentiation (^)
> Division and multiplication (/,*) (no order of precedence between the two)
> Integer division (\)
> Modulo arithmetic (Mod)
> Addition and subtraction (+,-) (no order of precedence between the two)

If the same arithmetic operator is used multiple times in a single line of code, the operators are evaluated from left to right.

The order of precedence of logical operators is:

> Not
> And
> Or
> Xor

If the same arithmetic or logical operator is used multiple times in a single line of code, the operators are evaluated from left to right.

APPENDIX D

Constants and Enumerations

This appendix consists of a reference for Visual Basic's built-in constants and enumerations.

VB.NET defines several enumerations in the Microsoft.VisualBasic namespace. For instance, the CompareMethod enumeration is defined as:

```
Enum CompareMethod
    Binary = 0
    Text = 1
End Enum
```

Thus, we can use the following expressions in our VB code:

```
CompareMethod.Binary
CompareMethod.Text
```

On the other hand, VB also defines two equivalent built-in constants in the Constants class of the Microsoft.VisualBasic namespace that serve the same purpose:

```
VbBinaryCompare
VbTextCompare
```

Note, however, that VB does not define built-in constants corresponding to every member of every enum. For instance, there are no built-in constants that correspond to the OpenMode enum members. This enum is used in the FileOpen procedure/statement:

```
Enum OpenMode
    Input = 1
    Output = 2
    Random = 4
    Append = 8
    Binary = 32
End Enum
```

In this appendix, we list all of the VB constants and enumerations.

Visual Basic Intrinsic Constants

Table D-1 contains an alphabetical list of VB's built-in symbolic constants. They are actually implemented as fields of the Constants class in the Microsoft.Visual-Basic namespace.

Table D-1: Visual Basic constants

Constant	Value
VbAbort	3
VbAbortRetryIgnore	&H00000002
VbApplicationModal	&H00000000
VbArchive	32
VbArray	8192
VbBack	Chr(8)
VbBinaryCompare	0
VbBoolean	11
VbByte	17
VbCancel	2
VbCr	Chr(13)
VbCritical	&H00000010
VbCrLf	Chr(13) & Chr(10)
VbCurrency	6
VbDate	7
VbDecimal	14
VbDefaultButton1	&H00000000
VbDefaultButton2	&H00000100
VbDefaultButton3	&H00000200
VbDirectory	16
VbDouble	5
VbEmpty	0
VbExclamation	&H00000030
VbFalse	0
VbFirstFourDays	2
VbFirstFullWeek	3
VbFirstJan1	1
VbFormFeed	Chr(12)
VbFriday	6
VbGeneralDate	0
VbGet	2
VbHidden	2
VbHide	0
VbHiragana	32
VbIgnore	5
VbInformation	&H00000040

Constant	Value
VbInteger	3
VbKatakana	16
VbLet	4
VbLf	Chr(10)
VbLinguisticCasing	1024
VbLong	20
VbLongDate	1
VbLongTime	3
VbLowerCase	2
VbMaximizedFocus	3
VbMethod	1
VbMinimizedFocus	2
VbMinimizedNoFocus	6
VbMonday	2
VbMsgBoxHelp	&H00004000
VhMsgBoxRight	&H00080000
VbMsgBoxRtlReading	&H00100000
VbMsgBoxSetFore-ground	&H00010000
VbNarrow	8
VbNewLine	Chr(13) & Chr(10)
VbNo	7
VbNormal	0
VbNormalFocus	1
VbNormalNoFocus	4
VbNull	1
VbNullChar	Chr(0)
VbNullString	
VbObject	9
VbObjectError	&H80040000
VbOK	1
VbOKCancel	&H00000001
VbOKOnly	&H00000000
VbProperCase	3
VbQuestion	&H00000020
VbReadOnly	1
VbRetry	4
VbRetryCancel	&H00000005
VbSaturday	7
VbSet	8
VbShortDate	2
VbShortTime	4
VbSimplifiedChinese	256

Constant	Value
VbSingle	4
VbString	8
VbSunday	1
VbSystem	4
VbSystemModal	&H00001000
VbTab	Chr(9)
VbTextCompare	1
VbThursday	5
VbTraditionalChinese	512
VbTrue	1
VbTuesday	3
VbUpperCase	1
VbUseDefault	&HFFFFFFFE
VbUserDefinedType	36
VbUseSystem	0
VbUseSystemDayOfWeek	0
VbVariant	12
VbVerticalTab	Chr(11)
VbVolume	8
VbWednesday	4
VbWide	4
VbYes	6
VbYesNo	&H00000004
VbYesNoCancel	&H00000003

ControlChars Class

The Microsoft.VisualBasic namespace includes a ControlChars class whose shared fields can be used for device control and outputting special characters. Most of the shared fields also have equivalent Visual Basic intrinsic constants, as the following table shows:

Field	Value	Intrinsic constant
Back	Chr(8)	VbBack
Cr	Chr(13)	VbCr
CrLf	\r\n	VbCrLf
FormFeed	Chr(12)	VbFormFeed
Lf	Chr(10)	VbLf
NewLine	\r\n	VbNewLine
NullChar	Chr(0)	VbNullChar
Quote	Chr(34)	none
Tab	Chr(9)	VbTab
VerticalTab	Chr(11)	VbVerticalTab

Note that these constants must be qualified with the class name, as in.

```
If str = ControlChars.CrLf Then
```

Visual Basic Enumerations

The following is a list of VB enumerations, along with the VB constants that can be used in place of individual enumeration members. In a few cases, there seem to be missing VB intrinsic constants. These are marked with a question mark (?).

Note that all enumeration members must be qualified with the name of the enumeration to which they belong.

AppWinStyle Enumeration

```
Enum AppWinStyle
    Hide = 0                    ' VbHide
    NormalFocus = 1             ' VbNormalFocus
    MinimizedFocus = 2          ' VbMinimizedFocus
    MaximizedFocus = 3          ' VbMaximizedFocus
    NormalNoFocus = 4           ' VbNormalNoFocus
    MinimizedNoFocus = 6        ' VbMinimizedNoFocus
End Enum
```

CallType Enumeration

```
Enum CallType
    Method = 1                  ' VbMethod
    Get = 2                     ' VbGet
    Let = 4
    Set = 8                     ' VbSet
End Enum
```

CompareMethod Enumeration

```
Enum CompareMethod
    Binary = 0                  ' VbBinaryCompare
    Text = 1                    ' VbTextCompare
End Enum
```

DateFormat Enumeration

```
Enum DateFormat
    GeneralDate = 0             ' VbGeneralDate
    LongDate = 1                ' VbLongDate
    ShortDate = 2               ' VbShortDate
    LongTime = 3                ' VbLongTime
    ShortTime = 4               ' VbShortTime
End Enum
```

DateInterval Enumeration

```
Enum DateInterval
    Year = 0
```

```
        Quarter = 1
        Month = 2
        DayOfYear = 3
        Day = 4
        WeekOfYear = 5
        Weekday = 6
        Hour = 7
        Minute = 8
        Second = 9
End Enum
```

DueDate Enumeration

```
Enum DueDate
    EndOfPeriod = 0
    BegOfPeriod = 1
End Enum
```

FileAttribute Enumeration

```
Enum FileAttribute
    Normal = 0              ' VbNormal
    ReadOnly = 1            ' VbReadOnly
    Hidden = 2              ' VbHidden
    System = 4             ' VbSystem
    Volume = 8             ' VbVolume
    Directory = 16         ' VbDirectory
    Archive = 32           ' VbArchive
End Enum
```

FirstDayOfWeek Enumeration

```
Enum FirstDayOfWeek
    System = 0             ' VbUseSystemDayOfWeek
    Sunday = 1             ' VbSunday
    Monday = 2             ' VbMonday
    Tuesday = 3            ' VbTuesday
    Wednesday = 4          ' VbWednesday
    Thursday = 5           ' VbThursday
    Friday = 6             ' VbFriday
    Saturday = 7           ' VbSaturday
End Enum
```

FirstWeekOfYear Enumeration

```
Enum FirstWeekOfYear
    System = 0             ' VbUseSystem
    Jan1 = 1               ' VbFirstJan1
    FirstFourDays = 2      ' VbFirstFourDays
    FirstFullWeek = 3      ' VbFirstFullWeek
End Enum
```

MsgBoxResult Enumeration

```
Enum MsgBoxResult
    OK = 1                              ' vbOK
    Cancel = 2                          ' vbCancel
    Abort = 3                           ' vbAbort
    Retry = 4                           ' vbRetry
    Ignore = 5                          ' vbIgnore
    Yes = 6                             ' vbYes
    No = 7                              ' vbNo
End Enum
```

MsgBoxStyle Enumeration

```
Enum MsgBoxStyle
    DefaultButton1 = &H00000000        ' vbDefaultButton1
    ApplicationModal = &H00000000      ' vbApplicationModal
    OKOnly = &H00000000                ' vbOKOnly
    OKCancel = &H00000001              ' vbOKCancel
    AbortRetryIgnore = &H00000002      ' vbAbortRetryIgnore
    YesNoCancel = &H00000003           ' vbYesNoCancel
    YesNo = &H00000004                 ' vbYesNo
    RetryCancel = &H00000005           ' vbRetryCancel
    Critical = &H00000010              ' vbCritical
    Question = &H00000020              ' vbQuestion
    Exclamation = &H00000030           ' vbExclamation
    Information = &H00000040           ' vbInformation
    DefaultButton2 = &H00000100        ' vbDefaultButton2
    DefaultButton3 = &H00000200        ' vbDefaultButton3
    SystemModal = &H00001000           ' vbSystemModal
    MsgBoxHelp = &H00004000            ' vbMsgBoxHelp
    MsgBoxSetForeground = &H00010000   ' vbMsgBoxSetForeground
    MsgBoxRight = &H00080000           ' vbMsgBoxRight
    MsgBoxRtlReading = &H00100000      ' vbMsgBoxRtlReading
End Enum
```

OpenAccess Enumeration

```
Enum OpenAccess
    Default = &HFFFFFFFF
    Read = 1
    Write = 2
    ReadWrite = 3
End Enum
```

OpenMode Enumeration

```
Enum OpenMode
    Input = 1
    Output = 2
    Random = 4
    Append = 8
    Binary = 32
End Enum
```

OpenModeTypes Enumeration

```
Enum OpenModeTypes
    Any = &HFFFFFFFF
    Input = 1
    Output = 2
    Random = 4
    Append = 8
    Binary = 32
End Enum
```

OpenShare Enumeration

```
Enum OpenShare
    Default = &HFFFFFFFF
    LockReadWrite = 0
    LockWrite = 1
    LockRead = 2
    Shared = 3
End Enum
```

TriState Enumeration

```
Enum TriState
    UseDefault = &HFFFFFFFE          ' VbUseDefault
    False = 0                        ' VbFalse
    True = 1                         ' VbTrue
End Enum
```

VariantType Enumeration

```
Enum VariantType
    Empty = 0
    Null = 1
    Short = 2
    Integer = 3                      ' VbInteger
    Single = 4                       ' VbSingle
    Double = 5                       ' VbDouble
    Currency = 6                     ' VbCurrency
    Date = 7                         ' VbDate
    String = 8                       ' VbString
    Object = 9                       ' VbObject
    Error = 10                       ' VbError
    Boolean = 11                     ' VbBoolean
    Variant = 12                     ' VbVariant
    DataObject = 13                  ' VbDataObject
    Decimal = 14                     ' VbDecimal
    Byte = 17                        ' VbByte
    Char = 18
    Long = 20                        ' VbLong
    UserDefinedType = 36             ' VbUserDefinedType
    Array = 8192                     ' VbArray
End Enum
```

VbStrConv Enumeration

```
Enum VbStrConv
    None = 0
    UpperCase = 1              ' VbUpperCase
    LowerCase = 2              ' VbLowerCase
    ProperCase = 3             ' VbProperCase
    Wide = 4                   ' VbWide
    Narrow = 8                 ' VbNarrow
    Katakana = 16              ' VbKatakana
    Hiragana = 32              ' VbHiragana
    SimplifiedChinese = 256    ' VbSimplifiedChinese
    TraditionalChinese = 512   ' VbTraditionalChinese
    LinguisticCasing = 1024    ' VbLinguisticCasing
End Enum
```

APPENDIX E

The VB.NET Command-Line Compiler

With the release of the .NET Framework Software Development Kit (SDK), Visual Basic for the first time features a command-line compiler that allows you to create and compile Visual Basic components and applications apart from Visual Studio. Ironically, this means that one of VB.NET's significant advances is the ability to use your favorite text editor, such as NotePad or WinEdit, to create VB.NET code. This appendix details the operation of the compiler, *vbc.exe*.

Compiler Basics

Syntactically, the compiler is fairly typical in that it uses command-line switches to control its operation. A command-line switch is designated by a slash or hyphen followed by a keyword. If the keyword takes an argument, it is separated from the keyword by a colon (:). For example:

```
vbc sample1.vb /target:library
```

supplies the **library** keyword as an argument to create a library file (that is, a DLL). If multiple arguments are required, they are separated from one another by commas. For example:

```
vbc sample1.vb /r:system.design.dll,system.messaging.dll
```

references the metadata in the *system.design.dll* and *system.messaging.dll* assemblies.

The minimal syntax required to compile a file named *sample1.vb* is:

```
vbc sample1.vb
```

This generates a console-mode application. You can specify the type of component or application you wish to generate by using the **/target** switch. To generate a Windows executable, you'd enter something like the following at the command line:

```
vbc sample1.vb /t:winexe /r:system.windows.forms.dll
```

Note the /r switch, which adds a reference to the assembly that contains the system.windows.forms namespace. You must explicitly add references to any assemblies your application requires, other than *mscorlib.dll* and *microsoft.visual-basic.dll*.

To compile multiple files, just list them on the command line using a space to separate them. For example:

```
vbc sample1.vb sample2.vb /t:winexe /r:system.windows.forms.dll
```

Since *sample1.vb* is the first file we listed and we haven't explicitly designated an output filename, the compiler will generate a Windows executable named *sample1.exe*.

Command-Line Switches

The VB.NET compiler supports the following command-line switches.

Output Filename and File Type

Switch	Description
/out:*<file>*	Defines the output filename. If not present, the output file will have the same root filename as the input file. *<file>* can be the root filename without a file extension.
/target:*<type>* or: /t:*<type>*	Defines the type of file to be generated by the compiler. *<type>* can be any of the following keywords: exe (to create a console application), winexe (to create a Windows application), library (to create a library assembly in a DLL), and module (to create a .NETMODULE file that can be added to an assembly). If the switch is not present, type defaults to exe, and the compiler attempts to create a console application.

Input Files

Switch	Description
/addmodule:*<file>*	Includes the .NETMODULE file named *<file>* in the output file.
/libpath:*<path_list>*	The directory or directories to search for metadata references (which are specified by the /reference switch) that are not found in either the current directory or the CLR's system directory. *<path_list>* is a list of directories, with multiple directories separated by commas or semicolons. Note that /libpath is additive; using multiple switches adds *<path_list>* to existing paths rather than replacing the existing ones.
/recurse:*<wildcard>*	Includes all files in the current directory and its subdirectories according to the wildcard specifications. For example:
| | ```
vbc /recurse:*.vb /t:library
      /out:mylibrary.lib
``` |
| | If you use the /recurse switch, you do not have to name a specific file to compile; however, if you do, it should not match the specification provided as an argument to the /recurse switch. |
```

Switch	Description
/reference:<file_list> or: /r:<file_list>	References metadata from the assemblies contained in <file_list>. Each filename in <file_list> must include a file extension.

Resources

Switch	Description
/linkresource:<resinfo> or: /linkres:<resinfo>	Links to a managed resource file without embedding it in the output file. <resinfo> has the form: <file>[,<name>[,public|private]] where <file> is the filename of the resource, <name> is the logical name used to load the resource, and the public and private keywords determine whether the resource is public or private in the assembly manifest. By default, resources are public.
/resource:<resinfo> or: /res:<resinfo>	Embeds the managed resource or resources named <resinfo> in the output file. <resinfo> takes the form: <file>[,<name>[,public|private]] where <file> is the filename of the resource, <name> is the logical name used to load the resource, and the public and private keywords determine whether the resource is public or private in the assembly manifest. By default, resources are public. The /resource switch cannot be used along with the /target:module switch.
/win32icon:<file>	Indicates the application icon is found in a Win32 icon (ICO) file.
/win32resource:<file>	Indicates resources are to be found in a Win32 resource (RES) file.

Code Generation

Switch	Description
/optimize[+|-]	Determines whether compiler output is optimized to produce smaller binary files that offer improved efficiency and performance. Optimized code, however, is more difficult to debug. Its default value is on (+). /optimize is equivalent to /optimize+.
/removeintchecks[+|-]	Removesinteger overflow checks. Its default value is off (-). Turning it on places the responsibility on the developer for ensuring that integers don't overflow their bounds. /'removeintchecks is equivalent to /removeintchecks+.

Debugging

Switch	Description
/debug[+-]	Determines whether debugging information is generated and included in the output file or files. The default value is /debug-, which suppresses the generation of debug information. /debug+ or /debug causes the compiler to generate debugging information.

Switch	Description
/debug:full or: /debug:pdbonly	Defines the form of debugging information output by the compiler. full generates full debugging information and allows a debugger to be attached to the running program; it is the default value if debugging is enabled. pdbonly generates a debug symbol (PDB) file only. It supports source-code debugging when the program is started in the debugger, but displays assembler only when the running program is attached to the debugger.

Errors and Warnings

Switch	Description
/nowarn	Disables warnings.
/warnaserror[+|-]	Treats warnings as errors, so that warnings prevent the code from compiling. Its default value is off (-). /warnaserror is equivalent to /warnaserror+.

Language

Switch	Description
/define:<symbol_list> or: /d:<symbol_list>	Declares global conditional compiler constants. <symbol_list> has the form name=value, with multiple values separated by commas.
/imports:<import_list>	Globally imports namespaces, eliminating the need to define them with individual Imports statements. <import_list> is a comma-delimited list of namespaces.
/optioncompare:binary	Specifies binary (case-sensitive) string comparison; this is the default value. The switch does not override any explicit Option Compare settings found in individual source-code files.
/optioncompare:text	Specifies case-insensitive string comparisons. The switch does not override any explicit Option Compare settings found in individual source-code files.
/optionexplicit[+|-]	Determines whether variables must be explicitly defined before they are used; the default setting is on. The switch does not override any explicit Option Explicit settings found in individual source-code files. /optionexplicit is the same as /optionexplicit+.
/optionstrict[+|-]	Determines whether implicit narrowing conversions and late binding are allowed; the default setting is off. The switch does not override any explicit Option Strict settings found in individual source-code files. /optionstrict is the same as /optionstrict+.
/rootnamespace:<string>	Defines a root namespace for all type declarations. This means that an Imports statement need not be used to import the root namespace, and that the relative path of a type (starting from the root namespace) can be used in place of its fully qualified name. Any Imports statements, however, must contain the fully qualified namespace name.

Miscellaneous

Switch	Description
/help or: /?	Displays help information.
/nologo	Suppresses the display of the compiler's copyright banner.
/quiet	Turns on quiet output mode; the compiler displays less information about errors than it does ordinarily.
/verbose	Turns on verbose output mode; the compiler displays more information about the file being compiled and about errors than usual.

Advanced

Switch	Description
/baseaddress:<number>	Specifies the base address at which a library or module should be loaded. If a single application or component uses multiple libraries, or if modules are loaded by a single application or component, the runtime attempts to load them at the same address and then maps them to new addresses. In this case, performance can be improved by specifying the base address of a project's additional libraries or modules. <number> should be a hexadecimal address.
/bugreport:<file>	Generates a file named <file> that contains information needed to report a bug.
/delaysign[+|-]	If on (+), signs the assembly using only the public portion of the strong name key; if off (-), the default value, generates a fully signed assembly. The /delaysign option must be used with either /keycontainer or /keyfile.
/keycontainer:<string>	Specifies a strong-name key container with the assembly's key pair. The name of the container is indicated by <string>; if <string> has embedded spaces, it should be enclosed in quotation marks.
/keyfile:<file>	Specifies the file containing a key or key pair that will be used to give an assembly a strong name. If the filename has embedded spaces, <file> should be enclosed in quotation marks.
/libpath:<path_list>	Specifies the list of directories to search for metadata references. By default, the global assembly cache is automatically searched for references.
/main:<class> or: /m:<class>	Specifies the class or module (or a class that inherits from System.Windows.Forms.Form) that contains *Sub Main*, which, if present, is a program entry point for applications and components. It is particularly useful if more than one class/module in a project has a subroutine named *Main*.
/utf8output[+|-]	Emits compiler output in UTF8 character encoding, which is useful when local settings prevent compiler output from being displayed to the console correctly. Its default value is off (-). /utf8output is the same as utf8output+.

Using a Response File

The Visual Basic compiler also allows you to specify command-line options and settings from a text file or *response file* when you compile your program. The syntax is:

```
vbc @<file>
```

where `<file>` is the name of the response file, including its path if it is not located in the current directory. The response file simply contains source filenames and compiler options; it is interpreted as if the filenames and compiler switches were entered at the command line.

The syntax of a response file is quite simple. Multiple filenames or switches can be included on a single line. However, a single switch, option, or filename cannot span multiple lines. In addition, # serves as a comment symbol.

For example, a response file named *mylib.rsp* might appear as follows:

```
# Build the library
/target:library
/out:mylibrary
/debug+
/debug:full
libfunc1.vb
libproc1.vb
libstrings.vb
```

The compiler can then be invoked by entering the following at the command line:

```
vbc @mylib.rsp
```

A response file can be combined with switches and filenames entered at the command line, and multiple response files can be used. The compiler processes these items in the order in which they are encountered. This means that settings in a response file can be overridden by later specifying command-line options or that command-line settings can be overridden by later specifying a response filename. For example, the command line:

```
vbc libnumeric.vb @mylib.rsp /debug-
```

compiles a file named *libnumeric.vb*, in addition to the three files already named in *mylib.rsp*. It also reverses some settings in *mylib.rsp* by preventing debugging information from being included in the output file.

APPENDIX F

VB 6 Language Elements Not Supported by VB.NET

This appendix provides an alphabetical list of language elements that are present in VB 6 but are not supported by VB.NET.

Element	Description
Array function	Returns a variant array whose elements contain the values passed as arguments to the function
AscB function	Returns an integer representing the character code of the first byte of a string
Atn function	Returns the arctangent of a number; replaced by the Atan method in the System.Math class
Calendar property	Determines whether a project should use the Gregorian or Hijri calendar
CCur function	Converts an expression into a Currency data type
ChrB function	Returns the character corresponding to an 8-bit character code
Close statement	Closes a file opened with the Open statement
CVar function	Converts an expression into a Variant data type
CVDate function	Returns a Date variant
CVErr function	Returns an error from a procedure
Date, Date$ functions	Return the current system date
Date statement	Sets the current system date
Debug.Print	Sends output to the Immediate window
DefBool statement	Defines all otherwise undeclared variables beginning with particular alphabetical characters as Boolean
DefByte statement	Defines all otherwise undeclared variables beginning with particular alphabetical characters as Byte
DefCur statement	Defines all otherwise undeclared variables beginning with particular alphabetical characters as Currency
DefDate statement	Defines all otherwise undeclared variables beginning with particular alphabetical characters as Date
DefDbl statement	Defines all otherwise undeclared variables beginning with particular alphabetical characters as Double

Element	Description
DefDec statement	Defines all otherwise undeclared variables beginning with particular alphabetical characters as Decimal
DefInt statement	Defines all otherwise undeclared variables beginning with particular alphabetical characters as Integer
DefLng statement	Defines all otherwise undeclared variables beginning with particular alphabetical characters as Long
DefObj statement	Defines all otherwise undeclared variables beginning with particular alphabetical characters as Object
DefSng statement	Defines all otherwise undeclared variables beginning with particular alphabetical characters as Single
DefStr statement	Defines all otherwise undeclared variables beginning with particular alphabetical characters as String
DefVar statement	Defines all otherwise undeclared variables beginning with particular alphabetical characters as Variant
Eqv operator	Represents a logical equivalence operator
Error function	Returns standard description of a particular error code
Get statement	Retrieves data from a disk file into a program variable
GoSub...Return statement	Passes execution to and returns from a subroutine within a procedure
IMEStatus function	Returns the state of the Input Method Editor
Imp operator	Represents a logical implication operator
Initialize event	Fires when an object is first used
Input, Input$, InputB, InputB$ functions	Reads a designated number of characters from a file opened in input or binary mode
Instancing property	Defines how instances of a class are created
InStrB function	Returns the position of a particular byte in a binary string
IsEmpty function	Determines if a variable has been initialized
IsMissing function	Determines whether an argument has been passed to a procedure
IsNull function	Indicates whether an expression contains Null data
IsObject function	Indicates whether a variable contains a reference to an object
LeftB, LeftB$ functions	Returns the leftmost n bytes of binary data
LenB function	Returns the actual size of a user-defined type in memory
Let statement	Assigns the value of an expression to a variable
Load statement	Loads a form or control
LoadResData function	Extracts a string containing a resource included in a resource project
LoadResPicture function	Assigns a graphic from a resource file to the Picture property of an object
LoadResString function	Retrieves a string from a resource file
MidB, MidB$ functions	Returns a specified number of bytes from a larger binary string
MidB statement	Replaces a specified number of bytes in a binary string
MTSTransactionMode property	Indicates whether a component is an MTS object and, if so, determines its level of transaction support
Name statement	Renames a disk file or directory
ObjPtr function	Returns a pointer to an object
On...GoSub statement	Causes program execution to jump to a subroutine based on the value of a control variable

Element	Description
On...Goto statement	Causes program execution to jump to a label based on the value of a control variable
Open statement	Opens a file
Option Base statement	Defines the default lower bound for arrays dimensioned within a module
Option Private Module statement	Restricts the scope and visibility of a module to the module's project
Persistable property	Determines whether a class in an ActiveX DLL project can be saved to disk
Property Set statement	Declares a procedure that assigns an object reference to a property
Put statement	Writes data from a program variable to a disk file
Right, Right$ functions	Returns the rightmost bytes from a binary string
Set statement	Assigns an object reference to a variable
Sgn function	Determines the sign of a number
Sqr function	Calculates the square root of a number
String function	Creates a string composed of a single character repeated a given number of times
StrPtr function	Returns a pointer to a BSTR (Visual Basic string)
Terminate event	Fired when an object is destroyed
Time function	Returns the current system time
Time statement	Sets the current system time
Type statement	Defines a user-defined type
Unload statement	Removes a form or a dynamically created member of a control array from memory
Width# statement	Specifies a virtual file width when working with files opened with the Open statement
VarPtr function	Returns a pointer to a variable

Index

Symbols

\ integer division operator, 616

< less-than comparison operator, 620

<= less-than-or-equal-to comparison operator, 620

- (minus) subtraction operator, 616

*= multiplication assignment operator, 618

. (period) in regular expressions, 106

+ (plus)
  addition operator, 616
  in regular expressions, 107
  string concatenation operator, 619

? (question mark) in regular expressions, 107

-= subtraction assignment operator, 618

_ (underscore) VB.NET line continuation character, 118

+= addition assignment operator, 618

& (ampersand) string concatenation operator, 619

* (asterisk)
  multiplication operator, 616
  in regular expressions, 106

@ (at sign) type identifier, 43

[] (brackets) in regular expressions, 106

^ (caret) exponentiation operator, 617

: (colon) and line numbers, 593

&= concatenation assignment operator, 619

{} (curly brackets) in regular expressions, 107

/= division assignment operator, 618

/ division operator, 616

$ (dollar sign) type identifier, 47

= (equals sign)
  assignment operator, 28, 618
  comparison operator, 620

! (exclamation point) type identifier, 47

^= exponential assignment operator, 618

> greater-than comparison operator, 619

>= greater-than-or-equal-to comparison operator, 620

<> inequality operator, 620

\= integer division assignment operator, 618

A

Abs function (Math class), 101, 149, 611

abstract classes, 82

abstract members, 82–84

abstraction in object-oriented programming, 63

access modifiers, 32
  class modules and, 69, 86–90
  declaring variables and constants, 35
  using in Property statement, 461
  using in Sub statements, 539

CustomColors property (ColorDialog class), 207
CustomMarshaler (UnmanagedType enumeration), 416

D

\d and \D in regular expressions, 106
data access with ADO.NET, 105
data, managed, 92
data members in class modules, 67
data types, 30, 36–51
    changes for VB.NET, 585–587
    converting, 49–51
        functions for, 179–184, 190, 196–198, 216–219, 605
            Option Strict statement and, 447–450
            System namespace and, 99
    simple, 41–49
    summary of, 39–41
    SystemTypeName function and, 545
    TypeName function and, 558–560
    for VB.NET, 9–11
    VbTypeName function and, 568
Date data type, 40, 43
    converting values to, 181
    VB 6 vs. VB.NET, 587
DateAdd function, 222, 605
DateDiff function, 224–227, 605
DateFormat enumeration, 629
DateInterval enumeration, 629
DatePart function, 227–229, 606
dates and times, 605
    Day function, 232
    formatting, 335
    GetTimer function, 351
    Hour function, 364
    IsDate function, 395, 609
    Minute function, 424
    Month function, 428
    MonthName function, 428
    Now property, 436
    predefined formats for, 329
    Second function, 502
    TimeOfDay property, 551
    Timer property, 552
    TimeSerial function, 552
    TimeString property, 553
    TimeValue function, 554
    Today property, 555
    user-defined formats for, 330
    Weekday function, 572

WeekdayName function, 573
    Year function, 580
DateSerial function, 229, 606
DateString property, 230, 606
DateValue function, 231, 605, 606
Day function, 232, 606
DBNull, evaluating to, 395, 609
DDB function, 233, 609
Debug class, 234, 611
/debug command-line switch, 636
Debug.Assert method, 235, 606
Debug.AutoFlush property, 236, 606
Debug.Close method, 237, 606
Debug.Flush method, 237, 606
Debug.Indent method, 237, 606
Debug.IndentLevel property, 238, 606
Debug.IndentSize property, 238, 606
Debug.Listeners property, 238, 606
Debug.Unindent method, 239, 606
Debug.Write method, 240, 606
Debug.WriteIf method, 240, 606
Debug.WriteLine method, 241, 607
Debug.WriteLineIf method, 242, 607
Decimal data type, 40, 43
    CDec function and, 50
    converting values to, 183
    ValDec function and, 564
declarations, function, 66
Declare statement, 242–246, 607, 614
declaring
    object variables using WithEvents, 576
    statements used for, 607
    variables and constants, 34–36
        changes for VB.NET, 587
        Option Explicit statement and, 446
default button constants, 431
default events, 113–115
Default keyword
    Property statement and, 461
    vs. DefaultMember attribute, 247
default properties, 600
DefaultEvent attribute, 117
DefaultExt property
    OpenFileDialog class, 444
    SaveFileDialog class, 497
DefaultMember attribute, 246–249
/define: command-line switch, 637
Deftype statements (not supported in VB.NET), 587, 596
/delaysign command-line switch, 638
Delegate class, 109

instance constructors (see class constructors)
instance members, 71
instantiating classes, 70
InStr function (String class), 384, 614
InstrRev function (String class), 385, 614
Int function, 386, 605, 612
Integer data type, 40, 44
   changes in VB.NET, 586
   converting values to, 190
   encapsulation and, 64
integer division assignment operator (\=), 618
integer division operator (\), 616
Intellisense, 55
interest payments, computing, 390
interest rates for annuities, calculating, 478
Interface keyword, 84
Interface statement, 387–389, 613
Interface (UnmanagedType enumeration), 416
InterfaceID property (COMClass attribute), 208
interfaces, 63, 65–67
   abstract members and, 82–84
   defining, 84
InterfaceShadow property (COMClass attribute), 208
internal rate of return, calculating, 391, 609
intrinsic constants, 625–628
   MsgBox function and, 431
InvokeMember method, 246
I/O functionality, providing, 104–106
IPmt function, 390, 609
IRR function, 391, 609
Is operator, 392, 613, 620
IsArray function, 394, 603, 609
IsCompliant property (CLSCompliant attribute), 197
IsDate function, 395, 609
IsDBNull function, 395, 609
IsEmpty function (not supported in VB.NET), 595, 597
IsError function, 396, 608, 610
IsError property (Obsolete attribute), 440
IsMissing function (not supported in VB.NET), 61, 592, 597
IsNothing function, 397, 610
IsNumeric function, 398, 610

IsReference function, 398, 610
Item method (Collection class), 56, 203, 603
Item property (Hashtable class), 360, 604
IUnknown (UnmanagedType enumeration), 416

J

Join function (String class), 400, 603, 615
Join method (String class), 102

K

/keycontainer: command-line switch, 638
/keyfile: command-line switch, 638
Keys property (Hashtable class), 361, 604
keystrokes, sending to active window, 506–509
Kill procedure, 400, 608

L

language elements not supported by VB.NET, 640–642
language reference, 143–581
LastDLLError property (Err object), 130, 291, 607
LastIndexOf method
   Array class, 100, 165, 603
   String class, 102
LastIndexOfAny method (String class), 102
late binding, 45, 55
   command-line switches and, 637
LBound function, 402, 603
LCase function (String class), 403, 615
Left function (String class), 403, 615
Len function (String class), 404, 614, 615
Length property
   String class, 102
   VBFixedArray attribute, 567
/libpath: command-line switch, 635, 638
lifetime of variables, 32–34
LIFO (last-in, first-out) data structures, 522
Like operator (String class), 405, 615, 620
Line method (not supported in VB.NET), 595, 597
line numbers
   colons must follow, 593
   Erl property and, 283
LineInput function, 407, 610

About the Authors

Steven Roman is a Professor Emeritus of mathematics at the California State University, Fullerton. He has taught at a number of other universities, including the Massachusetts Institute of Technology, the University of California at Santa Barbara, and the University of South Florida. Dr. Roman received his B.A. degree from the University of California at Los Angeles and his Ph.D. from the University of Washington. He has authored over 35 books in mathematics and personal computing.

Dr. Roman's other computing books include: *Access Database Design and Programming, Writing Word Macros, Writing Excel Macros, Developing Visual Basic Add-Ins,* and *Win32 API Programming with Visual Basic,* all published by O'Reilly & Associates, as well as *Concepts of Object-Oriented Programming with Visual Basic* and *Understanding Personal Computer Hardware,* published by Springer-Verlag. He has also written a number of software applications, including Object Model Browser, a browser that displays a structured view of virtually any type library. For more information on Dr. Roman's books, articles, and software, visit his web site at *http://www.romanpress.com.*

Ron Petrusha is the Visual Basic programming editor for O'Reilly & Associates. He began working with computers in the mid-1970s, programming in SPSS (a progammable statistical package) and FORTRAN on the IBM 370 family. Since then, he has been a computer book buyer, editor of numerous books on Windows and Windows programming, and a consultant on projects written in dBASE, Clipper, and Visual Basic. Ron also has a background in quantitative labor history, specializing in Russian labor history, and holds degrees from the University of Michigan and Columbia University.

Paul Lomax is Chief Technical Officer of NTWebhost (*http://www.ntwebhost.co.uk*), a leading web hosting company located in the United Kingdom. Paul is a longtime Visual Basic developer, having first begun VB programming with Version 1.0. Paul has written systems for financial derivations forecasting, satellite TV broadcasting, the life insurance industry, and the oil and gas industry. Paul is the author or co-author of a number of bestselling O'Reilly titles, including *VB and VBA in a Nutshell: The Language, Learning VBScript,* and *VBScript in a Nutshell.* When not sitting in front of a keyboard, Paul can usually be found behind the wheel of a racing car, competing in events around the U.K.

Colophon

Our look is the result of reader comments, our own experimentation, and feedback from distribution channels. Distinctive covers complement our distinctive approach to technical topics, breathing personality and life into potentially dry subjects.

The animal on the cover of *VB.NET Language in a Nutshell*, Second Edition, is a catfish. Catfish can be found all over the world, most often in freshwater environments. Catfish are identified by their whiskers, called "barbels," as well by as their scaleless skin; fleshy, rayless posterior fins; and sharp, defensive spines in the dorsal and shoulder fins. Catfish have complex bones and sensitive hearing. They are omnivorous feeders and skilled scavengers. A marine catfish can taste with any part of its body.

Though most madtom species of catfish are no more than 5 inches in length, some Danube catfish (called wels or sheatfish) reach lengths of up to 13 feet and weights of 400 pounds. Wels catfish (found mostly in the U.K.) are dark, flat, and black in color with white bellies. They breed in the springtime in shallow areas near rivers and lakes. The females hatch eggs in their mouths and leave them on plants for the males to guard. Two to three weeks later, the eggs hatch into tadpole-like fish, which grow quickly in size. The largest recorded wels catfish was 16 feet long and weighed 675 pounds.

Catherine Morris was the production editor and proofreader for *VB.NET Language in a Nutshell,* Second Edition. Ann Schirmer assisted with the copyedit. Sarah Sherman and Claire Cloutier provided quality control. Judy Hoer wrote the index.

Pam Spremulli designed the cover of this book, based on a series design by Edie Freedman. The cover image is a 19th-century engraving from the Dover Pictorial Archive. Emma Colby produced the cover layout with QuarkXPress 4.1 using Adobe's ITC Garamond font. David Futato produced the CD label with QuarkXPress 4.1 using Adobe's ITC Garamond font.

David Futato designed the interior layout, based on a series design by Nancy Priest. Neil Walls converted the files from Microsoft Word to FrameMaker 5.5.6 using tools created by Mike Sierra. The text and heading fonts are ITC Garamond Light and Garamond Book. The illustrations that appear in the book were produced by Robert Romano and Jessamyn Read using Macromedia FreeHand 9 and Adobe Photoshop 6. This colophon was written by Linley Dolby.

Microsoft .NET Programming

.NET Framework Essentials, 2nd Edition

By Thuan L. Thai, Hoang Lam
2nd Edition February 2002
320 pages, 0-596-00302-1

.NET Framework Essentials, 2nd Edition is a concise and technical overview of the Microsoft .NET Framework. Covered here are all of the most important topics—from the underlying Common Language Runtime (CLR) to its specialized packages for ASP.NET, Web Forms, Windows Forms, XML and data access (ADO.NET). The authors survey each of the major .NET languages, including Visual Basic .NET, C# and Managed C++.

C# Essentials, 2nd Edition

By Brad Merrill, Peter Drayton &
Ben Albahari
2nd Edition January 2002
216 pages, 0-596-00315-3

Concise but thorough, this second edition of *C# Essentials* introduces the Microsoft C# programming language, including the Microsoft .NET Common Language Runtime (CLR) and .NET Framework Class Libraries (FCL) that support it. This book's compact format and terse presentation of key concepts serve as a roadmap to the online documentation included with the Microsoft .NET Framework SDK; the many examples provide much-needed context.

COM and .NET Component Services

By Juval Löwy
1st Edition September 2001
384 pages, 0-596-00103-7

COM & .NET Component Services provides both traditional COM programmers and new .NET component developers with the information they need to begin developing applications that take full advantage of COM+ services. This book focuses on COM+ services, including support for transactions, queued components, events, concurrency management, and security.

VB.NET Framework Class Library in a Nutshell

By Budi Kurniawan
1st Edition May 2002 (est.)
640 pages (est.), ISBN 0-596-00257-2

With both a fast-paced tutorial and a reference, *VB.NET Framework Class Library in a Nutshell* meets the needs of two primary audiences: programmers who want a quick introduction to using the FCL, and those who want a comprehensive reference to the FCL in book form. This book is a sequel to *VB.NET Language in a Nutshell* in that it covers the classes in the .NET framework using VB syntax. It's a hardworking manual that belongs on every VB developer's bookshelf.

How to stay in touch with O'Reilly

1. Visit Our Award-Winning Web Site

http://www.oreilly.com/

★ "Top 100 Sites on the Web" —PC Magazine
★ CIO Magazine's Web Business 50 Awards

Our web site contains a library of comprehensive product information (including book excerpts and tables of contents), downloadable software, background articles, interviews with technology leaders, links to relevant sites, book cover art, and more. File us in your bookmarks or favorites!

2. Join Our Email Mailing Lists

Sign up to get email announcements of new books and conferences, special offers, and O'Reilly Network technology newsletters at:
elists.oreilly.com.
It's easy to customize your free elists subscription so you'll get exactly the O'Reilly news you want.

3. Get Examples from Our Books

To find example files for a book, go to:
http://www.oreilly.com/catalog
select the book, and follow the "Examples" link.

4. Contact Us via Email

order@oreilly.com
For answers to problems regarding your order or our products. To place a book order online visit:
http://www.oreilly.com/order_new/

catalog@oreilly.com
To request a copy of our latest catalog.

booktech@oreilly.com
For book content technical questions or corrections.

proposals@oreilly.com
To submit new book proposals to our editors and product managers.

international@oreilly.com
For information about our international distributors or translation queries. For a list of our distributors outside of North America check out:
http://international.oreilly.com/distributors.html

5. Work with Us

Check out our web site for current employment opportunites:
http://jobs.oreilly.com/

6. Register your book

Register your book at:
http://register.oreilly.com

O'Reilly & Associates, Inc.
1005 Gravenstein Hwy North
Sebastopol, CA 95472 USA
TEL 707-827-7000 or 800-998-9938
    (6am to 5pm PST)
FAX 707-829-0104

International Distributors

http://international.oreilly.com/distributors.html • international@oreilly.com

UK, EUROPE, MIDDLE EAST, AND AFRICA (EXCEPT FRANCE, GERMANY, AUSTRIA, SWITZERLAND, LUXEMBOURG, AND LIECHTENSTEIN)

INQUIRIES
O'Reilly UK Limited
4 Castle Street
Farnham
Surrey, GU9 7HS
United Kingdom
Telephone: 44-1252-711776
Fax: 44-1252-734211
Email: information@oreilly.co.uk

ORDERS
Wiley Distribution Services Ltd.
1 Oldlands Way
Bognor Regis
West Sussex PO22 9SA
United Kingdom
Telephone: 44-1243-843294
UK Freephone: 0800-243207
Fax: 44-1243-843302 (Europe/EU orders)
or 44-1243-843274 (Middle East/Africa)
Email: cs-books@wiley.co.uk

FRANCE

INQUIRIES & ORDERS
Éditions O'Reilly
18 rue Séguier
75006 Paris, France
Tel: 33-1-40-51-71-89
Fax: 33-1-40-51-72-26
Email: france@oreilly.fr

GERMANY, SWITZERLAND, AUSTRIA, LUXEMBOURG, AND LIECHTENSTEIN

INQUIRIES & ORDERS
O'Reilly Verlag
Balthasarstr. 81
D-50670 Köln, Germany
Telephone: 49-221-973160-91
Fax: 49-221-973160-8
Email: anfragen@oreilly.de (inquiries)
Email: order@oreilly.de (orders)

CANADA
(FRENCH LANGUAGE BOOKS)
Les Éditions Flammarion ltée
375, Avenue Laurier Ouest
Montréal, QC H2V 2K3 Canada
Tel: 1-514-277-8807
Fax: 1-514-278-2085
Email: info@flammarion.qc.ca

HONG KONG
City Discount Subscription Service, Ltd.
Unit A, 6th Floor, Yan's Tower
27 Wong Chuk Hang Road
Aberdeen, Hong Kong
Tel: 852-2580-3539
Fax: 852-2580-6463
Email: citydis@ppn.com.hk

KOREA
Hanbit Media, Inc.
Chungmu Bldg. 210
Yonnam-dong 568-33
Mapo-gu
Seoul, Korea
Tel: 822-325-0397
Fax: 822-325-9697
Email: hant93@chollian.dacom.co.kr

PHILIPPINES
Global Publishing
G/F Benavides Garden
1186 Benavides Street
Manila, Philippines
Tel: 632-254-8949/632-252-2582
Fax: 632-734-5060/632-252-2733
Email: globalp@pacific.net.ph

TAIWAN
O'Reilly Taiwan
1st Floor, No. 21, Lane 295
Section 1, Fu-Shing South Road
Taipei, 106 Taiwan
Tel: 886-2-27099669
Fax: 886-2-27038802
Email: mori@oreilly.com

INDIA
Shroff Publishers & Distributors PVT. LTD.
C-103, MIDC, TTC Pawane
Navi Mumbai 400 701
India
Tel: (91-22) 763 4290, 763 4293
Fax: (91-22) 768 3337
Email: spdorders@shroffpublishers.com

CHINA
O'Reilly Beijing
SIGMA Building, Suite B809
No. 49 Zhichun Road
Haidian District
Beijing, China PR 100080
Tel: 86-10-8809-7475
Fax: 86-10-8809-7463
Email: beijing@oreilly.com

JAPAN
O'Reilly Japan, Inc.
Yotsuya Y's Building
7 Banch 6, Honshio-cho
Shinjuku-ku
Tokyo 160-0003 Japan
Tel: 81-3-3356-5227
Fax: 81-3-3356-5261
Email: japan@oreilly.com

SINGAPORE, INDONESIA, MALAYSIA, AND THAILAND
TransQuest Publishers Pte Ltd
30 Old Toh Tuck Road #05-02
Sembawang Kimtrans Logistics Centre
Singapore 597654
Tel: 65-4623112
Fax: 65-4625761
Email: wendiw@transquest.com.sg

AUSTRALIA
Woodslane Pty., Ltd.
7/5 Vuko Place
Warriewood NSW 2102
Australia
Tel: 61-2-9970-5111
Fax: 61-2-9970-5002
Email: info@woodslane.com.au

NEW ZEALAND
Woodslane New Zealand, Ltd.
21 Cooks Street (P.O. Box 575)
Waganui, New Zealand
Tel: 64-6-347-6543
Fax: 64-6-345-4840
Email: info@woodslane.com.au

ARGENTINA
Distribuidora Cuspide
Suipacha 764
1008 Buenos Aires
Argentina
Phone: 54-11-4322-8868
Fax: 54-11-4322-3456
Email: libros@cuspide.com

ALL OTHER COUNTRIES
O'Reilly & Associates, Inc.
1005 Gravenstein Hwy North,
Sebastopol, CA 95472 USA
Tel: 707-827-7000
Fax: 707-829-0104
Email: order@oreilly.com

O'REILLY®

TO ORDER: 800-998-9938 • order@oreilly.com • www.oreilly.com
ONLINE EDITIONS OF MOST O'REILLY TITLES ARE AVAILABLE BY SUBSCRIPTION AT safari.oreilly.com
ALSO AVAILABLE AT MOST RETAIL AND ONLINE BOOKSTORES

O'REILLY & ASSOCIATES, INC. LICENSE AGREEMENT
VB.NET Language in a Nutshell
for Visual Studio .NET

This is a legal agreement between you and O'Reilly & Associates, Inc. ("O'Reilly"). Carefully read all the terms and conditions of this agreement prior to opening the CD envelope. Opening the CD envelope indicates your acceptance of these terms and conditions. If you do not agree to these terms and conditions, return the package and all components of this product to the point of purchase for a refund. If purchased from O'Reilly, upon return of the product within 30 days of purchase, a refund will be given. If purchased from another source, follow their return policy.

LICENSE: This License Agreement permits you to use one copy of the VB.NET Language in a Nutshell for Visual Studio .NET CD-ROM ("CD-ROM") you have purchased on any single workstation, provided the CD-ROM is in use on only one workstation at any time. If you have multiple licenses for the CD-ROM, then at any time you may have as many copies of the CD-ROM in use as you have licenses. You may not mount the CD-ROM nor download the contents onto a network or server.

COPYRIGHT: The contents of the CD-ROM are owned by O'Reilly. The CD-ROM is protected by United States and international copyright and other laws. You may not remove, obscure, or alter any notice of patent, copyright, trademark, trade secret, or other proprietary rights. You may not copy the written materials accompanying the CD-ROM, except by prior written permission from the owner of such material, as described above. This license and your right to use the product terminate automatically if you violate any part of this Agreement. In the event of termination, you must immediately destroy all copies of the product or return them to O'Reilly.

LIMITED WARRANTY: O'Reilly warrants the CD-ROM to be free from defects in materials and workmanship for 90 days after delivery. Defective media may be returned for replacement without charge during the 90-day warranty period unless the media has been damaged by acts or actions of the Licensee or while under its control.

O'REILLY MAKES NO OTHER WARRANTIES EXPRESSED OR IMPLIED WITH RESPECT TO THE SOFTWARE (INCLUDING ASSOCIATED WRITTEN MATERIALS), ITS MERCHANTABILITY, OR FITNESS FOR ANY PARTICULAR PURPOSE. IN NO EVENT WILL O'REILLY BE LIABLE FOR INDIRECT OR CONSEQUENTIAL DAMAGES, INCLUDING, WITHOUT LIMITATIONS, LOSS OF INCOME, USE, OR INFORMATION, NOR SHALL THE LIABILITY OF O'REILLY EXCEED THE AMOUNT PAID FOR THE CD-ROM. THIS LIMITED WARRANTY GIVES YOU SPECIFIC LEGAL RIGHTS. YOU MAY HAVE OTHERS, WHICH VARY FROM STATE TO STATE.

Without limitation, O'Reilly does not warrant that the CD-ROM is completely error free, will operate without interruption, or is compatible with any equipment or software configurations. The Licensee expressly assumes all risk for use of the CD-ROM. Repair, replacement, or refund (at the option of O'Reilly) is the exclusive remedy, if there is a defect.

GENERAL: You may not sublicense, assign, or transfer the license or contents, except as expressly provided in this Agreement. This Agreement constitutes the entire agreement between you and O'Reilly and supersedes any prior written or oral agreement concerning the contents of this package. This Agreement is governed by the laws of the State of California as if the parties hereto were both California residents; and you consent to exclusive jurisdiction in the state and federal courts in San Francisco in the event of any dispute.